PENGUIN REFERENCE BOOKS

THE PLAIN-LANGUAGE LAW DICTIONARY

Robert E. Rothenberg is a well-known editor whose many books have been widely distributed in the United States and in fourteen foreign-language editions throughout the world. He has edited three multivolume encyclopedias, two on medicine and one on child care, and a dictionary of medical terms. The main thrust of his endeavors has been to translate complicated technical material into easily understood language. The success of these efforts may be measured in part by the fact that his books have sold several millions of copies and have been offered for sale and as premiums by such organizations as the Book-of-the-Month Club, the World Book Encyclopedia, and others. Robert E. Rothenberg received a Bachelor of Arts and a Doctor of Medicine degree from Cornell University and is a Diplomate of the American Board of Surgery and a Fellow of the American College of Surgeons.

Stephen A. Gilbert is a member of the New Jersey and the Florida bars and holds a Bachelor of Arts and a Law degree from Cornell University. Presently, he is Vice President and Associate General Consel of the Motor Club of America Companies.

EDITORIAL CONSULTANTS

John J. DeLury, Member of the New York Bar and Acting Justice of the Supreme Court of the State of New York

Noel Arnold Levin, Member of the New York and Connecticut Bar

THE PLAIN-LANGUAGE LAW DICTIONARY

EDITED BY

ROBERT E. ROTHENBERG

STEPHEN A. GILBERT

ASSISTANT EDITOR

PENGUIN BOOKS

Penguin Books Ltd, Harmondsworth,
Middlesex, England
Penguin Books, 625 Madison Avenue,
New York, New York 10022, U.S.A.
Penguin Books Australia Ltd, Ringwood,
Victoria, Australia
Penguin Books Canada Limited, 2801 John Street,
Markham, Ontario, Canada L3R 1B4
Penguin Books (N.Z.) Ltd, 182–190 Wairau Road,
Auckland 10, New Zealand

First published 1981

LIBRARY OF CONGRESS CATALOGING IN PUBLICATION DATA
Main entry under title:
The Plain-language law dictionary.
(Penguin reference books)
1. Law—United States—Dictionaries. I. Rothenberg, Robert E.
II. Gilbert, Stephen A. III. Series.
KF156.P58 349.73'03'21 81-4327
ISBN 0 14 051.109 1 347.30321 AACR2

Printed in the United States of America by
Offset Paperback Mfrs., Dallas, Pennsylvania
Set in CRT Times Roman

ACKNOWLEDGMENTS

The task of converting complex legal terms and expressions into simple, understandable linguistic forms would have been much more difficult of accomplishment had it not been for the extraordinary cooperation of the editorial consultants and Stephen A. Gilbert, our assistant editor. These men took time out from their heavy schedules to engage in this endeavor, and to them this editor wishes to express his deep appreciation.

—R.E.R.

FOREWORD

More than 400,000 attorneys are licensed to practice law in America. Not only do most of them practice law, but they write the laws that govern us, and they hold most of our public offices. These men and women run our courts and judicial system; they control our personal and social conduct through rules, regulations, ordinances, and prohibitions. They come to our aid when we are in trouble; they prosecute us when representing our adversaries; and they advise us what to do before signing a lease, buying a home, entering into a contract, forming a business, or planning a marriage. Finally, they tell us how to dispose of our belongings when we die. But these good counselors communicate with us in a language all their own, and they compose documents that defy our comprehension.

It is true that the language of the law is obscure, complicated, and difficult even for educated and sophisticated lay people to understand. Most of us are resigned to our ignorance and reluctantly rely entirely upon our attorneys for interpretation and guidance. Similar relationships have existed between patients and their physicians. With blind faith that their physicians would take the right course of action to cure them, patients have assumed passive roles, taking little responsibility for medical decisions that greatly influenced their lives.

Times have changed. Today people want to understand as much as possible about technical subjects, whether they involve placing a man on the moon or the surgical procedures used in heart transplants. This expanded human curiosity applies as well to the field of law, and indeed such curiosity is warranted. To live knowledgeably and securely in these times when disputes and litigations are so commonplace, when almost every transaction entails extensive legal negotiation, when most business decisions call for familiarity with dozens of restrictive regulations, when every dollar earned must undergo the scrutiny of state and federal tax authorities, when personal relations so frequently require specially tailored legal documents, such as wills, trusts, partnership agreements, separation and divorce agreements—to live securely with all of these a person must have some understanding of ordinary legal procedures and must master the basic vocabulary of legal terms and phrases.

This dictionary is intended for the general public. Many of the words listed are also employed in everyday transactions, but the definitions given here are the legal meanings and relate only by coincidence to their usage in conversation. As examples, the word "suit" refers to a proceeding in a court of law, not to wearing apparel; an "instrument" means a written document, not a violin or piano; a "sentence" refers to a term in jail, not to a spoken or written passage containing subject, predicate, and object.

This book will have served its purpose if it enables the reader to protect his or her rights better when involved in a legal matter, or if it improves basic understanding of legal words and phrases. As a lawyer would say, you will be better equipped to understand the law after perusing these pages because, "*Res ipsa loquitur,*" which in plain language means, "The thing speaks for itself."

—R.E.R.

LIST OF ABBREVIATIONS

A.A.A. Agricultural Adjustment Administration
A.A.A. American Arbitration Association
A.B. Able-bodied, especially referring to a seaman
A.B. Bachelor of Arts
A.B.A. American Bar Association
A.B.R. *American Bankruptcy Reports*
A.C. Appellate court
A.C.L.U. American Civil Liberties Union
A.E.C. Atomic Energy Commission
A.G.Dec. *Attorney General's Decisions*
Am. Jur. *American Jurisprudence*
A.L.R. *American Law Reports*
A.M.C. *American Maritime Cases*
A.N.R. *American Negligence Reports*
A.P. The Associated Press

B.A. Bachelor of Arts
B.S. Bachelor of Science

C.A. Court of Appeals
C/A Current account
C.A.A. Civil Aeronautics Authority
C.A.V. "The Court will consider" (*Curia advisare vult*)
C.B. Common bench
C.C. Circuit court; criminal case
C.C.A. Circuit Court of Appeals
C.C.P. Code of civil procedure
C.F.R. Code of federal regulations
C.I.A. Central Intelligence Agency
C.J. Chief justice
C.L. Civil law
C.O. Commanding officer; common orders
Co. Company
C.O.D. Payable on delivery
C.P. Common pleas
C.P.A. Certified public accountant

D.A. District attorney
D.B.E. "To be decided later"; provisionally; matters taken up *ex parte*
D.C. District court; District of Columbia
D.J. District judge
D.O.A. "Dead on arrival"

D.T.s *Delirium tremens*
D.W.I. "Died without issue"; "driving while intoxicated"

E2 A fraction of a section (one square mile) of land
E.B.T. Examination before trial
E.C.G. Electrocardiogram
E.E.G. Electroencephalogram
e.g. "As an example"
E.K.G. Electrocardiogram (the same as E.C.G.)
E.M.G. Electromyogram
E.O.E. Errors and omissions excepted
E.S.P. Extrasensory perception
et al. And others
et seq. And as follows
et ux And wife
etc. And so forth
exr. Executor

F.A.A. "Insurance against total loss only" (*re* Maritime insurance)
F.B.I. Federal Bureau of Investigation
F.C.C. Federal Communications Commission
F.D.A. Food and Drug Administration
F.D.I.C. Federal Deposit Insurance Corporation
F.H.A. Federal Housing Administration
F.O.B. Free on board (no charge for loading an article for shipment)
F.P.A. Fair Practices Act
F.P.C. Federal Power Commission
F.R. Federal Register
F.S.L.I.C. Federal Savings and Loan Insurance Corporation
F.T.C. Federal Trade Commission
F.U.R. "A thief" (*Homo trium litterarum*)

G.A. General Assembly
G.A.O. General Accounting Office (federal)
G.L.O. General Land Office
G-Man A government man; agent of the F.B.I.
G.M. Grand Marshal
G.N.P. Gross National Product
G.O.P. "The Grand Old Party" (Republican Party)

H.A. "In this year" (*hoc anno*)
H.B. A bill in the House of Representatives
H.H.F.A. Housing and Home Finance Agency
H.E.W. Department of Health, Education & Welfare
H.R. House of Representatives
H.T. Under this title (*hoc titulo*)

I.C.C. Interstate Commerce Commission
id. The same (*idem*)
i.e. That is (*id est*)
I.M.F. International Monetary Fund
in. Inch

Inc. Incorporated
I.O.U. "I owe you"; a note promising to pay a debt
I.R.C. Internal Revenue Code
I.R.S. Internal Revenue Service

J. Journal
J.A. Judge Advocate
J.A.G. Judge Advocate General
J.D. Doctor of Juris
J.P. Justice of the peace
J.U.D. Doctor of Common and Canon Laws

Kg. Kilogram
Kv. Kilovolt
Kw. Kilowatt

L.C. Leading cases
L.J. Law journal; law judge
L.L.B. Bachelor of Law
L.L.D. Doctor of Law (often an honorary degree)
L.R.A. *Law Reports Annotated*
L.S. The place of the seal or official signature on a document
L.S.D. A hallucinatory drug
Ltd. Limited; a business company or corporation

M.A. Master of Arts
M.D. Doctor of Medicine
M.E. Master of Engineering
Miss Title prefixed before an unmarried female's name
ml. A milliliter; 1 cubic centimeter
M.O. Mode of operation
M.P. Military police
m.p.h. Miles per hour
Mr. Title prefixed before a male's name
Mrs. Title prefixed before a married female's name
M.S. Master of Science
Ms. Title prefixed before a female's name, whether married or not
Ms Manuscript
Mss Manuscripts

N.A. "It is not permitted" (*non allocatur*)
N.A.A.C.P. National Association for the Advancement of Colored People
NASA National Aero Space Agency
N.B. "Mark well"; observe (*nota bene*)
N.C.C.A. *Negligence and Compensation Cases Annotated*
N.C.D. "No one disagreeing or dissenting"
N.L. "It is not clear" (*non liquet*)
N.G. "Not good"
N.L.R.B. National Labor Relations Board
N.P. Notary Public; tried before one judge (*nisi prius*)

N.R. *New Reports*; nonresident
N.A.M. National Association of Manufacturers
nul None

O.C. Orphan's Court
O.T. Old terminology
Oz. Ounce

P.A. Annually (*per annum*)
Pat. Dec. *Patent Decisions*
P.C. Penal Code
Pfd. Preferred
P.H.A. Public Housing Administration
Ph.D. Doctor of Philosophy
P.H.V. "For this purpose" (*pro hac vice*)
P.J. Presiding justice
P.L. Public law
P.M. Postmaster
P.O. Public officer
Pol. Code Political code
P.P. "In his own person" (*propria persona*)
P.P.A. Per Power of Attorney
Prob. Code Probate code
Prob. and Mat. Code Probate and matrimonial code
P.S. Public statutes
Pub. Laws Public laws
P.U.R. *Public Utility Reports*

Q.E.D. "It is proved" (*quod erat demonstrandum*)
Q.E.N. "Execution should not be issued"
Q.M.G. Quartermaster general
Q.S. Quarter sessions; quantity sufficient
Q.T. Quietly, secretly; a suit in which plaintiff has acted as informer and will benefit along with authorities if money is collected; also known as "*qui tam*"
q.v. A direction referring a reader to another part of a document

R. Registered; patented
R.A. Regular appeals
R.C. Rolls of court
R.C.L. Ruling case law
R.E.A. Rural Electrification Administration
R.F.C. Reconstruction Finance Corporation
R.F.D. Rural Free Delivery
R.G. A general order or rule of a court (*regula generalis*)
R.L. Revised laws
R.S. Revised statutes
Rules Sup. Ct. Rules of the Supreme Court

S. Statute
S.B. Senate bill
S.Ct. *Supreme Court Reporter*
S.E.C. Securities and Exchange Commission
Sen.J. *Senate Journal*
S.F.S. "Without fraud on his part" (*sine fraude sua*)
S.L. Session laws

S.P. “The same principle” (*sine prole*)
Spec. Sess. Special session
St. Ch. Cas. *Star Chamber Cases*

T-Man A treasury agent
Tax L. Rev. *Tax Law Review*
T.M. *Tax Magazine*
T.M.R. *Trademark Reports*
T.R. Tons registered, referring to a ship
Ter. L. Territorial law

U.B. Upper bench
U.L.A. *Uniform Laws Annotated*
U.N. United Nations
U.S.C. United States Code
U.S.C.C. United States Circuit Court
U.S.C.S.C. United States Civil Service Commission
U.S.D.C. United States District Court
U.S.I.A. United States Information Agency
U.S.R. *United States Supreme Court Reports*
U.S.R.S. *United States Revised Statutes*
U.S.T.C. *United States Tax Cases*

V.E. “A sale must be made” (*venditioni exponas*)
viz. “That is to say”; namely (*videlicet*)
vs. Versus; against

Wash. C.C. *Washington United States Circuit Court Reports*
W.C. and Ins. Rep. *Workmen’s Compensation and Insurance Reports*
W.H.O. World Health Organization

The use of single and double arrows (> ≫) indicates, respectively, *see* and *see also*, where a point is either amplified or complemented in another entry.

Words or phrases which are printed in SMALL CAPITALS are themselves the subjects of definitions in their appropriate alphabetical places.

THE PLAIN-LANGUAGE LAW DICTIONARY

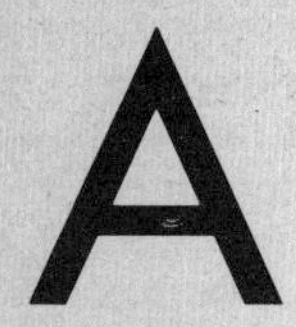

A fortiori. More effective; with greater reason (Latin).
A priori. To reason *a priori* is to conclude that from what has existed previously, certain effects must necessarily follow (Latin).
A tort. Unjustly; without reason (French).
Abandoned property. PROPERTY for which an owner has, without necessarily designating who shall take POSSESSION, given up all CLAIMS, RIGHTS, and possession.
Abandonment. The relinquishing of a thing or a PROPERTY without necessarily designating who shall take POSSESSION of it.
Abandonment of child. The DESERTION of a child with intention to cut off all relations and OBLIGATIONS toward the child.
Abandonment of copyright. Publication without first obtaining a COPYRIGHT.
Abandonment of spouse. Leaving a husband or wife without JUST CAUSE, and with the deliberate intention of causing lifetime SEPARATION.
Abandonment of trademark. Not only giving up the use of a TRADEMARK but also showing explicitly one's intention to give it up.
Abatable nuisance. A NUISANCE that can be readily corrected so as not to harm anyone; not a PERMANENT NUISANCE.
Abatement. A decrease; a reduction; an extinction.
Abatement of action. To put an end to a LAWSUIT. To pursue the same matter, a new SUIT (ACTION) must be brought.
Abatement of bequest. The PROCEDURE carried out when an EXECUTOR determines that an insufficient amount of money has been left in an ESTATE to pay off all debts, all costs of administering the estate, and still pay all the LEGACIES called for in the will.
Abatement of tax assessment. A decrease in the amount of TAX imposed upon an individual.
Abator. One who illegally takes POSSESSION of PROPERTY before the true HEIR has had the chance to take possession.
Abdicate. To disown; to relinquish completely; to renounce.
Abduction. The taking away, by force or persuasion, of a child, wife, or other person. It is a CRIMINAL OFFENSE.
Abettor. One who promotes or instigates the performance of a CRIMINAL ACT. ≫ INSTIGATION.
Abeyance, in. In expectation. An ESTATE is in abeyance when no one is at hand to claim the estate. However, the law anticipates that the rightful HEIR will be found and the estate will then no longer be in abeyance.
Ability to stand trial. Being physically and mentally able to defend oneself in a COURT of law. This ability often depends upon the findings of medical consultants appointed by the court.

Ability to support. The capacity to make enough money to SUPPORT a DEPENDENT, or to possess sufficient PROPERTY from which funds for support can be provided.
Abjudicate. To deprive by a JUDGMENT of the court; to take away by an adverse court DECISION.
Abjuration. The taking of an OATH to give up a RIGHT, such as swearing to give up ALLEGIANCE to a foreign country upon becoming a United States citizen.
Able-bodied. Capable of serving in the military. It does not necessarily mean that an individual is free of all defects.
Abnegate. To give up; to renounce.
Abolition. Destruction; elimination. The abolition of slavery did away with the practice completely.
Abortion. The spontaneous or artificial termination of pregnancy before the embryo or FETUS can sustain life on its own, outside the uterus.
Abortive trial. An incomplete TRIAL, one that has, for one reason or another, terminated before a VERDICT has been reached.
Abridgment of damages. The reduction of the amount of DAMAGES by a COURT ORDER. (In some cases, a JURY's award exceeds that which the court deems appropriate.)
Abroachment. Buying goods wholesale and selling them retail without offering them for sale in the open market.
Abrogation. The REPEAL of a LAW; an ANNULMENT; a cancellation of an existing AGREEMENT or STATUTE.
Abscond. To run away from the LAW; to absent oneself in an attempt to avoid legal PROCESS.
Absconding debtor. Someone who owes money and runs away from his CREDITORS, or who hides so they cannot find him.
Absente reo. In the absence of the DEFENDANT in a case (Latin).
Absentee landlord. An OWNER of PROPERTY who never visits or supervises it but leaves these tasks to another. Thus, the one who LEASES the property has no access to the actual owner.
Absenteeism. Purposeful absence from work in order to collect UNEMPLOYMENT INSURANCE, often practiced when there is no real or valid reason for not working.
Absolute. Unconditional; complete; final; without any restrictions or conditions.
Absolute acceptance. Unqualified and total AGREEMENT to accept a responsibility or LIABILITY.
Absolute assignment. A complete, outright transfer of TITLE.
Absolute conveyance. A DEED that transfers the TITLE (usually to land) from one person to another, without any conditions.
Absolute discretion. The total and final power of acting on one's own judgment, without outside influence or control.
Absolute divorce. A final and total DIVORCE, returning both the wife and husband to the status of single persons.
Absolute estate. Real estate, land, and/or buildings, over which the OWNER has complete

control, POSSESSION, and the total right of disposal.

Absolute guaranty. An AGREEMENT in which the borrower guarantees absolutely the repayment of a loan, or a CONTRACT in which one party guarantees absolutely the payment of certain monies that are due.

Absolute law. LAW that follows the rules of nature; law that is changeless. Although absolute law may be true in an abstract sense, it is not always exercised in actuality. ➤ LAW OF NATURE.

Absolute nuisance. Illegal interference with another person's enjoyment and use of his or her PROPERTY; the unlawful doing of a wrong to another, when that wrong could be corrected by the wrongdoer.

Absolute pardon. A PARDON without any conditions.

Absolute privilege. The PRIVILEGE that one enjoys in defaming the reputation of another when there is no way in which the person so defamed can bring SUIT.

Absolute rights. PRIVILEGES resulting from the ownership of PROPERTY; RIGHTS derived from a CONTRACT relationship; the right to make or to refuse to make a contract with someone else.

Absolute warranty. A GUARANTY in a sale to which no conditions are attached; a total and permanent WARRANTY.

Absolve. To ACQUIT; to release from an OBLIGATION.

Abstract of record. A brief but complete abbreviation of the records of a CASE in law.

Abstract of title. An abbreviated but complete history of the TITLE to land. Such an abstract should include all records of LIENS or LIABILITIES to the title, should they exist.

Abusive language. Language so hurtful that it causes mental anguish. Abusive language is sometimes used as a ground for DIVORCE.

Abuttals. The boundaries to a piece of PROPERTY, showing what properties are adjacent to it. ➤ BOUNDARY SUIT.

Abutting owner. An OWNER of PROPERTY that borders property belonging to someone else.

Acceleration clause. A STIPULATION in an AGREEMENT, a NOTE, or a MORTGAGE, stating that the whole debt will come due if there is failure to make annual interest payments or failure to comply with other provisions of the CONTRACT.

Acceptance of plea. The reception by the court of a PLEA OF GUILTY in a criminal case.

Acceptance of service. The acknowledgment by a DEFENDANT of a SUMMONS without going through the formalities of having someone serve it upon him/her.

Access. An approach to premises. (Access to land is sometimes granted by a person who owns land that would ordinarily interfere with ready passage.) Access also means the opportunity of a spouse to have sexual intercourse with a mate.

Accession. Acquiring a RIGHT or a thing; an addition; the rights to all that one's own property produces.

Accessory after the fact. An individual who knows that a crime has been committed and conceals that knowledge from the authorities, or who protects and aids the offender. > AID AND COMFORT.

Accessory before the fact. An individual who incites, stimulates, or aids in the commission of a crime, even though not present at the time the crime is committed. > AID AND ABET.

Accessory to a crime. A person who is connected to a crime, either before or after its commission, but is not present during its perpetration. > AID AND ABET.

Accident. An unexpected, unforeseen event. It may be a mishap or a fortunate occurrence.

Accidental cause. An unforeseen cause, one that cannot be avoided even by exercising extreme care and diligence.

Accidental death. Death due to ACCIDENT rather than to natural causes. An unexpected demise that was not anticipated.

Accidental killing. A death coming about as a consequence of a lawful act performed on the assumption that no harm will result. (It is different from INVOLUNTARY MANSLAUGHTER, which results from an unlawful act.)

Accommodation. A favor done without consideration of monetary or other reward. Also, a friendly solving of differences.

Accommodation note. A PROMISSORY NOTE (I.O.U.) on which someone other than the original borrower has placed his or her name. Such ENDORSEMENT, carried out without monetary consideration, assumes responsibility for payment in the event that the original borrower fails to meet his or her OBLIGATIONS. > ENDORSEMENT—ACCOMMODATION.

Accommodation paper. A NOTE that is signed by one person to help another obtain a loan.

Accomplice. One who consciously and willingly participates, either in a minor or major way, in a crime. > ACCESSORY TO A CRIME.

Accord. An AGREEMENT by two or more parties to settle their differences or CLAIMS.

Accord and satisfaction. A legal DOCUMENT testifying to the fact that a CLAIM has been settled and that SATISFACTION exists on the part of all those concerned.

Account. An unsettled CLAIM, based upon dealings that have created a DEBTOR and CREDITOR relationship.

Accountability. The state of being responsible and liable. > LIABILITY.

Accountable. Responsible; liable.

Accountant. An expert in bookkeeping and accounting; a CERTIFIED PUBLIC ACCOUNTANT is also expert in calculating taxes.

Accounts payable. Monies owed to an open account, that is, an account that is not yet settled.

Accounts receivable. Monies owed to an unsettled, open account.

Accredited. Recognized as worthy and approved. An accredited law school is one approved by the licensing agencies of the various states.

Accretion. The attainment of more PROPERTY by natural

causes, such as land being added by the deposit of dirt from a river.

Accrual basis. The keeping of records and the reporting of INCOME for TAX purposes according to the time of the right to receive payments, rather than the time payments are actually received.

Accrue. To increase, such as to gain interest that is added to principal.

Accrued compensation. Compensation that has been awarded and is due and payable.

Accrued depreciation. The lessened value of something because of its decreased ability to render a service.

Accrued interest. INTEREST that is accumulating, or has accumulated but has not yet been paid.

Accrued right. A RIGHT that has matured (has been established) and is backed by the legal authority to demand a remedy to any wrongs that have been committed.

Accumulated profit. Undivided profits, that is, those earned but not yet distributed.

Accumulated surplus. A fund resulting from undistributed earnings and profits of a COMPANY or CORPORATION, in excess of its CAPITAL STOCK.

Accumulation trust. A TRUST that holds on to its INCOME in order to increase its capital, rather than paying out that income to a beneficiary.

Accumulative judgment. A second or additional SENTENCE that is pronounced to go into effect after an individual has completed the serving of a previous sentence.

Accumulative legacy. An additional or second LEGACY.

Accumulative sentence. > ACCUMULATIVE JUDGMENT.

Accusation. A formal CHARGE, made in court, that a person is GUILTY of a punishable OFFENSE.

Accusatory instrument. A DOCUMENT charging someone with a crime.

Accusatory part. The part of a CHARGE or INDICTMENT that spells out the specific OFFENSE.

Accused. The accused is the DEFENDANT.

Accuser. One who claims that another is GUILTY of a punishable OFFENSE or crime. ≫ PLAINTIFF.

Acknowledge. To confess; to admit.

Acknowledged child. A child who is recognized by a parent as his own. (In a PATERNITY PROCEEDING, a man may deny that a child is of his creation.)

Acknowledged instrument. A DOCUMENT that is formally recognized before an authorized OFFICIAL. The person acknowledging the INSTRUMENT states that it is authentic and was executed voluntarily and freely.

Acquainted. Having knowledge of; familiar with.

Acquest. PROPERTY obtained through PURCHASE.

Acquiesce. To consent, usually without enthusiasm; to agree quietly.

Acquiescence. Quiet approval or, more accurately, lack of disapproval.

Acquire. To buy or gain POSSESSION of PROPERTY.

Acquired rights. RIGHTS that one

did not possess originally but that were procured through a person's own activity.

Acquisition. Something that one has purchased, been given as a gift, or has inherited.

Acquisition charge. A prepayment penalty; a charge made for paying off a loan before it is due.

Acquit. To declare NOT GUILTY; to set free.

Act. A STATUTE; a LAW enacted by a legislative body; a DEED.

Act of God. A happening resulting purely from nature, without the interference or participation of humans, such as flood, hurricane, fire due to lightning, etcetera. ➢ ACT OF PROVIDENCE.

Act of honor. When a person cannot or does not honor a bill, and a third person, who is not involved in the bill, agrees to honor it, this transaction is called an act of honor.

Act of law. An ACT that stems from the operation of existing laws or that is carried out under the authority of judges. (Acts of law are based upon fixed legal rules and facts.)

Act of providence. An ACCIDENT beyond the scope of prevention of humans. ➢ ACT OF GOD.

Acta publica. Matters of public concern and general knowledge (Latin).

Acting. Performing, such as acting as counsel; substituting for someone who is not performing, such as an *acting judge* or an *acting chairman*, etcetera.

Actio bonae fidei. An ACTION in GOOD FAITH; a group of actions in which the judge is authorized to take into account equitable considerations (Latin).

Actio in factum. An ACTION adapted to the particular case; an action in CIVIL LAW resembling an action in COMMON LAW (Latin).

Actio in rem. An ACTION for the recovery of something that is in another's POSSESSION (Latin).

Actio rescissoria. An ACTION to restore the right of TITLE that has been lost through a previous JUDGMENT. For example, a minor who was judged not ready for a title may sue to have that right restored upon reaching maturity (Latin).

Action. A legal action; a PROCEEDING in a court in which a PLAINTIFF claims against a DEFENDANT; a PROSECUTION in a court by one party against another.

Action ex contractu. An ACTION based upon a CONTRACT, usually because one PARTY has failed to live up to his contractual obligations (Latin).

Action pending. A LAWSUIT that is in progress.

Actionable fraud. A deception in which one PARTY tries to get another party to give up something that he or she rightfully possesses.

Actionable negligence. Failure, through carelessness or neglect, to perform a legal duty, thus damaging or injuring another; failure to exercise due care, thus causing harm.

Actionable nuisance. Knowingly doing something that interferes with another person's enjoyment of his or her PROPERTY. Also,

carelessly permitting something to injure or interfere with the lawful use of property by another.
Active concealment. Misleading and deceptive actions or words so as to conceal the truth.
Active negligence. Failure to exercise ordinary care, resulting in mental or physical harm to another; the opposite of *passive negligence.*
Active trust. > TRUST, ACTIVE.
Actual authority. AUTHORITY that a PRINCIPAL confers upon an agent (someone acting for the principal).
Actual cash value. The price that could be gotten if the product, PROPERTY, or item were sold in the open market.
Actual knowledge. Knowledge that is definitely and positively known, not presumed.
Actuarial solvency. The ability of a benefit society or an INSURANCE company to meet all of its obligations, especially those obligations to its policy-holders (insurance company) or members (benefit society).
Actuary. A specialist who is expert in calculating the cost of carrying a risk, such as determining what an INSURANCE PREMIUM should be for a particular type of policy.
Ad damnum clause. The clause in a PLAINTIFF's suit stating the amount of damages being claimed (Latin).
Ad diem. At the day (Latin).
Ad exitum. At the end; at issue (Latin).
Ad hoc. For this purpose. An ad hoc committee is one appointed for a special purpose, to perform a particular function (Latin).
Ad hominem. Personal, often referring to a personal argument; to the person (Latin).
Ad idem. On the same point (Latin).
Ad infinitum. Endless; going on and on—endlessly—in a discussion or argument (Latin).
Ad litem. For the purpose of the LAWSUIT (Latin).
Ad valorem. According to the value of (Latin).
Ad vitam. For life (Latin).
Added damages. DAMAGES added on to what is actually due; damages added as a punishment to the defendant. Added damages is sometimes referred to as *smart money.*
Addendum. An addition to a written DOCUMENT, often placed at the end of the main body of the document.
Addict. A habitual user of habit-forming drugs, such as narcotics, tranquilizers, amphetamines, hallucinatory drugs, etcetera.
Additur. **1.** The authority of a COURT OF APPEALS to deny the PLAINTIFF a new trial if the DEFENDANT agrees to pay a certain amount of money to the plaintiff. **2.** The authority of a court to increase the award given to a plaintiff by a JURY.
Adduce. To present; to introduce. The word is often used to refer to the presentation of EVIDENCE.
Ademption. The cancellation of a LEGACY, or a certain part of a legacy, by a person who has made a WILL.
Adequate consideration. A reasonable and fair price.

Adequate preparation. Adequate preparation refers to the proper preparation of a case by an ATTORNEY. It includes interviews with WITNESSES, knowledge of the facts, knowledge of the applicable laws, analysis of the probable handling of the case by the opposing attorney, and, of course, consultations with the client.

Adequate remedy at law. A remedy that brings complete relief in the controversy at hand. Adequate remedy defeats the defendant totally and permanently. ➢ REMEDIES.

Adjective law. Procedural law; the rules by which courts operate.

Adjournment. The suspension of a trial, either for a fixed period of time or indefinitely.

Adjournment sine die. Suspension of a trial or hearing without fixing another time for the next session (Latin).

Adjudge. To pass upon; to SENTENCE; to render JUDGMENT.

Adjudication. The determination of issues in a LAWSUIT; the JUDGMENT of a court, settling a matter deliberately and finally.

Adjudication of bankruptcy. The determination, through PROCESS, that a person or company is BANKRUPT.

Adjunction. The inclusion of one matter in another matter; an ACCESSION; an addition.

Adjuration. Swearing under OATH.

Adjustment. A SETTLEMENT of a CLAIM, often involving the determination of a mutually agreeable compromise sum.

Adjutant general. The chief ADMINISTRATIVE OFFICER of the Army.

Administrative officer. An OFFICIAL of the executive branch of the government, as distinguished from an official of the legislature or the judicial branch.

Administrative proceeding. A PROCEEDING that takes place before an administrative agency rather than in a COURT of law.

Administrative remedy. Obtaining REDRESS or enforcing one's RIGHTS by putting a matter before an administrative agency. If a remedy is not found by the GOVERNMENTAL AGENCY, then the matter is taken to COURT.

Administrative system. A system created by LEGISLATION, in which an AGENCY is empowered to make binding RULES and REGULATIONS.

Administrator. The personal representative of a deceased person's ESTATE. Also, a manager.

Admiralty law. LAW pertaining to maritime matters. (Maritime matters include shipping, navigation, civil and criminal infractions while at sea, etcetera.) ➢ MARITIME LAW.

Admissible evidence. EVIDENCE permitted to be introduced during a TRIAL.

Admission by demurrer. Material that is assumed to be true in a PLEADING solely for the purpose of demurring (objecting). If the OBJECTION (DEMURRER) is overruled by the judge, the material is not to be considered EVIDENCE in the case. ➢ DEMURRER TO EVIDENCE.

Admission to bail. The requiring of security by a monetary deposit or by a bond, in order to free the DEFENDANT temporarily. Admission to bail implies that the defendant will appear in COURT when the TRIAL is ready to start.

Admission to probate. The acknowledgment of the court that a WILL being presented is actually the will of the deceased person who executed it. (After a will has been admitted to PROBATE, it is still possible for someone to object to it or to certain of its provisions.)

Admission to the bar. An expression denoting the fact that an ATTORNEY has fulfilled all requirements to practice LAW in a particular JURISDICTION (state) and is free to do so.

Admonition. A reprimand from a judge to a person who has committed an OFFENSE. Such admonition usually warns the individual that any repetition of misconduct will be treated more severely.

Adopt. To take as one's own; to approve, such as adopting a law.

Adopted child. A child who is not the natural offspring of a parent but who, by legal ACTION, has become a true child. Sometimes, but not always, an adopted child is considered a legal HEIR.

Adult. In CIVIL LAW, a male who has reached 14 years of age and a female who has reached 12 years of age. In COMMON LAW, one becomes an adult now at 18 years of age in most states.

Adult children. Daughters or sons who have attained the age of an ADULT.

Adulteration. The act of placing an impure ingredient, or a cheaper ingredient, into another substance.

Adultery. Sexual intercourse by a married person with someone other than his or her spouse.

Advance payment. A payment made before it is due; a payment made early in anticipation of a future DEBT.

Adventitious. Accidental; not arising out of the ordinary course of events.

Adventurer. One who takes a risk in a business venture; a mine promoter, or one who owns shares in a mining venture.

Adversary. An opponent in a LAWSUIT.

Adversary proceedings. An ACTION in law in which there are opposing parties.

Adversary trial. A TRIAL in which there are opposing parties, with each one having the opportunity to present its side of the issues.

Adverse interest. INTEREST that displaces one's own interest, partially or completely.

Adverse party. A PARTY on the opposing side in a LAWSUIT.

Adverse possession. Taking POSSESSION of PROPERTY when it is known that someone else has laid CLAIM to it.

Advise. To counsel; to give advice; to give notice.

Advisement. A JUDGE takes a matter under advisement when he wants more time to consider all the facts before rendering a decision.

Advisory jury. A JURY appointed by a federal JUDGE to help decide questions of fact.

Advisory opinion. A written OPINION given by a JUDGE or a tribunal of judges upon a question of law. Such opinion is not ren-

dered during the consideration of a legal matter in progress.
Advocacy. Active espousement of a cause or support of an issue.
Advocate. An ATTORNEY AT LAW; one who gives legal advice and pleads for a client in a LAWSUIT.
Aeronautics and Space Act. A federal law establishing a national space program. The STATUTE also provides that space shall be used only for peaceful purposes that will benefit all of mankind.
Affair. A LAWSUIT; a matter. Also, a love relationship, usually nonmarital.
Affected with a public interest. Something that concerns the community.
Affiance. To PLEDGE, specifically for a man and a woman to agree that they will marry.
Affiant. One who makes an AFFIDAVIT; a DEPONENT.
Affidavit. A written STATEMENT of facts, sworn to and signed by a DEPONENT before a NOTARY PUBLIC or some other authority having the power to witness an OATH.
Affidavit of defense. An AFFIDAVIT stating that the DEFENDANT has a good defense; an affidavit of merit.
Affidavit of good faith. An AFFIDAVIT made by one who is appealing a case, stating that the APPEAL is based upon a true belief that the JUDGMENT should be overturned; an affidavit stating that the appeal has not been made for the purposes of delay.
Affidavit of merits. An AFFIDAVIT stating that the DEFENDANT has a good case, giving the facts substantiating the CLAIM.
Affidavit of demurrer. An AFFIDAVIT made by an ATTORNEY in which he objects to the court's DECISION, stating that the objection is not made for the purposes of delay.
Affidavit to hold to bail. An AFFIDAVIT made by a PLAINTIFF, clearly stating that the DEFENDANT is indebted to the plaintiff and that there is valid cause for a LAWSUIT; an affidavit required before a defendant can be arrested and held in custody.
Affiliation. A close association; an alliance, as with a business or political organization.
Affiliation proceeding. BASTARDY PROCEEDING, to determine the paternity of a child and to decide whether a certain man is liable for its support. ➤ PATERNITY PROCEEDING.
Affinity. The ties and relationship between a person and the blood relations of his or her spouse. (A judge is disqualified from a case if he is in any way related to, or has any affinity to, any one of the LITIGANTS.)
Affirm. To confirm or RATIFY; a COURT OF APPEALS affirms or disaffirms a decision of a lower court.
Affirmance. The confirmation of a LAW or DECISION made by another COURT or legislative body.
Affirmant. One who ATTESTS to a fact, or confirms something, without taking an OATH.
Affirmation of fact. A STATEMENT confirming the details of a CONTRACT or TRANSACTION, not merely an expression of opinion.
Affirmative action. Action taken by an authority to remedy a situa-

tion, rather than to punish anyone for a wrongdoing.

Affirmative charge. A CHARGE to a JURY that no matter what the EVIDENCE may show, the DEFENDANT cannot be CONVICTED under the existing INDICTMENT. Thus, the charge attempts to remove the issue from the jury's consideration.

Affirmative defense. A DEFENSE that introduces new matter which, even if the PLAINTIFF's contentions are true, constitutes a defense to the complaint. An affirmative defense goes beyond the mere denial of the plaintiff's ALLEGATIONS.

Affirmative relief. COMPENSATION (RELIEF) due to the DEFENDANT, not the PLAINTIFF. The defendant's relief may come through a separate suit other than the one that the plaintiff had instituted.

Affirmative statute. A law drawn up so that its provisions *must* be carried out.

Affirmative warranty. A WARRANTY that confirms the existence of a fact at the time an INSURANCE POLICY is entered into.

Affix. To attach to; to sign; to attach one's signature.

Affix a seal. To attach one's signature and stamp, or seal.

Afforce. To strengthen; to increase.

Affray. An argument or fight in a public place, resulting in INTIMIDATION of the public and DISTURBANCE OF THE PEACE.

Affreightment. An AGREEMENT by a ship owner to rent his ship for the carrying of cargo.

Affront. An insult.

Aforesaid. As already mentioned.

Aforethought. Premeditated; deliberate. A crime committed after planning and scheming is said to be carried out aforethought.

Against the evidence. Contrary to the weight of the EVIDENCE. (A VERDICT against the evidence is one that is not supported by the evidence.)

Against the peace. A term used often in claiming a BREACH OF PEACE.

Against the weight of the evidence. Contrary to the EVIDENCE, as a VERDICT that does not actually conform to the evidence that has been presented.

Against the will. A STATEMENT that something was done against someone's will, as RAPE, or ASSAULT, or ROBBERY.

Age of consent. The age at which a female is legally entitled to consent to sexual intercourse or to marriage. This age differs from state to state. In some states, an age of consent also exists for males.

Age of discretion. Usually fourteen years, the age at which a child is judged old enough to choose a guardian.

Age of nurture. A child under seven years of age.

Age prayer. A request by a minor, or his or her representative to delay action on a legal matter until reaching majority.

Agency by estoppel. A situation in which an AGENT (DEPUTY) of a PRINCIPAL exercises powers that were not actually granted to the agent. In such cases, even if the principal is unaware that the agent has exercised powers that were not granted, the principal is bound by the agent's actions.

Agency by necessity. An emergency situation in which an AGENT (DEPUTY) exercises powers not granted to him by the PRINCIPAL. In such cases, the agent is acting properly even though he has not received authorization to act.
Agency by operation of law. An agency existing because it conforms to the prevalent law, not because of an agreement between AGENT and PRINCIPAL.
Agency in fact. An agency that comes about from an AGREEMENT between PRINCIPAL and AGENT.
Agency-shop agreement. An AGREEMENT that permits an employee to join or not join a LABOR UNION. However, a prerequisite of employment is that he must pay the union initiation fees and the regular dues.
Agenda. Items to be discussed at a meeting.
Agent. An individual authorized by another to act for her or him; one entrusted with conducting another's business affairs.
Agent's lien. The legal right to payment from a PRINCIPAL for services rendered by an AGENT. This will include reimbursement for necessary expenditures, advances, and commissions due the agent from the principal.
Aggravated assault. An attack carried out with the intent to rob, rape, or kill. It is a more violent offense than *ordinary assault* or *common assault.*
Aggravation. Any circumstance that increases the gravity of an OFFENSE, such as an armed robbery in which the PERPETRATOR repeatedly threatens to maim or kill the victim.
Aggravation of damages. An increase in the amount of DAMAGES granted to the PLAINTIFF because of circumstances surrounding the INJURY. Also, increase in the amount of damages because the DEFENDANT displayed exceptional MALICE in carrying out the offense.
Aggravation of disability. An INJURY superimposed upon an original injury, often encountered in a WORKMEN'S COMPENSATION disability.
Aggregate. The total; the entire sum; the complete amount.
Aggregate liability. The total amount covered by a liability INSURANCE POLICY. It may cover a specific limited amount for one CLAIM and an aggregate amount for several claims of the same nature. ➤ INSURANCE, LIABILITY.
Aggressor. A person who starts a fight or other violent act.
Aggrieved party. The person who has suffered from an OFFENSE; the one whose legal RIGHTS have been threatened or damaged.
Agitator. An individual who incites or stirs up a situation, especially one who stimulates discontent.
Agrarian law. LAWS that break up large land holdings, distributing such land to a number of people. Also known as Agrarian Reform acts.
Agreed case. A CASE in which all parties concerned submit to the COURT an agreed-upon statement of the facts that are essential to the determination of the LITIGATION. Thus the court does not

have to decide questions of fact but may concentrate on matters of law.

Agreed order. An ORDER of the COURT made upon the AGREEMENT of the parties in the CASE.

Agreement. The meeting of minds on an issue. When opposing parties reach an agreement, the case is said to be settled.

Agreement of sale. A CONTRACT to purchase something to be carried out at some time in the future. The OWNER agrees to sell, and the purchaser agrees to buy.

Aid and abet. To help in the commission of a crime. The aid may be by words or acts. ➤ ACCESSORY TO A CRIME, ACCESSORY BEFORE THE FACT.

Aid and comfort. To give assistance; to support. Giving "aid and comfort" to an enemy during war is a crime. ➤ ACCESSORY AFTER THE FACT.

Aiding an escape. A CRIMINAL OFFENSE, whether committed by a jailer or other person.

Air piracy. The forceful or violent takeover of an aircraft. ➤ HIJACKING.

Air rights. The RIGHT to build above a piece of land or existing structure or building.

Aisne. The firstborn in a family.

Alcoholic. A person who is addicted to alcohol.

Alcoholic beverage. Any drink containing alcohol, such as beer, wine, whiskey, etcetera.

Alcometer. An apparatus that calculates the amount of alcohol that has been imbibed, frequently used by police to determine if someone is or is not intoxicated.

Alderman. A city OFFICIAL, serving in the government under a MAYOR.

Aleatory contract. A CONTRACT in which the outcome—benefits or losses—to the contracting parties depends upon an uncertain event or circumstance.

Alia enormia. A term used by the PLAINTIFF'S attorney to claim additional injuries, not specifically stated, that were sustained by the plaintiff. The Latin words mean "other wrongs."

Alias. A word indicating that someone was called by more than one name; otherwise (Latin).

Alias dictus. Otherwise called (Latin).

Alias execution. A second attempt to carry out an EXECUTION (a legal performance) after the first one has failed to accomplish its purpose.

Alias subpoena. A second SUBPOENA, issued because the initial one failed to accomplish its purpose.

Alias summons. A second SUMMONS, served because the original one was defective or improperly served.

Alias writ. A second WRIT, issued in the same case because the original one was ineffective.

Alibi. A STATEMENT OF CONTENTION by an individual that he or she was so distant when a crime was committed, or so engaged in other provable activities, that participation in its commission was impossible.

Alien enemy. A CITIZEN of a foreign country with whom one's own country is at war.

Alien friends. CITIZENS of a foreign country with whom one's own country is at peace.

Alien née. An individual who was born in a foreign country.
Alienable. Subject to being transferred.
Alienate. To transfer the TITLE to PROPERTY; to give up the OWNERSHIP of property voluntarily.
Alienation clause. A provision cancelling an INSURANCE POLICY if the insured PROPERTY is sold.
Alienation of affection. A wrongful act of an individual that interferes with the affection that one spouse has for another. (A husband deprived of his wife's love because she has fallen in love with another man has suffered alienation of affection. The same is true of a woman whose husband falls in love with another woman.)
Alieni juris. Under the control of another individual, such as a child who is under the authority of a GUARDIAN (Latin).
Alienist. A psychiatrist. In legal matters, alienists are often called upon to testify as to the mental condition of a defendant.
Alimony. The monetary support that one is entitled to from a spouse after a SEPARATION or DIVORCE. The COURT usually fixes the amount of such alimony.
Aliquot. A portion; a fraction. In establishing a TRUST, an aliquot is that percentage of the total that a beneficiary is entitled to.
Aliter. Otherwise; otherwise decided.
All and singular. The total and each of its component parts; all, without exception. (A term frequently used in the language of WILLS and other legal DOCUMENTS.)
All fours. Two similar law CASES, alike in the facts involved and in the DECISIONS arrived at.
Allegation. The CONTENTION of a PARTY in a LAWSUIT, including what he intends to prove.
Allegation of fact. The recitation of the factual details by a party in a LAWSUIT, setting forth what actually took place in dealings with the other party.
Alleged. Claimed; charged.
Allegiance. Loyalty to one's country and its government. Also, faithfulness to an individual, or to an inanimate thing such as an organization, or an abstract thing such as an idea.
Alliance. In INTERNATIONAL LAW, a close association or AGREEMENT for JOINT ACTION between two or more countries. A union or close relation between two people or two families.
Allocable. The breaking down of a lump sum and distributing it in several parts. (This term is often used in analyzing business accounts.)
Allocate. To allot; to ration; to assign.
Allocution. The questioning of a convicted person for the purpose of ascertaining whether there is any legal reason why the VERDICT of GUILTY should not have been pronounced. (In actuality, allocution is a mere formality of the court.)
Allograph. A signature made by one person for another.
Allotment. A distribution of shares, or of land, or of any other PROPERTY. A portion of something.

Allow. To permit; to give one his due; to approve; to concede; to accept as true.
Allowance. An assigned amount of money, usually paid on a regular, periodic basis. A deduction; the act of allowing.
Allowed claim. A DEBT that is legal and entitled to be paid.
Allurement. An exceptional attraction; something that entices. (A child may be allured to trespass on another's property by an attractive swimming pool, etcetera.)
Alluvion. Earth or sand that is added to property by the action of water. Waves may deposit solid material on lands bordering the sea.
Alter. To change, either by increasing or decreasing; an ASSESSMENT may be altered.
Alter ego doctrine. A DOCTRINE that treats the CORPORATION and those owning its stock as identical. This doctrine is applied without regard to the corporate entity, in order to further justice.
Altercation. A TRIAL by examination of WITNESSES. (In general usage, altercation means a fight or dispute.)
Alternate legacy. A LEGACY in which the TESTATOR (the person who has made the WILL) gives one of two or more things, without designating exactly which one.
Alternative contract. A CONTRACT in which the OBLIGATIONS of the parties involved may be fulfilled in one of several ways.
Alternating custody. A division of the CUSTODY of a child or children between the two separated or divorced parents. ➤ DIVIDED CUSTODY.
Alternative judgment. A JUDGMENT that permits SATISFACTION in one of several ways.
Alternative obligation. An OBLIGATION that can be satisfied in more than one way. (For example, an obligation could be satisfied either by turning over a certain thing *or* by paying a certain sum of money.)
Alternative pleading. A SUIT couched in such terms that the several facts presented leave doubt upon which particular fact the ATTORNEY will base his or her case.
Alternative relief. A request for a REMEDY in which the PLAINTIFF is not sure of the exact RELIEF to which he or she is entitled, thus permitting the court to direct one of several forms of relief.
Alternative remainders. Disposition of property in alternative ways, with one method to take effect only if the other does not. The second method of disposition then substitutes for the first.
Alternative remedy. A choice of REMEDY left open by the law. (A new STATUTE may create a new remedy without doing away with one that existed previously.)
Alternative writ of mandamus. A COURT ORDER commanding the person against whom it is issued to do a certain thing or else to show cause why he or she should not be forced to do it (Latin). ➤ MANDAMAS.
Altius tollendi. The right of an individual to build a house as high

as desired, unless there is a preexisting legal restraint (Latin).

Alto et basso. An AGREEMENT by two parties in a DISPUTE to submit all their outstanding differences to ARBITRATION (Latin, meaning "high and low").

Amalgamation. The merging or joining together of two or more different elements or things. (Two or more companies or organizations may amalgamate, thus forming one.)

Ambassador. A high-ranking diplomatic representative, sent by one SOVEREIGN STATE to another sovereign state; an ENVOY.

Ambiguity. A word, phrase, expression, sentence, or paragraph of unclear meaning. A STATEMENT that can be interpreted in more than one way. A statement that contradicts itself.

Ambulance chaser. A term for an ATTORNEY AT LAW of dubious reputation who solicits accident cases. (This kind of lawyer is said to "chase ambulances" so as to solicit the business of the injured party.) ➤ INDIRECT SOLICITATION.

Ambulatory jurisdiction. A JURISDICTION that is not limited to one area but can be effected in various places.

Ambulatory will. The right of a TESTATOR to change a WILL.

Amenable. Accountable; answerable to the law; liable to PUNISHMENT.

Amend. To correct; to change; to alter so as to correct defects in a DOCUMENT.

Amendment as of course. A change in a PLEADING (the written presentation of a case), made in such a manner and at such a time as to make permission of the court unnecessary.

Amendment by compulsion. A change in PLEADING ordered by the court because the original pleading was couched in such terms as to prejudice or delay the TRIAL.

Amendment of income tax return. Changes made by the taxpayer to his or her income tax return, usually done to correct defects in the original filing.

Amendment of pleading. Changing a PLEADING so as to correct errors and to make a more accurate presentation of the facts.

Amendments to the Constitution. Modifications to the UNITED STATES CONSTITUTION, which must first be ratified by three-quarters of the states in order to become Amendments, and thus part of the Constitution. (See pages 389–95 for the complete texts of the Amendments to the Constitution.)

Amends. SATISFACTION to an injured PARTY by the making of payments or reparations; the correction of a wrongdoing.

Amenity. Something that improves the desirability of a PROPERTY and enhances the enjoyment of its owners. (The construction of a swimming pool constitutes an amenity, or improvement.)

Amercement. A PENALTY or fine imposed by a COURT upon its own OFFICERS or employees for improper conduct. (A court may impose an amercement upon a sheriff for not turning in monies he has collected.)

American Arbitration Association. A voluntary, not-for-profit organization that maintains a panel of ARBITRATORS who will hear labor or other DISPUTES. (BINDING ARBITRATION requires the parties involved to accept the decision of the arbitrator.)

American Bar Association. An organization of members of the bar (ATTORNEYS AT LAW) from the various states.

American Civil Liberties Union. A voluntary, not-for-profit organization that helps to maintain the CIVIL RIGHTS of citizens whose rights are threatened, or may possibly be threatened.

American clause. A clause in a MARINE INSURANCE policy that the insurer is responsible for the full amount called for in the policy, even if the insured is covered by another similar policy.

American Federation of Labor-Congress of Industrial Organizations (A.F.L.-C.I.O). An organization composed of the two largest labor unions in the country, namely, the American Federation of Labor and the Congress of Industrial Organizations.

American Law Institute. A nonprofit organization whose main objective is to define and clarify the COMMON LAW principles that exist in our country. (The common law does not depend upon written STATUTES but rather upon the principles laid down by the courts in their decisions.)

American Law Reports. Series of books that print and annotate cases that were and are important in American LAW. The *Reports* are referred to frequently by ATTORNEYS involved in current LAWSUITS.

American Specialty Boards. These are organizations which qualify—through written and oral examinations—physicians as specialists. A diploma from a Specialty Board signifies that the physician is an expert in his or her particular field of medicine.

Amicable action (suit). A SUIT brought mutually by two parties for the joint purpose of obtaining the court's DECISION on a doubtful question of LAW.

Amicus curiae. A friend of the court (Latin). Someone not directly involved in a LAWSUIT who supplies information on some matter of law about which the court may be doubtful.

Amnesia. Loss of memory. It may be temporary or permanent, and it may be due to disease or to being in an emotionally disturbed state.

Amnesty. A PARDON, usually for some OFFENSE against the government. (Amnesty often carries with it the understanding that the offending party will return to duty and obedience to the government.)

Amortization. The paying off of an indebtedness through regular installments. (A MORTGAGE on PROPERTY is amortized over a period of years through regular payments.)

Amount covered. The sum for which the INSURER is liable should the INSURED suffer a loss.

Amount of dispute. The monetary value of something that is in dispute between two LITIGANTS.

An et jour. A year and a day, a frequent sentence meted out by a court (French).

Analytical jurisprudence. A philosophy of LAW that results from comparing and analyzing various legal concepts. Analytical JURISPRUDENCE does not depend upon any one theory or upon existing laws or principles.
Anarchy. Lawlessness; lack of government. Anarchy usually implies public confusion and disorder.
Ancestor. A person from whom one is descended; a progenitor. (Specifically, a parent, grandparent, great-grandparent, etcetera.)
Ancient deed. A true and valid DEED that is more than thirty years old.
Ancillary administration. A proceeding in a locality where a deceased person owned PROPERTY, but which is a different locality from the one in which the estate is being administered.
Ancillary jurisdiction. The RIGHT of a COURT to aid and regulate a DECISION reached in an original SUIT in another court. Through the ancillary process, relitigation (trying a case again) is avoided, and fraudulent attempts on the part of the defendant to escape responsibility are nullified.
Ancillary proceeding. A PROCEEDING that complements a proceeding in another court. Also, a proceeding that is secondary or subordinate to another action.
Ancillary suit. A SUIT that grows out of another suit, such as an ACTION for the enforcement of a JUDGMENT decided in another COURT or the same court. (An ancillary suit is sometimes brought to prevent a defendant from fraudulently transferring PROPERTY so as to avoid payment of a judgment against him.)
Anesthesia, consent for. Written permission given by a patient or by his or her parent, guardian, or spouse (if the patient is unable to act in his own behalf) for an anesthesiologist to render anesthesia for a surgical procedure. (In dire emergencies when the patient cannot act for himself, the anesthesiologist may proceed without consent.)
Animus. The mind or the soul; intention and design (Latin). A crime committed with animus is one in which the PERPETRATOR knows full well what he is doing and has planned it.
Animus quo. The intention or design that accompanies the performance of an act (Latin).
Annex. To join; to attach.
Anno domini (A.D.). In the year of our Lord (Latin).
Annotation. Notes and comments on the various points in a legal ACTION, intended to illustrate their meaning and importance.
Annual. Yearly; occurring once a year.
Annual depreciation. A yearly computation on the decreasing value of a PROPERTY, based upon the estimated life of such property.
Annuity. A yearly payment, usually paid by an INSURANCE company to an INSURED. The annuity may be for for a certain specified number of years or for life.
Annulment. The act of cancelling something; making it void. An annulment of marriage is a legal

decision that the marriage never existed. (An annulment is not a DIVORCE.)

Anomalous. Deviating from the common RULE. Something is anomalous when it cannot be related to anything in the ordinary.

Anomalous plea. A DEFENDANT's answer to an ACCUSATION that is partly affirmative and partly negative.

Answer. The reply of a DEFENDANT to the ALLEGATIONS and ACCUSATIONS of a PLAINTIFF. Often, it constitutes a denial of the charges made by the plaintiff.

Answer over. PLEADING again after defects in one's presentation have been made by the opposite party. Also known as a PLEADING OVER or RESPONDEAT OUSTER.

Ante-factum Before the fact (Latin). An act done before; a previous act.

Ante mortem. Before DEATH; words often used to describe a statement made prior to dying (Latin).

Antecedent debt. A previously contracted DEBT, one that was once binding but has become unenforceable.

Antedate. To date a DOCUMENT prior to its actual date of execution. (Antedating is sometimes done illegally to escape TAX or other OBLIGATIONS.)

Antenatal. Before birth; prenatal.

Antenuptial contract. An AGREEMENT made between a man and woman prior to their MARRIAGE, often including provisions for the disposal of their property should DIVORCE or DEATH ensue. ➢ ANTENUPTIAL SETTLEMENT; PREMARITAL AGREEMENT.

Antenuptial settlement. A CONTRACT made between a man and woman prior to marriage, determining the disposition of their PROPERTY rights and interests.

Anticipation. The RIGHT to pay off a MORTGAGE before it is due, without the payment of a PENALTY for such action.

Anticipatory breach of contract. Failure to perform a PROMISE in a CONTRACT even before the contract has gone into effect.

Antinomy. An inconsistency, such as a contradiction of ideas existing in various provisions of a law.

Antitrust acts. For example, the Sherman Antitrust Act and the Clayton Act, which are federal laws aimed at preventing individuals, CORPORATIONS, combinations of corporations, or TRUSTS, from gaining or maintaining monopolies and thus restraining free trade.

Antitrust affidavit. In some states, an AFFIDAVIT must be filed each year by CORPORATIONS doing business in the state, attesting to the fact that they are not part of a pool or combination of corporations that restrain free trade.

Apertura testamenti. A Latin term for proving the authenticity of a WILL by having WITNESSES appear before a judge and testifying that they had signed the DOCUMENT.

Apex rule. In mining law, the finder of a MINING CLAIM on PUBLIC LANDS can claim the RIGHT to mine everything beneath and perpendicular to the surface area of his claim. The finder can thus follow and mine any vein that lies within his boundaries.

Aphasia. An inability of a person to find and use words to express his ideas, even though he is completely capable of understanding what is communicated to him, and his judgment and other mental faculties are unimpaired. (This condition frequently occurs following a stroke involving the speech area of the brain.)

Apparent authority. The AUTHORITY granted by a PRINCIPAL to an AGENT to act in his behalf. Such authority must be traceable to the principal and includes the right of the agent to do only those things that are usually and ordinarily done.

Apparent danger. A danger that is known and recognized by both an employer and his employee on the premises where the employee works. In CRIMINAL LAW, apparent danger refers to the doctrine of SELF-DEFENSE in HOMICIDE. Apparent danger would make the homicide apparently necessary to self-preservation. ➤ JUSTIFIABLE HOMICIDE.

Apparent heir. An HEIR who, by his relationship, is certain to inherit the ESTATE of his relative. (Same as HEIR APPARENT.)

Apparent jeopardy. The JEOPARDY of a DEFENDANT in a CRIMINAL ACTION being tried before a court with proper JURISDICTION and a JURY that has been properly selected and sworn.

Appeal. The request for a REVIEW by a higher court of a VERDICT or DECISION made by a lower court.

Appeal bond. Money that must be set aside by the PARTY making an APPEAL, should the appeal to a higher court fail. The monies go to pay costs and damages of the unsuccessful appeal.

Appearance. The actual presence in court of the DEFENDANT and PLAINTIFF in a SUIT. (By making an appearance, the parties to the suit place themselves within the AUTHORITY of the court.)

Appearance by attorney. The substitution of a LAWYER, acting as an AGENT for a PARTY to a SUIT.

Appearance docket. A RECORD, kept by a COURT CLERK, showing who was present at various times during the course of a TRIAL.

Appellant. The PARTY who appeals a CASE from a lower to a higher court.

Appellate court. A COURT with the authority to REVIEW the handling and decision of a case tried in a lower court.

Appellate jurisdiction. The power of a COURT to REVIEW, to uphold, or overturn a DECISION of a lower court.

Appellee. The RESPONDENT; the PARTY against whom an APPEAL is taken.

Append. To attach or add.

Appendix. Something added to a legal BRIEF, placed at the completion of the text.

Applicable local law. A LAW that would determine the HEIRS of someone who died without making a WILL and designating his heirs.

Applicant. Someone who files a PETITION or makes an APPLICATION; a petitioner; a person who applies for a legal REMEDY to his problem.

Application. A request; a PETITION. (An application for INSURANCE is a preliminary step toward being given an INSURANCE POLICY.)

Appointee. Someone who has been selected for a particular OFFICE or TRUST.

Apportion. To distribute portions of something, such as land, or RIGHTS, or shares.

Appraisal. An evaluation of the worth of PROPERTY. When ordered by a COURT, such estimation of value may be carried out by one or more reputable, qualified, disinterested parties.

Appreciation in value. Increase in the worth of PROPERTY. (It usually does not include increased value due to renovations or improvements.)

Apprehend. To find and ARREST; to take a suspect into CUSTODY.

Appropriate process. An ORDER to appeal and to produce books and records, and further, to TESTIFY, such process issued by the INTERNAL REVENUE SERVICE.

Appropriation. The act of taking control of something, such as the taking over of PRIVATE PROPERTY for public use.

Appropriation bill. A proposed LAW to authorize the spending of money and detailing the amount and purpose of such expenditure.

Appropriation of land. The taking of land. In such APPROPRIATION, it is assumed that payment for such occupation will be made in due time.

Appropriation of water. A diversion of a river or other body of flowing water so as to put it to some beneficial use.

Approval. The act of agreeing and sanctioning.

Approved endorsed note. An I.O.U. An AGREEMENT to pay a DEBT, endorsed by someone whose credit is good.

Approximation. A situation in which a charitable gift is applied as nearly as possible to conform to the original intent of the DONOR. (In such instances, for one reason or another, the exact wishes of the donor cannot be carried out.)

Appurtenance. Something that is attached to or is part of another thing. (In PROPERTY law, a barn or garden is an appurtenance to the main house.)

Aquatic rights. RIGHTS that people have to use rivers, lakes, and the sea for purposes of navigation, fishing, and pleasurable pursuits.

Arbiter. An individual appointed to settle a controversy according to the rules of EQUITY and LAW; a REFEREE.

Arbitrage. A business TRANSACTION in which one profits from the difference in the rates of money exchange. For example, stocks are bought in one market and sold in another to make profit from a difference in the two markets.

Arbitrary discretion. A DECISION made wrongfully, possibly because of a whim, or for unsound reasons.

Arbitrary power. The AUTHORITY to act in any manner one sees fit.

Arbitrary punishment. PUNISHMENT that is completely up to the presiding judge and not subject to provisions of any law.

Arbitration. The submission by two contesting parties of their disagreement to an impartial ARBITRATOR, usually agreeing that his ruling in the DISPUTE will be binding and final.

Arbitration clause. A provision in a CONTRACT to submit any present or future disagreement to an ARBITRATOR, whose decision in the matter shall be final and binding.

Arbitrator. A disinterested person, chosen by the parties in a DISPUTE, who will hear the details of the dispute and who will render a DECISION as to how the dispute shall be settled.

Arguendo. For the sake of ARGUMENT, to assume that something is true even if one doesn't believe it to be true (Latin).

Argument. A presentation in a legal CASE that attempts to convince people that their CONTENTIONS are right.

Argument on appeal. A legal ARGUMENT set before a court to aid it in making a proper JUDGMENT. Such an APPEAL will submit facts and points of law to bolster its CONTENTION.

Argumentative instruction. Suggestion by the COURT to the JURY, urging it to pay special attention to certain facts in the case. Such INSTRUCTION may tend to influence the jury's decision, but it is permissible so long as it does not prejudice the VERDICT.

Armed force. A posse; a group of armed civilians authorized by the official PEACE OFFICER of the community to aid in the capture of criminals and the prevention of crime.

Armed robbery. A ROBBERY by one who carries a lethal WEAPON, thus threatening bodily harm to the victim.

Armistice. A TRUCE; a halt in combat between two or more nations.

Arms. A weapon. It may be carried legally for purposes of self-defense; or it may be carried illegally with intent to do harm.

Arm's-length transaction. An expression stating that a TRANSACTION was open and above board, not resulting from some inside manipulation or deal.

Arraignment. The act of bringing a DEFENDANT into COURT for the purpose of answering CHARGES against him.

Arrears. Money that is unpaid, such as unpaid rent; or a balance that is overdue on a loan.

Arrest. The taking of a person into CUSTODY by an OFFICER of the LAW. To deny an individual his personal liberty by placing him under the JURISDICTION of the law.

Arrest of judgment. A COURT'S delay in rendering a JUDGMENT because of some defect in the TRIAL that might result in a reversal of the VERDICT on APPEAL.

Arrest without warrant. An ARREST carried out by a PEACE OFFICER, or even a private citzen, under circumstances in which there is certainty or almost absolute certainty that a particular crime has been committed. (As an example, the arrest of a person seen as he is committing a crime.)

Arrogation. **1.** The act of claiming or taking more than is actually due, or taking something that is not rightfully due. **2.** The adoption of someone who has reached adulthood.

Arson. Willfully setting fire to PROPERTY.

Articles. The various provisions of a LAW, an ORDINANCE, or a CONTRACTUAL AGREEMENT. (A PARTNERSHIP AGREEMENT, for example, may contain many articles or CLAUSES making up the total arrangement.)

Articles of agreement. A written DOCUMENT specifying the several terms of the AGREEMENT.

Articles of impeachment. A formal, written CHARGE, outlining the reasons why IMPEACHMENT has been instituted. (Impeachment merely cites the ACCUSATION. After impeachment, a TRIAL must be held to prove whether or not the ACCUSED is GUILTY.) The term impeachment is used most often when referring to a public official who is suspected of wrongdoing.

Articles of incorporation. The DOCUMENT by which a CORPORATION is formed and organized under the CORPORATION LAWS of the state. (Each state has its own laws of incorporation.)

Articles of the peace. A sworn COMPLAINT made by a person who states he has been threatened with BODILY HARM. As a consequence, the COURT may order the person who has made the threat to give assurance that there will be no violent act. Failing this assurance, the court may take such an individual into CUSTODY.

Articles of war. The various provisions making up the CODES OF CONDUCT and justice governing the armed forces of our country. These ARTICLES include the disciplinary action to be taken upon violation of the articles of war.

Articulated pleading. A setting forth of the COMPLAINT or the DEFENSE against a complaint in separate CLAUSES (ARTICLES), each specifying a particular issue in the case.

Artifice. A trick; a cunning device. (A presentation made with artifice tries to trick the COURT and/or JURY into believing something that is not actually true.)

Artificial insemination. A method of causing a pregnancy in which semen, usually from an anonymous donor, is introduced by injecting it from a syringe into the vagina.

Artificial person. A COMPANY or CORPORATION.

Artificial presumptions. Also known as *legal presumptions.* An ASSUMPTION of truth based upon the LAW, as distinguished from an assumption that derives its effect from a natural tendency to believe.

As between. The relative position of two people in reference to a third person, with one party having a different relationship from the other in regard to the third person.

As is. An expression denoting the fact that goods are being sold in the condition the seller has stated they were in. Such goods are sold as is. (It is the purchaser's responsibility to discover if such goods are damaged.)

Ascertain. To find out; to make certain, without doubt.
Aspersions. Damaging criticisms. (To cast aspersions upon someone's reputation implies that the person is not honorable.)
Asphyxiation. Suffocation due to lack of oxygen or to too much carbon dioxide in the blood.
Assailant. Someone who ASSAULTS another person.
Assassination. A MURDER committed without cause or provocaton, such as a hired murder.
Assault. The infliction of BODILY HARM by one person on another, done willfully and illegally.
Assault and battery. A legal expression for an attack by one person against another, resulting in BODILY INJURY.
Assault with intent to murder. An attack carried out with MALICE AFORETHOUGHT and with the intent to kill.
Assault with intent to rape. An attack carried out with the intent of forcing SEXUAL INTERCOURSE against the will of the victim.
Assault with intent to rob. An attack causing BODILY INJURY, accompanied by an intent to commit ROBBERY.
Assay office. The governmental OFFICE that evaluates the various metals used in producing coins.
Assembly. **1.** A gathering and coming together of people to learn about and to discuss common issues. **2.** An Assembly in many states is the lower legislative body. (The State Senate is usually the upper legislative body.)
Assent. To agree; to comply; to express a willingness to do something.
Assert. To declare; to maintain; to charge as true.
Assess. To fix the value of something. (Private PROPERTY is assessed in order to determine the amount of TAXES to be paid.)
Assessed valuation. The precise value of PROPERTY upon which TAXES must be paid.
Assessment. The amount of money each person in a common enterprise must pay to receive his or her share of a common benefit. (Each owner in a COOPERATIVE APARTMENT, as an example, may be assessed a specific amount of money—according to apartment size—toward refurbishing the lobby or installing new elevators, etcetera.)
Assessment of damages. Fixing a VALUATION upon the amount of money a DEFENDANT must pay for DAMAGES he has caused the PLAINTIFF.
Assessment period. Taxable period.
Assessor. An OFFICIAL whose function is to evaluate the worth of PROPERTY.
Assets. Everything that is available, or can be made available, to pay a DEBT or debts. (A bank's assets includes all the money, SECURITIES, and PROPERTY that the bank can muster to pay its depositors and STOCKHOLDERS, should the need arise.)
Assets of a decedent's estate. Monies and PROPERTIES of a deceased person. Such monies and properties are made available to the estate's EXECUTOR for the

payment of outstanding DEBTS and for distribution to HEIRS.

Asseveration. A solemn STATEMENT, affirming the truth of something.

Assignable. Negotiable; transferrable.

Assignable error. An error occurring during a TRIAL that can be used and pointed out should an APPEAL become neccessary.

Assignable lease. A LEASE that can be transferred to someone else without getting permission from the LANDLORD.

Assigned risk. POLICIES issued by insurance companies only because state laws require them to issue such policies.

Assignee. The person to whom a RIGHT is assigned.

Assignment. The transfer of PROPERTY from one person to another.

Assignment for benefit of creditors. The transfer of a BANKRUPT individual's or company's assets to its CREDITORS.

Assignment of account. The transfer of money by a DEBTOR to an ASSIGNEE (CREDITOR) as such money becomes available.

Assignment of copyright. The transfer of a COPYRIGHT by the OWNER to another.

Assignment of counsel. A court-appointed ATTORNEY, usually for the purpose of serving as counsel to a DEFENDANT who lacks the money to engage his own attorney.

Assignment of errors. The STATEMENT of mistakes supposedly made in a TRIAL in a lower court. Such an assignment of errors is often used in the hope of obtaining a reversal of the verdict in a higher court.

Assignment with preferences. An ASSIGNMENT that specifies which CREDITORS should receive payment of their DEBT in full, before paying the claims of other creditors.

Assistant attorney general. A subordinate and aide to a state or federal attorney general.
> ATTORNEY GENERAL.

Associate. An ATTORNEY practicing with another attorney, or with a firm of attorneys, but not as a partner or member of the firm.

Association. A group of people who have formed an organization to pursue a common purpose.

Assumpsit. **1.** A PROMISE by one person to do something or pay a certain sum to another person. Such a promise may be written or oral, but has not been sworn to. **2.** In practice, assumpsit is a suit to recover damages for failure to carry out a contract (Latin, "he promised").

Assumption. The act of assuming responsibility; the act of taking for granted; the act of adopting an OBLIGATION.

Assumption of indebtedness. An AGREEMENT by one person to pay the DEBTS of another.

Assumption of mortgage. The AGREEMENT of a GRANTEE (one to whom a grant is made) of a mortgaged PROPERTY to pay the DEBT secured by the MORTGAGE.

Assumption of risk. A DEFENSE against a charge of NEGLIGENCE, based upon the fact that the

PLAINTIFF knew full well what the risks were, and therefore must assume those risks himself.

Assurance. > INSURANCE.

Assured. > INSURED.

Astipulation. An AGREEMENT. > STIPULATION.

Asylum. **1.** A SANCTUARY where a person is immune from ARREST. **2.** An outmoded term for a mental institution.

At any time prior to. Before such a date.

At arm's length. Dealing with someone strictly according to one's RIGHTS, without trusting another's PROMISES or seeming agreeableness; proceeding cautiously. > ARM'S-LENGTH TRANSACTION.

At large. **1.** Unrestrained; not in CUSTODY. **2.** Not representing any specific district or area. (A delegate-at-large may be chosen by an entire organization rather than by a restricted district.)

At law. According to LAW. (This implies that an issue depends upon an existing law, not upon EQUITY or fairness.)

Atheist. An individual who does not believe in the existence of God.

Atrocious assault. An attack characterized by cruelty and brutality.

Attach. To seize, such as to take over PROPERTY. Usually, such attachment is preliminary to a court PROCEDURE determining the fate of said property.

Attaching creditor. A CREDITOR who has attached, or taken over, the property of his DEBTOR.

Attachment execution. **1.** A PROCEDURE wherein PROPERTY or money is taken over to enforce a JUDGMENT rendered by a court. **2.** The taking of money from a salary in order to pay a DEBT that a court has judged must be paid.

Attachment of property. The taking of PROPERTY to be held by the COURT during a TRIAL. This is done so that the property serves as security should the case be decided against the DEFENDANT.

Attainder. The loss of CIVIL RIGHTS when someone has been convicted of a crime calling for the DEATH PENALTY.

Attainted. To have received a sentence of ATTAINDER, as a result of a conviction for high TREASON.

Attempt to evade taxes. An unlawful effort to avoid payment of TAXES due to the INTERNAL REVENUE SERVICE.

Attempted assault. An attempt to cause BODILY HARM to another, including acts to carry out the actual ASSAULT.

Attempted crime. Preparation for, planning for, and an actual effort to commit a CRIME. (It is a crime to attempt a crime.)

Attempted murder. A planned effort to kill someone. (Even though unsuccessful, an attempt at MURDER is a CRIME.)

Attempted robbery. A planned effort to commit a ROBBERY that has failed.

Attended by a physician. In an INSURANCE application, the above phrase refers to some serious illness or condition that required the services (attendance) of a doctor.

Attest. To state to be true; to bear WITNESS to.

Attestation. The witnessing of the

signing of a written DOCUMENT at the request of the maker of the document. Such attestation (as in making a WILL) includes signing the document as a WITNESS.

Attestation clause. A CLAUSE at the end of a WILL, whereby a WITNESS certifies as to the fact that the will was executed in his presence and was signed by him.

Attestation of a will. The witnessing of the signing of a WILL. (This is usually accompanied by the WITNESS signing an ATTESTATION CLAUSE.)

Attesting witness. Someone who signs his name to a DOCUMENT at the request of the maker or makers of the document, thus certifying its existence and identity.

Attorney (Attorney at law). A LAWYER; a COUNSEL; a member of the BAR; an OFFICER of the COURT who is engaged by a client to try a CASE.

Attorney-client privilege. The RIGHT of the client to have information he gives his attorney kept confidential.

Attorney general. The chief law officer of a state or of a nation.

Attorney in fact. A LAWYER who has received authorization, through a written DOCUMENT called a "POWER OF ATTORNEY," to act for a client, especially in specific legal matters.

Attorney of record. The LAWYER who has been specifically designated by a client to represent him in a legal matter.

Attorney's fee. The money paid to a LAWYER by his client for handling his legal problems.

Attorney's lien. The right of a LAWYER to retain the money he has collected for his client until such time as the client has paid his proper charges and fees.

Attorney's retainer. **1.** A preliminary fee paid to a LAWYER before he undertakes the job of handling his client's CASE. **2.** A yearly sum paid by an individual or COMPANY to a lawyer, or firm of lawyers, for handling their legal matters. ➤ RETAINER; RETAINER, GENERAL; RETAINER, SPECIAL.

Attractive nuisance doctrine. A PRINCIPLE stating that people who have on their premises something that is attractive to children, but which also has inherent dangers connected with it, are expected to take reasonable care that no harm comes to said children should they TRESPASS and utilize the attractive nuisance. (As an example, people with swimming pools are expected to have a fence around them or to cover them when they are not attended by an adult.)

Auction. A SALE, open to the public, of items and PROPERTY sold to the highest bidder.

Audit. To decide; to determine; to pass upon. An audit is an official review of accounts and records. Such a review may verify the accounts and records, or it may expose defects in them.

Auditor. **1.** An OFFICIAL of a governmental AGENCY whose job is to inspect and examine closely the records and disbursements of public monies made by duly appointed or elected authorities. **2.** An appointee of a COURT, assigned to inspect the records in a case where the accounts of the two parties to the action are in question.

Authentic act. An ACT that has been executed before a NOTARY PUBLIC.

Authority. JURISDICTION; power; a duly appointed or elected body given the power to carry out specific functions, such as a PORT AUTHORITY.

Authority by estoppel. Apparent AUTHORITY, not actual. The authority that a PRINCIPAL permits his AGENT to assume although he has not been actually granted such authority.

Authority of the court. The power granted to a COURT to act on certain types of legal matters.

Authority to execute a deed. The AUTHORITY to sign a written DOCUMENT transferring PROPERTY from one person to another.

Authorize. To empower someone to act; to give the AUTHORITY for someone to carry out a certain act.

Automatic continuance. When the term of a COURT ends before a CASE is settled, the case may be bound over automatically to the next session or term of the court. This is known as automatic continuance.

Automobile liability insurance. An INSURANCE POLICY guaranteeing payment to the INSURED for DAMAGES he must pay for personal injuries to other parties or for damages to someone's PROPERTY. Such policies usually specify the limits to which the insurance company is liable.

Autonomy. Freedom from control; independence. An autonomous country is free from influence or control by some other state.

Autopsy. Necropsy. The examination of a dead body by a pathologist for the purpose of finding the cause of death. Also known as a post-mortem examination.

Autopsy, testamentary authorization of. A STATEMENT in a WILL authorizing the performance of a post-mortem (AUTOPSY) examination.

Average and reasonable charges. Fees that are in line with those made by others in the area who have rendered a similar service.

Averment. A positive STATEMENT of a FACT, often made in a TRIAL in opposition to an argument by an ADVERSARY (an opposing party).

Avow. To make a solemn STATEMENT; to justify an act.

Avulsion. **1.** The loss of one's land due to the action of water, such as a flood or new direction of a stream or river that has washed away land. **2.** In medicine, the abrupt loss of tissue due to an accident, such as the loss of skin or muscle that has been torn away because of an accident.

Award. The decision of ARBITRATORS in giving monies to a PARTY who has claimed DAMAGES; the awarding of money to a worker injured during the course of his work. This latter award is said to be a *compensation award.*

B

Baby act. A PLEA in a contract DISPUTE that the action of the opposing party is not valid because the DEFENDANT was a MINOR when the CONTRACT was made.
Bachelor of Law. The degree given upon graduation from a college of law, abbreviated L.L.B.
Back taxes. Unpaid TAXES, due from ASSESSMENTS made in previous years.
Backing. Endorsement; guaranteeing the payment of.
Bad behavior. Bad CONDUCT of a criminal while serving a sentence; the opposite of GOOD BEHAVIOR, a condition necessary before receiving PAROLE.
Bad debt. A DEBT that cannot be collected.
Bad faith. CONDUCT in which there is a design of ill-will or an ulterior motive to commit DECEIT or FRAUD.
Bad faith cause of action. A LAWSUIT based upon the ASSUMPTION that the opposing party's CONDUCT showed reckless disregard of the suitor's RIGHTS and was unreasonable.
Bad title. A TITLE to PROPERTY that is defective, making a SALE to another unfeasible.
Badge of fraud. A FACT that throws suspicion upon a TRANSACTION, warning those involved to look deeply into the matter before completing it.
Bail. To release someone held in CUSTODY. Those who arrange bail undertake to see to it that the individual who is out on bail will appear in COURT when ordered to do so.
Bail bond. The posting of a BOND to release an individual who is being held in legal CUSTODY. The bond assures the COURT that the ACCUSED will appear at the proper time to answer CHARGES against him.
Bail bondsman. A person who puts up the BOND necessary to obtain the release of an ACCUSED. The accused pays the bail bondsman for rendering this service.
Bail in error. BAIL given by a DEFENDANT who intends to APPEAL a decision of the court and who wants to delay payment of a JUDGMENT until the appeal is heard.
Bail money. Money given as BAIL instead of a BAIL BOND.
Bailable. Someone who is capable of being bailed. Often, people accused of MURDER or TREASON are not permitted BAIL.
Bailable offense. A crime or OFFENSE that allows the ACCUSED to receive bail.
Bailee for hire. Someone to whom PROPERTY is delivered in TRUST for another. He receives COMPENSATION for so doing.
Bailiff. A GUARDIAN of PROPERTY; someone who is appointed to take charge of another's property or affairs; a person who is given authority by a SHERIFF to act as a DEPUTY in taking charge of prop-

erty for an OWNER who is involved in LITIGATION.

Bailiff errant. Someone appointed by a SHERIFF to perform acts such as serving SUBPOENAS, SUMMONSES, etcetera.

Bailment. The giving of PERSONAL PROPERTY by one person to another in TRUST. This is done for a specific reason, the property to be held until a CONTRACT is fulfilled. When the contractual OBLIGATION is fulfilled, the property is returned to the OWNER.

Bailor. Someone who delivers goods (bails) to another. He may or may not own the goods.

Bait. **1.** To anger or harass. **2.** Something used to entice.

Balance of convenience. In a doubtful CASE, the COURT must judge or balance out whether an INJUNCTION should be granted the PLAINTIFF against a DEFENDANT. The question is to balance the relief given the plaintiff against the INJURY the injunction will inflict upon the defendant.

Balance of power. In international matters, when a country wishes to protect itself against a country or countries that might attack it, it makes alliances with friendly countries so as to even out and balance the power that potentially unfriendly countries possess.

Balance sheet. A financial statement showing the ASSETS and LIABILITIES of a business.

Ballot. A piece of paper on which a voter records his vote.

Banishment. The DEPORTATION or expulsion of an individual from a country.

Bank a deal. To lend money to someone with whom one is making a CONTRACT, thus making the borrower into a CREDITOR.

Bank credit. The credit rating of a borrower at a particular bank with which he does business.

Bank of issue. A bank that issues its own NOTES, to be used as money. (This can be done only by governmental authorization.)

Bank robbery act. A federal LAW assuming JURISDICTION over crimes committed against a federal or national bank.

Bankable paper. DRAFTS, NOTES, or CHECKS, and other SECURITIES, of such high quality that they are treated by banks the same as cash.

Banker's acceptance. The giving of CREDIT by a bank by accepting a BILL OF EXCHANGE or DRAFT.

Banker's lien. The RIGHT of a bank to appropriate any PROPERTY or money of a customer to satisfy a LOAN that is due.

Banker's note. A NOTE that resembles a bank note but is issued by an unincorporated bank or private banker.

Bankrupt. Unable to meet one's OBLIGATIONS and pay one's CREDITORS. The term may apply to an individual, PARTNERSHIP, or CORPORATION. Legal BANKRUPTCY is decreed by a court.

Bankruptcy. The state of being unable to pay one's DEBTS. Such person or company is subject to being proceeded against by his CREDITORS, according to prevailing bankruptcy laws.
≫ INSOLVENCY.

Bankruptcy court. A court having JURISDICTION over BANKRUPTCY proceedings.

Bankruptcy laws. Laws passed to

aid CREDITORS in collecting money owed to them by a BANKRUPT person or company. Bankruptcy laws also can benefit those who are unable to pay their DEBTS. > CHAPTER ELEVEN; INSOLVENCY LAWS.

Banns of matrimony. Public announcement of an intended marriage, such proclamation often made in a church.

Bar. **1.** All the ATTORNEYS practicing in a community. **2.** Literally, the wooden railing separating the judge and the lawyers in a courtroom.

Bar association. An organization composed of ATTORNEYS. The various bar associations usually lay down the CODE OF ETHICS by which attorneys should practice their profession.

Bar examinations. Examinations that law school graduates must pass before being given the privilege to practice LAW in a particular state or before a FEDERAL COURT.

Bargain. An AGREEMENT between two or more PARTIES, such as occurs when one agrees to sell certain PROPERTY and the other agrees to buy such property.

Barratry. The practice of stirring up trouble between others, such as inciting LAWSUITS or quarrels.

Barred. Prevented. A LAWSUIT is said to be barred when the STATUTE OF LIMITATIONS expires.

Barren money. A DEBT that is owed without the payment of INTEREST.

Barrenness. Infertility; inability to bear offspring. (The term "sterility" was formerly used to denote barrenness.)

Barrister. A term used in English law to denote a legal COUNSELOR who pleads his case at the BAR.

Barter. To exchange one type of goods or PROPERTY for another. In former times, people often bartered for commodities rather than pay money for them.

Base. **1.** A foundation. **2.** Corrupt; evil.

Basic patent. A PATENT in a new field, often of great importance and recognized by the scientific community.

Bastard. A child BORN OUT OF WEDLOCK; an ILLEGITIMATE CHILD.

Bastardy proceedings. The legal action taken to compel the father to support his ILLEGITIMATE CHILD. > FILIATION PROCEEDING; PATERNITY PROCEEDING.

Battered child. A child injured as a result of the beatings by a parent.

Battery. Physical violence inflicted upon someone without his consent; unlawful INJURY to someone's body.

Bear interest. When making a LOAN, the lender usually asks that the money be augmented by the payment of INTEREST. Thus, a loan of $1,000 may bear interest of six percent per annum, or sixty dollars per year.

Bearer. The person who has a DOCUMENT in his possession and who will receive any payment that is due on said document. As an example, when a CHECK or NOTE is payable to bearer, anyone who presents the check or note will receive the payment therefrom.

Bearer paper. A NOTE or COM-

MERCIAL PAPER payable to the person who presents it for payment.

Become aware of. To have specific knowledge of.

Begging the question. An ARGUMENT that assumes that the QUESTION at issue has already been proved.

Behind closed doors. A conference held in secret.

Belligerent rights. RIGHTS to be exercised during the conduct of war. As an example, nations at war have laid down laws such as not killing innocent noncombatants, the humane treatment of prisoners of war, the medical care of enemy wounded, etcetera.

Belonging to. Legal ownership of.

Belongings. All PERSONAL PROPERTY, including OWNERSHIP of land or any other type of PROPERTY.

Bench. The JUDGE or judges of a COURT. An individual who "sits on the bench" is a judge.

Bench legislation. Decisions of judges that go contrary to the LAW, and which should have been left to the legislative bodies of the city, state, or federal governments to decide.

Bench trial. A TRIAL in which the judge will find the facts and apply the LAW, instead of letting the JURY do the job.

Bench warrant. A WARRANT for the arrest of someone charged with CONTEMPT or with some CRIMINAL OFFENSE. Such a warrant is issued by a judge, usually when the person accused has failed to appear to answer the charges against him.

Beneficial devise. A clause in a WILL that gives the DEVISEE (someone who inherits) a direct interest in the PROPERTY of the person who has made the will (the TESTATOR).

Beneficial estate. One in which the person inheriting the estate takes the property solely for his own use and benefit.

Beneficial interest. The right to profits from an ESTATE or PROPERTY, without owning the estate or property.

Beneficiary. An individual who receives BENEFITS granted to him by another. As examples, an HEIR is given money in a WILL by someone who has died; a person who is named to receive the monies from a LIFE INSURANCE POLICY. (Institutions, corporations, charitable organizations, etcetera, may all be beneficiaries.)

Benefit of cession. Immunity from imprisonment, granted to a DEBTOR who has turned over all his PROPERTY, as needed, to his CREDITORS.

Benefit of clergy. An outdated custom in which the clergy was exempt from TRIAL or PUNISHMENT in an ordinary (nonchurch) COURT. Today, the clergy are subject to the JURISDICTION of the same courts, for the same offenses, as laymen (nonclergy).

Benefit of counsel. The right of an ACCUSED to be represented by an ATTORNEY who will be given ample time to study and prepare a defense for his client.

Benefit theory. A theory that if one backs out of an AGREEMENT he must see to it that the opposite PARTY does not suffer.

Benevolent associations. Nonprofit organizations whose purpose is to help their members who are sick or who are visited by misfortune.

Bequeath. To leave something to someone, or to an organization, in a will.

Bequest. A LEGACY; a DEVISE.

Beseech. To ask for; to implore; to seek eagerly.

Best evidence. A DOCTRINE that the best available proof, and not a lesser proof, must be presented in COURT to prove a FACT.

Bestiality. **1.** The display of or acting out of inhuman qualities. **2.** Unnatural sex relations between a human and an animal.

Bestow. To grant; to bequeath.

Betrothal. A PROMISE to marry; an engagement.

Betterment act. A LAW that permanent improvements to PROPERTY which increase its value are recoverable, the occupant being paid by the real owner to the extent of the value of the improvements.

Beyond a reasonable doubt. The degree to which the PROSECUTION must prove its CASE in order to obtain a GUILTY verdict in a CRIMINAL ACTION.

Bias. PREJUDICE; a feeling of hostility and ill-will.

Bicameral. Having two legislative houses, such as a senate and a house of representatives, as opposed to a government having but one legislative parliament.

Bid bond. A BOND that a bidder must post when seeking a CONTRACT for construction of a public improvement.

Bid in. The act of bidding for one's own PROPERTY during an AUCTION sale. This is done so that the property is not sold for less than its real value.

Biennially. Once every two years.

Bigamy. A CRIMINAL OFFENSE whereby someone is simultaneously married to two people.

Bilateral contract. An AGREEMENT wherein both parties promise to perform certain acts and to fulfill OBLIGATIONS to each other.

Bilged. The condition of a ship in which water has leaked into the bottom through a hole or holes in the planks.

Bill. A COMPLAINT, a written STATEMENT of particulars in a SUIT, presented to a COURT of justice.

Bill for a new trial. In an EQUITY proceeding, a request is made of the COURT that an INJUNCTION (a STAY) be given so as to delay the carrying out of JUDGMENT already given. At the same time, a new TRIAL on the matter is requested.

Bill for foreclosure. A legal request by a MORTGAGEE (the owner) of a MORTGAGOR (the lender, usually a bank) to have the PROPERTY sold and thereby to get the money mortgaged, with costs and interest.

Bill for fraud. A statement that a DECREE of a court was based on FRAUD and that, therefore, the decree should be VACATED (declared nonexistent).

Bill not original. > DEPENDENT BILL.

Bill obligatory. A PROMISSORY NOTE; a BOND without any conditions attached to it. Also known as a *single bill.*

Bill of appeal. A written COMPLAINT in an APPEAL of FELONY.

Bill of attainder. > ATTAINDER.

Bill of certiorari. A BILL seeking the removal of a CASE from the JURISDICTION of a lower court to a higher court. It implies incompetency on the part of the lower court. A bill of certiorari applies to cases in courts of equity.

Bill of conformity. A bill in EQUITY wherein an EXECUTOR asks the help of the court in administering an ESTATE.

Bill of credit. Paper issued by a state or federal government to circulate and to be used as money. (Naturally, the "paper" is backed by the CREDIT of the issuing state or federal government.)

Bill of discovery. A written STATEMENT filed for the purpose of compelling a DEFENDANT to answer charges against him. Such bill would make the defendant answer all questions put to him and to produce all DOCUMENTS relative to the case.

Bill of entry. A listing and description of imported goods. The bill of entry is submitted to CUSTOMS officials. Also, a list of goods being exported.

Bill of evidence. A transcript of the TESTIMONY given at a TRIAL. Such written material is gathered from the notes of court stenographers.

Bill of exceptions. A written STATEMENT by a party in a TRIAL objecting to the RULINGS, INSTRUCTIONS, and DECISIONS of the trial JUDGE. Such a bill must state the circumstances and FACTS upon which the exceptions are based. The bill of exceptions is used as a device to obtain an appeal from the rulings of the lower court.

Bill of exchange. A written ORDER of one person upon another to pay money to a third person on demand, or on a specified date. Also known as a DRAFT.

Bill of health. A physician's certification that an individual is in good health. In MARITIME LAW, an official statement that a ship and its crew are in a healthy condition.

Bill of indictment. A criminal charge brought before a GRAND JURY prior to obtaining an INDICTMENT. If the grand jury indicts, the ACCUSED must stand TRIAL.

Bill of information. A written STATEMENT accusing someone of a CRIME and leading to a trial for the commission of said crime. Also known as a COMPLAINT.

Bill of interpleader. A written STATEMENT filed with a court to obtain a settlement in a dispute over PROPERTY or money between two opposing parties, each claiming the right to such property or money. The person filing the bill of interpleader wishes to free himself from possible LITIGATION concerning the money or property which he is holding, but in which he has no interest. By compelling a SETTLEMENT, the person filing the bill is freed from responsibilities relating to the property or money.

Bill of lading. A written memorandum acknowledging the RECEIPT of goods and acknowledging the responsibility of delivering such goods to their destination.

Within the bill, it is understood that payment will be made for rendering the service.

Bill of particulars. A written listing of the precise nature of the charges being leveled by the PLAINTIFF against the DEFENDANT. This information, when received by the defendant, will enable him to better prepare his defense. A bill of particulars can be obtained by the defendant on MOTION to the court.

Bill of peace. A bill filed for the purpose of doing away with repeated SUITS by various persons, at different times, on the same matter. A bill of peace is usually submitted to a COURT OF EQUITY.

Bill of review. One which requests a COURT OF EQUITY to review and revise or reverse its decision.

Bill of revivor. A bill submitted for the purpose of reviving a SUIT that has been terminated before a decision had been reached. Such a bill is often brought when either the PLAINTIFF or the DEFENDANT has died before the suit was concluded.

Bill of Rights. The guarantee of RIGHTS in the UNITED STATES CONSTITUTION. These rights are fundamental and include the basic privileges of all United States citizens. The Bill of Rights is contained within the first ten Amendments to the Constitution. (See pages 389–95 for the complete texts of the Amendments to the Constitution.) Most state constitutions also include a bill of rights, as written in the federal Constitution.

Bill of sale. A DOCUMENT giving evidence that PROPERTY has been sold to a purchaser by a seller.

Billy. A club or bludgeon. Police officers often carry a billy.

Bind. To cause a legal OBLIGATION. This obligation may come about as the result of a LAW, a CONTRACT, or a DECREE of a court. (One can bind himself as well as another person.)

Binder. A written memorandum which insures something immediately but temporarily, until an INSURANCE POLICY can be issued. (An insurance broker may see to it that a valuable ring, fur coat, etcetera, has a binder so that if it is lost or stolen before an insurance policy is issued, the purchaser will be covered.)

Binding. Obligatory; required.

Binding arbitration. An ARBITRATION in which the arbitrating parties *must* accept the findings and decisions of the ARBITRATOR or arbitrators.

Binding instruction. An INSTRUCTION by a JUDGE to a JURY that they are bound by certain existing laws in their deliberations and in their ultimate VERDICT.

Binding over. An act of a COURT ordering a DEFENDANT to furnish BAIL and appear at his TRIAL, or an act of a court freeing a defendant on his own recognizance with the understanding that he will keep the peace and appear at his subsequent trial.

Bipartite. In two parts.

Birth certificate. A CERTIFICATE filed with the proper authorities upon the birth of a child. Such certificate records the date and place of birth, the parents' names, etcetera. Birth certificates may be filed in local communities, counties, or seats of state governments.

Black Maria. An enclosed automobile, usually painted black, that transports prisoners or accused people to and from jails or prisons. Black Maria is a slang term.

Blackjack. A heavy metal WEAPON (often made of lead), covered with leather and having a flexible handle. Blackjacks are often carried by police officers, sometimes by criminals.

Blacklist. A list of persons to be avoided for one reason or another. (Employers occasionally make up a list of discharged employees that they send to other employers so that they will not hire them.)

Blackmail. EXTORTION. A CRIMINAL ACT in which an individual attempts to get money from another through threats. The threats may be of any nature, such as a threat to embarrass someone socially, or a threat to start a LAWSUIT unless certain monies are paid. Underlying all blackmail is the fact that the blackmailer is attempting to get money or property unlawfully.

Blacks. People of the Negro race.

Blank acceptance. An acceptance of a BILL OF EXCHANGE by writing one's name across its face. This signing is carried out before the bill is made and delivered.

Blank endorsement The endorsing of a PROMISSORY NOTE or BILL OF EXCHANGE by writing the name of the endorser, without stating the name of the PARTY to whom the note is to be paid.

Blanket policy. An INSURANCE POLICY covering a whole stock of merchandise. (This is necessary because goods are changing each day through sales and the receipt of new merchandise.)

Blasphemy. Malicious remarks or writings against God, usually aimed at influencing people to be irreverent.

Blockade. The act of preventing people from entering. Most often the term refers to prevention of shipping from entering a port or putting people or cargo onto land.

Blood feud. Ongoing hostility between two families, frequently resulting in violent attacks by one or the other, or both, families.

Blood money. Money paid as a reward for aiding in the capture and PROSECUTION of a person guilty of MURDER.

Blood tests. Most states require that couples undergo a blood test for syphilis prior to obtaining a marriage license. It is the duty, in most states, for the physician to report positive results to the health authorities.

Bludgeon. A dangerous WEAPON; a club of heavy wood, sometimes with lead or another metal hammered into its center.

Blue chips. Grade-A, high-class SECURITIES.

Blue laws. STATUTES or ORDINANCES banning certain activities on Sundays, such as certain athletic games or entertainment or the selling of merchandise in stores. These laws are now obsolete in many parts of the country.

(Originally, these laws were enacted so that people would attend religious services rather than go shopping or go to games or shows.)

Blue-ribbon jury. A specially selected JURY, composed of especially well-qualified individuals.

Blue sky law. A STATUTE to prevent the sale of STOCK of fraudulent COMPANIES. (The expression originates from the fact that some people are naive enough to buy "blue sky" if it is offered to them for sale.)

Board of aldermen. The governing body of a city or township.

Board of arbitration. A courtlike body, authorized to act in an impartial manner under the rules of ARBITRATION. The board hears the dispute and settles the controversy by rendering a decision.

Board of directors. A group of people who represent a CORPORATION and run its business.

Board of examiners. A state board with the AUTHORITY to approve or disapprove an applicant for a license to practice a profession that requires special knowledge and skills.

Board of fire underwriters. An association composed of people who are engaged in the fire insurance business.

Board of health. A group of people whose duties involve the safeguarding of the public's health. They have many functions, including overseeing the hygiene and sanitary conditions of a community, the administration of immunizations to prevent communicable disease, and the keeping of health statistics. (Boards of health may have county, city, or state JURISDICTION.)

Board of pardons. A state organization with the authority to grant PARDONS and to recommend CLEMENCY to criminals. The governor is usually a member of this board.

Board of parole. > PAROLE BOARD.

Board of review. An organization with the power to review the ASSESSMENTS made on PROPERTY. Also, a board that hears COMPLAINTS as to alleged excessive force and brutality by police officers.

Board of special inquiry. A board set up by the commissioner of immigration to investigate matters concerning immigration.

Board of supervisors. The governing board of a county.

Board of trade. A voluntary organization whose function is to promote and to protect business interests. Usually it is a citywide organization and functions for all commercial interests, although in some instances, its main purpose is to aid those interests of a particular trade.

Bodily harm. Physical force causing INJURY; an intentional attack against someone, resulting in injury to the body. > BODILY INJURY.

Bodily injury. Any harm coming to the body as the result of external force. Such INJURY may come from a blow or it may come from MALPRACTICE of a physician, or as the result of RAPE or attempted rape. > BODILY HARM.

Body execution. The confinement of an ACCUSED in JAIL; the arrest of an individual for the SATISFACTION of a JUDGMENT against him.
Body of laws. A collection of the statutes that are in effect.
Body of the offense. This phrase means that the crime charged has actually been committed by someone.
Body politic. The people as a whole; a situation in which each citizen agrees, with the entire citizenry, to be governed by common laws and rules and regulations. ➢ COMMONWEALTH; PUBLIC; STATE.
Bogus. Phony; fictitious. A bogus CHECK is one given by an individual upon a bank where he has no funds or no account.
Bona fide. True; honest; acting in good faith.
Bond. An OBLIGATION; a written DOCUMENT that states a certain sum of money is owed and will be paid on a certain date. Bonds carry INTEREST in most instances. There are many types of bonds, including *fidelity bonds, security bonds, corporate bonds, indemnity bonds, penal bonds,* and *investment bonds.*
Bondage. Slavery; involuntary servitude.
Bond-creditor. A CREDITOR who has taken a BOND to secure his DEBT. He will receive INTEREST on the money he has loaned.
Bondage. Slavery; involuntary servitude.
Bonded goods. Goods upon which a BOND has been issued to secure payment of the DUTY on them.
Bonded indebtedness. A DEBT secured by a BOND issue, the monies received to be used for corporate purposes. Such bonded indebtedness and bond issues must conform to the laws of the state in which they are issued.
Bonded warehouse. A building designated by the government as a storage place for imported merchandise. The BOND of the warehouse protects the government from possible losses, the bond being posted by the owner of the warehouse.
Bondsman. One who enters into a BOND as surety; a BAIL BONDSMAN issues a bond to arrange bail for an ACCUSED. If the accused fails to appear in court for trial, the bail money (put up by the bondsman) is forfeited.
Bonification. The forgiveness of TAXES, especially on merchandise to be exported; in effect, a method of enabling goods to be sold abroad as if they had not been taxed.
Bonis cedere. To surrender PROPERTY, as a DEBTOR does to a CREDITOR (Latin).
Bonus. A COMMISSION; money paid by an employer to an employee as a reward for good performance; an extra dividend; money paid by a MORTGAGOR to a MORTGAGEE for prepayment of a mortgage DEBT.
Boodle. Money received in an unlawful enterprise; money paid as a bribe, often referring to corrupt activity of a public official.
Book account. A ledger containing accounts of CREDITS and DEBITS, the entries based upon relations between a debtor and creditor.

Book value. The worth of a STOCK after deducting LIABILITIES from ASSETS; the value shown by the balance sheets of the COMPANY or CORPORATION.
Booked. Brought before a COURT to answer a CHARGE; bound legally to make an engagement. (An individual may be booked on charges of drunken driving.)
Bookmaker. A professional betting man who receives WAGERS from several people on sporting events and distributes the money, minus his COMMISSION, to the winners.
Books of account. Shop-books; books showing the transactions between a shop and a customer. Books in which merchants and traders keep their ACCOUNTS. (These books are often composed of cards or are loose-leaf sheets of paper.)
Bootlegging. The illegal selling of intoxicating liquors. This is often done to avoid payment of TAXES on the beverages.
Bootstrap sale. A device whereby an individual converts ordinary income into CAPITAL GAIN by selling corporate stock.
Booty. PROPERTY captured on land from an enemy during war.
Born alive. A newly delivered child, born with a heartbeat, but who never establishes breathing, and thus dies within minutes after being born.
Born out of wedlock. A child whose parents never married each other. > BASTARD; ILLEGITIMATE CHILD.
Borrow. To obtain a LOAN. Implied in borrowing is the intention and PROMISE to repay or to return.
Bottom hole contract. An AGREEMENT wherein the owners CONTRACT to pay the well drillers a certain sum of money when the well is drilled to a specified depth.
Bottomry. A CONTRACT in which a lender supplies money to repair a ship or to purchase necessary equipment for the ship. The OWNER of the ship agrees to repay the LOAN, with interest, on completion of its specified voyage. However, it is understood that if the ship should sink or not reach its destination, the lender shall lose the money he has loaned.
Bought and sold notes. Notes of a TRANSACTION by a BROKER. The note of a sale is called a *sold note*; the memorandum of the purchase is called a *bought note.*
Bound. Being controlled by an OBLIGATION. (Someone is bound to perform a certain act whether he wants to or not. Similarly, one is bound by the CLAUSES in a CONTRACT.)
Boundary suit. A LAWSUIT to determine the actual boundaries of adjoining lands; thus, a DISPUTE between two landowners re their boundary lines.
Boycott. A conspiracy among two or more people to interfere with the normal carrying on of business by another. Intimidation and threats may accompany boycotts, with active prevention of customers doing business with the boycotted party.
Breach. A violation of a LAW, either by COMMISSION or OMISSION.
Breach of confidentiality The failure to hold information confi-

dential. A LAWYER commits a breach of confidentiality if he reveals secret information a client has told him; similarly, a doctor commits this breach if he reveals CONFIDENTIAL INFORMATION his patient has told him.

Breach of contract. Failure to carry out the terms of a legal CONTRACT.

Breach of covenant. A failure to carry out the terms of a written AGREEMENT which has been duly witnessed and executed. The failure may be one of OMISSION or COMMISSION of an agreement.

Breach of faith. A violation of a moral DUTY, such as failure to carry out one's sworn PROMISE upon assuming a public office.

Breach of peace. Creation of a public disturbance. Loud, riotous, or other unsocial conduct may upset public tranquillity and thus constitute a breach of peace.

Breach of promise. A failure to go through with a PROMISE of marriage.

Breach of trust. A violation of a TRUSTEE to perform his duties properly. It may be willful or may be due to mere oversight or NEGLIGENCE. (A trustee is a person who is legally in charge of PROPERTY or money that ultimately will go to a BENEFICIARY.)

Breaking a case. An informal expression among judges of a court, expressed to one another, of their feelings in a CASE, with such views being given to find out if they are in sufficient agreement so as to render an OPINION or VERDICT.

Breaking a will. Contesting a WILL and succeeding in overturning its validity.

Breaking into. Illegally entering premises with intent to rob.

Breaking jail. Escaping from jail.

Breast of the court. A VERDICT of a COURT that has been decided but not yet announced is said to be in "the breast or bosom of the court." The expression also refers to the recollection and the conscience of the JUDGE in a specific matter brought before him.

Breviate. A short STATEMENT; an abstract; a BRIEF.

Bribery. An illegal act in which one offers, gives, or receives money or any other consideration in order to influence the actions of a public OFFICIAL or OFFICER. The corrupt giving or receiving of money as a price for official action.

Brief. A condensed, abbreviated written STATEMENT of a larger DOCUMENT. A brief is prepared by an ATTORNEY to serve as the basis for an argument in a LAWSUIT. It includes POINTS OF LAW that the lawyer intends to establish. ≫ BREVIATE.

Bring suit. The initiation of legal PROCEEDINGS; to start an ACTION.

Broker. A person employed as an AGENT for the purpose of buying or selling something at the request of another individual, in compensation for which he receives a COMMISSION. Also, a middleman; a negotiator between two parties; a dealer in securities; an individual who sells PROPERTY for an OWNER.

Broker's lein. The RIGHT of a BROKER to take his COMMISSION from the proceeds of a SALE made through his efforts, or commission from a purchase made by him for a PRINCIPAL.

Brought to trial. A SUIT is brought to trial when the TRIAL has actually started.

Budget system. A plan whereby expenditures are balanced against income so as to be sure that solvency is maintained.

Buggery. A broad term referring to out-of-the-ordinary forms of sexual intercourse, including that between a man and woman, man and man, or man or woman with an animal.

Building lien. A legal CLAIM for priority of payment for the value of work performed and the value of material supplied in repairing or building a structure. The LIEN may also apply to the land upon which the structure is built.

Building lines. Setback lines; the lines on a street beyond which the law prohibits one from building.

Building loan. A LOAN given to enable someone to erect a building. Banks often issue such loans,, receiving interest in return.

Building permit. A written DOCUMENT, issued by a town, city, or county allowing one to build a proposed structure. Without such a permit, it is illegal to build.

Building restriction. A REGULATION outlining the shape, form, and manner in which one can build and, frequently, prohibiting the construction of certain types of edifices. As an example, in some residential areas, there are building restrictions against erecting commercial structures.

Burden of evidence. Usually, the responsibility of the PARTY starting a LAWSUIT to produce evidence that will prove his CASE.

Burden of proof. The duty of establishing the truth of a CONTENTION in a LAWSUIT. Usually, this burden lies upon the PLAINTIFF or PROSECUTOR who has instituted the action.

Bureaucracy. A government run by appointed chiefs of bureaus, departments, and agencies rather than by OFFICERS, mainly elected officers, of government.

Burglary. The breaking and entering into another's home, office, or other property with the intent of committing a crime.

Business agent. A representative of a LABOR UNION. Usually he is a paid member of the union staff who visits various union shops to hear comments and grievances from the workers.

Business expense. Various legitimate expenses incurred during the conduct of a business enterprise. Such expenses are deductible from INCOME TAXES.

Business record exception. An exception to the rule barring the introduction of HEARSAY EVIDENCE in a LAWSUIT. This exception permits the introduction of routine business records in a case before a court.

Business trust. An arrangement in which PROPERTY is placed in the hands of trustees who control and manage it for the benefit of beneficiaries.

By due process of law. In accordance with fundamental principles of justice; in conformity with usual judicial PROCEEDINGS. > DUE PROCESS OF LAW.

Bylaws. Rules and regulations adopted by CORPORATIONS, associations, benefit societies, etcetera, to govern their ongoing activities. Such bylaws must be compatible with the charters of the various organizations and must be in conformity with their aims and goals.

Bystander. Someone who looks on but has nothing to do with the activity in progress. (A person may be standing innocently on a street, witnessing a bank robbery, and he is then termed a bystander.)

By virtue of. By AUTHORITY of; because of. (Payments made to a public official by virtue of his rightful function, according to law.)

C

Cadaver. A dead body; a corpse.
Caducary. Relating to the forfeiture of property.
Calculated risks. A term used in medical circles, especially surgical, in which the risks involved in operating upon a patient are reckoned and are weighed against the risks of not operating.
Calendar. The method of calculating time according to days, months, and years.
Calendar days. Consecutive days, including each day of the week and holidays.
Calendar of cases. A list of the cases read for trial and scheduled to be tried during the term of the court.
Call. **1.** In CONTRACT dealings, a call is a formal demand for payment. **2.** An OPTION to purchase additional STOCK in a CORPORATION at a stipulated price.
Callable bond. BONDS that can be redeemed (paid off) before their maturity date.
Calling the docket. The announcement of the various ACTIONS (SUITS, CAUSES) to be heard during the term of the COURT, and the setting of the times for such actions.
Calling the jury. Drawing the names of potential JURORS out of a box and examining them for suitability to serve, in the order that their names are picked from the box.
Calling the plaintiff. If a PLAINTIFF feels that he has not proved his case and that the VERDICT will go against him, he and his COUNSEL may not appear in court to hear such verdict. In such an event, the court clerk calls the plaintiff, and if he and his ATTORNEY are not present, the SUIT is dropped before the verdict is rendered.
Calling upon a prisoner. When an ACCUSED has been found GUILTY, it is customary for the clerk of the court to call upon the prisoner and ask him why JUDGMENT should not be passed upon him. (This is a mere formality, for judgment will be passed.)
Calumny. SLANDER; LIBEL; DEFAMATION OF CHARACTER or reputation.
Camera. A judge's chamber (Latin). > IN CAMERA.
Cancel. To strike out; to cross out; to ANNUL a document by erasure or by defacing it. When a DEBT is owed, it is cancelled upon payment.
Candidate. A person seeking an OFFICE. In politics, an individual who has been nominated by his party and who will stand election.
Canon. A LAW.
Canonical disability. Inability to have intercourse; impotence.
Capable. Competent; having legal power; qualified.
Capital assets. All property or money, plus surplus and undis-

tributed profits. For INCOME TAX purposes, all the property or money held by the taxpayer.

Capital crime. An offense that may be punishable by the DEATH SENTENCE, although the death sentence is not mandatory.

Capital expenditure. Monies spent to improve a company's PROPERTY or to construct a building for a company's use. Such expenditures are not deductible from TAXES as ordinary business expenses.

Capital gains. Profits from the sale of CAPITAL ASSETS in excess of costs and values. Such gains are subject to special taxation, as specified by tax laws.

Capital investment. Monies spent to increase the worth of an ASSET.

Capital outlay. Money spent in buying and promoting a business.

Capital punishment. The death penalty.

Capital stock. The shares of stock issued by a CORPORATION. They represent the liability of the company to the SHAREHOLDERS. The number of shares issued are authorized by the CHARTER of the corporation.

Capitalist. A person whose income is derived from INVESTMENTS. In ordinary usage, a capitalist is an individual of wealth who lives off PROPERTY he owns and from INTEREST and DIVIDENDS he derives.

Capitalization. The structure of a COMPANY in reference to the STOCKS and BONDS it has issued and their worth.

Capitalize. To estimate the value of a STOCK; to authorize the issuance of a certain number of stocks and BONDS in the CHARTER of a CORPORATION; to supply with capital.

Capitation tax. A poll TAX; a tax imposed upon each person.

Capitulation. Surrender.

Capricious disbelief. An unwarranted and purposeful disbelief of a dependable, believable witness.

Caption. The seizure or ARREST of a person. Also, the heading of a PLEA or LAWSUIT, naming the PLAINTIFF, DEFENDANT, the nature of the suit, etcetera.

Captive. A prisoner of war.

Capture. To seize. The right to possess that which is on one's own PROPERTY. Thus, an owner captures the oil which lies beneath his land.

Cargo. The goods and merchandise carried by a merchant ship.

Carnal abuse. STATUTORY RAPE; INJURY to the female genitals in an attempt to penetrate them and consummate intercourse.

Carnal knowledge. SEXUAL INTERCOURSE. In legal terms, the placing of the male organ at the entrance of the vagina, even if the organ does not penetrate the HYMEN (maidenhead), constitutes carnal knowledge.

Carnally knew. A technical term used in an INDICTMENT charging RAPE.

Carrying charges. INTEREST on a LOAN; the cost of owning PROPERTY, including the cost of TAXES, the cost of a mortgage, etcetera.

Carte blanche. Unlimited AUTHORITY. A blank DOCUMENT intended by the signer to be filled in and used by another, without restriction (French).

Cartel. An association of businessmen, usually financiers, whose purpose is to corner a market or to fix prices or to acquire a monopoly in a specific field. Cartels are often secret, and sometimes, illegal.
Case. A contested issue in a COURT of law; a controversy presented according to the rules of judicial PROCEEDINGS. An ACTION, a CAUSE, a SUIT.
Case dismissed. A controversy "thrown out of court" without being considered or tried. The disposal of a CASE by sending it out of COURT without a TRIAL.
Case in point. A decision of a POINT OF LAW based upon a previous DECISION of another COURT presenting the same legal problem.
Case law. The LAW on a particular subject based upon a group of similar issues decided by other COURTS. Case law is not based upon STATUTES, but upon experiences in similar situations in other actions.
Case reserved. A DECISION rendered as a matter of form in order to obtain the opinion of a higher court or the opinion of other judges serving in the same COURT.
Case system. The study of LAW through the examination, perusal, research, and knowledge of cases that are important. It is also known as the inductive method of studying law.
Cash contract. A CONTRACT that does not create a DEBT because the contract is fulfilled with the payment of cash.
Cash discount. A reduction in price if payment is made in cash within a specified period of time.
Cash flow. An accounting term for the total net income plus monies allowed for DEPRECIATION of equipment and plant.
Cash market value. The fair market value, or what something can be sold for in a free, open market, for cash.
Cash surrender value. The value of an INSURANCE POLICY at any specific time before the policy is due. This amount is calculated according to established rules. The insured who is cancelling his INSURANCE is entitled to a certain amount of money, determined by how much PREMIUM he has paid in during the life of the policy.
Cash value. The amount for which something can be sold in a free market. Also known as *market value, fair market value, clear market value.*
Casual evidence. Any EVIDENCE that happens to be brought up in a CASE which was not arranged beforehand to be the evidence of an event or FACT.
Casus major. A major ACCIDENT, such as a fire, earthquake, tornado, etcetera; an unusual event.
Catastrophe. A major disaster; something greater than casualty.
Categorical question. A question that can be answered by a "yes" or a "no."
Cattle rustling. The STEALING of cattle, a common crime during the settling of the West in the nineteenth century.
Caucasian. The white race.
Caucus. A meeting of people of the same political persuasion, conducted for the purpose of determining the opinion and position

of its members on particular issues.

Causa mortis. In contemplation of approaching death. Changes in wills and in bequests are sometimes made in expectation of early death (Latin).

Causa rei. Literally, the fruits of a thing. What a claimant would have had if a DEFENDANT had not withheld what rightfully belonged to him The ACCESSIONS or APPURTENANCES (Latin).

Causa sine qua non. An inevitable, unavoidable CAUSE; a cause without which something could not have happened (Latin).

Cause. A LAWSUIT or legal action; that which produces an effect; a CASE.

Cause célèbre. A sensational, celebrated CASE, one that attracts an unusual amount of attention because of the issues involved or the persons who are involved (French).

Cause of action. The CAUSE which gives a person the right to bring a suit for RELIEF (DAMAGES). Also, the FACTS that establish the right to bring an ACTION in court.

Cause of injury. That which produced the INJURY.

Cautionary instruction. An admonition and instruction from a judge to a JURY, cautioning them not to discuss the case with anyone outside the jury room while the TRIAL is in progress.

Cautionary judgment. A JUDGMENT placing a LIEN on the PROPERTY of a DEFENDANT so as to prevent him from fraudulently disposing of the property during the course of the TRIAL. If, in the event the outcome of the trial goes against him, the property will be available to SATISFY the PLAINTIFF.

Caveat. A warning or notice to beware or to be on guard; sometimes a notice of opposition to the probating of a WILL.

Caveat emptor. "Let the buyer beware" (Latin). In othr words, the buyer purchases at his own risk. In the COMMON LAW, warranties in the sale of PERSONAL PROPERTY are exceptions to this maxim.

Caveator. A person who files an objection, such as to the probating of a WILL.

Cease and desist order. An ORDER issued by an authority commanding that certain activities be stopped. Thus, an employer might be ordered by a labor board to stop unfair practices toward his employees.

Cede. To surrender; to give up. Often used when referring to territory that one country grants or surrenders to another country.

Cedent. Someone who transfers some RIGHT or interest

Celation. Concealment of a pregnancy or a delivery. A medical term.

Celibacy. The state of being unmarried. Also, abstention from SEXUAL INTERCOURSE. (In this connection, priests of the Roman Catholic Church maintain a state of celibacy.)

Censorship. Restrictions on the publication and presentation to the public of a book, article, play, motion picture, etcetera, that is obscene, immoral, or indecent, or incites to riot. In wartime, censorship is imposed in order to prevent information from reaching the enemy.

Censure. To criticize severely; to condemn. (Censure of a colleague by the Senate or House of Representatives is a most severe PUNISHMENT for misconduct.)

Census. An official calculation of the number of people in a city, town, county, state, or country. (In the United States a national census is conducted once every ten years.)

Central Intelligence Agency (C.I.A.). A federal AGENCY whose function is to conduct all intelligence activities and to obtain information essential to the security of the United States. The C.I.A. reports to the National Security Council and to the President.

Certainty. Without the shadow of a doubt; clarity; particularity; accuracy; distinctness. (The opposite of uncertainty.)

Certificate. A written STATEMENT serving as verification and authentication of the fact set forth. Such a DOCUMENT is often signed by a NOTARY PUBLIC.

Certificate of abstractor. A CERTIFICATE verifying the austractor of TITLES to PROPERTY, showing the records of title covered by his search. In addition, the CERTIFICATE will record the dates when the search began and ended.

Certificate of acknowledgment. The CERTIFICATE of an OFFICER, such as a JUSTICE OF THE PEACE, NOTARY PUBLIC, etcetera, attached to a DEED, MORTGAGE, or other DOCUMENT, stating that the parties thereto had personally appeared before him on a particular day and had acknowledged the document to be their voluntary act and deed.

Certificate of assize. A WRIT (a formal document) under which a second TRIAL on the same issue was held before the same JURY because of a mistake made by the COURT.

Certificate of authenticity. A CERTIFICATE verifying the authenticity of a DOCUMENT. Such certificate is usually made out by a CLERK OF THE COURT or some other officer of the court.

Certificate of conformity. A certificate made out by a CLERK OF THE COURT, or some other authorized officer of the court, stating that a DOCUMENT or AFFIDAVIT is in conformity with the law. A certificate of conformity is frequently combined with a certificate of authentication.

Certificate of deposit. A DOCUMENT issued by a bank acknowledging that it has borrowed money from a depositor, and stating that it will repay the LOAN on a specifed date and that the depositor shall be paid a certain amount of INTEREST on his loan.

Certificate of occupancy. A DOCUMENT certifying that a building has been satisfactorily completed, has conformed to zoning and other standards, and is ready to be occupied. Without this CERTIFICATE, a building cannot be legally occupied.

Certificate of partnership. A written STATEMENT naming all the partners in a COMPANY. Such certificates should be filed with the proper authorities.

Certificate of public convenience. A PERMIT to use public highways for specifically stated purposes. Also, a DOCUMENT from a PUBLIC SERVICE COMMISSION permitting the construction of a public utility plant.

Certificate of purchase. A DOCUMENT issued by an OFFICIAL to a successful bidder at a tax sale, giving the DEED to the bidder upon the confirmation of the SALE by the COURT.

Certificate of sale. Also known as CERTIFICATE OF PURCHASE. A DOCUMENT given by the SHERIFF or other OFFICER conducting a sale to a purchaser, giving him the RIGHT to a DEED should the OWNER fail to redeem the PROPERTY during the specified period of redemption.

Certification of question. A practice wherein a CASE, or a question of LAW, may be referred by a lower court to a higher court for DECISION.

Certification of record on appeal. The signing of papers by a judge attesting to the fact that this is an APPEAL based upon a BILL OF EXCEPTIONS.

Certification proceeding. An ACTION of the NATIONAL LABOR RELATIONS BOARD to determine if the employees of a COMPANY actually want a particular union to represent them.

Certified check. The signing of a CHECK by a bank officer showing that the depositor has adequate funds to cover the amount of the check.

Certified copy. A copy of a DOCUMENT signifying that it is a true copy. Such copy is certified by the OFFICER to whose CUSTODY the original document is entrusted.

Certified public accountant. A trained accountant who has passed a rigid set of tests of his knowledge and has received the degree of C.P.A.

Certify. To vouch for the authenticity of something. Certification is often carried out by signing a DOCUMENT, thus attesting to its validity.

Certiorari. A formal ORDER or WRIT issued by a superior to an inferior court, requiring the return of the record and PROCEEDINGS in order that the record may be corrected in matters of law. Certiorari is a writ of review and inquiry by one COURT of ACTIONS and PROCEEDINGS taken in another court (Latin).

Chain of title. The various transfers of TITLE to PROPERTY from one person to another, commencing from the earliest records of OWNERSHIP and terminating with the deed to the person presently claiming title.

Challenge. An OBLIGATION; an exception.

Challenge for cause. A challenge to a potential JUROR based on some reason or cause. This type of challenge is different from a PEREMPTORY CHALLENGE, which is not made for cause nor can it be debated or refused.

Challenge propter affectum. An OBJECTION to a potential JUROR based on alleged bias or partiality (Latin).

Challenge propter defectum. An

OBJECTION to a potential JUROR on the grounds that he is deficient in certain respects (Latin).
Chamber business. Judicial matters transacted by a judge in his private OFFICE (CHAMBERS).
Chambers. The private OFFICE of a judge.
Champertor. A person who backs a LAWSUIT at his own expense, in exchange for receiving part of the gains growing out of the suit.
Champerty. A bargain made with a PLAINTIFF to pay the costs of a LAWSUIT. In exchange, the one making the bargain (the CHAMPERTOR) will receive part of the award should the suit terminate successfully.
Chancery practice. EQUITY practice, that which concerns itself with JUDGMENTS based on fairness and right dealing rather than upon written STATUTES and matters of LAW.
Change of beneficiary. Switching a bequest or beneficial interest from one person to another.
Change of domicile. A change of principal residence or abode.
Change of title. The transfer of PROPERTY from one person to another, with the purchaser assuming the TITLE.
Change of venue. The removal of a SUIT from one location to another. Such changes are frequently made in order to assure the LITIGANTS a better chance for a fair trial.
Chapter Eleven. A common phrase used to describe a COMPANY, CORPORATION, or organization that has gone into BANKRUPTCY. Under bankruptcy laws, such a company may be permitted by the COURT to continue to do business for a time so long as it pays all its current debts. It must emerge from "Chapter Eleven" eventually, through reorganization, or it must cease doing business.
Character witness. A WITNESS who testifies as to the general reputation and character of the person on TRIAL.
Characterization. A term for determining the nature of the matter being brought before the COURT so as to decide which JURISDICTION should consider the issue.
Charge. The term for the STATEMENT of the alleged OFFENSE for which one is brought to COURT. It does not include specifications. Also, an instruction to a JURY to help them in their consideration of a case.
Chargé d'affaires. A diplomatic representative sent to another government; sometimes a substitute for an ambassador.
Charge of indictment. That part of an accusation which sets forth the facts making up the OFFENSE for which the defendant is being tried.
Charge-off. A term used in accounting when one eliminates an item from ASSETS. (Charge-offs are often made when an ACCOUNT RECEIVABLE has lost value or is worthless.)
Chargeable. Something which can be charged; legally liable to be charged.
Charitable bequest. A gift, legally carried out in a WILL, to an educational, religious, or other tax-

exempt organization. Such a bequest must be free from gain or profit to the giver.

Charitable corporation. An organization whose purpose is to serve mankind, without gain or profit to those who have formed the CORPORATION; a nonprofit or not-for-profit corporation.

Charitable institution. An institution organized for benevolent purposes, free from corporate profit or gain. Voluntary hospitals, organizations such as the Red Cross, etcetera, fall into this category.

Charitable organization. One that issues no capital STOCK and has nothing in its CHARTER providing for DIVIDENDS or profits.

Charitable trust. A TRUST whose ASSETS and INCOME shall benefit the general public, or a significant segment of the public.

Charter. An act of a legislature creating a CORPORATION and setting forth its franchise; also, a DOCUMENT defining the organization of a corporation.

Charter of pardon. A DEED, or CHARTER, pardoning a CRIMINAL for his OFFENSE.

Charter money. Money paid for the use (or CHARTER) of a ship. It may be a fixed sum or may be calculated according to the profit of the venture.

Chartered accountant. In Britain, a chartered accountant is the equivalent to a certified public accountant in the United States.

Chartered ship. A ship hired out to carry a cargo, or a group of passengers.

Chaste. Legal jargon for an unmarried female who has never experienced sexual intercourse.

Chattel. PROPERTY that is moveable and not part of the real estate.

Chattel mortgage. A MORTGAGE on CHATTELS, or PERSONAL PROPERTY rather than on REAL ESTATE. In other words, personal possessions are given as security against a LOAN or OBLIGATION.

Check. A DOCUMENT directing a bank to pay money to the person or organization named on the CHECK. Such a DOCUMENT must be signed by the person possessing the bank account, and sufficient funds must be in the account to permit payment.

Check-off sytem. The deduction of UNION dues by an employer from the wages of the employees. The monies so collected are turned over to the union.

Chicanery. FRAUD or trickery resulting in DAMAGES to an individual or individuals. Such an act is illegal.

Chief clerk. The principal employee charged with superintending the administration of the business of the OFFICE. (A chief clerk of a COURT supervises the CALENDAR and other matters to be brought before the court.)

Chief justice. The JUDGE who assigns cases and directs the running of a court where more than one judge, usually more than three, sit together. (There is a Chief Justice of the United States Supreme Court who is appointed by the President to preside over the entire COURT, numbering nine, including the Chief Justice.)

Child abuse. Violent and inhuman behavior by an adult, often a parent, toward a child. It is illegal for a parent to habitually beat or too strenuously punish a child, either physically or mentally.

Child custody. The support, control, and maintenance of a child, granted by a COURT ORDER when the parents are separated or divorced.

Child labor laws. Laws prohibiting the employment of MINORS under a specified age. (The age may vary from state to state.)

Choate. Complete; justifiable against other CLAIMS; the opposite of inchoate.

Chose. A case of ACTION; CHATTEL or PERSONAL POSSESSION; a personal RIGHT; a CHOSE IN ACTION.

Chose in action. The right of a CREDITOR to be paid by a DEBTOR; a right to possession, recoverable by bringing a LAWSUIT.

Chronic disease. An illness that lasts a long time, or one that will continue permanently such as diabetes or arteriosclerosis.

Circa. About; around; in the neighborhood of (Latin). A term often used in estimating the age of something ancient.

Circuit court. A COURT whose authority extends over several DISTRICTS or counties. In some instances, several judges preside at the same time, each handling a different CASE.

Circuit judge. A judge of a CIRCUIT COURT.

Circuit justice. A federal judge assigned to a CIRCUIT COURT or DISTRICT.

Circumduction. Cancellation; ANNULMENT.

Circumstantial evidence. Indirect evidence. Facts and circumstances surrounding an event from which a JURY may infer other related facts. Circumstantial, or INDIRECT EVIDENCE, tends to substantiate the main issues involved in a CASE, even if it falls short of proving the case.

Citation. A notice of a COURT proceeding; a WRIT commanding a person to appear in court on a certain day.

Cite. To summon to appear in COURT. This is usually carried out by serving the cited individual with a summons. Cite also means to quote or to refer to a preceding CASE.

Citizen. An inhabitant of a town, city, state, or country, entitled to all its privileges. There are two main types of citizens of a country, namely, the *native-born citizen* (one born in his country) and the *naturalized citizen* (one born in a foreign country but who has adopted the citizenship of his present country).

Citizen's arrest. An ARREST of a person by a citizen who is not an OFFICER of the LAW.

Citizenship papers. A certificate of citizenship, such as one issued to a person who has been born abroad.

Civil action. A SUIT entered into for the purpose of enforcing a civil or personal RIGHT. Not a criminal action. Civil actions are proceedings in which one party sues another party for a legal wrong or for the prevention of a wrong. (A suit of a CLAIMANT against a DEBTOR for nonpayment is a civil action.)

Civil damages. Monies awarded to a PLAINTIFF as COMPENSATION or SATISFACTION for a wrong committed by a DEFENDANT, such as a breach of CONTRACT, etcetera.

Civil law. 1. Written LAW. 2. Law prevailing as the result of ACTS or STATUTES. 3. Law dealing with civil rather than criminal matters. That law which has been established by a community such as a city or state. Also known as municipal law. Civil law should be distinguished from "laws of nature," or that type of law which has universal application (COMMON LAW).

Civil liability. A sum of money assessed against a DEFENDANT. It may be single, double, or treble the original amount of the actual DAMAGES.

Civil liberty. Political freedom. The freedom enjoyed by a member of a society that restrains its people only insofar as it is necessary to maintain the general welfare. Civil liberty recognizes the right of the individual to live his life with minimal restrictions so long as he does not interfere with the public order. > CIVIL RIGHTS.

Civil nuisance. Something done to annoy or hurt the PROPERTY of another.

Civil obligation. An OBLIGATION that can be enforced through a CIVIL ACTION or SUIT in court.

Civil responsibility. The LIABILITY to respond to a CIVIL ACTION for a DAMAGE or INJURY. It is not the same as criminal responsibility, which would be tried in a criminal court.

Civil rights. Those rights granted to every citizen by the UNITED STATES CONSTITUTION and its Amendments, particularly the guarantees of equal rights among all people, regardless of religion, race, color, or previous condition of servitude. They include the rights of PROPERTY, marriage, protection by the LAWS, freedom to worship, trial by jury, etcetera.

Civil rights laws. Those passed and adopted by Congress in 1866, 1957, and 1964 to implement the guarantees in the UNITED STATES CONSTITUTION and its Amendments. Civil rights laws guarantee equal protection to all people, regardless of race, color, or creed.

Civil service. All governmental services given to the people and paid for by the people by a town, city, county, state, or federal government, *not* including the services rendered by the military.

Civil suit. > CIVIL ACTION.

Civilian. One who is not a member of the armed forces.

Civilization. The state of society in which culture, industry, science, and government have developed to a high degree. It implies a recognition of the personal, civil, and public rights of the individual and groups of individuals. It shuns discrimination and enslavement because of race, sex, color, or creed.

Claim. A demand for PROPERTY or money, or its equivalent; an assertion that one is entitled to something or that one owns something.

Claim adjuster. A person who determines the validity and value of a CLAIM, especially a claim against an insurance company.

Claim and delivery. A SUIT for recovery of PROPERTY wrongfully taken or held, including damages for the wrongful act.

Claim in bankruptcy. Written proof that a valid DEBT is owed by a BANKRUPT person or company.

Claim jumping. Asserting one's RIGHT and filing a CLAIM to mine public lands in the same area where another person has placed a claim. Such claim jumping is often based upon the fact that the original CLAIMANT has not properly filed his claim according to LAW, or has not taken all steps he should have taken to establish his claim.

Claim of exemption. The RIGHT, given by judicial process, of a DEBTOR to retain certain of his personal property, free from seizure by the CREDITOR.

Claim of ownership. Entering land with intentions to CLAIM and hold it; a claim of RIGHT; a claim of TITLE.

Claimant. Someone who asserts a RIGHT; a person who has an interest in an ESTATE as an HEIR.

Clandestine. Secret; hidden. The word often implies that something is being kept secret for illegal or unworthy purposes.

Class action. A SUIT brought by one or more people (PLAINTIFFS) on behalf of a class or group of persons. Such a suit is entered upon for the benefit of other similarly situated persons.

Class legislation. STATUTES or LAWS that favor some and discriminate against others in a society.

Class representation. In a situation in which members of a class sue or are sued on behalf of other members, the JUDGMENT (court's decision) is binding for or against those members thus represented.

Class suit. > CLASS ACTION.

Classified information. Knowledge that can only be released upon the permission of the original source of the information, or knowledge made available only to a group of authorized individuals.

Clause. A part of a sentence, a sentence, or a paragraph contained in a legal DOCUMENT, such as a LAW, DEED, CONTRACT, etcetera.

Clause of devolution. A CLAUSE denoting the transfer from one person to another of a RIGHT, OBLIGATION, ESTATE, or TITLE.

Clause of return. A CLAUSE in a DEED providing that a RIGHT, under certain specified circumstances, shall return to the grantor.

Clean bill of health. A lay term denoting that a person is free from disease and is in a healthy condition. ≫ BILL OF HEALTH.

Clean hands. The PRINCIPLE that a court DECISION should not be in favor of a PLAINTIFF who has not conducted himself honestly. In other words, the complainant has not come into court with clean hands.

Clear and convincing proof. Proof beyond a reasonable doubt; evidence that has convinced an unbiased jury, composed of competent, reasonable jurors.

Clear and present danger. **1.** Phrase used to indicate that past behavior leads one to believe that violence is contemplated and expected. **2.** Behavior that is not protected by the constitutional guarantee of freedom of speech and press.

Clear annuity. An ANNUITY (an annual income) free from TAXES.

Clear evidence. EVIDENCE that is positive, beyond a shadow of a doubt.

Clear legal right. A RIGHT based upon a matter of LAW, determined by totally acceptable FACTS.

Clear proof. Certain PROOF; proof that can be seen and is acceptable to all.

Clear title. Absolute TITLE; a title free from any limitations or OBJECTIONS.

Clear value. Net value; the value after all payments of OBLIGATIONS and DEBTS have been satisfied.

Clearance. The right of a ship to leave port. (A term used in MARITIME LAW.)

Clearance card. A written note given by an employer to an employee stating why he left the job and stating his competence in the job that he performed. Such card (or note) is often used by the employee to present to the next employer from whom he seeks employment.

Cleared. Acquitted; forgiven; declared innocent.

Clearinghouse. An association of banks, organized at one place to exchange checks and other types of indebtedness held by one bank and due from another. It is a go-between for the DEBTS and CREDITS of its members.

Clearing the courtroom. The removal of all guests and onlookers from a COURTROOM. (This is a prerogative of the presiding judge.)

Clemency. Reducing the amount of PUNISHMENT that would normally be meted out to a CRIMINAL.

Clerical error. A mistake in the record of a TRIAL inadvertently committed by the CLERK OF THE COURT.

Clerk of the court. The official scribe whose job it is to make an accurate recording of the PROCEEDINGS of a TRIAL and to hold such recordings in his possession.

Clerkship. The period spent by a law student or recent law school graduate in the offices of a practicing ATTORNEY; a legal internship. Such clerkships are often served during the period between graduation from law school and the passage of the bar examinations.

Client. Someone who retains or employs an ATTORNEY.

Close. As a verb, close means to finish, wind up, terminate. As a noun, close means a parcel of land surrounded by a fence.

Closed. In referring to a real estate TRANSACTION, the deal is closed when final agreement is reached and one PARTY delivers the DEED and the other pays for it.

Closed corporation. A COMPANY in which the officers can fill vacancies on its board without asking the permission or vote of the STOCKHOLDERS; a family CORPORATION, in which most of the stock is owned by members of one family.

Closed hearing. A TRIAL conducted in private; the opposite of an open court.

Closed shop. A company in which an employee must be a member of the UNION before he can be hired.

Closed shop contract. A CONTRACT in which the employer agrees to hire only union members, and all employees agree, so long as they work for the COMPANY, to remain union members.

Closing. Completing a TRANSACTION for the PURCHASE or SALE of REAL ESTATE; making the final argument in a TRIAL.

Closing argument. The summation made by a lawyer in a trial.

Cloture. The procedure in a legislature wherein the debate on an issue is closed and, as a consequence, a vote is taken.

Cloud on title. Any issue which casts doubt on the validity of a TITLE.

Co-adventurer. An individual who joins others in a business enterprise and shares the risks of said venture.

Coaching. Instructing a WITNESS before he takes the stand to TESTIFY. This is sound legal practice so long as the ATTORNEY does not urge the witness to falsify the truth. Also, it is improper for an attorney to coach a witness or try to influence what he says during the time he is testifying.

Code. A collection of LAWS; the published STATUTES governing a certain area, arranged in a systematic manner, such as a *penal code, sanitary code,* etcetera.

Code of ethics. A system of RULES governing moral PRINCIPLES and good CONDUCT, usually formulated for a group of people or a profession. (Congress and the legal and medical professions all have codes of ethics for their members.)

Code of judicial conduct. RULES of CONDUCT for judges, recently adopted by the AMERICAN BAR ASSOCIATION.

Code of professional responsibility. The RULES that govern the professional conduct of LAWYERS, passed by the AMERICAN BAR ASSOCIATION and adopted by the states. Violations of this code may be punished by suspension or revoking of an attorney's license to practice the law.

Codicil. An addition or supplement to a WILL. It may also delete or modify various provisions of a will. (Codicils must be witnessed and signed in the same manner as the original will.)

Codification. Assembling and arranging the LAWS of a locality, such as a state, so that they form a system of laws that can be approved as a whole by the state legislature.

Co-equal. The same rank; the same value; equal to.

Coercion. Forcing someone to do something, often by physical force; compulsion; compelling someone to obey against his will.

Co-executor. One of two or more people designated to administer someone's ESTATE; JOINT EXECUTOR.

Cognation. Related by blood ties; a "blood" relationship.

Cognizance. Recognition; judicial examination of a matter; the AS-

SUMPTION of AUTHORITY by a judge to investigate or try a CASE.
Cognomen. A person's family name.
Cognovit note. > JUDGMENT NOTE.
Cohabit. To live together as husband and wife. The term applies even when no formal MARRIAGE has taken place.
Coinsurance. Two or more policies issued by different INSURANCE companies covering the same RISK. Also, a sharing of a risk by the insurer and the insured.
Cold blood. A MURDER committed in cold blood is a premeditated, willful murder.
Co-litigant. A person who joins someone else in suing a DEFENDANT.
Collapsible corporation. A CORPORATION purposely designed to be liquidated before it has accumulated sufficient monies to pay TAXES.
Collateral. PROPERTY held as SECURITY for an OBLIGATION. Also, *supplementary collateral* or *auxiliary collateral.*
Collateral attack. An attempt to upset a JUDGMENT, ORDER, or DECREE by some proceeding or action outside of the court in which the judgment was rendered. Also known as an *indirect attack.*
Collateral estoppel. ESTOPPEL by JUDGMENT; the doctrine of RES JUDICATA. In other words, the PRINCIPLE that an issue has been decided finally and decisively and no similar SUIT can be brought in another COURT by the same LITIGANTS in the same matter.
Collateral facts. FACTS that can not be put in EVIDENCE because they do not actually pertain to the issue involved.
Collateral limitation. A limitation which gives an interest in PROPERTY for a specified period of time but makes the right to possess the property depend upon some related (collateral) event.
Collateral power. The right to dispose of PROPERTY, given to someone who has no interest in the property. Also called, "naked power."
Collateral security. Additional security for a DEBT, subordinate to the original security. It is a kind of secondary guarantee that the debt will be honored.
Collateral source rule. This is a rule that a CLAIMANT may collect DAMAGES for medical or hospital care from a DEFENDANT even if he has been covered for these expenses by another source, such as medical or hospital insurance.
Collation. The mixing and blending of PROPERTY so as to divide it equally. This is frequently necessary when someone has died without a WILL and his property must be divided equally among several HEIRS.
Collation of advancements. The grouping of ASSETS of an ESTATE in which there has been no WILL for the purpose of determining the equitable distribution to the HEIRS, specifically by deducting assets that have already been distributed (advancements) to some of the heirs but not to others.
Collect on delivery (C.O.D.). This means that merchandise is to be given over to the purchaser only if he pays for it on delivery.
Collective bargaining. A proce-

dure provided for in the NATIONAL LABOR RELATIONS ACT. The aim of collective bargaining is to reach AGREEMENTS between employers and representatives of employees on wages, hours, fringe benefits, and other conditions relating to employment.

Collector. Someone appointed by a court to collect and hold the ASSETS of a deceased person's ESTATE until an EXECUTOR is appointed to administer it.

Collision clause. In MARITIME LAW, a provision in an INSURANCE POLICY covering the possibility of a collision between the insured vessel and another vessel.

Colloquium. A STATEMENT in an ACTION for SLANDER or LIBEL specifying what words were spoken or written by the DEFENDANT, and how they defamed the PLAINTIFF.

Collusion. An AGREEMENT between two or more people to defraud another, or to obtain something they are not entitled to.

Collusive action. A SUIT carried out to determine a point of LAW. In actuality, a collusive action is not a controversy between a PLAINTIFF and DEFENDANT.

Color of law. The appearance of a legal RIGHT, but not truly constituting a legal right.

Color of office. An act (or acts) carried out by an OFFICER of the LAW which is outside or beyond the AUTHORITY given him by his OFFICE.

Color of title. A just TITLE to PROPERTY; a title derived from a DEED or a court DECREE, but which may or may not be valid title; an apparent title.

Colorable claim. A CLAIM that appears to be valid but, in truth, is invalid. Also, an unjustifiable claim to PROPERTY made by a person who is in possession of said property against the demand of a trustee in BANKRUPTCY.

Colorable imitation. An imitation of a product made so cleverly that it deceives people.

Colorable transaction. A TRANSACTION that appears legitimate but, in reality, is calculated to deceive.

Co-maker. An individual who endorses a check or other negotiable DOCUMENT, promising to pay if the original signer of the CHECK or document does not fulfill his OBLIGATION to pay.

Combination. A conspiracy of people who have gotten together to carry out some unlawful act.

Combination in restraint of trade. An association of two or more individuals or CORPORATIONS whose purpose is to monopolize the market in their product, or to fix its price, to restrict its sale, or to otherwise deal in unfair practices.

Comes and defends. An expression commonly used in presenting a DEFENDANT's case. It means that the defendant has come to court and will defend the suit against him.

Comity. Courtesy; respect; a willingness to grant a privilege even though such privilege may not be due.

Command. An order, usually implying that some action *must* be taken, as directed.

Comment upon the evidence. An expression denoting that the judge is not privileged to give the JURY his personal opinion on the merits of the CASE.

Commerce power. The AUTHORITY given by the UNITED STATES CONSTITUTION to Congress in allowing it to control trade with foreign countries and trade between the states.

Commercial Code. A set of laws formulated through the efforts of various national organizations for the purpose of having uniform PRINCIPLES throughout all the states. The Commercial Code constitutes one of the uniform LAWS. (The American Law Institute has been most active in attempting to set up laws that will be applicable in most commercial transactions.)

Commercial corporation. A COMPANY engaged in trade and business transactions.

Commercial law. That LAW which applies to the rights and relations of people engaged in trade or commerce.

Commercial paper. A written DOCUMENT serving as money. Commercial paper includes bank CHECKS, PROMISSORY NOTES, and other NEGOTIABLE INSTRUMENTS for the payment of money.

Commingle. To put together into one fund monies from several different sources.

Commission. An AUTHORITY; an authorization; a directive from a COURT authorizing a person or group of persons to exercise some special function or to perform certain specific acts.
➤ COMMISSIONS.

Commission to examine witnesses. An authorization from a court for a COMMISSION to examine and obtain STATEMENTS from WITNESSES who are outside the JURISDICTION of the COURT.

Commission to take depositions. An AUTHORITY to a COMMISSION to take TESTIMONY from WITNESSES who cannot personally be produced in COURT.

Commissioner. An OFFICER who is charged with the administration of the LAWS relating to a particular area; the manager of a bureau or AGENCY of government. (In this country, there are Commissioners of Sanitation, Education, Welfare, Fire, Police, Fisheries, etcetera.)

Commissioner of deeds. A NOTARY PUBLIC; someone authorized to acknowledge deeds from outside the state to be used within the state.

Commissions. Monies paid to an EXECUTOR of an ESTATE, AGENT, BROKER, TRUSTEE, or RECEIVER for his or her services. Such monies are usually a percentage of the total amounts involved in the transaction or estate.

Commit. To send someone to prison, to a mental institution, a reformatory, etcetera, by authority of a COURT ORDER.

Commitment. In medical JURISPRUDENCE, it is the act of sending someone to a mental institution. In CRIMINAL LAW, it is the carrying out of a JUDGE's directive to take a prisoner to JAIL.

Committing magistrate. A JUDGE of a lower court who has the authority to conduct preliminary hearings of people charged with a crime. He may dismiss the charges if he finds insufficient EVIDENCE against them or he may place the accused in JAIL to await a TRIAL.

Commodity credit corporation. A federal government AGENCY whose function is to support prices of agricultural products through subsidies, PURCHASES or LOANS, and to help sell such products in the domestic and foreign markets.

Common belief. An opinion believed in by the great majority of people in a community. Although such belief is usually true, there are many instances wherein it is not true.

Common counts. The various forms of a SUIT to recover damages for the nonpayment of a contract. Includes an action of ASSUMPSIT.

Common jury. An ordinary JURY, not a special or GRAND JURY.

Common knowledge. A matter so generally accepted by the general public that a COURT will accept it without PROOF.

Common law. **1.** LAW declared by judges functioning in areas not controlled by governmental REGULATIONS, ORDINANCES, or STATUTES. **2.** Law originating from usage and custom rather than from written STATUTES. **3.** The unwritten laws.

Common-law action. A CIVIL SUIT, as distinguished from a CRIMINAL SUIT. Common-law actions include ASSUMPSIT, REPLEVIN, TRESPASS, DEBT, etcetera.

Common-law husband. A man living and cohabiting with a woman without having gone through the civil or religious ceremony of MARRIAGE. Implicit in the relationship is an understanding that a marital arrangement exists. Many states do not recognize common-law marriages.
➢ COMMON-LAW WIFE.

Common-law lien. A LIEN granted by the COMMON LAW, or by implication of law, not by a CONTRACT or AGREEMENT between two or more PARTIES.

Common-law replevin. A CIVIL SUIT in which an owner seeks to regain possession of PROPERTY that has been taken or is being held by another.

Common-law wife. A woman living and cohabiting with a man without having gone through the civil or religious ceremony of MARRIAGE. Implicit in the relationship is an understanding that a marital arrangement exists. Many states do not recognize common-law marriages.
➢ COMMON-LAW HUSBAND.

Common pleas. The name of the COURT which hears civil cases; also, a term for CIVIL SUITS, as distinguished from CRIMINAL PROSECUTIONS.

Common right. A RIGHT supported by the COMMON LAW. In other words, a right or privilege to which all people are entitled, equally and in common.

Common stock. Shares in a CORPORATION whose value fluctuates according to the profits, losses, or value of the COMPANY.

Common use. A phrase that refers to articles used by the general public. Such articles are sold widely and in many markets.

Commonalty. The great body of CITIZENS; the masses.
Commonweal. Public welfare; common good.
Commonwealth. The PUBLIC; the STATE; the BODY POLITIC. (The term applies to a democratic, republican form of government such as exists in the various states of the United States.)
Commune. A self-governing COMMUNITY; a small administrative unit of government. (This term has been adopted by many left-wing revolutionary governments.)
Communicable diseases, reporting of. The health codes of most communities require physicians to report to the local boards of health on the incidence of various communicable, contagious diseases. > CONTAGIOUS DISEASES, REPORTING OF. In addition to the ordinary contagious diseases of childhood, illnesses such as smallpox, polio, cholera, etcetera, and venereal conditions are reportable.
Communism. A socialist form of government in which PROPERTY is owned by the STATE and there is common OWNERSHIP of the agents of production, and supposed equal and equitable distribution of the products of production.
Community. A society of people living in a particular neighborhood or vicinity. It presupposes common interests.
Community of interest. An INTEREST applying to all parties embarking upon or engaged in a common enterprise.
Community property. A term applying to the PROPERTY rights of a husband and wife wherein their assets belong to both, rather than to husband or wife individually. Community property laws exist in some states but not in others.
Commutation. The act of changing or altering. Commutation of a SENTENCE means lessening it, such as changing a death sentence to a life imprisonment sentence.
Commutative contract. A CONTRACT in which each PARTY receives an equivalent or mutual OBLIGATION and BENEFIT.
Compact. A serious, important CONTRACT; an agreement setting forth RIGHTS and OBLIGATIONS. Compacts often refer to agreements between nations.
Company. A CORPORATION or PARTNERSHIP.
Company union. A UNION whose membership is limited to the employees of a single COMPANY.
Comparative jurisprudence. The comparison between different systems of LAW.
Comparative negligence. A PRINCIPLE in a suit to recover damages that compares the NEGLIGENCE of the DEFENDANT to that of the PLAINTIFF. In other words, if the plantiff was slightly negligent but the defendant was very negligent, the plaintiff may be awarded the damages. Or, if the plaintiff was grossly negligent and the defendant only slightly negligent, no award may be granted.
Comparison of handwriting. The comparing of two specimens of handwriting to see if they were both done by the same person.
Compendium. An abbreviated work or book; a synopsis.
Compensable death. DEATH caused by an accident or illness

arising out of employment. Such death is compensable under the WORKMEN'S COMPENSATION laws.

Compensable injury. INJURY that arises out of employment, such as a hernia resulting from lifting an unusually heavy object.

Compensation. Remuneration; payment for services rendered; money paid to an injured employee.

Compensation case. A CASE in which a worker claims that an ACCIDENT or illness is the result of his employment and that he is, therefore, entitled to money.

Compensation claim. The CLAIM made in a COMPENSATION CASE.

Compensatory damages. The precise loss suffered by a PLAINTIFF, as distinguished from PUNITIVE DAMAGES, which are over and above the actual losses sustained.

Competency. The presence of those attributes that makes a witness fit to give testimony; qualifications to perform; capability.

Competency to stand trial. The ability of a DEFENDANT to understand the charges against him. In MEDICAL JURISPRUDENCE, it implies that a defendant is sane, rather than so mentally sick or unbalanced so as not to be able to defend himself against the charges being brought against him.

Competent. Duly qualified; able; possessing the required legal qualifications.

Competent evidence. EVIDENCE required to prove a certain point. Also, relevant or ADMISSIBLE EVIDENCE, as opposed to evidence that is inadmissible or irrelevant.

Competent witness. A WITNESS who is legally qualified to TESTIFY in a CASE. The phrase does not necessarily imply that the witness will be truthful.

Competitive bidding. A PROCESS in which bids are sent to several bidders, all of whom are treated equally and are bidding under similar terms.

Complainant. A PLAINTIFF; the person who starts the SUIT. In a CRIMINAL ACTION, the prosecuting WITNESS or the state may be the complainant.

Complaint. The PLEADING by which a PLAINTIFF brings a SUIT and sets forth the reasons for his action.

Complete. Full; finished; not lacking in any particulars, such as a *complete copy* or a *complete legal title.*

Comply. To act in accordance with one's OBLIGATIONS; to yield; to carry into effect; to accommodate.

Compos mentis. Of sound mind. The opposite of NON COMPOS MENTIS (Latin).

Composition in bankruptcy. An agreement between a BANKRUPT (DEBTOR) and his CREDITORS which arranges for the settlement of CLAIMS at lesser amounts and for extension of the time in which the debt must be paid.

Compound a felony. > COMPOUNDING A CRIME.

Compound interest. INTEREST paid on interest that has been added to a PRINCIPAL. Compound interest pays on the principal plus accrued interest.

Compounding a crime. A situation in which an injured PARTY agrees not to prosecute the PERPETRATOR of a crime in exchange for a bribe or some monetary reward.

Compromise. An AGREEMENT to make concessions in a dispute or LITIGATION, thus settling outstanding CLAIMS. Such arrangement may take place out of COURT, or in court.

Compromise verdict. A VERDICT reached by a JURY by some members giving up some of their convictions in return for other jurors giving up some of their convictions. This type of verdict is improper and does not conform to the true ideal of TRIAL BY JURY.

Comptroller. A city or state OFFICIAL whose job is to look after monetary and fiscal affairs. His task includes the examination and audit of accounts, the keeping of records, and the supervision of those who collect public money.

Compulsion. The act of compelling; the application of mental or physical force to induce the performance or the OMISSION of an act.

Compulsory arbitration. In labor DISPUTES, some laws of some communities force the two sides, labor and management, to undergo ARBITRATION. These laws apply mostly when the possibility of a strike seriously affects the public interest. Some labor CONTRACTS make provisions for compulsory arbitration should the two sides fail to reach agreement through the ordinary system of collective bargaining.

Compulsory education. Education that a parent or guardian must see that a child receives. Compulsory education up to age 16 is provided by LAW in many states.

Compulsory insurance. Automobile liability INSURANCE that is required before one can operate a vehicle.

Compulsory process. A SUBPOENA, SUMMONS, or WARRANT of arrest to compel someone to appear in COURT. The PROCESS may want him to appear as a WITNESS or DEFENDANT, or otherwise.

Concealment. The active suppression of FACTS, or a neglect to disclose facts that a person knows and is duty-bound to communicate.

Concealment of cause of action. Hindering or eluding someone who has a legitimate LAWSUIT, or misleading or failing to supply him with information to which he is entitled.

Conception. The onset of pregnancy; the moment at which the sperm enters the egg; fertilization.

Concerted action. ACTION that has been conceived, planned, and agreed upon by two or more parties. (The employees of a company may meet and take concerted action, such as a STRIKE.)

Conciliation. The settlement of a DISPUTE in a civil, or friendly, manner.

Concluding argument. > CLOSING ARGUMENT.

Conclusions of law. The conclusions of the COURT, based upon the FACTS which form the basis for the DECISION of a CASE. Also, a court's STATEMENT of the LAW on a controversial point or issue.

Conclusive evidence. Indisputable, absolute EVIDENCE that establishes a FACT beyond any reasonable doubt.

Conclusive presumption. A belief or ASSUMPTION, based upon specific FACTS in EVIDENCE, which is so strong that it cannot be denied or rebutted, nor will the law permit it to be denied.

Concordat. A treaty or pact between two or more governments or countries.

Concubine. A woman who cohabits with a man in a nonmarital state.

Concur. To agree; to happen at the same time.

Concurrent jurisdiction. The AUTHORITY conferred upon two or more courts to hear and decide the same types of cases; or the JURISDICTION of both a court and a governmental agency over the same matter. > COORDINATE JURISDICTION.

Concurrent negligence. A situation in which both the PLAINTIFF and the DEFENDANT contributed toward the INJURY for which DAMAGES are sought.

Concurrent sentences. Multiple SENTENCES in which terms of imprisonment for more than one crime are ordered to run simultaneously, rather than with one sentence following another.

Concurring opinion. An OPINION given by a second AUTHORITY, upholding and agreeing with the opinion of the first authority.

Condemn. To judge GUILTY; to declare a building unfit for occupancy and to therefore order its destruction; to pass JUDGMENT upon someone convicted of a crime.

Condemnation money. An expression for the money a DEFENDANT must pay to the PLAINTIFF who has won a suit for damages.

Condemnation proceedings. The PROCESS in which PROPERTY of a private OWNER is taken over for public use. Equitable COMPENSATION must be paid to the owner.

Condition precedent. **1.** A condition that must exist prior to the conclusion of a CONTRACT or AGREEMENT. **2.** In laws governing ESTATES, a condition that must exist before an estate can rest or take effect.

Condition subsequent. A condition whose effect is not produced until after vesting of the ESTATE or the commencement of the OBLIGATION.

Conditional bequest. A LEGACY that is granted subject to some conditions.

Conditional contract. A CONTRACT in which the validity depends upon the fulfillment of a specified condition.

Conditional creditor. A CREDITOR with a future right of action.

Conditional dismissal. A discontinuance of a SUIT based upon the fulfillment of a specific condition. (An action to foreclose on a piece of PROPERTY is dismissed because the payments due are made.)

Conditional judgment. A JUDGMENT that goes into effect when a particular condition is fulfilled.

Conditional limitation. A CLAUSE in a LEASE which terminates said lease if a certain condition is not fulfilled.

Conditional pardon. A PARDON that takes effect only when a specified condition is met, or a pardon that terminates because a specified condition has not been fulfilled.

Conditional reversal. A reversal of a JUDGMENT with conditions, such as an AGREEMENT from the DEFENDANT that the original judgment shall stand, should he lose at a second TRIAL on the matter.

Conditional sale. A SALE in which the PURCHASER acknowledges that the PROPERTY is being sold only upon condition that he perform a specified act or that some specified event takes place.

Conditional stipulation. A PROMISE (STIPULATION) to do something upon condition that a specific event or happening takes place.

Condominium. The joint OWNERSHIP of a multiunit dwelling, each of whose owners has exclusive ownership of an individual unit, but in which all common elements (the lobby, the grounds, swimming pool, etcetera) are owned by the tenants in common with no single tenant having exclusive rights to such facilities.

Condonable offense. Misconduct that is forgiven, as a transgression of a spouse even though such transgression might be grounds for DIVORCE.

Condone. To forgive; to forget an OFFENSE.

Conduct. To regulate or to manage and direct. Also, a term meaning behavior, such as *good conduct* or *bad conduct.* (A criminal in jail may be given special consideration because of *good conduct.*)

Conference. A MEETING of several or more people to deliberate and decide upon an issue. Also, the meeting of two legislative bodies, such as the House and Senate, to iron out their differences on a pending BILL.

Confession. A voluntary STATEMENT of an ACCUSED person that he has committed the crime for which he is CHARGED. (No confession is valid if it is forced upon someone.)

Confession and avoidance. An admission of the PLAINTIFF's charges, accompanied by the introduction of new matters and facts that constitute a DEFENSE against the CHARGES. (Confession and avoidance goes beyond mere admission or denial of the plaintiff's ALLEGATIONS.)
≫ AFFIRMATIVE DEFENSE.

Confession of judgment. An admission by a DEBTOR that he owes money to a CREDITOR. Such CONFESSION sometimes is made following an ARBITRATION procedure in which an award has been made in favor of the creditor.

Confidence game. A swindle in which the swindler has gained the confidence of the victim.

Confidential communication. A communication made in confidence. Such a communication does not have to be revealed and is considered PRIVILEGED by the law. (Information that a CLIENT gives to his LAWYER may be judged to be a confidential communication.)

Confidential information. Information that is received in confidence and therefore should not and cannot be revealed, unless the giver of the information approves such revelation.

Confidential relation. A relationship between people wherein one of them is duty-bound to keep certain information secret, and is given the responsibility of acting in the best interests of the other. (The relation between CLIENT and ATTORNEY is a confidential relation.)

Confidentiality. The quality of being confidential, privileged, or secret.

Confinement. **1.** Physical restraint, such as a prisoner who is confined to JAIL or to an institution. **2.** In medical parlance, confinement means being in a hospital or home for childbirth.

Confirmation. A written DOCUMENT stating that certain outstanding matters have been agreed upon and made binding; an affirmation.

Confirmation of sale. An affirmation by a court that the conditions of a SALE have been approved. (The term is often used when a COURT approves an EXECUTOR'S sale of PROPERTY.)

Confiscate. To take PRIVATE PROPERTY from an individual for the use of the state.

Conflict of interest. A situation in which a person's individual interests are in opposition to the interests of his duty to others. As an example, an elected public OFFICIAL who owns real estate may approve a ruling or a change in zoning that would increase the value of his PROPERTY.

Conflict of laws. Differences of LAWS in different counties, municipalities, states, or countries, affecting people who have made AGREEMENTS OF CONTRACTS in two or more of those counties, municipalities, states, or countries. It is frequently necessary to reconcile the inconsistencies of the laws from one community to another.

Conflicting evidence. EVIDENCE from different sources which contradict one another. Thus, the evidence from a PLAINTIFF may be entirely different from that supplied by the DEFENDANT.

Conformed copy. A duplicate copy of a DOCUMENT. It differs from the original in that it is not actually signed by the maker of the document, but by someone who notes on the copy that it had been signed by the originator. A conformed copy of a document may also contain notations in the margins, placed there by someone other than the maker of the document.

Conformity. Resemblance; agreement; correspondence in form or use.

Confrontation. The face-to-face meeting of an ACCUSED and a WITNESS against him. This confers upon the accused the right to refute the TESTIMONY against him.

Confusion of debts. A method of doing away with a DEBT whereby the CREDITOR and DEBTOR become the same person. As an example, a debtor may become the heir of the creditor. Thus, by INHERITING the creditor's money or PROPERTY, he no longer has a debt to pay. (This frequently takes place when a parent is the creditor and an HEIR, a son or daughter, is the debtor.)

Confusion of rights and obligations. > CONFUSION OF DEBTS.

Confusion of titles. A merger of TITLES, as when two titles to the same PROPERTY become owned by the same person.

Conglomerate. A CORPORATION that is composed of several subsidiary corporations, some of which may be engaged in business in completely different industries. As an example, an oil company may own a publishing company, or a publishing company may own a lighting-fixture business.

Congress. **1.** In America, Congress is composed of the two legislative bodies, the Senate and the House of Representatives. **2.** In INTERNATIONAL LAW, a Congress is an assembly of representatives from different countries who meet to consider matters for their common good.

Congressional record. The printed daily record of what goes on in CONGRESS.

Conjectural evidence. The type of EVIDENCE that is based upon an estimate or guess, and is therefore not sufficient to form the basis of a reasoned conclusion.

Conjecture. A notion; an idea; a guess. Conjectures may have some slight significance in a TRIAL but they rarely determine the outcome or produce deep belief.

Conjoint will. A WILL granting money or PROPERTY that the makers of the will own in common. It takes more than one person to make a conjoint will.

Conjugal rights. Marital RIGHTS; included among them are the rights of a wife and husband to each other's company, affection, and physical and spiritual love. > MARRIAGE.

Conjunctive denial. A denial by a DEFENDANT of all the COMPLAINTS made against him by the PLAINTIFF. This term applies only when the plaintiff has made a series of complaints in his suit.

Connally Act. A federal law that aids those state laws that limit the amount of oil that can be produced by certain fields. The Connally Act makes it an offense to ship oil in excess of specified limits from the state of origin to another state.

Connivance. The secret permission or cooperation of one person to the COMMISSION of an unlawful act by another.

Consanguinity. Blood relationship; kindred; being descended from a common ancestor.

Conscience. The faculty of being able to distinguish between right and wrong, and the moral sense that wishes to make that distinction. Someone of *good conscience* wants, in his own way, to live a life that he feels is "right" and "fine" and "moral." These evaluations, of course, vary from person to person, from country to country, from decade to decade, etcetera.

Conscience of the court. When a matter of EQUITY is tried in court, after ascertaining all the FACTS, the court decides the ISSUE. In so doing, the conscience of the court is employed in making a fair, equitable DECISION.

Conscientious objector. A person who refuses to join the armed forces because of his religious beliefs and training.
Conscious minors. Routine treatment, both surgical and medical, cannot be given to a MINOR without consent of a parent, next of kin or guardian. However, in an emergency such treatment can be given without obtaining consent.
Consecutive sentences. Jail terms succeeding one after another, without an interval. (The opposite of CONCURRENT SENTENCES.) ≫ SENTENCE, CUMULATIVE.
Consensual. A CONTRACT is said to be consensual when both parties fully agree to its provisions.
Consensus. A general AGREEMENT, often derived by polling a group and finding the majority's OPINION; a general opinion.
Consent. To agree; to assent. Consent must be an AGREEMENT between two or more people. In rape cases, consent means that the female willingly assented to the sexual act.
Consent, by court order. An AGREEMENT reached by order of the court.
Consent, by sibling. In MEDICAL JURISPRUDENCE, if a brother or sister is the nearest available kin, he or she can give CONSENT for an operation or other procedure to be performed upon a sibling.
Consent, for autopsy. Permission, given by the nearest of kin, to perform a POST-MORTEM examination.
Consent, informed. In MEDICAL JURISPRUDENCE, a patient must be given all the facts concerning his illness and the procedure he is about to undergo before such procedure is embarked upon.
Consent, of minor. A MINOR cannot consent to a medical or surgical PROCEDURE to be performed upon him or her, unless no kin can be reached, or if an emergency exists that will not permit time to reach the nearest of kin.
Consent, of spouse. In MEDICAL JURISPRUDENCE, a spouse can give CONSENT for a medical, surgical, or other PROCEDURE to be performed if the patient is unable to do so.
Consent, oral. Spoken assent. Such consent is only sufficient, in MEDICAL JURISPRUDENCE, when it is impossible to obtain written CONSENT.
Consent, refusal of. The patient or nearest of kin may refuse CONSENT for a medical or surgical procedure to be performed. However, if the patient is a MINOR and it is the consensus of the attending physicians that the child's life is in danger as a result of such refusal of consent, a COURT ORDER may be obtained to force the parents' consent.
Consent, restrictions on. In MEDICAL JURISPRUDENCE, CONSENT for a PROCEDURE cannot be obtained if the patient is a MINOR or fails to understand the request for consent, or is of unsound mind, or is under the influence of drugs or alcohol. However, in dire emergencies, consent can be waived.
Consent, written. Consent forms are given to patients to study and read before undergoing a hospital medical or surgical PROCEDURE.

It is universal practice to make sure that the patient understands all the eventualities that may take place following a particular procedure and understands the risks involved. Such consent forms are signed and witnessed before the procedure takes place.

Consent decree. A DECREE entered into with the consent of both PARTIES to a SUIT. As an example, a consent decree of DIVORCE is granted in some states when both parties, or their representatives, are present in court and agree to the divorce. A consent decree can only be overturned if it is proved that one of the parties to the decree used FRAUD in obtaining it.

Consent judgment. A JUDGMENT (decision of the court) agreed to by the contending PARTIES. A consent judgment usually constitutes a compromise to settle a DISPUTE.

Consent rule. A RULE employed whereby an EJECTMENT suit (one to obtain possession of PROPERTY) is used as a REMEDY for determination of TITLE to property.

Consequence. The natural result that takes place from an event; that which one would expect to happen. A painful lump on the head is a consequence of a severe blow to the head.

Consequential damages. Loss or INJURY that results indirectly. As an example, a store owner who has a fire loses not only the goods and fixtures that have been burned, but he loses what he would have earned had there been no fire and he could have continued to sell his merchandise.

Conservation. The protection of PROPERTY or lands against misuse, exploitation, pollution, or other forms of desecration or depredation.

Conservator. A person put in charge of PROPERTY by COURT ORDER. It is this person's duty to protect and preserve such property; a custodian.

Consider. To think about; to study or ponder, to examine carefully.

Consideration. 1. A term applied when a matter has been heard and decided; consideration has been given. **2.** A matter of CONTRACT wherein one PARTY agrees to do something in return for something the other party agrees to give him, such as money, goods, PROPERTY, etcetera.

Considered opinion. An OPINION based upon study, thought, and reason. A JUDGE renders a considered opinion after adjudging all aspects of a CASE and coming to a reasoned determination of the ISSUES.

Consign. To give to the CUSTODY of a third person something belonging to a DEBTOR, but eventually going to a CREDITOR.

Consignment. The giving over of goods to the CUSTODY of another so that he may sell such goods for the benefit of the consignor. The consignee is the person who accepts and attempts to sell the goods. He receives money when the goods are sold. If the goods are not able to be sold, then they are returned to the consignor.

Consistent. In AGREEMENT with; not contradictory.

Consolidate. To unite or merge. In Congress, two or more BILLS are frequently consolidated into one bill.

Consolidation of actions. The act of uniting or merging several SUITS into one so that there will be just one TRIAL and one DECISION. The COURT often orders this to be done when there are several parties all suing on the same matter.

Consonant statement. When a WITNESS has given TESTIMONY that has been attacked and labeled false, the COURT may allow testimony from the person to whom the witness had originally made his STATEMENTS, in order to prove that the witness *had* given reliable, truthful testimony.

Consortium. **1.** The marital rights of both husband and wife toward each other. Loss of consortium would occur, for example, if a husband was so injured that he could not have SEXUAL INTERCOURSE with his wife. **2.** In the CIVIL LAW, the joining of several parties in one LAWSUIT action.

Conspicuous place. A place where many people will be able to observe something. A notice required to be posted by COURT ORDER must be placed where it can be readily seen by many interested or disinterested PARTIES.

Conspiracy. A group or combination of people who join together for the purpose of committing an unlawful act.

Conspiracy of silence. An AGREEMENT by two or more people not to reveal their knowledge of some unlawful act.

Constable. A city or town or county OFFICER whose duties are similar to those of a SHERIFF.

Constant. Uniform; fixed; invariable.

Constituent. Someone who gives authority to another to act in his behalf. The people whom a Congressman represents are called his constituents.

Constitution. A DOCUMENT containing the fundamental laws governing a political entity, such as a nation or state. Also, a document stating the PRINCIPLES and RULES by which a society or COMPANY or CORPORATION shall be governed. > UNITED STATES CONSTITUTION.

Constitutional law. The branch of the law that concerns itself with the interpretation and enforcement of the various provisions of the UNITED STATES CONSTITUTION and its Amendments. It also concerns itself with laws passed by the several states that might be in conflict or in violation of the Constitution or its Amendments.

Constitutional right. A RIGHT guaranteed by the UNITED STATES CONSTITUTION. Such a right cannot be violated by laws enacted by any state or by Congress.

Constraint. RESTRAINT; compulsion; an interference or restraint of free will or of liberty.

Construction. The process of determining the real meaning of a LAW, or a CONTRACT, when its real meaning is somewhat obscure and difficult to define.

Constructive assent. A CONSENT attributed to someone through an interpretation of CONDUCT rather than by a STATEMENT made. It is a conjectured rather than actual assent.

Constructive contempt. CONTEMPT OF COURT committed outside the COURT. Refusal to accept or obey a SUMMONS or SUBPOENA is constructive contempt, as is the intimidation of a WITNESS.

Constructive crime. An act constructed to be unlawful by a COURT, but not so obviously unlawful that PROSECUTION would ordinarily ensue. It is a crime "built up" by a court.

Constructive force. A crime in which the victim is menaced and placed in a position where he has good reason to be in fear for his safety, and cannot resist the PERPETRATOR.

Constructive malice. > LEGAL MALICE.

Constructive possession. Legal POSSESSION, as distinguished from actual physical possession, which may or may not be legal possession.

Constructive trust. A TRUST operative by LAW which, in fact, does not properly give the right to the possessor to hold PROPERTY. In other words, even though the law may permit someone to hold property, it does not justly belong to him nor should it be possessed by him.

Constructive willfulness. Complete disregard for the safety of others and a conscious unwillingness to safeguard people who might be endangered.

Construe. To interpret; to ascertain the meaning of, especially the language of a DOCUMENT.

Consul. An OFFICER of a country assigned to a foreign country to watch over its interests and the interests of its CITIZENS. Consuls also try to advance the business interests of their mother country.

Consul general. An OFFICER of a government who presides over a consulate of his government in a foreign country.

Consultation. A deliberation; a conference between two people; the act of seeking advice on some matter.

Consummation. The completion of an act. A marriage is said to be consummated when the husband and wife COHABIT.

Contagious diseases, reporting of. In most communities, the reporting of contagious diseases to the board of health is required. Among those diseases especially important to report are: diphtheria, poliomyelitis, smallpox, cholera, etcetera. Infectious diseases such as meningitis and encephalitis are also reportable. > COMMUNICABLE DISEASES, REPORTING OF.

Contemner. One who commits CONTEMPT OF COURT.

Contemplation of bankruptcy. Acts taken with the knowledge that one's business is about to fail and BANKRUPTCY will be declared.

Contemplation of death. The transfer of money or PROPERTY by one who, because of an illness, has knowledge that he will soon die. (Acts in contemplation of death are sometimes performed in order to avoid estate TAXES.)

Contemporaneous. Taking place at the same time as another occurrence.

Contempt of Congress. Failure to appear or to TESTIFY when ordered to do so by Congress or one of its duly appointed committees. Contempt also exists when a WITNESS conducts himself in a manner so as to show disrespect to Congress. A jail SENTENCE may be meted out for contempt of Congress.

Contempt of court. Any conduct or act which lessens the dignity of the court or which is calculated to obstruct justice or hinder the court proceedings. (A fine or a jail sentence may be meted out for contempt of court.)

Contention. An assertion; a CLAIM.

Contentious. Contested; argumentative. A TRIAL between two adversaries is said to be contentious.

Contest. To DENY and DEFEND against a PLAINTIFF in a court of law.

Context. Those parts of a spoken or written passage that precede or follow a specific word, phrase, or sentence. Taking words out of context often alters the meaning of the entire passage or text.

Contingency. The possibility of happening; an event that *may* occur.

Contingent claim. A CLAIM that has not happened but is dependent on an event that may or may not take place in the future.

Contingent fee system. A method of paying for an ATTORNEY'S services in which the CLIENT pays a certain sum, depending upon how much is awarded in the SUIT. Said sum is usually a percentage of the monies collected, rather than a flat, fixed fee. If the suit is lost, the client may pay nothing to the attorney.

Contingent fund. A fund set up by a city, or other political entity, to pay for necessary expenses that will, in all likelihood, occur during an ensuing year. Such a fund does not specify precisely what expense items will be paid for, since they may not be known at the time the fund is set up.

Contingent liability. An OBLIGATION or DEBT which is not presently fixed, but which will become fixed if a future event happens to take place. If the event does not take place, no liability exists.

Contingent right. A RIGHT depending upon the occurrence of some future event, or upon the performance of a particular act.

Continuance. The postponement or ADJOURNMENT of a case pending in COURT to some future date.

Continuing bail. BAIL that carries over from one term of COURT to another until the DEFENDANT is either acquitted or convicted.

Continuing breach. A VIOLATION of the LAW that persists for a prolonged period of time, or one that is repeated over and over again.

Continuing consideration. Acts which must, of necessity, take place over a prolonged period of time.

Continuing easement. An EASEMENT that is never-ending, such as the flow of a river. (An easement is the right of a nonowner to use adjacent land in a specific way.)

Continuing jurisdiction. The AUTHORITY of a COURT to try a case from its beginning to its termination.

Continuing offense. An unlawful act performed continuously or over and over again.
Continuing offer. An offer that is kept open for a specified period of time.
Continuing trespass. A wrongful act that persists over a prolonged period of time, involving damage to a person's PROPERTY or health.
Contra omnes gentes. Against all the people (Latin).
Contra pacem. Against the peace (Latin).
Contraband. Merchandise that is exported or imported contrary to law.
Contract. An AGREEMENT between two or more people, one PARTY (or parties) agreeing to perform certain acts, the other party (or parties) agreeing to pay for or give other consideration for said performance. A contract places an OBLIGATION on one party to do something and an obligation upon the other party to reward the doer.
Contract of record. A CONTRACT that has been declared through COURT action and has been entered in the court records.
Contract of sale. A CONTRACT in which there is an AGREEMENT on the part of seller to give over to the buyer certain PROPERTY in exchange for the payment of a specified sum of money.
Contract medicine. The rendition of medical services on a prepaid basis, rather than by payment of a fee for each service rendered. Full-time doctors are frequently employed by hospitals on a contractual annual wage basis. In such instances, the hospital is entitled to all or most of the fees such a physician may earn.
Contract price. The amount of money to be paid under a CONTRACT to render a service, such as to build a house. Also, the amount of money paid in a contract of SALE.
Contract with specialist. When a patient agrees to undergo a particular medical or surgical PROCEDURE and agrees upon a fee for such procedure, he is in actuality making a CONTRACT with the physician who agrees to perform the procedure.
Contractor's bonds. A BOND in which a contractor guarantees to do a certain job, and if he fails to comply, the OWNER will collect up to the limit of the bond.
Contractual obligation. A binding PROMISE (OBLIGATION) that arises out of an AGREEMENT (CONTRACT).
Contradiction in terms. A STATEMENT that contradicts itself.
Contradiction of witness. The presentation of EVIDENCE that disproves or is contrary to a witness' TESTIMONY.
Contrary to evidence. Contradictory to the EVIDENCE.
Contrary to law. Unlawful; in violation of a legal STATUTE or REGULATION.
Contravening equity. A RIGHT which is opposed to or inconsistent with a right being sought.
Contravention. Breaking a LAW; going against an established RULE or REGULATION.
Contributory. Supplementary; additional.
Contributory negligence. A failure on the part of the PLAINTIFF

to exercise ordinary, proper care, thus contributing toward an accident. Such contributory negligence on the part of the plaintiff in a DAMAGE suit often constitutes a DEFENSE for the DEFENDANT.

Controversy. A SUIT or CIVIL ACTION; an issue appropriate for determination in a court of LAW. Controversies take place between PLAINTIFFS and DEFENDANTS.

Contumacy. The failure or refusal of an individual charged as a DEFENDANT to appear in court to defend the CHARGES against him; failure to obey a SUMMONS.

Contumely. Insolence; rudeness; disdain.

Contusion. An INJURY beneath the skin without a break in the skin's surface; a bruise.

Convenience and necessity. An expression used when a carrier applies for a LICENSE to operate one or more vehicles commercially along a specified route or highway.

Convening order. A STATEMENT that the COURT was in session and did business at a certain time in a certain place.

Conventional lien. A LIEN (the legal RIGHT to hold PROPERTY or to have property applied for payment of a CLAIM) resulting from an AGREEMENT between two or more PARTIES, rather than one originating from the LAW.

Conversion. 1. The taking of another's PROPERTY without permission or cause. It is an unlawful act. **2.** In EQUITY, conversion is the exchange of property from real to personal, or vice versa.

Convertible bonds. BONDS that can be converted or turned into STOCK, usually COMMON STOCK.

Convertible term insurance. Term LIFE INSURANCE, which has no cash surrender value, but that can be turned into ordinary life insurance, which does have cash value.

Conveyance. 1. A DEED transferring the TITLE of land from one person to another. **2.** A transfer of title (to anything) from one person to another.

Conveyancing. The investigation of the TITLE to land or PROPERTY, and the composition of legal DOCUMENTS leading to the transfer of such property from the OWNER to another.

Convict. Someone who has been found GUILTY of a CRIME or MISDEMEANOR; to find an ACCUSED guilty.

Conviction. A JUDGMENT that an ACCUSED is GUILTY of a CRIME.

Convincing proof. PROOF that is sufficient to establish a charge BEYOND A REASONABLE DOUBT.

Cooling time. In the COMMISSION of a CRIME, it is important to know whether the PERPETRATOR committed the act in a state of intense emotional stress or whether he did it "in cold blood." Cooling time is that period during which the perpetrator has become completely composed and therefore performs his act in a calm state, fully comprehending what he is doing.

Cooperative apartment. An apartment unit in which the tenant has an interest in the OWNERSHIP of the building and a LEASE entitling him to continued occupancy of his particular apartment.

Cooperative association. A COM-

PANY or organization composed of a group of people who have banded together for the achievement of a common goal for their mutual benefit.

Coordinate jurisdiction. The AUTHORITY possessed by two or more COURTS of equal status, each having the right to try a certain type of CASE. Also called CONCURRENT JURISDICTION.

Cop. Slang for POLICE OFFICER or policeman.

Copping a plea. Pleading GUILTY to a lesser OFFENSE than the one charged, and having such PLEA accepted by the COURT.

Coprolalia. A medical term denoting the habitual use of foul and obscene language. Mentally unsound people often engage in *copralalia.*

Copyright. A RIGHT granted by law to the author of a literary or artistic work, giving him the exclusive privilege, for a period of years, to publish and sell his writings or productions.

Copyright law. That branch of the LAW which protects owners of copyrights from infringement, plagiarism, etcetera.
> INFRINGEMENT OF COPYRIGHT; VIOLATION OF COPYRIGHT.

Coram nobis. A WRIT of coram nobis is a request to set aside a VERDICT because of errors of fact that took place during the TRIAL (Latin).

Coram vobis. Essentially the same as CORAM NOBIS (Latin).

Co-respondent. A person named as an adulterer in a DIVORCE suit, such individual being charged by the PLAINTIFF who seeks the divorce.

Cornering the market. Buying up most of a particular commodity on the market so as to hold it to sell for a higher price.

Coroner's case. A DEATH that has occurred due to violence or under suspicious circumstances which is then referred to the coroner, resulting in examination and possible AUTOPSY.

Coroner's inquest. An investigation into the cause of a violent or suspicious DEATH. The INQUEST is held by a coroner with the help of a JURY. > MEDICAL EXAMINER.

Corporal punishment. Physical PUNISHMENT, such as whipping or lashing meted out to a convicted criminal. Such punishment is not intended to cause serious BODILY INJURY.

Corporate bonds. BONDS issued by a CORPORATION. Such bonds represent a written PROMISE of a corporation to pay certain INTEREST in return for a LOAN of money, plus a promise to redeem the bonds and pay back the money loaned.

Corporate entity. The CORPORATION, as distinct from its STOCKHOLDERS or OFFICERS.

Corporate medicine. In some states physicians can form professional CORPORATIONS to practice medicine. However, this does not free them from personal LIABILITY in the care of their patients. The letters "P.C.," after a physician's name, mean that the physician is incorporated.

Corporate practice of law. In

some states, ATTORNEYS are privileged to form professional corporations to practice law. However, this does not free them from personal LIABILITY in their relations with their CLIENTS.

Corporate reorganization. The PROCESS of reorganizing a COMPANY that is in financial trouble so as to make it into a profitable business.

Corporate seal. An emblem or symbol of a CORPORATION, often embossed on a corporation's stock or bond CERTIFICATES, or on a CONTRACT of the corporation.

Corporation. A legal entity composed, usually, of a number of people who have joined together for a common purpose. Such legal entities are formed under city, state, or federal laws. Some CORPORATIONS are public and some are private; some private corporations are organized for profit, others are nonprofit. Private corporations often issue STOCK to their owners in return for the money they invest.

Corporation de jure. A COMPANY organized strictly according to the LAWS governing the formation of CORPORATIONS (Latin).

Corporation law. LAWS governing the formation and activities of CORPORATIONS. A corporation LAW FIRM is one that specializes in handling legal matters concerning corporations rather than individuals.

Corporeal hereditaments. Tangible things that are inherited, as distinguished from incorporeal hereditaments, such as RIGHTS or PRIVILEGES.

Corporeal presence. Bodily presence, often required by a court. The need to be present in a COURT OF LAW, instead of being represented by an ATTORNEY.

Corpse. A dead body.

Corpus. The capital of an estate or fund; the main substance of a thing. (The term is of Latin derivation, meaning "body.")

Corpus delicti. The body upon whom a crime has been committed, such as the corpse of a murdered person (Latin).

Corpus juris. The substance or body of the LAW (Latin).

Correction officer. A prison guard; a jailer.

Corroborating circumstances. Facts that support the TESTIMONY of a WITNESS.

Corroborating evidence. Additional information that substantiates and supplements EVIDENCE already submitted to the COURT.

Corrupt intent. Doing something with full knowledge that it is illegal, such as charging INTEREST on a LOAN which is in excess of that allowed by law.

Corrupt practices acts. LAWS whose intentions are to prevent excessive monies being spent on the election of candidates for public office and to regulate how such monies may be spent. Also, these laws are aimed at preventing unfair methods of campaigning, such as making false accusations against one's opponent, etcetera.

Corrupting the morals of a minor. Any act by an adult that leads a child to participate in immoral activity or to witness immoral activities.

Corruption. Behavior that is in violation of the law; illegal; an attempt to interfere with the carrying out of the law.
Co-signer. Someone who signs a DOCUMENT along with another person or persons, often assuming OBLIGATIONS to be shared with the other signers.
Cost-plus contract. An AGREEMENT that fixes the amount of money to be paid a contractor for labor and costs of materials, plus a percentage of extra money paid as profit for carrying out the CONTRACT.
Costs. Monies ordered by a court to be paid by the loser to the winner after a civil trial is concluded.
Costs of administration. Monies owed to the receiver who has administered a BANKRUPT business. These costs take precedence over monies owed to the creditors.
Costs of prosecution. The same as "costs"; the monies expended in prosecuting a SUIT. If a PLAINTIFF wins the case, he may be awarded costs of prosecution.
Co-tenancy. The OWNERSHIP or POSSESSION of a PROPERTY by two or more people; tenants in common; joint tenancy.
Counsel. A LAWYER; and ATTORNEY; a COUNSELOR. To counsel means to advise.
Counselor, Counselor-at-law. An ATTORNEY who has been admitted to the BAR and is licensed to practice.
Count. To state or PLEAD a CASE in COURT; to argue a case; a particular CHARGE in an INDICTMENT.
Counterclaim. A CLAIM or cause of action by a DEFENDANT against a PLAINTIFF.
Counterfeit. The manufacture, distribution, or sale of false money, stamps, or other items having monetary value. Any forged DOCUMENT is, in reality, counterfeit.
Counter-injunction. An INJUNCTION that stops or countermands the enforcement of an injunction. An injunction is a COURT ORDER prohibiting someone from carrying out a specified act.
Countermand. To cancel an order previously given.
Counter plea. A PLEA placed on record in reply to another plea.
Countersign. An additional signature placed on a DOCUMENT for the purpose of authenticating it. A CONTRACT may insist that more than one concerned OFFICER of a COMPANY sign the AGREEMENT.
Countervailing equity. A RIGHT or EQUITY that is opposed to, or equal to, one which is being sought. Such an equity should be given equal consideration to the one being sought.
Counts. The sum total of the various charges brought against a DEFENDANT. A defendant may be found GUILTY on one or more counts, or INNOCENT of some counts and not others.
County. A subdivision of a state. Large states may have many counties, whereas small states have but few. The AUTHORITY of a county depends to a great extent upon whether a city or town is within its borders. Generally, the counties without important towns and cities within its borders

have greater JURISDICTION over the government in their area. Throughout the country, the powers of various counties vary greatly.

County clerk. > CLERK OF THE COURT.

County court. A state COURT whose seat is located in a particular county. Although its JURISDICTION may be limited, a county court may, in some states, have AUTHORITY throughout the entire state.

County jail. A JAIL for minor criminals or for criminals who are transient.

County line. The boundary between two counties. A crime committed on a county line, such as a highway, may be tried in either adjacent county.

County seat. The COMMUNITY in which the county administrative buildings and COURTS are located.

Coupons. CERTIFICATES, usually located on BONDS, for the collection of interest. "Clipping coupons" means cutting off the particular certificate and presenting it to a bank for payment or deposit.

Court. A place where justice is administered. There are dozens of different types of courts, each especially set up for the administration of a particular type of justice.

Court clerk. > CLERK OF THE COURT.

Court-martial. A military COURT for trying cases involving members of the armed services.

Court of appeals. A COURT having the power to review the law and the decisions of a lower court in particular types of cases. > APPELLATE COURT.

Court of common pleas. A TRIAL court; a COURT with general JURISDICTION OR AUTHORITY over CIVIL CASES.

Court of equity. A COURT having AUTHORITY over cases involving various rights or matters of EQUITY. Controversies in equity should be distinguished from those involving matters of the written laws or STATUTES.

Court of general sessions. A COURT having power to hear CRIMINAL CASES.

Court of inquiry. A COURT to inquire into the innocence or guilt of a member of the armed forces in the performance of his or her DUTIES.

Court of last resort. The highest COURT, the one whose decision is final and from which no APPEAL can be taken.

Court of probate. > PROBATE COURT.

Court of special sessions. A COURT that is not regularly in session but which is activated from time to time to hear particular cases.

Court order. A written direction of a JUDGE or a COURT. Legally, it must be obeyed.

Court record. The official, written documentation of what transpired during a HEARING or TRIAL.

Court reporter. The official stenographer, employed by the court to write down what has transpired, verbatim, during the trial. The reporter's recordings constitute the COURT RECORD.

Covenant. A written AGREEMENT, signed and notarized, between two or more people, in which one PARTY or parties promises to perform certain acts and the other party or parties agree to recompense him or them for such performance. In other words, a covenant is a binding CONTRACT between two or more people. Suits for VIOLATION of a covenant are EX CONTRACTU, arising out of a written contract.

Covenant to convey. A written, signed AGREEMENT by the one making the COVENANT (the covenantor) to give to the receiver (the covenantee) certain properties under certain circumstances.

Covenant to renew. A CONTRACT giving to the lessee (the one leasing the PROPERTY) the right to renew the lease under certain conditions outlined in the renewal CLAUSE of the lease.

Covenant to stand seised. A CONTRACT in which a man agrees to give up land for the use of his family. In essence, this transfers the right to the PROPERTY from himself to his wife, children, etcetera.

Cover up. To hide something that is unlawful; to evade or impede an investigation into the legality of certain questionable acts.

Covert. Secret; concealed. A covert act is one that is hidden, often because of fear of revelation, from public knowledge.

Coverture. The special legal RIGHTS that married women were once entitled to. In modern times, coverture is fast fading into nonexistence.

Craft union. A labor organization composed of members who are all in the same trade or occupation.

Crank. An emotionally disturbed person who acts erratically. Cranks frequently call the POLICE to tell them they know the CRIMINAL who performed an unsolved crime when in reality they have no knowledge of the matter at all.

Credentials. Written STATEMENTS showing who a person is and what official privileges he is entitled to. Ambassadors present their credentials when they take up their posts in a foreign country.

Credibility. The believability of a WITNESS; worthy of belief.

Credible. Believable.

Credit. The ability of someone to borrow, based upon the opinion of the bank, or other lender, as to his capability to repay and his reliability to repay.

Credit rating. An opinion concerning the reliability of an individual in the payment of his DEBTS. Someone with a high credit rating has both capability and reliability in the payments of monies he owes. There are organizations whose function is to assign credit ratings to various individuals and businesses. Such ratings are based upon present and past history of capability and reliability.

Credit union. A nonprofit CORPORATION organized under existing laws for the purpose of obtaining CREDIT for its members.

Creditor. A person to whom a DEBT is owed. (The one owing the creditor is known as the DEBTOR.)

Creditor's suit. An ACTION in COURT brought by a CREDITOR to force the payment of a debt that a court has already decreed should be paid. Such a suit frequently attempts to collect a DEBT from assets of the DEFENDANT that are not attachable by LAW. A creditor's suit is also called a *creditor's bill.*

Credits. OBLIGATIONS or monies due, or those that will become due.

Crime. A VIOLATION of an existing LAW or a failure to perform an act required by law.

Crime, common-law. A CRIME committed and punishable under the COMMON LAW, rather than crimes created by statutes. The common law is declared by JUDGES, as distinguished from laws resulting from statutes or existing ORDINANCES.

Crime, high. Unlawful act nearly equal to FELONY, which, however, does not fall within the category of a felony. A felony is more serious than a MISDEMEANOR and usually carries a SENTENCE in excess of one year.

Crime, infamous. A major CRIME, such as a FELONY or TREASON. An infamous crime is one for which a severe JAIL term may be imposed. GRAND JURIES investigate and INDICT those accused of infamous crimes.

Crime against nature. A "sex perversion," such as sexual contact between a human and an animal or, in the COMMON LAW, sexual acts between people that deviate from the so-called "normal." In recent years, society has altered greatly its concepts concerning what is or is not a "crime against nature" insofar as it applies to relations between human and human.

Crime of omission. An OFFENSE characterized by the failure of an individual to perform a required act. It may be just as serious as a CRIME of COMMISSION.

Crimen falsi. A CRIME containing the elements of FRAUD and DECEIT (Latin).

Crimes, statutory. CRIMES that are created by existing STATUTES rather than by the COMMON LAW.

Criminal. Someone who has committed a CRIME of a serious nature. The word also means "wicked."

Criminal act. A breaking of the LAW, either a MISDEMEANOR or a FELONY; a violation of a STATUTE or of the COMMON LAW.

Criminal action. A LAWSUIT that provides for bringing an offender to justice.

Criminal assault and battery. A physical attack resulting in BODILY INJURY, committed by an ASSAILANT. Such an act, if proven to be willful, is punishable by law, and the PENALTY imposed will be gauged by the extent of injuries and the wantonness of the act.

Criminal charge. An INDICTMENT against an ACCUSED, resulting in a trial for the COMMISSION of the crime.

Criminal contempt proceeding. An ACTION against a person who has disobeyed, acted contemptuously, or demeaned a COURT of LAW. Such PROCEDURES are adopted in order to preserve the dignity and enforce the power of the court.

Criminal court. A COURT in which criminal cases, as distinguished from civil cases, are tried.

Criminal gross negligence. An

act of COMMISSION or OMISSION in which one demonstrates a willful disregard for the RIGHTS of others, resulting in possible or actual harm or INJURY.

Criminal insanity. A mentally ill state in which one is unable to distinguish between right and wrong and, as a result, commits unlawful acts.

Criminal intent. The knowledge that one is performing an unlawful act; the intent to commit a crime.

Criminal jurisdiction. The right of a particular COURT (with its judges) to hear and decide cases of a criminal nature.

Criminal law. That branch of LAW that deals with CRIMES and their PUNISHMENT. In other words, this type of law concerns itself with public wrongs, such as ROBBERY, BURGLARY, FORGERY, HOMICIDE, etcetera.

Criminal negligence. Neglect or NEGLIGENCE of such a nature that it is punishable as a crime, such as MANSLAUGHTER due to failure of a person to do something that he should have done.

Criminal offense. An OFFENSE in which a CRIME has been committed, which will be tried in a CRIMINAL COURT rather than in a CIVIL COURT; an illegal act contrary to existing LAWS and STATUTES; an offense indictable by a GRAND JURY.

Criminal procedure. Methods in the law for the apprehension, TRIAL, and PUNISHMENT of one accused of having broken existing LAWS; a CRIMINAL PROSECUTION.

Criminal prosecution. A TRIAL in a CRIMINAL COURT on behalf of the general public for the purpose of bringing to justice a person or persons who have committed a CRIME. Thus, a suspected murderer is charged by the state for his crime; a person suspected of TREASON is charged by the federal government for his alleged crime.

Criminal responsibility. In MEDICAL JURISPRUDENCE, the mental capacity of an ACCUSED to understand the nature of the CHARGES being brought against him and his mental capability of behaving in a manner prescribed by the law. A totally unbalanced, mentally sick individual may have no knowledge that he is committing an unlawful act.

Criminally inflicted wound. A wound caused by an illegal attack upon a person's body.

Criminology. That branch of science devoted to the study of crime and criminals.

Crippling. Physically disabling.

Crook. A word in common usage denoting a thief, swindler, forger, or con man.

Cross-action. A suit brought by the DEFENDANT against the PLAINTIFF, growing out of the same subject matter as the plaintiff's suit.

Cross appeal. An APPEAL in which both parties to a CASE appeal the JUDGMENT that has been rendered.

Cross-claim. A CLAIM that is made by one PARTY in a SUIT in opposition to a claim that has already been made against him by the other party in the suit.

Cross-demand. > CROSS-CLAIM.

Cross-examination. The examination of a WITNESS brought into court by the opposing PARTY in a SUIT. In other words, the questioning of an opposing witness.

Cross-remainders. A situation in which land is willed to two or more people; if one or more of the LEGATEES should die, the PROPERTY crosses over to the surviving LEGATEE or legatees. The ultimate inheritor must await the death of all the original legatees before receiving the land.

Cross-suit. > CROSS ACTION.

Cruel and unusual punishment. Excessive, inhuman PUNISHMENT. In many states, the death penalty is now ruled to be cruel and unusual punishment. Beating or starving prisoners is also considered cruel and unusual punishment.

Cruelty. The act of causing severe physical or mental harm to another. The definition of cruelty varies from state to state, but the COMMISSION of physical violence or the infliction of severe mental anguish by a spouse often serves as grounds for divorce. *Extreme cruelty* and *intolerable cruelty* are often charged in divorce suits.

Cruelty to animals. The infliction of pain, suffering, or neglect by a human upon an animal. This constitutes an offense punishable by LAW.

Cuckold. A man whose wife has been or is unfaithful to him.

Culpable. At fault; indifferent to others' rights; blamable; worthy of censure.

Culpable negligence. Failing to do something that a reasonable, prudent person would do, or doing something that a reasonable, prudent person would not do. As a consequence of such behavior, harm is done to someone. Culpable negligence is more than ordinary NEGLIGENCE; there is a willful or wanton aspect associated with it.

Culprit. An ACCUSED; an individual brought to COURT to answer for the COMMISSION of a crime. A culprit is one who is accused but not yet convicted.

Cum gran salis. With a grain of salt (Latin).

Cumulative evidence. Additional EVIDENCE or corroborating evidence on a particular point in a TRIAL.

Cumulative offense. The repetition of the same OFFENSE, usually over a period of days or weeks.

Cumulative punishment. SENTENCES to run one after the other, as distinguished from CONCURRENT SENTENCES, which allows the serving of sentences for several crimes at the same time. Cumulative sentences are frequently meted out to second or third offenders and are greater than those meted out to first offenders. > CONSECUTIVE SENTENCES; SENTENCE, CUMULATIVE.

Cunnilingus. An oral-genital contact between the mouth and the female genitals.

Curator. Guardian.

Cure by verdict. An error in the TRIAL of a CASE is rendered harmless by the VERDICT when it goes in favor of the party who has suffered the error. Also known as *cure by judgment.*

Curfew. A particular time in the evening when all those without official duties shall remain indoors. Curfews are ordered by towns or municipalities during times of riot and public disorder.

Curia. COURT (Latin).

Current account. An account between parties that continually do business with each other; an open account. (The opposite of a closed account.)

Current liability. An existing DEBT; an indebtedness that should be paid off within a year's time.

Current value. The prevailing price or value; the common market price at the place where the commodity originates.

Custodian. An individual employed to safeguard and watch over somebody's PROPERTY.

Custody. The care and control of PROPERTY, or of a person or persons. Custody does not necessarily imply OWNERSHIP. A child may be given over to the custody of a parent or guardian; a prisoner may be held in custody by being placed in JAIL.

Custody of the law. The lawful holding or seizure of PROPERTY by an OFFICER of the LAW.

Custom. An oft-repeated mode of CONDUCT; a form of behavior acceptable to the majority of society, such as working five or six days a week. A custom, by its universal adoption and repetition acquires the importance and effect of a LAW in a particular COMMUNITY or country.

Customary. Usual; ordinary; according to custom; the general practice of the majority of people.

Customary practice. In MEDICAL JURISPRUDENCE, the common method of treatment in a given community, as practiced by the well-trained, ethical physicians of that community.

Customs. DUTIES payable on imported merchandise. Such items are inspected by CUSTOMS officers, and duties are levied, or not levied, according to existing customs LAWS.

Customs court. A federal COURT with JURISDICTION to review levies made by CUSTOMS collectors, and the authority to hear and act upon complaints from importers of goods and merchandise.

Customs law. LAWS governing the payment or exemption of DUTIES upon imported goods. (Some goods are dutiable, others are not, according to current customs laws.)

Customs lien. A LIEN (the right to hold) on PROPERTY by the government upon articles for which duty is due and not paid.

Cy Pres doctrine. A DOCTRINE that permits a donor's gift to be given to a similar type of charity if, for some reason, it cannot be given to the original charity named by the donor.

D

Daily wages. In COMPENSATION CASES, the payment awarded to an injured worker determined by his rate of pay per day, or per hour, if this latter method was used in calculating his wages.
Damages. Compensation that the law awards to someone who has been injured or suffers a loss because of the action of another.
> ADDED DAMAGES.
Damages, actual. Money awarded to a COMPLAINANT equal to his actual loss or INJURY; it does not include PUNITIVE DAMAGES. Also known as *general damages* or *compensatory damages.*
> DAMAGES, COMPENSATORY.
Damages, compensatory. An award that will just cover the actual loss and nothing more.
Damages, consequential. DAMAGES that are not directly the result of an act but flow from the consequences of an act. The damages to a vehicle may cost X number of dollars to repair, but there are consequential damages if that vehicle cannot be serviceable as the result of the accident, and the owner therefore cannot use it for gainful purposes.
Damages, double or treble. Double or triple the amount of *actual damages,* allowed by some JURIES in some states for injuries resulting from FRAUD, TRESPASS, or NEGLIGENCE. > DAMAGES, ACTUAL.
Damages, excessive. Monies awarded by a JURY that are far in excess of those warranted in a particular CASE.
Damages, exemplary. DAMAGES in excess of the actual loss, awarded sometimes when the wrong was aggravated by FRAUD or violence.
Damages, irreparable. DAMAGES that cannot actually compensate for the loss, as it is not possible to measure the loss in terms of monetary compensation.
Damages, nominal. An insignificant award to a PLAINTIFF who has not actually sustained a serious INJURY or loss.
Damages, permanent. An award based upon the knowledge that the DAMAGES are permanent and cannot be remedied.
Damages, proximate. Immediate DAMAGES that result from the act of the defendant; expected damages.
Damages, punitive. Compensation in excess of the actual DAMAGES, awarded to the PLAINTIFF as punishment to the DEFENDANT for the wrong he committed.
> DAMAGES, EXEMPLARY.
Damages, remote. Unexpected DAMAGES resulting from the original act. Such damages are beyond the control of the negligent PARTY.
Damages, speculative. DAMAGES that are anticipated in the future from similar acts of the negligent PARTY.
Damages, temporary. Occasional,

repeated DAMAGES that can be remedied by acts of the negligent party.

Damages, unliquidated. Compensation that has not yet been determined by the court, even though the PLAINTIFF has been successful in his SUIT.

Damages and costs. A phrase binding the DEFENDANT, who is appealing an award against him, to pay the amount of the JUDGMENT plus INTEREST if his APPEAL is unsuccessful.

Damages at large. An award for which there is no precise measurement, such as DAMAGES for pain, suffering, or mental anguish.

Damages for delay. Extra monies awarded to the PLAINTIFF for the delay in settlement, caused by the DEFENDANT's appeal of the JUDGMENT.

Damages for loss of use. Awards made to compensate for the loss of use of something that ordinarily earns money.

Damnum. DAMAGES (Latin).

Dangerous per se. Something that, in itself, is dangerous and may cause INJURY without human intervention, such as an avalanche or a rock slide.

Dangerous weapon. Anything that may inflict serious BODILY HARM or cause a fatality. It does not necessarily have to be a gun or knife. ➤ DEADLY WEAPON; LETHAL WEAPON.

Data. FACTS from which conclusions are drawn; information, collected in order to reach a conclusion.

Date of injury. The date on which an ACCIDENT occurred. Such a date is important in a COMPENSATION CASE to determine exactly when recompense should start.

Date of issue. Date upon which BONDS or other SECURITIES are offered and upon which INTEREST commences.

Day fixed for trial. The day upon which a SUMMONS must be answered in COURT and a date is set for the actual commencement of the TRIAL.

Day in court. The day when a DEFENDANT or ACCUSED appears in COURT and defends himself/herself against the charges brought by the PLAINTIFF.

Days of grace. Extra days, often thirty days, beyond the date on which a payment is due. INSURANCE carriers often permit thirty days of grace beyond the time when a PREMIUM payment is due. After the days of grace, the INSURANCE POLICY lapses.

De bonis non. A Latin expression meaning "of the goods or property not dispersed or taken care of." When an EXECUTOR of an ESTATE dies before the estate is settled, an ADMINISTRATOR is appointed to complete the task. He is said to be granted de bonis non, or the right to administer what has not yet been distributed. Also known as de bonis non administratis.

De die in diem. From day to day (Latin).

De facto. Actual; in fact. The expression is used to describe a COMPANY, a person, a CORPORATION, etcetera, that exists and is functioning in a certain capacity but has not been legally authorized to do so. De facto is the opposite of de jure, which means something that is according to law (Latin).

De facto government. A GOVERNMENT that is in power but has not been duly elected according to the laws of the country.

De jure. Legal; lawful, legitimate; duly authorized. The opposite of de facto (Latin).

De jure government. A GOVERNMENT that has been placed in power according to the laws of the land; a legally constituted government.

De minimis. Of trifling consequences; a matter so small the COURT does not wish to consider it (Latin).

De novo. Anew; again. A TRIAL de novo is a second trial on the same matter, starting afresh (Latin).

Dead body, right to bury or cremate. In MEDICAL JURISPRUDENCE, it must be ascertained that a person has died of natural causes before permission can be granted to bury or cremate the remains.

Deadlocked jury. A JURY that is unable to reach a DECISION.

Deadly weapon. Anything that can be used to cause serious BODILY HARM or death. In addition to guns and knives, there are clubs, axes, stones, and many other things that have, from time to time, been used as deadly weapons. ➤ DANGEROUS WEAPON; LETHAL WEAPON.

Deal. A TRANSACTION between two or more people; a business arrangement to attain certain desired results.

Dealing. Buying and selling. A STOCKBROKER is said to be dealing in SECURITIES.

Dealings. Business TRANSACTIONS.

Death. The termination of life. In medicine, this state is defined as one in which the heart has stopped beating, respirations have ceased, and brain waves (as determined by electroencephalography) no longer exist.
➤ DETERMINATION OF DEATH.

Death certificate. An official DOCUMENT attesting to the fact that a person has died. These CERTIFICATES are issued by lawfully constituted AGENCIES in a COMMUNITY.

Death duties. ESTATE TAXES.

Death sentence. CAPITAL PUNISHMENT for a crime, carried out according to local, state, or federal statutes. The sentence may call for hanging, electrocution, asphyxiation, or shooting.

Death warrant. AUTHORIZATION from an OFFICIAL stating the time and place for the carrying out of a DEATH SENTENCE.

Death trap. A building or structure that is dangerous to the lives of the occupants, even though on the surface it may appear to be safe.

Debauchery. A term with many meanings for sensual acts that are far in excess of average or normal behavior. Debauchery may consist of excess or immoral sexual acts, habitual drunkenness, corruption of innocent people, lewdness, etcetera.

Debenture. A CERTIFICATE issued by a CORPORATION acknowledging a DEBT and promising to repay the LOAN with interest; an unsecured BOND.

Debit. A bookkeeping term for

entries made on the left side of a ledger or account book, noting monies that are due or owing. (A debit is the opposite of a CREDIT.)

Debt. Money owed; money owed as the result of an AGREEMENT or CONTRACT, oral or written.

Debt, fraudulent. A DEBT wherein the person owing the money has deceived the CREDITOR, defrauding him.

Debt, privileged. A DEBT that is to be paid before any others should the DEBTOR become BANKRUPT.

Debtor. A person who owes money; someone liable by contract to pay a CLAIM.

Debtor in possession. An individual, individuals, or a COMPANY or CORPORATION that continues to occupy its property and to conduct business during the time when BANKRUPTCY proceedings are in progress. Such PROCEEDINGS may be geared to rehabilitating the individual or individuals, COMPANY, or CORPORATION, or they may be in the process of liquidating the remaining assets of the debtor in possession.

Deceased. A person who has died.

Decedent. A person who has died. (WILLS frequently refer to the decedent, the maker of the will.)

Deceit. FRAUD; misrepresentation; harming someone by deceiving him or her.

Decision. A JUDGMENT or DECREE issued by a judge or JURY; the deciding of a LAWSUIT; FINDINGS of a court.

Decision on appeal. The JUDGMENT of an APPELLATE COURT. It may be upholding, modifying, or reversing the decision of the lower court.

Decision on the merits. A court DECISION that is final, rendering it impossible for other SUITS to be brought by the same person on the same matter.

Decision reserved. A JUDGMENT not given immediately after conclusion of the TESTIMONY but reserved by the judge for later.

Declaration of dividend. A decision of a board of directors of a CORPORATION to pay its STOCKHOLDERS a certain amount of money for each share they own.

Declaration of Independence. A statement issued on July 4, 1776, by the thirteen American colonies declaring themselves free and independent from Britain. (See pages 379–81 for the complete text.)

Declaration of intention. A statement by a foreigner, made and recorded in COURT, that he intends to become a United States CITIZEN.

Declaration of trust. A STATEMENT by an OWNER of PROPERTY that he intends to set up a TRUST for said property, as the result of which the property will be for the use of another person or persons but the TITLE to the property shall remain with the owner.

Declaratory decree. A binding STATEMENT as to the rights in a CASE in EQUITY, not accompanied by an award or JUDGMENT.

Declaratory judgment. A STATEMENT of the COURT as to the RIGHTS in a CASE, not accompanied by any award of damages or relief. In other words, the court declares its OPINION and interpretation of the LAW.

Declaratory statute. A STATUTE enacted to clarify the LAW on a particular matter.

Decoy. To lure or entice. A *police decoy* is frequently used to catch a CRIMINAL in the act of committing a CRIME.

Decree. The DECISION of a COURT OF EQUITY. A JUDGMENT is a decision of a COURT OF LAW.

Decree, consent. A DECISION agreed to by both PARTIES, made and sanctioned by a COURT.

Decree, interlocutory. A DECISION made during the course of a SUIT to clarify and decide a particular point that has arisen. Such DECREE does not necessarily determine the outcome of a case.

Decree nisi. A provisional DECREE that will become final unless cause is shown why it should not become absolute.

Decree of divorce. A JUDGMENT, issued by a COURT, granting a DIVORCE.

Decree of interpleader. A DECREE ordering rival claimants in a suit to litigate between themselves to determine who is entitled to the CLAIM.

Decree of nullity. A DECISION for the ANNULMENT of a marriage. Annulment is different from divorce in that it decrees that the marriage never truly existed and is *null and void.*

Dedication by deed. A setting aside of land for public use via a DEED that specifies exactly to what use the PROPERTY shall be put.

Deductible expenses. Expenditures for business purposes that can be deducted from one's INCOME TAXES.

Deed. A written DOCUMENT transferring the OWNERSHIP of land, and the buildings thereon, to another person or persons.

Deed inter partes. A DEED for the transfer of PROPERTY, made between the owner of the property and the individual who will become the owner of said property (Latin). It is to be distinguished from a deed executed by an ATTORNEY or AGENT of one of the parties to the TRANSACTION.

Deed of release. A QUITCLAIM deed, releasing PROPERTY from the burden of a MORTGAGE upon the payment of certain specified conditions.

Deed of separation. A DOCUMENT spelling out the details of a SEPARATION wherein the husband may provide for the separate maintenance and support of an estranged wife.

Deed of trust. A DOCUMENT in which PROPERTY is placed in the hands of TRUSTEES whose duties include the payment of OBLIGATIONS due. This type of deed is in actuality a valid MORTGAGE.

Deem. To determine; to consider; to judge.

Defalcation. The misuse of money entrusted to someone; embezzlement; misappropriation.

Defamation of character. SLANDER or LIBEL; the stating or printing of material which damages someone's reputation and good name. One does not sue for defamation of character but rather for libel or slander.

Defamation of the dead. SLANDER or LIBEL of someone who is dead.

Defamatory per se. Written or printed material that is so obviously libelous and injurious that it will form the basis for a LAWSUIT.

Default. The failure of a person, persons, CORPORATIONS, or municipalities to pay their DEBTS; the failure to carry out an OBLIGATION.

Default day. The last day on which a DEFENDANT can appear in COURT to defend himself. Should the person fail to appear on that day, a DEFAULT JUDGMENT will be rendered against him.

Default judgment. An award given to a PLAINTIFF because the DEFENDANT fails to appear or to be represented in his own DEFENSE.

Defeasance. A CLAUSE in a MORTGAGE that states that the mortgage is VOIDED (ended) when all the payments have been made.

Defeasible title. A TITLE that is likely to be nullified and VOIDED.

Defect of parties. The ability of a COURT to hear and decide a case on its own because both PLAINTIFF and DEFENDANT fail to appear in COURT and give essential TESTIMONY.

Defect of substance. A flaw in the presentation of an INDICTMENT or PLEA, usually an important OMISSION, that is necessary for said plea or indictment to be acceptable in COURT.

Defective title. A flaw in a TITLE which makes it nonnegotiable; a title to property obtained through unlawful means, such as FRAUD, the use of force, etcetera.

Defend. To attempt to defeat a CLAIM or charge; to represent a DEFENDANT.

Defendant. The PARTY who refutes a claim made by a PLAINTIFF; the person ACCUSED in a LAWSUIT.

Defendant in error. This term refers to a PLAINTIFF who has won his case in a lower court and now becomes the DEFENDANT when the opposing party appeals the decision, creating another TRIAL on the same matter in a higher court.

Defense. The denial of CHARGES, brought by a PLAINTIFF against a DEFENDANT; an answer to a COMPLAINT.

Defense, frivolous. A DEFENSE that is obviously a pretense.

Defense counsel. A trial LAWYER who represents the DEFENDANT.

Deferred sentence. A delayed SENTENCE.

Defiance of the law. Refusal to obey the ORDER of a COURT; contemptuous conduct toward a court or legally constituted OFFICIAL.

Deficiency assessment. An extra TAX on INCOME, resulting from an audit in which it was found that insufficient tax had been paid originally.

Deficiency judgment. A court's DECISION that a DEFENDANT must pay more money than that secured by PROPERTY. In other words, if the PLAINTIFF wins a suit for $1,000 but the defendant only has property worth $400, the balance of $600 is the amount of the deficiency judgment.

Deficiency on foreclosure. The monies still due the CREDITOR after the FORECLOSURE of a MORTGAGE.

Deficit. Deficiency, especially in

money; the amount by which money falls short of a required amount.

Defile. To corrupt; to pollute; to deflower a female; to dishonor, such as burning a flag of the United States.

Definitive. Final; conclusive; the absolute end of a DISPUTE. (A definitive JUDGMENT is a final one, as distinguished from an INTERLOCUTORY judgment.)

Defloration. The act of taking a female's virginity; the act of deflowering. The term implies seduction. > DEFILE.

Deforcement. The situation wherein a person holds land to which another person is entitled; an intrusion; a DISSEISIN.

Defraud. To cheat; to deprive a person of something that rightfully belongs to him through DECEIT, cunning, trickery, or misrepresentation.

Defunct. Dead; deceased. When referring to an enterprise, it means "out of business."

Degree of crime. A consideration in the determination of a SENTENCE. Generally, the greater the degree and intent, the more severe the PUNISHMENT.

Degree of negligence. The determination as to whether NEGLIGENCE was slight, moderate, or willful. The more willful and severe the NEGLIGENCE, the greater the PENALTY imposed.

Degree of proof. The extent and measure of the EVIDENCE in a case, the main factor in a jury's VERDICT as to GUILTY or NOT GUILTY.

Delectus personae. The right of a PARTNER to approve or disapprove a potential, new partner (Latin).

Delegated power. That AUTHORITY bestowed by a higher authority.

Delegation of authority. The transfer of AUTHORITY from one person to another.

Deletion. The crossing out or removal of certain words, sentences, or clauses from a legal DOCUMENT.

Deliberate. **1.** An act that has been thought out and considered. (The opposite of spontaneous or impromptu.) **2.** To deliberate means to think about or consider, or to plan beforehand.

Deliberate and premeditated. An act that has been considered and planned before it has been carried out, such as a deliberate and premeditated ROBBERY or MURDER.

Deliberations of a jury. The PROCESS of sorting out the EVIDENCE and the FACTS in a case prior to reaching a DECISION.

Delict. A MISDEMEANOR; a wrong; a CRIMINAL OFFENSE. In legal language delict is a TORT.

Delictum (Latin). > DELICT.

Delinquency proceeding. An action in a JUVENILE COURT for the purpose of placing a child under the JURISDICTION of the court.

Delinquent. An individual who does not carry out that which is expected of him or that which he has promised to do; a DEBT that is due and has not been paid; neglectful of duty.

Delinquent child. A child who has committed an OFFENSE that is unlawful and would be punishable by law if the child were an adult.

Delirious. A person who acts irrationally because of a lack of awareness of reasonable conduct. (Severe illness is often accompanied by a delirious state.)

Delirium tremens. A mental illness resulting from the continued, excessive use of alcohol. The illness is characterized by tremors and intense hallucinations (Latin).

Delivery bond. A forthcoming BOND; a redelivery bond; a bond issued upon the seizure of merchandise subject to the conditions for its restoration to the DEFENDANT. Such bonds are frequently issued by REVENUE OFFICERS upon seizure of goods.

Delusion. A thought, idea, or concept that is irrational. Delusions are major characteristics of certain types of mental illness, such as paranoia, dementia praecox, and others. So-called "sane" individuals may also harbor occasional delusions but these seldom motivate their ongoing social conduct, nor occupy a major part of their thinking life.

Demand. A legal OBLIGATION; a CLAIM; to claim as one's right; to insist upon; a positive request that presupposes that there is no DEFENSE to the claim or RIGHT.

Demand, compulsory. The presentation by an OWNER of PROPERTY or an ARTICLE justifying the surrender of said property or article. Having thus proved his CLAIM, the item or items must be surrendered.

Demand in attachment. A DEBT in which the REMEDY of ATTACHMENT (the taking of PROPERTY into CUSTODY until a JUDGMENT is rendered) is available.

Demand in reconvention. A DEMAND that a DEFENDANT mounts in answer to a demand by a PLAINTIFF; a counterclaim.

Demand note. A NOTE that states it is payable on DEMAND, whenever the note is presented.

Demand paper. COMMERCIAL PAPER that is payable on DEMAND. The term implies that the DEBT is already due.

Demeanor. Appearance; the "look" and attitude. The term is often applied to a WITNESS, wherein his demeanor might be described as, "Well-dressed, pleasant, ready and willing to answer questions quickly and without hesitation," etcetera. On the other hand, a witness might display an exactly opposite demeanor.

Demented. Mentally ill; of unsound mind; unable to distinguish right from wrong.

Dementia praecox. A form of mental illness seen most often during the younger years of life. Also known as SCHIZOPHRENIA or, in nonmedical parlance, "split personality." A person with paranoid dementia praecox frequently has the false notion that he/she is being persecuted and may, as a form of DEFENSE, commit violent, unlawful acts.

Demesne. Own; his or her own; complete OWNERSHIP and control of one's land.

Demise. A DEED; a LEASE; a transfer of PROPERTY; a CONVEYANCE or creation of an ESTATE to someone else for life. In MEDICAL JURISPRUDENCE, demise is a DEATH.

Democracy. A form of government in which the AUTHORITY and power rests with all the CITI-

ZENS, who freely choose and vote their candidates into and out of OFFICE.

Demonstrative evidence. Real EVIDENCE; evidence that appeals directly to the senses, such as the sense of sight. (A gun shown to a JURY constitutes demonstrative evidence.) Also, evidence which does not depend upon TESTIMONY.

Demurrage. In MARITIME LAW, demurrage is the amount of money payable to a shipowner for the detention of his ship beyond the number of days agreed upon with the party who chartered the ship. (Such detention may have been occasioned by the extra time it took to unload or load the cargo.)

Demurrer. An OBJECTION, especially a PLEADING. A CONTENTION that the facts submitted by the opposite PARTY do not justify the LAWSUIT. In actuality, it is a motion to dismiss the CHARGES.

Demurrer to evidence. A DEFENDANT's objection to the PLAINTIFF's entire EVIDENCE, conceding the truth of certain of his facts but contending that the facts conceded do not constitute a right for him to win the CASE. A demurrer to evidence is a method of taking a case from the JURY.

Demurrer to indictment. An OBJECTION to an INDICTMENT based upon a defect in said indictment, such as failure to set forth clearly what the OFFENSE was supposed to have been.

Demurrer to interrogatory. An OBJECTION by a WITNESS to a question that is asked of him. In so doing, the witness offers his reasons for not responding.

Demurrer to jurisdiction. An OBJECTION to the AUTHORITY of the court to try a particular case. Such a demurrer is made by the DEFENDANT.

Demurrer to plea. A method whereby a PLAINTIFF tests the adequacy of a DEFENDANT's answer to his charges. Also, in CRIMINAL LAW, a method of objecting to the legal sufficiency of a defendant's PLEA.

Demurrer to the person. A DEMURRER raising the question of whether the PLAINTIFF is competent to pursue the LAWSUIT.

Denaturalize. To deprive someone of his or her citizenship.

Denial. A DEFENSE against a CHARGE; a contradiction; a TRAVERSE. (When a DEFENDANT answers a PLAINTIFF's charges, he or she often denies them. Even if it is stated that the defendant has insufficient information to respond to a COMPLAINT, this will constitute a denial.)

Denunciation. The condemnation of a person; the notification of the authorities that a crime has been committed.

Deny. To issue a denial; to contradict; to protest.

Departure. A changing of the CAUSE OF ACTION in a LAWSUIT, brought by the PLAINTIFF or, the changing of the DEFENSE by the DEFENDANT in a case.

Dependent. Someone who relies upon another for his partial or total support and maintenance. (A spouse or MINOR child is referred to as a dependent.)

Dependent bill. An ACTION in a COURT OF EQUITY relating to a matter already decided in the court. A dependent bill continues the former suit and seeks to obtain relief concerning some matter connected with the original suit. Also known as *bill not original.*

Dependent covenants. A written AGREEMENT or CONTRACT in which both parties agree to carry out certain acts, thus making the covenant dependent upon the performance of those particular acts or OBLIGATIONS.

Dependent relative revocation. The DOCTRINE that an old WILL prevails and is binding, *even* if the person (TESTATOR) making the will has stated an intention of making a new will but has not yet done so. In other words, until a new will has been duly executed, it is not valid or binding.

Depletion deduction. A special INCOME TAX deduction granted the owners of mineral deposits, such as oil, gas, etcetera, or forests whose trees are used for commercial purposes.

Deponent. Someone who gives TESTIMONY under OATH; a WITNESS; a person who gives a written STATEMENT attesting to the truth of a matter.

Deportation. The banishment of someone to a foreign country, along with the taking away of CIVIL RIGHTS and PROPERTY.

Depose. To deprive someone of a public office against his will; to give a written STATEMENT; to state something under OATH; to give written EVIDENCE.

Deposit insurance corporation. > FEDERAL DEPOSIT INSURANCE CORPORATION (F.D.I.C.).

Deposition. The written TESTIMONY of a WITNESS, given under OATH. Such a STATEMENT may be presented in a TRIAL, before a trial, at a HEARING, or in response to written questions put to a witness. A deposition is also called an AFFIDAVIT or a STATEMENT under oath.

Deposition, pre-trial. A written STATEMENT, attested to by OATH, presented before the beginning of a TRIAL.

Depreciation. A lessening of value of a PROPERTY. Such loss of worth may arise from several causes, including continued use, damage from weather, obsolescence, etcetera. The INCOME TAX laws permit deductions from wear and tear or diminished usefulness of property that is used in business for the production of income.

Depredation. The act of plundering, vandalizing, or robbing.

Deprivation without due process. The taking away or destruction of PROPERTY without going through the normal processes of LAW, as laid down through REGULATIONS of judicial bodies.

Deputize. To give the AUTHORITY to an individual to act in the capacity of another, usually a public OFFICER, such as a SHERIFF.

Deputy sheriff. An individual who acts for a SHERIFF, performing his duties.

Deranged. Of unsound mind; mentally incompetent.

Derelict. Failure to perform one's DUTY; an individual without a home or means of SUPPORT, such as a vagrant; an abandoned ship.

Dereliction. Neglect of DUTY; ABANDONMENT of PROPERTY.

Derivative action. A SUIT by a STOCKHOLDER against an OFFI-

CER of a CORPORATION. The suit seeks to prevent a wrong or remedy a wrong committed by the officer against the corporation.

Derivative evidence. EVIDENCE not admitted to COURT because it has been gotten by following up on evidence collected illegally.

Derogation. The passage of a LAW that abolishes or partially repeals or cuts down on the effect of a previous law.

Derogatory clause. A secret clause in a WILL wherein the maker of the will states that no subsequent will shall be valid unless it contains the derogatory clause, as written.

Descendant. A child, grandchild, great-grandchild, and so forth, down through the generations.

Descent. Inheritance from one's parents, grandparents, etcetera.

Desecrate. To treat sacrilegiously; to violate the sanctity of something sacred.

Desegregation. The removal of barriers based upon racist concepts. Desegregation LAWS have eliminated the separation of races in schools, public places, and opportunities for employment. Although desegregation laws have been enacted in this country, in many instances true desegregation has not yet taken place.

Desertion. The act of abandoning one's DUTY and OBLIGATION, such as a husband who abandons his family, a soldier who leaves his post, a captain who abandons his ship, etcetera.

Design to kill. A PREMEDITATED, thought-out plan to commit a MURDER.

Designation of beneficiary. A naming in an INSURANCE POLICY of the person who shall receive the value of the policy upon the policyholder's death.

Despoil. To take PROPERTY away illegally from a rightful OWNER. The term implies violence and/or criminal ACTIONS resulting in the taking away of the property.

Destitute. Without money to maintain SUPPORT; a person abandoned by those responsible for supporting him/her.

Detainer. **1.** Holding a person without consent. **2.** Withholding land from a rightful OWNER.

Detection. The finding of a CRIMINAL; the making of a discovery; the bringing out of some hidden facts.

Detective. A POLICE OFFICER whose duties are to detect and apprehend people who have committed crimes.

Detector. A device, electrically triggered, for hearing sound waves emitted through the air; a "bugging" apparatus.

Detention. Holding someone, such as a suspected CRIMINAL.

Detention of patient. The act of keeping a patient within the confines of a hospital or institution, such detention being carried out to safeguard the patient's health and well-being. A mentally ill patient with suicidal tendencies may be detained in a mental hospital.

Determinable. Capable of being terminated after a certain period of time, or if a certain event takes place.

Determinate obligation. An OBLIGATION in which a specific thing must be done, and no substituted act can satisfy the obligation.

Determination. The end of a LAWSUIT, terminated by a decision of the COURT. (A CASE is determined in favor of one or the other of the parties to the SUIT.)
Determination of death. DEATH is present when vital signs have ceased. These signs include brain waves, as determined by electroencephalography; heart action, as determined by electrocardiography; and respirations.
Detriment. 1. Harm or loss suffered to property or to a person. **2.** Giving up a benefit or right.
Device. A deceit or plan to trick. A *gambling device* may be a machine specially designed to cheat those who gamble.
Devise. A gift originating from a clause in a WILL, usually a gift of real estate. However, a devise may refer to a gift of PERSONAL PROPERTY.
Devise and bequeath. A phrase frequently used in WILLS denoting a gift of PERSONAL PROPERTY or REAL ESTATE, or both.
Devise and grant. Words used in WILLS denoting the transfer of PROPERTY and TITLE to an HEIR.
Devisee. Someone who receives a gift of land in a WILL.
Devolution. The transfer of PROPERTY from one person to another, according to regular legal processes.
Dialectics. The art of reasoning through logical discussion and arguments; logic.
Dictum. An OPINION, contained in a judge's DECISION, that is not essential to the determination of the case. A dictum is not binding on the COURTS in deciding future cases of a similar nature.
Die by his own hand. > SUICIDE.
Die without issue. To die without descendants.
Dies amoris. A day of grace; being granted an extra day. Also known as dies gratiae (Latin).
Dies juridicus. A day on which the COURTS are open and are hearing CASES (Latin).
Dilatory defense. A DEFENSE that obstructs or delays the progress of the CASE without touching upon the merits or lack of merits of the case.
Dilatory plea. An answer to a COMPLAINT that does not touch upon or consider the merits of the case. A dilatory plea may attempt to defeat the CHARGES by going into such issues as improper JURISDICTION or other matters or PROCEDURE. > DILATORY DEFENSE.
Diligent. Concerned; eager to carry out a responsibility; untiring; truly responsible; hard-working.
Diplomatic immunity. Freedom from some local RULES, REGULATIONS, and ORDINANCES, enjoyed by representatives of foreign countries who are residing and working in this country. However, diplomatic immunity does not confer the RIGHT to carry out espionage or crimes such as FORGERY, THEFT, ASSAULT, HOMICIDE, etcetera.
Dipsomania. Uncontrollable addiction to alcohol; a mental illness characterized by habitual intoxication.
Direct. 1. Immediate; proximate; the opposite of indirect and remote. **2.** To order; to guide; to command; to control; to regulate.
Direct attack. A face-to-face con-

frontation; a challenge to the validity and integrity of a court's DECISION with the express purpose of overturning the JUDGMENT.

Direct cause. The immediate cause of an INJURY or ACCIDENT; the legal cause; the proximate cause.

Direct evidence. TESTIMONY and PROOF that goes directly to the issue at hand; proof which requires no other evidence; testimony that arises from the WITNESS' own information and knowledge.

Direct examination. Examination of a WITNESS by the party who called him into COURT to TESTIFY, as opposed to cross-examination, which is conducted by the other side in the case.

Direct injury. The immediate result of a VIOLATION of a legal RIGHT.

Direct interest. A certain interest; interest about which there is no doubt.

Direct loss. An immediate loss, such as someone would suffer if his house were consumed by fire; the opposite of a REMOTE LOSS.

Direct tax. A TAX imposed directly upon PROPERTY, calculated according to the worth of the property.

Direct verdict. A situation in which a judge tells the JURY what its VERDICT must be.

Director. Someone who controls, regulates or directs, such as an administrator, a chief executive officer, or a member of a board of trustees.

Directory statute. A LAW or REGULATION directing that some act or actions be carried out, as distinguished from a MANDATORY STATUTE which directs that some action be taken and then goes on to spell out the consequences and penalties if the action is not taken.

Directory trust. A TRUST in which the funds are vested in a specified manner, as distinguished from a DISCRETIONARY TRUST in which the TRUSTEE or trustees have discretion as to how the funds are managed.

Disability. 1. The state of being legally incapable to perform an act; a lack of competence or power to perform. **2.** An INJURY or illness which incapacitates one from carrying out his usual DUTIES. Such a disability may be physical or mental, total or partial, temporary or permanent.

Disability, temporary. An incapacity from which one will recover.

Disability, total and permanent. An incapacity which now totally prevents one and will continue indefinitely to prevent totally someone from performing his duties or carrying out his job.

Disability insurance. An INSURANCE POLICY that will pay workers who are absent from work because of illness or INJURY. Most states have their own state-run disability insurance program in which the PREMIUM payments are shared by both the workers and their employers.

Disaffirmance. The repudiation of an AGREEMENT or CONTRACT. Such disaffirmance is legally correct if the original contract or agreement was voidable. (In other words, if the contract stated that

it could be repudiated under certain specified circumstances.)
Disagreement. Different opinions on the same subject, as among members of a JURY concerning the INNOCENCE or GUILT of an ACCUSED.
Disapprove. To disallow; to render an unfavorable JUDGMENT; to refuse to confirm a nomination or appointment of an OFFICIAL.
Disavow. To disclaim; to repudiate; to refuse responsibility for an unauthorized act of an AGENT or DEPUTY.
Disbar. To take away an ATTORNEY'S LICENSE to practice.
Disbarment proceeding. An ACTION to take away an ATTORNEY'S LICENSE to practice. Such PROCEEDING may be instituted by a CLIENT who believes he has been wronged by his attorney, or it might be instituted by a judge, a COURT, a committee of the bar association, or by a group of attorneys.
Discharge. The release of someone who has been held in CUSTODY; to free; to end an OBLIGATION by payment of the outstanding DEBT; to perform a DUTY.
Discharge, honorable. > HONORABLE DISCHARGE.
Discharge in bankruptcy. The release of a BANKRUPT from his DEBTS after CREDITORS have received all the payments available from the bankrupt's remaining ASSETS. Such discharge permits the person so discharged to start business again without being liable for his former debts.
Discharge of jury. The release of a JURY after completion of a CASE or their term of service. Also, the release of a jury because of a MISTRIAL.
Discharge of patient. The release of a patient from hospital confinement; the release of a patient when his illness has terminated.
Discharge of patient, against advice. Patients occasionally release themselves from a hospital against the advice of their physician. In such instances, the patient discharges himself.
Disclaimer. The refusal to accept responsibility or to recognize the existence of an OBLIGATION.
Disclosure. The making known of something; a revelation; the uncovering of something that had been kept secret.
Discontinuance. The failure of a PLAINTIFF to continue to press the SUIT. As a consequence, the case is dismissed.
Discounting commercial paper. The deducting of interest on a LOAN before the loan is given. (The DOCUMENT stating the loan is known as COMMERCIAL PAPER.)
Discovery, bill of. > BILL OF DISCOVERY
Discredit. To disbelieve the TESTIMONY of a WITNESS; to distrust; to destroy the credibility of a person, such as a witness.
Discrepancy. An inconsistency between the contentions of a PARTY to a SUIT and the actual FACTS; a variance; a lack of conformity.
Discretion of the court. The sound JUDGMENT of a COURT, allowing it the privilege of deciding

certain outstanding issues upon which there are no governing legal rulings.

Discretionary damages. DAMAGES awarded by an impartial JURY after due deliberation.

Discretionary divorce. A DIVORCE granted by a COURT for causes that it (the court) thinks sufficient. To grant this type of divorce, there must be a STATUTE giving the power to the court to use its own discretion.

Discretionary power. The power to do or not to do a certain thing.

Discretionary trust. A TRUST that permits the ADMINISTRATOR and/or TRUSTEE to use his own judgment in certain pertinent matters. It is *not* a trust wherein certain procedures *must* be carried out. In a discretionary trust, no direction is given to the trustee as to precisely how the monies are to be invested.

Discrimination. The denial of equal protection of the LAWS; the failure to treat all people alike despite differences in race, color, creed, sex, or social position.

Discumberment. The freeing of PROPERTY from a LIEN.

Disencumbrance. The release from a burden (ENCUMBRANCE), such as a MORTGAGE.

Disfigurement. An ACCIDENT or INJURY or other event resulting in impairment of one's beauty, appearance, or symmetry.

Disfranchisement. The taking away of a person's citizenship and his right to vote; the expulsion of a member of a CORPORATION.

Dishonor by nonpayment. A written PLEDGE to pay a LOAN is dishonored when the DEBTOR fails to make the payment which is due.

Disinherit. To exclude from an INHERITANCE. (In so doing, the maker of a WILL must state that one who ordinarily would inherit, such as an offspring, is not to receive any inheritance.)

Disinterested witness. A competent WITNESS who has nothing to gain or lose by the outcome of the CASE.

Disinterment. The removal of a body from a grave. This may be ordered by a COURT in order to examine the body to see if the DEATH was due to natural or violent cause.

Disjunctive allegation. A STATEMENT in an INDICTMENT charging that one of two things might have been committed, such as a CHARGE that an accused murdered *or* caused to be murdered an individual.

Dismissal. A termination of a CASE before it comes to a TRIAL of the ISSUES; a COURT's DECISION to dismiss a case because the PLAINTIFF has insufficient grounds for the suit; the freeing of a DEFENDANT by a PROSECUTING ATTORNEY before he comes to trial.

Dismissal agreed. A termination of a CASE agreed upon by the two contesting PARTIES, often resulting from a settlement of the outstanding ISSUES.

Dismissal compensation. A payment made by an employer to an employee upon the termination of his employment. Such payment is in addition to monies owed the employee as wages.

Dismissal of appeal. A refusal by a COURT OF APPEALS (an appellate court) to hear and try a case that has already been decided in a lower court.

Dismissal of judgment. A dismissal of a CASE without judging it and without preventing the bringing of a new SUIT on the same issue.

Dismissal with prejudice. A JUDGMENT dismissing a CASE because the PLAINTIFF's contentions have not been proved and, furthermore, the judgment bars the plaintiff from future ACTION on the same issue.

Dismissal without prejudice. A dismissal of a CASE not based on its merits and not preventing a future SUIT on the same issue.

Disorderly conduct. Behavior that is socially unacceptable or violates the law or disturbs the peace. Use of loud, obscene language in public, drunkenness associated with boisterous behavior, etcetera, are forms of disorderly conduct.

Disparagement. Discrediting someone or something, occasionally resulting in DAMAGES to reputation or to one's ability to earn a living.

Dispensation. Permission, granted by an AUTHORITY, to do something that is usually prohibited; an exemption from penalties usually imposed by law.

Dispensing power. The AUTHORITY of an AGENCY to excuse someone from performing a DUTY, or to refrain from prohibiting a regularly prohibited form of conduct or act.

Disposition. The final SETTLEMENT of a DISPUTE or CASE in COURT; the judge's final JUDGMENT.

Dispossess proceedings. The ACTIONS of a LANDLORD who wishes to regain POSSESSION of his leased PROPERTY, usually because of nonpayment of monies that are due.

Dispossession. Losing POSSESSION of a premise; ouster. ≫ EVICTION.

Disputable presumption. An ASSUMPTION of a FACT or facts, offered without positive PROOF, that can be defeated or overturned only by producing EVIDENCE that is convincing and positive.

Dispute. A CONTROVERSY; an argument. In LAW, a dispute arises when one PARTY presents an ARGUMENT or a point of view that he contends is factual and such point of view or argument is denied by the other party.

Disqualify. To render unfit; to make someone ineligible; to revoke qualification. A judge may disqualify himself from trying a case because he may have an interest in its outcome, or he may believe that he cannot be completely impartial.

Disregarding corporate entity. In considering an issue involving a CORPORATION, disregarding corporate entity means that no distinction is made between the individuals who make up the corporation and the corporation itself. Ordinarily, in legal matters, the corporation is considered separate and distinct from its OFFICERS and STOCKHOLDERS.

Disregarding testimony. Any TESTIMONY not relevant to the issues being considered, or testimony that should not have been admitted in the TRIAL, may cause the judge to advise the jury to disregard the testimony.

Disseisin. The wrongful DISPOSSESSION of an OWNER from his PROPERTY.

Disseisor. An individual who wrongfully dispossesses someone from property that rightfully belongs to him.

Dissenting opinion. Where more than one JUDGE sits in judging a case, such as a COURT OF APPEALS, there may be a difference of OPINION among the judges. Although the MAJORITY OPINION will decide the CASE, a judge who disagrees with the opinions of the majority of judges, may write a dissenting opinion.

Dissipation of funds. The squandering of money by someone in DEBT, without regard to his OBLIGATIONS to his CREDITORS.

Dissolute. Someone who disregards the accepted social standards and who behaves in a lewd, immoral, and unrestrained manner.

Dissolution. The cancellation of a CONTRACT or PARTNERSHIP; the act of revoking or cancelling a legal PROCEEDING, as when a COURT dissolves an INJUNCTION; the act of terminating a MARRIAGE; the dissolving of a CORPORATION.

Dissolve. To cancel or terminate.

Distort. To give a false meaning to something, such as to distort the truth; to misrepresent.

Distrain. To appropriate somebody's PROPERTY as a PLEDGE or guarantee that a certain OBLIGATION will be fulfilled. A hotel might hold or distrain a guest's luggage until the hotel bill is paid.

Distress. To take PROPERTY away from a wrongdoer and to give it to the party he has injured, in order to give satisfaction for the wrong.

Distress warrant. A DOCUMENT or WRIT authorizing an OFFICER to seize PROPERTY, often issued to a LANDLORD permitting him to take the property of a tenant who has not paid his rent for a long period of time.

Distribution. The transmission of the ASSETS of a deceased person's ESTATE to the HEIRS, after all DEBTS, CLAIMS, and TAXES have been paid.

Distribution of capital. The giving of a CORPORATION'S ASSETS to the STOCKHOLDERS, thus depriving CREDITORS of payment of their CLAIMS against the corporation.

Distributive finding of the issue. A VERDICT of a JURY in which it finds some issues in favor of the PLAINTIFF, and some in favor of the DEFENDANT.

District attorney. The PROSECUTING ATTORNEY of each federal district in the United States and its possessions. Also, each state, and some counties in some states call their prosecuting attorneys "district attorneys."

District court. A court of the federal government or of a state, having JURISDICTION over a particular geographic area. Such area may be a whole state, several states, or only part of a state, depending upon the size of its population.

District judge. A judge of a United States or state district court.
Disturbance of repose. The unauthorized removal of a body from its grave.
Disturbance of the peace. Boisterous, loud, and unruly behavior that upsets the tranquillity of a COMMUNITY or neighborhood.
Diversion. The unauthorized use of something; the turning aside of funds from their usual use.
Divest. To get rid of; to sell PROPERTY; to deprive of something; to DISPOSSESS.
Divestiture. The act of getting rid of something. A CORPORATION that sells one of its subsidiaries is undergoing divestiture. Such divestiture is frequently the result of a court decision, ordering the company to get rid of certain of its PROPERTY.
Divided custody. The sharing of the time a child will spend with separated or divorced parents. A child may spend weekdays with one parent and weekends with the other parent. ➤ ALTERNATING CUSTODY.
Dividend. A fund set aside by a CORPORATION composed of profits that will be apportioned to its various STOCKHOLDERS. When a corporation is profitable, its board of directors will usually declare a dividend. When the corporation fails to make money for any prolonged period of time, it may skip or fail to declare dividends.
Divisible contract. A CONTRACT having several components. Thus, if one part of the contract is not fulfilled, the other parts may continue in force. In this type of contract, a REMEDY for nonperformance can be sought only for that part of the contract which has not been fulfilled. ➤ SEVERABLE CONTRACT.
Divisible divorce doctrine. The concept that the DIVORCE is valid in that it has dissolved the MARRIAGE. However, the divisible divorce doctrine recognizes that the financial OBLIGATIONS of the divorced parties to one another may not have been resolved.
Division of fees. An ethical practice among ATTORNEYS who handle a case jointly, but an unethical practice when an attorney pays a fee to someone who has solicited business for him. (In medical practice, the division of fees between doctors is unethical. It is called FEE-SPLITTING.)
Division of powers. The system of government in the United States wherein certain POWERS are within the province of the federal government while other powers are within the province of the various state governments.
Divorce. A legal ending, by COURT ORDER, of a MARRIAGE. The legal basis for divorce differs from state to state; there is no national divorce law.
Divorce agreement. An AGREEMENT between a husband and wife as to the disposition of their PROPERTY upon obtaining a DIVORCE.
Divorce suit. A contest in COURT between a divorced couple in which one party has the role of PLAINTIFF and the other of DEFENDANT. In such a SUIT, the court decides the outstanding ISSUES.
Divulge. To make known; to reveal. The term is often used to de-

fine a situation in which a third party overhears a conversation between two parties and then divulges or reveals the contents of said conversation.

Docket. A written record of the PROCEEDINGS in a COURT. Also, a list of the cases to be tried during a specified term of the court.

Doctrine. A belief; a tenet; a GOVERNMENT policy, such as the doctrine that all people are created equal.

Documentary evidence. Objects that tend to prove the truth or falsity of an ISSUE, including written STATEMENTS and DOCUMENTS. Documentary evidence is the opposite of *spoken evidence* or *oral evidence.*

Documents. INSTRUMENTS; written STATEMENTS; anything containing a written message, such as a contract. A public document is one that can be seen and read by the general public.

Domain. Control and OWNERSHIP of PROPERTY.

Domestic bill of exchange. A written ORDER of one person upon another to pay money to a third person, executed between people who live in the same state.

Domicile. The place where someone has his main home, and even if he spends time elsewhere, he intends to use it as his principal residence.

Dominant estate. Land that controls and restricts the construction of a building within a certain distance from its boundaries; the opposite of a SERVIENT ESTATE.

Donee. Someone who receives a gift; a person who is granted with a POWER OF APPOINTMENT.

Donor. The giver; one who makes a gift or sets up a TRUST. In MEDICAL JURISPRUDENCE, one who gives blood or an organ to a recipient.

Dormant judgment. A JUDGMENT (an AWARD by a COURT) that is no longer active and enforceable because the party who has received the judgment fails to enforce it or, having died, is unable to enforce it. Such a judgment must be revived before it can be enforced.

Dossier. A bundle of DOCUMENTS containing detailed information on a particular subject. Someone who is suspected of being subversive may have a large dossier about his activities in the files of GOVERNMENT agencies such as the C.I.A. or the F.B.I.

Double damages. An AWARD that is twice as great as the *actual damages* incurred. Double damages are frequently awarded as a punishment to the wrongdoer. ➤ DAMAGES, ACTUAL.

Double indemnity. The receipt of twice the amount of money that an INSURANCE POLICY is supposed to give. Such indemnity and payment are usually based upon clauses in the policy that double payments shall be made for accidental death.

Double jeopardy. A second TRIAL for the same OFFENSE. It is against the law to try a person a second time for the same crime if he has been acquitted the first time. ➤ FORMER JEOPARDY; IN JEOPARDY; LEGAL JEOPARDY.

Double taxation. The taxing of a person twice for the same PROPERTY or, taxing one person for the property and then taxing another person for the same property.

Doubtful title. OWNERSHIP of PROPERTY that is in doubt. As a consequence, a purchaser of said property may find that his RIGHT to it may be questioned in COURT.

Dower. The RIGHT that a WIDOW has to her dead husband's PROPERTY. Dower rights vary from state to state in our country, as each state has its own LAWS on the subject.

Dower by common law. The RIGHT of a WIDOW to one-third of her husband's land. This LAW is in existence in some states but not in others.

Dowry. PROPERTY or money that a woman brings to her husband when she marries. In actuality, it is a gift to him.

Draconian law. A very severe or unusually harsh law (Greek).

Draft. A written INSTRUCTION from one person to another, ordering the payment of a specified sum of money to a third person on a specified date in the future. Also known as a BILL OF EXCHANGE.

Driving while intoxicated (D.W.I.). In order to determine that a person is intoxicated while driving, a breathing test is frequently given to determine the quantity of alcohol in his body. This test, performed with an ALCOMETER, should be carried out within an hour or so after the driver has been accosted by the AUTHORITIES, or the results will be valueless. However, a person can be found GUILTY of driving while intoxicated even without an alcometer test.

Drug addict. Someone who is habituated to and unable to cease taking a habit-forming drug. The most common addictions are to alcohol, heroin, morphine, cocaine, amphetamines, and others.

Drunk. Intoxicated; inebriated; someone so deeply under the influence of alcohol that he is unable to control his conscious faculties.

Dual citizenship. A status in which one individual is claimed as a CITIZEN by two countries. Such people often travel with two PASSPORTS.

Duces tecum. A SUBPOENA that orders someone to bring certain DOCUMENTS with him when he comes to COURT (Latin).

Due and proper care. Diligent, intelligent, sufficient care in preventing an ACCIDENT. An individual who drives a vehicle knowing that his brakes are not working properly is *not* exercising due and proper care.

Due-bill. A written acknowledgement of a DEBT. Such a DOCUMENT is often sold to a third party, permitting him to use the services of the DEBTOR so as to pay off the debt. Hotels, resorts, cruise ships, etcetera, sometimes issue due-bills to a CREDITOR. The creditor, in turn, sells the due-bill to someone who uses the facilities of the hotel or resort or cruise ship, thus cancelling the debt to the creditor.

Due care. The type of care that a sensible person exercises in a situation requiring carefulness. A good example would be when a person, prior to taking a long automobile trip, has his car checked out thoroughly before embarking upon the trip.

Due compensation. The RECOMPENSE to which a person is entitled. In the law of EMINENT DOMAIN, due compensation means payments that will fully repay the owner for the INJURY or appropriation of his PROPERTY.

Due course. In the ordinary course of events.

Due date. The date upon which a DEBT falls due; the date upon which TAXES should be paid; the date upon which a PROMISSORY NOTE is to be paid.

Due diligence. The degree of effort and care in carrying out an act or OBLIGATION that the average, sincere, energetic person would exhibit; conduct that is devoid of NEGLIGENCE or carelessness.

Due notice. Adequate information concerning an upcoming COURT ACTION, given far enough in advance, and given personally, to enable someone to appear in COURT and to be fully prepared to defend himself.

Due process of law. The regular course of events in the administration of justice, respecting the RIGHTS of every person, giving him the time and the right to defend himself without interference and without the fear that the law will be unfair to him.

Due proof. Sufficient EVIDENCE; adequate PROOF; proof backed up by incontrovertible FACTS.

Due regard. Fair CONSIDERATION; giving sufficient attention and weight to FACTS that are presented in a CASE.

Duly. Suitably; according to legal requirements; properly executed; according to law.

Duly qualified. Adequately trained and prepared to perform a certain task or to fill a certain office.

Duly sworn. To swear under OATH, such oath being administered by someone authorized to administer oaths. (Once having been duly sworn a person's TESTIMONY or statement must be true, or he may be prosecuted for PERJURY.)

Dummy corporation. A COMPANY functioning as a legitimate enterprise but, in actuality, having no real corporate purpose. Such CORPORATIONS are frequently organized by an individual who hopes, by establishing a corporation, to avoid personal LIABILITIES.

Duplicitous. A word used to describe the kind of PLEADING that combines two or more grounds of ACTION in an attempt to gain a single DECISION.

Duplicity. Double-dealing; the quality of being deceptive. In a SUIT, the mistake of joining two separate ACTIONS in one COURT.

Duress. Undue pressure by one person against another in order to get him to do something he does not want to do. This pressure might take the form of threats of BODILY HARM, or of exposure of information that the threatened person wants to keep secret, etcetera.

Duress of imprisonment. Arresting someone for good cause but without proper AUTHORITY; an ARREST for a wrong purpose without a just cause. Also, bad treatment of someone who has been imprisoned, whether for just or unjust cause.

Duress of property. The procuring of PROPERTY through undue pressure threatening the destruction of said property; a CONTRACT obtained through threats; the refusal of a person in POSSESSION of another's property to release it unless an unlawful demand is agreed to.

Duress per minas. An act agreed to because of the threat of BODILY HARM or a threat to imprison someone (Latin).

Duty. A legal OBLIGATION.

Dying declaration. The STATEMENT of a victim of HOMICIDE just prior to dying, naming the murderer and the circumstances surrounding the act. Such a declaration may be used in any subsequent TRIAL of the person accused of the crime.

Dying without issue. Dying without being the parent of a born, or unborn, child.

E

E pluribus unum. The motto of the United States, meaning "Out of many, one" (Latin). In popular translation, "One for all and all for one."

Earned income. Monies earned through one's labor or work, as distinguished from monies earned through INTEREST on INVESTMENTS or OWNERSHIP of PROPERTY.

Earning capacity. Monies that one is capable of earning as a result of training and skills. When someone is injured, the damages he or she seeks often are geared to earning capacity.

Earning power. > EARNING CAPACITY.

Easement. The RIGHT of a nonowner to use land. Such a nonowner may be a next-door neighbor, the general public, or the GOVERNMENT. An easement would be the right of an OWNER of property, who has no land on the street, to use another individual's property to reach the street. Easements must be negotiated and voluntarily agreed to by the owners of property.

Easement appurtenant. A proper or pure EASEMENT. An easement appurtenant is a right to use another's land which passes to a new owner who may buy or INHERIT the PROPERTY. This type of easement is to be distinguished from an *easement in gross,* which ceases when the person who acquired it sells the property or dies.

Easement by custom. The use of another's PROPERTY, not legally obtained but practiced because it has for many years been the CUSTOM to do so. Should an owner of property decide to discontinue the EASEMENT, he will have the legal right to do so.

Easement of access. The RIGHT of using a pathway or road to and from a PROPERTY that belongs to another, giving access to a street or roadway.

Eavesdropping. Listening secretly to a private conversation. This is a COMMON LAW offense, which is especially offensive when the eavesdropper reports said conversations to others.

Edict. A LAW or command issued by a head of state. It implies a nondemocratic form of GOVERNMENT in which a sovereign has the POWER to make laws without consulting a legislative body.

Effective franchise. The RIGHT of a CITIZEN to vote during an election.

Effective possession. Occupancy of a portion of land, continued for a prolonged period of time, to support a CLAIM of TITLE to the entire tract of land. Also known as *virtual possession.*

Efficient intervening cause. A CASE in which the DEFENDANT has done nothing wrong but, nevertheless, DAMAGES and INJURIES have resulted.

Eighteenth Amendment. The Eighteenth Amendment, which prohibited the traffic and sale of liquor, passed in 1919 and was repealed in 1933 by the Twenty-first Amendment. > UNITED STATES CONSTITUTION.

Ejectment. A LAWSUIT by a rightful title-holder to recover PROPERTY that is occupied by another whose TITLE to it is unjustified. Also, a SUIT by an OWNER to repossess his property from someone who has leased it and whose LEASE has expired.

Electoral college. Not an actual college, but a group of people chosen by the voters to cast their votes for President and Vice-President. In actuality, the electoral college is a mere formality, as the general public in each state decides the candidates for whom the votes shall be cast.

Electrocardiogram. An apparatus that records the electric current that passes through the heart as it beats. There is a normal pattern which is recorded and can be interpreted by the attending physician. Heart attacks, such as coronary thrombosis and other abnormal conditions, can be detected by noting changes in the recording of the electrocardiogram. However, not all heart conditions are accompanied by an abnormal electrocardiogram. Also called E.C.G. or E.K.G.

Electrocute. To put to DEATH in the electric chair.

Electroencephalogram. The recording of brain waves, obtained by attaching electrodes to various points on the scalp. Such tracings often give an accurate picture of brain disease.

Eleemosynary corporation. A private, not-for-profit CORPORATION established for charitable purposes or for benevolent purposes.

Eleganter. With due regard to form; accurately.

Eligible. Legally qualified.

Elopement. **1.** The abandonment of a husband by a wife who goes away with another man and COHABITS with him. **2.** The act of a couple who voluntarily go off and secretly wed.

Emancipation. Free, such as when a minor is freed from parental control when he or she reaches the age of maturity.

Emancipation Proclamation. The setting free of the slaves during the Civil War, as proclaimed by President Abraham Lincoln in 1863.

Embargo. An ORDER of the GOVERNMENT prohibiting the entry or departure of certain goods. Also, acts by the government's armed forces to prevent planes or ships of other countries from entering or leaving airports or shipping ports.

Embezzlement. The unlawful, fraudulent taking of money or PROPERTY by a person to whom said money or property had been entrusted. Embezzlement is a CRIMINAL OFFENSE. The term is synonymous with MISAPPROPRIATION OF FUNDS.

Embracery. An attempt to influence a JURY corruptly toward a desired VERDICT. An individual who commits this crime is known as an embraceor.

Emigration. The act of leaving one country for another. Upon arriving at the new country, the emigrant is called an immigrant.
Eminent domain. The AUTHORITY to take PRIVATE PROPERTY and to convert it for public use. Private land may be taken by right of eminent domain by a state government in order to use it for a state highway. The one who must surrender such property is justly compensated for it.
Emoluments. Monies received for services rendered; compensation arising out of one's office or employment; reimbursements.
Emphasizing facts. Taking certain EVIDENCE that has come up in a TRIAL and stressing its importance to a JURY, thus attempting to influence said jury toward a particular VERDICT. The FACTS emphasized may or may not be sufficiently important as to be decisive in a jury's deliberations and decision.
Employer's liability insurance. INSURANCE that an employer takes out to protect himself in the event of an on-the-job INJURY or DEATH of one or more of his employees. When such an injury or death occurs, the employee or his family will collect DAMAGES that are paid by the employer's liability insurance policy. In most states, employers are required by law to carry this type of insurance. ≫ WORKMEN'S COMPENSATION.
Empower. To grant AUTHORITY; to delegate; to commission.
Emptor. A buyer (Latin).
Enable. To give someone the power to do something.
Enabling clause. The provision in a LAW that gives the AUTHORITIES the POWER to put it into effect.
Enabling power. The RIGHT to approve something, especially something that will be regulated by LAWS or STATUTES.
Enabling statute. A LAW that gives the right to individuals or CORPORATIONS to do something that they were not previously permitted to do.
Enacting clause. A phrase in a new LAW stating which legislative body voted the STATUTE, and recording the fact that it was duly enacted at a certain time and place. The enacting clause signifies that the new law is now operative.
Encroachment. Extending one's PROPERTY onto that of another; a TRESPASS, such as building a fence that intrudes upon or obstructs a public highway.
Encumbrance. A LIABILITY that lowers the value of a piece of PROPERTY, such as a LIEN or a MORTGAGE.
Encumbrancer. **1.** One who has a legal CLAIM against an ESTATE, thus diminishing the value of the estate until the claim is paid. **2.** A person who has a LIEN or MORTGAGE on PROPERTY, thus depreciating the value of such property until such time as the encumbrance is removed.
Endorsement. Signing a CHECK or NOTE, or other negotiable DOCUMENT, so that the rights granted by the check or note are transferred to another person. (When someone endorses a check, it per-

mits the check to be cashed or deposited by another person.)

Endorsement—accommodation. An ENDORSEMENT made without any monetary consideration, but done as a favor.

Endorsement, blank. An ENDORSEMENT that specifies no one in particular, thus permitting anyone to negotiate payment.

Endorsement, conditional. An ENDORSEMENT in which the endorser attaches some condition to his liability.

Endorsement, full. An ENDORSEMENT in which the endorser names the particular individual to whom the money shall be paid.

Endorsement, qualified. An ENDORSEMENT that limits the LIABILITY of the person who has endorsed the check or other DOCUMENT.

Endorsement, special. An ENDORSEMENT that specifically names the person to whom the money is payable.

Endowment. **1.** Setting up a fund, the INTEREST from which will go to a BENEFICIARY. Endowments are often established for the benefit of educational institutions to enable them to carry out research or to hire certain teachers or professors, etcetera. **2.** The assignment of monies and/or properties to a woman upon her husband's death; the establishment of dower rights.

Enfeoffment. > FEOFFMENT.

Enforceable. In a CONTRACT, enforceable means to perform, to execute, or to put into effect that which the contract specifies should be done.

Enforceable legal right. A RIGHT recognized by LAW and one which can be carried out by law, if necessary.

Enforceable trust. A valid TRUST. Should a TRUSTEE fail to turn over funds from such a trust when requested, the beneficiaries can sue the trustee to force him to do it.

Enfranchise. **1.** To free; to grant the right to vote. **2.** To grant someone the right to sell his merchandise; to confer a FRANCHISE.

Engross. To write down in legal form; to make a draft of a legal DOCUMENT, often carried out in handwriting.

Enjoin. To forbid; to issue an INJUNCTION, thus restraining someone from carrying out a specific act; a COURT ORDER demanding that someone not do, or do, something.

Enjoyment. The exercise of a RIGHT, such as the right to free speech or to peacefully occupy one's own PROPERTY.

Enlarging statute. A LAW that remedies, by making it more comprehensive or extensive, a previous law. ➤ REMEDIAL STATUTE.

Enoch Arden laws. STATUTES that declare someone dead who has been missing for a certain period of years. As a consequence, a spouse may remarry after such a specified period of time has elapsed. ➤ LEGALLY DEAD; PRESUMPTION OF DEATH.

Enrolled bill rule. A rule that an enrolled bill, one which has been duly passed, signed, and filed by the proper AUTHORITIES, shall not be questioned by the COURTS as to its enactment.

Ensue. To follow or to come later. When one is given a large dose of sleeping pills, sleep ensues. The word implies that there is a direct connection between a certain act and what follows said act.

Entailment. A change, either an interference with or a curtailment, in the rules that usually govern how PROPERTY is inherited by the legal DESCENDANTS; a direction by which property descends differently from the usual order.

Entering judgment. The writing down in the records of the DECISION of the court in a particular CASE. It certifies the pronouncement of the court that was made orally.

Enterprise. A project; a business venture; an undertaking.

Entice. To lure; to wrongfully persuade; to tempt for ulterior motives; to get someone to do something he ordinarily would not do.

Enticement of child. An act in which a child is unlawfully taken from the CUSTODY of a parent who has been awarded the custody in a judicial ACTION.

Entitle. To give the RIGHT to a CLAIM; to grant a TITLE or right; to furnish sufficient grounds for a title or claim.

Entrapment. The act of public OFFICERS (policemen, government agents, etcetera) wherein they lure a suspected criminal into performing a criminal act. Entrapment is carried out against someone who is not actually contemplating the performance of a CRIMINAL ACT. However, once he does carry out the act, he is liable to PROSECUTION, but may be NOT GUILTY.

Entreaty. Supplication; begging; earnestly pleading.

Entry. The written record of a court PROCEEDING.

Entry book. A record book in which a register of TITLES is kept. This type of ledger is kept in the office of a recorder or registrar of DEEDS.

Entry of judgment. The written RECORD of a DECISION of a court in the permanent court records.

Enumerated. Mentioned specifically; specified.

Envoy. A diplomatic representative from one country to another. An envoy holds a rank beneath that of AMBASSADOR.

Equal and uniform taxation. TAXES that are the same for everyone in a particular area; taxes that show no favoritism toward any class but are at the same rate for everyone.

Equal protection of the law. This phrase grants everyone the equal RIGHT to the enjoyment of liberty and the pursuit of happiness, as well as the right to receive the same consideration as everyone else, under the laws of his COMMUNITY, his state, and the federal government. It implies that the same punishment shall be meted out to all violators of the law, regardless of their race, creed, or station in society.

Equal Rights Amendment (E.R.A.). An Amendment to the UNITED STATES CONSTITUTION proposed by Congress in 1972 but not yet, at this writing, passed by the required 38 states. In brief, it provides:

1. Equality of rights under the law shall not be denied or abridged by the United States or any state on account of sex.

2. The Congress shall have the power to enforce, by appropriate legislation, the provisions of this article. 3. This Amendment shall take effect two years after the date of ratification.

Equal rights statutes. Laws that state there can be no discrimination because of sex, race, color, or creed. For example, a woman seeking a LOAN has the same rights to that loan as a man, provided her CREDIT is good. In other words, she must be judged on her merits alone, not on her husband's or any other person's credit.

Equalize. To make uniform, such as equalizing the ASSESSMENTS that people pay in various districts under the same JURISDICTION; to make equal.

Equally divided. A common provision in a WILL that PROPERTY shall be "shared and shared alike"; in other words, it will be divided PER CAPITA and not PER STIRPES.

Equitable. Fair; just; according to the PRINCIPLES of justice. An equitable settlement of a DISPUTE is fair to both sides.

Equitable action. A LAWSUIT based on matters of EQUITY rather than upon existing STATUTES or LAWS. Such an action comes under the JURISDICTION of a COURT OF EQUITY, which settles the matter on the basis of specific laws that govern the situation.

Equitable assets. RIGHTS that require the aid of a COURT OF EQUITY for their determination.

Equitable assignment. An ASSIGNMENT that is not enforceable by existing laws, but which may be enforced by a COURT OF EQUITY. (An assignment is a transfer of PROPERTY from one person to another.)

Equitable chose in action. A personal RIGHT that a COURT OF EQUITY will recognize, such as a right against a TRUSTEE to enforce the execution of a TRUST.

Equitable construction. The INTERPRETATION of a STATUTE by either enlarging or narrowing the exact letter of the law. In interpreting CONTRACTS, COURTS OF LAW, and COURTS OF EQUITY must stick to the exact provisions laid down in the contract.

Equitable conversion. An alteration in the nature of PROPERTY whereby, in EQUITY, PERSONAL PROPERTY is considered as real estate, or real estate is considered as personal property.

Equitable defense. > EQUITABLE PLEA.

Equitable ejectment. Although EJECTMENT is a legal process, equitable ejectment is a REMEDY sometimes employed in certain cases.

Equitable estoppel. A situation in which justice forbids one from denying his own statements or acts; a form of prevention of a person, by his own act or conduct or silence, from asserting rights which might otherwise have existed. > ESTOPPEL IN PAIS.

Equitable execution. Procedures whereby a COURT OF EQUITY enforces its DECISIONS and DECREES. The appointment of a receiver with the power of sale is an equitable execution.

Equitable garnishment. An ACTION in which a CREDITOR, who has already won a suit against a DEBTOR but has not been paid by him, seeks to discover PROPERTY owned by the debtor and to take possession of it to SATISFY the judgment.

Equitable lien. A RIGHT to have a fund or PROPERTY, or its proceeds, applied to the payment of a particular DEBT. Such right exists in EQUITY but not in the LAW.

Equitable plea. A DEFENSE in a LAWSUIT which is based upon matters of EQUITY (fairness or justice), not upon written LAWS; the same as EQUITABLE DEFENSE.

Equitable recoupment. A reasonable and fair reduction of a CLAIM; a fair and equitable reduction of the amount of DAMAGES that have been awarded to a CLAIMANT.

Equitable right. A RIGHT that will be protected by EQUITY even though it is not a right existing under a STATUTE or LAW.

Equitable rule. A just, fair RULE, as one issued by a COURT OF EQUITY.

Equitable seisin. The POSSESSION of land, coupled with the RIGHT to possess it, according to rules of EQUITY and the knowledge that such possession will be sanctioned and protected by a COURT OF EQUITY.

Equity. **1.** A method of obtaining justice through evaluation of the merits of an ISSUE, rather than through reliance upon existing LAWS and STATUTES. **2.** Equity is often used to refer to fairness and justness, especially in regard to the settlement of DISPUTES between people. **3.** Matters in which no existent laws govern decisions, are submitted to a COURT OF EQUITY.

"Equity corrects errors." A popular expression defining a function of EQUITY.

"Equity delights in amicable adjustments." An expression defining the major purpose of a COURT OF EQUITY. Instead of relying upon written laws in its determinations, equity courts attempt to settle disputes by doing what is fair and just to all parties concerned.

"Equity does not make the law, but assists it." A popular saying explaining the function of EQUITY.

"Equity follows the law." A maxim that EQUITY will attempt to follow the principles of law even though no actual law governs its decisions.

"Equity is equality, and equality is equity." A self-explanatory expression.

Equity jurisdiction. An AUTHORITY based upon the fact that the matter at hand is one requiring deliberations of an equitable nature and one that will not lend itself to SETTLEMENT by recourse to written LAWS or STATUTES.

Equity of redemption. The right of a MORTGAGOR to redeem property after it has been forfeited by law because of a breach in the terms of the MORTGAGE. This is accomplished by paying the debt, interest, and costs.

Equity of statute. The spirit and intent underlying a law as an aid to its interpretation.

Equity pleading. Written statements (PLEADINGS) of CLAIMS presented before a COURT OF EQUITY or, written answers to a complaint set forth in a SUIT in a court of equity.

Equivocal. Something having a doubtful meaning, or a double meaning, or something of uncertain significance.

Erasure. The removal of words from a written DOCUMENT. (Erasure of a phrase or clause in a WILL, when performed by the maker of the will and so initialed, is sometimes considered a revoking of that portion of the will.)

Erroneous judgment. A DECISION or JUDGMENT issued by a COURT that had JURISDICTION to decide the case but the judgment so issued is contrary to existing law or is based upon a wrong application of legal principles. Such a judgment is subject to being overruled on appeal to a higher court.

Error. A mistake in LAW or in FACT; a mistake in a TRIAL, thus leading to the review of the JUDGMENT by a higher court.

Error coram nobis. A WRIT to be brought before a court that has rendered a JUDGMENT contending that the VERDICT should be set aside because of an error or errors in FACT that took place during the TRIAL (Latin).

Error in fact. Such an error occurs when a court renders a VERDICT or JUDGMENT, not knowing an essential fact. As a result, the judgment may be VOID or is voidable.

Error in law. Mistake made by the COURT in applying the LAW to the case at hand.

Error in vacuo. An error made by a presiding JUDGE which does not result in an erroneous JUDGMENT. Such an error does not subject the case to a retrial.

Escalator clause. A CLAUSE in a CONTRACT, or in a LEASE, made during a period of governmental price control regulations. This type of clause allows for increases in the terms of the CONTRACT or LEASE when a relaxation of price controls takes place.

Escape. The unlawful departure of a prisoner from his place of confinement.

Escape clause. A clause in a LEASE of a tenant-owner of a CO-OPERATIVE APARTMENT, allowing him to forfeit the stock and monies that the sale of the cooperative would bring, in exchange for a release of the OBLIGATION to pay the monthly maintenance on said apartment.

Escheat. This term stands for the right of the state to possess the PROPERTY of someone who dies and leaves no HEIRS, or of someone who abandons property during his lifetime.

Escrow. When two parties make an AGREEMENT or CONTRACT that will take a certain amount of time to perform, they may agree that the monies to be paid for the performance of the contract shall be held by a third person. Upon completion of the terms of the agreement of contract, the third person turns over the money or property to the person who has fulfilled the contract or agreement.

Espionage act. A federal STATUTE dealing with the punishment of spies. Its provisions apply both to spies of foreign nationalities and to CITIZENS who engage in treasonable acts.

Espousal. 1. A promise to marry; an engagement. 2. The adoption of a cause or principle. (The United States espouses democracy.)

Essence of a contract. The vital portion of a CONTRACT.

Essoign. The excuse a DEFENDANT gives for not appearing in COURT when he has been ordered to do so.

Establishment clause. A CLAUSE in the First Amendment to the UNITED STATES CONSTITUTION separating Church and State, providing that neither the federal government or any state can pass laws favoring a religion nor can it force any CITIZEN to profess a belief in any religion.

Estate. 1. PROPERTY in which someone has an interest; a person's RIGHT to property, such as real estate. 2. An estate is composed of a person's total POSSESSIONS, including money, securities, land, etcetera. (The word estate is synonymous with the word property.)

Estate at will. PROPERTY, such as land or houses, that are leased from the owner to another person, the lessee holding and occupying the property only so long as the owner wishes him to hold and occupy it.

Estate in bankruptcy. Assets that go to the TRUSTEE when BANKRUPTCY has taken place, such trustee having been appointed by a COURT acting under the bankruptcy laws.

Estate in severalty. An ESTATE held solely and completely by one individual as the only TENANT.

Estate tax. A TAX paid for the privilege of transferring PROPERTY from a deceased person to the HEIR or heirs of said property. (An estate tax is not a tax on the property itself, nor is it an inheritance tax.)

Ester in judgment. To make an appearance as a PARTY to a pending LAWSUIT.

Estimated tax. An INCOME TAX, the amount of which is based upon expected earnings, not upon income that has already been earned. Estimated taxes are usually paid in installments during the year. An employer withholds some of the employee's wages in order to turn the money over to the INTERNAL REVENUE SERVICE and have it credited toward the payment of the employee's income tax.

Estop. To prevent; to stop; to bar.

Estopped. Prevented; stopped; barred.

Estoppel. An estoppel exists when someone is forbidden by law to speak against his own deed or act; it is a bar against a person saying anything contrary to that which has been established to be the truth.

Estoppel by contract. A bar against renouncing or reneging on facts that have already been agreed upon in a CONTRACT.

Estoppel by deed. A bar preventing someone who is party to a deed from denying the existence of the deed or denying the truth of facts contained in the deed.

Estoppel by judgment. A bar against litigating again certain facts that have already been accepted as true. Also, a bar against relitigating an ISSUE or SUIT that has previously been decided.

Estoppel by oath. A bar againt denying, in a future LAWSUIT, something that has been sworn to under oath in a previous lawsuit.

Estoppel by silence. > ESTOPPEL IN PAIS.

Estoppel in pais. The bar to a person, because of some act or omission of something he should have done, to plead or prove an otherwise important fact; an estoppel by silence; an EQUITABLE ESTOPPEL.

Et al. An abbreviation for *et alia,* "and others" (Latin). Often used when there is a long list of people involved in a matter.

Et non. "And not" (Latin).

Et sic. "And so" (Latin).

Ethics. A code of good behavior; a system of moral principles. A CODE OF ETHICS governs how various people in a particular profession should behave, such as lawyers, doctors, congressmen, etcetera. Violations of the code of ethics may lead to various forms of censure.

Euthanasia. The act of painlessly putting someone to DEATH who has an incurable disease. Also called "mercy killing." Euthanasia is illegal at the present time.

Evasive answer. An attempt to evade a straightforward, complete, honest response during questioning in a TRIAL; a response that neither admits nor denies.

Eviction. The act of getting one to leave lands or quarters he has been occupying, such an act being authorized by a COURT OF LAW. > DISPOSSESSION.

Evidence. Everything that is brought into COURT in a TRIAL in an attempt to prove or disprove alleged FACTS. Evidence includes the introduction of exhibits, records, documents, objects, etcetera, plus the TESTIMONY of WITNESSES, for the purpose of proving one's case. The JURY or judge considers the evidence and decides in favor of one PARTY or the other.

Evidence of insurability. PROOF that one is in sufficiently good health so as to merit the issuance of a LIFE INSURANCE POLICY.

Evidence of title. A DEED proving the TITLE to OWNERSHIP of PROPERTY, such as land and/or a building.

Evidence to support the verdict. Legal EVIDENCE tending to support the FACTS in a case in which the PARTY who was given the favorable VERDICT had the BURDEN OF PROOF.

Evidentiary facts. Those FACTS that are essential in proving the matter at ISSUE; facts that are derived from TESTIMONY of WITNESSES or from other sources.

Ex cathedra. "From authority"; having the weight of authority (Latin).

Ex contractu. Arising out of a CONTRACT; founded on a contract (Latin). (It is the opposite of EX DELICTO.) This type of case is covered by the CIVIL and COMMON LAW.

Ex delicto. Arising out of a CRIME, or out of something that is contrary to law, or out of some wrong that has been committed (Latin).

Ex facto. Arising out of a FACT; arising as the result of an act or known fact (Latin).

Ex lege. As a matter of law (Latin).

Ex officio. A PRIVILEGE or RIGHT arising out of one's position in another capacity; by virtue of the OFFICE (Latin). An ex officio member of a committee is one who automatically is on the committee because of his holding another office or position, such as a mayor might be an ex officio member of the board of education in a particular community.

Ex parte. For the benefit of one party (Latin). An ex parte procedure is one carried out in COURT for the benefit of one party only, without a challenge from an opposing party.

Ex parte injunction. An INJUNCTION issued without giving notice to the opposing PARTY.

Ex parte motion. A MOTION made in court without notice being given to the opposing PARTY.

Ex post facto. After the thing has been done; after the fact (Latin).

Ex post facto law. A LAW that makes a crime greater than it was when it was committed. Also, a law that makes the PUNISHMENT greater than it was when the crime was committed.

Ex turpi causa. A CLAIM that arises from the breaking of a LAW (Latin).

Exaction. The unlawful demand of money by a public OFFICIAL for services rendered, when the services should have been carried out without any charge.

Examination. The questioning of an individual or individuals in connection with a legal matter.

Examination before trial. The questioning and TESTIMONY of a WITNESS, given under OATH, before the onset of a TRIAL. Results of such examination may be presented during a subsequent trial. Also known as an E.B.T., or a DEPOSITION.

Examination of witnesses. The interrogation or questioning of WITNESSES, carried out in COURT with the witnesses under OATH.

Excambium. An exchange of property (Latin).

Exception. The disagreement with a judge's refusal of a request made by one of the attorneys in a case. The request usually takes the form of an OBJECTION, and the refusal is stated by the judge in the words "OBJECTION OVERRULED." The exception is duly recorded and may possibly form the basis for a future appeal from the court's decision in the case.

Exception in deed. This type of exception takes back or withdraws from a deed something that has previously been granted.

Exception of misjoinder. An attempt to throw out a PLAINTIFF's claim because another party, who has no right to make a claim, is included in the action.

Exception of no cause of action. An OBJECTION to a PLAINTIFF's SUIT based upon absence of legal validity to the CLAIM and to lack of exhibits to support the claim.

Exception of no right of action. An OBJECTION to the right of a particular PLAINTIFF to press a

CLAIM. (The DEFENDANT in such an instance may argue that the plaintiff has no interest or right in the matter at hand.)

Exception to bail. An OBJECTION to the amount of bail.

Exceptor. Someone who OBJECTS to a ruling of the court. He may use his exception as a basis for a subsequent appeal.

Excess. **1.** Overreacting to a situation; using more force than is necessary in protecting oneself. **2.** The holding of more monies than is necessary by a CORPORATION. (Such excess monies, profits, might have been distributed to stockholders.) **3.** Too much.

Excess of jurisdiction. A CASE which originally proceeded in a COURT having proper JURISDICTION, but in which the judge went beyond his jurisdiction in rendering some JUDGMENT or in issuing a particular ORDER.

Excess of privilege. A STATEMENT that goes beyond the limits of PRIVILEGE in that it is violent or intemperate or irrelevant to the matter at hand, resulting thereby in defaming the person or persons about whom the statement was made or written.

Excess profits tax. An INCOME TAX computed on profits in excess of a certain percentage of the invested capital. Such a tax may or may not be imposed at a progressive rate.

Excessive assessment. A tax evaluation that is too high and not in conformity with other evaluations.

Excessive bail. BAIL that is greater than the amount necessary to ensure that the accused will appear in court and not "jump bail."

Excessive sentence. A SENTENCE of longer duration than the amount of time fixed by law.

Excessive verdict. A VERDICT that is out of proportion to the matter at hand, thus violating the conscience of the court. Also, a verdict that is unreasonable and appears to be motivated by prejudice.

Excise tax. A fixed and direct charge placed upon merchandise or commodities, unrelated to the amount of property belonging to the one upon whom the tax is imposed; a license tax; a PRIVILEGE tax.

Exclusion. The act of denying entry or admission.

Exclusionary clause. A PROVISION in a CONTRACT which restricts the actions that a PARTY can take if the other person fails to fulfill the contract.

Exclusionary rule. A DOCTRINE that prevents illegally gathered EVIDENCE from being presented in COURT.

Exclusive. **1.** Restrictive; controlled by one person alone. (An exclusive right to sell merchandise means that no one else may sell the product.) **2.** An exclusive organization is one that limits its membership strictly, according to its own rules and regulations.

Exclusive power. Sole power.

Exclusive remedy. A REMEDY is called exclusive when a LAW creates a new LIABILITY or a new RIGHT not previously in force, and then prescribes a remedy to enforce the new liability or right.

Exclusive right. A RIGHT or

PRIVILEGE that can be used only by the person who has been granted the right or privilege.

Exculpatory. Clearing or tending to clear of GUILT or FAULT.

Exculpatory clause. A CLAUSE in a TRUST which excuses the TRUSTEE of any LIABILITY for acts performed as the trustee, provided those acts were carried out in GOOD FAITH.

Excusable. Pardonable; something done that was not entirely without blame but which can be excused and freed from LIABILITY.

Excusable homicide. **1.** HOMICIDE committed in self-defense. **2.** A homicide committed accidentally, without any intent to hurt. ➤ HOMICIDE, JUSTIFIABLE; JUSTIFIABLE HOMICIDE.

Excusable neglect. A form of NEGLIGENCE in which the DEFENDANT was unable to control the circumstances that led to the negligence. In other words, the neglect is considered excusable because it was not the result of the defendant's carelessness or failure to take proper steps to avoid the negligence. Where a judge deems that excusable neglect exists, he may set aside the JUDGMENT against the defendant.

Excusable trespass. A TRESPASS that is PARDONED, thus doing away with any LAWSUIT.

Excuse. **1.** A reason given for doing, or not doing, a thing. **2.** A request to a court to forgive an unlawful act because of EXTENUATING CIRCUMSTANCES.

Execute. **1.** To carry out; to sign; to seal; to do; to complete. **2.** To put someone to DEATH who has been given the DEATH SENTENCE.

Executed oral agreement. An ORAL AGREEMENT that has been fully completed (executed) by both parties to the agreement.

Executed trust. A TRUST that has been completely declared and defined, thus requiring no further DOCUMENTS to complete it.

Execution. **1.** A carrying out of an JUDGMENT; the completion of an act or course of action. **2.** The putting to DEATH of someone who has been condemned to die.

Execution of instrument. The signing, sealing, and notarizing, if necessary, of a legal DOCUMENT.

Execution of judgment. Putting into effect the DECREE or JUDGMENT of a COURT. (To obtain a judgment from a court is one thing; to see that the judgment is carried out as ordered, is to ensure its execution.)

Execution sale. A SALE by a SHERIF or other public OFFICER of PROPERTY that has legally been seized by him. Such a sale is usually by public AUCTION.

Executive agent. An OFFICER of a COMPANY who acts for the board of directors.

Executive agreement. An AGREEMENT between the president of the United States, acting within the authority granted to him, and representatives of a foreign nation.

Executive capacity. A position in a business organization calling for the management and direction of operations of said organization.

Executive order. An ORDER given by the president or by the governor of a state.

Executive pardon. A PARDON for a crime, ordered by the president or by the governor of a state.

Executive power. The authority vested in the executive department of the federal government or the government of a state.
Executor. The person named by a maker of a WILL to carry out the directions as set forth in the will. The executor's duties include the payment of all outstanding DEBTS and the disbursement of PROPERTY to the HEIRS, as designated in the will. Also, the executor makes all bequests to charitable organizations, etcetera, as directed in the will.
Executor-trustee. An EXECUTOR of an ESTATE whose administrative duties extend beyond the period usually needed to pay all DEBTS and to make distribution of the ASSETS of the estate. This extension often consists of making a TRUSTEE of the executor.
Executorial trustee. Someone who is appointed to be an EXECUTOR (the person who carries out the directions set forth in a WILL) and also to be a TRUSTEE of the estate after the executor's duties have been carried out.
Executor's bond. A BOND that an EXECUTOR of an ESTATE must furnish in order to serve as the ADMINISTRATOR of an estate. Such bond is usually prescribed by law.
Executory. Not yet performed; something that will be carried out but has not yet been completed.
Executory judgment. A JUDGMENT (decision) rendered by court action but which has not yet been carried out; an ORDER to a DEFENDANT to pay which has not yet been obeyed.
Executory process. When a JUDGMENT (an order by a court) has not been carried out, such as a payment to a PLAINTIFF, an executory process is begun to seize property of the DEFENDANT and use it to pay his DEBT.
Executory trust. A TRUST in which the legal specifics have not been explicitly stated. As a consequence, it may become necessary to obtain help from a COURT OF EQUITY in order to carry out exactly what the maker of the trust had in mind when he set it up.
Executory use. A TRUST or an INTEREST that will come into being at some time in the future.
Executrix. A female EXECUTOR.
Exemplary damages. DAMAGES in excess of the actual loss that has occurred. Exemplary damages are usually ordered as a punishment to the DEFENDANT for poor or bad CONDUCT that permitted the damages to take place.
Exempt income. Income or monies that are exempt from INCOME TAX. Certain income may be exempt from federal taxes but not state taxes, or vice versa.
Exemption. The act of being freed from a certain OBLIGATION that would ordinarily prevail, such as an exemption from serving on a jury because of a house-confining illness.
Exemption from service of process. Freedom from being served with a SUMMONS or SUBPOENA while performing some public duty. Thus, a member of Congress while it is in session, or a LAWYER trying a case in court may be exempt from service of

process. Such exemption applies to CIVIL ACTIONS, not to matters of a criminal nature.

Exercise of judicial discretion. The DISCRETION or PRIVILEGE that a judge has in deciding a case. The term implies that the judge is not limited or governed in making his decision by existing LAWS and STATUTES.

Exercising an option. The right of having first choice in purchasing something, such as a piece of land or other PROPERTY. (Such OPTIONS are usually granted only for a specified period of time.)

Exhaustion of remedy. The PRINCIPLE that one should do everything possible to correct a situation before seeking the help of the courts.

Exhibit. A DOCUMENT or OBJECT offered in EVIDENCE and marked for identification. A written document such as a contractual AGREEMENT may be an exhibit; a revolver allegedly used in a shooting may be an exhibit, etcetera.

Exhibitionism. **1.** Actions aimed at attracting undue attention, such as loud, boisterous talk or the wearing of outlandish clothes. **2.** Undressing in public, or displaying one's genitals in public. This type of exhibitionism is punishable by law.

Exhume. To remove a body from a grave or vault; to disinter. Exhumation may be carried out by COURT ORDER to have the body examined by court-appointed physicians in order to discover whether foul play was the cause of death.

Exigency of a bond. The ACT or PERFORMANCE upon which a BOND is conditioned; the conditions of a bond. (A BAIL BOND is issued upon condition that the recipient of the bond will make an appearance in court when ordered to do so.)

Exigency of a writ. That part of a WRIT that directs what should be done.

Existing creditors. CREDITORS who have claims against a DEBTOR that are valid and in existence, whether or not the debtor has taken actions to make himself free from his OBLIGATIONS.

Existing debt. Existing indebtedness; a DEBT that is in existence even though the date for its payment has not yet arrived.

Existing equity. A RIGHT to future payment.

Existing liability. An OBLIGATION based upon some future condition, which may or may not result in a DEBT.

Existing person. An embryo or fetus growing within its mother's womb but not yet born is considered an existing person insofar as its legal rights after it is born.

Exitus. The last stage of a PLEADING or ACTION (Latin). (In medicine, exitus means "death.")

Exonerated. Absolved of a CHARGE; declared not responsible; NOT GUILTY; released from LIABILITY; exculpated.

Expatriation. The voluntary leaving of one's country in order to become a resident or CITIZEN of another country.

Expectant estates. An ESTATE not yet in existence but which will be possessed at some time in the future; estates in expectancy.

Expectant heir. An HEIR APPARENT; someone who, by blood relationship, is in line to inherit a person's PROPERTY should that person die without having made a WILL.

Expectant right. A RIGHT that depends upon the continued existence of present conditions until some event that will take place in the future. > EXPECTANT ESTATES.

Expedite. To speed up; to hasten to a conclusion; to accomplish promptly.

Experience rating. A practice carried out by many INSURANCE companies wherein they charge lower rates to insured groups who have regularly had fewer CLAIMS. In other words, the rates are based upon past experiences.

Experimental evidence. Proving a CONTENTION by performing an experiment in COURT.

Experimental testimony. TESTIMONY of a WITNESS who has carried out certain experiments to prove or disprove that a particular act took place. In court, the witness testifies as to his or her findings.

Experimentation. > NUREMBERG CODE OF ETHICS.

Expert testimony. TESTIMONY given by someone who has particular expertise in a technical or scientific or professional field, such as the testimony of a physician concerning a particular illness or disease.

Expert witness. A WITNESS with special knowledge in a particular sphere, such as a scientist, an engineer, etcetera. Such a witness gives EXPERT TESTIMONY.

Expiate. To atone for; to make amends or reparations for.

Expiration. The lapsing of an INSURANCE POLICY.

Expository statute. A STATUTE that contains words setting forth its true intent and meaning, and also stating what its limitations are.

Express. Unmistakable; indubitable; clear; definite; explicit; without doubt. (An express acceptance is clear and definite, leaving nothing to conjecture or implication.)

Express assumpsit. An AGREEMENT and OBLIGATION to do something, such as to pay money to someone, stated in explicit, EXPRESS terms.

Express authority. AUTHORITY granted to do a particular job or carry out an act, such authority being stated in explicit, clear terms that leave no doubt as to meaning.

Express emancipation. Freedom that a child obtains when his parents freely and willingly permit him to do as he pleases, including leave home, live on his own, and earn his own living.

Express malice. A willful, PREMEDITATED determination to harm another.

Express trust. A TRUST that comes into being out of a positive declaration made by the person owning the property that will make up the trust.

Expromissor. A person who takes over another person's DEBT or OBLIGATION, thus releasing the original DEBTOR. To do this, the CREDITOR must first agree to accept the new debtor.

Expropriate. **1.** To take over PRIVATE PROPERTY for public use, by a local, state, or federal government. **2.** To surrender a CLAIM to PROPERTY.
Expunge. To strike out completely; to OBLITERATE. (A false arrest may be ordered expunged from the records, so that it is as if it had never taken place.)
Expurgate. To cleanse; to purify. It may be required to cut out objectionable segments of a sexually graphic or highly violent motion picture so that it can be shown to the general public. Such a picture is said to have undergone expurgation.
Extension. A continuance; a prolongation; a lengthening of time to meet an OBLIGATION.
Extension of payment. The prolongation of time to meet an OBLIGATION must be agreed to by both parties, the OBLIGOR and the OBLIGEE.
Extenuating circumstances. Facts that tend to reduce the sentence in a CRIMINAL CHARGE or the DAMAGES in a CIVIL ACTION.
Extenuation. A FACT or facts that would tend to lessen the severity of a PENALTY or PUNISHMENT.
External, violent and accidental means. A term referring to a death that was not caused by natural means.
Extinguishment. Cancellation; destruction. The word is often employed when referring to the cancellation of a RIGHT, a CONTRACT, a POWER, an AUTHORITY, etcetera.
Extort. To compel against one's wishes; to coerce. CONFESSIONS are sometimes alleged to have been extorted—in other words, forced from an ACCUSED against his will. To extort money, such as in BLACKMAIL, is to make someone give it against his own wishes for fear of exposure.
Extortion. The illegal, unlawful obtaining of money from someone.
Extra legem. Beyond the protection of the LAW; outside of the law (Latin).
Extra viam rights. The RIGHT of someone to use adjoining property to travel over when the highway is impassable (Latin, "outside the roadway").
Extract. A segment or portion of a written DOCUMENT.
Extradition. The surrender of a person ACCUSED or CONVICTED of a crime to the JURISDICTION where the crime is alleged to have been committed. This may mean the transfer from one country to another, from one state to another, etcetera.
Extrajudicial. **1.** Outside of the court's JURISDICTION. **2.** Something that takes place outside of the COURT, such as an extrajudicial CONFESSION, or an extrajudicial OATH.
Extraneous evidence. **1.** EVIDENCE that comes from outside the COURT. **2.** Evidence that is not pertinent to the matter at hand.
Extraneous offense. An OFFENSE that has nothing to do with a present TRIAL, committed by the ACCUSED at another time. A person presently accused of FORGERY may have been convicted of ROBBERY in another trial.
Extraordinary. Above average;

out of the ordinary; unusual. A person accused of NEGLIGENCE may contend that he or she exercised extraordinary care.

Extraordinary grand jury. A GRAND JURY whose duty is strictly limited to the precise investigation of a particular issue; its questioning of WITNESSES must be confined to the immediate matter at hand.

Extraordinary motion for new trial. A MOTION that is out of the ordinary and seldom occurs.

Extraordinary remedy. A REMEDY that attempts to make possible RELIEF that cannot usually be obtained in an ordinary COURT ACTION. (WRITS of HABEAS CORPUS, MANDAMUS, etcetera, are extraordinary remedies.)

Extraterritorial. Outside the boundaries of a state or country.

Extraterritoriality. The operation of LAWS outside the boundaries of a state or country. A diplomat serving in a foreign country is given exemptions from certain laws of the foreign country, since he is judged still to be in his home country when serving abroad.

Extreme care. The care that a sensible peson is supposed to exercise when faced with dangerous circumstances or conditions.

Extreme cruelty. Conduct of one spouse leading to deep anxiety, fear, mental torture, or impairment of health of the other spouse. (Extreme cruelty implies a habitual form of behavior, not just one or two instances.) Extreme cruelty is a frequent ground for DIVORCE.

Extreme hazard. In MARITIME LAW, a situation in which a ship is in grave danger of sinking, despite all attempts to save her.

Extremis. In medicine, this term defines a patient in the terminal stages of a fatal illness. Such a patient is said to be in extremis.

Extrinsic ambiguity. An uncertainty in a CONTRACT, not stemming from a CLAUSE in the contract but from some outside but related matter.

Extrinsic evidence. EVIDENCE that does not appear in the body of a CONTRACT or other written DOCUMENT (PAROL or VERBAL EVIDENCE is considered extrinsic) but which has a bearing upon an issue.

Extrinsic fraud. DECEIT that will lay the groundwork for setting aside a JUDGMENT. Such FRAUD as is parallel or collateral to the ISSUES in a CASE while the case is being tried and the judgment rendered.

Eyewitness. A WITNESS who testifies to what he or she has seen. (Loosely applied, an eyewitness may also be a person who testifies to what he has heard or smelled, etcetera.

Eyewitness provision. A CLAUSE in an INSURANCE POLICY requiring proof of the circumstances of an accident, with such proof to be supplied by an eyewitness other than the CLAIMANT.

F

Fabricated evidence. EVIDENCE that is either false or so altered that it is deceitful; *manufactured evidence.*

Fabricated fact. A FACT not founded on truth; a fact that may be true but which has been given a false interpretation and been purposely misrepresented.

Face. Material that appears on a DOCUMENT or STATUTE without any explanation or modification.

Face of judgment. The amount of money granted by a JUDGMENT, without interest.

Face value. The total amount of money to be paid, including the PRINCIPAL and INTEREST, according to the terms of a CONTRACT or AGREEMENT.

Facsimile. An exact copy.

Fact. Something that took place; an act; something actual and real; an incident that occurred; an event.

Fact-finding body. A group of people authorized to find out the true FACTS in a matter and to render a DECISION based upon their findings.

Factor. An AGENT employed by a PRINCIPAL to sell his goods, who will receive a commission for making the sale.

Factoring. The business of buying ACCOUNTS RECEIVABLE at a discount. Outstanding accounts are bought by the FACTOR from the CREDITOR. The factor then proceeds to collect the full amount from the DEBTOR.

Facts in issue. The events (FACTS) upon which the PLAINTIFF bases his CLAIM, or the events upon which the DEFENDANT denies the claim.

Failure of consideration. Sometimes in making a CONTRACT, one PARTY agrees to give the other contracting party a certain thing of value. When, through no fault of the first party, the thing of value loses its worth, a failure of consideration has occurred. This is not considered fraud, but rather something that has taken place accidentally or by an honest mistake.

Failure of proof. The lack of sufficient EVIDENCE to prove an alleged FACT; failure to present sufficient PROOF to sustain and win a LAWSUIT.

Failure of title. The inability of an OWNER to prove beyond doubt that he or she is the rightful and unimpeachable owner of a certain property.

Failure to meet obligations. The failure of a bank to pay its depositors when they demand their money. Also, the failure of an individual or individuals to fulfill his or her commitments.

Failure to file taxes. The failure to file an INCOME TAX return within the time allotted to do so.

Faint pleader. A deceitful or false PLEADING, with the intention of deceiving people who are not participants in the LAWSUIT.

Fair and equitable. In a BANK-

RUPTCY, fair and equitable is a term used to signify that everything is being done to see that CREDITORS are paid fairly and reasonably, and that the STOCKHOLDERS are also treated equitably. Such treatment generally takes place during the reorganization of the bankrupt company.

Fair and impartial trial. A TRIAL in which the DEFENDANT's rights are safeguarded. In such a trial, the defendant should be tried by an impartial judge and JURY, and be protected by a competent ATTORNEY, who will have ample time to prepare the defense and who will insist upon the appearance of all necessary WITNESSES. ≫ FAIR TRIAL.

Fair and reasonable market value. The value of PROPERTY that a seller is willing to sell for and the value that a buyer is willing to buy for. This value must be determined when, under law, property has to be disposed of because of nonpayment of a MORTGAGE.

Fair and reasonable value. The value placed upon PROPERTY for the purpose of imposing a just TAX upon it. (This phrase frequently appears in STATUTES governing taxation on property.)

Fair and valuable consideration. The payment of a just amount of money for the sale or transfer of PROPERTY.

Fair book value. The price of STOCK determined by evaluating the worth of the ASSETS of a CORPORATION and deducting its LIABILITIES.

Fair cash value. The price that PROPERTY will bring if sold in an open, free market.

Fair competition. The maintenance of free competition among companies selling similar products. This involves the absence of such unfair practices as PRICE FIXING or the selling of a product below cost in order to force a competitor out of the market.

Fair damages. DAMAGES that not only compensate for a loss or INJURY but go beyond it. In judging such damages, an AWARD may take into consideration factors such as the inability of the PLAINTIFF to pursue his duties because of the injury, etcetera.

Fair employment practices act. Laws prohibiting discrimination in hiring because of race, color, creed, national origin, or sex.

Fair hearing. A HEARING that conforms to fundamental PRINCIPLES of justice but which is held outside of COURT. (Such hearings are often conducted by ADMINISTRATIVE AGENCIES.)

Fair labor standards act. The Wages and Hour Act, a federal law regulating the hours and wages of employees who work for companies that are engaged in INTERSTATE COMMERCE. (This STATUTE covers the great majority of businesses in this country.)

Fair market value. > FAIR AND REASONABLE MARKET VALUE.

Fair on its face. A tax DEED (a deed that transfers the OWNERSHIP of PROPERTY because of nonpayment of taxes) that is legal but may not conform in every respect to the precise wordage that should have been used in writing it.

Fair persuasion. Attempting to convince someone of something without resorting to threats of bodily harm or economic loss, or without molestation or harassment.

Fair return on investment. A RETURN that conforms more or less with the going rate for similar INVESTMENTS and that reflects fair payment for use of PROPERTY.

Fair trial. A TRIAL characterized by the presence of an impartial judge and JURY, and in which all EVIDENCE is heard before a VERDICT is reached. > FAIR AND IMPARTIAL TRIAL.

Fair valuation. Current market price. > FAIR AND REASONABLE MARKET VALUE.

False action. A SUIT brought on a pretended or fictitious right when the PLAINTIFF knows there is no just cause for the suit. Such an action is usually brought for some illegal purpose; *feigned action.*

False affidavit. PERJURY because of untruths contained in an AFFIDAVIT authorized by law.

False arrest. The unlawful restraint and/or imprisonment of someone by an officer of the law; *illegal arrest.* (False arrest can serve as the basis for a SUIT by the one so arrested.)

False claim. The conscious making of an untrue STATEMENT or CLAIM in order to obtain some benefit or reward. (A false claim is more than an excessive claim and constitutes a CRIMINAL OFFENSE.)

False entry. An untrue STATEMENT in books of account, made for purposes of deception. Such an entry constitutes a CRIMINAL OFFENSE.

False impersonation. The act of assuming another's identity, such as a person who poses as an officer of the law when he is not such an officer.

False imprisonment > FALSE ARREST.

False instrument. A counterfeit DOCUMENT.

False pretenses. A premeditated, calculated, thought-out MISREPRESENTATION of FACT or situation, frequently entered into to DEFRAUD someone of PROPERTY or money.

False statement. A deceitful, purposely untrue STATEMENT made for ulterior motives.

False swearing. Untrue STATEMENTS that are sworn to as true, often made before a court or public official. However, false swearing is not considered perjury unless it is done in court during a JUDICIAL PROCEEDING.

False verdict. A VERDICT that is not arrived at after thorough consideration of all the EVIDENCE; a verdict delivered by a JURY that fails to listen to and be guided by the instructions of the judge.

False witness. A WITNESS who consciously and willfully gives false TESTIMONY.

Falsify. To alter a DOCUMENT so that it does not adhere to the truth; to forge or intentionally change a document for one's own benefit.

Falsifying a record. Changing a RECORD or written DOCUMENT. Such an action is a CRIMINAL OFFENSE.

Falsus in uno. The right of a JURY to disregard *all* of a WITNESS's TESTIMONY if it is discovered that there has been false testimony in any part of the testimony (Latin).

Familiarity. Knowing someone through frequent contacts, not usually implying intimacy; more than a casual acquaintance.

Family arrangement. An AGREEMENT among members of a family on how inherited PROPERTY shall be distributed or divided, with methods of distribution or division differing from those spelled out by the law.

Family corporation. A CORPORATION whose STOCK is held exclusively, or in large part, by members of one family.

Family court. A COURT whose JURISDICTION extends to controversies and matters needful of solution among members of a family. Family courts consider many different matters, including fights between husbands and wives, problems of child CUSTODY or DELINQUENCY, fitness of parents to maintain their rights to control their children, nonsupport, etcetera.

Family settlement. An AGREEMENT as to how the ASSETS of an ESTATE should be distributed, made by members of a family without resort to the COURTS.

Farm Credit Administration. A federal agency in the Department of Agriculture, whose function is to aid farmers during times of stress through the extension of credit and aid in refinancing.

Fascist. A person who believes in a totalitarian dictatorship which stresses nationalism and racism; an advocate of fascism.

Fatal variance. A VARIANCE (a difference in two steps of a legal procedure which must agree before the legal procedure can become effectual) that misleads a DEFENDANT in preparing and pursuing his DEFENSE in an adequate manner.

Fault. NEGLIGENCE; a wrongful act; a departure from that which is expected of someone; a neglect of OBLIGATION or DUTY; mismanagement; bad faith.

Favored beneficiary. A BENEFICIARY who receives more in INHERITANCE than others who, according to relationship, would normally expect to receive equal inheritances. When a favored beneficiary exists, in some instances the other beneficiaries raise the question of "undue influence."

Feasance. The performance of an ACT; putting into effect.

Feasible. Capable of accomplishment; something that can be done successfully.

Fed. Abbreviation for the Federal Reserve System, the central U.S. bank that controls the nation's monetary supply (usually referred to as "the Fed").

Federal. In this country, federal refers to the U.S. government; national.

Federal Bureau of Investigation. Usually referred to as the F.B.I., it is the national U.S. investigative agency responsible for the maintenance of internal security. The agency is under the JURISDICTION of the Department of Justice and the Attorney General.

Federal common law. Federal COMMON LAW consists of those laws established by the federal courts, uninfluenced by laws and legal decisions made by state courts. Although there is no national common law, states recognize and adhere to those laws laid down by federal common law.

Federal courts. COURTS of the U.S. government, as distinguished from state, county, or city courts.

Federal Deposit Insurance Corporation. Known as the F.D.I.C., it is an agency of the U.S. government that insures bank deposits and the solvency of banks.

Federal grand jury. A GRAND JURY that hears matters pertaining to violation of federal statutory law.

Federal grant. A transfer of land by the federal government through an act of Congress; the giving of money by the federal government to an institution, or individual, for purposes of research.

Federal judge. A judge who presides over a U.S. FEDERAL COURT, as distinguished from a state, county, or city court.

Federal offense. An OFFENSE or crime defined by Congress and carrying punishments laid down by Congress. TREASON, INCOME TAX evasion, SMUGGLING, KIDNAPPING across state lines, etcetera, are just a few of the many federal offenses. (These offenses are tried in federal courts, not in state, city, or county courts.)

Federal rules of civil procedure. Uniform RULES governing procedure in DISTRICT COURTS of the United States. These rules originated from the United States SUPREME COURT, and are concerned with civil cases.

Federal rules of criminal procedure. Uniform rules governing procedure in CRIMINAL CASES in United States DISTRICT COURTS.

Federal rules of equity practice. Uniform rules governing procedure in equity cases in United States DISTRICT COURTS.

Federal statute. A national LAW enacted by Congress.

Federal taxes. Taxes, such as the INCOME TAX, levied by the United States. Such taxes are payable to the INTERNAL REVENUE SERVICE.

Federal tort claims act. A law passed by the government which gives the federal DISTRICT COURTS the authority to hear CLAIMS for DAMAGES against the United States.

Federation. **1.** An association of people organized for a common purpose. **2.** A combination of UNIONS, such as the American Federation of Labor.

Fee. A recompense for a service.

Fee simple. Total ownership of land and the buildings upon it, with the right to WILL such PROPERTY to HEIRS upon the death of the owner.

Fee-splitting. The division of legal fees between a referring ATTORNEY and the attorney who handles the matter. In the law, fee-splitting is a legitimate practice providing the referring attorney renders a service; in medicine it is unethical, and in many states it is unlawful.

Fee tail. A legal ESTATE of lands and PROPERTY which are to pass on to HEIRS by lineal descent only, that is, from father or mother to daughter or son.

Feigned accomplice. Someone who joins in the COMMISSION of a crime for the purpose of apprehending the criminal or criminals committing the crime. In other words, an UNDERCOVER MAN who makes believe he is a participant but who has in actuality been planted there by the police or other governmental authorities.

Feigned action. > FALSE ACTION.

Feigned issue. An issue presented by a COURT OF EQUITY, which does not have JURISDICTION to settle the matter, to a COURT OF COMMON LAW, which does have the proper jurisdiction. Such an issue is made up with the consent of both parties to a suit in a court of equity. The court of common law decides the issue and the court of equity then has a ruling upon which to base its decision.

Fellatio. The sexual act in which the male organ is taken into the mouth. Also known as fellation.

Felon. An individual who commits a FELONY.

Felonious assault. An attack upon another's person of a major nature, subjecting the one who commits the ASSAULT, if convicted, to a JAIL sentence.

Felonious homicide. Murdering someone without an excuse or justification. SUICIDE is also considered felonious homicide.

Felony. A major crime, as distinguished from a minor one or a MISDEMEANOR. Felonies include ROBBERIES, BURGLARIES, FELONIOUS ASSAULT, MURDER, etcetera.

Fence. Someone who receives stolen property knowingly and then sells it to another.

Feoffment. The DEED granting someone possession of LANDS or PROPERTY. > ENFEOFFMENT.

Fetters. Chains placed around the ankles in order to prevent CONVICTS from escaping; shackles.

Fetus. An unborn child beyond three months in its development. (Prior to that period, the unborn child is known as an EMBRYO.)

Fiat. A command or order originating from a source of AUTHORITY. In Latin, the word means "Let it be done!"

Fiction. An ASSUMPTION of LAW that something which is false is true, or the supposition that certain facts have existed when in actuality they haven't existed. Such fictions are assumed in law in order to accomplish justice.

Fiction of law. > FICTION.

Fictitious. Pretended; false; imaginary; counterfeit; not genuine.

Fictitious action. An ACTION brought solely for the purpose of obtaining the opinion of the court on a point of law; a *feigned action.*

Fictitious name. A false name; an ALIAS; an assumed name. A fictitious name is frequently taken to hide one's true identity.

Fictitious plaintiff. One who appears in court as the CLAIMANT, but who actually has nothing to do with the matter at hand. (Such an individual is guilty of CONTEMPT OF COURT.)

Fidei-commissum. A BEQUEST of PROPERTY to one individual, accompanied by a direction that the individual give the property to another individual who is not able to receive the bequest under the WILL (Latin).

Fidelity bond. A guarantee as to the integrity and honesty of someone who is entrusted with money or valuable property. The BOND guarantees payment of a loss should a bonded employee or officer of a company embezzle or abscond with money or valuables in his care.

Fiduciary. A person who acts as a TRUSTEE in the handling of a TRUST. (Such a fiduciary must be BONDED.)

Fiduciary capacity. One serves in a fiduciary capacity when handling money or property for, or transacting business for, the benefit of another party. ATTORNEYS AT LAW, GUARDIANS, BROKERS, EXECUTORS, and directors of CORPORATIONS all serve in fiduciary capacities when performing for the benefit of CLIENTS or others.

Fiduciary debt. A DEBT based on some CONFIDENCE or trust, not upon a contract.

Fiduciary relation. A relationship of an informal nature in which one person trusts fully and relies upon another; a confidential relationship.

Fifth Amendment. An amendment to the UNITED CONSTITUTION, included in the BILL OF RIGHTS. It is the privilege of not giving EVIDENCE that might lead to SELF-INCRIMINATION—in other words, refusing to answer questions because the answers might involve one in a crime.

File. 1. A record of the COURT; a place where DOCUMENTS are deposited. 2. To present a legal DOCUMENT to a public OFFICER for the purpose of having it placed on permanent record and preserved.

Filiation proceeding. A court PROCEEDING to force the father of an "ILLEGITIMATE" child to support it. Such an action is based upon proof of parenthood. > PATERNITY PROCEEDING.

Filing a brief. Presenting a written STATEMENT to a COURT, explaining the case to the judge. Such a BRIEF is filed by an ATTORNEY representing one of the PARTIES in a DISPUTE.

Filing a claim. Presenting a written STATEMENT of one's request for DAMAGES, RELIEF, or other demands against an opposing party in a LAWSUIT.

Filing articles of incorporation. Placing on record the details of INCORPORATION of a COMPANY, the material being deposited in a public office specified by law for such filings.

Filing date. The date upon which a CLAIM or demand must be presented and filed.

Final. Definitive; terminating; completed. The term final is used in contrast to the word "interlocutory."

Final decision. A DECISION that settles a matter completely, leaving nothing further to be discussed or acted upon.

Final hearing. A HEARING that will settle a case once and for all, through a final DECISION.

Final settlement. 1. An AGREEMENT that winds up all matters between partners who are dissolving their partnership. 2. The final settlement of outstanding OBLIGATIONS and the final DISTRIBUTION of all ASSETS of an ESTATE.

Final submission. The condition existing when the whole case, including the PLAINTIFF's and DEFENDANT's statements, has been presented and is submitted to the court for its DECISION or VERDICT.

Financial statement. A written STATEMENT that an individual submits to a bank prior to receiving a loan; a credit statement.

Financial worth. The net value of a person's PROPERTY and ASSETS, minus his LIABILITIES or DEBTS. > NET WORTH.

Finder's fee. Money paid to someone who puts together a business DEAL for another, resulting in the making of profits.

Finding of fact. A conclusion reached by a court after due CONSIDERATION; a DECISION reached by ARBITRATORS; a determination of the truth after consideration of STATEMENTS made by the opposing parties in a suit.

Findings. The results of the DELIBERATIONS of a COURT or JURY; the DECISIONS expressed by a judicial AUTHORITY after consideration of all the FACTS.

Fine. To impose a monetary PENALTY upon someone convicted of an OFFENSE.

Fine-force. Absolute necessity.

Fingerprints. The marks left by the pressing of the tips of fingers upon an object. Since no two persons' fingerprints are exactly alike, the prints left by a suspected criminal are of great significance. (A file of fingerprints maintained in the F.B.I. office, Washington, D.C., is often consulted in trying to identify a person who might have committed a particular crime.)

Firearm. A WEAPON, such as a revolver or gun, which acts as a result of the explosion of gunpowder.

Firebug. Someone who purposely sets fire to PROPERTY; a pyromaniac; a committer of ARSON.

Firm. A PARTNERSHIP or COMPANY that is unincorporated; a business concern.

First-class misdemeanant. Someone who has been found guilty of a MISDEMEANOR but who is thought to deserve lenient treatment.

First-class title. A TITLE to PROPERTY that is free from doubt; a title that is "clean."

First-degree burglary. The intentional breaking into a dwelling, presently occupied, with the intention of stealing items from it.

First-degree murder. A deliberate, premeditated, planned killing, or one that accompanies a crime such as RAPE, BURGLARY, or ASSAULT AND BATTERY.

First-hand evidence. EVIDENCE resulting from having witnessed an event or from being part of an event, as distinguished from *hearsay evidence.* > EYEWITNESS.

First conviction. The first conviction is often taken into CONSIDERATION when sentencing an HABITUAL CRIMINAL for a subsequent offense. (The sentence for a second conviction is often much greater than that given for the first conviction.)

First instance. A phrase referring to the TRIAL COURT in which a case was first tried, as distinguished from a later trial in a court of appeals.

First lien. A LIEN that takes precedence over all other CLAIMS against a piece of PROPERTY. After the first lien has been satisfied, other liens can be considered. > FIRST MORTGAGE.

First mortgage. A MORTGAGE having priority over any other LIEN upon the same piece of PROPERTY.

First publication. The COPYRIGHT by an author prior to publication of a manuscript; the date upon which the first copies of a work were placed on sale.

Fiscal. An adjective referring to financial matters in general. (Fiscal affairs are *financial affairs.*)

Fiscal officers. PUBLIC OFFICIALS charged with the responsibility of collecting and distributing public monies, such as those of a city, county, state, or federal government.

"Fishing trip." An expression denoting a loose and indiscriminate attempt to discover FACTS in questioning a WITNESS or in proceeding in a court ACTION.

Fitness of parent. In a DIVORCE suit, the court considers carefully the fitness, or ability of a parent to take care of a child or children, as well as the welfare of the child or children, before rendering a decision as to future CUSTODY. The welfare of the child is the prime consideration, but important secondary considerations are the morals of the individual parents and their financial status.

Fixed assets. ASSETS, or RESOURCES, essential to the undertaking or operation of a business. For example, the POSSESSION of vehicles is essential to the operation of a taxi business.

Fixed by law. Prescribed by an existing STATUTE.

Fixed charges. Expenses that must be paid whether or not a business is operating, such as rent, taxes, etcetera.

Fixed liabilities. Certain known DEBTS or OBLIGATIONS of a business.

Fixed prices. Agreed-upon prices. > PRICE FIXING.

Fixing a jury. An unlawful attempt to influence a JUROR or jurors to vote a certain way.

Fixing bail. Setting an amount of BAIL that must be deposited before a suspect can be released.

Flagrantly biased. Outrageously prejudiced.

"Flee to the wall." An expression denoting that a HOMICIDE was committed completely in SELF-DEFENSE, after all measures other than homicide had been exhausted.

Floating capital. *Circulating capital;* funds set aside to pay current expenses.

Floating security. A fair and equitable LIEN against a going concern, temporarily serving as security for a DEBT or OBLIGATION.

Flogging. Punishment for a crime consisting of lashing with a whip. This type of punishment has practically gone out of existence in this country.

Food and drug act. A federal law governing the INTERSTATE COMMERCE of foods, drugs, and cosmetics. Its provisions include regulations concerning purity of products, labeling that presents true facts about products, restrictions against false CLAIMS, and removal of dangerous products from interstate markets.

Footprints. Impressions made by the feet in earth, snow, sand, or other surfaces. Footprints can be presented as legitimate EVIDENCE.

For cause. Legal CAUSE; a cause recognized as sufficient by law, as distinguished from a cause based upon someone's discretion or opinion.

For that whereas. A phrase frequently used in introducing the PLAINTIFF's case before a COURT; the words used in a formal opening STATEMENT.

For value received. An expression denoting that a bill has been paid, acknowledging having received full value.

Forbearance. Waiting for a DEBT to be paid without taking action to collect the debt; a delay in enforcing one's rights.

Forbidding disclosure to parents. In MEDICAL JURISPRUDENCE, a MINOR's insistence that a physician not reveal medical information to a parent. (For example, a girl under 18 years of age may not want to reveal to her parents the fact that she is pregnant.)

Force and fear. An expression used in a situation in which a CONTRACT or AGREEMENT was made because one of the parties was forced into it, or became party to it, out of fear. Such a contract or agreement, if force and fear is proved, is VOID.

Force majesture. An "act of God," something resulting from floods, earthquakes, lightning, storms, etcetera (French); also *force majeure.*

Forced entry. Entering another person's premises by force, against the will of the occupant or owner of the PROPERTY.

Forced sale. A sale of property ordered by a court in satisfaction of a judgment against the owner of said property; a sale against the will of the owner.

Forcible detainer. The unlawful retention of PROPERTY, such as keeping out the person who rightfully owns the property. In so doing, threats of force, or force itself, is often exercised.

Foreclose. To take over OWNERSHIP of PROPERTY because of present owner's failure to pay the OBLIGATIONS of said property, such as failure to pay a MORTGAGE when due; to terminate; to bar.

Foreclosure sale. The SALE of PROPERTY on which the MORTGAGE has not been paid off; such a sale includes payment of the mortgage.

Foreign Agents Registration Act. A federal law requiring people who represent foreign countries to register with the U.S. government so that their activities in behalf of foreign countries can be observed. The law applies to public relations consultants, advertising agencies, as well as others who promote the interests of foreign countries. Such activities in behalf of foreign countries are not necessarily harmful to the United States, but registration of these individuals results in the opportunity to observe their activities more easily.

Foreign bill of exchange. A BILL OF EXCHANGE (an order of one person upon another to pay money to a third person) not drawn or payable in this country, but payable in a foreign country.

Foreign extradition. The surrender of a fugitive from justice from one country to another, where he will be tried for his alleged OFFENSE. ≫ EXTRADITION.

Foreign jurisdiction. The AUTHORITY to hear and try a case beyond one's own borders. Foreign jurisdiction is usually obtained by AGREEMENTS between sovereign nations.

Foreign tax credit. A ruling that attempts to eliminate double INCOME TAX obligations for those Americans who earn money abroad. In essence, a CREDIT is given by the United States INTERNAL REVENUE SERVICE against taxes paid to a foreign country.

Foreign trade. Import and export trade between countries.

Foreman of the jury. A JURY member designated by the jury to be their spokesperson.

Forensic. Adjective meaning belonging to courts of justice.

Forensic medicine. A science that deals with the application of various branches of medicine to the law. (≫ MEDICAL JURISPRUDENCE.) The law frequently relies upon medical facts in determining a case that affects life or PROPERTY.

Foreseeability. The ability to know in advance; a reasonable anticipation that INJURY might result from certain acts or failure to perform certain acts.

Forfeit. To lose the right to do something, especially because of defaulting an OBLIGATION or because of an OFFENSE.

Forfeiture of bond. Failure to meet a condition, the result of which is that a BOND is forfeited. As an example, if a DEFENDANT fails to show up at a trial, the BAIL BOND is forfeited.

Forgery. COUNTERFEITING or falsifying a DOCUMENT; to sign another person's name to a check or other legal document in an attempt to defraud. Forgery is a major CRIMINAL OFFENSE.

Form. The outline of an ACTION to take place in court, containing the appropriate words and phrases to make it formally acceptable. Form is the opposite of substance, with substance being the essential material of the action.

Form of the statute. The actual command or ORDER contained in a LAW, as stated in its words and language.

Former conviction. A previous TRIAL and CONVICTION for the same OFFENSE.

Former jeopardy. A PLEA that an accused cannot be tried twice for the same OFFENSE. In other words, once found INNOCENT, a person cannot be again brought to TRIAL for that same OFFENSE. ≫ DOUBLE JEOPARDY; IN JEOPARDY; LEGAL JEOPARDY.

Forms of action. Various kinds of suits brought in the COMMON LAW. Some of the most frequent forms are TRESPASS, TROVER (the appropriation of another's PROPERTY for one's own use), REPLEVIN (the recovery of stolen PROPERTY), DEBT, and ASSUMPSIT (recovery for a PROMISE that has not been carried out), etcetera.

Formula instruction. The complete STATEMENT and explanation of a law, given to a JURY by a judge to enable it to consider the case knowledgeably.

Fornication. Unlawful SEXUAL INTERCOURSE, either between two unmarried people or between people who are married, but not to each other; illicit sexual intercourse.

Forswear. To SWEAR to something that the swearer knows is untrue.

Forsworn. Having made a FALSE STATEMENT under OATH.

Forthwith. Promptly; immediately; without delay.

Fortuitous event. An *unforeseen event;* something happening by chance; an accidental occurrence.

Forum. A COURT; a place where legal controversies are heard and decided; a judicial tribunal.

Forum non conveniens. The DOCTRINE stating that a COURT, even though it has the AUTHORITY to try a case, may decide to turn the matter over to another court. This is sometimes done when a court feels that another court can more appropriately try the matter (Latin).

Forwarding fee. A part of an ATTORNEY's fee paid to another attorney who actually handles the case. Such a fee is often paid by an attorney, or a LAW FIRM, to another attorney or firm because he or they do not specialize in a particular type of law. Thus, an attorney specializing in tax law may send a homicide case to an attorney who specializes in criminal law. > FEE-SPLITTING.

Forwards and backwards at sea. Going from port to port during a voyage.

Foster parent. An adult who rears another's child.

Found guilty. A phrase denoting the CONVICTION of an ACCUSED.

Found innocent. A phrase denoting the ACQUITTAL of an ACCUSED.

Foundation. A charitable organization; an endowment of monies to a charitable organization. An individual can establish a fund or foundation, the earnings of which are designated to go for charitable purposes.

Four corners. The face of a DOCUMENT; the document itself.

Fourteenth amendment. This amendment to the UNITED STATES CONSTITUTION extends U.S. citizenship to everyone born in this country as well as to anyone who undergoes naturalization. Prior to this amendment, ratified in 1868, people were CITIZENS of individual states.

Fractional. An irregular division of land, either less or more than conventional amounts of acreage.

Frame-up. A plot to incriminate an innocent person in a crime.

Franchise. 1. A PRIVILEGE conferred by LAW, such as the privilege to vote. **2.** A grant of special privileges to a merchant to sell a product manufactured and/or owned by another.

Franchise tax. A TAX on the PRIVILEGE and RIGHT to carry on business as a corporation. Such taxes may be calculated according to the amount of business done, the amount of earnings or DIVIDENDS, or the total value of the STOCK issued by the CORPORATION.

Franchisee. A person or COMPANY that is granted a FRANCHISE by a FRANCHISOR.

Franchisor. A person or company that grants a FRANCHISE to a FRANCHISEE.

Franking privilege. A PRIVILEGE, issued to certain government OFFICERS, to send mail pertaining to their office and duties without payment of postage.

Fratricide. The killing of a brother or sister.

Fraud. An intentional distortion of the truth perpetrated upon someone in order to convince him to give up money, PROPERTY, some RIGHT, or other thing rightfully belonging to him; deception; DECEIT, trickery.

Fraud in the inducement. Trickery in getting one to sign a DOCUMENT.

Fraud in treaty. DECEIT in getting someone to sign a DOCUMENT that misrepresents the intended AGREEMENT, or a document whose contents are not in conformity with agreements reached.

Fraud order. An order by the postmaster general to return mail to a sender who is attempting to use the mails to defraud.

Fraudulent act. An act involving bad faith or dishonesty.

Fraudulent alienation. The transfer of TITLE to PROPERTY in order to prevent CREDITORS from collecting their just DEBTS. Also, the squandering of the ASSETS of an ESTATE so that it will have little or no value.

Fraudulent concealment. The hiding of a fact or facts that someone is morally and legally obliged to disclose.

Fraudulent conveyance. The TRANSFER of PROPERTY to another in order to deprive a CREDITOR from receiving what is rightfully due.

Fraudulent preference. The act of favoring a particular CREDITOR, in order to cheat other creditors.

Free. Unrestricted; not bound by legal restraint; having the power and right to do whatever one wishes; the opposite of enslaved, restrained, restricted, inhibited.

Free and clear. A "clean" TITLE; a title to property that is free of LIENS or other possible hindrances.

Free and equal. The right of every citizen to vote, incorporating the principle that every vote shall have equal weight; a term referring to a completely free election.

Free egress. The right to leave land or PROPERTY whenever one wishes.

Free enterprise. The right to enter into and conduct one's own business without governmental consent. Such ENTERPRISE is usually embarked upon in order to make profit. (In Communist states, one must receive government consent before starting a business, and the profit motive is suppressed or regulated by government decree.)

Free entry. The right to enter upon and travel on land as often as one wishes.

Free list. Imported articles or merchandise upon which no DUTIES are charged, such as antiques, original works of art, etcetera.

Free love. Cohabiting; having sexual relations without marriage.

Free passage. The ability to travel a road or highway without hindrance.

Free shareholders. Those who own stock in a BUILDING AND LOAN ASSOCIATION who are not borrowers from the association.

Freedom of assembly. The RIGHT of people in the United States to gather together in order to discuss issues of public importance, limited only by abuse of the right.

Freedom of religion. Guarantees, under the FIRST and FOURTEENTH AMENDMENTS to the UNITED STATES CONSTITUTION, of the right to worship as one pleases, without government regulation or restriction.

Freedom of speech. Guarantees, contained in the FIRST and FOURTEENTH AMENDMENTS to the UNITED STATES CONSTITUTION, of the right of people to speak what they please without government regulation or restriction, limited only by abuse of the right. Speech that advises the forcible overthrow of the duly elected government would constitute an abuse of the right to free speech.

Freedom of the press. Guarantees, contained in the FIRST and FOURTEENTH AMENDMENTS to the UNITED STATES CONSTITUTION, of the right of people to publish what they please without government regulation or restriction, limited only by abuse of the right.

Freehold. The OWNERSHIP of land. Upon one's death the TITLE passes on to one's HEIRS.

Frequenter. Someone who visits a place often; someone who is not an employee but who comes to a place frequently. A frequenter is not a TRESPASSER.

Friend of the court. Amicus curiae (Latin). Someone not directly involved in a LAWSUIT who supplies information upon some matter of law upon which the court may be doubtful.

Friendly suit. An ACTION in court brought mutually by two parties for the joint purpose of settling a point of law upon which there are differing opinions. > AMICABLE ACTION.

Friendly witness. A WITNESS called into COURT by one PARTY to a SUIT and who is expected to give TESTIMONY favoring the party who called him to court.

Frigidity. A lack of desire for SEXUAL INTERCOURSE; an inability to obtain satisfaction from intercourse.

Fringe benefits. BENEFITS received by employees in addition to their wages. HEALTH INSURANCE, LIFE INSURANCE, DISABILITY INSURANCE, and PENSION benefits are all classified as fringe benefits.

Frivolous action. A LAWSUIT that is legally untenable and worthless. Such actions are sometimes brought for the purpose of annoying or causing trouble for a DEFENDANT, without any real hope of the action being successful.

Frivolous appeal. An APPEAL that is without merit and which will undoubtedly be denied.
Frivolous demurrer. A MOTION to dismiss charges that are so flimsy and untenable that the judge will deny them out of hand.
Frivolous plea. A sham PLEA or DEFENSE, completely devoid of merit.
Frontage. The amount of PROPERTY one has facing the street or highway.
Fronting and abutting. A description of PROPERTY that borders on, or adjoins another.
Fruits of crime. Material things taken during the COMMISSION of a crime, such as the money stolen from a bank; loot; BOOTY.
Frustration. Inability to go through with one's intentions. (Frustration of a CONTRACT exists when both parties want to go through with their agreement but are prevented from doing so by events they do not control.)
Frustration of testamentary intention. The failure of a LEGATEE or HEIR to go through with a promise he or she made to the maker of a WILL during the deceased's lifetime. (The maker of the will may have relied upon the heir or legatee to give the inheritance to another party. Failure to do so constitutes frustration of testamentary intention.)
Fugitive. A person ACCUSED or CONVICTED of a crime who flees, thus evading the law and thereupon becoming a fugitive from justice.
Fugitive witness. A person wanted to TESTIFY in court who flees the JURISDICTION of the court, thus becoming a fugitive from justice.
Fulfillment of contract. The completion of an AGREEMENT with all promises on both sides fully met and all OBLIGATIONS fulfilled.
Full disclosure. The telling of *all* that one knows, not hiding or concealing anything that might be pertinent to the CASE.
Full faith and credit. A phrase pertaining to the following: the FEDERAL LAWS require that each state in the nation must treat the laws of other states as valid, and must, wherever possible, enforce those laws as if they were their own.
Full jurisdiction. Complete and total AUTHORITY to hear, try, and decide a particular type of CASE.
Full pardon. A total PARDON, so complete that the GUILTY party is restored to a state in which he is as innocent as if he never committed the OFFENSE.
Full particular. A STATEMENT to an INSURANCE COMPANY of all the circumstances surrounding a particular ACCIDENT. Upon receipt of full particulars, the insurer will be in a good position to evaluate its LIABILITIES.
Full settlement. Complete payment of all OBLIGATIONS, CLAIMS, and DEBTS, resulting in the termination of all outstanding ISSUES.
Functional depeciation. For tax purposes, PROPERTY may lessen in value, and therefore be taxed less, because it no longer functions efficiently.
Functionary. A public officer.
Fundamental law. The basic law of the land, such as the UNITED

STATES CONSTITUTION and its Amendments.

Fundamental rights and privileges. The rights of life, liberty and property, FREEDOM OF SPEECH and ASSEMBLY, FREEDOM OF THE PRESS, FREEDOM OF RELIGION, the right to DUE PROCESS of the law, and the right to the PURSUIT OF HAPPINESS. These rights are all guaranteed to Americans in the UNITED STATES CONSTITUTION and its Amendments.

Fungible. A thing that can be replaced readily by another similar thing. For example, a sack of potatoes can be replaced easily by another sack of potatoes.

Furnish. To provide, equip, or supply.

Further instructions. Additional INSTRUCTIONS given by a judge to a JURY after they have already begun their DELIBERATIONS.

Future earnings. Earnings that would have been acquired had it not been for an INJURY that prevented a person from participating in gainful occupation.

Future right. A RIGHT that will take place, according to STIPULATIONS or PROVISIONS of an existing CONTRACT.

Futures. AGREEMENTS made by dealers in commodities (such as wheat, barley, rice, cotton, beans, etcetera) to buy or sell said commodities at a future date at a set price. These agreements or CONTRACTS are made on promises to deliver, not upon actual present ownership of the commodities.

G

Gainful occupation. Working for a living; earning WAGES. (In COMPENSATION INSURANCE, one frequently considers whether the employee, because of job-connected injuries or illness, is able to perform his ordinary work.)
Gallows. The wooden apparatus constructed for hanging those sentenced to DEATH by hanging.
Game laws. Laws passed for the purpose of preserving wildlife. These STATUTES usually set forth the season of the year in which certain animals may be killed, as well as the number of such animals that can be killed by any hunter. (Game laws vary from state to state.)
Garnishee. A person against whom a GARNISHMENT has been declared, usually a DEBTOR whose money or property is being withheld until he pays his debt.
Garnishment. A legal proceeding in which a CREDITOR seeks to obtain payment from a DEBTOR out of money, salary, or property of the debtor. The procedure takes place *after* a JUDGMENT against the debtor has already been handed down.
General Accounting Office. The G.A.O., a federal agency headed by the comptroller general and responsible for accounting and auditing funds of the U.S. government.
General appraisers. Appraisers appointed by an act of Congress to help customs officials determine the value of imported merchandise, goods, art, etcetera.
General assets. Available money or PROPERTY; ASSETS in hand; assets that can readily be used to pay outstanding DEBTS.
General assignment to creditors. A transfer of a DEBTOR's title to property to a TRUSTEE, with authority given to the trustee to liquidate the debtor's affairs and to distribute the proceeds to the CREDITORS.
General assumpsit. A LAWSUIT based upon the implied promise of a DEFENDANT to pay a debt to a CREDITOR. Also called *common assumpsit.*
General court-martial. The type of COURT-MARTIAL held for a major violation or crime committed by a member of the armed forces. The COURT is presided over by five commissioned officers. (However, if the accused is a member of the noncommissioned personnel, he may demand that one member of the court also be of a noncommissioned rank.)

General creditor. A CREDITOR not entitled to priority; a creditor whose claim is not secured by a LIEN or MORTGAGE.

General damages. Those INJURIES (DAMAGES) resulting directly from the action, or failure to take action, of the DEFENDANT.

General demurrer. A statement by the DEFENDANT that the CLAIMS of the PLAINTIFF are insufficient to justify a suit against him, and that the claims are lacking in substance.

General devise. A gift, granted in a WILL, that does not limit itself to REAL ESTATE but may include other kinds of PROPERTY as well.

General exception. An objection to a PLEADING (a COMPLAINT) for want of substance, as distinguished from a *special exception,* which bases its objection on the form in which the pleading is presented.

General improvement. An improvement of an area for the benefit of an entire COMMUNITY, such as electrification or irrigation of a rural area.

General instruction. An instruction by a JUDGE to a JURY, setting down the salient points in the case that must be considered before bringing in a VERDICT. In this instruction, the judge will state that the merits of the case must be decided only on the EVIDENCE. The judge will also state the limitations of the ISSUES to be decided.

General lien. A right to retain another's PROPERTY until payment of a DEBT is made. Such a LIEN can originate only from a CONTRACT that was made between the CREDITOR and DEBTOR.

General objection. An overall objection to EVIDENCE, not specifying the reasons why the evidence is inadmissible.

General obligation bond. A BOND issued by a government, such as a city or state, payable out of general funds raised through taxes, as distinguished from a bond payable out of special funds put aside for the express purpose of paying off the bond.

General pardon. A PARDON given to a whole class or group of people who have been convicted of a crime, such as political prisoners. ➢ AMNESTY.

General restraint of trade. Methods of trading that tend to stifle COMPETITION and to lead toward MONOPOLY control, thus depriving the public of the advantages flowing from FREE COMPETITION. (RESTRAINT OF TRADE is an unlawful act.)

General retainer. The hiring of an ATTORNEY or firm of attorneys on a basis of a period of time, often a year. The attorney or attorneys will receive a certain set sum of money whether they do a little or a great deal of work during the period of the retainer.

General Services Administration. The G.S.A., a federal government AGENCY charged with the "housekeeping" duties of the government. It supplies all government bureaus and agencies with their physical necessities, providing everything from paper clips to new buildings.

Germane. Relevant; pertinent; apropos.

Gerrymander. Maneuvering and changing BOUNDARIES of an ELECTION DISTRICT or area, be it county or state, in order to give an advantage to one political party.
Ghost surgery. Surgery performed by a surgeon other than the one engaged by the patient, carried out without the patient's express knowledge and consent. This type of surgery is unethical and unlawful.
Gift causa mortis. A gift of PERSONAL PROPERTY given in anticipation of the donor's death (Latin), upon condition that the property shall belong completely to the DONEE if the donor dies as anticipated. Such a gift can be revoked should the donor not die as anticipated.
Gift deed. A gift of land or PROPERTY for an extremely small, trifling sum of money, for less than the real value of the property.
Gift in trust. A gift of PROPERTY to a recipient, minus the legal TITLE to it. In other words, the recipient will receive the benefits of the gift but will not own it outright and will not himself be able to sell it or give it to a DONEE of his choosing.
Gift over. An ESTATE created upon the expiration of a preceding estate.
Gift tax. A TAX on the transfer of property from one living person to another. The tax is levied on the transfer, not on the property transferred.
Gifts inter vivos. Gifts between living people (Latin), the gifts becoming final and irrevocable during the lives of the donor and the recipient.
Gist. The main ISSUE or point of the matter under discussion.
Give and bequeath. This phrase is used often in a WILL attesting to a LEGACY that will become effective upon the death of the maker of the will, and upon proof that the will is valid.
Give notice. To inform someone that a legal SUIT is about to take place. Such notice is usually served legally, although it may be informal notification.
Give time. To extend the time for a payment of a DEBT which is due.
Go-between. An AGENT who serves both parties in a TRANSACTION; an intermediary.
Go in evidence. Material is said to "go in evidence" when it has been presented and accepted as EVIDENCE in a trial.
Go quit. To be declared INNOCENT; to be exonerated; to be dismissed.
Go without day. To be dismissed by a COURT without instructions to return; to go *sine die* (Latin).
Going and coming rule. A rule concerning the rights of an employee to COMPENSATION BENEFITS should he be injured on his way to work or while returning home from work. In some instances, compensation is denied; in other instances it is granted.
Going concern. A business in operation, carrying out the activities for which it is organized. It usually refers to a profitable enterprise, but it may also refer to a full operation that is not making money.
Going price. The current market VALUE; the prevailing price at a particular time.

Going public. An expression used when a privately owned company issues shares which can be purchased by the general public.
Good behavior. Lawful CONDUCT. The phrase is often used in reference to the orderly conduct of a prisoner, and such good behavior is essential for PAROLE or for shortening a SENTENCE in jail.
Good cause. Sufficient grounds from a legal point of view; substantial and convincing reason.
Good conduct. > GOOD BEHAVIOR.
Good faith. Honest intentions: fairness; equity. (One deals in good faith when one attempts, without guile or deception, to settle a controversy.)
Good repute. A good reputation. (People who are generally known to be honest and forthright are frequently classified as being of good repute.)
Good Samaritan doctrine. This doctrine, in effect in more than 40 states, frees the doctor from LIABILITY and MALPRACTICE suits should he treat a patient in an emergency. Prior to this doctrine, physicians were reluctant to give first aid in accidents for fear of being sued for malpractice.
Good standing. Someone who is up-to-date in paying his dues or other obligations to a society or organization; someone not DELINQUENT.
Good title. A TITLE that is free from any doubt and can be sold with the full knowledge that it is "clear" and valid.
Goodwill. Something beyond the calculated worth of a company; the knowledge that the reputation of a company will ensure that regular customers will continue to patronize the firm; an intangible ASSET whose value is based upon the good name the business has developed over the years.
Goods and chattels. PERSONAL PROPERTY, as distinguished from REAL ESTATE. (Money is not considered as goods and chattels.)
Government. The complex of organizations, institutions, agencies, executive and legislative bodies, laws, and customs through which a political unit is directed and controlled.
Government bond. A LOAN to the federal GOVERNMENT by individuals, calling for the payment of a specified amount of INTEREST. Such bonds are free from federal taxes.
Government de facto. > DE FACTO GOVERNMENT
Government de jure. The true, lawful GOVERNMENT, as opposed to one set up by a dictator or ruling group that has taken over without free elections (Latin).
Governmental agency. An organization created for the purpose of carrying out a GOVERNMENT function. See Appendix.
Grace. A favor; dispensation; indulgence.
Grace period. An extra period of time granted to an insured person to pay a PREMIUM that is due. Insurance companies usually keep insurance in force for 30 days after the due date of premium payment. After that time, the insurance lapses.
Graded offense. A CRIME for

which a greater punishment is given than that ordinarily meted out.

Grades of crime. Crimes are usually specified according to grades of severity, that is, from a mere VIOLATION, to a MISDEMEANOR, to a FELONY.

Graft. The unlawful obtaining of money; defrauding an individual or the public of money. (The term is often used to describe the unlawful activities of a public OFFICER who takes public money for personal use.)

Grand jury. A group of citizens whose duties include inquiring into crimes in their area for the purpose of determining the probability of GUILT of a PARTY or parties. Should a grand jury conclude that there is a good probability of guilt, it will recommend an INDICTMENT of the suspects. Grand juries may be county, state, or federal, and the number of members varies anywhere from 6 to 23, according to locality and type.

Grand larceny. THEFT of money or property above a specified amount of value. (Theft of small amounts of money or of property of little value is known as PETTY LARCENY.)

Grandfather clause. An exception to a new RESTRICTION or new STATUTE which permits those already doing something to continue to do it even though the activity is contrary to the new restriction or statute.

Grant. **1.** A TRANSFER of property by DEED. **2.** To give; to bestow. **3.** A gift.

Grantee. A person to whom land is deeded or a GRANT is made.

Grantor. The person who makes a GRANT or who deeds over his land.

Grass widow. A slang expression for a woman who is living apart from her husband. (She may or may not be a divorcée.)

Gratis appearance. The voluntary appearance in court of a DEFENDANT without waiting for a SUMMONS or SUBPOENA.

Gratuitous. Without payment; without legal consideration.

Great bodily harm. A major INJURY. (The determination of the seriousness of a harm is usually left to a JUDGE and/or JURY to decide.)

Great bodily injury. > GREAT BODILY HARM.

Gross adventure. In MARITIME LAW, a loan on BOTTOMRY (a contract whereby an owner of a vessel borrows money to make a voyage, pledging the vessel as security).

Gross income. The total income of a person or business, prior to deducting expenses.

Gross neglect of duty. **1.** This term is frequently used in a suit for DIVORCE. It includes glaring violations of one's marital OBLIGATIONS. **2.** The term is used frequently when a public OFFICER is accused of major derelictions of his obligations, thus endangering the public welfare.

Gross negligence. **1.** Failure to act where duty demands that one act. **2.** Acting in such a manner that one ignores the safety of others. **3.** Willful neglect.

Gross profit. The excess of price received over price paid for a product, before deductions are taken for costs of production, plant operations, etcetera.

Ground for disbarment. Misconduct of an ATTORNEY, serious enough for him to lose his license to practice the law.

Ground for divorce. A legal cause for DIVORCE. Grounds for divorce differ from state to state.

Ground of action. The basis of a lawsuit; the facts upon which a suit rests.

Ground rent. Rental monies to be retained by an OWNER who has granted his land to another, or to the public.

Group insurance. An insurance CONTRACT between an insurance company and a group of people, often the employees of a company. Group insurance may be in the nature of HEALTH, ACCIDENT, DISABILITY, or LIFE INSURANCE.

Grub stake. In mining, an AGREEMENT in which one person supplies the tools, equipment, provisions, etcetera, to explore for minerals, and the other person agrees to carry out the exploration. If minerals are found, the two parties share the benefits of the find.

Guarantee. An individual to whom a guarantee is made. > GUARANTY.

Guaranteed annual wage. A labor AGREEMENT in which an employer agrees to pay an employee a certain basic sum of money each year, even though the employee has an hourly or weekly salary arrangement. The employee, by actual calculation, may earn less or more than the guaranteed annual wage.

Guaranteed title. A TITLE to property that a title insurance company will insure.

Guarantor. One who makes a guarantee. > GUARANTY.

Guaranty. 1. A STATEMENT by a producer that his product meets certain standards, and that if it proves to be defective, he will make restitution; a WARRANTY. **2.** To undertake the responsibility of paying someone's debt should he fail to pay it himself.

Guardian. A person who has been given the legal RIGHT and duty to take care of another individual and/or that individual's PROPERTY. Guardianships are granted when a person does not have certain legal rights, such as a MINOR, to take care of himself and his affairs, or a mentally ill or debilitated person not being capable of managing himself and his affairs.

Guardian's bond. A BOND required to be posted by a guardian who has been appointed by the court. Such bond is in the event the guardian does not look after the affairs of his TRUST properly, or in the event that he should divert money or property to his personal use.

Guest statute. A LAW, in some states only, prohibiting a guest riding in a friend's car to sue that friend if there is an ACCIDENT. However, he *can* sue if the driver has shown unusual NEGLIGENCE.

Guild. A union or association of working people engaged in the same craft, art, business, or profession.

Guilty. The opposite of INNOCENT; the VERDICT that is handed down when one has been CONVICTED of a crime or OFFENSE; the PLEA of admission that a defendant may make, be it guilty of a parking violation or guilty of a MURDER.

Guilty knowledge. Knowledge that unlawful circumstances exist but ignoring that knowledge. As an example, the acceptance of stolen goods is guilty knowledge.

Guilty with explanation. Admitting an OFFENSE but stating the extenuating circumstances surrounding the offense. As an example, a driver may be exceeding the speed limit in order to rush his injured child to a hospital. The motorist may then plead guilty with explanation.

Habeas corpus. A COURT ORDER to release a prisoner being held in CUSTODY. The habeas corpus WRIT orders the person before the court in order to determine his innocence or guilt (Latin).
Habendum clause. That CLAUSE in a DEED which describes the ESTATE to be granted.
Habitation. A place of abode; a domicile. Used to describe the RIGHT of a person to live in someone's house as a TENANT and to use it as a residence.
Habitual. Customary; repeated; addicted to a particular kind of behavior, such as an habitual drunkard.
Habitual criminal. A person convicted of a FELONY three or more times. The term varies in meaning from state to state.
Habitual criminal statute. A LAW that imposes more severe punishment for a crime committed two or more times.
Habitual drug users, reporting of. It is incumbent upon physicians to report known drug addicts to the appropriate authorities—in most areas, the police.
Habitual drunkenness. Repeated intoxication, due to the drinking of alcoholic beverages in excess, by one addicted to alcohol.
Haeriditas testamentaria. INHERITANCE of an ESTATE, as stated in the last WILL and testament of one who has died (Latin).
Half-brothers or sisters. Siblings who have the same mother but different fathers, or those who have the same father but different mothers.
Half-proof. PROOF by TESTIMONY of a single WITNESS or by a single DOCUMENT. Such proof seldom is sufficient to lead to a DECISION in a CASE.
Half-truth. A deceitful act in which one tells only part of the truth because the whole truth would have led to a different conclusion.
Hallucination. A mental distortion of the senses, especially those of sight and hearing. (As examples, a person may believe he has seen a ghost, or he may state positively that he heard the voice of someone who is dead.)
Hand down. A DECISION, OPINION, or VERDICT of a COURT is said to be handed down when such is rendered.
Handling charge. A fee charged by banks, BROKERS, etcetera, for rendering services to a CLIENT.
Handwriting expert. Someone specially trained in chirography, the art of determining whether or not a particular handwriting belongs to a particular person. Handwriting experts are extremely valuable as WITNESSES in many types of CASES.
Hanging. Suspending a person from the neck by a rope until dead; a common death PENALTY prior to the twentieth century.
Harboring a criminal. Hiding

someone being sought by the LAW for having committed a crime. Someone harboring a criminal becomes an ACCESSORY AFTER THE FACT, as it is unlawful to do so.

Harboring an alien. Hiding or aiding a foreigner to stay in the United States when he has no legal right to do so, an unlawful act.

Hard cases. CASES in which a fair DECISION can be reached only through very liberal interpretation of the LAWS governing the involved ISSUE.

Hard labor. A SENTENCE committing a person to work while in JAIL.

Hard money. Metal currency, such as copper, nickel, silver or gold, as distinguished from paper money.

Hardship cases. Those CASES in which the ordinary PUNISHMENT might, because of extenuating circumstances, be too severe. As a consequence, the court may be especially lenient.

Harmless error. An error in a TRIAL that is so unimportant that it will in no way influence the outcome of the CASE.

Harmonize evidence. An INSTRUCTION TO THE JURY, urging it to weigh conflicting EVIDENCE and attempt to determine the validity of all the evidence.

Hatch act. A federal law forbidding anyone employed by the executive branch of the government to engage in a campaign to elect a candidate for public OFFICE. However, such employees retain the right to vote for said candidate.

Hawking. Peddling goods on the streets, attracting attention by crying out in a loud voice. This practice is frequently against the law.

Hazard. **1.** A danger; a risk. **2.** To wager; to risk.

"He who seeks equity must do equity." An expression meaning that someone who seeks fair treatment in a legal CONTROVERSY must be fair in his treatment of his ADVERSARY.

Health insurance. An arrangement whereby an INSURANCE carrier, in return for the payment of a specified PREMIUM, agrees to pay for part or all of the medical expenses incurred by the insured when he, or a member of his immediate family, is ill or has met with an ACCIDENT. ➢ HOSPITAL INSURANCE.

Hearing. **1.** The ability to hear; the auditory sense. **2.** A PROCEDURE during which EVIDENCE is taken to determine an issue of FACT and to come to a decision based on that evidence. A hearing may take place out of COURT, but it must be presided over by someone with judicial AUTHORITY.

"Hear ye, hear ye, this court is now in session." The cry of the BAILIFF when a COURT is called in session.

Hearsay. Something not heard or witnessed personally but which is based upon what was heard or witnessed by another.

Hearsay evidence. Second-hand EVIDENCE; evidence that derives its value not directly from the testifying WITNESS, but from the believability of another person who has given information to the witness. Such evidence is often ruled to be inadmissible.

Heat of passion. Uncontrollable anger and rage provoking someone to commit an illegal and uncharacteristic act. If the anger and rage were justified, as from witnessing a rape or other crime, the court may act more leniently toward the offender who, in violent anger, killed the rapist.

Heave to. A command to a ship to stop its progress and head into the wind. A Coast Guard vessel may order a ship to heave to for inspection.

Heedless act. An act carried out without regard to the welfare and safety of others; reckless act.

Hegemony. The leadership of one sovereign state over other states having a more or less similar status.

Heir. A person who inherits money or PROPERTY, or who will naturally inherit property if someone dies without making a WILL.

Heir apparent. An HEIR who, by his relationship, is certain to inherit the ESTATE of his relative.

Heir at law. Essentially the same as HEIR; an heir recognized by LAW.

Heir conventional. An HEIR who inherits an estate as a result of a CONTRACT or AGREEMENT made previously between him and the DECEDENT (the owner of the estate who has died).

Heir presumptive. A person who would inherit an ESTATE if someone died under present circumstances, but who would not be the HEIR upon the birth of someone more closely related. Or if the heir presumptive died before the owner of the estate, his RIGHT to inherit would be destroyed.

Heir testamentary. A person who has been left money or PROPERTY by WILL.

Heirs and assigns. Words used customarily in the habendum clause of a DEED, stating exactly what is being passed on to HEIRS. > HABENDUM CLAUSE. ≫ FEE SIMPLE.

Held in trust. PROPERTY held by someone other than the OWNER, such as a TRUSTEE or an AGENT. Such trustee or agent is responsible to the owner and, for a fee, may manage the property and turn over to him any monies earned by the property.

Hereditaments. Anything that can be inherited, including money, PROPERTY, RIGHTS, etcetera.

Hereditary succession. Inheritance by DESCENT; the acquisition of TITLE by LAWS governing inheritance and descent.

Herein. An adverb referring to a certain phrase, sentence, CLAUSE, paragraph, or page in a DOCUMENT.

Heresy. A belief that is opposed to commonly held beliefs, such as that of an anarchist in a country with a democratic or socialist form of government. A heretic is one who expresses his beliefs openly, often publicly.

Heretofore. A word expressing time past, as distinguished from time present or time future. The term is used frequently in legal DOCUMENTS.

Heritable. Something which can be inherited.

Heritage. A culture handed down through the years from one generation to another; an inheritance.

Hermaphrodite. A person born with sex organs of both the male *and* the female. Usually, these organs are underdeveloped and incapable of functioning normally.
Hierarchy. An establishment of ranks from bottom to top, such as the ranks in the armed forces, the ranks in various government bureaus, etcetera.
High. **1.** A word used to express a superlative, as in the greatest degree. As examples, the HIGHEST COURT, high treason, high crimes. **2.** "High" is a slang expression describing someone under the influence of an intoxicating liquor, or someone who is under the influence of a drug, such as an amphetamine or marijuana.
High seas. Waters beyond the territorial JURISDICTION of any country; seas that belong to no nation and can be used freely by any nation.
Highest court. COURT of last resort; a court whose decision is final and cannot be appealed because there is no higher court to consider the matter.
Highwayman. A highway robber.
Highway robbery. Theft on a public roadway.
Hijacking. Stealing something that is in transit, such as commandeering a truck with merchandise and stealing said merchandise. Also, commandeering an airplane.
Hinder and delay. An expression used to denote unfair attempts to block the fulfillment of an existing AGREEMENT, OBLIGATION, or CONTRACT.
Hippocratic oath. A OATH taken by graduates of medical colleges outlining the code of ethical CONDUCT for a physician. This oath is thousands of years old but it is not a legally binding document required by medical licensing agencies.
Hiring-hall agreement. An AGREEMENT between labor and management that the UNION will maintain a hiring hall and that prospective employees will be given jobs through selection by the union's hiring methods.
His honor. A TITLE given to OFFICIALS such as mayors of cities, judges, etcetera.
Hitherto. A time already passed.
Hoc. This (Latin).
Hold. **1.** To possess, such as a title or a piece of PROPERTY. **2.** To judge, as a COURT holds someone to be innocent or guilty. **3.** To be a TENANT of another. **4.** To hold in CUSTODY, such as a prisoner. **5.** To administer. **6.** To keep.
Hold harmless. A term denoting "no responsibility." Someone held harmless is excused from LIABILITY and OBLIGATION.
Hold over. To maintain POSSESSION, as a TENANT who stays on after his LEASE has expired or as a public OFFICIAL who continues his duties after his term of OFFICE has expired.
Holder in due course. Someone who took a NOTE or CHECK in good faith, with the understanding that the check, note, or other DOCUMENT was BONA FIDE and contained no defects.
Holding. The judge's RULING or DECISION in a CASE.
Holding company. A CORPORATION that owns such a large share of other corporations so that it can dictate their policies and control their management.

Holding court. The presiding over an open court in session by a judge with AUTHORITY and JURISDICTION.
Holdup. A ROBBERY, usually involving use of a deadly WEAPON.
Holograph. A DEED, WILL, or legal DOCUMENT written in longhand by the maker.
Home rule. The RIGHT of local self-government, often granted by a state to an entity within its borders.
Homestead corporation. A COMPANY organized to buy a large tract of land for the purpose of improving it, subdividing it, and selling lots upon which homes can be built.
Homicidal mania. A mental sickness in which one has an irrational, uncontrollable desire to kill.
Homicide. MURDER; the killing of a human being by another human being. There are many types of homicide.
Homicide, accidental. Unintentional killing, as the mishandling of a hunting gun that fires and accidentally kills someone nearby. ≫ MANSLAUGHTER, INVOLUNTARY MANSLAUGHTER.
Homicide, by misadventure. The same as ACCIDENTAL HOMICIDE.
Homicide, culpable. Criminal MURDER.
Homicide, excusable. Killing someone in SELF-DEFENSE, or accidentally and unintentionally killing someone.
Homicide, felonious. Criminal HOMICIDE; wrongful homicide, be it out-and-out murder or MANSLAUGHTER.
Homicide, justifiable. The blameless killing of someone, such as a POLICE OFFICER who shoots and kills a criminal in the line of duty. SELF-DEFENSE is also JUSTIFIABLE HOMICIDE. ≫ EXCUSABLE HOMICIDE, JUSTIFIABLE HOMICIDE.
Homicide, self-defense. Killing someone to save one's own life; HOMICIDE, JUSTIFIABLE; JUSTIFIABLE HOMICIDE.
Homologation. Approval by a court.
Homosexual. An individual who has a physical attraction and love for members of his own or her own sex.
Homotransplantation. The taking of an organ, or part of an organ, from one person (dead or alive) and transplanting it in a live person. Written consent from a live DONOR, or from the next of kin of a dead donor, is essential for homotransplantation.
Honorable. A vague title of respect, given to various public OFFICIALS, JUDGES, etcetera, as "the honorable justice."
Honorable discharge. A written DOCUMENT, given to a person on completion of service in the Armed Forces, stating that he has conducted himself honorably during his service to his country. It differs from "a discharge without honor" or a "dishonorable discharge."
Honorarium. A gift freely given, not as a wage or salary; monies given without legal OBLIGATION to so do.
Honorary. A TITLE of honor given to someone who holds a position or OFFICE without recompense and without the need to render a service, such as an *hon-*

orary chairman. The title itself constitutes the reward.

Horizontal agreement. An AGREEMENT between different dealers in the same product whereby they attempt to control the price of said product.

Horizontal property acts. STATUTES governing and relative to CONDOMINIUMS.

Hornswoggle. A slang expression meaning to swindle or to cheat.

Hospital insurance. An INSURANCE POLICY that pays part or all of the costs of hospital care for a sick person. It is *not* the same as medical insurance, which pays part or all of the costs of medical bills submitted by physicians.

Hospital records. MEDICAL RECORDS of patients who are, or have been confined to a hospital. Such records belong to the hospital, but they can be subpoenaed and brought into court, if necessary.

Hostage. A person held in CUSTODY against his will by a person or persons who make demands that must be met before the hostage is released.

Hostile witness. A person who is antagonistic toward the PARTY who called him as a WITNESS. Such a witness can be treated as if he was summoned to court by the opposing party, and, as a result, he can be cross-examined.

Hotchpot. The mixing of PROPERTY owned by several people in unequal quantities in order to divide it again equally. > COLLATION.

House counsel. An ATTORNEY employed exclusively by one COMPANY or CORPORATION.

House of assignation. A whorehouse; a place used for prostitution. Also known as a bawdyhouse, a house of ill repute, etcetera.

House of correction. An institution for juvenile offenders; a REFORMATORY.

House of refuge. A house of correction; a REFORMATORY.

House of Representatives. Legislative body of the United States government to which members are elected every two years from various congressional districts, such districts being determined by population. Various states also have legislative bodies known as houses of representatives.

Housebreaking. BURGLARY; breaking into a house for the purpose of committing a crime, usually THEFT.

Household furnishings and effects. A common phrase in a WILL, usually including all the PERSONAL PROPERTY of the person making the WILL (the TESTATOR).

Household goods. Items in a home of a permanent nature. This phrase often appears in a WILL.

Housing administration. A federal AGENCY whose functions include measures to improve housing and to encourage home-building through helpful financing.

Humiliation. The sense of being disgraced, belittled, or made to look foolish. One can sue somebody for causing severe humiliation, but DAMAGES for same are difficult to compute.

Hung jury. A JURY in such disagreement that it cannot reach a verdict.

Hush-money. A bribe to keep silent.

Hymen. The membrane covering the entrance to the vagina in virgins. Rupture of this membrane occurs with first complete intercourse, rendering the female non-virginal. > MAIDENHEAD.

Hypothecation. The act of pledging something to someone without delivering anything. In MARITIME LAW, a ship may be hypothecated to someone who has given monies to supply the ship.

Hypothesis. A theory put forth by the prosecution in a criminal trial; an ASSUMPTION; a SUPPOSITION.

Hypothetical questions. Questions addressed to an expert WITNESS in a TRIAL, based upon theory or assumed FACTS. The witness is then asked to give his opinion should such assumed facts be actually true.

Hysteria. An extremely emotional state. During hysterical episodes people may perform acts they would never perform when more composed. Or, during hysterical episodes, people may lose control of some of their senses. As a consequence, one may suffer *hysterical blindness, hysterical paralysis,* etcetera. Such changes usually subside when the hysteria subsides.

I

Ibid. The same (Latin).
Idem. The same (Latin).
Idem sonans. Sounding alike (Latin). This term often refers to names that are confused with each other because they sound alike.
Identical. Exactly the same.
Identification. PROOF that a person, or a thing, is what it is represented to be.
Identity. The FACT that a person or thing is the same as he or it is claimed to be.
Ignoramus. A phrase used by a GRAND JURY when it decides that there is insufficient evidence for an INDICTMENT (Latin).
"Ignorance of the law is no excuse." A STATEMENT that prevails in criminal cases.
Illegal. Contrary to LAW; unlawful. ➤ ILLICIT.
Illegal consideration. An AGREEMENT OR CONTRACT which, if carried out, would be contrary to and harmful to the PUBLIC INTEREST.
Illegal entry. Entering of the United States by a foreigner without the approval of the immigration authorities.
Illegal interest. INTEREST on LOANS above the rates allowed by LAW; USURY.
Illegitimate. Having no legal authorization; contrary to the LAW.
Illegitimate child. A child born out of wedlock. Also, a child born to a married woman as a result of relations with a man not her husband. An illegitimate child is not an HEIR according to the laws of descent, unless it is specifically named as an heir. ➤ BORN OUT OF WEDLOCK; BASTARD.
Illicit. Forbidden by LAW; ILLEGAL; unlawful.
Illicit cohabitation. Living together by a man and a woman who are not married.
Illicit trade. Trade with a country that is forbidden by law. For many years, it was forbidden for Americans to trade with Red China.
Illiterate. Unable to read or write.
Illusory promise. A PROMISE which, on the surface, appears to be BINDING but on further examination has no real value or legal significance.
Immaterial. Not pertinent or of no consequence for use in a legal PROCEEDING. ➤ IMMATERIAL AND IRRELEVANT; IRRELEVANT.
Immaterial and irrelevant. Not important or relevant to the ISSUE at hand.
Immaterial facts. FACTS that are not essential to the ISSUES under consideration.
Immaterial issue. An ISSUE that is so IRRELEVANT and unimportant that it cannot influence the outcome of a trial or of a controversial matter.
Immediate cause. The final, determining cause of an outcome or event. An immediate cause may be preceded by many *contributory*

causes, none of which actually produced the ultimate event.

Immediate family. A term referring to one's parents, wife or husband, children, and brothers and sisters.

Immediately adjacent. Phrase describing PROPERTY that abuts or adjoins another's property; property having a common border with other property.

Immigrant. Someone who enters a country from a foreign country for permanent residence.

Imminent danger. A situation so dangerous and life-threatening that one must take immediate action, not awaiting help from others or from authorities. HOMICIDE in SELF-DEFENSE is said to result from imminent danger.

Immoderate. Unreasonable; beyond normal bounds; overreactive. Behavior that exceeds what could be expected from a sensible person confronted with similar circumstances.

Immoral consideration. A CONTRACT that is contrary to public MORALS; a CONSIDERATION that the public holds to be indecent.

Immoral purpose. Intention to commit an immoral act, such as bringing someone into the country for the purpose of prostitution.

Immunity. Exemption from; freedom from; a favor granting someone exemption from the law. A special privilege granted, such as being free from arrest in exchange for testifying in a case.
≫ IMPUNITY.

Immunity, waiver of. The renunciation by a WITNESS of the PRIVILEGE not to give TESTIMONY that might implicate himself as a PARTY to a criminal act.

Immunity clause. A provision that limits a TRUSTEE'S responsibility, confining it to LIABILITY for NEGLIGENCE or purposeful MISCONDUCT.

Immunity from process. The exemption or freedom from being served with a SUBPOENA, such as that accorded to WITNESSES while testifying in COURT or to members of a legislature or Congressmen who are in the act of performing their duties.

Immunity from suit. Freedom from legal ACTION accorded to someone for reasons of public policy. Also, freedom of a state or the federal government from a lawsuit, unless it agrees to such suit.

Immurement. Imprisonment.

Impairing the obligation of a contract. Any law which lessens the value of or decreases the enforceability of an agreement or contract. Such law is usually one that is enacted *after* the period during which the contract was entered into.

Impairment of future earning capacity. Interference with a person's ability to earn money. For example, an injury from an accident may diminish someone's earning capacity.

Impairment of memory. An inability to remember events; forgetfulness.

Impanel. To make a list of those selected for jury duty.

Impartial. Unbiased; unprejudiced; fair.

Impartial jury. A JURY that hears

a case without PREJUDICE and renders a fair VERDICT free from bias, and based solely upon the EVIDENCE.

Impartial medical panels. Groups of physicians who sit in judgment on MALPRACTICE claims. Their findings are not binding upon the PLAINTIFF or DEFENDENT, but are often accepted by both contesting parties, thus frequently avoiding court trials.

Impeach. To call the integrity of a public OFFICIAL into question. Impeachment does not mean conviction, but denotes a need to inquire into the integrity of the official.

Impeachment. The questioning of the credibility and integrity of a public OFFICIAL, leading to a TRIAL to determine if said individual should be discredited.

Impeachment of a verdict. The questioning of the validity of a VERDICT, based upon doubts that it was arrived at in a proper manner.

Impeachment of witness. The questioning of the believability of a WITNESS, based upon contrary TESTIMONY given by other witnesses.

Impediment. 1. An obstacle; a hindrance; something that stands in the way, such as the impediment of insanity, which bars someone from being responsible for his actions. **2.** A disability, such as an impediment of speech.

Imperative. Commanding; something that *must* be done; MANDATORY.

Imperfect. Defective; lacking in an essential detail, such as an *imperfect trust,* an *imperfect mortgage,* or an *imperfect obligation* (one not enforceable by suit).

Impersonate. To pretend to be someone else, such as a CIVILIAN who poses as a POLICE OFFICER. (It is unlawful to pose as a public OFFICER or government OFFICIAL when one is not.)

Impertinent. So out of place or IRRELEVANT that the matter should never have been brought into COURT.

Implead. To SUE; to bring into COURT. Also, to include an individual in a court ACTION who was not originally a part of the SUIT when it began.

Implication. Something that is assumed though not actually expressed. In a WILL, PROPERTY may pass to an HEIR by implication without the heir being specifically named.

Implied. Intended, but not expressed in words. An implied AGREEMENT is one that the parties intend to implement but have not declared in a written DOCUMENT.

Implied assent. An ASSENT that is understood and agreed to but has not been expressly stated.

Implied authority. The power that an AGENT possesses as delegated by a PRINCIPAL, or the AUTHORITY that, under given circumstances, a delegated AGENT would ordinarily possess.

Implied coercion. Inducing somebody to do something he does not want to do, because he is legally subject to another.

Implied consent. Failure by a woman to take the usual measures to oppose sexual advances, thus permitting the man to believe that there exists no sincere objection to intercourse. Implied consent frequently forms the basis of defense when a rape charge is brought.

Implied consideration. Payment or reward for an act performed at the request of another, without any express AGREEMENT as to monies that will be given for performing said act.

Implied contract. An AGREEMENT more or less agreed upon, but not put into words.

Implied easement. Permission granted by implication to the purchaser of part of an owner's holdings to cross or traverse PROPERTY still held by the OWNER.
> EASEMENT.

Implied malice. Acts that bear the stamp of ill-will, spite, vindictiveness, etcetera.

Implied powers. The AUTHORITY of public OFFICIALS that exists, not as a result of specific delegation of power, but as germane to the performance of their duties. In a sense, implied powers are *collateral powers* or *incidental powers.*

Implied rescission. The assumption by two parties making a new CONTRACT whose provisions differ markedly from the original that the old contract is VOID.

Implied waiver. A WAIVER, assumed to be in effect because of a person's behavior that shows he is waiving a particular RIGHT.

Importunity. Entreaty; begging; pleading earnestly and persistently.

Impose. To TAX; to levy; to place a burden upon someone, as in imposing a heavy fine.

Imposition. The act of taking advantage of someone; taking or imposing a burden.

Impossibility. Something that is physically unable to be performed.

Impostor. Someone who misrepresents himself or poses as another, usually for the purpose of perpetrating a FRAUD.

Impotence. Inability by a male to perform SEXUAL INTERCOURSE; technically, the inability to obtain and maintain an erection.

Impound. To take and hold funds in legal CUSTODY.

Imprimatur. A LICENSE to publish and print a book (Latin).

Imprison. To place a person in JAIL; to restrain a person's liberty, against his will.
> INCARCERATE.

Improbable. Difficult to believe, as an improbable ALIBI or TESTIMONY.

Improper conduct. Behavior that a sensible, prudent person would not indulge in; CONDUCT that is immoral.

Improper influence. Bringing undue pressure to bear upon someone in order to get him/her to do something he/she would not ordinarily do.

Improvement. Anything that increases the value of PROPERTY, such as installing air-conditioning in a building, etcetera.

Improvident judgment. An ORDER or JUDGMENT rendered by a COURT that is based upon erroneous information, or a judgment or order that is ill-considered.

Impulse. Something done without previous contemplation; a spontaneous act, carried out suddenly and on the spur of the moment.

Impunity. IMMUNITY from punishment or responsibility.

Imputation of payment. A partial payment to a CREDITOR applied toward fulfillment of the entire DEBT.

Imputed knowledge. Knowledge that someone should have because the FACTS were known to him; an AGENT'S knowledge to which the PRINCIPAL is bound because of his relationship with his agent.

Imputed negligence. That NEGLIGENCE for which a person is responsible because the negligent act was committed by someone acting in his behalf and under his direction.

In absentia. In the absence of (Latin).

In bank. Describing a COURT when all its judges are sitting (serving).

In being. In existence at a particular point in time.

In camera. In private, as with cases tried in COURT with the courtroom cleared, or others heard in a judge's private CHAMBERS (Latin).

In common. Something for the general use and enjoyment of all. The land, gardens, beaches, pools, etcetera, surrounding a CONDOMINIUM are in common, for the use of all tenant-owners.

In delicto. In the wrong; at fault (Latin).

In evidence. Before the COURT; EVIDENCE that has already been presented in a CASE.

In extremis. About to die, as a person who is in the last stages of a terminal illness (Latin).

In jeopardy. **1.** The status of a person who is on TRIAL before a COURT, having been charged with a crime. **2.** An expression sometimes used in claiming that a DEFENDANT is in DOUBLE JEOPARDY, that is, is being charged a second time for an OFFENSE that he has already been acquitted for. ➤ FORMER JEOPARDY; LEGAL JEOPARDY.

In judgment. In a COURT.

In jure. According to law (Latin).

In lieu of. Instead of.

In pais. An act taken informally, not through legal PROCEDURES (French).

In pari delicto. Equally at fault (Latin).

In perpetuity. Forever; for all time.

In person. An individual who acts as his own ATTORNEY in a CASE is said to appear in person.

In personam. Term used to describe a suit brought against a particular individual, as distinguished from one against a specific thing (Latin).

In place. In MINING LAW, a mineral that is in the position where it was placed by nature, undisturbed by man.

In propria. Term used to describe acting in one's own DEFENSE, or serving as one's own ATTORNEY (Latin).

In re. In the matter of; concerning (Latin).

In rem. Against the thing (Latin). This term refers to a SUIT against a "thing," as distinguished from a suit against a person.

In status quo. Without change; in the same situation as it was (Latin).

In stirpes. A term referring to a method of inheritance when someone dies without a WILL (INTESTATE), meaning inheritance by linear descent to the next of kin, or "according to the roots" (Latin).
In toto. Wholly; totally; completely (Latin).
In trust. The status of PROPERTY given over and entrusted to someone to guard and take care of. Money or property of an ESTATE is held in CUSTODY, or in trust, by a TRUSTEE until it is turned over to an HEIR.
In vacuo. Without any relation to anything else; in a vacuum (Latin).
In witness whereof. An expression making it clear that someone signing a legal DOCUMENT is signing as a WITNESS.
Inability to testify. Being unable to appear in COURT because of a mental or physical illness.
Inadequate consideration. A SETTLEMENT not equal in value to the loss; inadequate DAMAGES.
Inadequate remedy at law. A JUDGMENT or REMEDY that is defective in that it is not clear, practical, or sufficient.
Inadmissible evidence. EVIDENCE that under the rules of LAW cannot be presented in COURT.
Inalienable rights. PRIVILEGES that are fundamental, such as the RIGHTS of free speech, personal liberty, worship as one sees fit, ownership of property, access to due process of law, and freedom from discrimination because of race, color, creed, etcetera.
Inauguration. **1.** Putting into effect. **2.** Installation into office of an appointed or elected official, such as a president.
Incapacitated. Unable to perform one's usual functions or duties, due to a physical or mental disability.
Incarcerate. To confine one in a JAIL or PRISON; to IMPRISON.
Incendiary. An arsonist; one who deliberately sets fire to PROPERTY.
Incentive compensation. Payments in excess of agreed-upon WAGES; bonuses; profit-sharing. CORPORATIONS often offer executives or key employees incentive compensation for outstanding performance.
Incentive wages. > INCENTIVE COMPENSATION.
Inception. The beginning; the commencement, as the start of an AGREEMENT or CONTRACT.
Incest. SEXUAL INTERCOURSE between two members of the same immediate family, such as between siblings or a parent and child.
Inchoate. Unfinished; incomplete, as an AGREEMENT that has not been put into final form.
Inchoate lien. A LIEN that has not yet been put into effect, as a TAX LIEN prior to the time when a tax assessment has been made.
Incident. **1.** Anything that is connected with or is dependent upon another thing or event. **2.** An event, a happening.
Incident and appurtenant. Describing things that automatically go along with the transfer of PROPERTY or land, even though they may not be mentioned in the transfer. For example, trees on a piece of land are incident and appurtenant to the transfer of such

land from an OWNER to a PURCHASER.

Incidental. Depending upon something else; likely to happen; something happening in addition to another event.

Incidental proceeding. A course of action that stems from a main action or PROCEEDING.

Incidental relief. An AWARD in a COURT OF EQUITY that goes beyond that requested in the original COMPLAINT.

Incidental to employment. A natural risk that is inherent within a job that one has to do in order to fulfill his duties. Such risks need not necessarily occur on the premises of the employer.

Inciting to riot. Arousing people to unlawful, violent actions.

Included offense. A criminal act of lesser importance than the main OFFENSE set forth in the INDICTMENT. The ACCUSED may be CONVICTED of the included offense even if ACQUITTED of the main offense.

Incognito. Hiding one's real identity; appearing under an assumed name in order to avoid notice.

Income. The amount someone earns from a salary or from a business or profession. Gross income includes all monies earned before expenses and taxes; net income is that which is retained after payment of all expenses and taxes.

Income tax. A TAX on monies earned from one's business, profession, or PROPERTY. The federal government, certain states, and cities levy taxes on income.

Incommunicado. Term that describes being held without the PRIVILEGE of communicating with others, as with certain prisoners.

Incompatibility. Inability to live together, such as a husband and wife who find that MARRIAGE is no longer a tolerable state.

Imcompetency proceeding. An ACTION to determine whether someone is capable of taking care of himself and his affairs. Should an individual be found INCOMPETENT, others will be delegated by the appropriate AUTHORITY to guard the person and to run his affairs.

Incompetent. Incapable; inefficient; lacking the qualities necessary to discharge one's OBLIGATIONS and duties.

Incompetent evidence. EVIDENCE that is not permitted because it originates from an inadequate WITNESS or is otherwise defective.

Inconclusive. Subject to being disproved; readily rebutted and denied; insufficient to reach a conclusion, such as inconclusive evidence.

Inconsistent. Contradictory; contrary; repugnant.

Incontestable clause. A provision in a LIFE INSURANCE policy that the insurance company cannot contest a POLICY, or one of its provisions, after the insurance has been in effect for a specified period of time.

Incontinence. Lack of restraint in sexual activity; engaging in unlawful sexual relations.

Inconvenient forum. A DOCTRINE stating that a COURT may decide not to try a CASE if it feels that the PLAINTIFF should have brought the SUIT before another court with more appropriate JURISDICTION.

Incorporate. To form a CORPORATION. Each state has its own laws of incorporation.

Incorporated (Inc.). Functioning as a CORPORATION.

Incorporation by reference. The act of including another ISSUE in a single ACTION, merely by mentioning or referring to it. For example, it is permissible to include by reference a part or the whole of the ALLEGATIONS of another COUNT in the same SUIT.

Incorporeal hereditaments. RIGHTS or PRIVILEGES that are inherited, as distinguished from corporeal hereditaments (things or objects that are inherited).

Incorporeal things. RIGHTS or PRIVILEGES, as distinguished from tangible things that can be seen or handled.

Incorrigible. Unmanageable; uncontrollable, such as a perpetual criminal or a habitually delinquent minor.

Incorruptible. Unable to be bribed or made to do something unlawful; highly moral.

Increment. An increase; a steady growth; an enlargement.

Incriminating admission. A STATEMENT leading toward the establishment of GUILT.

Incriminating circumstance. A situation tending to prove that someone is GUILTY of a crime.

Inculpatory. Tending to establish GUILT; the opposite of EXCULPATORY.

Incumbent. An individual who is presently holding a public OFFICE.

Incumbrance. A LIABILITY that lowers the value of a piece of PROPERTY, such as a LIEN or a MORTGAGE.

Incurred. To have brought upon oneself; to have happen to oneself, such as a person who incurred an injury.

Indecent exposure. Exhibiting one's sex organs, such as the female breast or male genitals, in public.

Indecent liberties. A statutory OFFENSE in which an adult makes sexual advances toward a child. Such advances need not consist of attempts at actual intercourse.

Indefeasible. Referring to a RIGHT that cannot be taken away or revoked.

Indefinite imprisonment. Imprisonment for which no specified length of time is prescribed by law. As an example, a WITNESS who refuses to TESTIFY in a criminal case may be ordered to JAIL for an undetermined period of time until he/she signifies willingness to testify.

Indemnify. To protect and secure against damage or loss; to make good; to compensate for a loss.

Indemnity. INSURANCE against a possible loss; security with COMPENSATION for DAMAGES or loss.

Indemnity bond. A BOND to compensate for a loss to a person to whom an OBLIGATION has been incurred.

Indemnity contract. An AGREEMENT whereby someone will save another from the legal PENALTIES resulting from the CONDUCT of one or more of the parties involved in an ACTION.

Indenture. A DEED between two

parties transferring real estate, in which both parties assume OBLIGATIONS toward each other.

Indenture of trust. A DOCUMENT that states the specific conditions and terms of a TRUST, such as a pension trust, etcetera.

Independent advice. The confidential advice given by someone in a FIDUCIARY capacity to a person who is making a WILL giving money and/or PROPERTY to a LEGATEE (the person who inherits).

Independent contractor. Someone who is engaged to do a job or perform an act but who maintains control over how the job or act is to be carried out. In MEDICAL JURISPRUDENCE, a surgeon who agrees to perform a certain operation is an independent contractor.

Indeterminate sentence. A jail SENTENCE that does not specify the exact amount of time to be served. However, such time must, by law, fall between a minimum and maximum period.

Indian reservation. A portion of public lands set aside for the occupation and use of various tribes of American Indians.

Indictable. Appropriate for and subject to INDICTMENT, such as a FELONY that is punishable by imprisonment.

Indicted. Charged with a criminal OFFENSE.

Indictment. An ACCUSATION by a GRAND JURY, made after thorough investigation, that someone should be tried for a crime. When an indictment is handed down, the ACCUSED must stand trial for the alleged OFFENSE, but indictment in itself does not mean that the accused will necessarily be found GUILTY.

Indigent. An inability to support oneself; poor; needy.

Indirect evidence. CIRCUMSTANTIAL EVIDENCE; FACTS that merely tend to prove something but don't actually present incontrovertible EVIDENCE.

Indirect solicitation. A situation in which an ATTORNEY attempts to contact an injured person and get control of his claim. Indirect solicitation, also known as "ambulance chasing," is unethical and is practiced by only a small number of attorneys. ➤ AMBULANCE CHASER.

Indirect tax. A TAX not levied upon the actual value of a PROPERTY but upon some other CONSIDERATION, such as an "occupation tax."

Indispensable evidence. EVIDENCE essential to proving a FACT.

Indispensable party. A person who is essential to the determination of a SUIT; someone who must participate in a lawsuit if such suit is to succeed or to be judged.

Individual assets and debts. Monies or PROPERTIES owned or owed by a member of a PARTNERSHIP that are separate and independent of the partnership's properties or OBLIGATIONS.

Individual liability. The LIABILITY of a person, as distinguished from the OBLIGATIONS of a PARTNERSHIP, COMPANY, or CORPORATION.

Indivisible contract. An AGREE-

MENT that must be enforced completely, without division into its separate components. The completion of one part of such a CONTRACT is meaningless unless all parts of the contract are complied with.

Inducement. **1.** Anything that persuades an individual to do something, such as the PROMISE of reward if someone carries out a specified act. **2.** A BENEFIT that will accrue if someone agrees to a CONTRACT.

Indulgence. The granting of a favor, such as permitting a DEBTOR to take more time before paying a CREDITOR.

Industrial relations. The relations between employees and employers, or the relations between labor and management.

Inebriated. Under the influence of alcohol; INTOXICATED.

Ineligible. Not qualified; legally disqualified from holding a public OFFICE or TRUST.

Inevitable accident. An ACCIDENT that is unavoidable, such as an accident due to an act of God (floods, lightning, earthquakes, tornadoes, etcetera); an accident that could not have been prevented no matter what precautions one had taken.

Infamous crime. An OFFENSE punishable by imprisonment or the death penalty.

Infamy. Disgrace; evil reputation; the loss of honor and respect one is subject to after CONVICTION for an INFAMOUS CRIME.

Infant. A very young child.

Infanticide. The killing of an INFANT, usually the crime of murdering a newborn child.

Inferential fact. A deduction drawn not directly from EVIDENCE but from ASSUMPTIONS; conclusions based upon assumptions.

Inferior court. A lower COURT; a court of limited JURISDICTION; a court whose rulings can be overturned by a higher court.

Inferior equity. A RIGHT that can be superseded by, or is subject to another right.

Infidelity. Unfaithfulness on the part of a husband or wife.

Infirmative hypothesis. A theory used in trying a criminal case in which the DEFENDANT's innocence is assumed.

Infirmity. **1.** An illness or disease, usually of a permanent nature, often rendering an individual ineligible to take out a LIFE INSURANCE policy. **2.** A defect in a DOCUMENT or DEED.

Inflict. To cause, such as to inflict an INJURY; to impose as PUNISHMENT, such as to inflict a JAIL SENTENCE.

Influencing jurors. Wrongfully persuading JURORS in order to obtain a desired VERDICT.

Information and belief. A phrase stating that one believes something to be true, even though some of the facts may be lacking.

Informed consent. ASSENT given only after all the facts have been fully explained. Before undergoing surgery a patient should have all the possibilities explained to him/her. Then, informed consent can be given, or withheld.

Informer. An individual who notifies the AUTHORITIES of a violation of a LAW or a criminal act.

Infra annum clause. A CLAUSE in

an AGREEMENT that the fulfillment of the CONTRACT shall take place within a year's time (Latin).

Infraction. A violation; a breach, as of a CONTRACT or AGREEMENT; a violation of a LAW is also known as an infraction of the law.

Infringement of copyright. A violation of all, or substantial portions of, a copyrighted article, pamphlet, book, etcetera.

Infringement of patent. A violation of a RIGHT granted under PATENT LAW to an inventor; copying a patented article without authorization.

Infringement of trademark. Deceiving the public by copying, or devising an almost identical copy of, a TRADEMARK.

Inhabitant. A dweller; someone who resides in a particular locality; a resident. In some states, a person who lives within its confines for a half-year of every year is considered an inhabitant of that state.

Inherent power. The AUTHORITY to act and perform certain acts without having to consult anyone else.

Inherent right. A fundamental RIGHT or PRIVILEGE, such as those granted to all citizens. > INALIENABLE RIGHTS.

Inherit. To receive money and/or PROPERTY from someone who has died. Some may inherit as a result of a specific bequest in a WILL, or as a consequence of being a member of the family of a person who died without leaving a will.

Inheritance tax. A TAX levied on the transfer of money and/or PROPERTY from the LEGATOR (the one who has died and left money and/or property) to the LEGATEE (the one who INHERITS). An inheritance tax is not an actual tax on the money and/or property itself, but merely on its transfer.

Inhuman treatment. A CLAIM of unusual cruelty endangering health or life. Such inhuman treatment may be claimed by someone confined in JAIL, or it may be the claim of a spouse in a DIVORCE suit.

Iniquity. An error of a judge or COURT.

Injunction. A restraining order issued by a judge that a person or persons can or cannot do a particular thing. For example, a judge may order a labor union not to strike until a court hearing can be held. Injunctions may be temporary or permanent.

Injunction, final. A binding injunction issued after the rights of the concerned parties have been determined.

Injunction, interlocutory. A RESTRAINING ORDER issued before the RIGHTS of the concerned PARTIES have been determined.

Injunction, mandatory. An ORDER commanding that someone do a particular thing.

Injunction, permanent. An INJUNCTION that shall remain in force until the issues of the LAWSUIT have been settled.

Injunction, preliminary. A RESTRAINING ORDER issued at the beginning of a SUIT, mainly forbidding one of the PARTIES to carry out some act that is in dispute in the suit.

Injunction, preventive. An ORDER

forbidding someone from carrying out a particular act.

Injunction, temporary. A preliminary RESTRAINING ORDER.
> INJUNCTION, PRELIMINARY.

Injured party. A person who has been harmed by the act or acts of another.

Injury. Harm done to a person's physical or mental well-being; harm to one's pride or reputation; harm to one's RIGHTS and PRIVILEGES. Often the harm has resulted from the violation of one's legal rights by another.

Injustice. Failure of a COURT to deliver just treatment.

Inland waters. Waters separated from the ocean and within, or partly within, the territorial boundaries of the United States, such as lakes, ponds, rivers, etcetera.

Innocent. NOT GUILTY.

Innocent conveyance. A DOCUMENT that transfers merely the TITLE of the GRANTOR, not one that transfers a bigger ESTATE than the grantor has.

Innocent party. An individual who did not consciously or intentionally participate in a matter in DISPUTE.

Innocent trespasser. A person who accidentally or mistakenly crosses over or enters another's PROPERTY.

Innuendo. An indirect method of stating or writing material that is libelous or slanderous. In a suit for LIBEL OF SLANDER, an innuendo is the declaration by the PLAINTIFF of his CLAIMS against the DEFENDANT (Latin).

Inoperative deed. One which is not effective in transferring title to property, although it might be operative contractually.

Inoperative will. A WILL that cannot operate because its BEQUESTS and GRANTS are contrary to existing LAWS.

Inquest. **1.** An INVESTIGATION into the cause of DEATH of somebody who died violently or under suspicious circumstances; a CORONER'S inquiry; a MEDICAL EXAMINER'S investigation. **2.** An inquiry, such as an *inquest of office, inquest of title, inquest in lunacy,* etcetera.

Inquisition. An INQUEST; an INVESTIGATION, especially one initiated by a SHERIFF; any judicial inquiry.

Insanity. Mental illness; PSYCHOSIS; the condition of lacking the mental soundness to judge right from wrong or to manage one's affairs. Insanity may arise from a disease of the brain or from emotional causes. In LAW, insanity is represented by an inability to reason, to remember ordinary events, and to appreciate the nature of unlawful acts.

Inscription. **1.** The REGISTRATION or recording of a DEED, a MORTGAGE, or other DOCUMENT in a public RECORD OF REGISTRY. **2.** A writing on a substance of permanency such as stone or metal.

Insecurity clause. A provision in a contract permitting a CREDITOR to force the entire payment from the debtor.

Insinuation of a will. The production of a WILL and the submitting of it to PROBATE to prove that it is valid and genuine.

Insolvency. Inability to pay DEBTS, either by an individual, a

COMPANY, or a CORPORATION; BANKRUPTCY.

Insolvency laws. STATUTES providing that the ASSETS of an insolvent individual, COMPANY, or CORPORATION be surrendered to the creditor or creditors. Upon acceptance of the assets of the insolvent person, company, or corporation, the latter is freed from further obligations and liabilities.

Insolvent. Being unable to meet one's OBLIGATIONS and LIABILITIES.

Inspection laws. STATUTES granting the right of authorized public OFFICERS to enter and examine (inspect) PROPERTY in order to determine whether there is danger to the public health, danger of physical injury, or the possibility that police and fire regulations have not been carried out satisfactorily. Also, laws providing that property may be entered if it is thought to be used to defraud or impose on the public.

Inspection of documents. The RIGHT of a PARTY to a LAWSUIT to examine DOCUMENTS and other pertinent materials that are necessary to an adequate promotion of the lawsuit or to an adequate DEFENSE against charges of the opposing party. Such documents may be in the possession of the opposing (adverse) party or an OFFICER of the law.

Installment. A regular, periodic, partial payment of a DEBT. Goods bought on *installment plans* are usually paid for by regular monthly payments.

Instance and request. An earnest request that some information be supplied or that some thing be handed over. Instance and request, although "demanding," is not "commanding."

Instanter. Immediately; forthwith; at once.

Instigation. Incitement of another to do something, such as instigating someone to commit an unlawful act.

Institute. To start, such as to commence a LAWSUIT.

Instruct. To transmit information to another person or persons, as when a judge instructs a JURY, or an ATTORNEY instructs his CLIENT.

Instruction to the jury. The final CHARGES given by the COURT to the JURY prior to its DELIBERATIONS in a CASE. Such instructions explain the LAW and the important ISSUES that must be decided. The instructions do not tell the jury how it should decide, but merely offer guidance so that it can deliberate fairly.

Instrument. A written DOCUMENT, such as a DEED, a MORTGAGE, a negotiable SECURITY, a CONTRACT, a WILL, etcetera.

Instrument inter partes. A written DOCUMENT recording the TRANSACTIONS between two or more PARTIES (Latin).

Instruments of evidence. The DOCUMENTS—things as well as people who are WITNESSES—that are used to present FACTS to a judge and/or JURY.

Insubordination. Lack of respect and refusal to carry out an ORDER given by someone in AUTHORITY; refusal to obey directions.

Insufficient evidence. Inadequate EVIDENCE; not enough FACTS presented to convince a JURY to reach a VERDICT.

Insult. An indignity or affront to self-respect, often sufficient to warrant an AWARD of DAMAGES.

Insurable. Capable of being insured, as distinguished from a person or business that will not or cannot be insured because the risk is too high.

Insurable interest in life. A monetary interest in the continued life of another person.

Insurance. An AGREEMENT or CONTRACT in which an individual pays a PREMIUM (money) in exchange for a PROMISE (by an insurance company) of reimbursement should a loss occur. The COMPANY agreeing to pay for losses is called the insurance company or the INSURER; the person paying the premiums to guarantee against loss is called the INSURED.

Insurance, casualty. INSURANCE against loss or DAMAGE occasioned by ACCIDENT. It often pays medical expenses, loss of time for work, and COMPENSATION for suffering and physical INJURIES.

Insurance, commercial. INSURANCE against loss because of a BREACH OF CONTRACT or failure to perform something that has been formally agreed upon.

Insurance, employer's liability. The AGREEMENT by an insurance company to pay for the OBLIGATION of an employer to pay DAMAGES for an ACCIDENT causing INJURY or DEATH of an employee during the course of his employment.

Insurance, fidelity. INSURANCE that guarantees payment for a loss resulting from the dishonesty or lack of fidelity of an employee or OFFICER of a COMPANY.

Insurance, fire. An AGREEMENT by an insurance company to pay for losses resulting from a fire.

Insurance, fraternal. Life, accident, or disability insurance paid to an insured person who belongs to a fraternal organization. In these instances, the member of the fraternal association is the insured person who pays dues, and the fraternal association is the insurer who issues the policies.

Insurance, health. An arrangement whereby an insurance carrier, in return for the payment of a specified premium, agrees to pay for part or all of the medical expenses incurred by the insured person.

Insurance, hospital. > HOSPITAL INSURANCE

Insurance, indemnity. INSURANCE offering security or protection against loss, with AGREEMENT in the INSURANCE POLICY to pay for losses sustained.

Insurance, liability. INSURANCE in which a policy is issued that pays for DAMAGES or INJURIES to the person or PROPERTY of another.

Insurance, life. INSURANCE in which a policy is issued that pays a stipulated sum of money upon the DEATH of the INSURED, with such monies going to the ESTATE of the deceased or to a BENEFICIARY named in the INSURANCE POLICY.

Insurance, marine. INSURANCE involving a guarantee to pay for losses incurred to a ship or its cargo during a particular voyage, or for a stipulated period of time.

Insurance, mutual. A COMPANY in which the members are both the INSURED and the INSURER.
Insurance, term. INSURANCE limited to a specified period of time. Term life insurance develops no cash value.
Insurance, title. INSURANCE guaranteeing payment against a defect in a TITLE to a parcel of real estate.
Insurance adjuster. An individual who calculates the amount of loss from an INSURED'S CLAIM.
Insurance policy. A written AGREEMENT between an insurance company and an insured person. In the agreement, or policy, it is stipulated that the insured shall pay a certain amount of PREMIUM during each CALENDAR YEAR, in return for which he shall receive certain specified sums of money should he suffer a loss.
Insurance premium. The monies paid to an insurance company by the insured party in return for protection against a possible loss.
Insurance trust. An arrangement between an insured person and a TRUSTEE wherein the proceeds of a life insurance policy are paid to the trustee. He, in turn, will invest and/or distribute the monies to the BENEFICIARIES named in the WILL, according to the instructions given to him by the insured person prior to DEATH. Also known as a *life insurance trust.*
Insured. The person who takes out the INSURANCE POLICY.
Insurer. The insurance company, also known as the UNDERWRITER.
Insurgent. A person who revolts against his constituted AUTHORITY or government.
Intangible property. PROPERTY that has no value in and of itself but which represents value. FRANCHISES, STOCKS, BONDS, PROMISSORY NOTES, etcetera fall into this category.
Integrated contract. An AGREEMENT in which all the terms are recorded in writing.
Integration. 1. The bringing together of peoples of all races and creeds, with abandonment of all prejudices and discriminations. **2.** Integration of the bar results in an integrated bar to which all attorneys belong.
Integrity. Honesty; uprightness; of good moral character.
Intelligibility. Facts so stated that an individual of average intelligence can understand.
Intemperance. The use of alcohol to such an extent that one is habitually unable to conduct his affairs; the excessive use of intoxicating beverages.
Intended to be recorded. A common phrase in a DOCUMENT transferring PROPERTY (a CONVEYANCE) which mentions some other related property transfer that has not yet been recorded.
Intendment of law. The true meaning of the law; the common understanding of the law.
Intent. The purpose in carrying out a particular act, such as *criminal intent;* design; resolve.
Intentional. On purpose; willful; done with intent. The opposite of unintentional or accidental.
Inter alia. Among other things (Latin).

Inter partes. Between the PARTIES, such as a CONTRACT or AGREEMENT between two people (Latin).

Inter vivos. Between two living people, referring to the transfer of PROPERTY from one living person to another, rather than transfer of property through inheritance from a deceased to a living person (Latin).

Inter vivos trust. A living TRUST; a trust set up during the lifetime of the person who is settling money or PROPERTY upon another, as distinguished from a trust that leaves property or money after the DEATH of the GRANTOR (Latin).

Interchangeably. A term signifying that each PARTY to an AGREEMENT signs such agreement and hands the copy over to the other for his signature. They then exchange copies of the agreement.

Intercourse. **1.** Communication between two or more people; trade between two or more people. **2.** Commonly, the word is used to denote sexual relations between two people, i.e., *sexual intercourse.*

Interest. The RIGHT to benefit from something; a share of something; COMPENSATION payable on a regular basis, such as interest paid by a bank in exchange for the deposit or LOAN of money. There are many different types of interest, including *annual interest, compound interest, interest-bearing stock, legal interest, vested interest,* etcetera.

Interested person. A concerned person; someone having a share or interest in something, as opposed to a disinterested person. A judge who owns shares in a COMPANY appearing before his COURT may disqualify himself or be disqualified from presiding over a matter concerning such company because he is an interested person.

Interest suit. A LAWSUIT between two people interested in an ESTATE, each contending for the RIGHT to be the EXECUTOR of such estate.

Interference. **1.** A wrongful act by a person who prevents or disturbs another in the performance of his usual activities, or in the conduct of his business. **2.** In PATENT law, a situation wherein two people claim the rights to the same invention or discovery.

Interference proceeding. A HEARING before officials of the PATENT OFFICE wherein two people claim the right to the same discovery or invention.

Interim. Meanwhile; in the meantime; temporary (Latin).

Interim order. A temporary EDICT of a COURT, as a temporary INJUNCTION.

Interlineation. Writing in between the lines of a DOCUMENT.

Interlocutory. Temporary; not final or conclusive, as an INTERLOCUTORY DECREE of DIVORCE or an *interlocutory judgment.*

Interlocutory costs. Costs that are allowable while the CASE is still in progress and being determined.

Interlocutory decree. A temporary JUDGMENT or determination, made either before a matter has been determined in COURT or, during the course of a SUIT.

Intermarriage. In a strictly legal sense, intermarriage means merely the MARRIAGE of one person to another. However, in common usage, intermarriage refers to an individual of one race marrying someone of another race.
≫ MISCEGENATION.

Intermediary. Someone who negotiates a matter between two or more parties; a BROKER; a go-between.

Intermediate. Taking place during the middle of, or between the beginning and end of a LAWSUIT or other pending matter; intervening.

Intermediate order. An ORDER of a COURT that takes place during the progress of a CASE before it is ended. Such an order may render temporary relief to the PLAINTIFF while not deciding the case finally; an INTERLOCUTORY order; a temporary or provisional order.

Intermingling. The mixing together of goods or merchandise by an OWNER so that someone who makes claim to OWNERSHIP of some of them cannot distinguish and separate his own goods. This constitutes a wrongful deception.

Intern. 1. To apprehend and hold an enemy alien. **2.** To JAIL a political prisoner. **3.** In medicine, an intern is a physician-in-training in a hospital.

Internal revenue. Income the federal government receives from the collection of taxes.

Internal Revenue Service (I.R.S.). An AGENCY of the federal government which administers the TAX LAWS and codes, and receives monies paid in taxes.

International banking. Banking activities involving business TRANSACTIONS from one country to another. International banks engage in transactions in foreign countries, using either branches of their own bank or the facilities of banks in the foreign country.

International Court of Justice. The COURT set up by the United Nations to hear DISPUTES of an international nature.

International law. That LAW that governs and determines the rights of independent nations during peace or war; the laws of nations.

International Monetary Fund (I.M.F.). A fund contributed to by a large number of countries for the purpose of creating a ready supply of international CREDIT.

Interpellate. To ask a question; questions asked by a judge of an ATTORNEY during a DISPUTE.

Interpellation. An AGREEMENT by a party to be bound for a specific period of time, beyond which he will not be bound.

Interplead. 1. To LITIGATE against one another in order to discover who has the RIGHT to make a CLAIM against the third party. **2.** To file an INTERPLEADER in a pending lawsuit.

Interpleader. A BILL OF INTERPLEADER. When two or more people are making a CLAIM against a third PARTY, and when that third party does not know which of the claimants has the right to the PROPERTY, he files a bill against them, forcing them to LITIGATE among themselves to determine who has the actual RIGHT to make the claim. As a consequence, the third party who has no interest in the disputed property is not sued individually by rival claimants.

Interpolate. To alter a DOCUMENT by inserting words into it.

Interpretation. The explanation of the true meaning of a STATEMENT or written DOCUMENT; a translation.

Interpretation clauses. CLAUSES or sentences contained in various LAWS or STATUTES, explaining or defining certain of their terms and meanings.

Interpreter. A translator employed by a court to translate the TESTIMONY and EVIDENCE of a person who speaks no English, or who is unable to speak because of an infirmity, such as a deaf-mute. Interpreters must be sworn by the court to give accurate translations.

Interrogation. Questioning, as of a WITNESS or suspected CRIMINAL.

Interrogatories. A set of written questions presented to a WITNESS in order to obtain his written TESTIMONY (DEPOSITION) while he is under OATH to tell the truth. Interrogatories are part of the RIGHT OF DISCOVERY that a PARTY in a suit has in obtaining FACTS from his adversary. They often take place prior to the commencement of the TRIAL.

Interruption of possession. A situation in which the RIGHT OF POSSESSION is not enjoyed continuously.

Interruption of statute. An interruption in the normal period of the STATUTE OF LIMITATIONS, thus prolonging the period until the statute of limitations runs out.

Intersection. A crossing of two streets or highways that run in different directions.

Interstate. Between two or more states, such as *interstate commerce* or an *interstate highway.*

Interstate Commerce Act. A federal law governing CONDUCT in interstate TRANSACTIONS, ensuring that such conduct is fair, reasonable, and nondiscriminatory. The Interstate Commerce Commission oversees interstate commerce.

Interstate extradition. The surrender from one state to another of a person accused of a crime, such crime alleged to have been committed in a state not having JURISDICTION to try the case.

Interstate law. RULES and PRINCIPLES to be considered in SUITS between CITIZENS of different countries, taking into account the differences in the LAWS of individual countries.

Intervening act. A CAUSE of an INJURY or ACCIDENT that will erase the blame from the PERPETRATOR of the wrong who originally set things in action. A cause which begins operating to produce a result after the negligence of the defendant. Also known as *intervening cause* and *intervening force.*

Intervening agency. Same as INTERVENING ACT. An act that intervenes between (comes in between) cause and effect.

Intervening cause. > INTERVENING ACT

Intervention. An act wherein a third person seeks to become a PARTY to a SUIT between two other persons. He may wish to join the PLAINTIFF in pressing a

suit against a DEFENDANT or he may wish to join the defendant against the plaintiff.
Intestacy. Dying without having made a WILL; dying with having made a will that disposes of only part of an ESTATE.
Intestate. A state of INTESTACY, or dying without having made a WILL.
Intestate laws. STATUTES that stipulate how ESTATES shall be disposed of when no WILL exists.
Intimate relations. **1.** Close friendship. **2.** Confidential relations. **3.** SEXUAL INTERCOURSE, especially involving a man and woman who are not married to each other.
Intimation. The act of informing someone that a legal ACTION is soon to be undertaken; a notice to an opponent that an APPEAL from a court's DECISION will be taken.
Intimidation. Threatening someone; putting unlawful pressure upon someone; placing someone in fear in order to get him to do something he does not wish to do, such as forcing a person to perform an unlawful act. ⋙ THREAT.
Intolerance. Failure to respect different beliefs; narrow-mindedness; bigotry.
Intoxicated. Under the influence of alcohol to such an extent that one's normal faculties are impaired; drunk; INEBRIATED. There are blood and breathing tests to determine the quantity of alcohol in one's system. These tests are helpful in making determinations as to whether one was legally intoxicated at the time of the commission of an OFFENSE.
Intra vires. Within the power of (Latin). An act is intra vires when a person or business has the AUTHORITY to carry it out.
Intraliminal. A mining RIGHT to the minerals lying perpendicular to the borders of a CLAIM. It is the opposite of "extraliminal," which allows the mining to spread out underground beyond the borders of the claim.
Intramural. Within the walls of. A term designating the powers *within* the limits of a CORPORATION; the opposite of "extramural."
Intrinsic danger. A danger characteristic of a certain type of work; same as inherent danger; a danger unrelated to the competence of an individual, but one dependent upon the nature of the activity.
Intrinsic evidence. EVIDENCE derived from a written DOCUMENT.
Intrinsic fraud. DECEIT in obtaining a TRANSACTION; during a TRIAL, PERJURY, FORGERY, BRIBERY of a WITNESS, etcetera, constitute FRAUDS that might have been relieved by the COURT.
Intrinsic value. The actual, true value of a thing; the value that would be universally recognized.
Introduction of evidence. The bringing in of EVIDENCE during a TRIAL.
Intromission. **1.** In medical parlance, the placing of the penis within the vagina. **2.** The act of placing something within; the act of admitting.
Intruder. Someone who enters another's PROPERTY without the RIGHT to do so, particularly a person who has been forbidden to enter, for example, a burglar.
Intrusion. The act of one who in-

trudes (enters without the RIGHT or permission to do so). > TRESPASS.

Inure. **1.** To become effective; to come to one's benefit. **2.** To become accustomed to.

Inurement of title. The passing of TITLE to PROPERTY from one person to another without any formal DOCUMENT or writing.

Invading a trust. Using monies of a TRUST that had been set aside, usually not to be used. Under some circumstances, a trust may be legally invaded if it can be proved that use of some of its funds is necessary for the benefit of the beneficiaries of the trust.

Invalid. **1.** Not valid; illegal; void; having no effect. **2.** A permanently incapacitated person.

Invasion of privacy. A violation of one's RIGHT OF PRIVACY.

Invasion of trust. > INVADING A TRUST.

Invention. The creation of something new. Original inventions can be patented under the provisions of the PATENT LAWS.

Inventor. Someone who creates something new.

Inventory. An itemized list of goods and merchandise on hand, usually accompanied by notations of the value of such goods and merchandise.

Inverse condemnation. The taking of PROPERTY without actually entering onto it, such as by interfering with property RIGHTS.

Invest. To place money in a business venture in the hope of making more money; the giving of money in exchange for SECURITIES; to use money to make more money.

Investigation. Careful, intensive examination of circumstances and situations, to discover FACTS; questioning concerned parties; a legal inquiry.

Investment. A commitment of CAPITAL for the purpose of deriving an INCOME from it; a LOAN of money in return for INTEREST and a PROMISE to repay the loan.

Investment securities. STOCKS and BONDS sold on security and STOCK EXCHANGES, in accordance with standards laid down by the federal Securities and Exchange Commission (S.E.C.).

Investment trust. A CORPORATION that takes its ASSETS and INVESTS them in stocks and bonds, then distributes the INCOME and profits from these securities to the SHAREHOLDERS of the TRUST.

Inviolable. Not to be violated or invaded.

Invitation. The act of asking, specifically or by implication, people to enter your premises or PROPERTY. For example, a store owner issues an invitation to potential customers to enter his store.

Invoice. A list of merchandise sent to a consignee or PURCHASER containing the identities of the items sent and their prices.

Involuntary. **1.** Against the will; without consent. **2.** Unintentional, as an *involuntary twitch* of a muscle or an *involuntary movement* during sleep.

Involuntary discontinuance. The forcing of a CASE out of COURT because of some mistake in PLEADING or because of a technical error; also known as an *involuntary dismissal.*

Involuntary hospitalization. Confinement to a mental hospital against one's will.

Involuntary manslaughter. The unintentional killing of someone during an unlawful act of a lesser nature, such as the killing of a pedestrian by a driver who drives through a red light. Also, the killing of someone during the COMMISSION of a lawful act, which nevertheless results in death in an unlawful manner.
➢ MANSLAUGHTER; VOLUNTARY MANSLAUGHTER.

Involuntary servitude. Forcing someone against his will to work at a job, whether or not the person is paid for his labor; slavery.

Involuntary trust. A TRUST that comes into being by operation of existing LAWS. When a MINOR inherits money and/or PROPERTY, a trust is set up to administer it until the minor becomes of age.

Iota. The smallest possible quantity (Greek). A favorite expression of attorneys when attempting to discredit TESTIMONY is that there is not one iota of truth in the testimony.

Ipse dixit. He said it himself (Latin).

Ipso facto. By the act itself; by the mere fact itself (Latin).

Irrational. Absurd; ridiculous; mentally unsound; incoherent; unreasonable. A sane person may, under stress, have irrational lapses.

Irrecusable. A contractual OBLIGATION imposed on someone legally but without his CONSENT, and not caused by any act on his part. Such an obligation cannot be avoided.

Irregular judgment. A JUDGMENT that is contrary to the practice of the COURT and contrary to the established mode of PROCEDURE. Such a judgment may hold temporarily but usually can be reversed on APPEAL.

Irrelevant. Impertinent to an ARGUMENT or PLEADING; not applicable; not relating to; evidence that has no bearing on the issues.
➢ IMMATERIAL; IMMATERIAL AND IRRELEVANT.

Irreparable damage. INJURY of such a nature that it is impossible to calculate its extent by an award of money.

Irresistible force. An uncontrollable POWER; a force unable to be resisted, such as the force and actions of a rioting mob.

Irresistible impulse. An act of TEMPORARY INSANITY during which one commits a crime, such as a MURDER; an uncontrollable desire.

Irrevocable. Unable to be cancelled or nullified.

Issuable defense. A DEFENSE based solely on the merits of the CASE, calling for a VERDICT in favor of the DEFENDANT, as distinguished from a PLEA IN ABATEMENT (a defense that attempts to get the charges dismissed or attempts to lessen the severity of the charges). Also known as an *issuable plea.*

Issue. **1.** To come forth; to put out; to put into circulation. **2.** A point of LAW about which there is CONTROVERSY. **3.** A matter to be decided by a COURT. **4.** STOCKS, BONDS, or other SECURITIES that are offered for sale to the public. **5.** Descendants, such as children, grandchildren, etcetera.

Issue at law. A matter of CONTROVERSY or differing OPINION of LAW, submitted to a COURT for its ADJUDICATION (opinion and DECISION).

Issue in fact. A matter brought before a COURT in which ISSUES concerning the FACTS of the case are in CONTROVERSY, not matters pertaining to the LAW.

Issuing process or writ. The signing and delivery of a WRIT or PROCESS to a SHERIFF for his appropriate action.

Itemize. To record each item or article separately.

Itinerant vendor. Someone who travels from place to place selling his goods and wares.

J

Jactitation of title. A false CLAIM to TITLE to PROPERTY; the claim that someone's title to property is invalid; SLANDER of title.
Jail. A PRISON.
Jailbreak. An escape from JAIL, accompanied by force and violence.
Jail-house lawyer. A prisoner who studies the law while in JAIL in order to help himself and/or his fellow prisoners.
Jaywalking. Crossing a street in the wrong place, as diagonally at an intersection, or in the middle of the street. In most cities, jaywalking is unlawful.
Jeopardy. The danger of CONVICTION that anyone faces who is accused of a crime and is brought to TRIAL.
Jettison. To dump cargo overboard to lighten a ship when its safety is threatened. Also applies to an airplane that jettisons its fuel prior to making an emergency landing.
John Doe. The fictitious name often used in illustrating or arguing an ISSUE, or used as a substitute for a person's real name until the latter can be determined.
John Doe summons. A SUMMONS in which the DEFENDANT's name is unknown and which is therefore made out to JOHN DOE. After the true name of the defendant is known, it is substituted.
Joinder. Joining another person in a common SUIT, the acceptance by a party to an action of an issue tendered (formally presented).
Joinder in demurrer. An acceptance by the PLAINTIFF of a DEFENDANT's presentation of an issue of LAW (a demurrer). If the plaintiff does not accept the demurrer, he cannot continue his SUIT.
Joinder in issue. A PARTY's acceptance of the raising of an ISSUE of FACT by the opposing party in a LAWSUIT.
Joinder in pleading. Accepting the ISSUES raised by the opposing PARTY in a SUIT.
Joinder of actions. The uniting of two or more ISSUES, DEMANDS, or RIGHTS in one LAWSUIT.
Joinder of error. A written denial of errors alleged to have taken place.
Joinder of offenses. The uniting of several different CHARGES of criminal acts in one CASE.
Joinder of parties. The uniting of two or more people as coplaintiffs or codefendants.
Joint. Combined; united; coupled in a joint ACTION (SUIT).
Joint account. A bank account in more than one name, such as husband and wife, parent and child, etcetera.
Joint action. A SUIT brought or defended by two or more PARTIES.
Joint adventure. ➤ PARTNERSHIP.
Joint and several. An expression denoting unity, as distinguished from separate or individual.
Joint cause of action. A SUIT

brought by two or more people involving a single ISSUE.

Joint debtor's acts. Laws permitting the COURTS to render JUDGMENTS against one or more joint DEBTORS.

Joint enterprise. An ENTERPRISE engaged in by two or more people who have common interests and goals; a common enterprise. > JOINT ADVENTURE; PARTNERSHIP.

Joint executors. Coexecutors; two or more people who are charged with administering an ESTATE.

Joint liability. Equal responsibility, so that if one person in a JOINT ENTERPRISE is sued, the other or others are similarly sued and liable.

Joint tort. A wrong to be shared by two or more people, because they are jointly responsible.

Joint venture. > JOINT ADVENTURE.

Joint will. One WILL that contains the wills of two or more people, disposing of PROPERTIES jointly owned.

Judge. A public official, appointed or elected, authorized to hear and often to decide cases brought before a court of law.

Judge advocate. An OFFICER of a military COURT-MARTIAL who acts as the PROSECUTOR. However, his duties include protection of the ACCUSED, so that he is restrained from asking incriminating questions.

Judge advocate general. The chief legal adviser to the military. Each branch of the services, Army, Navy, Marines, Air Force, has its own judge advocate general.

Judge de facto. A JUDGE serving as a result of a legitimate election or appointment. In some areas a judge de facto is one who serves as a jurist under special circumstances, even if he has not been duly elected or appointed in the usual manner.

Judge pro tempore. A JUDGE appointed as a temporary judge, usually just to fill out a particular term of the COURT.

Judge's calendar. A listing of the CASES to appear and be tried before a certain JUDGE.

Judge's order. An order given by a JUDGE out of COURT, usually in his CHAMBERS.

Judgment. The DECISION of a COURT having the appropriate JURISDICTION to have tried the CASE; the final determination of a CASE; a ruling of the court.

Judgment, conditional. A DECISION rendered, providing one of the parties performs certain acts. The judgment becomes void if such acts are not performed.

Judgment, estoppel by. A bar against trying the case again, after certain facts have already been accepted as true.

Judgment, final. A JUDGMENT that positively determines a CLAIM and terminates it, as distinguished from an INTERLOCUTORY judgment.

Judgment book. A COURT record book in which JUDGMENTS are listed and kept on file.

Judgment by default. A JUDGMENT awarded to a PLAINTIFF because, given ample opportunity to do so, a DEFENDANT has not defended himself.

Judgment creditor. A person who has won his case against a DEBTOR but who has not yet collected his debt.

Judgment debtor. A person who has lost his case to a CREDITOR but has not yet paid his debt.

Judgment docket. A list of the DECISIONS rendered by a court, maintained by the CLERK OF THE COURT, and kept open for public inspection.

Judgment execution. A SUMMONS to a DEFENDANT who has lost his case, ordering him to explain why the DEBT (or goods or merchandise) should not be turned over to the PLAINTIFF.

Judgment in rem. A DECISION made by a COURT relative to the status of a particular thing or subject matter, as opposed to a judgment relative to a person or persons (Latin).

Judgment lien. A LIEN (the RIGHT to hold PROPERTY) against a JUDGMENT DEBTOR in favor of the JUDGMENT CREDITOR.

Judgment note. A NOTE a person who borrows money or who buys something on the installment plan. It gives the RIGHT to the CREDITOR to get a JUDGMENT against him in COURT if he fails to pay his DEBT or to pay for the thing he has purchased; also known as a *cognovit note.*

Judgment of his peers. An expression relating to TRIAL by a JURY of one's equals, usually composed of twelve men and women, but sometimes of a lesser number.

Judgment of respondeat ouster. A JUDGMENT against a DEFENDANT upon an ISSUE of LAW raised by his DEFENSE, resulting in the denial of the merits of his defense and forcing him to answer the ACCUSATIONS against him with a defense that is based on the merits of the involved issue or issues (Latin).

Judgment on merits. A DECISION of a COURT based upon the FACTS presented, rather than upon some technical legal PROCEDURE or practice.

Judgment-proof. Phrase describing people against whom a JUDGMENT of a COURT will have no effect because of their inability to pay their DEBT or to meet the demands of the judgment. Attempts, before or during a TRIAL, to make oneself purposely judgment-proof are illegal.

Judgment vacated. A DECISION of a COURT that is set aside; a new TRIAL is then ordered.

Judicial. Anything related to the administration of justice; anything that has to do with a COURT of JUSTICE.

Judicial action. A DECISION of a COURT, rendered after hearing the controversial ISSUES involved.

Judicial authority. The POWER granted to a judge, enabling him to hear a CASE and decide in favor of one or the other of the PARTIES engaged in the suit.

Judicial cognizance. Information upon which a judge must act, regardless of the FACT that it has not been proved in EVIDENCE.

Judicial comity. A courtesy of a COURT that respects the judicial decisions of another state, even though it is not obliged to do so.

Judicial decision. A DECISION made by judges in matters brought before them, especially matters brought before judges of a higher court who are reviewing decisions of lower courts.

Judicial errors. Mistakes of COURTS in rendering their DECISIONS. Such errors will, of necessity on APPEAL, be corrected by higher courts.

Judicial inquiry. An INVESTIGATION that looks into and enforces LIABILITIES that exist under the LAW.

Judicial notice. The act of a judge in recognizing certain truisms, thus doing away with the need to have one side put such FACTS in EVIDENCE. A judge may state his AGREEMENT to the fact that the earth is round.

Judicial opinion. The OPINION and DECISION (JUDGMENT) of a COURT.

Judicial order. An ORDER that is issued at a judge's discretion, often affecting the final outcome of a LAWSUIT.

Judicial proceeding. A matter brought before a judge who is exercising his judicial rights.

Judicial process. > PROCESS, JUDICIAL.

Judicial remedy. A court's DECISION settling a CLAIM in favor of one of the PARTIES to a SUIT.

Judiciary. That branch of the government whose duties include the interpretation and application of law; the BENCH; the system of COURTS to settle legal DISPUTES; the judges.

Judiciously. With sound judgment. An issue is decided judiciously when it is decided wisely and correctly.

Jumping bail. Disappearing before a TRIAL, in violation of BAIL that has been posted guaranteeing one's appearance in COURT.

Jural. Pertaining to legal rather than moral rights or obligations.

Jure in rem. Rights in a thing (Latin).

Juridical. Relating to a judge, or to a court system; conforming to LAW.

Jurisdiction. The POWER and RIGHT to administer JUSTICE; the geographic area in which a judge or a COURT has the right to try and decide a CASE.

Jurisdiction clause. In EQUITY CASES, that part of a COMPLAINT which gives the POWER to a COURT to hear and decide a DISPUTE. Without such help from a COURT OF EQUITY, the PLAINTIFF would have no way to have his complaint SATISFIED.

Jurisdictional dispute. A CONTROVERSY between LABOR UNIONS, each claiming the right to represent certain workers.

Jurisprudence. The philosophy of LAW; the science which deals with legal PRINCIPLES and relations.

Jurist. Someone who is expert in the LAW; a learned ATTORNEY or judge.

Juror. A member of a JURY; a person selected for JURY DUTY.

Jury. A specified number of men and/or women who are chosen and sworn to look into matters of FACT and, therefore, to determine and render a DECISION upon the EVIDENCE presented to them. Juries may be of different sizes in various JURISDICTIONS and in various categories. A GRAND JURY may have anywhere from 12 to 24 jurors.

Jury, common. An ordinary jury, as distinguished from a GRAND JURY or CORONER'S jury, etcetera.

Jury, grand. A JURY composed of 12 to 24 men and women whose duties include the hearing of ACCUSATIONS of criminal activities, taking preliminary EVIDENCE, and making INDICTMENTS (ACCUSATIONS that someone should be tried for an alleged crime) or determining that no indictment is indicated. If no indictment is brought in, a person is said to have been "cleared by a grand jury." > NO BILL.

Jury, hung. A JURY that, because of insoluble differences of OPINION, cannot bring in a VERDICT.

Jury, petit. An ordinary or common JURY that tries most civil and criminal cases.

Jury, special. A JURY picked with special care because of the importance of the matter before the court; a STRUCK JURY.

Jury, struck. A special JURY selected by a process in which 12, or sometimes fewer, people become jurors out of a total of 48 possible jurors. These jurors are supposedly the best qualified to hear the particular case to come before the COURT.

Jury box. The enclosed space in which a JURY sits during a TRIAL.

Jury duty. The time during which someone serves on a jury; an obligation of citizens, with the exception of certain classes of people such as ATTORNEYS, public OFFICIALS, physicians, dentists, the physically and mentally ill, who are excused in most states.

Jury list. A list of all possible and potential JURORS. Out of this list, an appropriate JURY is selected.

Jury process. The method by which a JURY is summoned and is compelled to attend COURT.

Jury selection. The process of selecting the individuals, out of the JURY LIST, who will serve on a particular JURY for a particular period of time.

Jury trial. A TRIAL by JURY, as distinguished from a trial by a judge alone.

Jury wheel. An apparatus or receptacle in which the names of all potential JURORS are placed, from which the names of those who will serve are blindly picked.

Jus. **1.** The LAW (Latin). **2.** The RIGHT (Latin). **3.** JUSTICE (Latin).

Jus ad rem. The RIGHT to a thing (Latin).

Jus naturale. > LAW OF NATURE

Jus non scriptum. The unwritten LAW (Latin).

Jus tertii. The RIGHT of a third party (Latin).

Just. That which is fair, legal, and lawful.

Just cause. A legal and fair CAUSE for carrying out an action, such cause being based upon good faith.

Just compensation. Fair payment for taking over PRIVATE PROPERTY and converting it to public use.

Just debts. Legal, valid obligations, such as the DEBTS owed by a deceased person's ESTATE.

Just title. A TITLE to PROPERTY that one has received from a person whom he believes to have been the OWNER; a title that may appear to be perfect but which is not absolute or perfect. > COLOR OF TITLE.

Just value. For TAX purposes, the fair value of PROPERTY; the market value.

Justice. 1. The attempt by judicial means to be fair and to give each party his due, under the law. **2.** The name given to a judge.

Justice department. The branch of the federal executive government headed by the ATTORNEY GENERAL. Among its duties are the tasks of handling all SUITS brought against or for the United States. Under the Justice Department is the Federal Bureau of Investigation (the F.B.I.), the Immigration and Naturalization Service, the Federal Prison system, etcetera.

Justice of the peace. A MAGISTRATE, a person serving as a judge in a small town, community, or county. He has limited AUTHORITY, his duties being specified by the town, community, or county that he serves.

Justifiable cause. A CAUSE based upon a well-founded belief.

Justifiable homicide. A killing of a person according to one's duties or out of necessity, without blame. (For example, executioner carrying out a DEATH SENTENCE commits justifiable homicide.) Also refers to a killing that takes place as a reaction to an attempted crime, as when a POLICE OFFICER is attacked by a person who is in the act of committing a crime. > EXCUSABLE HOMICIDE.

Justification. The reason for committing an act which appears on the surface to be unlawful but may then be judged excusable. Self-defense is sometimes ruled to be *justification* for killing.

Juvenile court. A COURT that hears matters pertaining to the OFFENSES of MINORS, juvenile delinquents, etcetera.

Juvenile delinquency. Wrongdoings of children and youths.

K

Kangaroo court. An unauthorized COURT, set up without legal AUTHORITY or POWERS, which takes the LAW into its own hands, often meting out undeserved punishments.
Keelage. Money paid for the privilege of anchoring a vessel in a harbor.
Keep. To hold; to maintain; to support; to retain in one's POSSESSION; to take care of.
Keep in repair. A CLAUSE in many LEASES, binding the lessee to keep the premises in good condition.
Keeping the peace. Maintaining public ORDER; preventing violence or other unlawful BEHAVIOR.
Keogh plan. A federal STATUTE permitting self-employed businessmen and professionals to set up pension and retirement plans for themselves. The plan is named after former Congressman Eugene J. Keogh.
Kickback. An unlawful act whereby an individual or individuals demand and receive part of the WAGES or payments made for the performance of a job or jobs done by another. The giving of kickbacks is punishable by FINE or IMPRISONMENT if it occurs in the performance of work for the federal government. FEE-SPLITTING among physicians also constitutes an unlawful kickback in some states.
Kidnapping. The taking away of an individual against his will. The term is usually applied to instances in which RANSOM is demanded for the return of the kidnapped person; abducting.
Kidnapping law. A federal OFFENSE in which a person is taken forcibly from one state to another, or to a foreign country. Also known as the Lindbergh Law.
Killed by misadventure. Accidentally killed, not during the performance of an unlawful act.
Kindred. Related by birth; blood relatives; consanguineous.
Kissing the book. Touching one's lips to the Holy Bible, as during the rendering of OATHS. It acknowledges that one swears to uphold one's PROMISES.
Kiting checks. Unlawfully covering an overdrawn CHECK by writing another check on another bank. When the second bank check also proves to be overdrawn, it is covered by writing an illegal check on a third bank, and so on.
Kleptomania. An uncontrollable desire to STEAL, motivated not by a need for the stolen money or goods, but by a psychological disturbance. Often, kleptomaniacs are well-to-do, and steal articles that are useless to them. They are best treated by psychiatrists rather than by ordinary legal punishments.
Knowingly. Consciously; with awareness; with knowledge; intentionally. The opposites are un-

knowingly; unconsciously; without knowledge.

Knowingly and willfully. A term applied to a crime carried out intentionally and with full awareness.

Knowledge. The perception of truth and facts; awareness of situations, circumstances, and facts; comprehension; understanding.

Known. Recognized, as a well-known person; understood, as a fact that has been comprehended; familiar, as a person who is known to another person.

Known heirs. Those who are recognized as having the RIGHT to inherit, as distinguished from unknown heirs.

L

Label. **1.** An addition to a written DOCUMENT or CLAUSE, such as a CODICIL. **2.** A slip of paper attached to a DEED so that a seal may be applied. **3.** A paper or cloth addition to an article of goods or merchandise, giving the name of the manufacturer, the materials out of which the goods are made, and other pertinent data.

Labor. **1.** To work; to toil. **2.** The work force; employees.

Labor dispute. A disagreement between employers and employees over such matters as wages, hours, working conditions, holidays, seniority, fringe benefits, hiring practices, firing practices, etcetera.

Labor relations acts. Laws, state or federal, that attempt to govern or regulate relations between employers and employees. These acts were put into effect in an attempt to lessen labor disputes, strikes, and lockouts.

Labor union. An organization of working people formed to protect their RIGHTS and to aid them in obtaining the best possible working conditions. The union acts in behalf of its members in NEGOTIATIONS and DISPUTES with management.

Lacey Act. A federal STATUTE enforcing GAME LAWS.

Laches. A DEFENSE which contends that RIGHTS that have not been enforced and have been neglected for a long time, cannot be enforced. Thus, the person who fails to enforce his rights over a long period loses those rights. This DOCTRINE applies particularly to PROPERTY, and is also known as the "doctrine of stale demand."

Lack of jurisdiction. Lack of AUTHORITY or POWER to act in a particular legal matter. For example, a municipal or state court lacks JURISDICTION over a case involving federal matters.

Land grant. The grant of land owned by the federal or state government to an institution, sometimes for educational purposes, such as a *land grant college,* or to a COMPANY that will serve the PUBLIC, such as a land grant to a railroad.

Land tax. A LEVY upon an OWNER of real estate, based on the assessed value of the land.

Land warrant. A GUARANTEE issued by a federal government land office to purchasers of PUBLIC LANDS. On presenting the WARRANT to the appropriate AUTHORITY in Washington, D.C., a deed to the land is given.

Landlord. An owner of a house, apartment, or land, to whom a tenant pays rent. One who leases PROPERTY; a LESSOR.

Landlord's lien. A claim by the LANDLORD to PROPERTY of a tenant who has not paid his rent. This LIEN may be upon furniture, or upon the produce raised by the tenant on the landlord's property.

Landmark case. A CASE of such importance that it establishes new LAW and sets new PRECEDENTS.
Landrum-Griffin Act. A federal law affording new RIGHTS to UNION members.
Language. A body of words which, when put together, offer a means of communication among people. There are many different languages, each used and understood by groups of people. Thus, there are languages of individual countries, or languages of different professions, such as the *language of the law.*
Lapsed policy. An INSURANCE POLICY that no longer is operative because the PREMIUM has not been paid.
Lapsus linguae. A slip of the tongue (Latin).
Larcenous intent. An intent or plan to STEAL.
Larceny. STEALING; thievery; taking something for one's own use that belongs to another. *Grand larceny* involves stealing something of major value; *petty larceny* means stealing something of relatively little value.
Lascivious. Lewd; lustful; arousing sexual desire, obscene; immoral.
Last clear chance. A doctrine that a party can recover DAMAGES, regardless of the existence of NEGLIGENCE, if the DEFENDANT could have avoided an INJURY after discovering that a danger existed.
Last resort. A term referring to a COURT OF LAST RESORT, a court from which there can be no APPEAL.
Last will and testament. The WILL that is valid and in force at the time of DEATH.
Latent ambiguity. A legal DOCUMENT, WILL, DEED, etcetera, which seems to be clear upon reading it, but which contains ambiguities (double, doubtful, or unclear meanings) when said document is related to external circumstances. For example, a will may leave "my house" as a bequest to a relative when, in fact, the maker of the will owns two houses.
Latent defect. A hidden defect; a defect not apparent on ordinary inspection.
Law. The RULES, REGULATIONS, ORDINANCES, and STATUTES, created by the legislative bodies of governments, under which people are expected to live. The law is interpreted by the COURTS; the FACTS are determined by JURIES. The laws of the land are the results of our moral thinking, the edicts of nature, and our experiences in living.
Law enforcement officers. The people responsible for KEEPING THE PEACE, such as the POLICE, SHERIFFS, etcetera.
Law of damages. The PRINCIPLES governing the size of an AWARD or VERDICT.
Law of evidence. The sum total of PRINCIPLES and RULES governing the presentation of EVIDENCE in a legal matter. The laws of evidence decide whether certain evidence of testimony can be admitted in a case, whether or not it is relevant to the issues under consideration, and how much or how little weight should be given to the evidence.

Law of nature. Laws that are based upon the "nature" of man, such as his supposedly inherent desire to do good and to reject dishonesty and irrational conduct. > NATURAL LAW.

Law of the case. The doctrine stating that when a point of LAW is decided by a COURT, that DECISION is binding in all subsequent stages of the CASE, until reversed by an APPELLATE COURT.

Law of the land. A LAW or laws that are in force throughout the entire country, such as the law that everyone in our land is entitled to equal protection under the law. > LEX TERRAE.

Law of torts. LAWS permitting individuals to recover DAMAGES for injuries.

Law Review. The periodical or magazine published by each individual law school, containing articles of legal interest. The law students with the highest grades are chosen to be members of the board of editors for the Law Review, making this a mark of high distinction and a reward for having done exceptionally well in one's work.

Law school. An institution of learning where students study to become ATTORNEYS.

Lawful. Legal; authorized by LAW; the opposite of unlawful.

Lawful discharge. The release of a BANKRUPT or DEBTOR from his DEBTS after he has done everything possible to pay his CREDITORS.

Lawful entry. The entry of someone onto real estate that he claims the RIGHT to POSSESS.

Lawful issue. DESCENDANTS; those who are entitled to inherit by virtue of kinship, such as the children of a deceased person.

Lawless. Ignoring or violating the LAW; not controlled by law; uncontrollable.

Lawsuit. A SUIT; a CAUSE; an ACTION; a DISPUTE between two or more PARTIES brought into COURT for a solution.

Lawyer. A man or woman licensed to practice LAW; an ATTORNEY; a COUNSELOR.

Layman. Someone who is not of the legal profession. Also, someone who has no particular profession.

Layoff. A dismissal from employment, usually a temporary loss of a job because there is insufficient work to be done. A layoff differs from being fired for JUST CAUSE.

Leading case. A suit of unusual importance, with the possibility that its DECISION may establish new law; a LANDMARK CASE.

Leading question. A question put to a WITNESS by an ATTORNEY that suggests the answer that the witness should give. In other words, a question that "puts words into the witness' mouth," and which will be disallowed by the presiding judge.

Lease. **1.** A CONTRACT or AGREEMENT between a LANDLORD and TENANT. The landlord is known as the LESSOR; the tenant is the LESSEE. **2.** To rent something for a specified period of time, such as leasing an automobile.

Lease in reversion. A LEASE that goes into effect at the expiration of the previous lease.

Leaseback. A sale of land or

PROPERTY with a lease given by the PURCHASER back to the original OWNER. Thus, the original owner stays on as a TENANT.

Leasehold. A lease of PROPERTY for a specified period of time, usually for many years. The United States had a leasehold on the Panama Canal Zone for 99 years.

Leave and license. The permission and CONSENT of the PLAINTIFF, used as a DEFENSE by someone accused of TRESPASS. For example, an OWNER of PROPERTY may have given permission for an owner of adjacent property to use an access road. Then, some time later, the owner claims that the owner of the adjacent property is trespassing on his property by using the access road.

Leave of absence. Temporary absence from work, possibly because of a prolonged illness or a prolonged holiday, with stated intention of return to the job. During a leave of absence, it is customary to suspend WAGES.

Leave of court. Permission of a COURT to take a particular action, without which the action would not be permissible.

Leaving scene of accident. Departing the site where an accident has taken place without first fulfilling one's obligations; this is what is done by the *hit and run driver*. It is a criminal act to leave the scene of an ACCIDENT in which one is involved.

Legacy. A gift granted in a WILL; a BEQUEST.

Legacy, absolute. A LEGACY without conditions.

Legacy, accumulative. An additional BEQUEST, granted by the same WILL or by another will.

Legacy, additional. A second or third LEGACY to a LEGATEE, contained in the same WILL or in a CODICIL contained in the will.

Legacy, alternate. A LEGACY that gives one of two or more things, without specifying which one or ones.

Legacy, conditional. A LEGACY that grants a BEQUEST provided certain things are done at some time in the future. If these things are not done, the bequest will not be granted.

Legacy, contingent. A LEGACY that may or may not take place at some time in the future.

Legacy, demonstrative. A BEQUEST of money that is designated from a specified fund.

Legacy, general. A BEQUEST of money taken from the general funds of the TESTATOR (the person who made the WILL).

Legacy, lapsed. A situation in which the LEGATEE (the person who is named to receive a BEQUEST) dies before the TESTATOR (the person who has made the WILL).

Legacy, pecuniary. A BEQUEST of money.

Legacy, residuary. A BEQUEST of all the rest of an ESTATE, after particular grants and bequests have been executed (carried out).

Legacy, specific. A BEQUEST of a specifically designated PROPERTY, such as a particular piece of jewelry, a painting, a parcel of land, etcetera.

Legacy, trust. A LEGACY to a TRUSTEE or trustees to be held in

TRUST, with the income earned from such a trust to go to specifically named BENEFICIARIES.

Legacy, universal. A WILL leaving all of the deceased person's ASSETS and ESTATE to one or more persons specified in the WILL.

Legal. According to the LAW; conforming to existing laws; lawful; the opposite of illegal.

Legal acumen. A PRINCIPLE stating that if a defect in a CLAIM to land is of such a nature that it requires legal skill and unusually keen insight to discover it, then the POWERS of a COURT OF EQUITY can be called upon to remove the "cloud" on the title.
> CLOUD ON TITLE.

Legal age. **1.** The age at which a person becomes old enough to transact business himself, such as making CONTRACTS, signing DOCUMENTS, etcetera; the age at which a person is considered an adult. Since the voting age has been lowered from 21 to 18 years, many states now consider 18 as a legal age. **2.** The legal age at which one could marry without parental consent used to be 21 years for a male and 18 years for a female. However, this age is now lower for both sexes in many states.

Legal aid society. A nonprofit organization that supplies legal help to those too poor to pay for it themselves.

Legal assets. That portion of a deceased person's ESTATE that is liable for the payment of DEBTS and for the payment of specified LEGACIES.

Legal assistants. PARALEGAL personnel; people who assist lawyers in their work, such as doing research, etcetera.

Legal cause. The real CAUSE of an INJURY or ACCIDENT; the IMMEDIATE CAUSE; the PROXIMATE CAUSE.

Legal consideration. Something legally sufficient to make a CONTRACT binding.

Legal counsel. **1.** The services rendered by an ATTORNEY. **2.** An attorney.

Legal cruelty. Cruelty of such a nature as to form the basis for DIVORCE. Conduct of a married person that repeatedly threatens the physical and psychological well-being of a spouse.

Legal defense counsel. An ATTORNEY who protects and attempts to ACQUIT a DEFENDANT in a LAWSUIT.

Legal dependent. An individual that one is obliged, by LAW, to support.

Legal detriment. A situation in which a person to whom a PROMISE has been made changes his position in a matter so that he assumes LIABILITIES not previously imposed upon him.

Legal duty. A DUTY that the LAW requires to be done.

Legal entity. An organization recognized by the LAW, such as a CORPORATION or a PARTNERSHIP.

Legal ethics. The code set up by members of the legal profession, detailing their moral and professional DUTIES toward CLIENTS and toward one another. Also, the OBLIGATIONS of ATTORNEYS toward the public and to the

COURTS. Violations of legal ethics are censurable by the BAR ASSOCIATIONS.

Legal evidence. TESTIMONY that is permitted to be presented during a TRIAL in the belief that such EVIDENCE will help to prove the FACTS in the matter in DISPUTE.

Legal fee. The money charged by an ATTORNEY for services rendered to a CLIENT.

Legal fraud. Actions that have a tendency to deceive and mislead, even though such actions may not have originated with a conscious intent to deceive and commit FRAUD.

Legal heirs. The nearest of kin; those entitled to inherit because they are the natural HEIRS and DESCENDANTS of the deceased person.

Legal insanity. Mental illness and incapacity of such a degree that the LAW recognizes it and frees the "insane" person from the responsibilities of someone in possession of his mental faculties. Thus, a legally insane person in a criminal case is committed to a mental institution rather than ordered to stand TRIAL.

Legal interest. The INTEREST that one is legally permitted to charge for a LOAN; interest charged in excess is USURY and is considered to be illegal, as a loan made by a LOAN SHARK.

Legal issue. Descendants; same as LAWFUL ISSUE.

Legal jeopardy. **1.** A situation in which an individual is brought to TRIAL and is in a position where he may be CONVICTED and found GUILTY. **2.** Also used as a term synonymous with DOUBLE JEOPARDY or PRIOR JEOPARDY, a situation in which an individual is tried more than once for the same OFFENSE. ≫ FORMER JEOPARDY; IN JEOPARDY.

Legal liability. The responsibility that two opposing parties in a LAWSUIT have toward each other, as recognized and enforced by the COURT.

Legal malice. The intentional performance of a wrongful act, without cause or provocation; constructive MALICE; malice in LAW.

Legal name. One given, or first, name and one family, or second, name. The possession of a middle name or names, or of middle initial or initials, is IMMATERIAL. The first name is also known as the *Christian* name; the second or family name is the *surname.*

Legal notice. Notice that conforms to the requirements of the LAW, as applied to any specific CASE.

Legal obligation. A DUTY or OBLIGATION that can be enforced by a COURT OF LAW; a DEBT; the legal responsibility to carry out what the law requires.

Legal proceeding. An ACTION taking place in COURT.

Legal process. > PROCESS, LEGAL.

Legal rate of interest. The maximum rate that can be charged for a LOAN, as prescribed by LAW. Such rate might vary from state to state.

Legal reporting. In MEDICAL JURISPRUDENCE, physicians and hospitals are required to report criminally inflicted INJURIES to the POLICE. This STATUTE overrides the usual confidential nature of a patient-physician relationship.

Legal representative. EXECUTOR; ADMINISTRATOR; a person who takes care of another's legal matters.

Legal reserve. Funds that INSURANCE companies must, by law, set aside so as to be able to pay CLAIMS against them.

Legal residence. The place where an individual spends most of his time; the home as recognized by LAW; the place from which a person perennially votes. Although a person may have several homes in several states, or foreign countries, only one domicile can be recognized as his legal residence. Usually, it is the place where he spends most of the time during the course of the year.

Legal right. Any PRIVILEGE or RIGHT which, if challenged, would be supported in court.

Legal separation. An AGREEMENT, sanctioned by a COURT, between a husband and wife, detailing the conditions and responsibilities of each while living apart. Such separation agreement will also include provisions for living conditions, visitation rights, and support of MINOR children.

Legal subrogation. The PRINCIPLE stating that when someone has been forced to pay a DEBT which should have been paid by somebody else, he is entitled to use all the REMEDIES the CREDITOR possesses against that other person. In other words, legal subrogation is a device to force the person who really owes the debt to pay it.

Legal tender. Money, whether it is made of paper or metal (coins); the type of money that the LAW recognizes as adequate for the payment of a DEBT. Jewels, property, or art objects, while they may have more value than the amount of money that is owed, are not legal tender.

Legal title. OWNERSHIP to PROPERTY that is recognized as sufficient under the RULES of LAW, as distinguished from a TITLE recognized under rules of EQUITY.

Legalese. A recently coined word describing the complicated, technical language employed in writing LAWS, STATUTES, CONTRACTS, WILLS, and other legal DOCUMENTS.

Legalism. Strict adherence to the letter of the LAW, often implying that heretofore there has not been strict adherence to the spirit of the law.

Legality. A matter or question of agreement or disagreement with the LAW. A matter may be brought into court to establish the legality of an outstanding question.

Legalize. To make something legal that otherwise might be illegal. People who have been living together without being married who register and marry according to the laws of a state, are said to legalize their relationship.

Legalized nuisance. A structure or erection which would ordinarily constitute an illegal NUISANCE (an annoyance or interference with the enjoyment of one's PROPERTY) but which has been declared legal by LAW. The residents of an area may consider the erection of a PRISON in their neighborhood a nuisance, but it is, nevertheless, built there by enactment of a STATUTE permitting such a structure.

Legally adopted. The ADOPTION of a child according to the LAWS of the state.

Legally committed. **1.** Being held by a COURT, as ordered by a JUDGE who has sufficient information to believe that a defendant *might* be GUILTY. **2.** Being placed in a mental institution after two expert physicians have filed papers attesting to a person's mental illness.

Legally competent. Fit and qualified to serve, especially in a capacity provided for by LAW, such as an EXECUTOR or ADMINISTRATOR.

Legally contributing cause. Not the major CAUSE of an INJURY, but one which had an important part to play in it.

Legally determined. Decided by process of LAW.

Legally dead. The same as PRESUMPTION OF DEATH, whereby a person can be declared legally dead when his whereabouts have been unknown for a period of years, usually 7, and all attempts to find him have failed. ➤ ENOCH ARDEN LAWS.

Legally liable. Responsible under LAW.

Legally sufficient evidence. Adequate EVIDENCE presented in a CASE, sufficient to allow the COURT to come in with a decisive VERDICT.

Legally sworn. Being bound by OATH. A person who is legally sworn before giving TESTIMONY swears to tell only the truth.

Legatee. The recipient of a LEGACY; an individual who inherits something.

Legation. **1.** The residence of a foreign minister in a foreign country. **2.** The staff of representatives who carry out their diplomatic functions in a foreign country. Such a staff includes ministers, attachés, secretaries, military aides, etcetera. **3.** An embassy.

Legator. A person who makes a WILL and leaves LEGACIES to HEIRS.

Legislation. **1.** The making of LAWS by a legislative body, such as the Senate, the House of Representatives, the various state and municipal bodies, parliaments, etcetera. **2.** In general terms, the product of any legislative body.

Legislative act. An act that describes and prescribes what the future LAW shall be in cases arising under it; the act of lawmaking.

Legislative intent. A term referring to what the lawmakers really meant when they passed a particular STATUTE or LAW. This is vital when statutes are open to varying interpretations.

Legislative power. The AUTHORITY of that branch of government charged with the responsibility of making and enacting LAWS.

Legislator. A member of a legislative body, such as an assembly, senate, house of representatives, city council, parliament, etcetera.

Legislature. A legislative body. The people who make the laws are members of the legislature.

Legitimate. That which is recognized as LEGAL.

Legitimate child. A child born from parents who are legally married to each other; a child BORN OUT OF WEDLOCK who has acquired legitimacy through LEGITIMATION.

Legitimation. The act of converting an ILLEGITIMATE CHILD into a legitimate one. This is sometimes accomplished by STATUTE, or by the subsequent marriage of the child's parents.

Legitime. That part of a parent's estate that must be inherited by his/her children, unless there is a legal CAUSE not to permit such inheritance.

Lesion. **1.** A disease or injury causing a change in the structure of a bodily organ. **2.** Hurt; INJURY; loss.

Lessee. Someone who LEASES or rents something, such as an apartment or an automobile.

Lesser included offense. A crime of less severity which is, nevertheless, included in the INDICTMENT of a more serious OFFENSE. This is done so that if the accused is acquitted of the more serious offense, he can still be convicted of the lesser offense without a separate TRIAL. An ACCUSED may be charged with both MURDER and MANSLAUGHTER, and if he is acquitted of murder—the more serious offense—he may still be convicted of manslaughter.

Lessor. The person who grants a LEASE to a LESSEE.

Let. **1.** To rent or lease. **2.** To award a contract to one of the bidders, as "to let a contract."

Lethal weapon. An instrument or WEAPON capable of causing DEATH, not necessarily a gun. It may be a knife, a pick, a bludgeon, a rock, etcetera. ⋗ DANGEROUS WEAPON; DEADLY WEAPON.

Letter of credit. A DOCUMENT given to a depositor by a bank. This official bank document authorizes payment of monies to the depositor by another bank or lender of money. When one travels abroad, he may take a letter of credit with him authorizing a bank in a foreign country to pay up to a certain limit of money to him, upon presentation of the letter.

Letter of the law. An expression used to denote the exact, strict interpretation of a STATUTE, ORDINANCE, REGULATION, or LAW.

Letter rogatory. A request from a COURT trying a CASE to a court in another state or in a foreign country, asking that the court take TESTIMONY from a WITNESS residing in the other state or foreign country, and that they forward such testimony to the court that is conducting the TRIAL.

Letters testamentary. Communications from a PROBATE COURT officially recognizing that a person has been designated as the EXECUTOR or ADMINISTRATOR of an ESTATE.

Letting out. Awarding a CONTRACT, such as a contract to perform construction on a building.

Leviable. Something that is subject to a TAX; taxable.

Levy. **1.** A TAX; an ASSESSMENT. **2.** To tax; to assess; to collect upon; to impose, such as a FINE.

Lewd. Indecent; obscene; pornographic; lascivious.

Lewd and lascivious conduct. Continued and repeated behavior of an indecent nature, not meant

to include cohabitation and intercourse out of wedlock.
Lex. The LAW (Latin).
Lex communis. The COMMON LAW (Latin).
Lex loci contractus. The LAW of the place where a CONTRACT was made (Latin).
Lex loci delicti. The LAW of the place where the wrong was committed (Latin).
Lex non scripta. The unwritten or COMMON LAW; LAW originating from custom and usage (Latin).
Lex scripta. Written LAW; STATUTE law; law originating from legislative enactments (Latin). Opposite of LEX NON SCRIPTA.
Lex terrae. The LAW OF THE LAND (Latin).
Liability. Legal responsibility; the OBLIGATION to do or not do something; an obligation to pay a DEBT; the responsibility to behave in a certain manner.
Libel. Any STATEMENT in print maliciously attacking someone, thus inflicting damage to his reputation, causing him humiliation, and exposing him to public ridicule. Also, statements that defame the memory of someone who is dead. > DEFAMATION OF CHARACTER; DEFAMATION OF THE DEAD.
Libelous. Defamatory; maliciously expressed STATEMENTS tending to injure someone's reputation.
Libelous per quod. STATEMENTS that are made or printed which appear to be slanderous and injurious, but which must be proved to be so. Also, statements that do not appear on the surface to be defamatory but which, in a legal SUIT, can be proved to be so.
Libelous per se. Publication of written material that must, by the very nature of the STATEMENTS, cause INJURY to the person against whom it is directed.
Liberal construction. The interpretation of a LAW OF CONTRACT in a manner so as to discover its true meaning, without quibbling over or arguing about its words, and without adhering to a strict interpretation of its words and phrases. Liberal construction of the UNITED STATES CONSTITUTION sticks to the major intent of its provisions and disregards strict interpretations of its words and phrases. ➤ LITERAL CONSTRUCTION.
Libertarian. A person who advocates great freedom in regard to social conduct and thought.
Liberties. The basic PRIVILEGES and RIGHTS of all Americans, as guaranteed by the UNITED STATES CONSTITUTION and its Amendments. *Indecent liberties* are those that society would judge as immoral and improper, especially sexual liberties.
Libertine. An individual who is sexually and morally unrestrained.
Liberty. Freedom from body and mind control; freedom from restraints; the ability to enjoy, without interruption or interference, the fundamental RIGHTS of every citizen, as guaranteed by the UNITED STATES CONSTITUTION and its Amendments.
License. 1. A RIGHT granted by one person (or COMPANY) to an-

other giving permission to the other person to do something that he could not legally do without such permission. The person granting the right is the LICENSOR; the one receiving the right is the LICENSEE. **2.** Unrestrained conduct, as the LICENSE to act in a certain manner. **3.** A special PRIVILEGE, such as a license to pilot a plane or drive an automobile, granted after qualifying by meeting certain specified tests.

License fee. A charge for issuing a LICENSE; a license TAX.

License tax. > LICENSE FEE.

Licensee. One who is granted a license.

Licensor. Someone who grants a LICENSE.

Licentious. Unrestrained by LAW or by acceptable moral codes; lewd; arbitrary; exceeding proper and customary bounds. The term is used in describing a person's habitual behavior.

Licentiousness. A mode of CONDUCT in which one indulges himself in whatever he wants to do, without regard for others.

Lien. A claim on another's PROPERTY.

Lienee. Someone whose PROPERTY is subject to a CLAIM.

Lienor. The individual who owns a LIEN.

Lieu. Instead of (French).

Life annuity. An INSURANCE AGREEMENT or CONTRACT in which the policy holder receives a certain sum of money each year for the rest of his life.

Life expectancy. The number of years that a person in relatively good health, and of a particular age, can expect to live, according to recognized mortality statistics. Life expectancy tables are published by many of the large life insurance companies and are statistically most reliable.

Life interest. An INTEREST in PROPERTY that persists for one's entire lifetime. However, life interest does not constitute OWNERSHIP.

Life of a writ. The period of time that a WRIT (a COURT ORDER) remains effective. At the expiration of a writ, another writ may be issued.

Life or limb. An expression meaning that no person shall be put in JEOPARDY, that is, in danger to life or limb, a second time for the same OFFENSE.

Life policy. A life insurance policy wherein an insurance company agrees to pay a certain sum of money upon the DEATH of the policy holder. > INSURANCE, LIFE.

Like benefits. Similar BENEFITS.

Limit. The extent of; the boundary of; the point beyond which there is no OBLIGATION, such as the limit of LIABILITY that an insurance company assumes.

Limitation. A limit; a restriction; a specified period of time during which a LITIGATION can take place and after that period, the STATUTE OF LIMITATIONS has expired; a time limit.

Limitation title. Full and claim-free TITLE.

Limited appeal. An APPEAL from a specific part of a DECREE or JUDGMENT, not from the entire decree.

Limited authority. POWER and AUTHORITY restricted to certain specified functions, duties, and acts, as opposed to unlimited authority.

Limited company. 1. A business enterprise restricted to specified joint ventures, as opposed to a general partnership. > PARTNERSHIP, GENERAL. **2.** A CORPORATION whose SHAREHOLDERS are liable only for the amount of money they have invested. In countries of the British Commonwealth, "Ltd." after a firm's name indicates that it is a limited company, or corporation.

Limited guaranty. A GUARANTY restricted to one TRANSACTION; a guaranty that limits the extent of CREDIT that will be granted.

Limited jurisdiction. The JURISDICTION or AUTHORITY of a lower court, as distinguished from the more general and greater jurisdiction of higher courts.

Limited liability. Restricted LIABILITY, as the responsibilities of SHAREHOLDERS of a CORPORATION (stock company).

Limited partnership. A financial agreement under which a contributor to a PARTNERSHIP is liable, if the company should fail, only for the sum of money he invested. (Other partners in the same enterprise, however, may not be *limited partners* but are general partners and have much greater obligations and liabilities.)

Line of credit. The maximum amount of CREDIT a bank or businessman will give to a customer.

Line of descent. > LINEAL DESCENT.

Lineal consanguinity. The blood relationship that exists between people who descend in a straight line, as son, father, grandfather.

Lineal descent. A descent in a direct line, such as grandfather, son, and grandson. Lineal descent is legally important when someone dies without leaving a WILL (INTESTATE).

Lineup. A PROCEDURE used by the POLICE wherein a WITNESS or victim of a crime attempts to identify a suspect from a group of people standing in a line. Also called a POLICE LINEUP.

Liquid assets. Monies, PROPERTIES, SECURITIES, etcetera, that can be made readily available for payment of a DEBT or debts.

Liquidated. Paid, settled; wound up, as a COMPANY that has gone out of business.

Liquidated account. An ACCOUNT in which the amount of money is fixed and agreed upon by the PARTIES or is fixed by LAW.

Liquidated debt. 1. A DEBT, the amount of which is fixed and certain. **2.** A DEBT that has been paid.

Liquidated demand. A DEMAND in which the amount has been agreed upon.

Liquidation. Winding up a business' affairs; the payment of a DEBT, thus ending an OBLIGATION.

Literacy test. A test of a person's ability to read and write, usually given to one who is attempting to qualify as a voter.

Literal construction. An interpretation of law that is according to the letter and is strict and narrow, as opposed to a LIBERAL CONSTRUCTION. A term often applied to the interpretation of the UNITED STATES CONSTITUTION. ≫ NARROW CONSTRUCTION.

Literal proof. PROOF offered in the form of written EVIDENCE.

Literary property. A manuscript that is to be published or has been published, the rights to which are owned by the author and/or publisher and the earnings from which go to the publisher and author.

Litigant. A person engaged in a LAWSUIT; a PLAINTIFF or DEFENDANT.

Litigation. A LAWSUIT; a legal ACTION; a SUIT.

Litigious. 1. A matter that is the subject of CONTENTION, such as a *litigious right.* **2.** Eager to enter into a LAWSUIT; prone to SUE.

Living trust. A TRUST that is in effect while the maker of the trust is still alive, as opposed to a trust set up by a WILL. Also known as an INTER VIVOS TRUST.

Loan certificate. A CERTIFICATE issued by a CLEARINGHOUSE to one of its associated banks. Such loan certificates may total as much as 75 percent of the collateral deposited by the associated bank.

Loan on life insurance policy. An advance made by an insurance company to an insured person, such monies to be deducted from the amount that will eventually be paid by the insurance company. If the LOAN is repaid, the policy resumes its full OBLIGATION to the insured person.

Loan shark. A usurer; someone who lends money and charges more INTEREST than the LAW allows. ≫ USURY.

Lobbying. The practice of attempting to influence LEGISLATION in favor of special-interest groups, frequently done by soliciting members of LEGISLATURES.

Lobbyist. Someone whose occupation includes attempts to influence LEGISLATORS to vote in favor of certain LEGISLATION.

Local law. LAW whose application is limited to certain restricted areas, such as MUNICIPAL ORDINANCES.

Local option. A PRIVILEGE granted to a local area, such as a town, city, or county, to pass a LOCAL LAW.

Locality. A COMMUNITY; a neighborhood; a vicinity; a geographic area.

Locality rule. In MEDICAL JURISPRUDENCE, a physician is expected to maintain the standards of other physicians who practice in the same community or locality.

Locative calls. Landmarks marking the BOUNDARIES of a piece of PROPERTY, such landmarks having been placed after the property has been surveyed.

Locking up a jury. Keeping a JURY out of touch with everyone during its consideration of a case. This is done so as not to expose it to the influence of the media or to people, other than fellow JURORS, who might try to influence their thinking.

Lockout. An employer's dismissal of employees because of a labor DISPUTE, such lockout resulting in the closing of the plant.

Locus criminis. The place where a crime was committed (Latin).

Lodging a complaint. Making a COMPLAINT.

Logrolling. **1.** A practice whereby one LEGISLATOR will vote for a BILL sponsored by another legislator, in return for which the other legislator votes for a bill his colleague is sponsoring. **2.** The inclusion of extraneous provisions to a pending bill in order to gain passage. In other words, the inclusion of these unrelated provisions will gain the affirmative votes of legislators who would not have otherwise voted for the measure.

Loiter. To idle; to lounge in a public place, doing nothing. The term implies that the loiterers are interfering with the activities in the area where they are idling.

Long-arm statute. A LAW of a state giving its COURT JURISDICTION over PROPERTY or persons outside the state.

Lookout. **1.** In maritime matters, a lookout is someone whose function is to see that navigation is unimpeded, clear, and safe. **2.** In criminal terms, a lookout is an accomplice of criminals who watches to see whether the police are approaching.

Loss of citizenship. Being deprived of citizenship for having given false information when applying for citizenship, such as not reporting a criminal conviction.

Loss of right to vote. Taking away of the voting RIGHTS of someone who has been convicted of a major criminal act, such as MURDER or TREASON, or a dishonorable discharge from the military.

Loss of use. In COMPENSATION law, the loss of use of an organ or part of the body such as a finger, hand, leg, etcetera. Such loss may be partial or total.

Lower court. A trial court, or one from which an APPEAL may be taken, as distinguished from a court from which no appeal can be taken; an inferior court.

Lucid interval. A period during which an otherwise irrational or mentally unbalanced person acts sensibly and rationally. This is characteristic of many forms of PSYCHOSIS, the symptoms and signs of which are intermittent.

Lump sum payment. A one-time payment, as opposed to payments made in installments.
> INSTALLMENT PLAN.

Lump sum settlement. A SETTLEMENT based upon the payment of one lump sum, instead of an existing arrangement wherein payments are being made periodically.

Lunacy. INSANITY; PSYCHOSIS; impairment of mental faculties to a point where someone is acting irrationally.

Lying in wait. Concealing oneself so as to take a victim by surprise; ambushing for the purpose of inflicting bodily harm.

Lynch law. The illegal taking of the LAW into one's hands for the purpose of lynching a suspected criminal. Such actions are almost invariably mob actions, taken outside the law.

Machination. The act of scheming and planning to do something, usually for some evil purpose.
Magisterial. Relating to the duties of a MAGISTRATE.
Magistrate. 1. A judge of a LOWER COURT; a JUSTICE OF THE PEACE. The duties of a magistrate include trying MISDEMEANORS and hearing EVIDENCE in more serious CASES. **2.** In broader terms, a magistrate is someone charged with administration of the LAW. For example, a governor is the chief magistrate of the state in which he serves.
Magna Carta. The Great Charter (Latin). The charter was propounded in England in 1215 A.D. and forms the basis of the English system of constitutional law and liberty. Much of American law is based upon principles contained in Magna Carta.
Maidenhead. The HYMEN; the unruptured membrane covering the entrance to the vagina. An intact maidenhead signifies that a female is a virgin.
Maim. To cripple; to INJURE so as to deprive someone of the use of part or all of a limb; to mutilate.
Maintain an action. To keep a LAWSUIT going until its final conclusion.
Majority. 1. The major portion of; more than one-half. **2.** The age at which someone is legally regarded as an adult, and therefore able to consummate a contract, vote, and marry without parental consent. > MINORITY.
Majority opinion. The DECISION of more than one-half of the JUDGES hearing and trying a case. > DISSENTING OPINION.
Majority rule. The DECISION and RULE of more than one-half of those who vote, disregarding the choice of those who do not vote.
Mala fides. In bad faith (Latin).
Maladministration. Bad ADMINISTRATION; misadministration. The term is often applied to the efforts of a public OFFICER who is thought to be doing a bad job in performing his duties. > MALCONDUCT.
Malconduct. Misconduct; maladministration; dishonest behavior, such as a public officer accepting a bribe.
Malefaction. A crime; a criminal OFFENSE.
Malefactor. A person who has been CONVICTED of a crime; a criminal.
Malfeasance. The perpetration of an unlawful act. (A public officer who commits a wrongful act or acts is said to be guilty of *malfeasance in office.*) > MISCONDUCT, MISFEASANCE.
Malice. Hatred; ill will; the intentional carrying out of a hurtful act without cause; hostility of one individual toward another. > MALICE IN LAW.
Malice aforethought. With planned MALICE. The term is often used in an INDICTMENT.

Malice in law. The intentional carrying out of an injurious, harmful act without CAUSE or justification.
Malicious. With hurtful intent; with MALICE.
Malicious abandonment. Desertion by a spouse without JUST CAUSE.
Malicious act. An intentionally wrongful act.
Malicious arrest. An ARREST intentionally made on the basis of false charges.
Malicious injury. A hurt arising from hate, jealousy, or spitefulness, carried out intentionally.
Malicious mischief. Purposeful destruction of another person's PROPERTY.
Malicious prosecution. A LAWSUIT begun out of MALICE in order to upset the DEFENDANT, usually started with full knowledge that the action will fail.
Malinger. To pretend that one is sick, in order to avoid work or the performance of some other obligation or duty.
Malpractice. Professional MISCONDUCT; immoral behavior in the performance of one's professional duties; neglect of one's duties toward a client by an attorney, or toward a patient by a physician; unusual lack of skill in the performance of one's professional activities.
Malpractice insurance. INSURANCE taken out against possible MALPRACTICE suits. Such insurance policies are issued to attorneys, physicians, dentists, and other professionals.
Managing agent. A person or agency representing the PRINCIPALS in the management of a company.
Mandamus. "We command" (Latin). A WRIT originating from a court of higher JURISDICTION and handed down to a LOWER COURT, ordering a certain thing to be done. Also, an order of a COURT to a CORPORATION or COMPANY, or one or more of its OFFICERS, or to a municipal corporation or a judicial officer, commanding the performance of a particular act.
Mandate. An ORDER or COMMAND (oral or written) that must be obeyed; a judicial command directing ENFORCEMENT of the court's decision.
Mandatory. Compulsory; something one *must* do; not a matter to be acted upon only if one wishes to; obligatory.
Mandatory injunction. An INJUNCTION that impels the recipient to take some specific action to change existing conditions and restore things to the way they were.
Mandatory statute. A LAW that demands compliance and leaves nothing to DISCRETION.
Mania. Mental illness associated with violence, obsessions, or periods of uncontrolled excitement.
Manic-depressive psychosis. A form of mental illness in which there are prolonged periods of great excitement and of great depression; *manic-depressive state.*
Manifest. Obvious; discernible; evident to one's understanding and to one's senses; unmistakable; clear.
Manifesto. A written declaration, published and spread among the peoples of a nation, stating the

reasons for a particular act, such as a declaration of war.

Mann Act. A federal LAW making it unlawful to transport a female across state lines or to a foreign country for purposes of engaging in such activities as prostitution, immoral sex, etcetera. Also known as the White Slave Traffic Act.

Manslaughter. The killing of a person without DELIBERATION, planning, or PREMEDITATION, but during the commission of some illegal, unlawful act. Manslaughter may be voluntary or involuntary, and often is carried out in the heat of the moment. Manslaughter differs from MURDER in that MALICE and premeditation appear to be lacking, these two elements being present in murder. > VOLUNTARY MANSLAUGHTER; INVOLUNTARY MANSLAUGHTER.

Mantrap. A mechanical device to entrap trespassers.

Manual labor. Physical labor, as distinguished from professional or nonphysical labor.

Marauders. Bandits and other lawless people who make it a practice to engage in felonious crimes such as ROBBERY, PLUNDER, and MURDER.

Margin. The actual amount of money one must pay toward the purchase of a STOCK when buying on margin. Such sum is only part of the total cost of the security, with the broker having the right to receive the balance should the value of the stock decline markedly.

Marine insurance. INSURANCE against loss of a ship or its cargo.

Marital deduction. The amount of money a wife or husband can inherit without paying ESTATE TAXES. For federal tax purposes, such deduction is equal to no more than one-half of the gross estate.

Marital share. That portion of a spouse's estate to which a husband or wife is entitled.

Maritime contract. A CONTRACT having to do with business transacted on navigable waters, especially concerned with the preservation of a ship and its crew.

Maritime law. That branch of the law dealing with NAVIGATION and COMMERCE transacted on the waters and the seas. It also relates to laws governing harbors, seamen, duties and rights of ship masters, cargoes, freights, salvage of ships, etcetera.

Maritime tort. A TORT (a civil wrong) committed at sea.

Mark for identification. A phrase often used when an EXHIBIT is produced in a TRIAL and the court clerk is asked to mark the material with a number or letter so that it may be recognized and identified.

Market price. The price at which a seller is willing to sell and a buyer is willing to buy.

Marriage. A contractual arrangement between a woman and man that they shall live together as wife and husband. The proof of such a union is usually certified by registering a MARRIAGE CERTIFICATE in a public hall of records.

Marriage certificate. A DOCUMENT that is EXECUTED (signed) by the person performing the marriage ceremony. It is *not* the same as a MARRIAGE LICENSE.

Marriage license. A DOCUMENT that is EXECUTED by a PUBLIC AUTHORITY, giving permission for a couple to marry. The marriage license is then submitted to the magistrate or member of the clergy who will perform the marriage ceremony. (The person performing the marriage ceremony must be authorized to do so by state law.)

Marriage settlement. A written AGREEMENT in which one spouse details the PROPERTY that will go to the other spouse. Such a settlement may be made prior to a MARRIAGE or during the marriage, or it may provide for the disposition of property after a spouse dies or the marriage is dissolved through separation or divorce.

Marshal. An OFFICER of the court, whose duties consist of carrying out the court's ORDERS, DECISIONS, and JUDGMENTS. Marshals may be federal, state, city, or county officers; they have much the same jobs as SHERIFFS or CONSTABLES.

Marshaling assets. The placing of ASSETS in order of value, so that they can be distributed fairly among those claiming them (CREDITORS).

Martial law. LAW that prevails during an emergency, in which the military assumes governmental controls and duties in a time of crisis.

Mass picketing. The use of large numbers of pickets to demonstrate outside the premises of a plant, factory, or other organization that is on strike. > PICKETING.

Master of the ship. The captain of a ship; the chief commanding officer of a ship.

Master-servant rule. In law, it is called *respondeat superior* (Latin), which means that the master (employer) must answer for the actions of his servant (employee).

Material allegation. A vital portion of a CASE, without which there is no case. A material allegation may be a major part of the PLAINTIFF'S claim against a DEFENDANT, or it may be a major part of the defendant's DEFENSE against the plaintiff's ACCUSATION.

Material evidence. Legitimate, pertinent EVIDENCE; evidence that is so important and so related to the issues being disputed that a judge or JURY may consider it as the vital, decisive factor in the CASE.

Material fact. **1.** A FACT that is essential to a case, either to the PLAINTIFF or DEFENDANT.
2. The fundamental reason for a CONTRACT.

Material fraud. Deceit or trickery that convinces someone to enter into a CONTRACT or AGREEMENT that he would never have entered into had there been no FRAUD.

Material witness. A WITNESS who can supply information that no one else can supply. In some CRIMINAL CASES, a material witness is so important to the PROSECUTION that he or she is held by the authorities until TESTIMONY has been given.

Maternity. Motherhood; the state of being a mother.

Matricide. The killing of one's mother.

Matter. The subject of a legal DISPUTE or LAWSUIT; the substance of the issues being litigated; the FACTS that go into the PROSECUTION or DEFENSE of a CLAIM.
Matter of fact. Phrase used to describe an undecided issue that can be answered by the TESTIMONY of reliable WITNESSES.
Matter of law. Phrase used to describe an undecided issue that can be answered by applying the LAW to the FACTS in the case.
Matter of record. Some DECISION or MATTER that has been written down in the records of a court and is there for anyone to see and examine. In a matter of record, one can prove the existence of something merely by checking the court record.
Matter of substance. A MATTER in which material goes to the very essence of an issue, as opposed to a matter of form, which is concerned merely with the technical aspects of the manner in which an issue is presented and discussed.
Maturity. 1. The end of the time period agreed upon for a LOAN or OBLIGATION, after which time the loan or obligation is due and must be paid. **2.** The attainment of adulthood. A child is said to reach maturity when he or she attains 18 or 21 years of age.
> MAJORITY; LEGAL AGE.
Maxims. PRINCIPLES and RULES generally recognized and accepted because they have been in use and have proved to be fair and reasonable over long periods of time.
Mayhem. The purposeful infliction of BODILY HARM to another, sometimes resulting in a disabling or disfiguring injury. Someone commits mayhem when he intentionally assaults another person.
> MALICIOUS INJURY.
Mayor. The head of a city government; the person who is responsible for the administration of a municipality. (In Hawaii, a mayor is the executive head of one of the state's counties.)
Measure of damages. The rules governing the determination of the amount of money a PLAINTIFF is entitled to in a given case.
Measure of value. A relative value; the measure of the value of something in comparison with the worth of other things.
Mechanic's lien. A CLAIM on a building, or the land it is built on, by someone who has constructed or repaired the building and has not been paid for his work.
Mediation. The settlement of DISPUTES between two parties by the intervention of a third PARTY, who acts impartially and attempts to reconcile differences. This third party is known as a mediator.
> ARBITRATION.
Medicaid. A program of hospital and medical INSURANCE for low-income and poor people, financed by federal, state, and local funds.
Medical evidence. TESTIMONY given by physicians, usually as EXPERT WITNESSES, in a suit.
Medical examiner 1. A coroner; a public medical officer. A physician is appointed to this position by a local GOVERNMENT. Duties of the medical examiner include the determination of the causes of death when the causes are obscure or are thought to be due to violence or an accident. **2.** A physician employed by an insurance

company to examine applicants for life insurance and determine their insurability.

Medical jurisprudence. The branch of medicine that concerns itself with questions of law; MEDICOLEGAL matters.

Medical records. Written material about the patient, including office and hospital charts, X rays, laboratory data, etcetera, detailing a patient's medical history and past and present illnesses. Medical records are the property of the physician or hospital, *not* the patient. However, medical records are subject to subpoena in cases involving medicolegal matters.
≫ HOSPITAL RECORDS.

Medical records, release of. MEDICAL RECORDS consist of confidential information and cannot be released without the patient's consent, or the consent of a parent or guardian if the patient is a minor. However, in a MEDICOLEGAL court ACTION, medical records are subject to SUBPOENA.

Medicare. A federally funded social security program providing hospital and medical INSURANCE for citizens over 65 years of age and for some totally disabled people under 65 years of age. The federal government pays most of the costs, with the Medicare recipient paying just a small portion of the total costs.

Medicolegal. Concerning both medicine and the law. A MALPRACTICE suit against a physician is a medicolegal matter.

Meeting. The gathering together of a group of people to discuss matters in which they share common interest; an assembly; a convention.

Meeting of minds. The conclusion of an AGREEMENT or CONTRACT after each participant has fully expressed himself and made known his thinking.

Megalomania. A mental illness in which the patient has delusions that he is someone of great importance.

Melancholia. A mental illness in which the patient is deeply depressed and melancholy. Such a state is often conducive to suicide.

Melioration. Improvement; betterment. Someone who improves substantially another's property is entitled to compensation for having made such meliorations.

Membership corporation. A not-for-profit corporation; a nonprofit company, such as the American Red Cross.

Memorandum. A written NOTE, usually recorded so that one is reminded to do something. (In Latin, memorandum means "to be remembered.")

Memorandum articles. The CARGO or goods specifically covered by INSURANCE during a particular voyage of a ship. Unless these articles are listed, they will not be insured by the underwriter.

Memorandum of association. The written DOCUMENT by which a corporation is formed and organized, under the corporation laws of the state; ARTICLES OF INCORPORATION.

Memorandum of understanding. A written NOTE detailing the points upon which two or more people are agreed.

Mental anguish. Fear; severe anxiety; grief; intense fright; the mental distress caused by a physical injury.

Mental competence. A state in which one is in possession of one's mental faculties and capable of the usual normal ability to express oneself. A mentally competent person recognizes right from wrong, is well-oriented, and is able to stand TRIAL or to serve as a WITNESS.

Mental cruelty. Behavior of one spouse to the other, causing danger to emotional and physical health. Mental cruelty is usually repeated or continuous, and does not consist of just one episode of cruelty. In some states, mental cruelty serves as GROUNDS FOR DIVORCE.

Mental defect. A cerebral deficiency; an inadequacy of thought processes. (Someone with a mental defect cannot serve as a JUROR.)

Mental illness. A disorder of the mind, whether of physical or emotional origin.

Mental incompetence. The opposite of MENTAL COMPETENCE.

Mental reservation. An unexpressed thought about a CONTRACT, held by one of the parties to the contract. This RESERVATION may be used as an excuse not to carry out fully all the provisions of the contract. In this sense, a mental reservation is not completely frank or honest.

Mercantile law. The RULES and REGULATIONS by which merchants deal with one another and carry out their transactions; COMMERCIAL LAW. Mercantile law is frequently governed by custom and usage, although some mercantile law may be governed by STATUTES and legal regulations.

Merchant seamen. Employees who work on privately owned ships, as distinguished from those who work on Navy or government-owned vessels.

Mercy killing. Terminating someone's life in order to end pain and suffering. Such KILLINGS are forbidden by LAW.

Meretricious. Sexually immoral; lewd; acting in a deceptive manner; tawdry.

Meretricious union. The living together in a supposedly married state of a couple who cannot legally be married to each other, usually because one or both parties is still married to another person, or because one party is not of a legal age to marry, etcetera.

Merger. 1. The joining together of two or more companies or corporations into one organization. 2. The uniting of two alleged OFFENSES into one ACTION. As a consequence, the defendant must defend himself against both charges.

Meritorious. Having legal worth, as a meritorious defense.

Merits. The significant ISSUES in a lawsuit. A JUDGMENT "on the merits" is a decision based upon all the EVIDENCE in a case.

Mesne. Between two opposites; intermediate; things that take place in between the beginning and the end, such as court orders that occur between the beginning and the end of a suit.

Mexican divorce. A DIVORCE decree obtained in Mexico, often very quickly. In some states, a Mexican divorce is recognized; in others it is not. (In former usage, the term Mexican divorce was used to describe any divorce obtained through the mails, without the appearance of the parties in person. This was also a "mail-order divorce.")
Middleman. A businessman who buys directly from the manufacturer and then sells to the consumer. He makes his living by "marking up" the wholesale price he paid the manufacturer and charging the consumer the higher retail price.
Military court. A COURT that investigates and conducts TRIALS of offenders who are in military service and are accused of having committed military OFFENSES. Such trials are called COURT-MARTIALS.
Military jurisdiction. The authority of MILITARY LAW falls into four categories: (1) when the United States is at peace or in war; (2) when the United States is engaged in a war outside its boundaries; (3) when there is rebellion within the United States; and (4) when the United States is invaded by a foreign country. Military jurisdiction is outlined in the UNITED STATES CONSTITUTION.
Military law. The law that governs the conduct of personnel in the military services. (It contains many RULES and REGULATIONS that differ markedly from CIVIL LAW.)
Military offenses. OFFENSES that take place entirely within the military service, such as absence without leave, desertion, sleeping on duty, insubordination, etcetera.
Militia. A group of citizens who can be called to active military duty in an acute crisis, to serve just for the duration of the crisis. The militia may be called to quell a RIOT or insurrection, or to protect property from being looted after a flood or earthquake, etcetera.
Mineral deed. A DOCUMENT transferring an owner's interest in minerals lying beneath the land he owns. In a sense, he no longer owns what lies under the surface of his PROPERTY.
Mineral lease. The granting of the RIGHT to mine one's PROPERTY, with the understanding that a specified ROYALTY will be paid if certain minerals are found and mined.
Mineral right. A RIGHT to take minerals from a certain area of ground, or the right to receive a ROYALTY resulting from the sale of minerals from this area.
Minimum charge. A base rate that a person is charged for the use of a UTILITY, such as a telephone or electricity, whether or not the utility is used.
Minimum sentence. The shortest jail term permitted by law for the commission of a particular crime.
Minimum wage laws. Federal STATUTES fixing the least amount of money that can be paid a worker for an hour's work.
Mining claim. A CLAIM involving the APPROPRIATION of public land upon which, or under which, minerals exist, the land having

been appropriated by private individuals who are acting according to law. Consequently, the minerals that are found belong to the prospector who has mined them.

Minister plenipotentiary. A diplomatic envoy with full power to carry out certain functions, second only in authority to an ambassador.

Ministerial duty. A specified duty carried out by a person in a public position. Such duty leaves nothing to the discretion of the minister.

Ministerial officer. An OFFICER whose duties are specifically prescribed by superiors, leaving nothing to judgment or DISCRETION.

Ministerial powers. The powers of a TRUSTEE or MINISTER that are detailed and specific, leaving nothing to DISCRETION.

Minor. A male or female who is under the age of legal COMPETENCE and RIGHTS, usually considered to be 21 years old but now frequently regarded as 18 years; a person too young to make a legal CONTRACT.
> LEGAL AGE.

Minor fact. An unimportant finding, fact, or circumstance in a case.

Minority. **1.** The state of being a child or youth who is less than the legal age. **2.** Less than one-half, especially when referring to the votes of people attempting to solve an issue. The opposite of MAJORITY.

Minors, medical treatment of. Underage individuals must receive the consent of parents before undergoing medical or surgical treatment, except in emergencies or in situations where the parent cannot be reached.

Mint. A federal plant where metals are converted into coins.

Minutes. A recording of what takes place during a trial, made by the court clerk, or the record of proceedings of a grand jury, etcetera.

Misadventure. An accident; an unintentional injury inflicted by one person upon another.

Misapprehension. The act of misunderstanding; a mistaken idea.

Misappropriation of funds. The unlawful taking of money entrusted to one's care.

Misbehavior. Unlawful conduct; intentional wrongdoing.

Misbranding. Labeling a product fraudulently so as to imitate another, usually well-known product. Also, stating the wrong amount of a substance, or incorrect ingredients, on the label.

Miscarriage. **1.** Termination of a pregnancy prior to full development or the ability of the fetus to sustain life on its own. **2.** A wrongful act for which the doer can be held liable.

Miscarriage of justice. An unfair DECISION of a court or judge that violates the RIGHTS of a party involved in a lawsuit.

Miscegenation. INTERMARRIAGE or cohabitation of people of different races, formerly unlawful in several states of the United States.
> MIXED MARRIAGE.

Misconduct. Improper behavior; CONDUCT that breaks a LAW or is contrary to established practice.

Misconduct in office. Unlawful behavior of a public OFFICER relating to the duties of the office.

Miscreant. A bad person; a depraved or villainous individual.

Misdemeanor. An OFFENSE of a minor order, less than a FELONY. Misdemeanors may be punishable by imprisonment in a county jail, whereas felonies are punishable by commitment to jail in state or federal penitentiaries. Most misdemeanors, however, are punishable by fines only.

Misdirection. An error by a COURT in instructing or charging a jury. > CHARGE; INSTRUCTION TO THE JURY.

Misfeasance. MISCONDUCT IN OFFICE and performance of unlawful acts while in office (misfeasance in office). ≫ MALFEASANCE.

Misjoinder. The joining in one LAWSUIT of parties or matters not permitted to be so joined, mainly because they lack consistency and the court DECISION will not affect all the parties to the suit in the same manner.

Misleading. Deceiving; calculated to lead people astray and to incorrect conclusions.

Misnomer. The wrong name (used in giving the wrong name to an individual involved in a suit or action); a mistake in designation of a party.

Mispleading. A basic and important error in trying or defending a LAWSUIT.

Misprision of felony. An OFFENSE wherein one fails to notify the authorities that he or she has WITNESSED a crime. In federal law, it is misprision not to report one's knowledge of TREASON or some other offense against the federal government.

Misreading. FRAUD in concluding an AGREEMENT, in which a person pretends to be reading a clause in the written CONTRACT but actually is reading something else. As a consequence the other party to the contract signs something he has not agreed to.

Misrepresentation. A STATEMENT that is untrue and not consistent with the facts. Misrepresentation may be innocent if a person thinks he is telling the truth; it is termed *negligent misrepresentation* if someone fails to find out the truth. Misrepresentation is fraudulent if there is intent to deceive and not tell the truth.

Mistake of fact. An unintentional error in knowing or recalling a FACT, not done with a will to deceive.

Mistake of law. A knowledge of the true FACTS but a mistake in concluding what the legal effect of those facts will be.

Mistaken identity. Phrase used to describe an error in identifying someone, often an accused person who resembles the real wrongdoer.

Mistrial. A TRIAL that a judge cancels while the trial is in progress. A mistrial may be declared because of some fundamental error in PROCEDURE, or because it is discovered that the court lacks JURISDICTION over a case, or because JURORS were selected improperly, or because of some misconduct that prevents a fair trial from continuing, etcetera. Declaration of a mistrial means that a new trial must be held in the same MATTER.

Mitigate. To lessen, as in reducing the punishment of a convicted person or decreasing the amount of DAMAGES a PLAINTIFF may have been awarded. Also, to reduce the charges, such as from first-degree murder to manslaughter, because of extenuating circumstances.

Mitigating circumstances. FACTS that reduce the severity of a CRIME and its punishment.

Mixed marriage. A marriage between people of different races. > MISCEGENATION.

Moderator. An individual who presides over a meeting, usually one in which controversial matters will be debated and decided.

Modification. A change or alteration in matters under discussion and at issue. Modification may take the form of addition or deletion of new elements in the involved issue, but it usually does not change the main thrust of the involved issue or matter under consideration.

Modus operandi. Method of operation (Latin).

Modus vivendi. The mode of living, an expression used in describing the way people work or get along or live together (Latin).

Moiety. One-half of anything.

Molestation. The act of HARASSING or annoying someone. The term is often used to describe the conduct of an adult who makes physical advances toward, or otherwise annoys, a child.

Momentum. Speed of movement; force of movement, as in, "The momentum was so great that the vehicle could not stop before it hit the other vehicle."

Monetary. Referring to money; PECUNIARY.

Money changer. An individual whose business is the exchanging of one kind of currency for another. Such a person earns his living by getting a commission for carrying out this kind of transaction, such as exchanging dollars for francs or pounds, etcetera.

Money had and received. An expression used by a PLAINTIFF claiming that he has given money to a DEFENDANT and that the defendant, in good conscience, should return that money.

Money order. An order for the payment of money, as issued by one post office or bank to another post office or bank. (A person in one city may obtain money from a bank or post office in another city if the bank or post office in the original city issues a money order.)

Monogamy. Marriage to just one person at a time, as opposed to BIGAMY or POLYGAMY, in which a person has two or more spouses at the same time. Bigamy and polygamy are unlawful in the United States.

Monomania. A form of mental illness in which someone focuses on just one irrational idea or group of ideas. The monomaniac may be sane and rational in all other matters.

Monopoly. Total control of a commodity, product, or service in a particular market; a means of doing away with competition. Monopoly is unlawful in a free-enterprise society such as the United States.

Monroe Doctrine. The principle expressed throughout American history that the United States will oppose any European takeover or interference in the political affairs of any government in the western hemisphere. This doctrine was first expressed during the presidency of James Monroe.

Moonlighting. The holding of a second job by a public employee who is supposed to work full time at his public job.

Moorage. A fee charged for the privilege of docking a ship or boat at a marina or wharf. (In essence, garaging a vessel.)

Moot. An open question; something that is debatable; unsettled; a subject for argument.

Moot question. A hypothetical question; a question that cannot be answered by referring to established RIGHTS and FACTS.

Moral. A PRINCIPLE for deciding what is right and what is wrong; virtuous; law abiding; adhering to society's concept of righteousness.

Moral certainty. A conviction or degree of certainty sufficiently strong to justify a conclusion, such as a moral certainty that an accused is guilty. (Moral certainty is somewhat less than *absolute certainty,* although it may be enough to convince someone to reach a firm conclusion.)

Moral coercion. Exerting extreme pressure upon someone to do or not to do something; excessive persuasion.

Moral considerations. CONSIDERATIONS based on moral rather than legal grounds; things that one wants to carry out because they are just and equitable, even though they may not be required by LAW.

Moral duress. Undue influence imposed by one person upon another, taking advantage of the other person's distress or weakness.

Moral evidence. A type of EVIDENCE that tends to support the truth or FACTS without actually establishing these with certainty.

Moral fraud. Deceit that involves a wrong of a moral nature.

Moral law. The law that deals with matters of conscience and concepts of proper and acceptable behavior.

Moral obligation. A duty arising from conscience rather than from any existing law which would force a certain OBLIGATION to be fulfilled.

Moral turpitude. An OFFENSE or CRIME that is not only illegal but demonstrates one's baseness, depravity, and lack of acceptable standards of social behavior.

Moratorium. A suspension of legal OBLIGATIONS and DEBTS; a delay granted in meeting one's debts, usually because of a crisis situation. For example, a debtor may be desperately sick and therefore be granted a moratorium until he recovers and is able to handle his affairs again.

Morgue. A building in which unidentified bodies are held until family or friends come to identify and claim them.

Mortal wound. A fatal wound.

Mortgage. The putting up of land or a building, or both, as SECURITY against a LOAN of money. Should the person who obtains the mortgage fail to pay off the loan as prescribed in the mortgage CONTRACT, the lender will take title and possession to the property. > MORTGAGE, FIRST; MORTGAGE, SECOND.

Mortgage, amortization of. The paying off of indebtedness through regular installments, usually over a period of many years.

Mortgage, chattel. A mortgage on PERSONAL PROPERTY rather than upon REAL ESTATE, in which personal possessions are given as security against a loan.

Mortgage, conventional. A CONTRACT in which a person binds part or all of his PROPERTY to another should he fail to pay off a loan on this property. During the period of paying off the loan (MORTGAGE), the borrower remains in possession of the property.

Mortgage, equitable. A LIEN on property that would be recognized by a COURT OF EQUITY, despite the fact that no legal mortgage exists. An equitable mortgage is based upon a firm AGREEMENT between the lender and the borrower.

Mortgage, first. A LIEN upon PROPERTY that takes precedence over any other lien or claim to the property. A first mortgage must be paid off first, taking precedence over a second mortgage or any other claim against the property. > MORTGAGE, SECOND.

Mortgage, general. A *blanket mortgage,* one that covers all the PROPERTY of the DEBTOR, as opposed to a *special mortgage,* which involves only a specified, limited property.

Mortgage, second. A LIEN or MORTGAGE that ranks beneath a first mortgage on the same property. Until the first mortgage is paid off, nothing is paid to the holder of a second mortgage. > MORTGAGE, FIRST.

Mortgagee. A person or lending institution to whom a MORTGAGE must be paid; in many instances, the mortgagee is a bank.

Mortgagor. The person who mortgages his property.

Mortis causa. In contemplation of death (Latin). Changes in BEQUESTS and in WILLS are sometimes made in expectation of an early death.

Mortuus exitus non est exitus. A Latin phrase used to mean "A child born dead is not considered to be a legal issue entitled to any of the usual rights of an offspring or descendant." (Latin).

Most favored nation clause. A CLAUSE in an AGREEMENT between nations, stating that the representatives of the two countries are entitled to all the RIGHTS and PRIVILEGES granted by them to other nations who hold the most favored positions in existing treaties. In other words, the countries agree to treat each other in the same manner as those countries that they treat best.

Motion. An oral or written application to a COURT or a JUDGE for a RULING or ORDER. In most instances, the motion requests a ruling to be made in favor of the one making the motion (the applicant).

Motion for a directed verdict. An application to a JUDGE or COURT that a particular VERDICT be rendered.

Motion for decree. An application to a court for a final DECISION in a suit.

Motion for judgment. An application for a court to render its DECISION and to grant a JUDGMENT in favor of the maker of the motion.
Motion in arrest of judgment. > MOTION TO SET ASIDE JUDGMENT.
Motion in error. A MOTION to review a court's decision to see if an error has been made. > WRIT OF ERROR.
Motion to adjourn. A proposal to end a MEETING or a court session.
Motion to set aside judgment. An application to overturn or set aside a court's VERDICT or DECISION. Such a MOTION is proposed by a party who is dissatisfied with the end result of the case. A motion to set aside a judgment must be based upon some vital error in the court's handling of the trial.
Motive. The reason underlying an action, such as the motive behind fraud is to take something that doesn't belong to one.
Mouthpiece. A slang expression for an attorney.
Movable estate. PERSONAL PROPERTY or belongings; personal estate.
Move. To move is to make a MOTION before a court, an application for a court to take a certain action.
Moving papers. DOCUMENTS that serve as the basis of a MOTION made during a court procedure; AFFIDAVITS presented in support of a motion; motion papers.
Mugging. **1.** Robbing someone by approaching from behind and throwing an arm around the neck, thus preventing the victim from defending him or herself. **2.** Any type of street holdup, no matter how performed.
Multifariousness. The joining together of two complaints or actions not connected with each other; a MISJOINDER. (Multifariousness improperly joins issues that should have been separate.)
Multiple damages. DOUBLE or TRIPLE damages; a court award of more than the actual damage. > PUNITIVE DAMAGES.
Multiple sentence. A punishment much greater than that imposed upon a first offender. HABITUAL CRIMINALS often receive sentences two or three times greater than first offenders.
Multiplicity of actions or suits. A term applied to a situation in which a PLAINTIFF improperly brings several actions in the same matter.
Municipal. Pertaining to the local government of a city or town.
Municipal bond. A bond issued by a town, city, or county. Such bonds are usually for the purpose of local improvements and are tax exempt.
Municipal corporation. A public CORPORATION; the corporate entity of a town or city, allowing it to do business under existing CORPORATE LAW. (Municipal corporations are nonprofit.)
Municipal courts. City COURTS, charged with administering the LAW within the city.
Municipal ordinance. A RULE, REGULATION, or LAW enacted by a town or city. Such ordinances must be permissible under the state laws in which the town or city is located.

Municipality. A political body such as a town or city, legally incorporated under the laws of the state in which the municipality is situated.

Murder. The killing of a human being, carried out with MALICE or planned in advance; PREMEDITATED MURDER.

Murder in the first degree. The killing of a human being that has been planned in advance and is carried out with MALICE; deliberate HOMICIDE. Also, killing that accompanies other crimes such as robbery, assault and battery, rape, etcetera.

Murder in the second degree. HOMICIDE that is not associated with MALICE or premeditation but which, nevertheless, is the result of a desire to inflict bodily harm. Murder in the second degree is without excuse or justification, and is therefore a more serious crime than MANSLAUGHTER.

Murder in the third degree. In a few areas of the country murder in the third degree is judged as a crime distinct from MURDER IN THE FIRST DEGREE or MURDER IN THE SECOND DEGREE. It is a crime in which there is no design or attempt to kill, but killing nevertheless takes place during the commission of a felony.

Mutation. A change. In a *mutation of libel,* a change is made as to the substance of the libel.

Mutatis mutandis. An expression indicating that changes have been made in terms of details, but that the general matter at issue remains the same (Latin).

Mutilation. Altering a DOCUMENT, such as a COURT RECORD, CONTRACT, or WILL, etcetera, to the extent that the document loses its value and is rendered imperfect.

Mutiny. The unlawful taking over of a ship by a crew, thus denying the captain his RIGHTS and control; an insurrection, whether at sea or on land.

Mutual. Agreeable to both PARTIES; reciprocal; carried out together; the exchanging of similar DUTIES and OBLIGATIONS by two or more people.

Mutual account. An ACCOUNT in which there are transactions between two people that are permitted to run freely, until a specified time when DEBITS and CREDITS are balanced.

Mutual assent. Agreement between two people; a MEETING OF THE MINDS.

Mutual benefit society. A non-profit organization set up to benefit its members, financially and otherwise. Such societies often provide benefits for sickness, life insurance benefits, etcetera. Members of mutual benefit societies pay regular dues.

Mutual company. A CORPORATION in which the customers are also the owners, such as a mutual insurance, etcetera. Members of mutual benefit societies pay regular dues.

Mutual fund. A COMPANY that takes its investors' contributions and buys shares in many companies.

Mutuality of contract. The AGREEMENT and assent of both parties to a CONTRACT, with each party agreeing to perform some act or acts to promote the contract.

Mutuality of estoppel. An AGREEMENT in which neither party is bound unless both parties are bound. (An estoppel is a bar against saying or doing something.)

N

Naked power. > COLLATERAL POWER.

Narcotic drug act. A federal STATUTE making it unlawful to buy, dispense, or sell certain NARCOTIC drugs without a federal license.

Narcotics. Drugs such as morphine, heroin, etcetera, that produce stupor or sleep, simultaneously relieving pain. Many narcotics are habit-forming, and addiction to them is extremely difficult to overcome.

Narcotics addict. An individual dependent upon a NARCOTIC drug, who suffers withdrawal symptoms when no longer taking the drug.

Narrow construction. Strict interpretation of a LAW, STATUTE, or DOCUMENT, as opposed to a LIBERAL, comprehensive interpretation; LITERAL CONSTRUCTION. Some federal judges adhere to a narrow construction of the meaning of certain passages in the U.S. CONSTITUTION, while others may give a broad, nontechnical interpretation of the same passages.

Nation. A country; a body politic; a people united under the same GOVERNMENT and LAWS; a country occupying a certain limited territory, over which it has independent control.

National bank. A bank authorized to conduct business under the laws of the United States, as distinguished from a state bank.

National currency. Money issued by the federal government, to be used as legal tender. Notes issued by national banks are also national currency.

National debt. Money owed by the United States government to those members of the public who have lent it money. INTEREST on such loans is paid by the federal government with money it collects in taxes.

National defense. The creation of various federal agencies to secure the nation against attack from its enemies. The Army, Navy, Marines, Air Force, Coast Guard, etcetera, are given the specific task of insuring the defense of the country.

National emergency. A crisis involving the safety and security of the entire country. A state of war constitutes a national emergency. However, a national emergency may be declared solely on the basis of a threat of an impending war or other crisis.

National government. The federal government; the governing body of the entire country, as distinguished from a state, territorial, or local government.

National Guard. An organization created under the U.S. CONSTITUTION in which reserve members of the armed forces can be summoned on short notice to active duty. The National Guard usually serves the individual states, aiding in the control of disaster, civil disturbance, or other emergency. A member of the National Guard is actually enrolled to serve a state and, as such, he is not a member of the federal armed services.

National Labor Relations Act. > WAGNER ACT.

National Labor Relations Board. (The N.L.R.B.) A federal agency set up to handle disputes between management and labor, especially those controversies involving businesses that operate in several states or throughout the whole country.

Nationality. The status of a person who is a citizen of a particular country. An individual may bear the nationality of the country in which he was born or he might abandon his original nationality and become "a national" of another country, whose citizenship he has adopted.

Native. A natural-born CITIZEN; one who was born in the country of which he is a citizen.

Natural. Pertaining to nature and to the operation of NATURAL LAW. (*Natural law* does not originate from enacted laws and statutes but from the inner instincts and desires of human beings.) ≫ LAW OF NATURE.

Natural-born. Having been born in the country in which one is a citizen.

Natural consequence. A result that follows an act and was expected to follow that act.

Natural daughter. A female child who has come into being by NATURAL ISSUE (born of her parents), as distinguished from an adopted daughter.

Natural death. Death from causes other than accident or violence. Also called death from natural causes.

Natural gas. A mineral in the form of vapor, found in the depths of the earth; a greatly utilized source of energy.

Natural issue. Children born of their parents, as opposed to adopted children.

Natural law. That law which originates from the nature of man and which is based upon the usual, natural conduct of human beings; the law that conforms to man's innate, basic desire to act sanely and rationally; the law without which society could not exist in an orderly, peaceful state. ≫ LAW OF NATURE.

Natural resources. Things of value that originate from nature, such as land, water, and minerals within the land.

Natural son. A male child who has come into being by NATURAL ISSUE (born of his parents), as distinguished from an adopted son.

Naturalization. The act of converting a foreigner into a citizen.

Naturalized citizen. An individual who was born in a foreign country but, conforming to our laws, has been granted citizenship. He or she is entitled to all the rights of people born in this country, except that he or she cannot become President.

Naval law. The RULES and REGULATIONS that govern men and women who are in the naval branch of the armed forces.

Navigable waters. Rivers, lakes, and oceans through which ships are able to pass and conduct their business.

Ne exeat. A COURT ORDER that forbids a person involved in a legal matter to leave the country or the state or whatever area is considered in the JURISDICTION of the court (Latin). Such a WRIT is usually issued so that a defendant cannot escape the court's authority.

Necessaries. Things that are needed to subsist, such as shelter, food, clothing, etcetera. In a DIVORCE settlement, necessaries are those things judged to be necessary for the wife and children, according to their mode and manner of living during the marital period.

Necessary diligence. The amount of earnest effort that most people expend in conducting their affairs, businesses, or professions.

Necessary inference. A conclusion or deduction that is unavoidable when all the facts are considered in a reasonable light.

Necessitous condition. A condition in which one is lacking in the essentials, such as food, shelter, clothing, and money to pay rent and other necessary items.

Necessity. A situation in which one is forced to do something. Someone who has had no chance but to act in a certain unlawful manner may be excused from this behavior if necessity was the cause of carrying out the act.

Necrophilism. Inordinate and uncontrollable attraction to corpses, a form of psychotic (insane) behavior; desire to make love to a dead body.

Necropsy. AUTOPSY; POSTMORTEM examination.

Née. A word added after a married woman's name, to indicate the name of her family before she was married. For example, Mrs. Mary Jones, née Smith (French).

Negative averment. A positive STATEMENT made in a negative way; for example, an accusation that someone is not performing his duties. The burden of proof in a negative averment is upon the person making the accusation.

Negative evidence. TESTIMONY that denies, rather than confirms, a fact. This type of EVIDENCE is frequently just as important as positive evidence. As an example, a WITNESS may testify that a certain event or act did *not* take place.

Negative pregnant. A denial that in actuality affirms or admits important facts. A negative pregnant is thus beneficial to the opponent in a lawsuit.

Neglect. Lack of care and failure to carry out one's DUTIES or OBLIGATIONS. > NEGLIGENCE.

Neglected child. A MINOR who does not receive the care he is entitled to from parent(s) or guardian.

Negligence. Failure to do what a reasonable, careful, conscientious person is expected to do; doing something that a reasonable, careful conscientious person would not do. ≫ NEGLIGENCE, ACTIONABLE; NEGLIGENCE, COMPARATIVE; NEGLIGENCE, CONCURRENT; NEGLIGENCE, CONTRIBUTORY; NEGLIGENCE,

CRIMINAL; NEGLIGENCE, CULPABLE; NEGLIGENCE, GROSS; NEGLIGENCE, WANTON.

Negligence, actionable. Failure, through carelessness or NEGLECT, to perform a legal DUTY, thus damaging or injuring another.

Negligence, collateral. NEGLIGENCE attributed to an employer as a result of some negligent act or omission by an employee.

Negligence, comparative. A term that is used in a suit to recover DAMAGES, in which the NEGLIGENCE of the DEFENDANT is compared to that of the PLAINTIFF. In other words, if the plaintiff was slightly negligent but the defendant was grossly negligent, the plaintiff may be awarded the damages. Or, if the plantiff was grossly negligent and the defendant only slightly negligent, no award may be granted.

Negligence, concurrent. A type of NEGLIGENCE in which both the PLAINTIFF and the DEFENDANT contributed toward the injury for which DAMAGES are sought.

Negligence, contributory. NEGLIGENCE in which there has been a failure on the part of the PLAINTIFF to exercise ordinary, proper care, thus contributing toward an accident.

Negligence, criminal. NEGLIGENCE of such a nature that it is punishable as a CRIME.

Negligence, culpable. NEGLIGENCE in which one fails to do something that a reasonable, prudent person would do, or in which one does something that a reasonable prudent person would not do. Culpable negligence is more than ordinary negligence, as it implies that the negligence was purposeful.

Negligence, gross. Conscious disregard of one's DUTIES, resulting in INJURY or DAMAGE to another. Gross negligence exists when an individual, by exercising ordinary good conduct, could have prevented injury or damage.

Negligence, hazardous. Reckless behavior that threatens someone or exposes someone to serious harm.

Negligence, legal. NEGLECT that is contrary to the ordinary conduct of reasonable, prudent persons. In other words, legal NEGLIGENCE can serve as the basis of a SUIT for DAMAGES. ≫ NEGLIGENCE PER SE.

Negligence, ordinary. NEGLIGENCE that could have been avoided if only one had exercised ordinary, reasonable, proper care. Ordinary negligence is not willful or purposeful, but rather, "unthinking."

Negligence, wanton. Careless, reckless lack of concern, resulting in INJURY or DAMAGE to another.

Negligence, willful. Conscious, knowing NEGLECT of DUTY, with knowledge that such conduct will result in INJURY or DAMAGE to another.

Negligence case. A LAWSUIT to collect DAMAGES from a person who has been NEGLIGENT and has thus caused INJURY or harm.

Negligence per se. NEGLIGENCE by law, in that a party has violated a STATUTE or ORDINANCE while displaying negligent conduct. Negligence per se is so obvious that it requires little or no proof in a court of law.

Negligent homicide. KILLING someone without intent to kill, but where the killing takes place while the person is performing a negligent act or is failing to exercise reasonable, prudent care. (A driver of an automobile who far exceeds the speed limit, or who drives while under the influence of alcohol, is guilty of negligent homicide if he runs down and kills someone.)

Negligent offense. An OFFENSE that results from negligent behavior, such as failing to perform a duty or doing something one should not have done.

Negotiable. Able to be transferred from one party to another, such as a check which, by endorsement, can be cashed by the person to whom it has been given. The opposite of NONNEGOTIABLE. > NEGOTIABLE INSTRUMENT.

Negotiable instrument. DOCUMENTS such as SECURITIES, CHECKS, BILLS OF EXCHANGE, etcetera, which are signed or endorsed, thus allowing for the payment of the stipulated amount that the security, check, or bill of exchange calls for, on demand or at some specifically designated time in the future. (On the other hand, a "NONNEGOTIABLE instrument" cannot be transferred by endorsement and delivery.)

Negotiations. Discussions leading to the conclusion of a business transaction or AGREEMENT. (Management and labor undergo negotiations in order to reach an agreement on labor contracts.)

Nemo. No one; nobody (Latin).

Nepotism. Favoritism shown by a public official who appoints a relative to a paid job, such as a lawmaker who gives his wife or daughter a position as his secretary.

Net assets. The net worth of a company after subtracting its OBLIGATIONS, DEBTS, and LIABILITIES from its gross ASSETS. (This is generally a bookkeeping maneuver.)

Net earnings. Net profits; the monetary receipts of a company after deducting the business and operating expenses.

Net income. Earnings after deducting all expenses from income. Income may be in the form of money from sales or services, from interest on investments, etcetera.

Net loss. A deficiency resulting from the fact that income is less than operating expenses.

Net proceeds. Gross income, minus deductible expenses.

Net profit. Money remaining after deduction of all EXPENSES, LIABILITIES, TAXES, etcetera.

Net worth. The value of a company, or the amount of money an individual is worth, after subtracting all LIABILITIES and OBLIGATIONS.

Neurosis. An emotional disorder accompanied by intense feelings of anxiety, compulsive behavior, symptoms of a physical nature when no disease exists, and other deviations which cause the neurotic to be unhappy. Neurosis differs from psychosis or insanity in that the neurotic person is aware that he or she is unstable and in need of help, whereas the psychotic often is unaware.

Neutral. Not taking sides, as a

country not at war views two neighboring countries at war with each other.

Neutrality. Maintaining impartiality in a DISPUTE, as between two people or two nations, etcetera.

New cause of action. A LAWSUIT based upon a new set of FACTS, differing from the original facts in a previous ACTION (suit) between the same LITIGANTS.

New evidence. Material that has come to light after a trial has been concluded. Such new evidence may become the basis for a new trial.

New matter. Material brought up by a DEFENDANT that goes beyond the PLAINTIFF's accusations. New matter attempts to show that the plaintiff's CLAIMS were never valid or true and that there never was just cause for the LAWSUIT. Such material is presented during TRIAL, not having been brought up by either party at the commencement of the suit.

New trial. A reexamination and reevaluation of a MATTER in the same court after a VERDICT has already been rendered. A new trial often has as its purpose the correction of errors made during the original trial.

Next friend. Someone who acts for a child in a court action.

Next of kin. The closest relatives. The term is frequently used to describe the closest blood relations who will inherit PROPERTY from a person who dies without making a WILL.

Nihil. Nothing (Latin). The word is used by a sheriff when he attempts to attach the PROPERTY of a DEFENDANT and discovers that he has no possessions.

Nihil est. "There is nothing" (Latin). The statement of a sheriff who has been unable to serve a SUMMONS upon a DEFENDANT.

Nil. The same as NIHIL (Latin).

Nineteenth Amendment. The Amendment to the U.S. CONSTITUTION giving women the right to vote. It was ratified in 1920.

Nisi. "Unless" (Latin).

Nisi prius. A TRIAL heard originally by a JUDGE and a JURY, as distinguished from a trial conducted on appeal before an appellate court (Latin).

No bill. A decision by a GRAND JURY that there is no justification for an INDICTMENT.

No consideration. A DEFENDANT's response to a court, stating that a CONTRACT sued on is not valid and enforceable because it had no legal foundation.

No-fault insurance. A form of automobile or accident INSURANCE in which each party's insurance company pays a certain share of the DAMAGES no matter whose fault the accident was.

No recourse. No assumption of responsibility; denial of LIABILITY for reimbursement for a loss or DAMAGES.

"Nol. prossed." The termination of a case by a PROSECUTING ATTORNEY during a TRIAL. Also called *nolled* (Latin).

Nolle prosequi. The discontinuance or termination of a case by the PROSECUTING ATTORNEY. Nolle prosequi takes place during the TRIAL (Latin).

Nolled. > NOL. PROSSED.

Nolo contendere. An AGREEMENT by a DEFENDANT to accept the punishment for an alleged OFFENSE while not directly admitting GUILT. In Latin, the term means, "I will not contest it." A plea of nolo contendere frequently leads to a punishment that is lighter than usual.

Nominal consideration. A token award, such as an award of one dollar. Nominal consideration may be given to a PLAINTIFF by a COURT just to show that he or she was right but also to show that no real monetary DAMAGES are justified.

Nominal damages. An award in favor of a PLAINTIFF showing that his claim was justified. However, since there was no true monetary loss, the award is not substantial.

Nominal defendant. A person named as a DEFENDANT not because he is really responsible for the DAMAGES but because the SUIT would be deficient if he were not made a party to it.

Nominal parties. Those people who are included in a SUIT merely because their presence is required because of the rules of PLEADING (the written statements containing the contentions of the PLAINTIFF or the DEFENDANT). Such parties do not have an interest in the issues of the dispute.

Nomination. The selection of a candidate to run for a political office.

Nonappearance. The failure of a DEFENDANT to appear in court to defend him or herself in a LAWSUIT.

Non assumpsit. An ASSERTION by a DEFENDANT that he did *not* promise to do something or pay something to the PLAINTIFF, as the plaintiff claims (Latin).

Nonbailable. A term referring to the allowability of bail. Nonbailable means that the accused is not permitted to post bail, as in the case of an accused murderer.

Noncancellable policy. A type of health and accident INSURANCE POLICY containing provisions forbidding the insurer to cancel the policy so long as the premiums are paid regularly. Thus, even if the insured is permanently disabled by illness or accident, the insurer is obliged to continue to pay the benefits for an indefinite period of time.

Non compos mentis. Mentally incompetent (Latin). Included in this group are people who are mentally defective from birth; people who were of sound mind but have been senile or have otherwise lost their faculties; people who have a mental illness such as PARANOIA, MANIC-DEPRESSIVE PSYCHOSIS, etcetera, and those who are of unsound mind because of the use of drugs or chronic alcoholism.

Nonconclusive judgment. A DECISION of a court that is subject to APPEAL, as opposed to a final or conclusive judgment, issued by a COURT OF LAST RESORT, which cannot be challenged.

Nonconforming uses. ORDINANCES that restrict the type of building that may be erected in a zoned area, or RULES that restrict land for certain uses in a certain area are referred to as nonconforming uses.

Nonconformist. One who disagrees and dissents from established, accepted practices and modes of behavior. (Nudists might be classified as nonconformists.)

Noncontestable. A provision in an INSURANCE POLICY that the insurer cannot cancel the policy after premiums have been paid for a certain period of time. In other words, if the insured person originally took out the policy without the insurance company knowing all necessary facts, it is the responsibility of the insurer to discover these facts within a specified time, or the policy automatically is valid.

Non cul. An abbreviation for NON CULPABILIS (Latin).

Non culpabilis. Not guilty (Latin).

Nondescript. Not capable of being classified, unclassifiable; indescribable.

Nondisclosure. Failure to reveal to the COURT an important fact. Such nondisclosure may be purposeful or without any intent to conceal.

Nondiscrimination clause. A provision in a public CONTRACT with a private contractor that he will not discriminate in hiring employees because of race, creed, color, or national origin, and that he will treat all employees without discrimination.

Non est. The return of a sheriff's WRIT or SUMMONS when the person to be served cannot be located (Latin).

Non est factum. A DEFENSE that denies the execution of the DOCUMENT upon which the suit is brought (Latin).

Nonfeasance. Failure by a public OFFICER to perform his duties. Such failure may be willful or due to incompetence or oversight.

Non fecit. A DEFENSE which claims that the DEFENDANT was not the maker of the INSTRUMENT upon which the SUIT is brought. In Latin, non fecit means, "He did not do it."

Nonforfeitable. Something that cannot be taken away, as opposed to something that can be forfeited.

Nonfunctional. Having no use; lacking usefulness.

Nonintervention will. A WILL that does not require an EXECUTOR to post a bond, freeing him or her from the necessity of reporting the administration of the ESTATE to the court.

Nonissuable plea. A DEFENSE that raises no issue of the FACTS in the case.

Nonjudicial day. A day upon which the COURT is not in session, such as a legal holiday or a Sunday.

Nonjury trial. A trial conducted before a JUDGE, without a JURY. In such trials, the judge alone decides the issues involved and renders JUDGMENT.

Nonleviable. Something exempt from TAXATION; nontaxable.

Nonnavigable waters. Bodies of water through which ships cannot pass.

Nonnegotiable. Not transferrable, as a CHECK, BILL OF EXCHANGE, or SECURITY that does not permit endorsement and delivery to another.

Non obstante veredicto. A Latin expression for a situation in which a JURY decides a case in favor of one party but the JUDGE reverses the jury's VERDICT and rules in favor of the other party; "notwithstanding the verdict."

Nonoccupational. A term referring to an injury or illness not incurred during, or as the result of, one's work.

Nonpayment. Failure to pay a DEBT, according to an AGREEMENT. Nonpayment may serve as the basis for a SUIT to recover.

Nonpecuniary damages. DAMAGES that cannot be calculated accurately in terms of money. Nonpecuniary damages thus must rely upon the JUDGMENT of the JURY that makes the award.

Nonperformance. A BREACH OF CONTRACT; failure to carry out the terms of an AGREEMENT or CONTRACT.

Nonprofit. To engage in an activity without intent to make a profit.

Nonprofit corporation. A COMPANY organized and operating for charitable purposes or for the good of the public, without the intent of making money. Also known as a *not-for-profit corporation.*

Non prosequitur. A MOTION to dismiss a CASE; a JUDGMENT in favor of the DEFENDANT, given because the PLAINTIFF fails to pursue the SUIT. In Latin, the term means, "He does not follow up."

Nonresident. A person staying in a locality where he is not a permanent resident. (An American living for a few months in a foreign country is a nonresident.)

Nonresponsive answer. An answer by a WITNESS that evades the issue or does not relate to the question that has been asked.

Non sequitur. "It does not follow" (Latin). A response unrelated to a question; a conclusion that does not logically follow the reasoning.

Non sui juris. A term referring to someone incompetent to act in his own behalf, unable to defend himself even if aided by an attorney. "Not his own master" (Latin).

Nonsuit. The termination of a SUIT because the PLAINTIFF has not carried out necessary steps toward concluding the suit.

Nonsupport. FAILURE to provide for those who, by law, one is OBLIGED to support, such as a spouse and child or children.

Nontenure. A DEFENSE in a REAL ESTATE action in which a defendant denies that he is a TENANT.

Nontestamentary assets. ASSETS that are not distributed through a provision in a WILL, even though the person who has died has made a will and has distributed other PROPERTY through a will. In other words, property that has purposely been left out of a will.

Normal. Conforming to an accepted standard. In law, a normal person is a MENTALLY COMPETENT person, able to defend himself and to act as a WITNESS or member of a JURY.

Not-for-profit corporation. > NONPROFIT CORPORATION.

Not guilty. A VERDICT of innocence; ACQUITTAL; a PLEA of innocence.

Not transferable. When referring to an INSTRUMENT OR DOCUMENT, this term means that the document cannot be given over to someone else by endorsement and delivery.

Notarizing. Having a signature on a DOCUMENT authenticated by signing in the presence of a NOTARY PUBLIC. The notary then signifies in writing that the signing has taken place.

Notary public. A public official who is authorized to WITNESS signatures on DOCUMENTS, to administer oaths, and to perform other tasks, such as attesting to the genuineness of various papers.

Note. A written promise to pay a specified amount of money to another; a PROMISSORY NOTE; COMMERCIAL PAPER.

Notice. Knowledge of the existence of a state of affairs or knowledge of certain facts. When an individual has received notice, it means he has been made aware of certain facts of a certain state of affairs.

Notice, averment of. A STATEMENT in a pleading recognizing that notice has been given.

Notice, constructive. Inferred or implied NOTICE, which cannot be contradicted legally.

Notice, immediate. A specified period of time given to an insured person in which to report a LOSS OF DAMAGES to an INSURANCE COMPANY.

Notice, legal. NOTICE that conforms to the requirements of the LAW, as applied to any specific case.

Notice, personal. NOTICE given personally, in writing or orally, directly to the person being charged or affected by the legal matter.

Notice, presumptive. Implied NOTICE, which is subject to being contradicted.

Notice, public. NOTICE given "to all whom it may concern"; notice given to the entire general public.

Notice, reasonable. Transmission of information or NOTICE that one would consider reasonable under the circumstances.

Notice in pais. NOTICE that is not in writing or on the record.

Notice of action. The act of making someone aware that he is to be involved in a LAWSUIT.

Notice of appeal. NOTICE that a decision of a court will be appealed to a higher court.

Notice of appearance. NOTICE to a court that an involved person is present and will appear in the case.

Notice of claim. NOTICE, required by law, that a person is suing a PUBLIC CORPORATION (town, city, state, etcetera) for DAMAGES. Unless such notice is given, the suit cannot proceed.

Notice of forfeiture. NOTICE to owners of PROPERTY to appear in court and to show why said property should not be forfeited. Such notice states the day and the time to appear in court.

Notice of judgment. NOTICE to a party against whom a JUDGMENT has been rendered that the judgment is being recorded.

Notice of motion. NOTICE from one party to another in a suit that a MOTION will be made in court at a certain date and time. The nature of the motion will be described in the notice of motion.
Notice of pendency. In REAL ESTATE, this term is used to indicate NOTICE that a certain piece of PROPERTY has a LIEN against it and that one should exercise care before taking title to it.
Notice of trial. NOTICE from one party to another of an intention to SUE and to bring the case to TRIAL as soon as convenient.
Notice to plead. NOTICE from a PLAINTIFF to a DEFENDANT to defend himself in a LAWSUIT. Failure to do so will lead to a JUDGMENT BY DEFAULT.
Notice to produce. Written NOTICE, requiring a party to produce in COURT a certain DOCUMENT or paper.
Notice to quit premises. Written NOTICE given by a landlord to a tenant, asking and requesting departure from the leased premises. Such a request must be within the provisions of the lease CONTRACT. Also, notice from a tenant to a landlord that he intends to quit the premises.
Notify. To give NOTICE; to make facts and circumstances known to someone.
Notoriety. The state of being widely recognized and known. In reference to CRIMINAL LAW, notoriety implies being widely known in an unfavorable light.
Notorious possession. Possession of PROPERTY that is well-known to the PUBLIC; property not secretly held.
Novation. The creation of a new CONTRACT or AGREEMENT to replace an old contract or agreement, the switch being agreeable to all persons concerned.
Nude contract. A CONTRACT in which no payments will be made. > NUDUM PACTUM.
Nudum pactum. A nude pact (Latin). An AGREEMENT in which there is no OBLIGATION to pay money, yet a promise to perform and an agreement does exist. The same as NUDE CONTRACT.
Nuisance. **1.** Anything that disturbs, annoys, or interferes with the use of one's PROPERTY. Nuisance implies an unreasonable or inconsiderate act or acts, often repeated or continued for prolonged periods of time, and creating a degree of unhappiness to the person suffering the interference. **2.** Anything that jeopardizes the public's safety and health. Nuisances are frequently the cause of lawsuits.
Nuisance, abatement of. The removal of a NUISANCE. The law permits the aggrieved party to remove the nuisance but not to retaliate by creating DAMAGE to the perpetrator's property.
Nuisance, actionable. Knowingly doing something that interferes with someone else's enjoyment of his own PROPERTY. Also, carelessly permitting something to injure or interfere with the lawful use of property by another.
Nuisance, common. A NUISANCE affecting the general public, as distinguished from a private nuisance affecting an individual.
Nuisance, continuing. A NUISANCE that persists indefinitely,

or is repeated so often that it is almost continuous.

Nuisance, permanent. A NUISANCE that will continue and cannot be remedied without going to great expense.

Nuisance in fact. A NUISANCE resulting from the location of the premises, or the manner in which the nuisance-creating activity is operated.

Nuisance per se. A NUISANCE that exists at all times and under all circumstances, as distinguished from a nuisance that exists because of its location or because of particular circumstances.

Nul. No; no one (Latin).

Nul tort. A DEFENSE in which the defendant claims he has committed no wrong; "no wrong" (Latin).

Null. Void; of no legal effect or consequence; nonexistent.

Null and void. Cancelled; of no legal effect; not binding.

Nullity. Something having no legal effect; the state of being null.

Nullity of marriage. A suit for the ANNULMENT of a marriage. Also known as a "nullity suit."

Nunc pro tunc. Back-dating something so that it goes into effect at an earlier date (Latin).

Nuncupative will. An oral WILL, not valid in most states.

Nuremberg Code of Ethics. This code governs medical research upon human beings. Briefly, it states: **1.** The subject must consent voluntarily. **2.** The experiment must give promise of yielding fruitful results that will benefit others. **3.** The experiment should be preceded by animal research. **4.** The experiment must not involve physical or mental suffering. **5.** No experiment should be conducted if there is a possibility of a disabling injury or death. **6.** The degree of risk of the experiment should not exceed the importance of the problem. **7.** Preparations and facilities for conducting the experiment should safeguard against even the most remote possibilities of injury or death. **8.** The experiment should be conducted only by scientifically qualified people. **9.** The subject of the experiment must have the right to terminate the experiment whenever he wishes. **10.** Those in charge of the experiment must terminate it at any stage if they foresee the possibility of an untoward effect upon the subject.

Nymphomania. Excessive, uncontrollable sexual desire in a woman. Nymphomania may be so severe as to constitute psychotic behavior but usually occurs in women who appear to be normal in most other respects.

O

Oath. A PLEDGE to tell the truth; a sworn PROMISE to perform a duty; a calling on God to WITNESS a statement.
Oath, assertory. **1.** An OATH relating to a past or present fact, as distinguished from a PLEDGE to do something in the future. **2.** An OATH required by law but not in a judicial proceeding, such as an oath that one makes before a custom-house official relative to imported goods.
Oath, corporal. > OATH, SOLEMN.
Oath, false. PERJURY; telling an untruth while under OATH to tell the truth. An oath, if proved to be false, may lead to a prison sentence.
Oath, judicial. An OATH taken in court, before a JUDGE or other court officer, as distinguished from a nonjudicial oath taken out of court.
Oath, official. A sworn STATEMENT by a public OFFICIAL, usually taken on assumption of office, that he or she will carry out duties conscientiously, honestly, and faithfully.
Oath, promissory. A sworn STATEMENT that one will carry out something in the future. Officials who take office issue promissory oaths to fulfill their duties and obligations faithfully.
Oath, purgatory. A sworn STATEMENT by which someone purges himself, or attempts to clear himself of some wrongdoing or misconduct.
Oath, solemn. A sworn STATEMENT given while placing one's hand on the Bible or while raising one's hand to "swear to God"; a corporal oath.
Oath, voluntary. An OATH taken voluntarily, not in court and not related to judicial matters, such as one may make when swearing to another person that one will perform a certain act or do a certain thing for that person.
Oath in litem. In CIVIL LAW, a PLAINTIFF'S OATH as to the value of the thing in dispute.
Oath of allegiance. An OATH in which one swears allegiance to a particular country and promises to uphold its PRINCIPLES and its CONSTITUTION.
Oath of calumny. An OATH in which a PLAINTIFF swears that his suit against the DEFENDANT is based on truth, and is not being instituted deceitfully or because of MALICE.
Oath of Hippocrates. An OATH taken by graduates of medical schools all over the world to uphold the teachings and high principles of Hippocrates, the ancient Greek who was the so-called "Father of Medicine." The Hippocratic Oath is not a legal, binding oath, but merely a PLEDGE by young physicians to perform their duties and obligations in a conscientious and ethical manner.
Oath of office. A specified OATH,

usually written and recorded, that an official must recite upon taking office. (The President of the United States takes an oath of office, swearing to uphold the U.S. CONSTITUTION.)

Obiter dictum. STATEMENTS by a JUDGE in rendering a DECISION that have no real bearing on the case in hand; remarks made aside. In Latin, the word *obiter* translates as "By the way."

Obit sine prole. Died without any ISSUE, such as children or grandchildren (Latin).

Object. To disagree; to pose an OBJECTION; to protest. ATTORNEYS in trials frequently object to TESTIMONY or procedures.

Object of an action. The purpose of a suit, such as to correct a wrong, to collect damages, etcetera.

Object of a statute. The purpose of a law, or what a law is supposed to accomplish.

Objection. A PROTEST against a RULING or ACTION, or failure of action. In a TRIAL, an attorney sometimes raises an objection which is either upheld or overruled by the judge. If the objection is overruled, the attorney may take an EXCEPTION to the judge's ruling and such exception is recorded.

Objection overruled. The term used by a JUDGE when he disagrees with an attorney's OBJECTION.

Objection sustained. A term used by a JUDGE when he upholds and agrees with an attorney's protest.

Obligation. Something a person is bound to do or bound not to do; a moral or legal DUTY. Penalties may be imposed upon people who fail in their obligations. ➤ OBLIGATION, ABSOLUTE; OBLIGATION, CONDITIONAL; OBLIGATION, CONJUNCTIVE; OBLIGATION, CONTRACTUAL; OBLIGATION, EXPRESS; OBLIGATION, IMPLIED; OBLIGATION, JOINT; OBLIGATION, MORAL; OBLIGATION, PERFECT; OBLIGATION, PERSONAL; OBLIGATION, PRIMARY; OBLIGATION, PRINCIPAL; OBLIGATION, PURE; OBLIGATION, SECONDARY.

Obligation, absolute. An OBLIGATION without conditions; an obligation that must be met exactly according to an AGREEMENT.

Obligation, conditional. An OBLIGATION that will be fulfilled by one individual provided another person fulfills a previously agreed-on obligation.

Obligation, conjunctive. An OBLIGATION containing several connected parts and objects.

Obligation, contractual. An OBLIGATION that arises from a firm AGREEMENT or CONTRACT.

Obligation, express. An OBLIGATION in which a person is bound by express terms to carry out a certain promise.

Obligation, implied. An OBLIGATION that is inferred to be a DUTY by the nature of the agreement. Such an obligation can be upheld by law.

Obligation, joint. An OBLIGATION in which two or more people bind themselves to perform an obligation.

Obligation, moral. A DUTY that should be carried out as a matter of conscience. However, a moral obligation cannot be enforced by LAW.

Obligation, perfect. An OBLIGATION that can be upheld by existing law and legal right.
Obligation, personal. An OBLIGATION that an individual binds himself personally to fulfill, being solely liable to carry it out.
Obligation, primary. An OBLIGATION that is the primary reason for an AGREEMENT or CONTRACT.
Obligation, principal. The main OBLIGATION.
Obligation, pure. An OBLIGATION that has no conditions attached to it.
Obligation, secondary. An OBLIGATION that is to be fulfilled if a principal obligation cannot be fulfilled.
Obligee. An individual to whom an OBLIGATION is owed.
Obligor. An individual who binds himself to perform an OBLIGATION.
Obliterate. To cancel out or erase written material in a legal DOCUMENT.
Obscene. Indecent; something that stimulates lewd reactions; immodest. "Obscene" has become a word with many interpretations; what is judged to be obscene by one court in one area may not be so judged by another court in another area.
Obscure. Difficult to understand; unclear; poorly expressed.
Obsession. A thought which persists in one's conscious thinking, no matter how hard one may try to forget it. Although this cannot be classified as normal behavior, it does not constitute insanity.
Obsolescence. The state of being outmoded, such as a factory that no longer serves its original purpose or an airplane that is no longer up to date.
Obstruct. To make difficult; to hinder; to interfere with.
> OBSTRUCTION OF JUSTICE.
Obstructing an officer. Interfering with the duties of a POLICE OFFICER, as when he is in the process of arresting someone.
Obstructing easement. Purposeful, unwarranted interfering by an owner of PROPERTY with the use of an EASEMENT by a nonowner. (An easement is the use by a nonowner of adjoining land, such as an access road.)
Obstructing navigation. Unnecessary, unwarranted interference with the free movement of ships; obstructing a waterway.
Obstructing process. An active attempt to prevent the carrying out of lawful PROCESSES.
Obstruction of justice. Interfering with, preventing, or attempting to prevent unlawful proceedings and the carrying out of justice. Obstruction of justice is a CRIMINAL OFFENSE.
Obvious. Apparent; easily understood; readily seen, such as an obvious danger, an obvious risk, etcetera.
Occupant. A TENANT; a person who takes possession of PROPERTY that belongs to no one.
Occupation. **1.** A situation in which someone takes possession and control over land, such as when a country is victorious in war and takes over the defeated enemy's land. **2.** A person's profession or line of business.
Occupational disability. An inability to work, caused by an inju-

ry or disease incurred during the performance of one's job. > OCCUPATIONAL DISEASE.

Occupational disease. An illness contracted because of the hazards of a particular type of employment, such as a miner who contracts silicosis (a serious lung disease) as the result of inhaling coal dust over a long number of years.

Occupational duties. Those responsibilities that one assumes as a regular, ordinary part of one's OCCUPATION.

Occupying claimant. A person who attempts to recover for improvements made while he has occupied PROPERTY, has paid for the improvements, and has thought that he would eventually take over TITLE to the property. The CLAIM is made after the claimant learns that he will not become the owner of the property he has improved.

Occurrence. An event; an incident; something that takes place without prior planning.

Occurrence witness. A WITNESS who was present and saw a particular event take place.

Odium. Hatred; MALICE.

Of counsel. A term applied to an ATTORNEY who has been engaged to help another attorney prepare and try a case. The "of counsel" attorney is not the ATTORNEY OF RECORD.

Of record. Entered on the RECORD; duly recorded.

Offender. A person who, according to law, is GUILTY of a CRIME or MISDEMEANOR.

Offense. A CRIME; a MISDEMEANOR; a breaking of the law; a transgression punishable under CRIMINAL LAW.

Offense, continuing. A series of unlawful acts carried out intermittently or continuously by the same person or persons, with the same motive or motives in mind.

Offense, criminal. MISDEMEANOR and FELONY. > CRIMINAL OFENSE.

Offense, quasi. An unlawful act attributed to someone who did not actually commit the act but who stimulated and influenced another to commit the OFFENSE.

Offense, second. An unlawful act committed by a person who has already been convicted of another OFFENSE.

Offensive language. Statements of a hurtful, derogatory, or obscene nature, made by one person to another.

Offer. An attempt to conclude an AGREEMENT through making specific proposals; a TENDER.

Offer and acceptance. An expression denoting that there has been AGREEMENT among two or more parties concerning the terms of a CONTRACT.

Offer for the record. A term used in court when presenting EVIDENCE in a LAWSUIT, such evidence to be placed in the official RECORD of the trial; offer of proof.

Offered evidence. EVIDENCE presented in a LAWSUIT.

Offer of compromise. A proposal to end a DISPUTE, thus doing away with the need for a LAWSUIT. An offer of compromise often leads to a SETTLEMENT OUT OF COURT.

Offer of proof. A presentation to a COURT stating the PROOF and TESTIMONY that will be introduced in order to prove the case. Such offer of proof is made by the attorneys for the parties engaged in the suit.

Office. **1.** A place where business is transacted; a place where someone practices a profession. **2.** A position held by an officer. (The presidential office is held by the President.)

Officer. One who holds a public position; a person charged by a local, state, or federal government to carry out certain duties and functions.

Officer de jure. A person who has been legally chosen to carry out certain duties and who is qualified to perform them.

Official. **1.** An officer. **2.** Pertaining to an OFFICE, such as the official duties of a mayor, a judge, a governor, etcetera.

Official act. One carried out by an OFFICER in line with his prescribed duties and functions.

Official misconduct. Misbehavior and unlawful acts committed by a public OFFICIAL in the performance of his duties. Such misconduct may be willful, or may be due to NEGLECT of OFFICE; a breach of faith by a public official.

Official notice. > JUDICIAL NOTICE.

Official seal. The seal or imprint placed upon an official DOCUMENT by a public OFFICIAL. Mere writing upon a document docs not constitute a seal.

Offset. A CLAIM made by an opposing party in a SUIT, such offset tending to cancel out the original claim of the PLAINTIFF; a COUNTERCLAIM.

Offspring. Issue; children or grandchildren.

Old-age assistance. Financial aid given to poor and needy elderly people. Such assistance is funded jointly by the state and the federal governments, under existing STATUTES.

Oligarchy. A government that rules through the power of just a few people, as opposed to a democratic form of government controlled through elected representation by a great number of people.

Olographic testament. A WILL written in longhand by the maker of the will (the TESTATOR). > HOLOGRAPHIC TESTAMENT.

Ombudsman. A person appointed by a local, state, or federal government to hear complaints from private citizens against their governments (Swedish). Such complaints are frequently transmitted to the appropriate governmental authority.

Omission. Failure to act; failure to do something one should do; failure to perform what the law requires one to do.

Omission, crime of. An OFFENSE characterized by the failure of an individual to perform a required act. (It may be just as serious as a CRIME OF COMMISSION.)

Omne. Anyone; any man; any woman (Latin).

Omnibus bill. A legislative bill that includes many provisions and subjects; some may be related to each other, while others may contain matters unrelated to each other. An omnibus bill, when presented to a governor or president for signing, may force approval of undesired provisions in order to get approval of desired provisions, since failure to sign such a bill would cause the whole enactment to be inoperative.

Omnibus motion. A MOTION containing many separate motions, some related, others totally unrelated to each other.

On account. A part payment, as distinguished from "payment in full"; to be charged to one's CREDIT.

On all fours. A case resembling another case in all aspects is said to be on all fours. In trying a case it is frequently helpful to point out that a similar case considered the same questions of law.

On call. A DEBT payable whenever demanded; a debt to be paid immediately; ON DEMAND.

On demand. An existing DEBT, payable when requested by the CREDITOR.

On or about. A phrase used in an accusation when the exact time that a CRIME was committed is not known.

On the merits. A DECISION of a court based upon the FACTS presented, rather than upon some technical legal procedure or practice.

On trial. A person is on trial while the CASE is being tried in a COURT of LAW; a case that is listed on a court DOCKET as being on trial is one that is being tried presently.

Once in jeopardy. A DEFENSE or PLEA that claims that the DEFENDANT has already been tried in another trial for the same OFFENSE; PRIOR JEOPARDY.
≫ DOUBLE JEOPARDY.

One-man-one-vote rule. A ruling in most democratic governments that one person can only have one vote. In essence, it means that no one person shall have greater voting power than any other person.

Onerous. Burdensome; having OBLIGATIONS or responsibilities that outweigh the advantages that might occur or accrue from those obligations or responsibilities. A CONTRACT or AGREEMENT may be onerous if the disadvantages of the arrangement are greater than the advantages.

Onus of proof. The BURDEN OF PROOF. In other words, the accuser or PLAINTIFF has the responsibility to prove his or her CLAIM or charges against the DEFENDANT.

Onus probandi. BURDEN OF PROOF (Latin).

Open account. An account that has not been settled because continuing transactions are in progress or will take place in the future.

Open contract. An AGREEMENT for the sale of land that provides that the seller must give proof of TITLE.

Open corporation. A COMPANY that sells its stock and shares to the general public, as distinguished from a CLOSED CORPORATION.

Open court. A COURT in session, open to the public. Certain sessions of a court may be closed or may take place privately in a JUDGE's chambers.

Open-end agreement. A SETTLEMENT made in a WORKMEN'S COMPENSATION case in which the payments for disability from injuries continue as long as the employee is unable to work.
Open-end contract. An AGREEMENT in which the exact amount of goods to be bought is not specified, but the provider agrees to deliver as much goods as the purchaser will require to meet his needs.
Open-end investment trust. A TRUST (monies given over to a TRUSTEE for the benefit of third parties) in which the shares owned by the trust may be sold and new shares purchased, if the trustees so decide.
Open-end settlement. > OPEN-END AGREEMENT.
Open hearing. An INVESTIGATION, often conducted by a governmental agency, which is open to the public; the opposite of a CLOSED HEARING.
Open shop. A shop (a factory or plant) in which nonunion as well as union workers are employed; the opposite of a CLOSED SHOP.
Open trust. An active TRUST.
Open will. An oral WILL; a NUNCUPATIVE WILL.
Opening a judgment. Reviewing a decision of a court to see whether it should stand as is, be modified, or set aside (VACATED).
Opening case. A further TRIAL after a DECISION for the introduction of additional argument or new EVIDENCE; an opening statement.
Opening statement. The initial STATEMENT of an ATTORNEY to a JUDGE, or to a judge and JURY, telling of the FACTS that he intends to present in order to prove his CASE.
Operation of law. A term referring to the determination of RIGHTS and OBLIGATIONS merely through application of the existing laws covering a situation. As an example, if a person dies without having made a WILL, the heirs automatically inherit the PROPERTY through the operation of law governing INHERITANCE.
Operative part. That portion of a DOCUMENT in which the main purpose of the transaction is spelled out, as distinguished from introductory or concluding sections of the document.
Opinion. **1.** The reasons given for a court's JUDGMENT, frequently pointing out the law that governed the court's conclusions. **2.** A belief; a judge's or court's reasoning in a particular matter.
Opinion, concurring. An opinion written by a JUDGE who agrees with the final decision in a case but who disagrees with the reasoning that led to the final decision.
Opinion, dissenting. > DISSENTING OPINION.
Opinion evidence. EVIDENCE given by EXPERT WITNESSES, such as a physician's TESTIMONY on what he thinks caused a death or a handwriting expert's testimony on whether a particular sample of script was written by a particular person. Ordinary witnesses are not usually permitted to give their opinions while testifying but are required to testify as to exactly what they saw or heard.
Opinion of court. A written

STATEMENT by a COURT giving its reasons for its DECISION in a case.

Opposite party. An ADVERSARY in a LAWSUIT.

Oppression. The unlawful deprivation of one's rights under the UNITED STATES CONSTITUTION; the unjust use of power or position in order to impose one's will upon another.

Oppressive litigation. A suit brought for malicious purposes, more to hurt an opponent than to win the case.

Opprobrium. The disgrace invoked by shameful behavior; shame.

Optical illusion. A thought that one sees something that is not actually there, such as a mirage.

Option. An AGREEMENT in which one pays for the privilege of buying something from or selling something to another person at a fixed price, within a specified period of time.

Option to purchase. The granting of a RIGHT to a potential purchaser, to be privileged to buy a certain PROPERTY for a specified price, within a specified period of time.

Option to renew. A RIGHT to renew a LEASE.

Option to terminate. The right of a TENANT, or of a LANDLORD, to terminate a LEASE under certain prescribed conditions.

Optional bond. A BOND that can be called for payment at a date prior to maturity.

Optional writ. A command to a DEFENDANT to do a certain thing or to SHOW CAUSE why he should not have to do it.

Oral contract. A spoken CONTRACT; a written contract that is incomplete but has been completed by oral (spoken) agreements. ➤ PAROL CONTRACT; VERBAL AGREEMENT; VERBAL CONTRACT.

Oral deposition. Spoken TESTIMONY from a witness, taken out of court but on INSTRUCTION of the court.

Oral will. A WILL not in writing; a spoken will; a NUNCUPATIVE WILL.

Ordain. To ENACT a law; to establish.

Order. A command; a direction; a demand by a JUDGE or a COURT that certain action be taken, or that a certain action not be taken (RESTRAINING ORDER). ➤ COURT ORDER.

Order nisi. An ORDER requesting that a certain thing should be done within a specified period of time, and that if the thing is not done within that time, then the order becomes absolute and the thing *must* be done.

Order of continuance. An ORDER of a COURT to continue a case.

Order of interpleader. An ORDER in favor of the PLAINTIFF, commanding that the defendants settle the controversy between themselves. Such an order is rendered when a dispute arises between two or more defendants in a lawsuit.

Order of reference. A direction of a COURT appointing a REFEREE to decide the case.

Order to show cause. An ORDER from a COURT commanding that a party appear in court to show why a certain thing should not be done.

Ordinance. A local LAW; a law

passed by a legislative body of a city or township or other local government; a STATUTE; a rule.

Ordinary. Usual; normal, as opposed to extraordinary.

Ordinary care. The degree of DILIGENCE one must exercise in order to avoid injury or damage to others. The exercise of less than ordinary care may lead to a charge of NEGLIGENCE.

Ordinary conveyance. A transfer of PROPERTY carried out voluntarily, not by a COURT ORDER that deprives an individual of TITLE to property.

Ordinary dangers. The dangers inherent in a particular job or OCCUPATION, such as the dangers involved in working at great heights or in mines; dangers that are not created by NEGLIGENCE. > ORDINARY HAZARDS OF OCCUPATION.

Ordinary diligence. That degree of care and attention that an average, conscientious, prudent person would exert in the performance of his tasks or job. Such diligence is the opposite of NEGLIGENCE.

Ordinary hazards of occupation. Those dangers inherent in the type of work one does, not resulting from NEGLIGENCE on the part of the employer. > ORDINARY DANGERS.

Organic law. CONSTITUTIONAL LAW; the fundamental, basic laws of a society or government.

Organize. **1.** To establish; to make something functional. **2.** To form a union out of unorganized, nonunion working people.

Organized labor. Unionized workers.

Original bill. A PLAINTIFF'S SUIT in a COURT OF EQUITY that is new and is unrelated to any previous SUIT on the same matter in the same COURT.

Original entry. The first entry made in an account book on a particular account, as distinguished from an entry made and copied from another account book.

Original evidence. **1.** An original DOCUMENT or material introduced into a TRIAL, as distinguished from a copy of a document or other material. **2.** First-hand EVIDENCE; the very best evidence that can be submitted in a case.

Original jurisdiction. The AUTHORITY of a COURT that originally tried a case, as distinguished from a court that has heard a case on appeal.

Original patent. A basic PATENT; a patent that constitutes a brand-new discovery in a new field.

Original process. The method and PROCEDURE used in commencing a lawsuit.

Ostensible. Obvious; apparent.

Ostensible authority. The power that a PRINCIPAL supposedly grants to his AGENT, thus leading a third party to believe that the agent has such power and authority.

Ouster. DISPOSSESSION; EVICTION; DISSEISIN. The term frequently implies a forceful eviction from PROPERTY.

Ouster by abatement. A situation in which a person dies, and before the heirs can inherit and take over the PROPERTY, someone who has no right to the property takes possession of it.

Ouster judgment. A court DECISION against a DEFENDANT, ordering him to abandon PROPERTY that he occupied wrongfully and turn it over to the PLAINTIFF.
Out of court. **1.** A case is thrown out of court when the PLAINTIFF has not presented a legitimate, valid, or believable complaint; a MATTER not before a court. **2.** A SETTLEMENT made out of court is one that the LITIGANTS make prior to the matter being tried and settled in court, or one that is made while the trial is in progress.
Outlaw. **1.** A notorious CRIMINAL, especially one who is a fugitive from the law. **2.** A person deprived of the protection of the law.
Out-of-pocket expenses. Money that one must pay to defray expenses while carrying out the usual DUTIES and OBLIGATIONS in the performance of a job.
Outrage and indignity. Injury to one's body, as well as serious harm to one's emotional stability.
Overcome. To overcome EVIDENCE presented by one party to a suit, the opposing party must present more convincing evidence; to outweigh.
Overdraft. An overdrawing of one's bank account; the making out of a check for more money than one has on deposit in a bank.
Overdue. Past due; unpaid.
Overreaching. Taking fraudulent advantage of someone through cheating, lying, or cunning.
Overriding veto. Passing a law again that has already been vetoed (turned down and left unsigned) by a government OFFICIAL such as a governor, president, etcetera. In the federal government, a bill vetoed by the President must receive two-thirds majority in Congress to override the veto and enact the measure into law.
Overrule. **1.** To overturn a decision made in a lower court. This occurs sometimes when a higher court reviews a case tried in a lower court. **2.** To deny; to reject. A judge frequently overrules an OBJECTION by an attorney.
Overruling a verdict. Rejecting a decision of a lower court. This happens sometimes when a case is brought on appeal before a higher court.
Overt act. An intentional, open, unconcealed act, as opposed to a covert, secret act; an act committed with a purpose and with intent. In CRIMINAL LAW, an act carried out with intent to cause harm.
Overture. A PROPOSAL; an opening move toward advancing NEGOTIATIONS.
Owing. An unpaid DEBT; an OBLIGATION that is due; due; unpaid.
Owner. A person who has the legal TITLE to PROPERTY; a proprietor.
Owner, equitable. A person who is recognized as the OWNER of PROPERTY but who has a TRUSTEE to administer the property for his or her benefit.
Owner, general. A person who has the primary TITLE to PROPERTY, as distinguished from a special OWNER who may have a bailee's LIEN upon the property.
Owner, joint. An individual who

owns PROPERTY with one or more other people.

Owner, legal. A person recognized by law to be the rightful OWNER of a PROPERTY.

Owner, reputed. A person who supposedly owns a property. In actuality, he or she may or may not be the legal owner.
> OWNER, LEGAL.

Owner, riparian. A person who owns PROPERTY bordering a body of water, such as a river, lake, or sea. Such an OWNER does not own the water bordering his property unless he owns all the land surrounding a private lake.

Owner of record. The true OWNER according to the public RECORDS.

Owner's risk. A term used by shippers of goods stating that the OWNER assumes the risks of DAMAGES to the goods while they are in transit.

Ownership. The RIGHTS of an OWNER in controlling his PROPERTY, including the right to hold and enjoy it, the right to lease or sell it, etcetera.

Oyez. "Hear ye"; an expression often used to alert those in the courtroom that the COURT will be in session momentarily. In most courts, the word is said twice by a court OFFICER, i.e., "Oyez, oyez."

P

Pact. A CONTRACT; an AGREEMENT; a TREATY; a COVENANT.
Pais. > IN PAIS.
Palm off. A slang expression meaning to sell or get rid of something under false pretenses. As an example, one may palm off a used car for a high price, stating it is in good condition when in reality it is in a very poor state of repair.
Palpable. Obvious; readily detected; easily felt.
Panderer. A pimp; a procurer.
Panel. A list of potential JURORS who might serve in a particular TRIAL; the members of a commission.
Paper. A legal DOCUMENT; an INSTRUMENT; a written STATEMENT or memorandum.
Paper credit. CREDIT based upon a written DOCUMENT giving SECURITY for a loan.
Paper money. The money prevalently in use. In actuality, paper money is a PROMISSORY NOTE issued by the government against its own CREDIT. Paper money is a substitute for mineral money, such as gold, silver, nickel, or copper.
Par. Equal; average; normal.
Par delictum. Equal guilt; equal fault; equal wrong (Latin).
Par value. The value of a DOCUMENT, such as a stock or bond, according to the amount stated on the face of the document. As an example, the par value of a bond as stated on its face may be $100, yet the bond may be selling at the time for considerably more or less than $100.
Paralegal. A person specially trained in legal work, but who is not a lawyer. Paralegal personnel have become important individuals in the carrying out of research and other important matters for attorneys. > LEGAL ASSISTANTS.
Paramount equity. An equitable CLAIM that comes first, and is superior to any other right or claim.
Paramount title. A CLAIM to ownership of property that is better than any other claim to the title.
Paranoia. A form of mental illness characterized by feelings of persecution, accompanied by hallucinations and delusions.
Parcels. Real estate PROPERTIES, with specifications as to their location and boundaries.
Pardon. A release from an unlawful OFFENSE; exemption from paying the penalty for a criminal act; the removal of guilt so that the offender is as free as if he had never committed the offense.
Parens patriae. The right of the government to take care of those who cannot take care of themselves, including children and the mentally incompetent (Latin).
Parent. A mother or father.
Parent corporation. A COMPANY that owns another company, said company being a SUBSIDIARY of the parent corporation.

Parental consent. The consent that a MINOR must obtain from a parent before marrying or undertaking other legal OBLIGATIONS.
Parentheses. Punctuation marks, ( ), used in the middle of a sentence to insert a word, phrase, or other sentence which relates to the main sentence. Such words, enclosed by parentheses, do not destroy the grammatical meaning and construction of the main sentence.
Paresis. **1.** Partial or complete paralysis. **2.** A brain disease, also known as dementia paralytica, caused by a syphilitic infection.
Pari causa. An equal cause; an equal right; on the same basis (Latin).
Pari delicto. Equally at fault (Latin).
Pari ratione. By the same reasoning (Latin).
Parliamentary rules. REGULATIONS adopted by a legislative body to control how meetings shall be conducted.
Parol arrest. An arrest made without a written, official, legal document; a verbal arrest, such as a police officer may perform when he seizes an offender in the act of committing a crime.
Parol contract. An oral, nonwritten agreement. > VERBAL AGREEMENT; VERBAL CONTRACT.
Parol evidence. Testimony given orally, as distinguished from written evidence.
Parole. Being let free from serving a sentence conditionally, the condition being that the parolee must behave lawfully and must obey all parole rules and regulations. Violation of parole results in the prisoner being returned to prison.
Parole board. A commission, provided by law, to consider applications for PAROLE. The parole board stipulates the conditions under which a prisoner may be paroled.
Parole system. A system wherein prisoners with indeterminate sentences (those without a fixed length of time) are paroled. If they act well while on parole, the parole continues; if not, they return to prison.
Parricide. The act of killing one's parent.
Part. A division of a COURT that specializes in the trying of certain types of cases.
Partial account. An accounting from an EXECUTOR covering a limited period of his activities in behalf of an ESTATE, as distinguished from a final account.
Partial dependency. The state of a person who is partially self-supporting but must depend upon others for a portion of his or her support.
Partial disability. The inability to perform all of one's duties, but with the ability to carry out some functions. (An individual with a chronic back injury may be able to do light but not heavy manual labor.)
Partial disclosure. A deceit in which one tells only part of a story or recites only some of the facts in a case, usually in an attempt to conceal important details.
Partial distribution. The granting to LEGATEES of a portion of an ESTATE, before final SETTLEMENT is made.

Partial evidence. EVIDENCE that tends to establish a relatively unimportant fact in a case. Such evidence may or may not have a bearing upon the major issue in a dispute.
Partial intestacy. The situation that occurs when someone leaves a WILL that disposes of only part of his total assets.
Partial loss. **1.** PARTIAL DISABILITY; partial loss of a part of the body, such as the loss of a tip of a finger. **2.** Loss of some part of a whole, such as a fire in which only a part of a structure is burned out.
Partial pardon. Forgiveness of only part of a crime or transgression, leaving the offender to pay the penalty for the remainder of the OFFENSE.
Partial probate. The filing of only the valid portions of a WILL that contains some invalid clauses.
Partial verdict. A VERDICT in a criminal case that acts upon only some of the charges made against the defendant.
Partible lands. Lands that can be partitioned or divided.
Participate. To have a share in; to join with others in a common enterprise or endeavor.
Participation in crime. An individual who is one of several who have committed an OFFENSE; also, one who has stimulated, instigated, aided, or conspired to commit a crime.
Particular. Specific; relating only to a portion of a whole; individual; not general.
Particular lien. A CHARGE against a specific piece of PROPERTY, by which it is held for the payment of a DEBT.
Particular malice. Hatred and ill will directed against a specific person or group of people.
Particulars. A BILL OF PARTICULARS; a written listing of the precise nature of the charges being leveled by the plaintiff against the defendant. This information, when received by the defendant, will enable him to better prepare his defense.
Particulars of sale. When PROPERTY is being sold at AUCTION, it is usually described in a written DOCUMENT known as the particulars of sale. It lists all the details about the property to be auctioned.
Parties in interest. A term that refers to everyone concerned in a BANKRUPTCY proceeding, including the bankrupt person or company, all CREDITORS, and others who have a stake in the bankruptcy.
Parties to a judgment. All those having an interest in a LAWSUIT.
Partition. A division of PROPERTY, whether it is land, merchandise, or other, belonging to co-owners. If property cannot be amicably divided by co-owners, then it is sold and the money derived therefrom distributed to the various co-owners.
Partition deed. A DEED (document) that effectively divides REAL ESTATE property.
Partner. An individual who is joined by another or several other people in a joint enterprise; a member of a firm or business; a member of a professional firm, such as a partner in a law firm.
Partner, dormant. A SILENT PARTNER; one who is not general-

ly known as a co-owner of a firm or business yet is entitled to all the rights of partnership. > PARTNER, SILENT.

Partner, limited. A person who has contributed funds to a PARTNERSHIP but is not actively engaged in the running of the business. His responsibilities as to the DEBTS and OBLIGATIONS of the partnership are limited to the amount of money he has contributed.

Partner, liquidating. A PARTNER who is given the task by his fellow partners of terminating and winding up the affairs of a firm that is going out of business.

Partner, nominal. A PARTNER who is publicly thought to be an active member of a PARTNERSHIP but in reality has no interest in it.

Partner, ostensible. A person who is publicly thought to be a member of a PARTNERSHIP. He may or may not actually have an interest in the business.

Partner, secret. The same as a dormant or silent partner.

Partner, silent. A dormant or secret partner.

Partner, special. A PARTNER who is not totally involved in a business; a person who is liable only up to the amount of money he has invested in the firm; a member of a "limited partnership." > PARTNER, LIMITED

Partner, surviving. A PARTNER who settles the affairs of a PARTNERSHIP when the business is dissolved because of the death of a co-partner.

Partnership. An agreement between two or more people to invest their money, time, and skill in a common endeavor, with the prior understanding that profits or losses will be shared in a prescribed manner; a CONTRACT in which two or more people are co-owners. > JOINT ADVENTURE; PARTNERSHIP, GENERAL; PARTNERSHIP, LIMITED; PARTNERSHIP, PARTICULAR; PARTNERSHIP ASSETS; PARTNERSHIP ASSOCIATION; PARTNERSHIP AT WILL; PARTNERSHIP DEBT; PARTNERSHIP GOODWILL.

Partnership, general. An ordinary PARTNERSHIP, one in which the PARTNERS are fully committed to conduct all their business for the joint benefit of all the partners, as distinguished from a limited partnership. > PARTNERSHIP, LIMITED; PARTNER, LIMITED.

Partnership, limited. A PARTNERSHIP that involves financial agreement under which a contributor to the partnership is liable, if the company should fail, only for the sum of money he invested.

Partnership, particular. A joint enterprise, or PARTNERSHIP, formed for the purpose of conducting one transaction, such as a purchase of a tract of land or real estate.

Partnership, universal. > UNIVERSAL PARTNERSHIP.

Partnership assets. PROPERTY belonging to the PARTNERSHIP, not to the individual members of the partnership. Such ASSETS are available to pay partnership debts.

Partnership association. An ASSOCIATION formed under existing laws that limits the responsibility of each partner to the amount of money he has invested. In other words, a partnership association is composed solely of special partners. > PARTNER, SPECIAL; PARTNER, LIMITED; PARTNERSHIP, LIMITED.

Partnership at will. An ASSOCIATION of two or more persons in a joint enterprise that shall continue only so long as the PARTNERS wish it to continue. A partnership at will can be dissolved at any time by a partner or partners dropping out without giving prior notice of their intentions.

Partnership debt. An OBLIGATION of the PARTNERSHIP, not of an individual partner.

Partnership goodwill. An intangible ASSET whose value cannot be precisely determined, obtained through the high regard and satisfaction of the PARTNERSHIP's customers. When selling a business, an attempt to compute value to goodwill is often made. This sum is then added to the worth of the property, merchandise, and other assets of the company.

Parturition. The act of giving birth; childbirth.

Party. **1.** A person engaged in a LAWSUIT, either a PLAINTIFF or a DEFENDANT. **2.** A person who has taken part in a transaction, such as a party to an AGREEMENT or CONTRACT.

Party aggrieved. A person who feels he has been wrongly treated in a COURT ACTION and whose legal rights have been damaged. Such a party has the right to appeal.

Party and party. A term referring to both the PLAINTIFF and the DEFENDANT; the two litigants in a LAWSUIT.

Party injured. A person who has been harmed by the act or acts of another person or persons.

Party of record. A person who has been formally designated as one engaged in a SUIT or an APPEAL.

Party structure. A partition; a wall or other structure separating PROPERTIES of different owners.

Party to be charged. A person against whom an ACCUSATION is brought in court; a person who, through legal procedure, is being forced to fulfill an AGREEMENT or CONTRACT that he has failed to fulfill.

Party wall. A wall built on the line between two adjoining pieces of land belonging to different persons, for their mutual benefit.

Pass. **1.** To pronounce or declare, such as to pass JUDGMENT or to pass SENTENCE. **2.** To be approved, such as a tax declaration that is passed by the revenue authorities. **3.** A DOCUMENT (usually a slip of paper) allowing a prisoner a temporary leave, such as a weekend pass.

Pass for cause. To permit a JUROR to go unchallenged for CAUSE, thus allowing the opportunity for an absolute. > PEREMPTORY CHALLENGE.

Passage. **1.** The enactment of a legislative bill, as opposed to the defeat of a bill (not passed). **2.** The crossing of a body of water; sea travel.

Passbook. **1.** A book in which a depositor records his bank deposits. **2.** A book in which a merchant records his sales to customers, especially sales on credit.

Passion. In reference to a crime

such as MURDER or ASSAULT, the element of passion often is an important consideration. An individual who commits a crime in sudden passion usually has not planned or premeditated the act. As an example, a man who finds his wife in the arms of a lover may commit a murder out of passion. ➤ SUDDEN PASSION.

Passive. Inactive; silent; submissive.

Passive concealment. The act of being silent about a fact; passive concealment does not imply active hiding of a fact or event.

Passive negligence. NEGLECT resulting from failure to act or perform something that one is legally obligated to do.

Passive participation. Silent CONSENT and AGREEMENT to the performance of an act or acts, usually illegal ones. Someone who stands by while others initiate a conspiracy to which he has agreed is known as a passive participant.

Passive trust. A TRUST in which the beneficiary performs all the duties that a trustee would ordinarily perform.

Passport. **1.** A legal DOCUMENT issued by a state or country attesting to and certifying an individual's citizenship. A passport is presented as EVIDENCE when entering a foreign country that one is a citizen of a particular country. ➤ VISA. **2.** A license to safe-conduct, issued during time of war.

Past consideration. One given before a CONTRACT is made, as distinguished from a present or future consideration. A past consideration is not essential to an AGREEMENT or contract that is about to be made.

Past due. Overdue, such as a payment of an OBLIGATION or DEBT.

Patent. **1.** The right of monopoly over the manufacture, sale, and use of a device or process that one has discovered or invented, such patent being granted by law or statute. **2.** A grant of MINERAL RIGHTS to public land. **3.** As an adjective, patent means "obvious" or "evident."

Patent danger. Obvious peril or danger.

Patent defect. An obvious fault or defect in an article of merchandise.

Patent infringement. The violation or encroachment upon someone else's patent.

Patent law. The branch of the law that deals with the obtaining of PATENTS, maintaining patents, infringement of patents, PATENT RIGHTS, etcetera.

Patent office. A subdivision of the U.S. Department of Commerce. Its duties include the issuance of PATENTS to inventors of new devices or processes and other matters relating to PATENT RIGHTS.

Patent right. A PRIVILEGE secured by PATENT, giving one the exclusive right to manufacture and sell a particular patented article, process, or device.

Patent suit. A LAWSUIT involving the validity of a PATENT or one dealing with an alleged violation of a PATENT RIGHT. > INFRINGEMENT OF PATENT; PATENT INFRINGEMENT.

Patentable. Meeting the requirements necessary to obtain a patent, such as the originality, uniqueness, and usefulness of a new article, device, or process.

Patentee. The person to whom a PATENT is granted.

Paternal. Relating to the father; originating from the father.

Paternal power. The legal AUTHORITY a father has over his children who are MINORS.

Paternal property. PROPERTY that one has inherited from his or her father.

Paternity. Fatherhood.

Paternity proceeding. A COURT ACTION to establish the PATERNITY of a child born out of wedlock and to force the father to support it. ➤ BASTARDY PROCEEDING; FILIATION PROCEEDING.

Paternity tests. Various blood tests performed to establish the fact that a particular man is or is not the father of a particular child. Such tests are done by comparing various blood groups and subgroups of the child's and alleged father's blood. (These tests have a very high degree of accuracy.)

Pathology. The medical science dealing with the nature of disease on the basis of the examination of diseased tissues and organs.

Patient consent. Permission given by a patient to a physician, dentist, or hospital to carry out a specified operative procedure or other form of treatment. (Such consent is not valid when obtained from a MINOR or patient whose mind is not clear, unless in an emergency situation.)

Patient consent in emergencies. PATIENT CONSENT does not have to be obtained in situations where life and death are involved. As an example, it is not necessary to obtain consent to perform a tracheotomy when one is choking to death, nor must preoperative consent be obtained when an immediate procedure must be performed to stop a life-endangering hemorrhage.

Patient forbearance rule. The rule that one spouse is not agreeing to or forbearing cruel marital treatment merely because he or she takes no immediate action against the other. In other words, the legal right to sue for SEPARATION OR DIVORCE is not impaired because someone put up with cruel treatment in the hope of saving the marriage.

Patricide. KILLING one's father.

Patrimonial. Pertaining to PROPERTY inherited from one's father or grandfather.

Patrolman. A policeman whose duties include patrolling a particular area or "beat."

Patron. **1.** A benefactor; a protector; a customer. **2.** A patron of the arts is one who helps to support enterprises such as museums, operas, ballets, etcetera.

Patronage. The power of making appointments to government positions. In some instances, patronage is dispensed without too great consideration of merit. As an example, an individual may be appointed as an ambassador mainly because he contributed large sums of money to a political party, rather than upon his qualifications as a diplomat.

Patronage dividend. A DIVIDEND, or REFUND, paid out of

the profits of a cooperative association to a customer of the association. The amount of the dividend is calculated according to the extent that the patron (customer) has used the facilities of the association.

Patronize. **1.** To favor; to encourage. **2.** To act in a condescending manner. **3.** To use the facilities of a store, such as a regular customer.

Pauper. An individual without means of self-support; an indigent person; a person dependent upon public assistance.

Pawnbroker. A person who takes goods (jewelry, musical instruments, and other items of value) in exchange for the advancement of money. If the money is returned to the pawnbroker, the goods are returned; if the money is not returned within a specified period of time, the goods are sold.

Pawnee. An individual to whom merchandise is pawned.

Payable. Due; a legally enforceable DEBT.

Payable on demand. Phrase used referring to a BILL that must be paid on the date due, without a GRACE PERIOD or extension of time.

Payable to bearer. Phrase used referring to a BILL that is payable to anyone who presents it, not necessarily to a specific person; a BEARER INSTRUMENT.

Payable to bills payable. Phrase used referring to the designation of an impersonal PAYEE when creating a BEARER INSTRUMENT.

Payable to cash. Phrase used referring to a PROMISSORY NOTE endorsed in blank by the maker, thus in reality creating a PAYABLE TO BEARER document.

Payable to holder. Phrase used referring to a BILL to be paid to whomever presents it. In other words, PAYABLE TO BEARER.

Payee. The person to whom a bill is to be paid.

Payment in due course. Payment made by the DEBTOR when the BILL is due, or within a few days thereafter.

Payment into court. Monies paid to a court (to its clerk) in accordance with an ORDER OF THE COURT. Such monies are distributed to the interested parties when they make application for payment.

Payoff. The time for a settlement of a debt; a reckoning.

Peace and quiet. The right to security, tranquillity, and freedom from violent disturbances, as guaranteed by the law.

Peace bond. A bond given by a person to a court pledging that he will not violate the law and he will "keep the peace."

Peace of the state. The protection that the state or nation provides for its citizens and those who reside within the law in its boundaries.

Peace officers. Police officers, sheriffs, deputy sheriffs, marshals, constables, and others whose duties involve the keeping of the peace.

Peaceable entry. Entering onto lands peaceably, without the use of force, as opposed to FORCIBLE ENTRY.

Peaceable possession. The uncontested taking POSSESSION of PROPERTY, as opposed to taking possession in spite of a suit against such possession.

Peaceful assembly. The RIGHT of people to meet peacefully and discuss matters important to them. The right of peaceful assembly is guaranteed by the U.S. CONSTITUTION.

Peaceful picketing. The right of workers on strike to picket without violence and without physical obstruction of the entrances to the premises.

Peculation. The unlawful taking over of government PROPERTY or FUNDS for personal use by an individual who has had such property or funds entrusted to his care.

Peculiar. **1.** Special; particular. **2.** An adjective describing someone whose actions or life-style is eccentric or strange.

Pecuniary. **1.** Involving money; monetary; financial. **2.** Capable of being evaluated in terms of money.

Pecuniary benefits. BENEFITS that can be evaluated in terms of how much money they are worth.

Pecuniary condition. Financial condition; the wealth of a person, including PROPERTY and earnings. The pecuniary condition of a person is frequently considered when extending CREDIT.

Pecuniary damages. DAMAGES that can be determined accurately in terms of money, as opposed to damages suffered by humiliation, shame, impairment of reputation, etcetera, which are impossible to calculate accurately in monetary terms.

Pecuniary injury. > PECUNIARY DAMAGES.

Pecuniary legacy. A LEGACY to be paid in money, often after conversion of the deceased person's PROPERTY into cash.

Pecuniary loss. **1.** A loss that can be evaluated monetarily. **2.** Money that a dependent loses when a person who supports him or her dies.

Pederasty. **1.** Sexual intercourse between male and male. **2.** Sexual intercourse between an adult male and a boy. **3.** A form of sodomy.

"Peeping Tom." A person who habitually peeps into windows, especially to see women in the nude.

Peer. An equal. A man judged by his peers is one who is tried or investigated by people of equal status and rank.

Penal. A term implying PUNISHMENT, imposed for violating the law. The punishment or PENALTY may be a monetary fine or may involve imprisonment.

Penal action. A suit that involves the payment of a PENALTY for violating the law. (The penalty may be a fine or imprisonment, or both.)

Penal bond. A BOND paying a specific sum of money if a specific act or performance is not carried out as promised.

Penal code. The set of laws governing criminal actions, as set forth by a state or a country. Such a code may describe the penalties to be enforced for certain crimes. (A model code has been proposed by the American Law Institute for application throughout the country.) > PENAL LAW.

Penal law. A penal code; a penal statute.

Penalty. **1.** The PUNISHMENT meted out to someone who has violated the law. **2.** A sum to be paid for not carrying out a CONTRACT or other act that one is obligated to perform.

Pendency of action. Phrase used to describe the status of a LAWSUIT from the time it was commenced until its final determination; the active life of a lawsuit.

Pending. Not yet decided; often used to refer to a suit that has been started but not yet finished.

Pending action. A LAWSUIT that is in the process of being determined.

Pending litigation. > PENDING ACTION.

Penetration. In cases of alleged RAPE, penetration is the insertion of the penis into the vagina. Complete insertion and/or ejaculation are not essential in determining penetration.

Penitentiary. A prison; in some areas, a penitentiary can be a local or county place of detention, as distinguished from a state prison.

Pension. A sum of money paid periodically to a retired employee, with such funds derived from accumulated contributions made over the years by the employee and employer, or by the employer alone.

Pension fund. Money set aside through employer and employee contributions, or by employer contributions only, and invested so that it will be available for periodic pension payments after retirement. Such funds are exempt from taxation.

Pension trust. A FUND put in trust with trustees, the monies to be safely invested so that they will be available to pay fixed sums to retired employees.

Pensioner. A person who receives a PENSION, usually a retired worker or government employee.

People. The citizens; the state; the nation; the constituted government. A CRIMINAL prosecution is stated as the "People against______," meaning that all the people are prosecuting an alleged perpetrator of a crime.

Per annum. By the year. Interest due per annum means interest due each year (Latin).

Per capita. By the individual; by the head. A per capita tax is one paid by each individual; share and share alike (Latin).

Per curiam opinion. An opinion rendered by a court composed of more than one judge, rather than one rendered by a single judge.

Per diem. **1.** Each day (Latin). **2.** A per diem is a payment made to someone for each day's work or services, as distinguished from payments made on a weekly, monthly, or yearly basis.

Per procuration. By proxy. The term means that someone, often an attorney, is authorized to act in another's behalf in a certain matter.

Per quod. Whereby (Latin); by means of which. This term is often used to preface a recitation of the harmful results caused by a wrongdoing.

Per quod defamatory. Statements that are made or printed which appear to be slanderous, but whose injurious consequences must be proved.

Per se. By itself (Latin); taken alone; simply stated.
Per stirpes. By representation (Latin). This term is used in WILLS to denote the share that a DESCENDANT has in a deceased person's ESTATE. As an example, if someone dies and leaves $10,000, half of which is to go to a son and the other half to a daughter, and the son dies leaving two children, then each child would inherit $2,500, or half the money their father would have inherited.
Percentage. A portion of 100.
Percentage commission. Monies received by a BROKER, based upon a PERCENTAGE of the price he obtains for the sale. Such COMMISSION is paid by the person who employs the broker.
Percentage compensation. Monies paid to a TRUSTEE based upon a PERCENTAGE of profits earned by the business he administers.
Percentage depletion. A PERCENTAGE of a taxpayer's gross income derived from oil or gas wells, or other natural deposits.
Perdurable. Existing or enduring forever. This term is often used when referring to an estate.
Peregrine. An alien; a foreigner.
Peremption. The quashing or putting an end to a LAWSUIT.
Peremptory. Conclusive; final; not to be challenged; absolute.
Peremptory challenge. A CHALLENGE to the seating of a JUROR by an ATTORNEY. A peremptory challenge is one given without cause or reason, but it is final and positive. In other words, a juror subjected to a peremptory challenge cannot be impanelled or seated in the jury. ➤ CHALLENGE FOR CAUSE.
Peremptory defense. A DEFENSE that denies the right of the PLAINTIFF to sue.
Peremptory exception. A DEFENSE that denies the right of the PLAINTIFF to sue and that seeks dismissal of the charges without trial. A peremptory exception usually raises a question of the law and the legal validity of the suit.
Peremptory instruction. An INSTRUCTION by a JUDGE to a JURY, pointing the direction of the VERDICT.
Peremptory rule. An order of the COURT to make its ruling absolute and complied with immediately; a RULE ABSOLUTE.
Peremptory undertaking. An attempt by a PLAINTIFF to see that his CLAIM is brought to trial at the very next session of the court.
Peremptory writ of mandamus. An ORDER commanding a PARTY absolutely to do a certain thing.
Perfect equity. The interest or equity of a buyer of REAL ESTATE who has fulfilled all his obligations to the owner, including full payment for the PROPERTY, but has not yet received the DEED to the property.
Perfect instrument. A DEED or INSTRUMENT is perfect when it has been recorded and filed for record in the appropriate bureau of records.
Perfect right. A right according to LAW, as distinguished from a MORAL RIGHT.
Perfect title. A clear TITLE; a title that is totally free from any cloud or LITIGATION or doubt.

Perfecting bail. Justifying BAIL; assuring the court that one has the PROPERTY and qualifications to be eligible for bail.

Perfecting transfer. The completion of the transfer of ASSETS in a BANKRUPTCY case.

Perfection of appeal. The completion of all the things necessary to be done in order to APPEAL a case.

Perfidy. Breach of TRUST; treachery; disloyalty; breach of confidence.

Performance The fulfillment of a CONTRACT or AGREEMENT, thus terminating an OBLIGATION.

Performance bond. A BOND guaranteeing that a CONTRACT will be fulfilled, and if it is not fulfilled, a sum of money will be paid as a PENALTY.

Performance test. A provision in a CONTRACT calling for determination that the CONTRACT has actually been fulfilled and the contractor is entitled to his money.

Peril. Danger; exposure to injury or loss; the risks insured against in an INSURANCE POLICY.

Perishable commodity. Items that deteriorate rapidly, such as vegetables or fruit.

Perjury. False TESTIMONY; the telling of an untruth when acting as a WITNESS in a COURT proceeding; the making of a false statement in an affidavit; the willful swearing to a falsehood in a matter before a court. Perjury occurs when someone has taken an oath to tell the truth and then knowingly tells an untruth; lying under oath. Perjury is punishable by severe fines and/or imprisonment.

Permanent abode. A legal RESIDENCE; a home where one spends most of his time and where one intends to continue to reside.

Permanent alimony. An allowance granted by a court to a spouse who is legally SEPARATED or DIVORCED. In actuality, such alimony may not be permanent as it may terminate under special circumstances, such as the death of one of the parties, the remarriage of a spouse, the misconduct of a spouse, etcetera. The situation varies from state to state, according to the different marital and divorce laws.

Permanent disability. A physical or mental incapacity that appears to be permanent and irreversible.

Permanent improvement. An improvement to land or other PROPERTY that will remain indefinitely and has become an integral part of the land or property.

Permanent injury. INJURY that appears with reasonable certainty to be ongoing and will not disappear.

Permanent nuisance. A DAMAGE to PROPERTY that will continue indefinitely; a nuisance that cannot be removed.

Permanent receivership. The management and administration of a business or property after the court has rendered a JUDGMENT, as opposed to a RECEIVERSHIP established merely to afford temporary relief.

Permanent support order. A court edict that a man or woman must support spouse and child or children permanently and indefinitely.

Permission. Legal CONSENT to perform an act, without which consent, the act would be illegal; the license to do something; sufferance.

Permissive. Permitted; allowable.

Permissive counterclaim. A SUIT brought by a DEFENDANT against a PLAINTIFF who is suing him. However, the permissive counterclaim has nothing to do with the matter that the plaintiff has brought up in his suit.

Permissive possession. The occupation of PROPERTY by an individual who has the CONSENT of the owner to so occupy it.

Permit. **1.** A license; a permission given in writing. **2.** To tolerate; to license; to grant permission.

Permutation. The act of exchanging or bartering.

Perpetrator. The individual who carries out a crime.

Perpetual annuity. Annual payments to continue for an unlimited period of time, including time after the death of the BENEFICIARY; an annuity to continue indefinitely, without interruption.

Perpetual easement. The right of a nonowner to use adjoining land (an EASEMENT) forever. The granting of the right of way across PROPERTY forever would constitute a perpetual easement.

Perpetual franchise. A PRIVILEGE that shall continue forever.

Perpetual succession. The continuous, uninterrupted existence of a CORPORATION even though its officers and personnel may change over the years.

Perpetuating testimony. Preserving TESTIMONY of a WITNESS so that it may be used in future LAWSUITS. A written, sworn DEPOSITION is taken so that if the witness dies or disappears, the testimony will still be on the record and will be usable.

Perpetuity. **1.** Something which lasts forever. **2.** Any attempt to control the disposition of PROPERTY by WILL that is supposed to continue longer than the life of someone who is alive when the maker of the WILL dies, plus 21 years.

Perquisites. Compensation above that of one's ordinary salary. Such benefits or monies are received properly and not in violation of one's position or duties, such as the free use of a telephone or car paid for by the employer.

Person. An individual, MINOR or adult, female or male; a corporation; a body of persons or individuals.

Persona non grata. **1.** An unaccredited person; someone who is not acceptable. **2.** In diplomatic terms, an individual who is not acceptable to a country to which he has been sent as a representative. **3.** A person in disfavor (Latin).

Personal. Pertaining to an individual; the opposite of impersonal.

Personal assets. Things owned by an individual, such as goods, real estate, securities, jewelry, furniture, houses, apartments, insurance policies, legacies, etcetera. Personal assets can be used to pay off DEBTS owed by an individual during his lifetime or after he dies.

Personal bias. PREJUDICE against one of the parties in a LAWSUIT, as expressed by a JUDGE hearing a case.

Personal chattel. PERSONAL EFFECTS; PROPERTY that is movable; articles of PERSONAL PROPERTY.

Personal effects. The same as PERSONAL CHATTEL; distinguished from property that is nonmovable, such as REAL ESTATE.

Personal holding company. A CORPORATION in which five or fewer people own at least half the stock and at least 80 percent of the corporation's income in any one year is derived from interest. Personal holding companies are subject to especially high federal income taxes, to avoid the use of the company as a means of escaping payment of taxes.

Personal indignity. The suffering of continued or repeated humiliation and ridicule, frequently a GROUNDS FOR DIVORCE. Personal indignity implies intolerable living conditions, but not bodily harm.

Personal injury. **1.** Damage (INJURY) to the body. **2.** A personal wrong or violation of a personal right. Such personal injury is frequently the basis for a LAWSUIT against the wrongdoer. Personal injury is not limited to physical bodily harm.

Personal knowledge. Firsthand knowledge; knowledge derived from one's having felt, seen, heard, or known about something himself. (Personal knowledge is *not* something one has learned from another person.)

Personal liability. An OBLIGATION of a person, as distinguished from an obligation enforceable against property. Also, the personal responsibility of an agent while acting in someone else's behalf.

Personal liberty. The RIGHT of a person to travel and to live wherever he wants within the confines of the country. Personal liberty is, of course, denied to prisoners, to people against whom a CRIMINAL ACTION is pending, and to those on PROBATION or PAROLE.

Personal property. Movable objects owned by individuals, such as securities, jewelry, furniture, clothing, money, etcetera. Personal property is also called *chattel property.* > PERSONAL CHATTEL; PERSONAL EFFECTS.

Personal representative. An administrator or executor of an ESTATE; a TRUSTEE; a RECEIVER.

Personal security. A GUARANTEE of a DEBTOR's personal pledge to pay his DEBT.

Personal service of process. The direct hand-to-hand delivery of a SUMMONS to the person being summoned.

Personal tort. A wrong perpetrated against another. It may take the form of a physical attack or it may be an attack against one's reputation or feelings.

Personal use trust. A TRUST created for a particular individual's sole use, in which the BENEFITS or INTEREST cannot be transferred.

Personally known. A legal STATEMENT acknowledging that one's identity is known and recognized. A NOTARY's certificate states that the person appearing before him is actually the person whose name is being signed to the DOCUMENT he is notarizing.

Personalty. Chattels; movable property; PERSONAL PROPERTY.
Persuade. To influence someone so that he will come to a particular conclusion or determination; to induce one to do something through argument and entreaty.
Pertain. To relate to; to belong to.
Pertinent. Relevant; directed toward the issue being discussed; apropos; related; germane.
Perturbation. A breach of the peace; a disturbance.
Perverse verdict. A decision of a JURY which fails to follow the INSTRUCTIONS of the JUDGE on a point of law.
Petit jury. A small JURY (French); a TRIAL jury, as distinguished from a GRAND JURY; a *petty jury.*
Petit larceny. The unlawful taking of another's PROPERTY, the worth of the property stolen being less than an amount specified by local statutes; same as *petty larceny.* (Petit larceny is distinguished from GRAND LARCENY because of the relatively small value of the articles stolen.)
Petition. A written, formal request for a particular thing to be done or a certain act to be carried out. In EQUITY PROCEEDINGS, a petition is in actuality a COMPLAINT.
Petition for certiorari. An application for a WRIT OF CERTIORARI. In other words, a request that there be a review and inquiry by a HIGHER COURT of proceedings that have taken place in a LOWER COURT (Latin).
Petition in bankruptcy. A written request, filed in a court, starting a proceeding in BANKRUPTCY.
Petitioner. One who presents a PETITION to a court seeking relief in a controversial matter. The person against whom the petition is leveled, is called the RESPONDENT.
Petitioning creditor. A CREDITOR who starts BANKRUPTCY proceedings against a DEBTOR.
Petitory action. A legal proceeding in which the PLAINTIFF seeks to establish his title to REAL ESTATE property. A petitory action occurs when TITLE to property is in dispute and the plaintiff wishes to establish in court that he is the rightful owner of the property.
Pettifogger. An ATTORNEY who engages in small and inconsequential affairs, or one whose activities are below the high standards one expects of an attorney at law.
Petty jury. > PETIT JURY.
Petty larceny. > PETIT LARCENY.
Philadelphia lawyer. A popular expression for an ATTORNEY who uses crafty, sly methods in practicing law.
Philanthropy. The act of donating money and/or property to worthy causes, such as hospitals, museums, colleges, charitable organizations, etcetera.
Physical cruelty. A basis for DIVORCE. It involves acts of violence of such a nature that they endanger health, or even life.
Physical depreciation. Decrease in the value of PROPERTY brought about by age and constant use. Such DEPRECIATION affects buildings and other structures.
Physical fact. As evidence in a CRIMINAL SUIT, a physical fact is one that exists as a result of hav-

ing been seen, heard, or felt. Seeing a person attack another is a physical fact; hearing a scream is a physical fact; feeling a gun pressed against one's body is a physical fact.

Physical impossibility. Being in two different places at the same time is a physical impossibility. In CRIMINAL CASES, the DEFENSE frequently claims that a crime could not have been committed by a particular person because of the physical impossibility that he could have been at the scene of the crime when it occurred. Also, a physical impossibility would exist if it were presumed that a 250-pound man could crawl through a window just eight inches wide.

Physical incapacity. In matters pertaining to DIVORCE, inability to perform the sex act is considered to be a physical incapacity.

Physical injury. 1. DAMAGE to one's body. **2.** In reference to PROPERTY, physical injury exists when something interferes with one's ability to use and enjoy one's own property. As an example, physical injury exists when one is denied access to one's own property because of blockage of a road leading to it.

Physical necessity. A situation in which one is forced to take a particular action, such as a situation in which one must inflict bodily harm on another in order to protect one's own physical safety.

Physical violence. An act in which bodily harm is inflicted upon someone. Physical violence is not infrequently presented as a reason that a DIVORCE decree should be issued.

Physician partnerships. Agreements in which two or more doctors agree to practice together, collect their fees together, and share them according to agreement. Also, they agree to share responsibilities for the outcome of the various cases that are treated by one or more of the partners.

Physician-patient privilege. The right to keep secret certain aspects of the patient's accident or illness before the commencement of a TRIAL. Often, this privilege is waived, and the physician and patient reveal all the details to the opposing attorney.

Physician's obligation to treat. Contrary to common belief, a physician is not legally OBLIGATED to treat a patient, even in an emergency.

Picketing. The practice of workers on strike posting union members at the entrances and exits of the workplace. Among other DUTIES, pickets see and note the workers who enter the struck premises to perform work. However, it is forbidden by law for pickets to interfere with those who wish to continue to work despite the existence of a strike.

Picketing, lawful. PICKETING that is carried out quietly and without demonstrations or violence.

Picketing, unlawful. Picketing that misrepresents the facts or is based upon false statements; dishonest picketing.

Pickpocket. A THIEF who steals valuables or money directly from one's pocket or pocketbook.

Pilferage. STEALING, especially taking a portion rather than all that one could take, in order that the theft not be discovered; filching.

Pilferer. A person who steals things of relatively small value, or one who just takes a small part of something.

Pillage. Plundering; the violent taking of things which do not belong to one.

Pillory. An outmoded form of PUNISHMENT in which the head, arms, and legs are placed through holes in a board and locked in place. This form of punishment for a CRIME was used extensively in Colonial days in the United States. The criminal was pilloried where all could see him; thus they were made aware of his unsocial behavior.

Pimp. A person who procures prostitutes for others. The pimp earns his living by extracting a portion of the fee paid to the prostitute.

Piracy. **1.** A robbery carried out on the high seas. **2.** The stealing and unlawful reprinting of a book, pamphlet, or other copyrighted material.

Place of contract. The geographic location in which an AGREEMENT has been concluded. Such place of contract frequently determines how the CONTRACT shall be fulfilled, because contracts often are subject to the laws of the place where the contract has been concluded.

Placer claim. A mining claim made by a private person or persons on public lands, wherein the minerals lie on the earth's surface, not in the rocks beneath its surface.

Plagiarism. Stealing the ideas, words, and language of another author and passing them off as one's own.

Plaint. A COMPLAINT; the presentation of a plaintiff's CLAIM in a LAWSUIT.

Plaintiff. The party who is bringing a LAWSUIT against a DEFENDANT; the person or persons who are suing. ➤ COMPLAINANT.

Plan. **1.** A procedure designed to reorganize a COMPANY so as to pay off DEBTORS and to continue the operations of a business, such a plan taking place in a BANKRUPTCY proceeding. **2.** A sketch or outline of something to be done.

Plant. A factory; a place where a business is conducted, most often including machinery for manufacturing a product.

Plea. The response by one who is accused of a CRIME; the answer the law requires of a DEFENDANT who is accused.

Plea, affirmative. An answer to a charge containing a FACT that destroys the plaintiff's case. Usually the fact in the affirmative plea has not been included in the charges presented by the plaintiff.

Plea, anomalous. A response to a charge, the PLEA containing both positive and negative facts.

Plea, bad. A PLEA that is deficient both in FACTS and in its form of presentation.

Plea, dilatory. An answer to a COMPLAINT that does not touch upon or consider the merits of the case.

Plea, double. A defective PLEA that contains separate, unrelated matters that are erroneously applied to one issue. This type of plea will not be permitted by the court.

Plea, equity. An answer stating reasons why the SUIT should be dropped or dismissed. Such a PLEA includes all the facts as seen by the DEFENDANT, and it answers all the questions raised by the PLAINTIFF.

Plea, false. A sham PLEA; a plea made in bad faith, with full knowledge by the pleader that he is not stating true facts.

Plea, foreign. A PLEA that challenges the AUTHORITY of the JUDGE to preside over the case.

Plea, negative. A PLEA that denies the substantial charges and specifies one fact that makes the PLAINTIFF's position untenable.

Plea, peremptory. PLEAS made to the merits of the issues between the two parties. Thus, the DEFENDANT specifically answers the PLAINTIFF's charges.

Plea, pure. A PLEA that introduces new material for the DEFENSE, such as a plea for release when the DEBT, the basis for the suit, has been paid. A pure plea refers to a matter or circumstance not mentioned in the PLAINTIFF's charges.

Plea, sham. A false PLEA; a plea so worded as to deceive and entrap.

Plea, special. > PLEADING, SPECIAL.

Plea bargaining. A procedure wherein bargaining takes place between the PROSECUTOR and the ACCUSED as to the disposition of the charges. Usually, such bargaining results in an AGREEMENT whereby the accused, by admitting the crime, receives a lighter sentence.

Plea in abatement. A PLEA that objects to the time, place, and mode of trying the case, but at the same time does not go into the merits of the PLAINTIFF's claims. Thus this type of plea gives the right of the plaintiff to renew the suit at another time, or in another place, or in another form.

Plea in bar. A DEFENDANT's response to charges that sims to defeat the PLAINTIFF's claims completely and finally.

Plea in discharge. A PLEA that admits the PLAINTIFF had a right to sue but that states that the DEFENDANT has already fulfilled his obligations to the plaintiff.

Plea in reconvention. A PLEA that sets up new material, not for the purposes of defense but to institute a cross-complaint.

Plea of confession and avoidance. An answer to a PLAINTIFF's charge granting that the plaintiff had a right to SUE, but stating that his cause of action has already been discharged by some subsequent matter.

Plea of guilty. A confession of GUILT made in an answer to a formal charge. A plea of guilty is a voluntary PLEA.

Plea of limitations. An answer to a charge that attempts to obtain the protection of the STATUTE OF LIMITATIONS. In other words, the PLEA seeks to have the charges dismissed because too long a period of time has elapsed since the commission of the alleged wrongdoing.

Plea of nolo contendere. In a sense, this is a plea of GUILTY, in that it states the DEFENDANT will not contest the charges brought against him. This type of plea anticipates that a less severe punishment will be meted out. A plea of nolo contendere does not free the defendant from the responsibilities of a civil action brought against him.

Plea side. The section of the court where CIVIL CASES are tried, as distinguished from the section where CRIMINAL CASES are tried.

Plead. To deliver the DEFENDANT's answer to the charges brought against him. Pleading is usually undertaken by an ATTORNEY AT LAW, although an accused is privileged to plead his own case.

Plead issuably. To answer CHARGES in such a manner as to raise questions as to the facts or the LAW, as they apply to the charges.

Plead over. To ignore purposely a particular statement or misstatement made by a DEFENDANT in his answer to the charges against him.

Plead to the merits. A PLEA that considers the main issues involved in the case, as distinguished from a plea that skirts or avoids the issues. A plea to the merits will permit a fair and full trial to proceed.

Pleader. A person who prepares PLEAS and files them in COURT, usually an ATTORNEY.

Pleading. The written statements of each side of a LAWSUIT, including the PLAINTIFF's claims and the DEFENDANT's responses.

Pleading, articulated. A PLEA that sets forth in separate, numbered paragraphs, responses to each of the facts or issues involved in the suit.

Pleading, special. A PLEADING is special when it includes material that goes beyond the mere denial of the PLAINTIFF's charges, including special matters of DEFENSE.

Pleading over. Introducing a new PLEA prepared by a DEFENDANT after his original plea has been rejected by the court for inadequacy or for not going to the merits of the case. Pleading over means that an amended or new plea will be introduced.

Pleadings. The formal ALLEGATIONS by the opposing parties as to their CLAIMS and DEFENSES. These pleadings will form the basis for the trial to be held to decide the case.

Plebiscite. The vote of an entire population on a proposed LAW or ACTION, usually one of major proportions. A plebiscite might be held to decide whether an entire people wanted to remain in status quo or whether they want to become united with or become part of another nation.

Pledge. The granting of physical possession of goods or PERSONAL PROPERTY to a person to whom one owes a DEBT. The CREDITOR holds such property as security until the debt is paid.

Plenary. Complete; full.
Plenary action. A SUIT in which the merits of the case are fully investigated and discussed, and the DECISION reached is unrelated to any other suit or action. A plenary action follows formal presentation of all the issues to the COURT by both parties.
Plenary confession. A full and complete confession.
Plenary suit. PLENARY ACTION.
Plenipotentiary. **1.** A diplomatic officer with full power and authority to act on behalf of another; the other is usually the ambassador. A diplomat with a plenipotentiary rank is usually the second-ranking diplomat, just under the ambassador. **2.** Full authority; full power.
Plevin. A warrant; an assurance; security.
Plunderage. The stealing of cargo or goods aboard ship.
Plurality. In elections, the candidate who receives the greatest number of votes is said to have a plurality. If there are only two candidates running for the office, the plurality will constitute a majority of the votes cast. However, if more than two candidates are running, the candidate who wins may have less than a majority of all votes cast. In such a circumstance, he will have merely a plurality.
Plurality of trust. A situation wherein a person in a single DOCUMENT creates more than one TRUST, but names the same person to be the TRUSTEE (administrator) of all the trusts he has created.
Pluries writs. Multiple COURT ORDERS of execution or ATTACHMENT, issued in the same suit or upon the same JUDGMENT of the court.
Pocket veto. The vetoing of a bill by an executive, such as a president or governor, by not acting upon it within the time prescribed by law. Thus, if the law says a bill should be signed within ten days to be valid, and the executive fails to sign it within the ten days, the bill is said to have received a pocket veto.
Point of law. A matter of law in a case is one that depends upon the existing STATUTES governing the situation, as distinguished from a MATTER OF FACT. Thus, despite the FACTS in a particular case, the court's ruling must follow what the law has already decided in other, similar cases. > MATTER OF LAW.
Point reserved. When a difficult POINT OF LAW is presented during a TRIAL, the JUDGE may want to weigh the matter and study it for a while. He will then state that interpretation and conclusion concerning the particular point will be forthcoming at a later time in the trial. In other words, point reserved.
Police court. A LOWER COURT that hears and tries minor OFFENSES and MISDEMEANORS. Such a court usually has a limited JURISDICTION.
Police lineup. > LINEUP.
Police officer. A law enforcement OFFICER employed by a township, county, municipality, or state. His or her duties are many and var-

ied, as outlined by the community served.

Police record. A court file in which records are kept of those who have been convicted of a crime or crimes. Other records are kept of those who have been arrested but are awaiting trial for alleged crimes.

Policy. **1.** A course of action to be followed or avoided. **2.** The programs and aims of a GOVERNMENT in caring for its people. **3.** A DOCUMENT issued by an insurance company.

Policy, blanket. An insurance policy that covers a class of PROPERTY rather than a particular article or thing. As an example, a blanket policy may cover all the art a man owns, whether it is located in one or many places.

Policy, endowment. A life insurance policy that after a specified number of years will start paying money to the insured if he is still alive, or to his heirs if he is dead. > INSURANCE, LIFE.

Policy, insurance. > INSURANCE POLICY.

Policy, paid-up. A life insurance policy on which no further premium is due. > INSURANCE, LIFE.

Policy, public. The aims and goals of the law in promoting the general welfare of the people.

Political. Pertaining to government; pertaining to the establishment of policies for governing a community, state, or nation.

Political crime. An OFFENSE against the government, such as treason or an attempt to overthrow a constituted government through illegal activities.

Political office. A government office obtained through elections. Not included in a political office are CIVIL SERVICE jobs or jobs dealing with the administration of justice, which should be free of political influence.

Political party. A voluntary, nongovernmental association formed for the purpose of proposing certain candidates for office and working toward their election. Each political party has its own ideas on how the government should be administered, what policies it should follow, and who would be the best people to be elected to carry out its principles and ideas.

Political process. The method by which candidates for public office are nominated and elected. In a democracy, the people are responsible for this process.

Political rights. PRIVILEGES of citizens established by the UNITED STATES CONSTITUTION; such privileges and RIGHTS grant them the power to participate in the establishment and administration of the government. Political rights enable one to speak his or her mind freely on government affairs and to vote freely for anyone he or she chooses.

Politics. The art and science of administering public affairs and government.

Poll. **1.** A list of people who are entitled to vote in an election. **2.** To question each JUROR to hear whether he agrees with the VERDICT. > POLLING A JURY. **3.** To take a poll is to ask a number of people their opinion on a certain question. The poll only questions a fragment of the sum total of those who have an opinion on the subject. However, a good sample poll of a relative few may supply the same information as if everyone had been polled.

Poll tax. 1. A tax on each head (individual) who resides in a specified area, regardless of occupation or amount of property owned. 2. The 24th Amendment to the UNITED STATES CONSTITUTION makes it illegal to levy a tax as a prerequisite to voting in a federal election.

Polling a jury. Asking each JUROR if he or she concurs in the VERDICT that has been presented to the COURT.

Polls. A place where people go to cast their vote.

Polyandry. The ancient practice of a woman having more than one husband at one time. Polyandry is still practiced in some remote regions of the Himalayas.

Polygamy. The practice of having more than one spouse at the same time. It is illegal in the United States and other Western countries but is still practiced in some regions of Asia and the Orient.

Polygraph. 1. A LIE DETECTOR apparatus. 2. A machine which makes copies of DOCUMENTS.

Pool. 1. An ASSOCIATION of merchants who jointly buy or sell a certain COMMODITY or commodities. 2. An illegal ASSOCIATION of merchants who agree to refrain from competing against one another in a free market, thus causing RESTRAINT OF TRADE. Such a pool usually agrees to price fixing and to dividing the profits of their activities.

Pooled semen. In ARTIFICIAL INSEMINATION, the semen of the husband is pooled with that of one or more donors. As a consequence, one is never certain exactly whose sperm has impregnated the woman, should the woman become pregnant.

Pooling. Commingling funds of several sources or TRUSTS in order to invest in SECURITIES.

Poor debtor's oath. A swearing by a DEBTOR that he has no money or PROPERTY with which to pay his DEBT.

Popular action. A SUIT to recover a PENALTY, the CAUSE being given to the people in general; an ACTION to recover a penalty, given to anyone who will SUE for it.

Popular government. Government controlled by the people through the FREE ELECTION of executives and legislators; a representative democracy.

Port authoriy. An ADMINISTRATIVE AGENCY with powers to maintain and control a port. Airports have within the past few decades been considered as "ports" and therefore may be under the JURISDICTION of a port authority.

Port of departure. A clean bill of health that a ship must carry before entering a United States port. Such a DOCUMENT is issued by the officials at the port from which the ship departed for the United States.

Port of entry. A port at which there are a customshouse and customs officers to examine and levy taxes upon ships and their cargo.

Portal to Portal Pay Act. A federal law governing the matter of payment to employees who are on the employer's premises but who have not yet begun to work.

Portion. **1.** A share; a part. **2.** The part of a parent's estate that is given to a child.

Positive evidence. **1.** EYEWITNESS' TESTIMONY **2.** TESTIMONY by a witness that he has himself seen or heard something take place.

Positive law. Rules of conduct established either by laws passed by legislatures or by the customs and practices of a people.

Positive wrong. A willful, premeditated, wrongful act, done with the intention of causing harm.

Posse. A group of men deputized by a SHERIFF to help him find and detain a CRIMINAL.
➢ ARMED FORCE.

Possess. To have in one's control; to have and to hold; to own; to have possession of.

Possession. Exclusive control and occupancy of PROPERTY; the RIGHT to live on and enjoy, without interference, land or other property.

Possession, actual. A situation in which one occupies the PROPERTY he possesses.

Possession, adverse. The occupancy of PROPERTY when the RIGHTS and TITLES to it may be contested by another person or persons.

Possession, constructive. POSSESSION assumed to exist. The one claiming TITLE to the PROPERTY is not actually occupying it although he claims the right to do so.

Possession, derivative. Occupancy of PROPERTY not from ownership of the TITLE but by the consent and arrangement with the owner. Such POSSESSION could be that of a person who has leased the property from another.

Possession, exclusive. Occupancy of land solely for one's own benefit and use, with exclusive CLAIM to the TITLE to said PROPERTY.

Possession, hostile. POSSESSION and occupancy of PROPERTY by one who denies any other person's RIGHTS or CLAIMS to the property.

"Possession is nine-tenths of the law." This aphorism implies that one who claims TITLE to and POSSESSION of property must have a very good case in order to oust the occupant, because "possession is nine-tenths of the law." (The saying should not be taken literally.)

Possession, natural. Physically occupying property without actually having title to it.

Possession, vacant. PROPERTY that has been totally abandoned and vacated by a person formerly in POSSESSION.

Possession, writ of. A COURT ORDER granting the RIGHT of someone to take over and occupy PROPERTY that is being occupied by another person.

Possessor, bona fide. One who occupies PROPERTY with the true conviction that he is the rightful and sole owner. When he faces a SUIT by someone who claims that he is not the owner of the TITLE, he ceases to be a bona fide possessor.

Possessor, mala fide. One who occupies and controls PROPERTY as if he were title-holder, when he is fully aware that he does not own the title to the property.

Possessory action. A SUIT to obtain actual POSSESSION and occupancy of PROPERTY, as distinguished from a suit that merely attempts to prove that one owns the TITLE to the property.

Possessory lien. One in which the CREDITOR has the right to occupy and use the PROPERTY until the DEBT is paid.

Possibility of issue extinct. This phrase refers to the doctrine that a woman, so long as she is alive and no matter what her age, is considered capable of bearing children. Thus, one cannot in legal matters invoke the conclusion that there will be no more children in the family to inherit money or property from an ESTATE that makes bequests to ISSUE.

Possibility of reverter. The possibility that an ESTATE will be returned to the grantor, if some particular event occurs at some time in the future. Such an estate is actually disposed of conditionally and may, under special circumstances, revert to the owner and not be disposed of at all.

Post-concussion syndrome. Chronic headaches suffered by some people who have sustained a head injury. Such symptoms may persist for weeks or months after the original accident.

Postdate. To date a DOCUMENT, CHECK, or other INSTRUMENT as some time later than it was actually signed. Postdating takes place when a person makes out a check, let us say, in July, but dates it for September.

Postdated check. A CHECK given to someone at an earlier date than is shown on the face of the check. Such a check does not become valid until the date on its face occurs.

Post diem. After the day (Latin). A request for payment post diem is a request for payment of a DEBT that is already due or overdue.

Post disseisin. The wrongful DISPOSSESSION of a property owner, committed again, after the rightful owner has regained POSSESSION of his property.

Post facto. After the fact (Latin). After the commission of the crime.

Post-mortem. An AUTOPSY; an examination of a dead body carried out to determine the cause of death. In Latin, post-mortem means "after death."

Post-nuptial settlement. A SETTLEMENT of money or property made after MARRIAGE, usually by a father for the benefit of his wife and/or children.

Post obit bond. A guarantee to pay off a LOAN out of money the borrower will receive from INHERITANCE at some time in the future (Latin).

Post rem statement. A declaration made after a TRANSACTION has been completed.

Post roads. Highways or sea routes over which mail was carried. Today, because almost all but local mail is transported by air, the term post road has become obsolete.

Post-trial motions. MOTIONS made in court after a TRIAL has ended.

Posterity. The DESCENDANTS of

a person, such as a child, grandchild, great grandchild, etcetera.

Posthumous child. A child born after the death of a father, or one born by Cesarean section immediately after the death of the mother.

Postmaster general. The head of the post office department.

Postpone. To delay; to put off to a later date; to defer.

Postponement. The delay or DEFERMENT of a TRIAL to a later time in the same day or to another day.

Potential. Possible, as distinguished from actual; capable of coming into being; a latent possibility, such as a person who has great potential to become successful but has not presently achieved success.

Pourover will. A WILL that leaves PROPERTY or money into an existing TRUST.

Poverty affidavit. A sworn STATEMENT, filed in COURT, that one does not have the money to pay the costs of a LAWSUIT.

Power. The authority and ability to do something; the right and capability of carrying out some act; the right of JURISDICTION.

Power, executive. The AUTHORITY vested in the executive department of the federal government.

Power, general. A POWER OF APPOINTMENT to be exercised without restrictions or limitations by the person granted the power.

Power of appointment. The AUTHORITY of a person to dispose of an interest that is vested in another person, or the authority to dispose of an interest that he himself possesses. Also, the authority conferred by WILL by one person upon another to select the person or persons who are to receive an ESTATE or an estate's income after the donor's death.

Power of attorney. 1. A written DOCUMENT stating that one appoints another to act in his behalf as an agent, giving him the authority to carry out certain specified acts. 2. A written DOCUMENT giving an ATTORNEY the authority to appear in court in someone's behalf.

Power of disposition. > POWER OF APPOINTMENT.

Power of revocation. The power to get rid of, divest, or sell PROPERTY or an ESTATE.

Power of visitation. The power of the directors or TRUSTEES of a nonprofit institution to run its affairs, including the AUTHORITY to appoint officers, faculty, etcetera.

Powers, collateral. The powers given by an owner to a person having no interest in a PROPERTY, to dispose of said property.

Powers, implied. The AUTHORITY of public officials that exists not as a result of specific delegation of power but is germane to the performance of their duties.

Powers, special. The AUTHORITY given to an AGENT to perform a specific act or acts, as distinguished from the authority to act in the PRINCIPAL's behalf in all matters.

Practicable. Something that can

be accomplished; feasible; workable.

Practical construction. The meaning and interpretation of a law or statute not by court decisions but by general consent and practice.

Practice. **1.** The way things are usually done; custom; habit. **2.** A method of proceeding in courts for the enforcement of rights or the correction of wrongs. **3.** A continuing occupation, such as the practice of law or the practice of medicine.

Practice act. A law that regulates and defines PROCEDURE in COURTS. Such acts are frequently supplemented with rules of practice.

Pragmatic. **1.** Pertaining to the practical point of view; practical. **2.** Officious; overly forward or aggressive.

Prayer. A request, such as is usually contained in a COMPLAINT asking for relief occasioned by a wrong committed by the DEFENDANT.

Preamble. A statement at the beginning of a LAW, act, or group of laws such as the U.S. CONSTITUTION, explaining why the law or laws are being enacted and what it is hoped they will accomplish; a preface.

Preappointed evidence. EVIDENCE that is submitted in advance as necessary for the proof of certain FACTS, as distinguished from CASUAL EVIDENCE that develops during the course of the case.

Precarious circumstances. The circumstances that exist when an executor's conduct and administration of an estate appear to be unwise, reckless, or imprudent, as judged by prudent observers.

Precarious possession. POSSESSION (the right to occupy and enjoy PROPERTY) that is dependent upon the pleasure of another and can be terminated at any time.

Precatory trust. A TRUST created with words of entreaty, such as "wish and request," rather than by words of command and direction. At times, a trust's validity is questioned because it was created with words of entreaty (PRECATORY WORDS) rather than words of command. However, such a trust's validity can frequently be upheld because the precatory words are interpreted as words of command.

Precatory words. Words of suggestion, recommendation, request, or entreaty, as distinguished from words of command.

Precaution. Measure taken in advance, in order to avoid a mishap or to produce a good result; foresight; prevention or preventive measures.

Precedence. The RIGHT to precede or to go before; to take precedence means the privilege of going ahead of, rather than after; to consider first.

Precedent condition. > CONDITION PRECEDENT.

Precedents. Court DECISIONS that are thought worthy to serve as models in future cases.

Precept. A written ORDER from a court commanding that certain things be done; a WARRANT; a direction of a court to an OFFICER or officers to carry out a certain act, such as to bring a person before the court.

Precinct. A police district; an election district.

Preclude. **1.** To make impossible; to estop; to prevent. **2.** To exclude; to rule out.

Precognition. The preliminary examination of WITNESSES by a PROSECUTING ATTORNEY before the beginning of a TRIAL.

Precondition. A CONDITION PRECENDENT; something that must happen before another thing can take place.

Predated instrument. Dating a CONTRACT or other DOCUMENT at a date earlier than the date on which it is executed (signed and notarized).

Predecease. To die before another person dies.

Predecessor. A person who precedes, or goes before, another person. (President Ford was President Carter's predecessor in office.)

Predicate. To use as a basis for a DEFENSE or an ACTION; to imply; to affirm; to base.

Predominant. A superior force or influence or power. (A predominant motive is one that prevails over other motives.)

Preemption claimant. Someone who claims PROPERTY before others, has occupied it, and is proceeding according to law to acquire TITLE to the property.

Preemption entry. The entering onto and occupation of public lands for the purpose of creating a homestead.

Preference. The RIGHT of one person over another. The term is often used in stating the order of descent for INHERITANCE purposes, that is, a surviving child has preference over a niece or nephew.

Preferential assignment. **1.** The right to be paid first, before all other creditors. **2.** An assignment of PROPERTY for the benefit of CREDITORS, made by a DEBTOR in BANKRUPTCY.

Preferential debt. A DEBT that is to be paid first, before debts owed to other CREDITORS.

Preferential transfer. A transfer of PROPERTY by an insolvent DEBTOR to one CREDITOR, with the exclusion of transfer to other creditors.

Preferred stock. Part of the capital of a CORPORATION, the nature of which is that profits are paid to holders of preferred stock before distribution of profits is made to holders of COMMON STOCK.

Prejudice. Actions favoring one side in a LITIGATION, not based upon the merits of the case but upon the bias and prejudice of a judge. Such an attitude of favoritism displayed by a JUDGE would render him or her unqualified to preside over the matter.

Prejudice of judge. Favoritism shown by a JUDGE toward one party in a LAWSUIT.

Prejudice of juror. A preconceived conclusion of a JUROR, formed before hearing all the facts in a case; an attitude of favoritism toward one side in a case, not based upon the merits of the case, but upon bias and prejudice.

Prejudicial error. A mistake in handling a TRIAL that results in substantial harm to the complaining PARTY. On review by a higher court, the court may find that a prejudicial error was of such substance as to entitle the complaining party to a new trial.

Prejudicial evidence. EVIDENCE introduced merely to influence the JURY wrongly. Such evidence should be ruled inadmissible.

Preliminary examination. An INQUIRY by a COURT to see whether there actually has been a crime committed and whether there is reasonable likelihood that a particular person committed the crime; a hearing; a *preliminary hearing.*

Preliminary hearing. > PRELIMINARY EXAMINATION.

Preliminary injunction. A RESTRAINING ORDER issued at the beginning of a LAWSUIT, mainly forbidding one of the parties to carry out some act that is in dispute in the case.

Premarital agreement. An AGREEMENT made between a man and woman prior to their MARRIAGE. It often includes provisions for the disposal of property should separation, divorce, or death ensue; an ANTENUPTIAL SETTLEMENT; a PRENUPTIAL AGREEMENT; an ANTENUPTIAL CONTRACT.

Premature judgment. A JUDGMENT BY DEFAULT, issued prior to the time DEFENDANT is supposed to appear in court to defend himself.

Premeditated design. In MURDER cases, the term means that the murderer planned the act beforehand and then consciously, willfully carried out his crime. > DESIGN TO KILL.

Premeditated murder. MURDER that was planned in advance and willfully carried out.

Premeditation. The thinking out of something in advance; forethought; consciously reflecting upon some thought or idea or act.

Premises. **1.** The basis or bases for an argument presented to a COURT; the real substance of a LAWSUIT; the introductory proposition that should lead to a conclusion. **2.** PROPERTY.

Premium. A reward for some act that has been performed; an amount paid by a borrower in order to receive preference in obtaining a loan; a bonus.

Prenuptial agreement. > ANTENUPTIAL CONTRACT; ANTENUPTIAL SETTLEMENT; PREMARITAL AGREEMENT.

Prepaid. Paid in advance.

Prepare. To make ready, such as to prepare a case for trial.

Preponderance. The weight, superiority, and credibility of a thing, as "the preponderance of evidence clearly shows the accused to be innocent."

Prerequisite. A requirement; something that is required beforehand.

Prerogative. Special PRIVILEGE; something which takes precedence, such as a prerogative writ; the inherent RIGHTS of the people.

Prerogative court. A PROBATE court where WILLS are filed.

Prerogative writ. A special COURT ACTION issued only under special circumstances, such as a WRIT of HABEAS CORPUS, a writ of MANDAMUS, or a writ of CERTIORARI. > HABEAS CORPUS, CERTIORARI, MANDAMUS.

Prescription. 1. A means of acquiring a RIGHT through continued POSSESSION and use over a prolonged period of time. As an example, a person who has used a right of way across another person's land for the past ten to twenty years may be said to have become entitled to that right of way through prescription. 2. A written order by a physician, given to a patient for presentation to a pharmacist. Such prescription orders a medication or medications that the pharmacist will prepare and contains information on dosages and use.

Prescriptive acts, easement, license, title, etcetera. Acts, easements, license, title, etcetera, obtained by way of PRESCRIPTION.

Prescriptive rights. PRIVILEGES obtained by way of PRESCRIPTION.

Presence of an officer. An OFFENSE, VIOLATION, or CRIME committed within view of a law enforcement officer. Such an offense, violation, or crime permits arrest without obtaining a WARRANT.

Presence of the court. A phrase used to describe CONTEMPT OF COURT, committed within the sight and/or hearing of the court.

Presence of the testator. A signing of a WILL within the sight of the TESTATOR. This implies that WITNESSES are present and that the testator is conscious and knows what he is signing.

Present. 1. Being at a certain place at a certain time. 2. To lay a motion or case before a COURT for consideration and action.

Present enjoyment. Something to be used and enjoyed now, as distinguished from something to be used and enjoyed at some future time.

Present interest. An interest that entitles a person to receive something immediately, such as a gift of income which commences now and continues on for a prolonged period of time.

Present worth rule. A rule sometimes observed in awarding a plaintiff DAMAGES based upon reduced earning capacity resulting from an injury. As an example, if a man has lost 25 percent of his earning capacity and his expectancy of work is for ten years, damages may be calculated by reducing this amount to its present worth. An annuity table is then used to determine what the plaintiff's dollar earnings are worth over a period of ten years, and that amount is awarded in damages, figuring the 25 percent loss of earning power.

Presentment. An informal CHARGE, in writing, made by a GRAND JURY. The charge, or presentment, stems from the grand jury's own investigation and knowledge of a possible OFFENSE or crime, not from information supplied to it by a PROSECUTING ATTORNEY. The presentment is given by the grand jury to the prosecuting attorney, who may then formally INDICT (charge) the ACCUSED person.

Preservation. The act of keeping something in good condition and safeguarding it from damage or harm; the act of preserving.

President. The chief executive officer of the United States; a presiding or managing officer of a legislative body, business, organization, committee, etcetera.
President pro tem. A person who acts as a president temporarily, often during the absence of the regular president.
Presiding judge. The JUDGE who hears and presides over a TRIAL. When a case is APPEALED, the request for the appeal bears the name of the judge who presided over the original trial.
Presumably. To be assumed as true.
Presume. To believe; to accept as true, even before conclusive evidence has been presented; to assume.
Presumption. An assumption; a conclusion drawn by inference; a presumption exists when a fact is thought to be true because another related fact is known to be true.
Presumption of death. An assumption that someone is dead, with such a conclusion based upon the fact that the individual has not been seen or heard from in many years. Also, an assumption that someone is dead because humans do not have such long life spans. Presumption of death would exist if it were known that a particular person was born 125 years ago. ≫ LEGALLY DEAD.
Presumption of fact. A logical conclusion based not upon direct, conclusive EVIDENCE in a case, but upon proved FACTS that are related to the matter. In other words, a reasonable conclusion that because one fact is known to be true, another fact must be true.
Presumption of innocence. In a CIVIL OF CRIMINAL CASE, the assumption that a person is innocent until proved guilty. Thus, the burden of proof that someone is guilty lies with the prosecutor.
Presumption of law. An assumption that has been created by an existing LAW OF STATUTE, thus forcing the COURT to a particular conclusion.
Presumption of survivorship. **1.** An assumption that one person has survived another, when in actuality they died in a common accident. **2.** An assumption that someone is still alive although he or she may not have been seen or heard from for some time.
Presumptions, mixed. Inferences or assumptions recognized by law because of their frequent occurrence, importance, and believability.
Presumptive death. ≫ PRESUMPTION OF DEATH.
Presumptive evidence. EVIDENCE considered to be factual unless proven otherwise; CIRCUMSTANTIAL EVIDENCE; INDIRECT EVIDENCE; FACTS and circumstances surrounding an event from which other facts are inferred.
Pretenses. Acts of pretending or making believe; a false pretense is a calculated, thought-out misrepresentation of facts.
Preterition. The failure of a person making a WILL to include or to provide for someone who would, by relation or descent, be entitled to an INHERITANCE if the deceased person had died INTES-

TATE (without having made a will).

Pretext. Something that is presented in order to conceal a true purpose; a cover-up, subterfuge.

Pretrial discovery. A BILL OF DISCOVERY presented to the opposing party before the beginning of a TRIAL. The procedure is frequently carried out to get important information from the opposing party before the actual trial begins. > BILL OF DISCOVERY.

Pretrial hearing. A preliminary meeting between LITIGANTS and their ATTORNEYS before the commencement of the actual TRIAL.

Prevailing party. The person who wins the LAWSUIT. It may be the PLAINTIFF who succeeds in his action, or it may be the DEFENDANT who successfully defends himself.

Prevarication. The act of deliberately speaking falsely in an attempt to mislead or deceive; telling an untruth.

Preventive injunction. An ORDER restraining someone from performing a specified act or acts, as distinguished from an affirmative injunction, which requires someone to perform a specified act or acts. > RESTRAINING ORDER.

Preventive justice. Justice that requires security measures in order to preserve the peace.

Preventive remedy. A REMEDY that prevents a violation of a RIGHT from being carried out. In other words, an injunction is a preventive remedy.

Previous question. A parliamentary procedure carried out to end debate and cause a question to be voted upon immediately. As an example, someone "moves the previous question." If the legislative body approves such a motion, then the issue must be voted without further debate.

Price control. A STATUTE of the federal government regulating the price of a COMMODITY or commodities. Price control frequently is enacted along with wage control in times of emergency.

Price discrimination. The act of charging one person more than another for the same service or article. This is illegal in interstate commerce.

Price fixing. An unlawful conspiracy among producers and/or distributors to fix the price of a product or products at a specified level.

Prima facie case. A CASE or ACTION that will win unless the other side produces strong evidence to contradict it; a case with sufficient positive evidence to convince a JUDGE and/or JURY.

Prima facie evidence. EVIDENCE that is obviously good and convincing; TESTIMONY sufficient on its face to convince JUDGE and/or JURY.

Primary. **1.** Chief; first; principal. **2.** A convention, meeting, or voting of voters to select a candidate who will represent their political party.

Primary boycott. A BOYCOTT carried out directly against an alleged offender, such as boycott against a particular supermarket because its owners are thought to give bad service to their customers.

Primary evidence. The best EVIDENCE available; evidence that is sufficient to establish a certain FACT.

Primary obligation. An OBLIGATION imposed by the law, such as an obligation on the grounds of public policy.

Primogeniture. The state of being the firstborn of a family; seniority by virtue of being the firstborn child.

Principal. Main; chief; most important. The main person, as distinguished from an agent.

Principal fact. The main fact in dispute in a case.

Principal in first degree. An individual who commits a criminal act.

Principal in second degree. An individual who witnesses and encourages the commitment of a criminal act by another or others.

Principle. A doctrine; a fundamental belief; a clear truth, universally accepted, such as the principle of law that one should be punished for committing a crime.

Prior conviction. A previous CONVICTION. When a repeated offender is convicted, the punishment is almost always greater than for a person who has had no previous convictions.

Prior jeopardy. > DOUBLE JEOPARDY.

Prior lien. A LIEN that has priority over other liens. In some instances, there is more than one CLAIM against property. When such a situation exists, the prior lien (claim) must be met first.

Priority. The right to take PRECEDENCE over another; the state of being ahead in time, therefore, having priority; a legal preference.

Prisoner at the bar. A phrase describing an ACCUSED person who is on trial for an alleged crime.

Privacy, right of. The RIGHT of a person to go his way and live his life without being subjected to outside interference, publicity, or other annoyances.

Private bill. A BILL that deals only with the personal interests of an individual, as distinguished from a public bill that may affect an entire community.

Private communication. > PRIVILEGED COMMUNICATION.

Private enterprise. A business or a professional activity carried out freely, without governmental interference or control, as distinguished from public enterprise regulated and conducted by a government.

Private law. Law pertaining to individuals, such as law dealing with an individual's attempt to recover DAMAGES for an injury to one's PERSON or PROPERTY.

Private property. > PROPERTY, PRIVATE.

Private rights. Basic RIGHTS that individuals are entitled to enjoy, such as the right to privacy, the right to own property, the right to go where one wants to go, etcetera.

Private ruling. A ruling of a court affecting an individual or individuals, not the community as a whole. > PRIVATE LAW.

Private wrong. A wrong committed against one or more individuals, as distinguished from a wrong against a local community, a state, or a country.

Privilege. A BENEFIT or RIGHT enjoyed by an individual, a group of people, a company, etcetera, not enjoyed by others; special dispensation; an exemption from the performance of some act that others are required to perform; an immunity.

Privilege, special. An IMMUNITY or POWER granted to some person or persons not granted to others. A diplomat representing a foreign country in this nation is granted certain exemptions, immunities, and privileges not granted the ordinary citizen.

Privilege, writ of. A court ORDER to enforce a PRIVILEGE.

Privilege against arrest. An exemption from ARREST granted to diplomats of foreign nations serving in this country. No matter what their status or rank, certain crimes, such as murder, do not allow for privilege from arrest.

Privilege against self-incrimination. The RIGHT granted by the 5th Amendment to the UNITED STATES CONSTITUTION whereby a person is privileged to refuse to answer a question or give TESTIMONY against himself.

Privileged communication. A communication of such privacy that the law exempts the person receiving such information from the duty of disclosing it. Communications from client to attorney, from patient to doctor, from penitent to priest, fall into the category of privileged communications. As a matter of fact, it is a violation of trust for an attorney, doctor, or priest to disclose such information or communication publicly.

Privileged communication, waiver at trial. During a TRIAL, a defendant may voluntarily decide to give up his RIGHT to keep certain information or communication secret.

Privileged communication, waiver by court order. Under special circumstances, a court has the right to order someone to reveal a PRIVILEGED COMMUNICATION.

Privileged communication, waiver of. The RIGHT to release the receiver of private information from keeping said information secret. Thus an ATTORNEY may be told by his client to reveal certain privileged information which had hitherto been kept confidential.

Privileged information. Information that is given only to certain persons, with the understanding that the information will not be revealed to others.

Privileges and immunities. The RIGHT of every United States citizen to protection by the government, the right to possess property, the right to pursue happiness, the right to safety, all within the laws of the country. These rights, known as privileges and immunities, are guaranteed in the 14th Amendment to the U.S. CONSTITUTION.

Privity. Private or "inside" information.

Privity in law. Identical interest of two people; the mutual relationship that exists toward the same PROPERTY. Thus, an heir is in privity with the ancestor from whom he inherits property, while someone who leases property is in privity with the person leasing it to him, etcetera.

Privy. 1. Private. **2.** An individual who is part of, or has an interest in, a SUIT, an ACTION, or other legal matter.

Privy token. A forged, false DOCUMENT, put together in order to obtain fraudulent possession of PROPERTY.

Privy verdict. A written, sealed VERDICT handed to a JUDGE out of court. Such a verdict becomes official only when announced publicly by the judge.

Prize law. The international codes of laws governing the capture of property at sea.

Pro and con. In favor of and against (Latin). A phrase that describes the arguments confronting each other from both sides in a legal DISPUTE.

Pro bono. An expression, derived from PRO BONO PUBLICO, meaning that free legal work has been done for some charitable or nonprofit organization (Latin).

Pro bono publico. For the good of the public (Latin).

Pro forma. A mere formality; as a matter of form (Latin).

Pro rata. According to percentage; proportionately (Latin).

Pro tem. Temporary, such as the appointment of a person to serve as a chairman only during the absence of the regularly appointed chairman (Latin).

Probability. Likelihood; something that may be true or may have happened has a probability of truth or fact. Probability may be great or small.

Probable cause. A reasonable cause, one that has a good chance of being true; a good ground for suspicion that a crime has been committed.

Probable consequences. Those results or consequences that have a good likelihood of taking place following a particular act or event; outcomes that a reasonable person could have foreseen.

Probable expectancy. Things that people have a right to expect.

Probable reasoning. Logic based upon a probable or supposed fact that one is attempting to prove.

Probate. The legal process of recording a WILL in the appropriate place, generally a PROBATE COURT, and proving that it is valid.

Probate bond. The bond of an EXECUTOR, GUARDIAN, or ADMINISTRATOR of an ESTATE, required by law to be given to the PROBATE COURT.

Probate court. The special COURT that handles matters concerning WILLS and ESTATES, such as the distribution of PROPERTY and money to those named in the will.

Probate judge. A judge of a PROBATE COURT.

Probate proceeding. Any COURT ACTION dealing with matters concerning WILLS and ESTATES. It may be a proceeding contesting the validity of a will, or merely one to carry out the orderly disposition of PROPERTY as set forth in the provisions of a will.

Probation. **1.** A trial period to test the fitness of a person to hold down a particular job or position. **2.** The act of proving. **3.** The permission given to a convicted criminal to remain out of jail under certain specific conditions and under the supervision of the court permitting the probation.

Probation officer. **1.** A court-appointed OFFICER whose duties include the supervision of criminals on PROBATION. He must see that the conditions of probation are being strictly observed. **2.** A public officer attached to a JUVENILE COURT who supervises the activities of juvenile delinquents.

Probationer. A criminal who is free on PROBATION.

Probative facts. Evidentiary FACTS; facts that tend to prove the matter at issue.

Procedural law. Law that follows certain rules and prescribes the methods for enforcing rights and correcting wrongs.

Procedure. RULES governing the conduct of a LAWSUIT, including the presentation of EVIDENCE, the making of MOTIONS, PLEADINGS, etcetera. In essence, it is the method of PROCEEDING in order to prove a legal RIGHT.

Proceeding. **1.** The presentation and prosecution of a LAWSUIT before a COURT. **2.** A CASE in court.

Proceeding, collateral. A PROCEEDING in which a particular question is involved incidentally; it is not a proceeding instituted for the purpose of deciding said question.

Proceeding, legal. Any ACTION, or CASE, being tried in COURT.

Proceeding, ordinary. A SUIT carried on in the usual manner, according to law.

Proceeding, special. Any ACTION in court that does not follow the ordinary, usual measures for trying a case; the opposite of an ORDINARY PROCEEDING.

Proceeding, summary. A CASE that is solved and settled quickly in COURT, without the aid of a JURY, without INDICTMENTS, and without other lengthy PROCEEDINGS.

Proceeding, supplementary. A PROCEEDING in which the DEBTOR, already ordered by the COURT to pay the CREDITOR, is questioned by the court to see if he has the means to carry out the decision of the court and pay the creditor.

Proceeding in error. A court PROCEDURE to have a LOWER COURT's decision appealed to a higher court, such PROCEEDING alleging that the lower court's decision was in error.

Proceedings in bankruptcy. COURT ACTIONS covering questions and matters between the BANKRUPT person or company (or the TRUSTEE or RECEIVER of the bankrupt person or company) and the CREDITOR or creditors. Such PROCEEDINGS include all matters, from the initial request of the conditions for SATISFACTION through the final distribution of the bankrupt's ASSETS to the creditors.

Process. **1.** A SUMMONS to appear in court to defend oneself; a WRIT; a WARRANT; a COURT ORDER; a SUBPOENA. **2.** All the acts of a court, from the commencement to the conclusion of a LAWSUIT. In other words, the court's regular method of operating (DUE PROCESS OF LAW). **3.** A written, formal ORDER of a COURT, issued under its authority as granted by law.

Process, final. The last COURT ORDER in a particular LAWSUIT, such as a WRIT OF EXECUTION (an order of the court that its decision be carried out).

Process, irregular. A COURT ORDER (WRIT) not issued in strict conformity with the established law.

Process, judicial. **1.** A SUMMONS or ORDER from the COURT informing the DEFENDANT of the ACTION against him and to compel him to appear in court to answer CHARGES. **2.** All the acts of the court, from the beginning to the end of a LAWSUIT.

Process, legal. A COURT ORDER; a WRIT; a WARRANT.

Process, mesne. A WRIT or COURT ORDER issued during a trial, as distinguished from a final process, which is issued after the trial's end.

Process, original. A WRIT or COURT ORDER issued before the commencement of a CASE, such as one ordering a DEFENDANT to appear in court to defend himself.

Process of interpleader. A PROCEDURE for determining the right to property claimed by more than one person, such property being in the POSSESSION of a third person.

Process server. A person who hands a SUMMONS or SUBPOENA upon a WITNESS or DEFENDANT.

Proclamation. A public declaration, such as one issued by a president or governor, usually set forth in written form. A very famous proclamation was the EMANCIPATION PROCLAMATION.

Proclamation of Emancipation. > EMANCIPATION PROCLAMATION.

Procreation. The production of children; reproduction.

Proctor. Someone who acts in another's behalf; a procurator.

Procuration. The act of granting AUTHORITY to another person to act in one's behalf. This is usually carried out in written form, such as a person giving POWER OF ATTORNEY to a lawyer.

Procurator. A person who acts in another's behalf, as an ATTORNEY who has been given POWER OF ATTORNEY; a PROCTOR.

Procure. **1.** To start something, as to institute a LAWSUIT; to effect; to contrive. **2.** To get or obtain something for oneself or for someone else.

Procurer. A pimp; a panderer.

Prodigal. A person who, despite being an adult, is incapable of managing his or her own affairs because of lack of good sense, failure to realize OBLIGATIONS, and extravagance; a spendthrift. In order to remedy such situations, courts often appoint GUARDIANS (CURATORS) for the prodigal.

Produce. **1.** To exhibit; to show; to place before one's view, as the promise of an ATTORNEY to produce a particular WITNESS in COURT. **2.** To yield, as a security is expected to "yield" a certain dividend. **3.** To procreate, such as to produce offspring. **4.** As a noun, produce means things that grow out of the soil or that come out of the ground, as gas or oil.

Production payment. A right to a payment of a specified share of the monies earned from minerals that have been mined.

Profanity. Irreverence toward sacred things, such as STATEMENTS that are scornful or contemptuous of God.
Profert. Producing a DOCUMENT in COURT for the purpose of having the opposing party examine and read it.
Profess. To declare publicly; to acknowledge openly.
Professional conduct. 1. The accepted manner of behavior of a professional, such as an ATTORNEY or physician. An attorney who demonstrates CONTEMPT OF COURT, or one who fails to keep the confidences of his client, is not exhibiting good professional conduct. 2. The way a LAWYER who has been admitted to the bar is supposed to behave and conduct his practice.
Professional corporation. A CORPORATION created for the practice of a profession, such as the law, medicine, dentistry, etcetera. Under recent STATUTES, individuals may incorporate. When they do this, they append the letters "P.C." after their names.
Proffer. An offer; to offer.
Profit sharing. An arrangement in a COMPANY or CORPORATION whereby employees and officers share in the profits of the business. Such profit sharing usually constitutes only part of the pay the employees receive for their work.
Profiteering. The practice of making an excessive amount of profit, usually in an underhanded or unprofessional way.
Prognosis. The probability of recovery from an illness.
Progressive tax. A TAX that taxes the wealthy more than the poor.
Prohibit. To prevent or forbid by legal means.
Prohibition. 1. An order by a higher court (one of greater JURISDICTION) for a lower court to stop trying a particular case on the grounds that it belongs in another court. 2. The name given to the VOLSTEAD ACT, the 18th Amendment to the U.S. CONSTITUTION. The Amendment forbade the sale of intoxicating beverages. The Amendment was repealed in 1933.
Prolix. Speaking or writing at great length, often boringly or tediously.
Prolixity. The habit of talking too much and giving unnecessary STATEMENTS, especially in pleading a case in court; verbosity.
Promise. A STATEMENT that binds a person to do something. A promise may be a matter of law, of conscience, or of honor; it may be written or verbal.
Promise to pay. An undertaking of a DEBTOR toward a CREDITOR, often in the form of a PROMISSORY NOTE, although it may be a verbal promise.
Promissory estoppel. A PRINCIPLE in EQUITY CASES that a promise is binding only if injustice can be prevented by enforcement of the promise.
Promissory note. A written DOCUMENT stating that a certain DEBT will be paid at a specified time or within a specified period of time. The NOTE will bear the signature of the DEBTOR and will state to whom and when the money will be paid.

Promissory oath. The swearing to God that a particular promise will be fulfilled.

Promote. To advance; to further; to sponsor; to aid the development and growth of an enterprise.

Promulgation. The making known to the public of a new LAW or RULE of the COURT.

Pronouncement of judgment. The rendition of a DECISION of the COURT, along with instructions to duly record the court's decision.

Pronouncement of sentence. The declaration of the COURT in a CRIMINAL CASE, stating the PUNISHMENT that the convicted criminal must undergo.

Proof. The establishment of truth through EVIDENCE; the effect of evidence; a conviction of the mind that a certain FACT in issue has been established as true.

Proof, affirmative. EVIDENCE that establishes a disputed fact.

Proof beyond a reasonable doubt. PROOF of such a forceful and convincing nature that there can be no REASONABLE DOUBT concerning the guilt of an accused. This is the type of proof necessary before declaring an accused to be GUILTY of a crime.

Proof evident. An expression meaning that the presumption is great and the PROOF overwhelming that a particular person has committed a particular CRIME. If such crime is a CAPITAL OFFENSE, such as MURDER, the accused will not be allowed bail because there is such great proof, proof evident, that he is the one who actually committed the crime.

Proof of claim. A written, documented CLAIM against a person who has died, such claim being filed in a PROBATE COURT. Also, a verified, written claim against someone who has gone into BANKRUPTCY.

Proof of death. EVIDENCE of death. A death certificate, filed in the appropriate place, is considered proof of death.

Proof of loss. A written, sworn STATEMENT by an insured person that he has sustained a particular loss. Such statement is presented to the INSURANCE COMPANY for reimbursement for the loss.

Propagate. **1.** To reproduce. **2.** To spread information.

Proper evidence. EVIDENCE that is relevant, pertinent, and admissible in COURT, as opposed to improper evidence.

Proper independent advice. Advice from someone who is competent to advise and who has nothing to gain or lose by giving advice.

Proper party. Any individual who is materially interested in the outcome of a LAWSUIT, and who is bound by the COURT DECISION in the case. However, the court decision in the particular matter can be rendered without him. In other words, he is not essential to the outcome or JUDGMENT in the case.

Property. **1.** Anything that can be owned, such as land, buildings, stocks, securities, jewelry, money, patents, copyrights, various rights, etcetera. **2.** The legal right to OWNERSHIP of a thing or things.

Property, community. A term applied to the property RIGHTS of a husband and wife when their AS-

SETS belong to both, rather than to wife or husband individually. Laws governing property rights vary from state to state.

Property, literary. > LITERARY PROPERTY.

Property, personal. > PERSONAL PROPERTY.

Property, private. PROPERTY belonging exclusively to an individual or individuals, as opposed to property owned by the PUBLIC; chattels; property that an individual has the RIGHT to possess, occupy, sell, or give to another.

Property, public. PROPERTY that is owned by a local, state, or federal community; the opposite of PRIVATE PROPERTY.

Property, real. Land and anything that is upon it, such as buildings, or anything that is in the ground beneath it or grows from its soil.

Property, special. An interest in or part OWNERSHIP of PROPERTY; special property is that which a mortgagee possesses on a piece of real estate, a house, etcetera.

Property act. A STATUTE enacted to make uniform the laws of PROPERTY throughout the country, especially to define rules for judging the validity of TITLE to property.

Property settlement. An AGREEMENT between a husband and wife who are getting a DIVORCE as to the distribution of their jointly owned PROPERTY.

Property tax. A TAX on the OWNERSHIP of PROPERTY, calculated according to the value of the property.

Proponent. A person who proposes something, such as a MOTION, in COURT; a person who ALLEGES or CLAIMS something; someone who places a WILL for probate in a PROBATE COURT; a person who supports a particular cause.

Proportional representation. A system of voting, not according to a strict majority of all the individual voters, but based upon the voting of various groups of people. The purpose of proportional representation is to ensure that minority groups, as well as the majority, are represented in a legislative body.

Proposal. **1.** A suggestion put forth for the purpose of obtaining acceptance. **2.** A measure put before a LEGISLATIVE body. **3.** An offer.

Proposition. **1.** A proposed STATUTE, RULE, or ORDINANCE put before the voters for their acceptance or rejection. **2.** An offer, with details explaining why it would be advantageous to accept it.

Propound. **1.** To offer a WILL for PROBATE. **2.** To set forth.

Proprietary articles. Merchandise manufactured under an exclusive RIGHT to produce and sell it.

Proprietary lease. A LEASE issued by a cooperative apartment association. Such leases grant the association the right to occupy the apartment under certain circumstances, such as nonpayment of maintenance charges.

Proprietary rights. RIGHTS and PRIVILEGES of an OWNER of PROPERTY.

Prorate. To divide and distribute monies proportionally; to ASSESS or TAX proportionally. (If someone owns 10 percent of the stock of a company and the company is sold, said person would receive 10 percent of the net proceeds from the sale.) > PRO RATA.

Prorating attachments. The act of placing all CREDITORS in equal status. Thus, when a settlement of DEBTS is made, each creditor receives his proportional share of the monies distributed.

Prorating claims. A distribution of ASSETS to CREDITORS proportionally, in relation to the size of their claims.

Prorating taxes. A division of tax LIABILITIES between the seller and buyer of PROPERTY.

Proration. The act of apportioning something, such as a computation of one's share in TAXES or of one's share in an ESTATE; apportionment.

Proration statute. A law requiring TAXES to be paid prior to the distribution of monies from an ESTATE, and the calculation of each person's share according to his interest in the estate.

Prorogation. An agreement to extend the time previously fixed.

Prosecute. To proceed and to maintain a LEGAL ACTION, such as a PROSECUTING ATTORNEY who tries in court to prove an ACCUSED person to be GUILTY; to attempt to enforce by legal action.

Prosecuting attorney. A LAWYER, appointed or elected, whose duties include conducting and maintaining suits on behalf of the state, or a district of the state. (The term usually refers to CRIMINAL CASES.)

Prosecution. A TRIAL carried out according to law before a JUDGE and a properly qualified JURY for the purpose of deciding the guilt or innocence of an accused person. (In CRIMINAL ACTIONS, the "people" or the "state" are stated as the one responsible for the prosecution.)

Prosecutor, public. A DISTRICT ATTORNEY or a STATE'S ATTORNEY whose job is to conduct criminal proceedings against an accused person.

Prosecutrix. A female who brings an ACTION, such as a charge of rape, etcetera.

Prospective earnings. Anticipated earnings; future earnings.

Prospective law. Law applying to situations that will arise after the time of enactment of the law. Most law is prospective, or in other words, it is not retroactive.

Prostitution. Indulgence in sexual acts in exchange for payment of money. (Prostitutes may be female or male.)

Protection order. A COURT ORDER delaying the showing of DOCUMENTS to the opposing party in a case, even though the request for the documents was made correctly.

Protective theory. The doctrine that more land or PROPERTY can be condemned and appropriated by a local, state, or federal governments than is actually needed for an intended project. Such extra land is taken for the purpose of enhancing and beautifying the area surrounding the project such as highway, and thus protecting the value of neighboring property.

Protective trust. A TRUST set up so that the TRUSTEE, fearful that the BENEFICIARY will not handle his monies wisely, can use discretion on how he disburses monies to the beneficiary.

Protectorate. A country whose international affairs, especially those involving security, are handled by another country. A protectorate may retain sovereignty over its internal affairs and thus continue to be an independent state.

Protest. **1.** Dissent; disapproval; a written STATEMENT, by someone making a payment, that he thinks the payment is illegal, exorbitant, unwarranted, etc., thus reserving the right to get the money back. **2.** An OBJECTION to a legal RULE or JUDGMENT.

Protestation. A DEFENDANT's indirect denial or acceptance of a CHARGE, made in such a way as to leave the matter open for further consideration during the course of the SUIT.

Protocol. **1.** Accepted methods of PROCEDURE among diplomats, heads of state, etcetera; ceremonial rules and procedures. **2.** A rough draft of an AGREEMENT or CONTRACT, or of a TREATY between nations.

Provable. Something that lends itself to being proved as true; susceptible of PROOF.

Provided by law. A phrase denoting that something has been prescribed (provided for) by an existing STATUTE (law).

Provisional. Temporary; preliminary.

Provisional court. Federal COURTS set up temporarily, such as those courts established in conquered territory during war.

Provisional injunction. A temporary INJUNCTION; a preliminary RESTRAINING ORDER.

Provisional order. A COURT ORDER made during the course of a TRIAL or LAWSUIT, such order being only of a temporary nature and not constituting the final JUDGMENT of the court.

Provisional remedy. The obtaining of a temporary ORDER from a COURT to prevent the opposing party from disposing of the PROPERTY in dispute, during the course of a trial.

Proviso. A qualification; a clause in a CONTRACT that imposes a condition, usually implying that if the condition (proviso) is not met, the contract is no longer valid or binding.

Provocation. The act of influencing or inciting someone to perform a particular act; the act of so enraging another person that he/she commits an act he/she would not ordinarily commit. For example, a husband could be so cruel to a wife that, in a rage, in response to his provocation, she stabs or shoots him.

Proximate. Direct, as opposed to indirect; immediate, as opposed to delayed.

Proximate cause. The immediate cause of an injury or accident; the legal cause; the real cause; a direct cause.

Proximate consequence. An outcome that proceeds from the ordinary course of events; an expected result or outcome.

Proximity. Nearness; closeness. The term applies to closeness and nearness in time, space, kinship, etcetera.

Proxy. A person who is authorized to act in another's behalf, such as an OFFICER of a CORPORATION who, in writing, is authorized to vote for a particular SHAREHOLDER; a CREDITOR who is authorized to vote for another creditor at a creditor's meeting.

Prudent. Exercising good judgment; wise; sensible; reasonably cautious; judicious; exercising prudence.

Prudent person doctrine. A rule that a TRUSTEE of an estate shall invest the ESTATE's funds only in low-risk, safe investments.

Pseudohermaphrodite. An individual born with the internal genitals of one sex but whose external genital characteristics resemble the opposite sex. The sex organs are usually incompletely formed and developed.

Psychiatrist. A physician who specializes in and treats disorders of the mind and mental disease.

Psychoneurosis. Mental and emotional imbalance associated with anxiety states but not accompanied by loss of insight or appreciation of reality.

Psychosis. Insanity; loss of contact with reality and loss of insight; loss of normal function of the mind; mental illness; a disease of the brain causing loss of mind function.

Public. **1.** Belonging to an entire community, whether it is a town, city, county, state, or nation. **2.** The citizens of a town, city, county, state, or country. **3.** The body politic. **4.** Owned by a government, as distinguished from something that is privately owned.

Public accountant. An individual who performs accounting services, audits books, oversees bookkeeping, etcetera, for a fee. Such a person may work on a yearly retainer fee or may be employed by the day. A CERTIFIED PUBLIC ACCOUNTANT (C.P.A.) is one who performs similar services but has passed certain rigid licensing examinations.

Public affair. **1.** A matter relating to government, whether local, state, or national. **2.** An event open to the general public. **3.** Something that is well-known to the general public.

Public auction. A sale, open to the general public, of PROPERTY or items to the highest bidder.

Public beach. A beach open to the public, as distinguished from a private beach.

Public corporation. A CORPORATION formed and operated only for the benefit of the general public, as distinguished from a private corporation; a MUNICIPAL CORPORATION; a political corporation.

Public defender. An ATTORNEY employed by a local, state, or federal government to defend people too poor to pay a private lawyer.

Public domain. Free from PATENT or COPYRIGHT, therefore open to the public for use; government property, as opposed to PRIVATE PROPERTY.

Public easement. A public right of way.

Public enemy. **1.** A citizen of a country against whom another country is at war. **2.** A criminal-at-law who threatens the safety of a community or a government.

Public grant. A gift of land from a government.
Public housing. Housing financed out of public funds for the purpose of furnishing low-cost living quarters for people of limited incomes.
Public institution. A school, home for the aged or mentally ill, a courthouse, college, library, hospital, or any other facility organized and run by public authority or created by law for the good of the public. Such institutions do not come into being for the purpose of making money; the opposite of a private institution.
Public interest. Matters concerning the welfare of *all* the people in a COMMUNITY, state, or nation.
Public land. Land owned by a government entity, such as a community, state, or nation. Such lands may from time to time be sold to private owners.
Public law. That which governs a whole public, such as statutes or ordinances that apply to everyone, no matter how trivial or serious.
Public nuisance. A violation of a public right, either by committing a certain act or acts, or failing to commit a certain act or acts. Such a nuisance may lead to common injury or harm.
Public offense. Conduct in violation of existing laws, punishable by law.
Public property. PROPERTY that is owned by and is devoted to the use of the general public.
Public record. A register in which records of legal TRANSACTIONS, PROCEEDINGS, STATUTES, RULES, REGULATIONS, LAWS, etcetera are kept on file and can be referred to from time to time.
Public relations. The art of creating favorable public opinion about a product, a company, an idea, a political candidate, a legislative proposal, a country, a city, etcetera.
Public ruling. A RULING affecting the entire public.
Public service commission. A body of men and women who regulate PUBLIC UTILITIES, such as the electric, power, telephone companies, etcetera.
Public trust. **1.** A public office. **2.** A trust whose ASSETS and INCOME shall benefit the general public; a charitable trust.
Public utility. A company rendering service to the whole public, such as providing electricity, gas, telephones, or other similar services.
Public welfare. The good of the society, including health, economic, social, and moral well-being.
Publish. To let it be known to the public; to print for general circulation; to give publicity to; to print a manuscript.
Puerility. **1.** The state of being a child; the state of being between childhood and adolescence. **2.** Foolish, childish conduct on the part of an adult.
Pundit. A wise man; a sage; an authority or expert.
Punishment. A PENALTY, a FINE, a jail SENTENCE, or other sentence pronounced upon a person who has committed an OFFENSE or a CRIME.
Punishment, capital. The death PENALTY.
Punishment, cruel and unusual.

1. Torture; barbarous or degrading conduct toward a prisoner. 2. A PENALTY that is out of all proportion to the OFFENSE committed.

Punishment, cumulative. Added PUNISHMENT given to someone who has committed the same type of crime on previous occasions; the kind of punishment meted out, by law, to habitual criminals.

Punitive damages. An award to a PLAINTIFF beyond actual possible loss. Such DAMAGES are by way of punishing the defendant for his act.

Punitive power. The authority of the government to punish those convicted of a CRIME.

Punitive statute. A LAW that imposes a PENALTY.

Purchase. To acquire TITLE to a PROPERTY, by the sale of said property by the OWNER; to buy.

Purchase on margin. The buying of a SECURITY (STOCK) without paying the full price to the BROKER, with intent either to pay the full price at a later date or to hold the stock for speculation, selling it when the price goes higher.

Purchase price. A price agreed upon by OWNER and buyer for the transfer of PROPERTY.

Pure accident. An accident caused by an unavoidable event. In other words, neither party to the accident was NEGLIGENT or at fault.

Pure plea. A PLEA that introduces new material for the DEFENSE, such as a plea for release when the DEBT, the basis for the suit, has been paid.

Purgation. A cleansing of GUILT; exoneration of oneself from suspicion of having committed a CRIME.

Purging a tort. Condemning oneself for having committed an acknowledged wrong. Also, assuming responsibility for a wrong committed by another. (Purging a tort implies that one will correct a wrong that he has committed.)

Purging contempt. The act of atoning for CONTEMPT OF COURT. This is usually done by apologizing to the court and/or by paying a fine for the misconduct.

Purloin. To steal; to pilfer.

Purport. To imply; to CLAIM; to mean; to convey.

Purposely. Something done with conscious intent; knowingly; intentionally.

Pursuant to. Conforming to; done in consequence of; following; according to.

Pursue. To follow through, as to pursue a claim until it is finally established; to continue actively a cause of action until its final conclusion.

Pursuit. 1. An occupation; a profession. 2. To chase or follow someone until he or she is captured.

Pursuit of happiness. A basic RIGHT guaranteed under the U.S. CONSTITUTION. It includes the right to go wherever one wants to go, the right to worship as one sees fit, the right to own property, the right to security and safety, and the right to live one's own life happily.

Purview. The main substance of a STATUTE that has been enacted, as distinguished from the PREAMBLE (opening explanation) of the law; the full scope of an enacted statute.

Putative. Supposed; reputed; alleged; commonly regarded as such. A putative father is a man supposed and reputed to be the father of a child born out of wedlock.

Putative marriage. A marriage that was contracted in good faith, but in ignorance of the FACT that it was actually an unlawful MARRIAGE. As an example, a divorced woman might remarry without knowing that her DIVORCE from her previous husband was not VALID.

Put in fear. Intimidated; placed in a position of being afraid not to perform an act one was urged to carry out.

Putting in evidence. Placing before a COURT.

Put out of court. The status of a CASE after its final determination.

Pyromania. An uncontrollable desire to set fires. Pyromania is a form of mental illness.

Q

Qua. In and of itself; for example (Latin).
Quack. A fake physician, one who practices medicine without having been trained and licensed.
Quae est eadem. A Latin phrase meaning that two things that appear to be different on the surface are in actuality the same matter.
Qualification of juror. The possession of those attributes by a potential JUROR that are essential for him to be able to qualify. These qualifications include soundness of mind, citizenship, residence in the area of the trial, lack of prejudice, etcetera.
Qualifications. The possession of those attributes essential for one who wishes to fill a particular public office or to carry out a specified job. For example, it is necessary for someone to have studied law before he can sit as a Supreme Court judge.
Qualified acceptance. An acceptance that modifies the original offer. In other words, a counteroffer.
Qualified denial. A semidenial; an inadequate DENIAL of a charge; a denial lacking positive force.
Qualified discharge. Partial RELEASE from an OBLIGATION.
Qualified endorsement. An ENDORSEMENT in which the endorser attaches some QUALIFICATION (condition) to his LIABILITY; a conditional endorsement.
Qualified nuisance. A negligently, carelessly, yet lawfully created NUISANCE that might cause INJURY. (It differs from an unlawful nuisance.)
Qualified oath. An OATH taken under circumstances that modify and reduce its forcefulness.
Qualified privilege. A conditionally PRIVILEGED COMMUNICATION; a limited privilege.
Qualified refusal. A conditional REFUSAL to hand over PROPERTY that lawfully should be handed over, such refusal based upon an outstanding OBLIGATION or LIEN. The implication is that when the obligation is fulfilled, the refusal will be withdrawn.
Qualified voter. A person who fulfills all the QUALIFICATIONS to vote.
Qualify. To possess the attributes necessary to occupy an office or to do a job.
Qualifying clause. A conditional clause in a CONTRACT.
Quantum meruit. As much as he deserved (Latin).
Quarantine. **1.** The RIGHT of a widow or widower to use the deceased spouse's PROPERTY until the ESTATE is settled. **2.** The isolation of patients who have communicable diseases. **3.** A regulation forbidding the transportation of infected or diseased livestock or goods from one area to another.
Quare. Wherefore; for example (Latin).
Quarrel. **1.** A DEBATE; a contro-

versy, such as takes place between the opposing parties in a LAWSUIT. **2.** An altercation; a scrap; a dispute, often vehement or violent.

Quarter-section. A measurement of land, usually 160 acres. As nearly as possible, a whole section (about 640 acres) is divided into quarters in order to make a quarter-section.

Quarterly. Every three months; one-quarter of a year.

Quash. To make VOID; to ANNUL; to SUPPRESS. For example, a court may quash (throw out) an INDICTMENT.

Quasi. Almost like it; sort of; similar to; analagous to (Latin). The term is frequently used when a matter seems to be the same as another matter but, in actuality, there are essential differences between the two.

Quasi admission. An ADMISSION by making inconsistent STATEMENTS.

Quasi estoppel. A legal principle that bars an individual from taking inconsistent positions in a LAWSUIT (Latin).

Quasi judicial. A term applied to "judicial" acts taken by AGENCIES and AUTHORITIES that are not really constituted as COURTS of law. As an example, a ruling handed down by a state or national labor board is a quasi judicial ruling.

Querulous. Full of complaints; the quality of being an habitual complainer; fault-finding; peevish.

Question. **1.** A query put to a witness. **2.** A matter about which the opposing parties in a SUIT are not agreed. **3.** A matter of investigation, examination, or debate. **4.** A problem.

Question, categorical. A QUESTION that can be answered by a "yes" or a "no."

Question, hypothetical. > HYPOTHETICAL QUESTIONS.

Question, judicial. A matter that should be decided by a COURT OF LAW, as opposed to a question that might be decided by a legislative body or by the executive branch of the government.

Question, leading. A QUESTION put to a WITNESS by an ATTORNEY that suggests the answer that the witness should give.

Question of fact. The QUESTION of the truth, such question to be decided after hearing evidence from both sides in a case. It is the JUDGE's or JURY's function to decide questions of fact.

Question of law. A matter for the courts to decide, based upon INTERPRETATION of existing laws pertaining to the matter at hand.

Qui tam action. A legal ACTION to collect a PENALTY through information supplied by an informer. If the penalty is collected, the informer receives part of it, and the government receives the remainder (Latin).

Quia timet. Because he fears (Latin). The name of a BILL filed in court by a party who wants some restraining action (an INJUNCTION) to be taken "because he fears" INJURY to his RIGHTS or interests in a pending case.

Quibble. To use evasive language in order to avoid an issue.

Quickening. The "feeling of life" within the uterus by a pregnant woman. These feelings should commence somewhere around the middle of pregnancy and are caused by the fetus's movements.

Quid pro quo. A Latin expression meaning "you do something for me and I'll do something for you"; in a CONTRACT, a CONSIDERATION that one party gives in exchange for a consideration from the other party.

Quieting the title. A court PROCEEDING for the purpose of removing a cloud from a title on property. > CLOUD ON TITLE.

Quitclaim. A DEED in which the owner passes on all the RIGHTS he possesses on his PROPERTY to the purchaser.

Quittance. Exoneration; a RELEASE.

Quo warranto. A court PROCEEDING questioning the RIGHT of an individual to take a certain ACTION. In Latin quo warranto means "by what authority."

Quod cum. Whereas (Latin). A term used in PLEADINGS.

Quod recuperet. That he recover (Latin). When a JUDGMENT has been rendered in favor of the PLAINTIFF, it is often called a judgment quod recuperet.

Quorum. A MAJORITY; the number of people who must be present to permit an organization, a group, a body, etcetera, to conduct its business and reach valid decisions.

Quota. **1.** The proportional part of a whole that is owed to a person, or to a group of people or to a particular district or state. **2.** The limited number of people that are permitted to emigrate to this country from various foreign countries. Each country has its own number, or quota, allotted to it.

Quotation. A STATEMENT to a COURT giving the exact language of a LAW or STATUTE, the exact ruling of a previous COURT, or the exact basis upon which a similar case was decided. Such quotations are usually made as a means of supporting one's arguments in a SUIT.

Quotient. The result of division.

Quotient verdict. An award of money to a PLAINTIFF, arrived at by adding the sum total of all the JURORS' awards and dividing by twelve.

R

Race statute. A LAW in some states that a person who first files a CLAIM has the right to the claim.
Racketeer. An individual who makes his living in enterprises and in a manner that go contrary to law.
Railroad right of way. The narrow strip of land used by railroads, usually owned by them. If not owned outright, the railroad has been granted the use of the land. (In other words, the railroad has been granted an EASEMENT.)
Railroad Unemployment Insurance Act. A federal law providing UNEMPLOYMENT INSURANCE for employees of railroads.
Raise a presumption. To do something that will cause someone to assume or presume a FACT. As an example, a person's silence may raise a presumption that he approves of what is being done.
Raising an issue. The bringing up of an issue by one side or another in a legal DISPUTE.
Raising portions. When an oldest son has inherited an ESTATE, it is customary for him to give a portion of it to his brothers and sisters. This PROCEDURE is termed raising portions.
Ransom. Money demanded by kidnappers in return for returning a captured and detained person or persons.
Rape. In the common usage of the term, rape is the forcing of sexual relations by a man upon a woman against her will. Also, in certain states, it is STATUTORY RAPE when a male has sexual relations with a female who is under the age of consent, even if she is a voluntary and willing participant in the sexual act. In recent years, several courts have ruled that rape exists when a woman forces sexual relations upon a man against his will or, in some instances, when a female has relations with a male who is under the age of consent, even if he is a voluntary and willing participant in the sexual act.
Ratable distribution. A distribution of monies on a proportional basis. As an example, when money is distributed to CREDITORS in a BANKRUPTCY proceeding, and ten cents is paid on each dollar owed, then each creditor will receive ten cents on each dollar owed to him.
Rate fixing. The authority of a state agency to set the rates a company, often a PUBLIC UTILITY, may charge its customers.
Rate of exchange. The rate at which money from one country can be exchanged for money of another country. The rates frequently fluctuate from day to day.
Ratification. Confirmation of an act already performed, such as congressional ratification of a TREATY made by the president with a foreign country. Also, when an AGREEMENT or CON-

TRACT has been made by a MINOR, it often is ratified by him when he reaches maturity.

Ratify, confirm, republish, redeclare. To approve, to confirm, to reconfirm. A legal expression denoting absolute ratification.

Ratio. Proportion; the relation between two numbers of the same kind; the relation that exists by dividing one quantity by another.

Rational. Reasonable; of sane mind; capable of reasoning.

Rational doubt. > REASONABLE DOUBT.

Rational interpretation. A clarification of the language of a written DOCUMENT so as to convey its true meaning and intent better. A JUDGE occasionally may indulge in rational interpretation when a document before the court is poorly constructed and unclear in its meaning.

Ravish. To RAPE; to force sexual relations against someone's will.

Real assets. PROPERTY, including land and real estate, left to an heir subject to payment of the TESTATOR's (the person who willed the property) DEBTS.

Real contract. An AGREEMENT concerning real estate, such as a land contract.

Real estate broker. An individual who acts as a go-between in the sale of real estate. For consummating the sale and transfer of property, the real estate broker receives a COMMISSION.

Real estate investment trust. A TRUST formed by a group of people who are investing their money for the purpose of buying and selling real estate.

Real estate syndicate. A joint enterprise of a group of people who pool their money for the purpose of buying or selling real estate.

Real evidence. EVIDENCE that can be seen in a courtroom by the JUDGE and/or JURY, such as the gun that caused the MURDER, or an injured limb for which the plaintiff is seeking damages. Real evidence differs from evidence given by a WITNESS in that it can actually be viewed.

Real party in interest. The person who stands to benefit from the SUIT, if he wins it.

Real property. Land; immovable PROPERTY on land, such as a building, an apartment house, etcetera.

Real release. A DOCUMENT signed by a CREDITOR and given to his DEBTOR when he considers his debt as fully paid, or when the creditor decides to release the debtor from any further claim.

Real value. The worth of something on an open, competitive market; the FAIR AND REASONABLE VALUE.

Reapportionment. The making of new district lines, usually carried out to give a fairer representation to the population in the area. A school district may be reapportioned to give better racial balance, or a congressional district may be reapportioned because of shifts in population.

Reargument. **1.** A REHEARING of a case in a higher court as the result of an APPEAL. **2.** A rehearing of a MOTION based upon new material or upon the fact that important material had been overlooked when the motion was originally argued.

Rearraignment. The bringing back of an ACCUSED into court after changes and amendments have been made in the charges against him.

Reason. 1. The mental ability to know good from evil, right from wrong, truth from falsehood; the ability to think. **2.** The motive for an act.

Reasonable act. A fair, sensible, just form of behavior; an act based on reason, not carried out in an extreme or arbitrary manner; the opposite of an unreasonable act.

Reasonable and probable cause. A suspicion so strong that it convinces a sensible person that there are good grounds for believing someone to be GUILTY of a particular CRIME.

Reasonable certainty. In deciding the amount of DAMAGES to be paid an injured party, one must be reasonably certain of the extent and permanence of the INJURY. Reasonable certainty must be distinguished from CONJECTURE, or from possible or probable outcome of an injury.

Reasonable diligence. The type of care and watchfulness one must expect of a reasonable, sensible, diligent, conscientious person. In judging whether or not NEGLIGENCE exists, one must ascertain whether reasonable diligence was exercised to avoid INJURY or accident.

Reasonable doubt. A lack of sufficient certainty from the EVIDENCE that an accused person is actually GUILTY of a particular CRIME; a fair doubt based on rational, sensible thinking.

Reasonable man. Someone who acts with common sense and has the mental capacity of the average, normal sensible human being, as distinguished from an emotionally unstable, erratic, compulsive individual. In determining whether NEGLIGENCE exists, the COURT will attempt to decide whether the DEFENDANT was a reasonable person.

Reasonable probability. EVIDENCE that tends to support a CONTENTION. Reasonable probability is less than certain PROOF, but it is helpful in deciding a CIVIL SUIT for DAMAGES. However, an accused would not be convicted of murder merely on the reasonable probability that he committed the act.

Reasonable rate. A charge that is in line with the service rendered. As an example, a charge of ten to twenty cents for a local phone call might be designated as a reasonable rate. However, a charge of ten to twenty dollars for an ordinary local call would not be so designated.

Reasonable time. A period of time that is in line (CONFORMITY) with the provisions of an AGREEMENT or CONTRACT; a period of time not accompanied by an unreasonable delay.

Reassignment. The transfer of PROPERTY (an ASSIGNMENT) by an ASSIGNEE (the person to whom the property has been transferred).

Rebate. The returning of a portion of monies paid, usually at the conclusion of a CONTRACT or TRANSACTION.

Rebut. To deny; to defeat. When

a PLAINTIFF makes a charge against a DEFENDANT, and the defendant denies the charge, he rebuts it.

Rebut an equity. To deny and defeat what seems to be a just CLAIM by producing EVIDENCE showing that, in actuality, the claim is unjustified.

Rebuttable presumption. An assumption that on the surface appears to be conclusive, but can be overcome by presenting contrary evidence.

Rebuttal. The presentation of facts to a COURT demonstrating that TESTIMONY given by WITNESSES is not true.

Rebuttal evidence. TESTIMONY and EVIDENCE showing that the evidence presented by the opposing party is not true.

Rebutter. A DEFENSE by a DEFENDANT in response to a SURREJOINDER by the PLAINTIFF. In other words, the plaintiff makes a charge, the defendant answers the charge, the plaintiff then denies the defendant's defense, and finally, the defendant issues a rebutter denying the surrejoinder (the past statement) of the plaintiff.

Recall. **1.** To call back, as a WITNESS is recalled to the witness stand. **2.** To vote a duly elected public official out of office by holding a new vote.

Recall a judgment. To cancel or reverse a JUDGMENT by a court because of a matter concerning the FACTS in the case.

Recant. To take back; to withdraw a statement one has made previously; to repudiate.

Recapitalization. The reorganization of the structure of a CORPORATION by increasing or decreasing its shares of STOCK, or by issuing PREFERRED STOCK where none had existed before, etcetera.

Recaption. The taking back of something that has been taken away; reprisal. It is considered recaption to take back a stolen vehicle.

Receipt. Written acknowledgment that one has received something, such as a receipt for goods delivered or for a bill paid.

Receiver. A disinterested outside individual appointed by a COURT to manage and administer PROPERTY or money that is in dispute in a LAWSUIT. Often when an apartment building or a hotel goes into BANKRUPTCY, the COURT will appoint a receiver to manage the building until the bankruptcy PROCEEDING has been concluded and the CREDITORS have been paid. The receiver is responsible to the court for the administration.

Receiver's certificate. A DOCUMENT issued with the court's authority, granting a FIRST LIEN upon the PROPERTY of a DEBTOR corporation in the hands of a RECEIVER.

Receivership. The turning over to a RECEIVER of property that is under LITIGATION. The property is administered under the receivership until legal determination is made as to its legitimate disposal.

Receiving stolen goods. A CRIMINAL OFFENSE when PROPERTY is held with knowledge that it has been stolen. In some areas, receiving stolen goods is punished as a crime separate and distinct from the theft itself; in other areas, one is punished for receiving stolen goods as an accessory to the crime of stealing.

Recess. A stoppage of COURT PROCEEDINGS for a short period of time. The court is not adjourned during the recess.

Recession. The giving back of PROPERTY to the person from whom it was originally received.

Recidivist. An HABITUAL CRIMINAL; a repeater.

Reciprocal contract. A bilateral CONTRACT; a contract in which both parties have OBLIGATIONS to perform, and the contract depends upon each party carrying out his promises.

Reciprocal demands. Legal OBLIGATIONS between two parties; CLAIMS that one person has against another and the other person has against him.

Reciprocal negative easement. An EASEMENT originating from restrictions limiting the use of PROPERTY for residential purposes.

Reciprocal trusts. TRUSTS that a husband and wife each set up for the other's benefit. They may also be trusts set up by two people who are not related or members of the same family. However, this is not a very usual occurrence.

Reciprocal wills. WILLS executed by two people, each naming the other as BENEFICIARY. Such wills usually are constructed in a similar manner and contain many identical provisions.

Reciprocity. A relationship between two people, corporations, countries, etcetera, in which privileges or favored positions granted by one are returned by the other. In other words, reciprocity means "I do for you and you do for me."

Recital. The written STATEMENT in the beginning of a DOCUMENT or DEED, explaining the reasons for the document or deed and for the TRANSACTION behind it.

Reckless. Careless; indifferent to the outcome of one's actions; heedless; negligent; acting without due caution.

Reckless driving. Operating a vehicle without regard to essential and necessary precautions and care.

Reclaim. To ask for the return of property that rightfully belongs to one. One would insist upon the return of goods that were taken under false pretenses.

Reclamation. **1.** The act of insisting upon the return of one's PROPERTY. **2.** A PROCEEDING wherein an owner of property obtains it from the TRUSTEE in a BANKRUPTCY. **3.** The act of taking land that lies fallow and turning it into land that can be cultivated or used for building purposes. Reclamation may entail draining water off the land, getting rid of swamps, etcetera.

Recognition. Acknowledgment; confirmation; AGREEMENT that an act carried out by another was performed with one's CONSENT and AUTHORITY.

Recognizance. An OBLIGATION, written and recorded in the COURT RECORD, to perform a certain act. As an example, an ACCUSED may be freed "on his own recognizance" if he formally agrees in writing to show up at his TRIAL. Thus, being freed upon one's own recognizance takes the place of posting a BAIL BOND. Failure to fulfill the obligation will mean forfeiture of a certain amount of money to the court.

Recommend. To advise; to suggest; to counsel; to speak in favor of.

Recommitment. Sending back to prison a CONVICTED person who has violated the terms of his PAROLE or the provisions of his PARDON.

Recompense. Payment for services rendered; REMUNERATION; COMPENSATION; a reward for services rendered.

Reconciliation. The act of coming together again after a DISPUTE; forgiveness of two parties, each for the other. The term is used frequently in describing a married couple who have been separated but agree to attempt to live again with each other harmoniously.

Reconstruction. The act of rebuilding. The Reconstruction Acts after the Civil War were enacted in an attempt to rebuild the South.

Recontinuance. The restoration of inherited RIGHTS and PRIVILEGES (known as incorporeal hereditaments) to someone who had been wrongfully deprived of those rights and privileges.

Reconvention. The act of instituting a COUNTERCLAIM; an ACTION brought by the DEFENDANT against the PLAINTIFF.
> COUNTERCLAIM.

Reconveyance. The return of TITLE papers, as when a MORTGAGE has been fully paid.

Record. A written DOCUMENT attesting to an EVENT, a TRANSACTION, AGREEMENT, CONTRACT, ACT, etcetera, drawn up under the authority of the law. A record is permanent EVIDENCE that some event, transaction, agreement, contract, act, etcetera, has taken place legally.

Recordation of verdict. The reception by the COURT CLERK of the jury's VERDICT, thus ending the TRIAL. Such verdict will be placed by the clerk in the court records.

Recoupment. The right of a DEFENDANT to have the PLAINTIFF's award of DAMAGES against him reduced; a reduction; a discount; a deduction.

Recourse. **1.** The seeking of assistance and help. **2.** The RIGHT of a person to get his just due by taking legal actions toward that end.

Recovery. The award of money given by a court to the person or persons who win the LAWSUIT.

Recrimination. **1.** An ACCUSATION by a DEFENDANT against the PLAINTIFF. For example, a wife may claim extreme cruelty by a husband. Then the husband may claim extreme cruelty on the part of the wife. **2.** A countercharge.

Recross-examination. An additional CROSS-EXAMINATION of a WITNESS. Cross-examination is the questioning of an opposing witness, brought into court by the opposing party.

Rectify. To correct; to amend an incorrect STATEMENT; to explain something that has previously been poorly explained.

Recurrent insanity. A mental illness that is of a temporary nature but that tends to recur from time to time. In between episodes of INSANITY, the person may be completely sane. (MANIC-DEPRESSIVE PSYCHOSIS is one of the illnesses which falls into this category.)

Recusatio testis. The rejection of a WITNESS on the grounds that he is incompetent (Latin).

Recusation. The act of DISQUALIFYING a JUDGE, or the judge disqualifying himself, from hearing a case. Such recusation may be based on the judge's prejudice or personal interest in the matter.

Reddendum. **1.** A clause on a transfer of PROPERTY, in which the grantor of the property reserves for himself some new thing out of that which he had already granted. **2.** Yielding; rendering (Latin).

Reddition. A COURT'S acknowledgment that something belongs to the person who is demanding it, not to the person who is surrendering it.

Redeem. **1.** To purchase back; to buy back. **2.** To reclaim PROPERTY by paying off the MORTGAGE or some other OBLIGATION.

Redeemable bond. A BOND that may be paid off before it matures. This is frequently done when the interest rate on the bond is much higher than the current rate at the time of redemption. However, many bonds are not redeemable until they reach maturity.

Redelivery bond. A BOND issued upon the seizure of merchandise, subject to the conditions for its restoration to the DEFENDANT; a delivery bond.

Redemption. The act of redeeming; turning in something, such as a BOND, for cash.

Redhibition. The act of not selling something because it is defective.

Redirect examination. The EXAMINATION of a WITNESS by the party who brought him into court, such examination taking place after the opposing party has concluded his CROSS-EXAMINATION of the witness.

Redress. **1.** The receiving of SATISFACTION for an INJURY one has sustained. **2.** COMPENSATION; REPARATIONS.

Reductio ad absurdum. A method of argument showing how ridiculous the opposing position is, and what absurd conclusions would follow if the opposition's position was upheld. In Latin the term means "reducing to absurdity."

Reduction of sentence. Lessening the severity of a PUNISHMENT, such as a jail SENTENCE.

Redundancy. The insertion of irrelevant and superfluous material into a legal DOCUMENT or PLEADING.

Reenact. To carry out again. In a trial, the prosecutor may reenact, for the benefit of the COURT, how a particular CRIME could have taken place.

Reentry. The act of taking POSSESSION again of one's PROPERTY that had been leased; or that one previously vacated but did not surrender the RIGHT to return to.

Reexamination. Examining a WITNESS again, after he has undergone CROSS-EXAMINATION by the opposing ATTORNEY.

Referee. An OFFICER of the COURT, appointed by the court to take TESTIMONY and to report his findings back to the court. Under certain circumstances the referee is authorized not only to hear the case but to render a DECISION. ➤ ARBITER.

Referee in bankruptcy. An OFFICER appointed by the COURT to hear matters pertaining to a BANKRUPTCY and to take care of the administrative matters that arise. Any act of a referee in bankruptcy is subject to the review and supervision of the court.

Reference. **1.** The act of sending a matter to a REFEREE for his CONSIDERATION and DECISION. **2.** An AGREEMENT between two parties to place their DISPUTE before an ARBITRATOR or REFEREE for his consideration and decision.

Reference statutes. Laws that refer to older existing laws and make them apply to new legislation.

Referendum. **1.** The reference of proposed new laws to the people for their vote of approval or disapproval. **2.** The power of the people, by their vote, to approve or disapprove an act of the legislature.

Refinance. The act of taking NOTES (signed AGREEMENTS to pay) and giving them over to a finance company that specializes in buying notes at a discounted price. In other words, if someone is holding a note for $1,000, he may turn that $1,000 note over to a company who will pay him $900 for it.

Reform. **1.** To correct, amend, or modify a DOCUMENT. **2.** To abandon evil conduct and become a better citizen.

Reformatory. A prison or correctional institution where people who have committed lesser crimes are sent. In a reformatory, great attention is paid toward rehabilitating and reforming the inmates so that they become good citizens upon their release.

Refreshing memory. Attempts by an ATTORNEY to get a WITNESS to remember facts or circumstances that he has forgotten.

Refund annuity contract. An AGREEMENT that if monies are still due at the time of the death of the person owning the annuity, such monies shall be paid to his ESTATE.

Refunds. Repayments to people who have overpaid an OBLIGATION, such as a TAX or a DUTY.

Refusal. **1.** The denial of a demand or a request. **2.** A negative response to comply with an ORDER of a COURT.

Refusal to plead. **1.** Defaulting in a LAWSUIT by not defending oneself. **2.** Remaining silent when ACCUSED.

Register. **1.** To record something formally. **2.** To list one's name as a voter. **3.** To enroll.

Register of deeds. A recorder of DEEDS; a public official whose duty is to keep on file legal DOCUMENTS such as DEEDS, MORTGAGES, etcetera.

Register of patents. A public official who records and keeps on file various PATENTS. Reference to the register will inform an inventor whether or not his idea is new or has already been patented.

Register of wills. A PROBATE COURT clerk who records WILLS.
Registered bond. A BOND that is payable to a particular person named on the face of the bond; a nonnegotiable bond.
Registered trademark. A TRADEMARK recorded and registered in the United States Patent Office, such registration giving the owner exclusive use of the trademark.
Registered voter. An individual who has recorded his name in the voting register and is legally entitled to vote.
Registration. The act of recording one's name; filing; enrollment.
Registry. A book, recognized by law, kept for the purpose of recording FACTS and DOCUMENTS.
Regular process. A WRIT or COURT ORDER issued in strict conformity to the established law.
Regulation. A RULE for controlling public affairs, such as a LAW, a STATUTE, or an ORDINANCE; a governing principle.
Rehabilitate. To restore someone to good health; to influence a criminal or delinquent to behave as a good citizen; to organize and make profitable again a money-losing or bankrupt business.
Rehearing. HEARING a case for a second time, usually to determine whether some error had been committed during the first hearing of the case.
Reimburse. To pay back; to restore monies that have been taken.
Reinstate. To restore to a position once occupied but from which one has been removed; to reestablish.
Reinsurance. An AGREEMENT between an INSURANCE COMPANY and another insurer, insuring the original insurer from possible loss or LIABILITY. In other words, reinsurance shares the risk taken by the original insurer.
Rejoinder. The second PLEADING (DEFENSE) of a DEFENDANT, in answer to a PLAINTIFF's reply to his first pleading (defense).
Relative convenience doctrine. A principle considered by COURTS when asked to issue an INJUNCTION (an order of RESTRAINT). The principle is that the court will not be bound to issue an injunction that will create greater INJURY than the wrong it is asked to correct.
Relative fact. A FACT having importance because of its relation to another fact; a circumstance.
Relative rights. The RIGHTS of individuals when considered in reference to the rights of other individuals.
Release. **1.** To give up a RIGHT or CLAIM; to relinquish. **2.** A discharge from DUTY or OBLIGATION. **3.** The freeing of a prisoner, such as a release from custody.
Release, deed of. **1.** The receiving back of full title to PROPERTY upon the payment of all outstanding DEBTS. **2.** A DEED relieving one of outstanding debts and OBLIGATIONS.
Release and satisfaction. A SETTLEMENT of a case in which the PLAINTIFF signs a statement releasing the DEFENDANT from any further LIABILITY for DAMAGES.
Release of dower. The giving up of a RIGHT or CLAIM by a spouse to PROPERTY owned by his or her mate.

Release on own recognizance. R.O.R.; setting someone free from custody on a PLEDGE that he will appear in COURT at a certain time and place to answer CHARGES against him. Such release is sometimes granted instead of posting BAIL.

Relevancy. The quality of being appropriate and applicable, such as EVIDENCE that bears directly on the issues being disputed or discussed.

Relevant evidence. TESTIMONY and EVIDENCE that bear directly on the issues being discussed or disputed.

Relict. A survivor, such as a widow who survives a husband, or vice versa.

Relicta. The giving up of a DEFENSE by a DEFENDANT (Latin).

Relief. **1.** An award of DAMAGES; the receiving of a favorable JUDGMENT; the winning of a LAWSUIT; a decree of a COURT granting the PLAINTIFF part or all of his CLAIM or claims against a DEFENDANT. **2.** The help that a poverty-stricken family receives for support from a governmental agency.

Religious liberty. Freedom to worship in any way that one sees fit, without interference. This is a basic RIGHT granted by the U.S. CONSTITUTION.

Relinquish. To abandon; to give up; to renounce a CLAIM or RIGHT.

Remainder. **1.** The rest; the portion remaining after a part has been taken away; the residue. **2.** The portion of an ESTATE or PROPERTY which is to be distributed after other portions have been disposed of. **3.** An estate to take effect and be enjoyed after another estate has been determined.

Remainder, contingent. A portion of an ESTATE that *might* be distributed if certain events take place.

Remainder, cross. A STIPULATION that when portions of an ESTATE are given to two or more people, the share given to one shall pass to the other or others upon his or their deaths.

Remainder, executory. > REMAINDER, CONTINGENT.

Remainder, vested. An ESTATE given to a particular person, to be enjoyed by him or her at some time in the future upon the happening of a certain event.

Remainderman. Someone who holds interest in an ESTATE in the future.

Remand. To send back, such as the sending back to JAIL of a prisoner until such time as his TRIAL is completed. Also, the sending back to a COURT of a matter that another court thinks should be further deliberated and decided.

Remediable. Capable of being corrected, rectified, or redressed.

Remedial law. That part of the LAW which details methods for enforcing one's rights.

Remedial statute. A LAW, the purpose of which is to correct an existing law that is not working, or has caused harm instead of good.

Remedies. The means employed by the law to correct INJURIES or to enforce legal RIGHTS.

Remedy over. A person who is responsible for a DAMAGE or an

ACT, but who can, in turn, blame someone else and obtain REDRESS from that person for the damages, is said to have a remedy over.

Remission. A PARDON; a release from a DEBT or OBLIGATION; an exoneration; the act of REMITTANCE (payment).

Remittance. Money sent from one person to another.

Remitter. An act whereby a person who has a valid TITLE to PROPERTY, and enters upon the property with less than his original title, is restored to his original VALID title.

Remittitur. In DAMAGE or MALPRACTICE awards, the amount of the award may seem to the COURT to be excessive. In such cases, the court may order a new TRIAL or may avoid a new trial by getting the PLAINTIFF and DEFENDANT to agree upon a lesser award. This practice is known as remittitur (Latin).

Remittitur of record. The sending back by a COURT of APPEALS of the records of a CASE that had been referred to it. The record may be sent back with a new DECISION, or with an upholding of the lower court's decision, or it may be sent back with recommendation that the case be tried over again.

Remonstrance. A PROTEST against the passage of a certain LAW, or a protest urging that certain actions of a public body not be taken. A remonstrance implies that several people, or large groups of people, are united in their protest.

Remote cause. In matters concerning NEGLIGENCE, a remote cause is one that would not lead to the event that happened. Thus, there would be no justification for awarding DAMAGES. A remote cause is in contradistinction from a DIRECT CAUSE.

Remote possibility. Something that might come to pass if several other events take place; something that might happen if several other unlikely things happen.

Remoteness of evidence. The status of EVIDENCE that does not have an obvious, plain connection with FACTS one is trying to establish.

Removal. A change in residence; the depriving of one's position, such as taking one's job away, the transfer of a thing or person from one place to another.

Removal of cause. The transfer of a LAWSUIT from one court to another, usually done because the original court lacks the JURISDICTION to try the case.

Removal, order of. A COURT ORDER transferring a pending case from one court to another.

Removing cloud from title. A PROCEDURE in which doubts as to the VALIDITY of a TITLE to PROPERTY are removed, thus rendering the title clear; quieting the title.

Remuneration. Payment for services rendered; salary; REWARD; RECOMPENSE.

Render. To perform, such as to render a service; to deliver; to yield; to give up.

Render judgment. To pronounce or give forth a VERDICT or DECISION.

Rendered account. A STATE-

MENT of CHARGES given by a CREDITOR to a DEBTOR; an ACCOUNT rendered.
Rendering a decision. The giving forth of a JUDGMENT by a COURT.
Renewal. The giving of more time for the payment of a DEBT or the fulfillment of an OBLIGATION; the revival or reestablishment of an issue that is in dispute.
Renounce. To abandon; to make a statement giving up a CLAIM; to relinquish a RIGHT.
Rent. **1.** To pay for the temporary use of a PROPERTY, such as the renting of an apartment or an automobile. **2.** Monies paid in exchange for the use of PROPERTY.
Renunciation. The act by which someone gives up or abandons a RIGHT or the CLAIM to a right. It does not necessarily mean that the right is transferred to another person.
Reopening a case. The granting of a new TRIAL, often resulting from the introduction of new, important EVIDENCE; permitting the parties in a case to present new evidence after RESTING A CASE.
Reorganization. The process of planning anew and of making changes, frequently referring to the reorganization of a CORPORATION that is in financial trouble so as to make it into a profitable business.
Reparation. The act of making amends for an INJURY or for DAMAGES that have been committed; the making good of a wrong.
Repatriation. The act of regaining one's citizenship after it has once been lost. Repatriation is a term applying to the coming home of an individual who has been forced to flee, or who has been ousted from, his country.
Repeal. The ANNULMENT of an existing STATUTE or LAW; to revoke a law and to substitute a new one in its place.
Repetition. The attempt to recover payments that have been made under mistaken conditions.
Repleader. A COURT ORDER issued after a VERDICT has already been given, ordering the parties to try the case again because the true, outstanding issue or issues have not really been settled by the TRIAL. Such a repleader is ordered on MOTION of the unsuccessful party in the case.
Repleader, judgment of. An ORDER of the COURT to try the CASE again because the real issue or issues in dispute have not been settled.
Replevin. A SUIT in which an owner seeks to regain PROPERTY that has been taken or is being held by another.
Replevin, writ of. A COURT ORDER authorizing an OFFICER to seize and hold the PROPERTY involved in a suit of REPLEVIN.
Replevy. To give back goods or PROPERTY that have been denied a rightful owner.
Replication. The PLAINTIFF's reply to the DEFENSE of the DEFENDANT.
Reply. A replication; the PLAINTIFF's answer to the DEFENSE by the DEFENDANT of CHARGES he has leveled against him.
Reporting a crime of violence. It

is the duty of physicians to report to the authorities all injuries that have arisen as a result of a violent act.

Repossession. Taking back something because installment payments have not been made on it.

Represent. **1.** To make an appearance in place of another, such as an ATTORNEY who appears in behalf of his client. **2.** To state as factual.

Representation. A STATEMENT of fact; the act of saying that something is true and factual.

Representation, estoppel by. An act by which a person, through silence or admissions, leads another to believe certain FACTS to be true when, in actuality, they are not true.

Representative. A person given the AUTHORITY to act in another's behalf, such as a TRUSTEE, an EXECUTOR, an OFFICER of a COMPANY, an elected member of a legislative body, etcetera.

Reprieve. The staying or delay of the EXECUTION of a SENTENCE, such as a reprieve from the DEATH PENALTY. A reprieve only postpones the carrying out of a sentence; it does not change the sentence.

Reprimand. A formal censure or scolding for having done something wrong, such as the reprimand of a LAWYER for misbehavior in COURT.

Reprisal. Retaliation against a wrongful act or against an unfriendly act, such as a nation seizing the property of a foreign country because its citizens have been mistreated in the foreign country, or because the foreign country has failed to keep its TREATY agreements; a RECAPTION.

Republic. A democratic form of government in which the citizens freely elect their officeholders, and governmental affairs are openly conducted by representatives of the people.

Republication. A second publication of a WILL; the reestablishment of a will that the will-maker (TESTATOR) has at one time revoked.

Repudiation. The act of disclaiming, renouncing, or rejecting; refusal to accept a RIGHT or PRIVILEGE; refusal to accept an OBLIGATION or DUTY.

Repugnancy. > REPUGNANT.

Repugnancy doctrine. The principle that the first clear STATEMENT in a DEED, WILL, or other DOCUMENT shall be held binding, despite the fact that subsequent clauses in the document are unclear or ambiguous, or cast some doubt on the VALIDITY of the first clear statement.

Repugnant. Contrary to what has been stated before; the quality of being inconsistent, such as stating contradictions in presenting facts that one wants to prove.

Reputable. Honorable; worthy of respect; in good repute; having a good reputation.

Reputed. Accepted by general public opinion, such as a man who is reputed to have a good reputation. The fact that someone or something is reputed to be as he or it is represented to be, does not necessarily coincide with the true FACTS.

Request for admission of facts. Asking the COURT for permission to introduce certain EVIDENCE.

Request for dismissal. Asking the court to dismiss or terminate the CASE, usually asked by the ATTORNEY for the DEFENDANT because he feels there is insufficient EVIDENCE against his client.

Request for new trial. Asking the COURT for a new TRIAL because of dissatisfaction with the JUDGMENT of the initial trial, or because of a belief that errors were made in the conduct of the initial trial.

Requirement contract. An AGREEMENT in which one party agrees to purchase all his requirements of a product from the other party.

Requisition. A written demand for PROPERTY; the seizure by government of property, such as may take place during time of war.

Requisitory letter. A request from a COURT trying a CASE to a court in another state or country. The request asks that the court take TESTIMONY from a WITNESS residing in the other state or country, and that they forward such testimony to the court that is conducting the trial. The same as LETTER ROGATORY.

Res. A thing; things (Latin).

Res accessoria. Something which belongs to or is connected with the principal thing (Latin).

Res adjudicata. > RES JUDICATA.

Res controversa. A point in question; a matter being contested (Latin).

Res derelicta. Abandoned property (Latin).

Res immobiles. Immovable things, such as land, buildings, etcetera (Latin).

Res ipsa loquitur. "The thing speaks for itself" (Latin). A legal phrase meaning that the facts, TESTIMONY, and circumstances are so clear that one can conclude, without doubt, that a certain act, or omission of an act, caused a particular DAMAGE or INJURY.

Res judicata. "The matter has been settled" (Latin). A term denoting that a JUDGMENT has been rendered and the CASE has been disposed of. The phrase indicates that the matter cannot be tried again.

Res mobiles. Movable things, such as furniture, paintings, etcetera, as opposed to RES IMMOBILES, such as land or buildings (Latin).

Res nova. A matter not yet settled or decided; a new matter (Latin).

Rescind. To cancel, such as an AGREEMENT; to ANNUL; to make VOID.

Rescission of contract. The cancellation of a CONTRACT or AGREEMENT, with both parties resuming the status they had before making the contract.

Rescue. The freeing of a prisoner without any attempt on the part of the prisoner to free himself.

Rescue doctrine. A principle stating that the person who causes an INJURY may be held LIABLE for injuries sustained by a third person who intervenes to help (rescue) the injured party.

Reservation. 1. The setting aside of a point in a suit for further

CONSIDERATION. A JUDGE often states "decision or judgment reserved." This means he has reservations about the point and wishes time to study it before rendering an OPINION. **2.** A clause in a DEED or other DOCUMENT in which the grantor reserves for himself certain RIGHTS, PRIVILEGES, PROFITS, BENEFITS, etcetera.

Reserve an exception. The PROCESS by which an EXCEPTION to the judge's ruling is recorded during a trial. The ATTORNEY who takes the exception may use it at a later time in appealing a decision to a higher court.

Reserve an objection. To ask the RIGHT to make an OBJECTION at a later time during a TRIAL. Such a right must be granted by the presiding JUDGE.

Reserve system. A system of banks, supervised by governmental agencies, whose function is to promote sound banking practices throughout the country and to aid the orderly flow of money and credit essential to the economic health of the nation.

Reserved option. A CLAUSE in a CONTRACT giving one or both of the parties the right to cancel the contract at some future time.

Resettlement. Reopening a court DECREE in order to insert a provision that was accidentally omitted at the time of the original SETTLEMENT.

Residence. The place where one lives. It may be a temporary or a permanent residence.

Resident alien. A foreigner who intends to live in the United States on a permanent basis. The status of resident alien must be approved by the immigration authorities.

Residential restriction. A local REGULATION defining the type of buildings or residences that can be constructed in particular areas or neighborhoods. > ZONING LAWS.

Residuary bequest. The disposition by WILL of all of a deceased person's ESTATE that has not been specifically disposed of. In other words, a will may give away money or PROPERTY to several specially named people or organizations, and then may state that all the rest of the money and property go to the deceased's spouse, children, etcetera.

Residuary clause. A clause in a WILL disposing of all the rest of a deceased person's ESTATE after all DEBTS have been paid and all specific BEQUESTS have been made.

Residuary devise. A residuary gift; a gift of all that remains of an ESTATE after all DEBTS and specific DEVISES (gifts) have been made.

Residuary estate. That which is left of an ESTATE after all DEBTS, legal expenses, gifts, and LEGACIES have been taken care of.

Residue. That which is left after the DEBTS and LEGACIES of an estate have been taken care of.

Residuum. A RESIDUE (Latin).

Resist. To oppose; to put up resistance.

Resisting an officer. Opposing an officer of the law who is attempting to carry out his authorized duties; trying to prevent an arrest.

Resolution. 1. An expression of opinion, usually after voting, issued by a legislative body, a group, or other organization. **2.** The solving of an outstanding problem or issue.

Respite. A delay in the EXECUTION of a SENTENCE.

Respondeat ouster. > JUDGMENT OF RESPONDEAT OUSTER.

Respondeat superior. A PRINCIPLE stating that the "master" is responsible for the wrongful conduct or act of his "servant." Also, the doctrine that a principal is responsible for the act or acts of his agent.

Respondent. **1.** A person who answers for or is SECURITY for another. **2.** In EQUITY, the person who answers a PLEADING or other BILL. **3.** A person against whom an APPEAL is brought.

Responsive. Answering; a relevant, complete answer to a question.

Responsive pleading. An answer to a COMPLAINT; a response to a CHARGE that answers the charges completely and may enter a COUNTERCLAIM.

Resseiser. The taking back of lands by one who has been ousted from those lands.

Resting a case. A term used when all the EVIDENCE has been presented and the party, or parties, are willing for the court to consider and render a JUDGMENT on the issues; the ATTORNEY often will state, "The case rests."

Restitution. The act of restoring something to its owner; the act of making good.

Restoration in kind. To repay; to restitute.

Restoration of status quo. The act of restoring a party to the position he was in before he made an AGREEMENT or CONTRACT. The term is used frequently when a contract is cancelled.

Restorative remedies. The placing of a PLAINTIFF in the same situation he was in before his RIGHTS, PRIVILEGES, or PROPERTY had been interfered with by the DEFENDANT. Such restorative remedies are carried out after a successful suit in a COURT OF EQUITY.

Restrain. To limit; to prohibit, to restrict; to impede; to obstruct; to hold back physically, such as restraining a person from attacking someone.

Restraining order. An ORDER issued by a COURT without notice to the opposing party, usually granted temporarily to RESTRAIN him until the court decides whether an INJUNCTION should be ordered. In actuality, a restraining order is a form of an INJUNCTION.

Restraint. Confinement; limitation; the act of depriving, such as depriving one of his liberty. > CONSTRAINT.

Restraint of trade. Practices that interfere with or do away with free trade, such as might occur when a MONOPOLY exists or when several companies conspire to interfere with unrestrained, free competition. > HORIZONTAL AGREEMENT; PRICE FIXING.

Restrictive covenant. A written AGREEMENT limiting the use of PROPERTY to specified purposes and regulating the type of strictures that may be placed upon such property.

Restrictive endorsement. An EN-

DORSEMENT specifying the person, persons, or company to whom a DEBT must be paid, thus converting a DOCUMENT into a nonnegotiable document. An endorsement on the back of a check that states "Pay to John Doe only" is a restrictive endorsement.

Restrictive interpretation. A narrow, precise, limited construction of the meaning of a LAW or other legal DOCUMENT. The opposite of liberal interpretation. ➤ LIBERAL CONSTRUCTION; LITERAL CONSTRUCTION.

Resulting trust. A TRUST arising out of implication by LAW and out of the intentions of the parties concerned. As an example, if money is given by one person to be held by another in trust, but for some legal reason the trust fails, then the money is still held by the second person in a resulting trust for the benefit of the first person.

Retainer. 1. The act of a client in retaining an ATTORNEY. 2. The fee paid by a client to an ATTORNEY when retaining him to act in his behalf.

Retainer, general. The hiring of an ATTORNEY on a basis of a period of time, often a year. The attorney will receive a set sum of money whether he does a great deal or little or no work during the period of the retainer.

Retainer, special. The hiring of an ATTORNEY for a specific purpose to perform a specific task.

Retaining fee. The fee given to an ATTORNEY at the time he is engaged by the CLIENT.

Retaliatory statute. A LAW passed by one state to counter a law passed by another state. In other words, if a state passes a law imposing certain TAXES on products imported from another state, then the other state may pass a similar law imposing taxes of its own.

Retirement. 1. The voluntary fulfillment of an OBLIGATION or payment of a DEBT. 2. The giving up of one's work, position, or professional activities.

Retirement of securities. The calling in and paying off of a BOND or other security; the redemption of a security; the repurchase of its own outstanding STOCK by a CORPORATION.

Retract. To withdraw, such as the withdrawal of an offer before it has been accepted; to take back, such as to retract a statement already made.

Retreat to the wall. A phrase used when claiming that a MURDER was committed in SELF-DEFENSE. It means that everything was done to escape the attacker before resorting to violent countermeasures.

Retroactive. A rule of law relating to something that has already been decided in the past; RETROSPECTIVE LAW; EX POST FACTO (after the thing has been done); effective as of a past date.

Retroactive statute. A law that imposes a new OBLIGATION on things already past; a law that is operative as of a past date.

Retrocession. The restoring of an old TITLE to a rightful OWNER, as opposed to granting a new title.

Retrospective law. Same as RETROACTIVE STATUTE.

Retry a case. To try a case again, as after a mistrial or after a HUNG JURY fails to bring in a VERDICT.

Return. 1. The act of an OFFICER of the COURT, such as a SHERIFF, in bringing back to the court the process (SUMMONS, SUBPOENA, etcetera) that he was ordered to serve, along with a report of his activities. **2.** A written report of one's earnings, expenses, etcetera, as recorded in a tax return. **3.** The amount of interest or profit one earns from an investment of money. **4.** To give back; to bring back; to place in the custody of.

Return day. The day, designated in a COURT ORDER or PROCESS or WRIT, on which the DEFENDANT must appear in COURT to defend himself.

Return nulla bona. The report of a COURT OFFICER stating that he has searched for the particular PROPERTY to be taxed and has not found it.

Return of indictment. The bringing of an indictment (a CHARGE) into COURT before a JUDGE.

Return of process. A written report of a COURT OFFICER detailing his activities in serving a PROCESS or carrying out an ORDER of the COURT.

Return of writ. > RETURN TO WRIT.

Return to writ. The report and response of a COURT OFFICER, such as a SHERIFF, to a WRIT or PROCESS. As an example, a response to a WRIT OF HABEAS CORPUS stating the facts relating to the detention of a prisoner. Same as *return of writ.*

Returnable. To be returned, such as a WRIT or COURT ORDER that is returnable on a specified day.

Returnable process. A WRIT on which the OFFICER of the COURT is required to give a report on his attempts to carry out the PROCESS. In other words, he must report whether or not he was successful in carrying out the court's order to serve the process.

Revendication. The act of reclaiming something that belongs to you but is in another's POSSESSION; to demand back.

Revenue. The return on an investment; profit; income on capital; income of a government derived from taxes or other sources.

Revenue officer. An agent of the INTERNAL REVENUE SERVICE whose duties include the enforcement of the Internal Revenue code of the United States.

Reversal. The ANNULMENT or voiding of a court's JUDGMENT or DECISION. Such reversal usually results from a higher court overruling a lower court's action or decision.

Reversible error. An error of a lower court of such a substantial nature as to cause a higher (APPELLATE) court to overrule the JUDGMENT of the lower court.

Reversion. The returning of PROPERTY to the owner after a grant has expired. In other words, property may have been temporarily granted to others for a specified period of time. When that time has passed, there is reversion of the property of the grantor.

Reversionary lease. A LEASE that goes into effect when the present lease expires.

Revert. To return to; to go back to a former owner.

Review. **1.** To reexamine; to reconsider. **2.** The CONSIDERATION by a higher (APPELLATE) court of a decision made by a lower (inferior) court.

Revision of statute. The EXAMINATION and review of an existing law with the possibility of restating the law or revising it so as to improve it and clarify its meaning and intentions.

Revival. The reactivation of a JUDGMENT that has not been carried out. Such a revival may entail the issuance of a new COURT ORDER.

Revivor, bill of. A PROCEEDING to revive a LAWSUIT that has been inactive because of the death of one of the parties.

Revocation. The voiding, annulling or revoking of a thing.

Revocation of license. The taking away of a license, such as the denial of the PRIVILEGE of a doctor to practice medicine because he has been guilty of MALPRACTICE, or the taking away of an ATTORNEY's privilege to practice the law.

Revocation of probate. The recall of a WILL that has been granted PROBATE, usually occasioned by the finding of a newer will or by some other substantial cause.

Revocation of will. The ANNULMENT or voiding of an existing WILL by the person who has made that will. Such revoking is usually followed by the making of a new will.

Revoke in its entirety. A phrase denoting that something has been cancelled completely and totally; the ANNULMENT of all and everything, leaving nothing still valid.

Revoke in part. A phrase denoting that some portions of a DOCUMENT are still VALID and in existence, as distinguished from REVOKE IN ITS ENTIRETY.

Revolving fund. A fund of a CO-OPERATIVE ASSOCIATION in which all or part of the profits of the association are retained for the benefit of its members. Each member is credited with his share, according to the amount of his investment in the association.

Reward. RECOMPENSE that is given for some outstanding accomplishment; monies that are given to someone who has aided in the APPREHENSION of a CRIMINAL.

Rider. **1.** A clause or provision that is attached to a DOCUMENT and should be considered as part of the document. **2.** An extra provision added to a legislative BILL.

Right. **1.** Something that is legally fair and just. **2.** Something that is ethically and morally fair and just. **3.** A PRIVILEGE. **4.** Something to which a person has a valid claim. **5.** Something to which a person is entitled.

Right and wrong test. A test given to an ACCUSED to find out whether he knew right from wrong at the time he allegedly committed his crime. If it has been determined by this test, and by TESTIMONY given by qualified PSYCHIATRISTS, that the accused was not of sound mind and did not know the difference between right and wrong, he may be excused from criminal prosecution.

Right in action. A right to POSSESSION, recoverable by bringing a LAWSUIT; the same as CHOSE IN ACTION.

Right of action. The RIGHT to bring suit in a particular matter; the right of a PLAINTIFF to seek SATISFACTION from a DEFENDANT.

Right of appeal. The RIGHT to appeal to a higher court for review of the JUDGMENT of a lower court. It is not a basic, inherent right, as a higher court, under some circumstances, may refuse to review a lower court's DECISION.

Right of approach. The right of a nation at war to stop and search a ship of another nationality. Such rights are specifically spelled out by various conventions of war.

Right of domicile. The RIGHT to dwell in a particular place.

Right of domain. The RIGHT to the OWNERSHIP and POSSESSION of land.

Right of entry. The right to peaceably enter upon and take POSSESSION of one's PROPERTY.

Right of first publication. A COPYRIGHT. > FIRST PUBLICATION.

Right of possession. The RIGHT to occupy one's own PROPERTY and to oust any occupant from same.

Right of privacy. The RIGHT of a person to go his way and live his life without being subjected to outside interference, publicity, or other annoyances. > INVASION OF PRIVACY.

Right of redemption. The RIGHT to free PROPERTY from any CLAIMS against it. Such right is exercised by paying off LIENS, DEBTS, MORTGAGES, etcetera, against the property, thus restoring it free and clear to the rightful owner.

Right of search. According to international law, the right of a ship of one nationality during wartime to stop a ship of a neutral nation to make sure it is not carrying cargo to a belligerent nation.

Right of visitation. The RIGHT of a parent to visit a child who is in the custody of an estranged (separated or divorced) spouse, or in the custody of a GUARDIAN.

Right of way. The RIGHT of passage over PROPERTY belonging to another; the right to lawfully use a highway or road belonging to the public.

Right to bear arms. A RIGHT defined in the 2nd Amendment to the UNITED STATES CONSTITUTION (see pages 389–95 for the complete texts of the Amendments to Constitution).

Right-to-work law. A state law, existing in some states only, forbidding UNIONS from insisting that a worker join the union in order to work.

Rights of accused. These RIGHTS consist of: **1.** The right to due process. > DUE PROCESS OF LAW. **2.** The right to the assistance of an ATTORNEY. **3.** The right to equal protection under the law. > EQUAL PROTECTION OF THE LAW. **4.** The right to a fair, impartial, speedy, public TRIAL.

Rigor mortis. The time at which

the muscles of a dead person become hard and firm. It used to be thought that one could fix the time of death by noting when rigor mortis set in, but this has been termed a very unreliable method by medical authorities (Latin).

Riot. An unlawful, violent, public disturbance caused by three or more persons, resulting in a BREACH OF THE PEACE and endangerment of nonparticipants.

Riparian rights. The RIGHTS of owners of property bordering waterways, including their right of access to the water, their right to use the water, etcetera. These rights do not include the PRIVILEGE of diverting or polluting the waterway.

Rising of court. The final ADJOURNMENT of a COURT; the end of the last day of a court TERM.

Risk. In insurance law, the danger and its extent, of a loss of the property insured. If an INSURANCE COMPANY judges a risk too general, it may decline to issue an insurance policy. A person may be judged a poor risk if he or she has had several losses under circumstances that seem to indicate carelessness on the part of the insured.

Robbery. The unlawful taking of PROPERTY from a person or in his presence, forcibly, against the person's will, and in a manner that causes fright and fear. Robbery involves a direct confrontation between the person being robbed and the robber.

Rogatory letter. > LETTER ROGATORY.

Roll. 1. A record of COURT or other official PROCEEDINGS. **2.** A list of taxable PROPERTIES or persons.

Royalty. 1. A payment to an author by a publisher, usually based upon a percentage of the retail price at which a book is sold. **2.** A payment made by a person or company who leases oil, mineral, or natural gas rights to the owner of the land above the oil, gas, or minerals.

Rule. 1. A REGULATION, ORDINANCE, or principle set up by an AUTHORITY, such as a local, state, or federal government. **2.** A regulation or order of a COURT concerning the manner in which its business shall be conducted.

Rule, absolute. A RULE that should be enforced forthwith, without delay; a PEREMPTORY RULE. Such a rule is issued by a court when a LITIGANT fails to show sufficient cause why the order should not be carried out.

Rule, general. Standing ORDER of a COURT.

Rule against perpetuities. A RULE against an attempt to control the disposition of PROPERTY that is supposed to continue longer than the life of someone who is alive when the maker of the WILL (the TESTATOR) dies, plus twenty-one years.

Rule nisi. A RULING of a COURT which becomes final unless one or both parties to a LAWSUIT show cause why it should not be made final (Latin).

Rule of law. A legal PRINCIPLE of general application, approved by the AUTHORITIES and used as a guide to conduct. A rule of law is expressed as a logical PROPOSITION.

Rule of property. A RULE OR REGULATION governing the ownership or transfer of PROPERTY, such a rule often based upon past procedures in similar matters.

Rule to plead. A court RULING ordering a DEFENDANT to enter a DEFENSE, and warning that if he fails to do so within a specified period of time, a JUDGMENT will be rendered in favor of the PLAINTIFF.

Rule to show cause. A RULE ordering a party to show why he has not performed a certain required ACT, or why the act should not be carried out.

Rules, cross. A situation in which both parties in a lawsuit obtain a RULE NISI. A rule nisi is a COURT ORDER making a ruling final unless either or both parties SHOW CAUSE why it should not be made final.

Rules of court. REGULATIONS governing the conduct of business and practice of the various courts. The presiding JUDGES carry out the rules of court as the need arises.

Rules of practice. Various ORDERS of a COURT regulating the methods used in presenting actions and conducting business.

Rules of procedure. REGULATIONS of a legislative body in conducting its business; rules of order.

Running account. An ACCOUNT of current dealings; an open account, as opposed to a closed account.

Running days. Successive days, including Saturdays, Sundays, and holidays. Running days are different from "working days."

Rusticum jus. Simple justice (Latin).

Rustler. A cattle thief.

S

Sabotage. Purposeful, intentional damaging of another's PROPERTY.
Sadism. Pleasure, or sexual gratification, obtained through hurting someone mentally or inflicting physical pain upon someone.
Safe investment rule. A calculation of the probable future earnings of one who has died. This information frequently forms the basis of a JURY's award to the SURVIVOR or survivors who are the heirs.
Safe-pledge. A guarantee that a particular person will appear in COURT at a particular time and date.
Sale. A CONTRACT between a seller and buyer agreeing to the TRANSFER of PROPERTY under certain conditions, including the amount of money to be paid, the date on which the property is to be transferred, the condition of the property at the time of transfer, etcetera.
Sale, bill of. A DOCUMENT giving evidence that PROPERTY has been sold to a PURCHASER by a SELLER.
Sale, exclusive. An AGREEMENT between an OWNER and a BROKER, such an agreement being that the owner will not sell his property except through the broker. EXCLUSIVE RIGHTS are usually given only for a limited period of time, after which the owner can make other arrangements to dispose of his property.
Sale, executory. A SALE that has been agreed upon, but one in which details have not yet been worked out.
Sale, forced. A SALE ordered by a COURT, against the wishes of the OWNER. Such sales are frequently ordered to satisfy outstanding OBLIGATIONS and DEBTS of the owner. Included in forced sales are foreclosures for failure to meet MORTGAGE obligations.
Sale, fraudulent. A SALE made to avoid legal OBLIGATIONS to CREDITORS. An owner may dispose of his property during a time when creditors are attempting to collect monies owed to them, thus perpetrating a fraud in that he no longer will own the PROPERTY that could have satisfied his obligations.
Sale, judicial. A SALE ordered by a court. > SALE, FORCED.
Sale on approval. A SALE that is conditioned or tentative, depending upon the intended purchaser's SATISFACTION with the thing he is buying.
Sale on credit. A SALE in which the property is transferred to the POSSESSION of the new owner but payment is put off to a future date.
Sale under power of sale. Foreclosing a MORTGAGE without resorting to COURT ACTION.
Sales tax. A TAX based upon a percentage of the RECEIPTS of a SALE.
Salvage. Payments allowed to

those who help to save something that is in danger of being totally lost, such as the salvage of a sinking or sunken ship and its cargo. Maritime law specifies conditions in which salvage charges are warranted.

Salvage lien. A maritime LIEN (a CLAIM against PROPERTY) by those who have assisted in saving a ship, part of a ship, and/or its cargo. Maritime law recognizes these liens as legitimate.

Same offense. The DOCTRINE that no one should be tried twice for the same CRIME, if he was once ACQUITTED of its commission. > DOUBLE JEOPARDY.

Sanction. **1.** A PENALTY imposed for the purpose of obtaining COMPLIANCE and obedience to the LAW; a coercive measure. **2.** Approval.

Sanctuary. A place where someone can go to avoid ARREST, such as a house of worship, or a foreign embassy or consulate building; a refuge.

Sane. The state of having MENTAL COMPETENCE and soundness of mind; knowing right from wrong, being capable of intelligent reasoning, and generally acting in a normal, socially acceptable manner. The opposite of INSANE or MENTALLY INCOMPETENT.

Satisfaction. **1.** The payment of a DEBT; the fulfillment of an OBLIGATION, such as the payment of a MORTGAGE or, the completion of one's obligations under a CONTRACT. **2.** The act of satisfying.

Satisfaction and accord. > ACCORD AND SATISFACTION.

Satisfaction piece. A written memorandum stating that the matter in DISPUTE between PLAINTIFF and DEFENDANT has been settled.

Satisfactory evidence. VALID, believable, credible, pertinent TESTIMONY; EVIDENCE of such a nature as to convince the COURT of its truth; convincing PROOF.

Satisfy. To fulfill a request; to pay off a DEBT; to discharge an OBLIGATION. > SATISFACTION.

Saving clause. **1.** A PROVISION in a LAW stating that certain important clauses will remain VALID even if the remainder of the law is overturned by subsequent judicial ACTIONS. **2.** A RESTRICTION in the repeal of a law, saving those provisions which preserve certain important RIGHTS and PRIVILEGES.

Saving property doctrine. The doctrine that a DEFENDANT who, through his NEGLIGENCE, has caused DAMAGE to another's PROPERTY is also liable for any personal INJURIES suffered by the OWNER of that property in his attempts to save it.

Saving the statute of limitations. Suing for the recovery of a DEBT or for DAMAGES before the STATUTE OF LIMITATIONS runs out. The statute of limitations is a specified number of years from the time the debt was incurred or the damage was inflicted.

Scale-down agreement. An AGREEMENT in which the CREDITORS agree to accept less than the full amount due them as full payment for their CLAIMS.

Schedule. **1.** An inventory; a list, such as a list of all ASSETS and LIABILITIES of a person or company that is filing for BANKRUPTCY. **2.** To prepare a timetable for the carrying out of particular acts; to prepare a list or inventory.

Schedule of exempt property. The listing by a person who is in BANKRUPTCY of those PROPERTIES which he claims cannot be held or taken by his CREDITORS.

Scheme to defraud. A planned attempt to deceive and cheat; a CONSPIRACY to carry out a FRAUD.

Schizophrenia. A form of mental illness in which there is a withdrawal from reality. It occurs most often in adolescents and young adults. ➤ DEMENTIA PRAECOX.

Sciendum est. It should be known (Latin). The term is used frequently in law books at the beginning of chapters, denoting that an explanation will be given.

Scienter. With knowledge; knowingly. The term is applied to someone who supposedly is aware of his GUILT (Latin).

Scintilla of evidence. A particle of EVIDENCE; an insignificant bit of evidence. DEFENSE ATTORNEYS often state, "There is not a *scintilla* of evidence to back up this claim."

Scire facias. **1.** A COURT ORDER (WRIT) most often used to revive a case in which a JUDGMENT has been issued but has never been carried out (executed) (Latin). **2.** A court command that someone appear in COURT and tell why a RECORD in his POSSESSION should not be destroyed.

Scope of a patent. The extent of a PATENT must be determined by principles of patent law if the patented article or invention does not lend itself to imposing specific limits upon it.

Scope of authority. The powers of an AGENT given to him by the PRINCIPAL, including not only the authority specifically designated but implied or inferred authority, too. In such instances in which there is doubt, the agent may claim that the scope of his authority to act for and in his principal's behalf is greater than that which is written down and recorded.

Scramming contract. A mining contract in which a person is given the right to mine a pit that is open and has already been mined before.

Scrip. **1.** A certificate indicating the RIGHT of the holder to receive PAYMENT in the future in the form of money, land, or goods. **2.** Paper currency.

Scurrilous. Vulgar; foul; indecent, obscene language. Scurrilous behavior is a MISDEMEANOR, when it takes place in public.

Seal, corporate. The official seal of a CORPORATION, usually affixed to its legal DOCUMENTS.

Seal, public. A seal affixed to a DOCUMENT issued by a local, state, or federal government. Such seals attest to the VALIDITY of the document.

Sealed and delivered. A phrase placed at the end of a CONTRACT or AGREEMENT, just above the place where the parties sign the DOCUMENT and have it witnessed by others.

Sealed verdict. A VERDICT that is placed in an envelope and sealed, to be delivered to the COURT when it is next in session.
Search, unlawful. A search conducted without legal authority, thus violating one's constitutional rights.
Search a title. To investigate a TITLE to PROPERTY to make sure it truly belongs to the alleged OWNER.
Search and seizure. Methods used in detecting and punishing CRIME, including the search for and the taking of PROPERTY and data which can be used in the prosecution of the criminal. Such search and seizure must be authorized by a court WARRANT, unless the crime is committed in the presence of an OFFICER of the law.
Search and seizure, unreasonable. 1. An unlawful search, conducted without legal authority. 2. A search that is so harsh and intense that it violates the rights of the citizen under investigation. A search in which the searchers, although authorized by law, destroy PROPERTY and intimidate unnecessarily the individual under investigation.
Search warrant. A written ORDER of a COURT permitting the search of premises thought to contain stolen goods, illegal drugs, or other materials or documents that have been obtained unlawfully.
Seat of government. The county seat; the capital of a state or federal government.
Seaworthy. Able to sail the seas safely. This is a term applied to ships, implying that the vessel is equipped and manned properly so as to be able to take the voyage it intends to take.
Secession. Withdrawal from membership in a group or organization. In the Civil War, secession was a word used by those Southern states that left the Union.
Second arrest. Rearresting a CONVICT who has escaped.
Second-degree murder. HOMICIDE that is not associated with MALICE or PREMEDITATION but which, nevertheless, is the result of a desire to inflict bodily harm. It is a more serious crime than MANSLAUGHTER.
Second mortgage. A MORTGAGE that is subject to or is junior to the first mortgage.
Secondary boycott. A BOYCOTT against a company that does business with one that is having a dispute with its union. A secondary boycott is a form of indirect pressure to get the labor-struck business to come to terms.
Secondary evidence. EVIDENCE which is not the best evidence. It may be admitted in court if PRIMARY EVIDENCE is not available. For example, a WITNESS may TESTIFY as to the contents of a particular DOCUMENT *if* that document is destroyed or unavailable. Such TESTIMONY is secondary evidence.
Secondary liability. A responsibility that is secondary to the PRIMARY LIABILITY. In other words, the LIABILITY one assumes when the primary liability is not completely fulfilled.
Secondhand evidence. HEARSAY

EVIDENCE; EVIDENCE that one has learned from someone else, not seen, heard, or learned himself. It differs from FIRSTHAND EVIDENCE, which one saw, heard, or learned all by himself.

Secret. Something not made known to other people or to the public; hidden; completely confidential; concealed.

Secret hearing. A closed HEARING OR TRIAL, not open to the public.

Secret trust. A plan by which the maker of a WILL bequeaths a certain amount of money or PROPERTY to an individual, with the secret understanding that he will take that money and give it to some charitable enterprise. This is sometimes done to avoid paying taxes on money given to charity in amounts greater than those permitted as tax exempt.

Secretary of state. The ranking cabinet officer in the U.S. government. His equivalent in foreign countries is the foreign minister.

Sectarian. Relating or pertaining to a particular sect or religion, as opposed to nonsectarian, which has no relation to religion or sect.

Section of land. One square mile, or 640 acres of land.

Secular. Unrelated to religion or things that are religious.

Secundum. In accordance with; following; next to; in favor of (Latin).

Secured creditor. A person who is owed money and whose CLAIM is secured by a LIEN OR MORTGAGE on the debtor's PROPERTY.

Security. 1. PROPERTY that has been pledged by a LIEN OR MORTGAGE, thus guaranteeing that the CREDITOR will be paid if the DEBTOR defaults. Security makes the promise to pay more than a personal OBLIGATION. **2.** A STOCK OR BOND that signifies that the borrower (the CORPORATION) owes a specified amount of money to the stock or bond holder. **3.** Measures to protect people against attack, robbery, danger, etcetera.

Security, collateral. Additional SECURITY for a DEBT, subordinate to the original security. It is a kind of secondary guarantee that the debt will be honored.

Security, personal. 1. A GUARANTEE of a DEBTOR's personal PLEDGE to pay a DEBT. **2.** The RIGHT that all people have to live safe, happy, secure lives.

Security Council. The governing committee of the United Nations. Its major objective is to see that all nations live together happily, healthily, and peaceably. It is composed of five permanent members—the United States, the Soviet Union, France, the United Kingdom, and China—and ten temporary members, each serving for a term of two years.

Security deposit. A deposit of money by a TENANT with a LANDLORD, given at the onset of a LEASE. It is held so as to insure payment to the landlord for any DAMAGES the tenant may do to the PROPERTY during the tenure of the lease. In many areas, landlords are now required to keep these monies in separate interest-bearing accounts, and to return the monies with interest on the termination of the LEASE.

Security laws. Federal REGULA-

TIONS whose purposes are to protect the country from subversive activities and from attacks from abroad.

Sedition. Any illegal action that tends to overthrow the government by force. Such ACTIONS or pronouncements present a definite danger to the peace, advocating departure from the orderly, peaceful methods of changing governments through free elections.

Seduce. To lead astray; to induce someone to surrender his or her body to the physical advances of another. Whereas the meaning of seduction formerly applied to a situation in which a woman was influenced to have sexual relations with a man, it is now recognized that a female may also be responsible for seducing a male.

Segregation. The act of separating, such as segregating the races in a school. Segregation of races in public places of all kinds is illegal in the United States and violates federal laws.

Seise. The legal TITLE and OWNERSHIP of property, such as real estate.

Seisin. OWNERSHIP, complete and full, of land.

Seisin in deed. Actual POSSESSION of land; the same as *seisin in fact* and *actual seisin.*

Seisin in law. The right to immediate POSSESSION of land.

Seizure. To take forcible POSSESSION of a thing; to ARREST and take a prisoner into CUSTODY.

Selection of jurors. The picking of people to serve on a JURY.

Self-dealing. Buying SECURITIES on insider's information, which affords a favorable position not granted to the general public. As an example, an officer of a CORPORATION may buy large blocks of stock on the inside, secret information that his corporation is about to complete a very profitable deal.

Self-defense. The process of defending oneself or one's property from an attack by another. Self-defense is an inherent RIGHT, but if the assailant is injured or killed in the act of self-defense, PROOF must be offered that the violence did come about only because it was necessary to save one's own life.

Self-executing judgment. A DECISION of a court requiring no action of the court to see that the JUDGMENT is carried out.

Self-incrimination. TESTIMONY given by oneself against oneself, which will tend to convict one of a CRIME. > PRIVILEGE AGAINST SELF-INCRIMINATION.

Self-insured. To act as one's own INSURANCE CARRIER, such as an employer who obligates himself to pay directly those employees who suffer injuries while on the job. Those who self-insure their companies or organizations are still subject to the supervision of the state insurance departments of their particular state.

Self-preservation. A basic instinct to protect one's health, body, and life.

Self-serving statement. A STATEMENT made to serve one's own purposes.

Semper. Always (Latin).

Senate. The upper chamber of the Congress of the United States, numbering two selected representatives from each state. At present there are one hundred senators.

Senator. A member of the U. S. Senate, or of a state senate. There are two senators elected from each state to the U. S. Senate. States each have their own rules concerning the election of state senators. U.S. senators serve for a term of six years.

Senile. A decline of mental faculties occasioned by old age. However, the number of years one has lived does not necessarily indicate whether a person is senile. An individual may not be senile at 80 years of age, or he may display great senility at 60 years of age.

Senile dementia. Loss of mental faculties because of hardening of the arteries and decreased blood supply to the brain. Such people are often MENTALLY INCOMPETENT.

Senior counsel. The ATTORNEY in charge of a LAWSUIT when there are two or more attorneys representing the same client.

Seniority. A PRINCIPLE among labor organizations that the employees who have worked the most number of years are entitled to be advanced first, rehired first, and laid off last.

Sentence. The JUDGMENT pronounced by a COURT after the CONVICTION of a criminal; a term in JAIL or a FINE, or both. Also, PROBATION.

Sentence, concurrent. A SENTENCE running at the same time as another sentence, as distinguished from a CUMULATIVE SENTENCE. > CONCURRENT SENTENCES.

Sentence, cumulative. One sentence after another, not running at the same time. Such punishment is often given to a criminal convicted on several counts. > CONSECUTIVE SENTENCES.

Sentence, indeterminate. A SENTENCE for a nonspecified period of time. Such sentences state "for not less than" or "not more than" so many months or years. Good behavior, with this type of sentence, may lead to earlier PAROLE.

Sentence, interlocutory. A temporary SENTENCE, awaiting the decree of a FINAL SENTENCE. Also, a sentence arising out of a cause related to the main cause in the case.

Sentence, suspended. > SUSPENDED SENTENCE.

Sentences to run concurrently. A CONCURRENT SENTENCE; a sentence to run at the same time as another sentence. Such sentences are given frequently when the convicted person is found guilty on several charges of wrongdoing.

Separable controversy. A separate claim contained within a single LAWSUIT. Such a CLAIM may be separated from the pending suit and undergo TRIAL in another action.

Separate acknowledgment. An acknowledgment of a DEED or other DOCUMENT by a married woman, separate and apart from her husband's acknowledgment.

Separate counts. Two or more CHARGES contained within one INDICTMENT, each count, in actuality, constituting a separate indictment for which the DEFENDANT may be tried.

Separate defense. When two or more people are being charged with the same offense, one DEFENDANT may offer a defense separate and distinct from the other defendants.

Separate estate. PROPERTY owned and controlled solely by a spouse, over which the mate has no control or rights.

Separate maintenance. Money paid by a married person for the support of a spouse from whom one is separated.

Separate property. PROPERTY owned and controlled by a married person, the spouse having no RIGHTS concerning it at all. The OWNER of such property can dispose of it at will, without the CONSENT of the spouse.

Separate trials. In a LAWSUIT against several DEFENDANTS, one or more of the defendants may request a separate trial and may offer a separate, different defense from the others.

Separation. The living apart of a husband and wife. If such a separation is ordered by a court, it is a "legal separation," in which event the details of SUPPORT and maintenance are often spelled out specifically in a DOCUMENT issued by the court.

Separation agreement. An agreement by a husband and wife to live apart. Such an AGREEMENT usually contains provisions for support.

Separation of powers. The balancing of AUTHORITY among the three main branches of our government, namely, the EXECUTIVE (presided over by the President), the JUDICIAL (presided over by our courts, with the Supreme Court being the highest judicial power), and the LEGISLATIVE (presided over by Congress). Each branch of the government has separate powers, independent of the powers of the other branches.

Sequester. To put aside and hold; to isolate, such as to sequester a jury during its DELIBERATIONS or to hold PROPERTY until a LAWSUIT concerning it is settled.

Sergeant at arms. A person appointed by a body such as the House of Representatives, the Senate, or some other legislative organization, to keep order and to see that the meetings are carried out in an orderly manner, according to existing rules.

Seriatim. One by one, as in *ad seriatim* (Latin).

Serious and willful misconduct. Improper behavior of major proportions, carried out intentionally.

Service by mail. Serving a SUMMONS by mailing it to the person's address, sometimes done when it is impossible to give the summons directly.

Service of a subpoena.
> SERVICE OF PROCESS.

Service of a summons.
> SERVICE OF PROCESS.

Service of a wife. The assistance, aid, comfort, companionship, and physical relations, etcetera, that a wife customarily affords a husband. In various LAWSUITS, a husband may claim that he has lost the services of his wife as a result of DAMAGES caused by the opposing party.

Service of execution. The acts of a SHERIFF or other COURT OFFI-

CER in carrying out the JUDGMENT of the court. This may include sale of the DEFENDANT'S PROPERTY in order to raise the money to pay the JUDGMENT.

Service of notice. The giving of information to a person entitled to receive it. As an example, the informing of a person of the CHARGES being brought against him by a PLAINTIFF. Service of notice must be carried out according to law, in such a manner that a person cannot deny he has received it.

Service of pleading. The formal delivery, to the PLAINTIFF or his ATTORNEY, of the answer to CHARGES. According to common legal practice, the DEFENDANT, or his attorney, serves the PLEADING (defense to plaintiff's charges) upon the plaintiff, or his attorney, in a written STATEMENT.

Service of process. The delivery of a SUMMONS, SUBPOENA, WRIT, or other legal DOCUMENT to the opposing party in a lawsuit.

Servient estate. A RESTRICTION placed on land wherein the DEED forbids the placing of a building within a certain distance from another's property.

Servitude. **1.** The state of being a servant or slave. **2.** When applied to land, servitude means that the land cannot be used for the CONSTRUCTION of a building within a specified distance of the neighboring property. > SERVIENT ESTATE.

Session. The period during any one day, or periods of days, during which a COURT, TRIBUNAL, LEGISLATIVE BODY, etcetera, conducts its business. When such a body is "in session," it means that it is not on vacation or has not terminated its usual period during which it conducts its business.

Set aside. To cancel, to ANNUL; to revoke. The expression is used frequently when a higher court overrules a DECISION or JUDGMENT of a lower court, or when an INDICTMENT is dropped.

Setoff. A COUNTERCLAIM by a DEFENDANT against a PLAINTIFF. The setoff may have nothing to do with the plaintiff's original claim.

Setting aside a verdict. The ANNULMENT of a court decision, often by a higher court.

Settle. To agree to a SETTLEMENT of a dispute; the coming together of opposing parties in a LAWSUIT; to resolve a difference.

Settle a bill of exceptions. To approve a BILL OF EXCEPTIONS. > BILL OF EXCEPTIONS.

Settle a document. To amend, correct, and put a DOCUMENT into its proper legal language and form.

Settle property. To determine the future of PROPERTY so that it will not be impaired or harmed by its present occupant.

Settled account. An account that has been paid.

Settled insanity. A legal (not a medical) term for recurrent or habitual mental illness.

Settlement. **1.** The ending of a dispute through an AGREEMENT. **2.** The PAYMENT of an OBLIGATION. **3.** The occupation of and building upon land.

Settlement out of court. AGREEMENT between opposing parties outside of COURT, before the controversy has been decided by the court.

Seventh Amendment. The Amendment that gives the right to a TRIAL BY JURY in a common LAWSUIT. (The COMMON LAW involves CIVIL, not CRIMINAL, matters.) The matter in dispute must be more than twenty dollars in value to have the right to trial by jury in a civil lawsuit.

Seven years' absence. When a person has been missing and his whereabouts unknown for seven or more years, he is presumed by law to be dead.

Severable. The quality of being able to exist independently. A severable law is one that continues to hold even if one clause or PROVISION is held not to be VALID.

Severable contract. One that contains many parts, thus really being several CONTRACTS in one. In a severable contract, some PROVISIONS may be fulfilled while others are not.

Several. More than two; distinct and separate.

Severalty estate. An ESTATE that is owned by one person only.

Severance. **1.** The act of separating and dividing. **2.** When there are two or more DEFENDANTS in the same case, one may wish to defend himself alone and not join with the others. This is termed severance.

Severance of prosecution. Separation into individual TRIALS in a case, often occasioned because one DEFENDANT wants to confess, turn STATE'S EVIDENCE, or wishes to offer a different defense than the other defendants.

Sexual assault. Physical advances of one person toward another, accompanied by threats of harm if resistance is put up to the advances; INDECENT ASSAULT. It is not necessary for complete sexual intercourse to occur in a sexual assault.

Sexual intercourse. Contact between the male and female organs, with penetration of the penis into the vagina; coitus.

Sham conviction. A situation in which a DEFENDANT pleads guilty to a minor OFFENSE in order to avoid TRIAL on a major offense.

Sham pleading. A DEFENSE that is obviously false and presented in bad faith.

Shanghai. To get a person drunk or to drug him and then place him on a ship about to go to sea. When the person awakes from his drunkenness or recovers from the drug's effects, he is pressed into service, against his will, as a seaman.

Share and share alike. Equal shares; equal proportions.

Shareholder. A STOCKHOLDER; an individual who owns a share in a corporate enterprise or in a business.

Sheriff. A law OFFICER whose duties include the keeping of the peace, the serving of SUMMONSES, SUBPOENAS, and other legal DOCUMENTS, the calling of JURORS, and the carrying out of JUDGMENTS issued by the COURTS. Sheriffs serve one county, to which their authority is limited.

Sheriff, deputy. A person appointed by the SHERIFF to aid him in his work, or to aid him in a particular task.

Sheriff's jury. A JURY summoned by a SHERIFF to carry out a questioning or an inquest (an INVESTIGATION as to the cause of death of someone who died violently or under suspicious circumstances). A sheriff's jury may have twelve members, or it may be composed of fewer or more than twelve.

Shield law. A LAW that protects an informant's right to conceal his source of information.

Shifting clause. A clause that permits a different distribution of PROPERTY than that originally prescribed.

Shifting the burden of proof. Transferring the BURDEN OF PROOF from one side of the case to the other. This can happen when the DEFENDANT makes a clearcut, convincing, obvious denial of the CHARGES against him. The PLAINTIFF in such instances, in essence, then assumes the role of the DEFENDANT.

Ship's husband. An individual appointed by the OWNERS of a ship to manage the affairs of the ship for the benefit of all the owners.

Ship's papers. DOCUMENTS carried by all ships on the high seas showing nationality, port of origin, ports of call, nature of cargo, and proof of compliance with laws of navigation.

Shock. A sudden severe disturbance of the mind or body. Shock is often accompanied by a lack of sufficient blood circulating in the blood vessels, thus leading to fainting, unconsciousness, or other manifestations of inadequate blood supply to the brain and other vital organs. The condition can be caused by marked blood loss, excruciating pain, overwhelming infection, extensive injuries to tissues, or by emotional factors.

Shock, mental. A state of sudden agitation brought on by an emotional upheaval, such as learning of the death of a dear one. Extreme joy can also precipitate a state of SHOCK, but recovery from this type of shock is rapid.

Shock, physical. A sudden severe injury, such as a blow on the head or a crushing injury to a limb.

Shoot. To use firearms, such as a revolver or shotgun, against someone, thus causing the person to be struck by a bullet.

Shop right rule. The PRIVILEGE of an employer to manufacture and sell an invention of one of his employees, without the payment of a ROYALTY. Also, the OBLIGATION of an employee who owns a PATENT on an invention to permit his employer to license and use the INVENTION. This rule is based upon the assumption that the invention came into being while the employee was employed and while using materials and the assistance of the employer.

Shore lands. Lands between the high and low water marks; lands bordering lakes, rivers, seas, etcetera.

Short cause. A case that will take but a short time for a JUDGE to hear and to decide.

Short notice. Less than the usual, ordinary time. An ATTORNEY may ask for a postponement of a trial because he has received short notice, not permitting sufficient time for him to prepare his case adequately.

Short sale. The SALE of STOCK not owned by the seller. Such sales are based upon the belief that the price of the stock will go down, thus benefiting the "short" seller.

Short summons. A SUMMONS that must be answered within a shorter than usual period of time. Such summonses are sometimes issued when it is feared that the person will attempt to leave town so as to avoid the JURISDICTION of the court.

Show cause. An ORDER of a COURT for an individual to appear in court and tell why he thinks the court should not take a certain action. Should a show-cause order not be answered, the court will proceed in taking the intended action.

Shyster. An unscrupulous lawyer whose practices are on the borderline of the illegal and unethical.

Sic. So; thus (Latin).

Sick benefits. Monies paid to employees while they are out of work because of illness. Such payments are made through HEALTH INSURANCE policies, either taken out by employers or through local or state-administered disability programs.

Sick leave. A leave of absence, sometimes accompanied by pay, occasioned by illness. When sick leave is granted, it is assumed that the employee will return to his job if and when he recovers from his sickness.

Signature. One's name, written in one's own handwriting. A signature at the end of a legal DOCUMENT attests to its authenticity and validity.

Signed and sealed. An expression denoting that a DOCUMENT has been duly EXECUTED.

Silence, estoppel by. A situation in which a person is obligated to speak in another's behalf but doesn't. Such silence is, in essence, dishonest and damaging.

Silent partner. A PARTNER not generally known as a co-owner of a firm or business, yet is entitled to the rights of partnership; a dormant partner; a secret partner.

Similar description. Being the same in many or most respects. A term often used when imposing an import TARIFF on goods from a foreign country.

Simple assault. **1.** An ASSAULT that was not provoked or aggravated. **2.** An assault that caused no bodily harm to the person assaulted.

Simple negligence. INJURY resulting from failure to take ordinary precautions, as distinguished from NEGLIGENCE that is willful and deliberate.

Simulated. Made to look like something it is not, sometimes with the intent to defraud; counterfeited; pretended.

Simulated contract. A CONTRACT that appears to be bona fide, but in actuality is not. Such a contract is not VALID.

Simulated fact. An untruth that is made to look like a truth in order to deceive; a false, invented fact.

Simulated judgment. A JUDGMENT which appears to be in good faith but actually is for the purpose of defrauding someone.

Simulated sale. An apparent SALE, not an actual sale, of PROPERTY in an attempt to put it out of reach of one's CREDITORS.

Simultaneous. Occurring at the same time or instant, such as simultaneous deaths.

Simultaneous Death Act. A LAW, universal in this country, governing situations in which two people die at the same time, as in an airplane crash. The law states that the PROPERTY of each person, such as a husband and wife, shall be disposed of as if the spouse had survived. This law's application is subject to clauses in the WILLS of people who die simultaneously, which might provide otherwise.

Sine die. A final ADJOURNMENT of a court is called sine die, meaning in Latin "without day"; an ADJOURNMENT without assigning another day for a further HEARING.

Sine qua non. An indispensable, essential requirement or condition. In Latin, sine qua non means "without which there is nothing."

Single. One only; unattached; standing alone; unmarried; individual.

Singular. 1. One only; individual; each; unique. **2.** The opposite of plural.

Sit-down strike. A strike in which the employees stay within the plant but do not work. Their presence, however, prevents others from working.

Sit in camera. To hold a private court HEARING or session, often in the judge's CHAMBERS.

Site. A location; a place where an event took place; land upon which one intends to build.

Sittings after term. Sessions of a COURT after the term of the court has ended; occasionally done to dispose of matters requiring early solution.

Situated. Physically located.

Situation of danger. A position from which one cannot escape. > LAST CLEAR CHANCE.

Skill, reasonable. Such knowledge and ability as is ordinarily possessed and exercised by the average, competent person.

Skilled witness. An EXPERT WITNESS; a WITNESS who possesses special knowledge in a particular field and can therefore give TESTIMONY on matters of OPINION.

Skipping bail. Not showing up in court when one is out on BAIL. This leads to forfeiture of the bail money.

Slander. Language used to defame a person, leading to his embarrassment, tending to hurt his reputation, or interfering with his business or livelihood. Implicit in slander is the fact that the accusatory or DEFAMATORY remarks are false. It is *not* slander to say that a person is a thief when he has been tried and convicted as a thief.

Slander of title. A false STATEMENT, in writing or made orally, which casts doubt upon or disparages a person's TITLE to PROPERTY. Slander of title is a purposeful, malicious act, done to hurt the value of the property.

Slanderer. An individual who knowingly makes false remarks about another person with intent to damage that person's reputation and/or ability to conduct his affairs in his usual manner.

Slanderous per quod. STATEMENTS that appear to be slanderous and DEFAMATORY, but whose injurious consequences must be proved.

Slanderous per se. Slanderous in itself (Latin). This type of SLANDER is present when a person makes false remarks that another has commited some criminal act, has violated accepted MORAL CODES, has some infectious, communicable disease, or is unfit to hold an OFFICE or perform his DUTIES because of dishonesty.

Slip sheet. A copy of a DECISION of the Supreme Court issued immediately after the decision has been reached; a "slip decision"; a "slip opinion."

Slowdown. The intentional slowing down of productivity by employees. Such a slowdown is often carried out instead of a strike, for the purpose of getting the employer to give in to employee requests or demands.

Slum. A rundown, dilapidated area where poor people live in poverty in inferior housing.

Slumlord. An OWNER of dilapidated, rundown tenements where impoverished people are forced to live.

Small Business Act. A federal law enacted for the purpose of aiding small business enterprises, to protect them from being put out of business by large CORPORATIONS.

Small claims court. COURTS set up for the express purpose of settling small CLAIMS. Decisions in such LITIGATIONS are made by a JUDGE within a short period of time, thereby avoiding a prolonged trial.

"Smart money." Monies (DAMAGES) a DEFENDENT must pay that are over and above the actual damages he has caused. Also called PUNITIVE DAMAGES.

Smith Act. A federal STATUTE making it unlawful to attempt to overthrow the government by force.

Smuggling. An unlawful act in which one attempts to bring prohibited articles into the country, or in which one brings in dutiable articles without paying DUTIES on them.

"So help me God." A STATEMENT concluding the swearing process; the words ordinarily concluding an OATH.

Sober. **1.** Not under the influence of an intoxicating beverage. A person may have imbibed an intoxicating beverage in moderation and still be quite sober. **2.** The opposite of drunk or intoxicated. **3.** A sensible, sedate person is often termed a "sober person."

Social club. An ORGANIZATION whose main function is social, unrelated to money-making; a club organized for getting people together in order to stimulate companionship. Such clubs are exempt from federal INCOME TAXES.

Social Security Act. A federal law providing for the establishment of universal federal and state insurance benefits, UNEMPLOYMENT INSURANCE, and other benefits for citizens who are in their later years.

Socialism. A form of government and social existence advocating the OWNERSHIP and control of capital and industry by the community as a whole. In other words, by the national government.
Society. A body of people living as members of a community, all subject to the same LAWS and REGULATIONS.
Sodomy. Unnatural ways of SEXUAL INTERCOURSE. In legal parlance, this includes intercourse between a human and an animal, anal intercourse, intercourse between an adult and a child, etcetera; buggery. Sodomy laws vary from state to state.
Sole. Exclusive; only one; single.
Sole possession. OWNERSHIP vested in one person only; exclusive possession.
Solemn occasion for advisory opinion. A situation in which LEGISLATURES or public OFFICERS are uncertain as to their AUTHORITY to take a particular action. They therefore seek advice from an outside advisor or advisory body.
Solemn will. A written WILL.
Solicit. 1. To seek, to plead; to entreat; to implore; to ask for. **2.** To lure or tempt, such as a prostitute who attempts to seduce a potential customer.
Solicitation. 1. The act of soliciting or seeking. **2.** The act of luring or tempting someone to commit an unlawful act.
Solicitor general. The assistant to the U. S. Attorney General, whose main function is to represent the United States in cases that come before the Supreme Court.
Solidarity. A situation in which several people bind themselves to the performance of a CONTRACT and in which each binds himself to the other. Should the contract not be fulfilled, any one party to the contract may be forced to pay the full sum due. Upon so doing, the others are freed from any OBLIGATION
Solitary confinement. The total and complete isolation of a prisoner in jail, with denial of any contacts with others. This is frequently a punishment for bad behavior in jail.
Solvency. Having sufficient funds so as to pay one's DEBTS; the opposite of INSOLVENCY.
Sound. 1. Free from defect; financially strong and secure; competent; healthy; able to function satisfactorily, such as a person who is sound of mind or has sound judgment. **2.** A noise.
Sound health. In robust physical condition.
Sound judicial discretion. Good JUDGMENT and DECISIONS of a COURT or a JUDGE.
Sound mind. In good mental health; SANE; free from mental illness.
Sound value. Good and fair value.
Sounding in damages. A LAWSUIT in which more than one remedy could have been sought, but the PLAINTIFF chose to sue for DAMAGES (monetary return for the wrong committed).
Source of income. The origin of income. The Internal Revenue Service frequently inquires into how and where a person came by certain income or monies.

Sources of the law. The origins of the LAW, such as cases already tried and decisions handed down, legal textbooks, law journal reports, and existing LAWS and STATUTES from which existing principles are derived.

Sovereign people. The entire citizenry who possess the power of electing their representatives and public OFFICERS and who live as a people within a SOVEREIGN STATE.

Sovereign power. The AUTHORITY and POWER to make and enforce the law of the land; INHERENT POWER. > INHERENT POWER.

Sovereign rights. The RIGHTS and PRIVILEGES of the state (nation).

Sovereign state. A nation; an independent country that governs itself.

Speaker. The presiding officer of the House of Representatives. Other legislative bodies, such as state legislatures, may also have speakers.

Special authority. The POWER of an AGENT to carry out only a specific act or acts that his PRINCIPAL has authorized him to carry out.

Special calendar. A list of pending LAWSUITS containing dates of HEARINGS or TRIALS.

Special counsel. An ATTORNEY employed to assist a state or federal ATTORNEY GENERAL in the PROSECUTION of a case.

Special damages. Extra DAMAGES awarded to a PLAINTIFF beyond the mere loss of PROPERTY; damages awarded after considering the peculiar circumstances of a particular case.

Special demurrer. An OBJECTION to a PLEADING of a DEFENDANT aimed especially at a particular defect in his DEFENSE, such as a defect in form in the pleading.

Special exception. An OBJECTION to the way in which a cause of action is presented.

Special executor. An EXECUTOR with limited POWERS in the administration of an ESTATE, such powers possibly being restricted to the administration of only one part of an estate.

Special facts rule. The RULE that a director of a COMPANY is duty-bound to reveal certain information to the STOCKHOLDERS, and that withholding such information is fraudulent.

Special jurisdiction. A COURT that is empowered to handle only certain types of cases, specified by LAW, is called "a court of special JURISDICTION."

Special matter. In defending himself, a DEFENDANT may include material of a special nature related to the main issues in CONTROVERSY. Notice to the PLAINTIFF is given that the special matter will be put in evidence.

Special motion. A MOTION that is up to the discretion of the COURT, rather than a motion that must be granted.

Special pleading. A DEFENSE that goes beyond the mere denial of the PLAINTIFF's charges. The PLEADING may include justification of or excuse for certain alleged acts, in addition to denial of PLAINTIFF's accusation.

Special privileges. RIGHTS granted to a person or group of people that are not granted to all people universally.

Special proceeding. Any REMEDY that is not an ordinary action; a PROCEEDING to be distinguished from an ordinary proceeding. > PROCEEDING, ORDINARY.

Special prosecutor. An ATTORNEY retained by a prosecuting lawyer to assist in the trying of a case. > SPECIAL COUNSEL.

Specialty. **1.** A CONTRACT under seal; an AGREEMENT signed, sealed, and delivered. **2.** The field in which a professional practices his profession. An ATTORNEY's activity may be limited to a particular specialty, such as criminal law, real estate law, etcetera.

Specific bequest. A LEGACY of a specified PROPERTY (CHATTEL) to a particular person, as precisely detailed in a WILL. > SPECIFIC LEGACY.

Specific intent. Premeditated, conscious intention to perform a certain act. The term is used frequently to describe the intentions of a person to carry out a particular CRIME or prohibited act.

Specification. A detailed STATEMENT listing the various points that will be brought up in a forthcoming LAWSUIT or LITIGATION.

Specimen. A sample; a part of something, displaying what the whole looks like.

Speculative damages. DAMAGES that depend upon future developments; QUESTIONABLE DAMAGES; damages that are mainly conjectural.

Speedy execution. The carrying out of the JUDGMENT of the court within a short time after the completion of the TRIAL.

Speedy trial. The RIGHT to a speedy trial is guaranteed by the U.S. CONSTITUTION. It means a TRIAL without unreasonable delay, taking place according to accepted RULES and REGULATIONS.

Spendthrift trust. A TRUST set up especially to protect the BENEFICIARY against his own spendthrift tendencies or against his own incompetence to handle money or PROPERTY.

Spin-off. A CORPORATION set up by a parent corporation, the stock of the new corporation being given to owners of shares in the parent company.

Spite fence. A fence built on the edge of one's property primarily for the purpose of annoying one's neighbor.

Split sentence. A SENTENCE consisting of a FINE and a term in JAIL, but suspending the jail sentence and collecting the fine.

Splitting a cause of action. Bringing separate LAWSUITS against the same person instead of joining all the complaints in one suit.

Splitting fees. The dividing of fees by two or more ATTORNEYS who serve the same client and who each render a service to the client. This is an acceptable practice in the law but is considered unethical in the practice of medicine.

Spoliation. Changes made in a DOCUMENT, such as a WILL or other legal INSTRUMENT, by an unauthorized person. Such spoliation will not change the VALIDITY of the document.

Spoliator. One who alters or attempts to destroy a legal DOCUMENT by making significant changes in it.

Sponsor. An individual who gives SECURITY for another or promises to be responsible for another.
Spouse. A person's wife or husband.
Spurious. 1. Fake; not genuine. 2. An illegitimate birth.
Squatter. A person who settles and inhabits land that he doesn't own, often PUBLIC LANDS.
Squatter's rights. The so-called RIGHT of a person to own a piece of land because he has occupied it for a long period of time. Such rights are not usually recognized by LAW.
Stakeholder. A person who holds money for others, pending the outcome of a TRANSACTION or WAGER. He is not involved in the transaction or wager.
Stale check. A check that has been held too long before cashing it, thus resulting in failure of a bank to recognize its VALIDITY.
Stale claim. A long-delayed CLAIM; a claim that has not been made for so long a period of time that a COURT will find great difficulty in determining the merits of the claim.
Stand. 1. The place where a WITNESS sits (or stands) to give TESTIMONY. 2. To remain in force; to appear in court; to stay unchanged.
Stand, to take the. To go to the place in a COURTROOM where one is sworn and gives TESTIMONY.
Stand, witness. The place where a WITNESS gives his or her TESTIMONY.
Stand mute. To refuse to plead either GUILTY or INNOCENT. On such an occasion, the court usually judges it as a NOT GUILTY plea.
Standard. Generally recognized as conforming to established practice, such as "standard order of procedure."
Standard of care. The type of care that is usually given by prudent, sensible people; the opposite of substandard or NEGLIGENT care.
Standing aside a juror. The temporary placing aside of a JUROR by a PROSECUTING ATTORNEY in a CRIMINAL CASE. Such juror is neither accepted nor rejected until the entire panel of potential jurors has been examined.
Standing by. The act of "standing by" and not transmitting information that would be most important in resolving a legal DISPUTE. It is the DUTY of someone who possesses valuable information to communicate it so as to help in the solution of a LAWSUIT.
Standing seised to uses. An AGREEMENT or COVENANT by an OWNER of PROPERTY to hold such property for the use of another person, usually a relative.
Star-chamber. A COURT that tried major crimes without the benefit of a JURY. This type of procedure has been outlawed for hundreds of years.
Stare decisis. A RULE that once a COURT decides a legal ISSUE, it should stand by that RULING when future cases of a similar nature come before it (Latin).
State. 1. A nation. 2. A state within the United States. 3. A situation or condition, such as a state of temporary insanity. 4. To declare; to say; to record.
State Department. The agency, headed by the Secretary of State,

that handles matters pertaining to our relations with foreign countries and governments.

State grand jury. A JURY, authorized by the various states, whose duties include inquiring into CRIMES for the purpose of determining the probability of GUILT of a party or parties. Should the grand jury conclude that there is a good probability of guilt, it will recommend an INDICTMENT of the suspected party or parties.
> GRAND JURY.

State insurance fund. A fund created and managed by a state for the purpose of paying WORKMEN'S COMPENSATION benefits and awards.

State secret. Information concerning matters of government that cannot and should not be revealed, even by a WITNESS in a COURT PROCEEDING.

State tax. A TAX levied by a state, as distinguished from a federal or local tax.

State trial. A TRIAL for a political CRIME or OFFENSE.

Stated term. An ordinary term or session of a COURT, as distinguished from a special term.

Statement. An exact, precise declaration of FACTS; an ALLEGATION; a presentation, as the opening statement by an ATTORNEY in behalf of his client.

Statement of case. **1.** An informal presentation of facts by a PLAINTIFF. **2.** A declaration required in some states when making a MOTION for a new TRIAL.

Statement of demand. A written declaration of the demands being made by the PLAINTIFF. It should include the details of the amounts of money due, or other REMEDIES that are sought.

State's attorney. An ATTORNEY representing the state, such as a state's ATTORNEY GENERAL or a state's DISTRICT ATTORNEY.

State's evidence. The TESTIMONY given by a WITNESS, in a CRIMINAL CASE, who has been a participant in a crime. Such testimony is given to aid the state in its CONVICTION of a fellow criminal. The purpose of the evidence is to get a lighter sentence or to avoid prosecution of oneself. State's evidence must be given voluntarily.

Status. The relation of an individual to the community in which he resides; rank; position; a position in regard to family relationships, such as "married," "divorced," etcetera.

Status quo. Without change; in the same situation as it was; stable (Latin).

Statute. A law passed by the legislative branch of a government.

Statute, criminal. An act of a legislative body relating to CRIME and its various forms of PUNISHMENT.

Statute, declaratory. A LAW passed by a LEGISLATURE to put an end to confusion or doubts about what the legal RULINGS are in a particular matter.

Statute, enabling. A law that gives the RIGHT to individuals or CORPORATIONS to do something that they were not previously permitted to do.

Statute, expository. A STATUTE that contains words setting forth its true intent and meaning.

Statute, general. A LAW applying

to everyone, as distinguished from a law that applies only to a few, or to a special circumstance.

Statute, local. One passed by a county or city LEGISLATIVE BODY, applying only to the area of their AUTHORITY.

Statute, negative. A LAW that states what *cannot* be done; a law prohibiting something, such as walking the streets unclad.

Statute, penal. A LAW providing a PUNISHMENT for an OFFENSE or CRIME, such as the punishment for committing a robbery, murder, etcetera.

Statute, perpetual. A LAW that will stay in effect permanently, without limitation as to the time when it shall remain in effect.

Statute, personal. A LAW affecting one person, rather than a whole community; the opposite of a general statute. > STATUTE, PRIVATE.

Statute, private. A LAW that concerns individuals or particular groups of individuals. > STATUTE PERSONAL.

Statute, public. A LAW affecting an entire community; the opposite of a personal or private STATUTE.

Statute, punitive. A LAW which imposes a PENALTY.

Statute, real. A LAW involving matters of PROPERTY rather than people.

Statute, remedial. A LAW whose purpose is to correct an existing law that is not working, or has caused harm instead of good.

Statute, revised. A STATUTE that has been altered, changed, updated, and reenacted.

Statute, special. A personal or special STATUTE. The opposite of a general or public statute. > STATUTE, PERSONAL.

Statute, temporary. A LAW remaining in force for only a limited period of time.

Statute, validating. A LAW enacted for the purpose of correcting past errors and omissions, thus making VALID something that was not valid.

Statute of limitations. A law establishing a specified period of time during which a LITIGATION (LAWSUIT) can take place, after that period, the suit can no longer be brought.

Statutory. Created by the enactment of a LAW, relating to a STATUTE or law; existing as the result of a statute.

Statutory action. A SUIT or ACTION based upon the existence of a LAW or STATUTE, or upon the violation of a particular statute or law.

Statutory bond. **1.** A BOND that meets the requirements of an existing STATUTE or LAW. **2.** A bond required by law.

Statutory crime. A CRIME specified by LAW, as distinguished from an OFFENSE that has not been declared CRIMINAL in an existing STATUTE. (The latter is a COMMON LAW offense.)

Statutory discovery. The REMEDY of discovery, as provided in an existing STATUTE. > BILL OF DISCOVERY.

Statutory exposition. An explanation in a subsequent STATUTE of a confusing or ambiguous PROVISION in a preceding statute.

Statutory foreclosure. The FORECLOSURE of a MORTGAGE or LIEN on a piece of PROPERTY without a LAWSUIT, such foreclosure being based upon an existing STATUTE.

Statutory interpleader. The REMEDY of INTERPLEADER as provided by an existing STATUTE.
> INTERPLEADER.

Statutory obligation. An OBLIGATION that must be met because it is spelled out in an existing LAW and therefore must be SATISFIED, as distinguished from an obligation that is founded upon AGREEMENTS or ACTS between parties.

Statutory pardon. A PARDON granted by an act of a LEGISLATIVE BODY.

Statutory rape. SEXUAL INTERCOURSE with a person under the legal age of consent, whether or not consent for intercourse has been granted. For example, if a man has intercourse with a willing partner who is under 16 years of age, it is considered statutory rape.

Stay. 1. A postponement; a moratorium. **2.** To stop or halt, usually temporarily, a legal PROCEEDING.

Stay of action. The POSTPONEMENT of a CASE, usually until such time as a pending matter is taken care of.

Stay of execution. A POSTPONEMENT of the carrying out of a JUDGMENT, such postponement being ordered by the COURT. A stay of execution may be granted by the same court that issued the original judgment, or it may be granted to give the DEFENDANT more time to satisfy the judgment, or it may be granted pending the defendant's appeal of the judgment to a higher court.

Stay of proceedings. A temporary suspension of a TRIAL, ordered by the COURT. There are many situations that might influence a court to halt the PROCEEDINGS, such as the promise of one of the parties to perform some act that he has omitted performing.

Stealing. Thieving; robbing; the act of LARCENY.

Stepchild. A child of one's wife or husband by a former marriage.

Stepfather. The husband of one's mother by virtue of a marriage subsequent to the death or divorce of one's natural father.

Stepmother. The wife of one's father by virtue of a marriage subsequent to the death or divorce of one's natural mother.

Sterilization. The act of making reproduction impossible. This may be accomplished in many ways, in the female, by removing surgically the ovaries; ligating or destroying the passageway through the Fallopian tubes, or by giving large doses of X rays to the ovaries; in the male, sterilization can be carried out by tying off the vas deferens (VASECTOMY) or by removing the testicles.

Stick up. A holdup; a robbery.

Stifling a prosecution. Not going ahead with a PROSECUTION, often because the PLAINTIFF has received certain monies in exchange for not PROCEEDING.

Stillborn. Dead at birth. If a child takes even one breath at birth, it is not considered a stillborn child.

Stipulation. An AGREEMENT between the opposing parties in a LAWSUIT in respect to some matter or matters that are connected with the suit. Such stipulations are made in order to avoid delays or expense in the conducting of the trial. Many stipulations consist of admissions of FACTS to which both parties agree. Stipulations are often recorded in writing, and are signed by the ATTORNEYS for the two sides in a PROCEEDING.

Stirpes. > PER STIRPES.

Stock broker. A person who buys and sells STOCKS for his clients.

Stock corporation. A CORPORATION that issues SHARES to STOCKHOLDERS. Stock corporations pay dividends to shareholders from their earnings and profits. Stock corporations must be authorized by the laws of the state in which they are incorporated.

Stock dividend. A fund set aside by a STOCK CORPORATION composed of profits that will be apportioned to its various STOCKHOLDERS, usually in the form of additional shares of STOCK.

Stockholder. Someone who owns SHARES in a STOCK CORPORATION. He is not responsible, merely by owning stock, for the actions of the corporate entity.

Stockholders' meeting. A MEETING of the STOCKHOLDERS of a corporation for the purpose of electing officers and conducting business requiring their action or consent.

Stockholder's suit. A legal ACTION instituted by a SHAREHOLDER in behalf of the CORPORATION. In other words, the STOCKHOLDER serves as the representative of the corporation.

Stock option. The granting to an individual the right to purchase STOCK at some future time at a specified price, rather that at its actual price at the time of purchase.

Stock split. The issuing of additional STOCK by splitting the value of the presently issued stock. Thus, if a company has one million shares outstanding, valued at $100 per share, it may split the one million shares to two million, each share then being valued at $50.

Stolen goods. The receiving and holding of stolen goods is a CRIMINAL OFFENSE when the person is aware that the goods have been acquired illegally.

Stonewall. A slang expression meaning that one should hold a certain position or tell a certain story steadfastly and continuously, even if he knows the position to be false or the story to be untrue.

Stowaway. Someone who hides in a vessel or airplane in order to obtain a free trip.

Stranding. The running aground of a ship.

Strangers. People who are not part of a TRANSACTION, or those who are not part of an AGREEMENT, nor can they be bound by it.

Straw bail. BAIL posted by a BONDSMAN who is irresponsible. Such bail is termed a "straw bond."

Straw man. **1.** A man whose name is used as a "front" for a TRANSACTION; a "dummy." **2.** ARGUMENTS brought up in a BRIEF solely for the purpose of debunking them.

Strict construction. A literal, narrow INTERPRETATION of a CONTRACT or other DOCUMENT, as opposed to a liberal construction or interpretation. Those who are strict constructionists of the U. S. CONSTITUTION interpret its meanings according to the exact language used in writing it, rather than interpreting it broadly and liberally.

Strictly construed. When referring to a STATUTE, it means that the COURT must make its JUDGMENT based plainly upon the language used in the writing of the statute. This affords no opportunity for the court to make its own interpretations as to what the lawmakers *might* have had in mind when they enacted the statute.

Strike. 1. To strike a word or passage, means to delete it. **2.** A work stoppage by employees for the purpose of obtaining better wages, working conditions, or fringe benefits from an employer.

Strike suit. A suit by a minority group of STOCKHOLDERS against a CORPORATION. Some such suits are brought to obtain a SETTLEMENT from the company or to obtain large fees for ATTORNEYS who handle the case. Strike suits are not undertaken to actually benefit the CORPORATION.

Strikebreaker. A "scab"; one who takes the place of an employee who is out on strike.

Striking a jury. The selecting of twelve jurors out of a list of many potential jurors.

Striking evidence. The excluding of improper EVIDENCE from a JURY's consideration.

String citation. The naming of CASE REFERENCES that were consulted in reaching a conclusion, the cases referred to being used to back up one's conclusion.

Strong-arm provision. A provision in the federal BANKRUPTCY LAW that gives the bankruptcy trustee all the POWERS of the most powerful CREDITOR or creditors, thus affording him the strong-arm to control the bankrupt's PROPERTY and ASSETS.

Struck jury. A special JURY; a jury chosen by striking off the names of other potential JURORS on a panel.

Stultify. An attempt by a DEFENDANT to show that he was not competent or rational when he carried out a CRIME or agreed to a CONTRACT.

Suable. Capable of being sued; an ISSUE that lends itself to a LAWSUIT.

Sub curia. Under the law (Latin).

Subcontract. An AGREEMENT between a CONTRACTOR and a third party to perform certain duties that the contractor has been hired to perform. As an example, a contractor, hired to build a building, may engage a subcontractor to dig the site and put in the foundation for the building.

Subcontractor. Someone who makes a CONTRACT with a CONTRACTOR to perform some work for the original contractor.

Subdivide. To divide PROPERTY into separate lots or acres in anticipation of building multiple structures on the property.

Subject matter. The matter in DISPUTE; the material over which there is LITIGATION.

Subject to. Governed by; subordinate to; provided that; contingent upon.

Subjection. The OBLIGATION of an individual to behave or act according to the WILL or JUDGMENT of another individual.
Sublease. The PRIVILEGE of a person who has leased a premise to LEASE it to another person. In leases, the privilege to sublease must be stated specifically or the LESSEE will not be permitted to sublease.
Submission. **1.** The act of surrendering or yielding. **2.** The act of a COURT in handing over a matter to a JURY for its CONSIDERATION and DECISION.
Submission bond. A BOND in which the disputing parties agree to submit their dispute to an impartial ARBITRATOR and agree to abide by his decision.
Submortgage. A situation in which the holder of a MORTGAGE obtains a LOAN from a third person, using the mortgage as SECURITY.
Subordination. A LIEN or CLAIM that is weaker than another lien or claim, and admittedly will be honored only after the stronger lien or claim has been satisfied.
Suborn. **1.** To influence someone to give false TESTIMONY or to commit a CRIME. **2.** To procure or provide something in an underhanded, dishonest manner.
Subornation of perjury. To convince someone to take a false OATH and to give false TESTIMONY.
Suborner. A person who induces another to commit PERJURY, or some other CRIME.
Subpoena. A DOCUMENT ordering an individual to appear in COURT and give TESTIMONY. Failure to appear, without good reason, may lead to the imposing of a PENALTY.
Subpoena duces tecum. A SUBPOENA that orders a person to bring certain DOCUMENTS into court when he answers the subpoena.
Subrogation. **1.** The act of substituting a CLAIM against one person for a claim against another person. **2.** The substitution of one individual for another in claiming a DEBT or RIGHT.
Sub rosa. Secretly; privately; clandestinely (Latin).
Subscriber. **1.** An individual who buys STOCK in a CORPORATION. **2.** A person who signs his name and agrees to the contents of a DOCUMENT.
Subscribing witness. A person who sees a DOCUMENT signed and affixes his name to the document, thus TESTIFYING in writing that the event has taken place.
Subsequent. An EVENT that takes place afterward; succeeding; happening at a later time or date.
Subsequent condition. A condition in a CONTRACT that cancels the LIABILITY of one party if the other party fails to comply with the terms of the contract. (Same as CONDITION SUBSEQUENT.)
Subsidiary corporation. A COMPANY that is owned and controlled by another company, often termed the PARENT COMPANY.
Subsidy. A grant of money, usually by the government, to aid in the development and success of an enterprise which the government thinks will promote the common good.
Substance. The true, basic mean-

ing of something; the real thing, as opposed to something imaginary or unrealistic.

Substantial performance. The carrying out of the major provisions of a CONTRACT, even though each and every OBLIGATION may not yet have been fulfilled.

Substantive evidence. EVIDENCE that tends to prove a fact in DISPUTE.

Substantive felony. An independent OFFENSE, not dependent upon the acts of others.

Substantive law. That part of the LAW which lays down and explains one's RIGHTS, as opposed to REMEDIAL LAW.

Substitute defendant. A person who assumes the role of DEFENDANT for another person in a SUIT or CONTROVERSY.

Substituted executor. An individual named to succeed an EXECUTOR should he die or not qualify as the executor for an ESTATE.

Substituted service. The serving of a SUMMONS by mailing it or by leaving it with a suitable individual at one's office or residence. In some areas, a substituted service is held to be just as VALID as a summons served directly by hand; in other areas, substituted services are not recognized as valid.

Substitution. SUBROGATION. The putting of one person or one thing in place of another.

Substitution by will. **1.** A CODICIL (clause) in a WILL that substitutes a new BENEFICIARY for a beneficiary originally designated; the insertion of a new provision giving the original beneficiary a new bequest, in addition to the original bequest. **2.** A GIFT OVER, such as the giving of a bequest to some person or organization *if* the original bequest does not take place.

Substitution of attorney. The changing of LAWYERS during the trying of a CASE.

Substitution of parties. The changing of a PLAINTIFF, or of a DEFENDANT, during the course of a LAWSUIT. This is sometimes done, with the court's permission, when the PLEADING or PROCESS has been amended.

Subtenant. A person who rents a LEASED premise from a TENANT. The original lease must specifically provide permission for the tenant to sublease the premises.

Subtraction. The withdrawing or withholding of services that one person owes to another, such as the NEGLECT of a tenant to properly maintain property, or the neglect to pay rent, etcetera.

Subtraction of conjugal rights. The living apart of a husband and wife without legal cause.

Subversive. To attempt to destroy or overthrow a government that has been established legally.

Succession. **1.** The act of following another, or succeeding to the RIGHTS of another. **2.** The acquiring of PROPERTY after the former owner dies and leaves it to a "successor."

Succession, testamentary. SUCCESSION (succeeding another) as the result of a clause in the WILL of a deceased person; succession according to will.

Succession, vacant. A situation

in which there are no known heirs or CLAIMANTS to PROPERTY left by a deceased person.

Succession tax. A LEVY upon the RIGHT of someone to receive property left to him in a WILL. It is not a TAX upon the value of the property left in the ESTATE.

Sudden emergency doctrine. A PRINCIPLE stating that one may be cleared of NEGLIGENCE when he has encountered a situation of great, sudden danger, not of his own making. Under a normal situation, where no sudden emergency exists, the individual would be held to be LIABLE for negligence.

Sudden passion. A phrase used to describe a violent act, such as MURDER, committed without PREMEDITATION but under circumstances of great emotional disturbance, such as fright, rage, anger, or terror. A person who finds a spouse unfaithful may, in sudden passion, commit a violent act.

Sudden peril rule. > SUDDEN EMERGENCY DOCTRINE.

Sue. To start a CIVIL LAWSUIT.

Sufficient cause. Sufficient legal reasons for removing an official from OFFICE, such as proving that he is not competent or fit to continue in the job.

Sufficient evidence. EVIDENCE adequate enough to justify the bringing of a LAWSUIT.

Suffocate. To cut off one's breathing by strangling, by making it impossible to breathe, or by using an asphyxiating gas.

Suffrage. The RIGHT to vote.

Suggestion of error. The request for another HEARING, based on the assumption that an important ERROR has taken place at a previous hearing.

Suggestive interrogation. The posing of a LEADING QUESTION. In other words, asking a question that suggests the answer.

Sui generis. One of a kind; unique; peculiar (Latin).

Sui juris. **1.** Having the capability (both mentally and physically) to manage one's own affairs. The Latin translation is literally. "Of his or her own rights." **2.** Possessing full political and CIVIL RIGHTS.

Suicide. Taking one's own life; self-destruction.

Suit. A LAWSUIT; a LITIGATION; an ACTION; a civil, rather than a criminal PROCEEDING; a proceeding taking place in a court of law where one person or persons takes ACTION against another person or persons.

Suit in equity. A LAWSUIT or case to be determined according to the court's JUDGMENT as to what is fair and equitable, rather than a SUIT whose outcome will depend upon existing laws or REGULATIONS.

Sum payable. The amount that is required to be paid in order to fulfill (discharge) one's OBLIGATION, as stated in a DOCUMENT that has recorded the obligation.

Summary. Immediate; brief; concise.

Summary contempt proceeding. An immediate HEARING to determine whether CONTEMPT OF COURT has been committed, conducted without presentation of formal CHARGES or a formal

PLEADING by the one accused of contempt. However, the one so accused may be entitled to a hearing and may be permitted to explain his conduct.

Summary conviction. A CONVICTION without a TRIAL. Such convictions are usually for minor offenses, such as passing a stop sign, etcetera, and are heard and decided on by a MAGISTRATE or other PEACE OFFICER, without the summoning of a JURY.

Summary court-martial. A COURT-MARTIAL of a military person for a minor OFFENSE. Such proceedings are judged by a commissioned officer, the accused being below the rank of a commissioned officer.

Summary judgment. A means of obtaining the COURT's decision without resorting to a formal TRIAL BY JURY. Such JUDGMENTS are sought when the opposing parties are in agreement on the FACTS in the dispute but wish to obtain a RULING as to the QUESTION OF LAW that is involved.

Summary jurisdiction. The authority of a COURT to give a JUDGMENT immediately, without requiring a TRIAL or any other AUTHORITY. The right of a JUDGE to hold someone in CONTEMPT OF COURT constitutes summary jurisdiction.

Summary proceeding. A matter before a court which can be cleared up quickly, without the need for a JURY and a formal, lengthy TRIAL. Such PROCEEDINGS are frequently used in BANKRUPTCY cases, cases for ARBITRATION, landlord-tenant disputes, etcetera.

Summary process. PROCESS that is immediate; an ACTION in court that can take place without going through the usual delays and lengthy PROCEEDINGS.

Summing up. The final STATEMENTS to the jury by the ATTORNEYS for each side, summing up their EVIDENCE and telling the JURY why the case should be decided in their favor. Following each attorney's summations, the JUDGE may issue his own observations to the jury in order to help it to a fair VERDICT.

Summons. A written notice (a WRIT) informing a person of a LAWSUIT against him or her. A summons tells the individual when and where to appear in COURT to DEFEND him or herself. Failure to observe a summons may lead to the loss of a case by DEFAULT.

Summons and severance.
> SEVERANCE.

Sumptuary laws. STATUTES that restrain the extravagant expenditures of money for unnecessarily luxurious and lavish living on the part of public officials.

Sunshine laws. A popular term for various state STATUTES that provide for the media and general public to view or be present during the deliberations of their LEGISLATIVE BODIES. Sunshine laws sponsor open debates and hearings, and frown upon secret and closed decision-making caucuses or meetings.

Superior court. A higher court than an INFERIOR COURT, but one

which has less authority than an APPEALS COURT. The exact status of a superior court differs from state to state.
Supersede. To replace; to ANNUL; to take the place of; to render VOID; to set aside.
Supersedeas. 1. A COURT ORDER or WRIT prohibiting the carrying out of a JUDGMENT of a court, pending its appeal to a higher court. 2. A JUDGE's order which temporarily suspends the PROCEEDINGS in another court.
Supervening cause. A legal action that intervenes and stops another CAUSE OF ACTION from being pursued and determined.
Supplemental affidavit. An AFFIDAVIT presented in addition to an original affidavit, setting forth additional FACTS to support one's CONTENTION.
Supplemental answer. An additional answer given for the purpose of altering, adding to, or deleting answers already given.
Supplemental bill. Additional material, presented during an EQUITY TRIAL, to support one's CAUSE OF ACTION or one's DEFENSE, or to correct a defect in the original cause of action or defense.
> EQUITY.
Supplemental claim. The filing of an additional CLAIM, after the submission of an original CLAIM.
Supplemental injunction. An INJUNCTION issued during the course of a TRIAL in order to ensure that the court's JUDGMENT at the conclusion of the trial will be effective. > INJUNCTION.
Supplemental pleading. An additional PLEADING in support of the original pleading.
Supplementary proceedings.
> PROCEEDING, SUPPLEMENTARY.
Support. 1. The supplying of a means of livelihood; subsistence, including a home, food to eat, and money for everyday necessities. 2. The OBLIGATION to provide for one's family.
Supposition. A guess or conjecture that something is true and factual, without positive PROOF that it is.
Suppress. To prohibit or to forbid; to put an end to something that already exists; to keep EVIDENCE from being presented by showing it to be irrelevant or gathered illegally.
Suppression of evidence. The act of keeping EVIDENCE from being presented because it was obtained illegally.
Supremacy clause. A STATEMENT in Article VI of the U.S. CONSTITUTION stating that its laws are the laws of the land and that all other laws, enacted by the states or other local governments, are subservient to and are bound by the laws as laid down by the Constitution.
Supreme court. 1. A high court, in some states, the highest court; in other states the state supreme court is inferior to the COURT OF APPEALS. 2. The U.S. Supreme Court is the highest in the land.
Surcharge. An additional CHARGE; a charge beyond and over what is expected as the correct, just, and expected charge; a charge on something already charged.

Surety. 1. An individual or COMPANY who GUARANTEES to answer for a DEBT, OBLIGATION, or failure of another person or company. 2. A GUARANTOR.
Surety company. A COMPANY whose business is to assume responsibility and guarantee payment for the OBLIGATIONS of another individual or company. In reward for this service, the surety company is paid a certain amount of money, calculated according to the amount of SECURITY required and supplied.
Suretyship. A CONTRACT in which one person or company undertakes to be responsible for the DEBT or DEFAULT of another person or company. In exchange for assuming this risk, the SURETY is paid a fee.
Surgical operation. A procedure in which a surgeon cuts into the body of a patient to remove diseased tissue or to remedy a bodily defect.
Surgical operation, consent for. Before undergoing surgery, a patient must give INFORMED CONSENT, based upon a full explanation by the surgeon of what he intends to do. In the event that the patient is a minor or is an incompetent adult, the next of adult kin must sign for consent to the surgery. In the event of a life-threatening emergency, consent for surgery need not be obtained.
Surname. The family name; the last name, as distinguished from the given or first name.
Surrejoinder. A STATEMENT (PLEADING) by the PLAINTIFF in answer to the pleading (statement in DEFENSE) made by the DEFENDANT in a LAWSUIT.
Surrender. The giving up of something; to yield; to return.
Surrender of a criminal. The transfer of an accused person from a JURISDICTION where he was apprehended to the JURISDICTION where he allegedly committed his crime.
Surrender of a preference. The giving up of a LIEN or assignment by a CREDITOR to the trustee in a BANKRUPTCY case, in order to make the CREDITOR's claim allowable.
Surrender of franchise. The VOLUNTARY act of giving up a FRANCHISE to the grantor of said franchise.
Surreptitious. Done fraudulently, deceitfully, or stealthily.
Surrogate. A JUDGE or judicial officer in charge of matters affecting WILLS and their PROBATE (legal matters concerning the VALIDITY and filing of wills), GUARDIANSHIPS for minors, adoptions, etcetera.
Surrogate's court. A state court having authority over WILLS and their PROBATE, the establishment of GUARDIANS, matters pertaining to adoptions, etc. > PROBATE COURT.
Surrounding circumstances. Related circumstances that may shed light on whether someone was, or was not, responsible or NEGLIGENT in causing an accident.
Surtax. An additional TAX on something already taxed.
Surveillance. The keeping of a suspect under OBSERVATION; supervision.

Survivor. A person who outlives another. (The term is often used in WILLS to designate what shall transpire when a particular LEGATEE survives, or fails to survive, another legatee.)

Survivorship. Being alive after someone else has died, often entitling the person to PROPERTY because he or she has survived another who had an INTEREST in the property.

Suspended sentence. **1.** The withholding of the execution of a jail SENTENCE upon certain conditions which the convicted person must meet. Failure to abide by these conditions will lead to the enforcement of the sentence. **2.** A sentence given by a COURT, but not actually served.

Suspension of a right. The temporary loss of a RIGHT or PRIVILEGE, such as the RIGHT TO AN ESTATE or the RIGHT OF VISITATION to children of a divorced spouse.

Suspension of a statute. A temporary stoppage in the operation of a LAW or REGULATION.

Suspension of license. The taking away of a LICENSE for a specified period of time, such as the license or RIGHT to practice law or medicine, or the license to operate a vehicle.

Suspensive condition. A provision in an AGREEMENT or CONTRACT where the OBLIGATION does not take effect until a certain event takes place.

Suspicious character. A person who, for good reasons, is suspected of being a CRIMINAL or is suspected of preparing to commit a CRIME. Such a person may be required by law-enforcement OFFICERS to give an accounting of himself and supply information that he is not engaged in an impending criminal act.

Sustaining demurrer. Upholding an OBJECTION in a legal matter; deciding in favor of the DEMURRER (objector).

Sustaining a ruling. Upholding a DECISION, INTERPRETATION, or RULING of a court.

Sustaining a verdict. Upholding a VERDICT; a ruling by a HIGHER COURT agreeing with the verdict of a LOWER COURT.

Swearing-in. The taking of an OATH upon being elected or appointed to a PUBLIC OFFICE. The taking of an OATH by a WITNESS in a LAWSUIT.

Sweatbox. A term used to describe a situation where an ACCUSED person is subjected to continuous questioning, without being permitted to eat, drink, rest, or sleep. Such interrogations are conducted in the hope of obtaining a CONFESSION.

Sweating. Receiving the THIRD DEGREE; submitting a prisoner to SWEATBOX treatment.

Swindling. Cheating one out of his PROPERTY; carrying out a fraudulent deal.

Sworn. Having taken an OATH; verified; attested to as being true.

Sworn testimony. TESTIMONY given under OATH. Such TESTIMONY, if proved to be false, can lead to a charge of PERJURY.

Syllogism. A method of logical reasoning consisting of a major and a minor premise (CONTEN-

TION) and a conclusion. In the law, the major premise is the PROPOSITION of the law involved, the minor premise is the proposition of FACT, and the JUDGMENT (DECISION) is the CONCLUSION.

Sympathy strike. A strike carried out not because of grievances against one's employer but by way of aiding and supporting brother workers who are on strike against their employers.

Synallagmatic contract. An AGREEMENT in which the contracting parties bind themselves to mutual OBLIGATIONS to perform certain acts; a RECIPROCAL CONTRACT.

Syndicate. An association of individuals formed for the purpose of carrying out various business TRANSACTIONS, each member of the syndicate having money invested in the project or projects.

Synonymous. Having the same idea or ideas; the same in meaning, such as "truthful" and "honest."

Synopsis. A brief summary of a DOCUMENT.

T

Tacit acceptance. An act upon the part of an HEIR to an ESTATE, demonstrating that he intends to accept his INHERITANCE.
Tacit law. A LAW that is accepted by the consent of the people rather than by the enactment of a legislative STATUTE by a LEGISLATURE or other governing body.
Tacit understanding. An implied, unstated, unexpressed AGREEMENT; something quietly agreed upon, without having been committed to writing.
Taft Hartley Act. A federal LAW enacted in 1947 that gives certain rights to employees and employers, including provisions under which a strike cannot be legally called, the forcing of employees to join a union, etcetera. The law also lists several unfair labor practices and attempts to regulate relations between capital and labor.
Tail, estate in. An estate which passes from parent to children or grandchildren only, in a direct line of descent. > FEE TAIL.
Taint. Someone convicted of a crime (FELONY).
Taking a plea. Pleading guilty to a lesser OFFENSE than the one charged, and have such a plea accepted by the court; copping a plea.
Taking case from jury. Directing a VERDICT; a situation in which a COURT grants a MOTION to sustain a JUDGMENT.
Taking the Fifth. Refusing to answer a question as a WITNESS on the grounds that the TESTIMONY may tend to incriminate oneself; the same as pleading the Fifth Amendment. > FIFTH AMENDMENT.
Talesman. Person chosen as JUROR when the panel of potential jurors has been exhausted and an insufficient number have been chosen to make a full jury. Often, a talesman is chosen from among bystanders in a courtroom.
Tam quam. "As well as" (Latin).
Tampering with a jury. Attempting to corrupt or intimidate a JURY so that it decides in favor of the PLAINTIFF or DEFENDANT. Jury tampering is a CRIMINAL OFFENSE.
Tangible property. PROPERTY that can be possessed physically, such as land, goods, jewelry, furniture, etcetera.
Tariff. A TAX or duty placed on imported goods.
Tax. A payment of money made to help support a government, such as an INCOME TAX, a SALES TAX, a PROPERTY TAX, etcetera. Such LEVIES are compulsory and are determined by the size of one's income, the value of merchandise sold, the value of the land, etcetera.
Tax court. A federal COURT of LAW which hears matters concerning TAX disputes, especially CONTENTIONS on the part of taxpayers that LEVIES upon them are exorbitant or incorrect.

Tax credit. Money owed a taxpayer who has overpaid his taxes.
Tax evasion. Filing false TAX RETURNS in the attempt to avoid paying all of one's tax OBLIGATIONS.
Tax exempt. Nontaxable INCOME, such as income earned through OWNERSHIP of state or municipal BONDS, COMPENSATION paid for INJURIES or illness, monies from life insurance policies, etcetera.
Tax ferrets. Public employees who look for and find properties that have not been assessed taxes, and who place such properties on a list to be assessed taxes.
Tax-free. > TAX EXEMPT.
Tax lawyer. An ATTORNEY who specializes in legal matters concerning taxes.
Tax lien. A CLAIM against PROPERTY as security for the payment of TAXES. Such a lien is authorized by LAW and may be executed if taxes are not paid.
Tax return. A written, signed STATEMENT declaring one's income and the taxes due upon said income; also, a statement of taxes due as the result of SALE of PROPERTY, inheritances, gifts, etcetera. Tax returns include information concerning deductions due to expenses and exemptions.
Taxable. Liable to TAXATION, such as income minus exemptions and deductions.
Taxation. The PROCESS whereby a local, state, or federal government assesses and collects revenues from its citizens and their professions or businesses in order to defray the costs of running the government and providing BENEFITS for its CITIZENS.
Taxing power. The AUTHORITY and POWER of a government to LEVY TAXES. Such power is accompanied by the authority to collect those taxes that have been levied.
Taxpayer. A person who pays TAXES.
Tearing of will. The revoking of a WILL by tearing the paper on which the will is written.
Temperance. Restraint; moderation; the refraining from excesses. A temperate person is one who acts without undue passion, who drinks only in moderation, and who observes those forms of behavior that society finds acceptable.
Temporary custody. The awarding of CUSTODY of a child to a parent temporarily, pending the outcome of a SEPARATION or DIVORCE suit.
Temporary injunction. A PRELIMINARY RESTRAINING ORDER, stopping somebody from doing something until the COURT reaches a DECISION on the matter.
Temporary insanity. Loss of one's mental faculties and ability to reason for a short period of time, followed by a return to sanity. Shock, severe illness, a head injury, drugs, and alcohol are all capable of producing temporary insanity. ≫ IRRESISTIBLE IMPULSE.
Temporary observation. In medicine, the placing of a patient in a hospital where his mental and physical actions and reactions can be monitored and observed so as to determine whether or not he is mentally or physically competent.
Temporary restraining order. **1.** A temporary or PRELIMINARY IN-

JUNCTION, pending a final determination by a COURT. **2.** An order by a judge that a person not carry out a particular act until the court has heard and decided the matter before it.
> RESTRAINING ORDER.

Temporary stay. A postponement for a limited period of time, such as the postponement of a SENTENCE, or of a TRIAL.

Tenancy in common. The possession of PROPERTY by two or more people wherein each PARTY possesses an undivided interest in the entire property. This is different from a situation in which each party owns a designated portion of the property, such as land.

Tenancy in fee. A LEASE renewable indefinitely, provided the rent is paid regularly.

Tenancy in tail. > FEE TAIL.

Tenant. A person who has leased or rented an apartment, home, land, or other PROPERTY.

Tenant, sole. The only TENANT; one person only signing a lease; an exclusive tenant.

Tenant at will. An individual who had a LEASE on PROPERTY, the lease having expired but the person continues to occupy the premises with the consent of the owner.

Tenant for life. A TENANT who holds land or buildings for life, provided he honors the provisions of the LEASE.

Tenant in common. > TENANCY IN COMMON.

Tenant in dower. A WIDOW who holds property by virtue of the rights of a wife to her husband's property. > DOWER RIGHTS.

Tenant in fee simple. Someone who possesses lands or buildings for his life and the lives of his heirs, forever.

Tenant in severalty. Someone who possesses PROPERTY in his own right only; the opposite of a JOINT TENANT; a sole tenant
> TENANT, SOLE.

Tenant-owner. Someone who owns shares in and possesses PROPERTY in a CONDOMINIUM or COOPERATIVE APARTMENT.

Tenants in common. > TENANCY IN COMMON.

Tender. To offer, especially money; to offer PROPERTY; to make an offer to settle an OBLIGATION.

Tender of amends. The offer by someone who has committed a wrong to right the wrong by paying a sum of money to the person he has wronged.

Tender of issue. The final phrase of a DEFENDANT'S PLEA in which he offers to submit the controversy to the COURT and JURY for its decision.

Tender of performance. An offer by an individual who has bound himself to fulfill a CONTRACT, to carry out his OBLIGATIONS according to the terms of said CONTRACT.

Tender offer. The offer to buy outstanding STOCK at a certain price, usually done to get a controlling INTEREST in a CORPORATION.

Tennessee Valley Authority. (T.V.A.) A federal board established for the purpose of developing the Tennessee River and its tributaries to promote cheap sources of electric power and irrigation for the state of Tennessee and surrounding states.

Tenure. The right of public employees and OFFICERS to retain their jobs, unless removed for some dereliction of duty or for some prescribed cause.

Tenure in office. The right to hold office for a designated term.

Term. **1.** A fixed period of time, such as the four-year term of a president. **2.** A time period given to a DEBTOR to pay his CREDITOR. **3.** The period of time during which a COURT holds a session.

Term bailment. BAIL for a limited, specified period of time.

Termination. The end; a cancellation; the act of concluding something.

Territorial courts. Courts in United States possessions, such as Samoa, Guam, and the Virgin Islands. They serve as state as well as federal courts.

Territorial property. The water and land over which a state has JURISDICTION, including seas out to a stipulated number of miles from a state's shores.

Territorial waters. The seas extending out from the coast of a state. The various states claim JURISDICTION over events taking place within those waters. (Formerly, a three-mile limit was accepted as territorial waters, now, many countries claim JURISDICTION over waters extending out as far as two hundred miles.)

Test action. A test suit, brought by one PLAINTIFF against one DEFENDANT, with the SUIT (ACTION) selected out of a number of similar suits that are pending before the COURT. The decision of the COURT in the test action, by AGREEMENT, will bind the other parties with similar cause for suit.

Test case. A CASE being tried for the purpose of determining the LAW involved.

Testament. A WILL disposing of PROPERTY of a deceased person.

Testament, mutual. A WILL in which two people leave their property to the survivor.
> MUTUAL WILL.

Testamentary. Relating to a WILL.

Testamentary capacity. Having the mental ability to make a valid WILL. Wills made when a TESTATOR is mentally incapable are subject to challenge.

Testamentary disposition. The disposal of PROPERTY as a gift, after the one making the WILL dies.

Testamentary guardian. A guardian, named in a parent's will, to look after a child's inheritance and matters originating therefrom, until the child reaches the age of MATURITY.

Testamentary instrument. A DOCUMENT left by a deceased person that is in the nature of a WILL, but which has not been formalized and sworn to in the presence of WITNESSES. Such an INSTRUMENT, if clear in its intent and language, may have the effect of a will.

Testamentary power. The POWER to make a WILL, as prescribed by LAW.

Testamentary trustee. A person appointed by a court to act as a TRUSTEE to carry out the provisions of a TRUST that was created by a WILL. Such a trustee may have been specifically named in the will or, a court may appoint someone to fulfill that role.

Testate. A person who dies leaving a WILL; the opposite of INTESTATE.

Testator. Someone who has made or is making a WILL (TESTAMENT).

Teste. To bear WITNESS; a declaration at the conclusion of a COURT ORDER (WRIT) bearing witness to the official character of the DOCUMENT (Latin).

Teste of a deed. > TESTIMONIUM CLAUSE.

Teste of a writ. > TESTE.

Testes, trial per. A TRIAL in which the judge makes the DECISION and issues the VERDICT, after hearing the case. Such trials are quite common when both sdes to the controversy waive their RIGHTS to a TRIAL BY JURY.

Testify. To give EVIDENCE as a WITNESS, under OATH. False TESTIMONY, given under oath, is a serious offense known as PERJURY.

Testimonial proof. PROOF derived through the testimony of WITNESSES, as distinguished from proof derived through the submission of written DOCUMENTS; the same as PROOF EVIDENT.

Testimonium clause. A CLAUSE at the conclusion of an official DOCUMENT, meaning, "in witness whereof."

Testimony. EVIDENCE given under OATH by a WITNESS, as distinguished from evidence derived from written DOCUMENTS.

Testimony, expert. TESTIMONY given by a person who has particular expertise in a technical, scientific, or professional field. The testimony of a physician concerning a particular operation, illness, or disease falls into the category of expert testimony.

Testimony, impartial. EVIDENCE that favors neither side in a CASE, it being offered by a completely disinterested PARTY.

Testimony, negative. TESTIMONY showing that a particular event could not possibly have taken place; testimony that denies rather than affirms a fact.

Testimony, positive. Direct EVIDENCE that an event did take place; also, TESTIMONY that a certain event did not happen.

Theft. > STEALING.

Theory of case. Facts upon which a LAWSUIT is founded, thus forming the basis for the RIGHT to SUE.

Therapy, consent for. The giving of permission by a patient, or his guardian, for a physician to carry out a specificed operation or form of treatment. INFORMED CONSENT means that the patient, or his next of kin if the patient is a MINOR or is incompetent, has been told precisely what form of treatment—or therapy—is to be instituted and the risks involved.

Thievery. > STEALING.

Things in action. The right of a CREDITOR to be paid by a DEBTOR; a RIGHT to POSSESSION, recoverable by bringing a LAWSUIT. > CHOSE IN ACTION.

Things personal. Personal belongings that are movable, such as merchandise, goods, money, jewelry, etcetera.

Things real. Fixed, immovable belongings, such as land, buildings, etcetera.
Third degree. Illegal method of trying to force a CONFESSION from a suspected criminal. It includes continuous questioning without permitting the ACCUSED to rest, sleep, eat, drink, or to have benefit of COUNSEL (ATTORNEY).
Third mortgage. A MORTGAGE that is subject to a second and first mortgage.
Third party. 1. Someone who is not directly connected with a CONTRACT, a DEAL, a LAWSUIT, an occurrence, etcetera, but who may be affected by its outcome. **2.** Persons other than the PLAINTIFF or DEFENDANT who are brought into a CASE.
Third party action. A situation in which a DEFENDANT brings into the CASE (ACTION) a third person because he believes that the third person is involved with him in the SUIT. The defendant does this so that the COURT may decide whether the third party is LIABLE in the CASE, rather than the defendant himself.
Third party beneficiary. A person who is not part of a CONTRACT, but for whose benefit the contract was entered into.
Third party claim. A CLAIM to PROPERTY by a third person who is not party to a DISPUTE in COURT relative to said PROPERTY.
Third party complaint. An attempt by a DEFENDANT to bring a THIRD PARTY into a case on the grounds that the third party is LIABLE to him.
Third party liability. The responsibility of a third person, not the original PLAINTIFF or DEFENDANT.
Third party plaintiff. A DEFENDANT in a case who attempts to bring a third person into the action because he believes this person is *liable.* > LIABILITY.
Third party practice. The practice which permits a DEFENDANT to bring a THIRD PARTY into a case.
Third person. A bystander; someone not involved in a LAWSUIT; a disinterested party.
Thirteenth Amendment. The Amendment to the UNITED STATES CONSTITUTION that abolished slavery.
Threat. A STATEMENT of intention to harm, intimidate, or INJURE another by carrying out some unlawful act. If the statement of intention is not through the carrying out of an unlawful act, then it is not considered legally as a threat. As an example, a CREDITOR may threaten to sue a DEBTOR in court, this being a legal right; it is not considered a threat. ≫ INTIMIDATION.
Threatened cloud. A possible blemish upon a TITLE, thus threatening to interfere with the attainment of a CLEAR TITLE.
Three-judge court. An APPEALS COURT with three judges sitting in on one case; usually a federal court that hears cases in which INJUNCTIONS are sought to the carrying out of a STATUTE claimed to be UNCONSTITUTIONAL.
Three-mile limit. > TERRITORIAL PROPERTY and TERRITORIAL WATERS.
Ticket. 1. A slip of paper issued

by a law enforcement OFFICER for a traffic violation (slang). **2.** The slate of a political party, naming people who seek election to office. **3.** A slip of paper entitling a person to a seat in a theater, admission to a train or plane, etcetera.

Time immemorial. Ever since the memory of man.

Time is the essence of contracts. A phrase meaning that one PARTY to a CONTRACT must carry out his OBLIGATIONS within the time period specified in the contract before he can require the other party to perform his obligations under the contract.

Time, reasonable. A period of time that is in line with the PROVISIONS of an AGREEMENT or CONTRACT; a period of time not accompanied by prolonged and unreasonable delay.

Timely notice. Notice given in time for someone to make alternate PROVISIONS. As an example, a physician should tell a patient under treatment well in advance of the time he intends to be out of town and unavailable.

Title. 1. The right of OWNERSHIP of PROPERTY; the just POSSESSION of one's own property. **2.** The word or name by which someone or something is known. **3.** The name for a portion of a STATUTE. **4.** The name of an ACTION in COURT or of a petition, consisting of the names of the involved parties, and other pertinent data.

Title, absolute. An exclusive RIGHT of OWNERSHIP, such as the sole ownership of land.

Title, adverse. A TITLE set up in opposition to another title.

Title, clear. A TITLE free from any limitations or objections.

Title, doubtful. OWNERSHIP of PROPERTY that is in doubt. A PURCHASER of such property may find that his right to it may be questioned in COURT.

Title, equitable. OWNERSHIP of PROPERTY that has been recognized in a COURT OF EQUITY as being based upon equitable, fair principles, as opposed to formal legal TITLE. An equitable title is an enforceable one.

Title, examination of. An INVESTIGATION made in behalf of a person who intends to buy PROPERTY to discover the history of the PROPERTY and to make sure that a clear, uncontested TITLE can be obtained. Such investigation is conducted in the OFFICES where public RECORDS are kept. Also called a *title search.*

Title, imperfect. A TITLE that does not grant total, complete, clear RIGHT to OWNERSHIP of PROPERTY.

Title, legal. OWNERSHIP of property that is recognized as sufficient under the RULES of LAW, as distinguished from a title recognized under rules of EQUITY.

Title, perfect. A TITLE that vests the absolute RIGHT of OWNERSHIP in an individual, without question.

Title, presumptive. A presumed OWNERSHIP of PROPERTY, such presumption being based on occupancy of the property rather than upon a legal right to the title.

Title, quiet. A suit in a COURT OF EQUITY to settle all claims to the rightful OWNERSHIP of PROPERTY.

Title by descent. TITLE obtained through inheritance, upon the death of the OWNER.
Title deed. A DOCUMENT showing the RIGHT of OWNERSHIP of PROPERTY.
Title defective in form. A TITLE bearing some defect on its face, not necessarily meaning that the title itself is defective.
Title in fee simple. Unconditional, complete, total ownership of property.
Title insurance. INSURANCE that a PURCHASER of PROPERTY takes out in order to insure himself against loss should the TITLE in some way prove defective.
Title of an act. The name of a STATUTE or LAW, or a brief description of its nature and purpose, such as "The Fair Labor Practices Act."
Title of declaration. A preliminary CLAUSE stating the name of the COURT and the date on which a matter is to be heard and tried.
Title retention. A LIEN or MORTGAGE to secure the purchase price of PROPERTY.
To assume and pay and save harmless. A phrase used in the transfer of PROPERTY, the new OWNER agreeing to assume the MORTGAGE and to secure the former owner against loss should the mortgage not be paid off.
To do time. To serve a term in jail (slang).
To have and to hold. Words used in a transfer (conveyance) of PROPERTY from one person to another, meaning that the property is to pass to that person, to be owned by him, and to pass on to his HEIRS when he dies.
To knowingly misrepresent. To intentionally falsify facts in order to gain something for one's benefit; to defraud.
To take an appeal. To APPEAL a decision of a LOWER COURT to a HIGHER COURT.
To take title. To gain and hold POSSESSION of PROPERTY legally.
To wit. Namely; that is to say.
Tolerance. **1.** Fair attitude toward the OPINIONS and actions of others, even though they may differ from one's own opinions and standards of CONDUCT. **2.** The ability to endure. **3.** Freedom from prejudice and bigotry.
Toll. **1.** To postpone the effect of a STATUTE OF LIMITATIONS, thus permitting a legal ACTION to be undertaken after a longer than normal period of time. **2.** A fee paid for use of a bridge, tunnel, etcetera.
Tonnage duty. A TAX levied upon ships according to their weight and capacity for carrying cargo; a tax upon a vessel.
Took and carried away. Words used in a SUIT against a person accused of STEALING.
Tort. A wrong committed by one person against another; a CIVIL, not a criminal wrong; a wrong not arising out of a CONTRACT; a violation of a legal DUTY that one person has toward another. (NEGLIGENCE and LIBEL are torts.) Every tort is composed of a legal OBLIGATION, a BREACH of that obligation, and DAMAGE as the result of the breach of the obligation.
Tort, personal. A wrong to a person, such as ASSAULT, or a wrong resulting in damage to a person's

feelings or reputation, such as LIBEL or SLANDER.

Tort, property. An interference by one person with the enjoyment by another person of his own property.

Tort, willful. A wrong intentionally committed.

Tort-feasor. A wrongdoer; a term formerly applied to a DEFENDANT who has injured a PLAINTIFF.

Tort liability. Responsibility for having committed a wrong (TORT) to another person. (A surgeon has tort liability if, through his NEGLIGENCE, harm comes to one of his patients.)

Tortious. Hurtful; wrongful; harmful; injurious; in the nature of a TORT.

Total disability. Complete inability to work or to carry out any of the duties of one's job or profession, even though one's body may not be totally disabled. A person who has been blinded is totally disabled if he is engaged in riveting or other kinds of work requiring him to function high up on the steelwork of a construction job.

Total loss. **1.** The complete loss of PROPERTY, as in an explosion that has totally demolished a building. **2.** In medicine, the complete loss of a part of the body, such as in amputation.

Totten trust. Putting one's own money in a bank under one's own name as TRUSTEE for another person.

Towing service. Bringing to port a ship that is unable to reach port under its own POWER, or to aid a functioning vessel in reaching port more quickly.

Township. **1.** A division of land six miles square. **2.** The name given to a COMMUNITY located within the confines of one county, such township having its own CIVIL GOVERNMENT.

Toxic. Poisonous fumes or vapors that can cause BODILY HARM, such as chlorine, are called toxic.

Toxicology. That branch of medicine which studies poisons, denoting their character, formulae, recognition, and their effects upon people and animals.

Trade association. An organization for the promotion of a trade, composed of members engaged in the same occupation. The exchange of information, the improvement of product quality, and the dissemination of new data all aid the members in selling their product.

Trade commission. A federal agency established to ensure FAIR TRADE practices and to see that the public is not defrauded or treated in an illegal manner, or that unfair competition among producers does not exist.

Trade dispute. A CONTROVERSY between employees and their employer as to WAGES and working conditions.

Trade secret. A process or compound known only to its owner and manufacturer, although the process or compound is not PATENTED.

Trade union. A grouping of working people who band together for the purpose of improving their working conditions and WAGES. Trade unions elect their own delegates and officers who meet with employers in the hope of resolving disputes. By united action, unions frequently reach agreements that will benefit all the workers in a particular trade or craft. > LABOR UNION.

Trademark. A name, marking, sign, or motto that a company can, by law, use exclusively in identifying and selling its product. > INFRINGEMENT OF TRADEMARK.

Traditionary evidence. EVIDENCE based upon what a deceased person said many years ago. Such evidence is often referred to in disputes over BOUNDARIES to land.

Traitor. An individual who has betrayed his country; one GUILTY of the act of treason.

Transaction. The act of conducting business; a DEAL; in a broad sense, a CONTRACT; something which takes place or has taken place; a dealing between two or more PARTIES.

Transcript of record. A written or typewritten copy of a COURT REPORTER's notes taken during a TRIAL. Such transcripts of records are frequently transmitted to a HIGHER COURT when a CASE is appealed.

Transcripted judgment. A JUDGMENT entered into in a county different from the one in which the CASE was tried and the DECISION was rendered.

Transfer in contemplation of death. A transfer of PROPERTY by a person who anticipates an early death; a gift INTER VIVOS (given during one's lifetime.)

Transfer of a cause. The switching of a CASE from the JURISDICTION of one COURT to another court.

Transfer of jurisdiction. The transfer of a case from a state to a federal court.

Transfer tax. A LEVY upon the passing of PROPERTY from the estate of a deceased person to an HEIR.

Transferable. Able to be transferred; negotiable, as opposed to a DOCUMENT that cannot be transferred from one person to another.

Transferred intent. A PRINCIPLE stating that one is still GUILTY of a crime if he attacks or INJURES a person he did not intend to injure. A person who ASSAULTS or shoots a person about whose identity he was mistaken, is still GUILTY of the crime.

Transgressive trust. A TRUST that violates the RULE AGAINST PERPETUITIES.

Transient person. An individual who has no fixed residence in the state in which he is found; a person passing through a state on his way to another destination.

Transit in rem judicatam. An expression denoting that a JUDGMENT has been made on a particular matter and that the matter is no longer open for questioning (Latin).

Transitory. Passing from place to place; fleeting, temporary; the opposite of permanent.

Transitory crime. A crime tried in a location other than the one in which the crime was committed.

Transmission. The RIGHTS of HEIRS to pass along inherited PROPERTY to their heirs, providing they die without designating how they wish to dispose of their property.

Transvestite. A person who poses as, and wears the clothes of, a person of the opposite sex.

Trauma. An INJURY, either physical or mental, caused by external violence.

Traveler's check. In actuality, a cashier's check of the issuing bank. Upon its issue, the person receiving the check signs it; when he cashes it, he signs it again in the presence of the person who will cash it or give merchandise in exchange for it. Traveler's checks are particularly valuable as they are not negotiable when lost. The person obtaining traveler's checks from his bank usually pays a small fee to the issuing bank for the service.

Traverse. **1.** To deny, such as a DEFENDANT'S denial of a PLAINTIFF'S CLAIM. **2.** To postpone a TRIAL until another term of the COURT.

Traverse, common. A flat denial of the CHARGES of the opposing side.

Traverse, general. A blanket denial covering all CHARGES.

Traverse, special. A qualified, nontotal denial of CHARGES accompanied by the presentation of additional FACTS which tend to prove the charges wrong.

Traverse jury. A TRIAL JURY, as distinguished from a GRAND JURY which merely offers an INDICTMENT but does not try the case.

Traverse of indictment. The denial of conclusions made by a GRAND JURY that has brought in an INDICTMENT.

Traverse upon a traverse. A denial of one PARTY growing out of a denial by the opposite party in a SUIT.

Treason. An act which betrays one's own country. HIGH TREASON, committed against the United States during wartime, may be punishable by LIFE IMPRISONMENT or DEATH.

Treasury note. A bill issued by the United States government, circulated as legal money (TENDER).

Treatise. A major, comprehensive book on a particular subject.

Treaty. An AGREEMENT in writing between two or more independent nations embarked upon for the benefit of the people of the countries that are signers of the DOCUMENT.

Treble costs. An AWARD, made according to an existing STATUTE, wherein the person receiving the award gets the ordinary costs, then half the ordinary costs, and finally, half of the latter.

Treble damages. An AWARD of DAMAGES, according to an existing STATUTE, consisting of the actual damages, tripled. A JURY usually awards merely the actual damages and the judge triples them. This large award is sometimes given as punishment to the defendant, but in other cases is awarded solely because the law in the matter calls for treble damages.

Treble penalty. A SENTENCE three times longer than the usual sentence, imposed upon an habitual criminal.

Trespass. **1.** Performing an unlawful act resulting in INJURY to a person or to his PROPERTY.

Trespass is often associated with violence. **2.** Illegal entry onto another's property. ➤ INTRUSION.

Trespass de bonis asportatis. A SUIT for recovery of damages from someone who has taken PROPERTY, not land, that doesn't belong to him (Latin).

Trespass for mesne profits. A SUIT against someone who has been ejected from PROPERTY that didn't belong to him. The suit is for recovery of DAMAGES the trespasser caused to the property and for any profits he may have made while he was in wrongful POSSESSION of the property.

Trespass on the case. A LAWSUIT for INJURIES received as the result of a wrongful act of another, even though the wrongful act was not caused by physical force; a SUIT for injuries caused by NEGLIGENCE.

Trial. A PROCEEDING in a COURT to decide a CONTROVERSY. A trial may be for a CIVIL ACTION or CRIMINAL ACTION.

Trial, fair and impartial, A TRIAL characterized by an impartial judge and/or JURY, one in which all EVIDENCE is heard before a VERDICT is reached. In such a case, the DEFENDANT's rights are safeguarded and he is represented by a competent ATTORNEY.

Trial, new. A re-trying of the same issues in the same COURT, before another jury, conducted after the court has already handed down its VERDICT. Such new trial may be initiated on the basis of an issue of FACT or facts.

Trial, nonjury. A TRIAL in which a judge, or a panel of judges, hands down the decision without a JURY. It is also known as a "trial by the court."

Trial, public. An open TRIAL, conducted in the presence of the public, as opposed to a closed trial.

Trial, separate. In a lawsuit against several DEFENDANTS, one or more of the defendants may request a separate trial and may offer a different, separate DEFENSE from the others.

Trial amendment. An answer that a DEFENDANT files during the course of a trial, the additional PLEADING (DEFENSE) arising out of some new situation, such as EVIDENCE, that has developed in the CASE.

Trial by jury. A TRIAL in which the VERDICT will be brought in by a JURY after hearing all the EVIDENCE in the CASE. ➤ TRIAL, NONJURY.

Trial by proviso. A situation in which a DEFENDANT proceeds to have his CASE tried because the PLAINTIFF has not pursued his charges and is lax in pushing the SUIT.

Trial counsel. A trial LAWYER. He may be the sole lawyer in a particular case or he may assist the ATTORNEY OF RECORD in trying the CASE.

Trial de novo. A new trial, to be conducted in a HIGHER COURT than the one which handed in the preceding VERDICT; a new trial in a COURT OF APPEALS (an appellate court).

Trial judge. The judge who presides at the TRIAL.

Trial jury. The JURY that hears and decides the case, as distinguished from a GRAND JURY

which merely hands in an INDICTMENT.
Trial lawyer. > TRIAL COUNSEL.
Trial term. That portion of a COURT'S work which is concerned with JURY trials.
Tried. Having had a TRIAL in COURT.
Tried separately. > SEPARATE TRIALS.
Triers. > TRIORS.
Triors. People appointed by a court to determine whether a potential JUROR who has been challenged, is indeed qualified to be a member of the JURY.
Tripartite. Having three parts; a CONTRACT involving three separate people with three distinct roles to play in the contract.
Triple damages. > TREBLE DAMAGES.
Triple damages. Same as TREBLE DAMAGES.
Trover. 1. A SUIT to regain PROPERTY that was lost, the suit being against the person who found and has held on to the property. **2.** A suit for DAMAGES against a person who found property and wrongfully converted it to his own use.
Truant. A minor who is absent from school without his parent's permission.
Truce. An agreement between opposing forces to stop fighting temporarily. > ARMISTICE.
True bill. The AGREEMENT of a GRAND JURY with the PROSECUTING ATTORNEY that an INDICTMENT should be made against an ACCUSED person. The grand jury endorses the indictment by stamping the words true bill on the document.
True man doctrine. The PRINCIPLE stating that a person under attack has the right to stand his ground and repel force with force, and if, in his defense he kills his assailant, he is not considered guilty of an offense. > JUSTIFIABLE HOMICIDE.
True verdict. A VERDICT of a JURY in which each JUROR has considered the case carefully and has come to his own conclusion, without persuasion or influence of outside parties.
Trust. 1. The handing over of PROPERTY or money to one person, to be held for the benefit of another person or persons. **2.** A monopoly, composed of a number of corporations.
Trust, active. A TRUST in which the TRUSTEE actively participates in the handling of the ASSETS of the trust, such as selling or buying SECURITIES, selling or buying PROPERTY, etcetera.
Trust, charitable. A TRUST in which the beneficiaries are public, nonprofit organizations, such as museums, schools, or charitable institutions.
Trust, constructive. > CONSTRUCTIVE TRUST.
Trust, contingent. A trust whose operation depends upon some future event.
Trust, direct. A clear, express, definite trust, as distinguished from an implied or CONSTRUCTIVE TRUST.
Trust, directory. A trust that is not yet complete, but merely outlined in its general intent and purpose.
Trust, dry. A TRUST that names a trustee but does not require him to perform any active duties.

Trust, educational. A TRUST that benefits an educational institution, or gives its money or property toward the establishment of an educational institution.

Trust, executed. A TRUST that states precisely and completely what its assets are to be used for.

Trust, executory. A TRUST that requires further action on the part of the originator of the trust or its TRUSTEE in order for the trust to become fully effective and meaningful.

Trust, express active. A TRUST in which the TRUSTEE, governed by provisions in the will creating the trust, gives over the income of the trust to the beneficiaries.

Trust, implied. A TRUST that comes into being as the result of the intention to create a trust as a matter of LAW; a trust assumed by prevailing circumstances.

Trust, inter vivos. A living TRUST; a trust set up during the life of the person who is settling money or PROPERTY upon another, as distinguished from a trust which leaves money or property after the death of the GRANTOR.

Trust, involuntary. A trust that comes into being as the result of a law which enforces its creation.

Trust, naked. A TRUST in which the trustee has no function other than to turn over the property or money to the beneficiaries.

Trust, passive. A TRUST in which the trustee has no active role to play or duties to perform.

Trust, precatory. > PRECATORY TRUST.

Trust, private. A TRUST for the benefit of a designated individual or individuals, as distinguished from a trust for the benefit of charitable organizations or public institutions.

Trust, public. A charitable TRUST; the opposite of a private trust. A trust for the benefit of the general public.

Trust, resulting. > RESULTING TRUST.

Trust, secret. A situation in which a writer of a WILL gives money or property to a person, with the distinct understanding that he will hold it in trust for another person.

Trust, shifting. A TRUST that is so set up that it may function for the benefit of substitute beneficiaries, or additional beneficiaries, under certain prescribed circumstances that may occur in the future.

Trust, simple. A TRUST in which money or property is given over to a trustee for the benefit of another person, as prescribed by laws governing the activities of trustees.

Trust, special. A TRUST in which the trustee is obligated to carry out specific intentions of the creator of the trust. For example, a trustee may be obliged to pay off the debts of the creator of the trust before handing over monies to a beneficiary.

Trust, spendthrift. > SPENDTHRIFT TRUST.

Trust, totten. > TOTTEN TRUST.

Trust, transgressive. A TRUST that violates the rules concerning perpetuities. > PERPETUITY.

Trust, voluntary. A TRUST in which the TRUSTEE willingly agrees to serve as a trustee for the benefit of another; the opposite of an involuntary trust in which the trust comes into being as the result of the operation of law.

Trust, voting. The RIGHT vested in one or several people to vote large shares of various stockholders' stock, for the purpose of electing officers or controlling the activities of a corporation.

Trust company. A corporation engaged in the banking business, the corporation acting as trustee of funds that investors and depositors have placed with the company; a bank that manages trusts.

Trust deed. A document wherein property is placed in the hands of trustees whose duties include the payment of obligations due. This type of deed is in actuality a valid mortgage.

Trust fund. The PROPERTY or money that is in a trust; the money or property that the trustee administers.

Trust fund doctrine. The principle that a corporation must pay off its debts before distributing its assets to stockholders.

Trust indenture. A DOCUMENT that states the specific conditions and terms of a trust, such as a trust to create pension funds, etcetera.

Trust legacy. A LEGACY to a TRUSTEE to be held for the benefit of specified beneficiaries.

Trustee. An individual who holds property or money for the benefit of another individual; a fiduciary.

Trustee, conventional. An individual appointed by a court to be a TRUSTEE, rather than one named by the creator of the TRUST.

Trustee, joint. Two or more people who are named to administer a TRUST.

Trustee, judicial. An officer of a court who serves as a trustee, his activities as trustee being limited by prescribed rules and regulations.

Trustee, quasi. A person who obtains personal benefit from a breach of trust, and therefore becomes answerable as if he were a trustee.

Trustee, testamentary. One named by a will to serve as a trustee.

Trustee ex maleficio. A TRUSTEE who acts wrongly in administering his duties and who may benefit from such wrongful actions, but is held liable for his conduct so that he does not profit personally (Latin).

Trustee in bankruptcy. The individual who holds the ASSETS and PROPERTY of a BANKRUPT, for the benefit of his CREDITORS.

Try. To argue a case in court; to hear and decide a case.

Turning state's evidence. > STATE'S EVIDENCE.

Turnkey. A person who holds the keys to a jail or prison.

Turnover order. **1.** A court order directing a bankrupt to turn over his property and assets to the trustee in bankruptcy. **2.** A court order to a defendant who has lost his case, to turn over the necessary money or property to the plaintiff who has won the case.

Turnover proceeding. A court proceeding to force the bankrupt person or company to turn over property to the trustee, which property the bankrupt has been concealing or trying to conceal.

Turpitude. Indecent; depraved; lack of good moral principles; unjust; baseness.
Turpitude, moral. Violation of honest, decent, moral behavior; an act of vileness or depravity.
Tutelage. Guardianship; the status of a person who is under the supervision of a guardian.
Twice in jeopardy. > DOUBLE JEOPARDY; PRIOR JEOPARDY.
Two-issue rule. A principle stating that where there are two or more issues in controversy in a court case, the verdict on one of them will stand even if there has been an error in the trying and deciding of the other issue or issues.
Two-witness rule. A requirement in some states that two or more witnesses must testify to the guilt of an accused before a conviction can take place in a crime calling for the death penalty.
Tying in. The practice of insisting that a second product must be purchased before being able to purchase a product one really wants to buy. (In some situations, this practice is a violation of antitrust laws.)
Tyranny. The rule of a dictator; a government ruled by one man or a small group of men, without representation and free vote of the public.

U

Ubi. Where (Latin).
Ubi supra. Where above mentioned (Latin).
Ukase. An official decree or order, usually originating from a monarch or dictator.
Ulterior motive. A concealed motive; an intention purposely kept secret; an undisclosed purpose.
Ultimate facts. FACTS that are essential to present in order for a court to reach a decision in a case.
Ultimatum. A final proposition offered to conclude an agreement or contract (Latin).
Ultimum supplicium. The ultimate punishment for a crime; the death penalty (Latin).
Ultra. Above; going beyond what is usual or ordinary, such as "ultrasound"; in excess of; beyond (Latin).
Ultra vires. Acts of a corporation going beyond its authorization by its charter or its acts of incorporation (Latin).
Unable to stand trial. A person who, because of mental incapacity or extremely poor physical health, is unable to defend himself in a court of law. (Such judgment is made after thorough examination by psychiatrists or physicians.)
Unaccrued. Not yet due.
Unanimous verdict. A VERDICT in which all the jurors agree.
Unauthorized practice. Practicing law without a license.
Unavoidable accident. An accident that could not have been avoided despite all parties having exercised due care and diligence.
Unavoidable casualty. An injury which could not have been avoided despite the fact that due care and diligence was exercised by all those involved in the accident or occurrence.
Unavoidable cause. An accidental cause, not occasioned by negligence or lack of diligence.
Unavoidable danger. In maritime law, an accident to a ship which could not have been avoided by the exercise of due care and diligence on the part of those operating the vessel.
Unclean hands. A doctrine stating that a decision should not be made in favor of a plaintiff who, himself, has not conducted himself honestly. In other words, he has come into court with unclean hands. This doctrine applies mainly to matters of equity.
Unconditional pardon. A PARDON that frees a criminal without any conditions attached to the pardon.
Unconscionable conduct. Unbelievably bad conduct; outrageous conduct; behavior displaying a total lack of conscience.
Unconscious adults. In medicine, it is within the law for a physician to treat an unconscious patient even without consent. However, if next of kin is available, he must first obtain consent.
Unconscious minors. In medicine, it is within the law for a

physician to treat an unconscious minor if a parent or next of kin or guardian is unavailable.

Unconstitutional. Contrary to the UNITED STATES CONSTITUTION; a local STATUTE that bars freedom of speech or freedom to worship would be considered unconstitutional.

Uncontestable clause. A provision in a life insurance policy that prevents the carrier from contesting a claim if the policy has been in force for a certain number of years, usually two years. > INSURANCE, LIFE.

Uncontrollable impulse. A desire to do something which is so intense that a person is unable to resist doing it. (The existence of an uncontrollable impulse is frequently used as a defense for the performance of a criminal act.)

Uncontrolled discretion. The power of a trustee to take a particular action without having to receive authorization from a court.

Undefended defendant. A DEFENDANT who does not appear in court to defend himself against the PLAINTIFF; a defendant who has no ATTORNEY to represent him is sometimes referred to as undefended.

Under control A phrase denoting that a driver is in complete command and control of his vehicle, is proceeding with adequate vision at a normal rate of speed, and can stop the vehicle within a reasonable distance and period of time.

Under the influence of alcohol. Having absorbed sufficient alcohol into the bloodstream so as to render one incapable of sound judgment, discretion, rational behavior, and, especially, incapable of operating a motor vehicle properly. (Various breathing tests and blood tests will demonstrate the quantity of alcohol in the body, and can determine whether a person is intoxicated or unduly under the influence of alcohol.)

Under the influence of drugs. A state in which one has taken sufficient drugs as to interfere with sound judgment, discretion, and/or rational, acceptable behavior. (Various blood and urine tests exist to determine the quantity of drugs in one's system.)

Undercover man. A person, usually an officer of the law, who is engaged in spying and obtaining information about criminal activities. An undercover man, or woman, may pose as a criminal and may go along with unlawful activities for a sufficient period of time so as to get evidence which he/she then turns over to the police.

Undersigned, the. The individual or individuals who sign a DOCUMENT.

Understand. To know; to comprehend; to be aware of the nature and consequences of an act; to have knowledge of.

Understood. Agreed; an understanding; assented to.

Undertake. To guarantee; to set about to do; to engage in; to promise; to perform; to enter upon.

Underwrite. To bind oneself to support a project, usually by investing money; to insure; to sign one's name to a DOCUMENT, thereby assuming an OBLIGATION.

Underwriter. A person who has assumed an obligation by signing his name to a document; an insurer.

Undisclosed principal. A person for whom an agent carries out a transaction without revealing his identity. As an example, an agent may purchase a piece of property without informing the seller who the buyer is.

Undisputed fact. An admitted FACT; a fact about which there is no controversy.

Undistributed profits. Surplus monies that a corporation has not distributed as dividends or placed in a surplus account.

Undivided profits. > UNDISTRIBUTED PROFITS.

Undue influence. An improper amount of pressure which influences someone to do something he would not do if left to his own devices. As an example, if it can be proved that someone persuaded a maker of a will to leave him money that he would not have received except for his undue influence, then the will might be set aside and nullified.

Unearned income. Monies that are received as a result of investments in property or securities, rather than money earned as wages, from practicing one's profession, or from operating one's business.

Unearned increment. Increased value of property resulting from the ordinary course of events, not from any effort on the part of the owner. As an example, a piece of real estate may go up in value merely because the neighborhood has become popular.

Unemployment insurance. A fund for the payment of benefits to unemployed persons. Such insurance is part of the federal Social Security System. Employers and employees contribute toward this insurance, which is administered at the state level, although the funds are supplemented by the federal government.

Unequivocal. Without doubt; clear; unmistakable; certain.

Unethical conduct. Behavior or actions that violate the standards of one's profession. Such unethical conduct may lead to the suspension or revoking of one's license to practice his profession. (There is a Code of Professional Responsibility that all lawyers are expected to adhere to.)

Unexpired term. The length of time yet to go in a prescribed term of office. (If a judge is elected for a ten-year period and has served six years, then he has an unexpired term of four years.)

Unfair competition. Dishonest, fraudulent practices and rivalry in a trade. Such unfair competition is restricted by various LAWS and STATUTES, and those guilty of it may be forced to answer in a COURT OF EQUITY. One of the major elements in unfair competition is that it injures the business reputation and good will of a rival organization.

Unfair hearing. A court HEARING in which all the elements of due process are not present. (The results of such a hearing may be that justice is not properly served.) > DUE PROCESS OF LAW.

Unfair labor practice. Failure

upon the part of an employer or a union to abide by the regulations of the National Labor Relations Act. This would include attempts by employers to prevent workers from joining or organizing a union, or discrimination against employees because they belong to a union, etc.

Unfair trade practice. The same as UNFAIR COMPETITION, especially the practice of selling merchandise camouflaged as if it were the merchandise of another manufacturer or merchant.

Unforeseen cause. A delay in giving notice of an injury received while at work which is understandable, and thus should not interfere with the worker's claim to compensation for the injury.

Unforeseen event. An event that could not be predicted as likely to occur.

Uniform commercial code. A set of laws, adopted by most states, that are uniform (similar) insofar as they relate to almost every type of business law.

Uniform laws. Laws that have been adopted by many states and are similar in their implications. Such laws were originally proposed by a national commission under the auspices of the Commissioners on Uniform State Laws.

Uniformity. The state of being the same; conformity; one thing being like another thing.

Unilateral contract. An AGREEMENT in which only one side to the contract makes a promise to perform or carry out some act; the opposite of a bilateral contract.

Unilateral mistake. A misunderstanding on the part of one party to an AGREEMENT.

Unimpeachable witness. A WITNESS whose expertise in a special field is so great that the judge and jury believe his testimony implicitly, despite contrary testimony by other witnesses.

Unincorporated assocation. A group of people acting together for a common purpose in a common enterprise, without being formed into a corporation.

Unintelligible. Something which cannot be understood; not intelligible.

Union shop. A factory or plant or company in which only union members can work. A worker may be permitted to work even if he is not already a union member, provided an agreement is made to join the union.

Unit rule. A rule that the majority vote of a delegation to a political convention shall be voted as a unanimous vote, thus giving the entire delegation's support to one candidate.

Unitary award. An award to a divorced woman, including support for herself and for her children.

United in interest. A term referring to co-defendants in a lawsuit, meaning that each one of the defendants will be affected in the same way by the verdict in the suit.

United Nations. An organization composed of most of the countries in the world for the purpose of promoting the welfare of all nations and to solve international problems and controversies in a peaceful manner.

United States Attorney General. The chief law enforcement officer of the United States. He is a cabinet member appointed by the President, and approved by the Senate of the United States. His duties include being in charge of the Department of Justice and the Federal Bureau of Investigation (F.B.I.).

United States of America The union of all the states, under the U. S. CONSTITUTION, with governmental control vested in the people of the various states.

United States commissioner. An officer of a federal district court whose duties include the bringing into court of persons who are accused of federal offenses. (He is not a judge.)

United States Constitution. The DOCUMENT containing the fundamental laws governing our nation, along with the principles of a free, representative democracy. The Constitution was adopted by the Convention of 1787 and ratified by the several states. Over the past years it has been amended 26 times. (See pages 382–95 for full Constitution and Amendments.)

United States courts. Federal courts. The Supreme Court was established by the Constitution and is the highest federal court. Courts of lesser federal authority are established by acts of Congress.

United States Senator. > SENATOR.

Unity of interest. Identical interest in PROPERTY that is held jointly, with each person having the same rights in the property.

Unity of possession. The principle stating that where property is held jointly, each person owns the whole property. In other words, the property is not broken down into shares or parcels.

Universal military service. Active service in the military required of every fit citizen.

Universal partnership. A PARTNERSHIP in which each PARTNER has contributed all of his property to the partnership.

Unjust enrichment, doctrine of. The principle stating that if one obtains property or money unfairly, even if it is not done unlawfully, he should return it.

Unlawful act. An act that is contrary to or violates an existing law.

Unlawful assembly. A gathering of three or more people which will disturb the peace because those assembling intend to perform unlawful or violent actions.

Unlawful conspiracy. A CRIMINAL OFFENSE in which two or more people get together and plan an illegal act. > CONSPIRACY.

Unlawful contract. An AGREEMENT in which one or more of the contracting parties performs an act that the law prohibits, or fails to perform an act that the law requires.

Unlawful detainer. The continuing possession of PROPERTY (land) that was once legally possessed after lawful possession of the property has ended. An example of unlawful detainer would be when a person continues to occupy premises he has been leasing after his lease expires, despite a landlord's request that the premises be vacated.

Unlawful detention. In MEDICAL JURISPRUDENCE, keeping a patient in a hospital when he requests discharge.

Unlawful entry. TRESPASS. Entering someone's PROPERTY without permission; a burglary.

Unlawful picketing. Riotous or violent picketing; picketing that does not serve the purposes of labor; dishonest picketing which distorts the facts of the labor dispute.

Unless lease. A lease to drill for oil or gas which specifies that the lease will terminate *unless* the person leasing the property begins to drill by a certain date, or failing the start of operations by a specified date, continues to pay rent for the lease rights.

Unlimited authority. Total, unrestricted, complete authority.

Unliquidated demand. A demand for damages, the exact amount of damages having not yet been determined.

Unmarried. Not married. (The term also applies to those who are divorced or widowed.)

Unnatural act. > CRIME AGAINST NATURE.

Unnatural offense. > CRIME AGAINST NATURE.

Unnatural will. A WILL in which the maker fails to provide for his wife or their children.

Unnecessary hardship. A zoning regulation that is so unreasonable that it deprives an owner of his basic RIGHTS concerning private property, and interferes with his economic use of his property.

Unprecedented. New; never having occurred before; without precedence. (An unprecedented action is one that has never taken place previously.)

Unprofessional conduct. Dishonorable or immoral behavior; conduct that violates the code of ethics of one's position or profession.

Unreasonable rates. Fees that are out of line with the ordinary, accepted charges for rendering a service; exorbitant rates, as judged by standards of others rendering a similar service.

Unreasonable restraint of trade. Practices that interfere with or do away with free trade, such as might occur when a monopoly exists or when several companies conspire to interfere with free competition.

Unreasonable search. Unlawful search, conducted without legal authority. As an example, breaking into one's premises and searching it without a search warrant. It is an unreasonable search even if carried out by law enforcement officers.

Unreasonable seizure. The taking of property without the legal right to do so. It is an unreasonable seizure, under the above circumstances, even if the property is taken by law enforcement officers.

Unresponsive answer. An answer by a witness which does not respond to the question asked of him.

Unseaworthy. A ship that is not capable of withstanding the usual stresses, strains, and perils of an ordinary voyage; a ship that has been declared untrustworthy by examining authorities.

Unsound mind. An individual who is incapable of managing his own affairs; a person who is mentally ill; insane; psychotic.

Unwritten law. **1.** All law which has not been enacted by statutes, rules, or regulations, but despite this, is recognized as the usual and normal law governing human conduct. **2.** Unwritten law is often observed and administered in the courts. **3.** The law as established by cases, rather than by reference to statutes that have been enacted.

Upset price. A minimum price below which property will not be sold. (A term frequently used when property is being auctioned.)

Urban easement. The RIGHT OF a person, whose property faces a street, to access to light, air, and entrance to and exit from his property.

Use. **1.** The right to enjoy one's property. **2.** To make use of; to employ.

Using mail to defraud. The conscious utilization of the U. S. mails to send out fraudulent material in the hope of receiving some financial gain. This is a federal crime, punishable by severe penalties.

Usual course of business. The regular, normal course of operations of a business, according to the customs of the particular trade.

Usufruct. The right to enjoy all the benefits of something that belongs to someone else, providing that the substance of the thing is not altered.

Usurious contract. A contract in which interest, greater than that which the law permits, is charged.

Usurp. To seize and hold something that one has no right to seize and hold, the implication being that the thing is taken forcibly.

Usurpation of enterprise. Taking over a FRANCHISE that one is not entitled to.

Usurpation of office. Unjustly seizing and taking over an office, especially a public office.

Usurper. A person who takes over a government by force.

Usury. The act of charging an exorbitant, excessive, illegal rate of interest for a LOAN; an unlawful contract for the loan of money. > ILLEGAL INTEREST; LOAN SHARK.

Ut supra. As stated above (Latin).

Utility, public. A company rendering service to the whole public, such as an electric, gas, telephone, or other type of corporation. It may be privately or publicly owned and operated.

Utmost care and skill. Phrase used denoting the greatest diligence and aptitude (skill) that can be exercised in the performance of a particular act. (A surgeon performing a delicate operation is expected to exercise the utmost care and skill comparable to the skills of those who are experts in the same field.)

Utter. **1.** Total; absolute; complete. **2.** To say; to speak words.

Uxor. Wife (Latin).

V

Vacate. To cancel; to annul; to set aside.
Vacating a judgment. Cancelling or rescinding a court DECISION (JUDGMENT).
Vacation. The ANNULMENT of a previous JUDGMENT OR DECISION; the act of setting aside or cancelling.
Vacation of award. The setting aside of an ARBITRATION award.
Vagrancy. The status of a person who loiters or travels from place to place, does not work, and has no money or means of support. Vagrancy implies that the person is physically and mentally capable of working.
Vagrant. A person who is liable to become a public trust because he maintains an idle, indolent state, loiters, and makes no attempt to find work to support himself.
Valid. Legally binding; sufficient; justifiable; complying with necessary regulations and formalities.
Validating statute. A law that corrects, adds to, alters, or deletes material from a previous law (statute), thus making the amended law valid.
Validity. The state of being legally sufficient and valid.
Validity of a statute. The effectiveness of a law insofar as it relates to its constitutionality. (An invalid statute may be thrown out because it is not in conformity with the Constitution.)
Validity of a will. The legal adequacy and sufficiency of a WILL that is being contested. (If it is held to be VALID, it means the will is a genuine one.)
Valuable consideration. A matter of CONTRACT in which one party agrees to do something in return for something the other party agrees to give him, usually money or property. The term implies that the person promised something has the right to enforce the promisor to pay him.
Valuation. The estimated worth of something; the price placed upon something.
Value, cash. The worth of a thing in terms of money; the market value; the salable value; the fair value; etcetera. > VALUE, FAIR; FAIR AND REASONABLE MARKET VALUE.
Value, clear. The value of an ESTATE after all CLAIMS have been paid. This value is used as the basis for judging the amount of inheritance tax that is due.
Value, face. > FACE VALUE.
Value, fair. The value that a seller is willing to sell for and the value that a buyer is willing to buy for.
Value, fair and reasonable market. > FAIR AND REASONABLE MARKET VALUE.
Value, market. > VALUE, FAIR.
Value, net. An insurance term referring to the reserve that an insurer must put aside from the annual premium to meet his obligations to the insured person.

The net value of the policy is then determined by the amount of money that has, over the years, been set aside for the particular insured's policy.

Value, true. The value at which property would be assessed if the owner were to sell it to a willing buyer.

Value received. A term frequently used in a PROMISSORY NOTE, meaning that a lawful consideration (a situation wherein one party agrees to do something in return for something the other party agrees to give him) has been given for the note.

Value rule. A RULE in building CONTRACTS in which the owner is entitled to receive the difference in values between the building as built, and the building as it should have been built, according to the contract.

Valued policy. An insurance policy in which the exact monies to be paid out, in the event of a loss, are stipulated on the face of the policy.

Vandalism. The senseless, willful destruction of or injury to property.

Variance. 1. A difference in two steps of a legal procedure which must agree before the legal procedure can become effective. **2.** A difference between what is charged and what is actually proved in a trial. **3.** Permission to use buildings or land in a way that would ordinarily go contrary to zoning regulations.

Vasectomy. The cutting of the vas deferens in the male. The vas deferens is the channel through which sperm travels from the testicles to a point where it can be ejaculated. The operation of vasectomy causes the male to be infertile (unable to impregnate a female) but in no way interferes with his potency or ability to engage in sexual intercourse.

Vehicular homicide. The killing of a person by a vehicle; an accidental HOMICIDE.

Venal. Acting in a courrupt manner; open to bribery.

Vendetta. A private feud, usually associated with violence and a desire to revenge a wrongdoing.

Vendor's lien. An OWNER's claim on land against a purchaser who has not yet fully paid for the lands, the owner retaining title until the PURCHASE PRICE is paid.

Venereal disease. An infection transmitted through sexual contact, such as syphilis, gonorrhea, etcetera.

Venire. 1. To appear in court (Latin). **2.** A COURT ORDER (WRIT) to summon JURORS into court.

Venire facias. 1. A COURT ORDER summoning JURORS (Latin). **2.** The whole jury panel, out of which a trial jury is chosen.

Venireman. A person who is summoned to act as a juror; a person who has received a writ known as a venire facias.

Venture. A new business enterprise, embarked upon to make profit. It is implicit that a venture carries with it the possibility of losing money, as well as making money.

Venue. The locality where a case is tried; a neighborhood.

Venue, change of. Change in the locality where a trial is held, often taking place because the new locality will offer better opportunity for a fair trial. Requests for a change of venue are often made by lawyers for defendants when they fear that the jurors in the locality where the crime was supposed to have been committed, might be prejudiced.

Venue facts. **1.** FACTS that, by law, do away with the right of a defendant to be sued in the locality or county where he lives. **2.** Facts to be established at a hearing.

Verbal agreement. An AGREEMENT reached orally, not committed to writing; a PAROL CONTRACT. ➤ ORAL CONTRACT; VERBAL CONTRACT.

Verbal contract. An oral, nonwritten AGREEMENT; a PAROL CONTRACT. ➤ ORAL CONTRACT; VERBAL AGREEMENT.

Verdict. The finding or DECISION of a JURY, duly sworn and impaneled, after careful consideration, reported to and accepted by the court.

Verdict, adverse. A VERDICT in which a person gets a verdict in his favor, but for a less amount than had been originally allowed.

Verdict, compromise. A VERDICT resulting from an improper "giving in" or compromising of one or more of the jurors on a matter of principle, in exchange for another juror or jurors' compromising on another issue in the case. Such compromises frequently produce a result that does not gain the approval of the entire panel of jurors.

Verdict, directed. A VERDICT directed by a JUDGE to the JURY. In criminal cases, a judge may direct a verdict of innocent, but cannot direct a verdict of guilty.

Verdict, estoppel by. A VERDICT that is barred because the same issues have already been settled between the same parties in a previous lawsuit.

Verdict, excessive. A VERDICT that is out of proportion to the matter at hand, thus violating the conscience of the court. Also, a verdict that is unreasonable or prejudiced.

Verdict, false. A VERDICT that is not in line with the principles of justice. Such verdicts are usually set aside (declared INVALID) by the presiding JUDGE, who then orders a new TRIAL.

Verdict, general. A VERDICT that merely specifies which party won the case. This is the ordinary type of verdict.

Verdict, guilty. A VERDICT that declares the DEFENDANT to be GUILTY of having committed the crime for which he has been charged.

Verdict, not guilty. A VERDICT that declares that the DEFENDANT has not been proved guilty of the crime for which he has been accused. ➤ NOT GUILTY.

Verdict, open. A VERDICT in which a CORONER'S JURY is unable to decide whether a deceased person died from natural causes or died as the result of a criminal act.

Verdict, partial. A VERDICT in which a JURY finds a DEFENDANT to be GUILTY of one or more parts of the accusations, but NOT GUILTY of other parts of the accusations against him.

Verdict, privy. A VERDICT given privately to a JUDGE after the court has adjourned. To be legal, the verdict must be given again publicly when the court is in session.

Verdict, public. A VERDICT given by a JURY in open court, as distinguished from a privy verdict. > VERDICT, PRIVY.

Verdict, quotient. A VERDICT consisting of an award of money to a PLAINTIFF arrived at by adding the sum total of all the JURORS' awards and dividing by the number of jurors impaneled.

Verdict, sealed. A VERDICT that is placed in an envelope and sealed, to be delivered to the COURT when it is next in session.

Verdict, special. A VERDICT that rules on each particular fact that is at issue before the court, as opposed to a general verdict, which merely rules in favor of one or the other opposing parties in the case. > VERDICT, GENERAL.

Verdict contrary to law. A VERDICT that the JURY was not, by law, entitled to render.

Verdict of guilty but insane. A VERDICT that finds the DEFENDANT mentally incompetent, yet GUILTY of having committed the crime. Such a verdict amounts to an acquittal, since an insane person cannot be convicted of a crime.

Verdict of no cause of action. A verdict in favor of the defendant on the grounds that the plaintiff had no right to bring charges against him.

Verdict of not guilty. A VERDICT that declares that the case against the DEFENDANT has not been proven. (This verdict differs from a verdict of "innocent.")

Verdict subject to opinion of court. A VERDICT that is subject to and dependent upon the DECISION of the COURT as to various points of law.

Verification. Confirmation as to the truthfulness of something, either by swearing under OATH or by offering an AFFIDAVIT as to validity.

Verified copy. A copy of a DOCUMENT authenticated by the person who created the original document.

Verified names. Names authenticated by an OFFICER OF THE COURT (a court clerk) after checking them against an official list.

Verify. To substantiate or confirm under oath.

Verity. Truthfulness; in conformity with the actual FACTS.

Vested. Something not subject to being taken away, such as vested rights; complete; settled; absolute; not dependent upon conditions, such as the complete, vested ownership of property.

Vested interest. An existing RIGHT or TITLE to something, even though the right of POSSESSION or enjoyment may not take place until some future time.

Vested remainder. An ESTATE given to a particular person, to be enjoyed by him or her at some time in the future upon the happening of a certain event.

Vested right. A PRIVILEGE or RIGHT guaranteed by the government, which cannot be taken away arbitrarily without performing an injustice.

Veterans' Administration. A federal government agency that administers the various BENEFITS that the government has voted for veterans of the armed services and their dependents. Such benefits include medical care, monetary benefits for injuries or illnesses incurred when a member of the military service, benefits to widows or minors of deceased veterans, etcetera.

Veto. To refuse to sign a law enacted by the legislative branch of government. The word means "I forbid" in Latin.

Veto, pocket. The nonapproval of a law passed by a legislative body, carried out merely by failing to sign the law. If the President takes no action on a law passed by Congress within ten days, and if Congress has adjourned during those ten days and therefore cannot override the veto, the law is not approved and is said to have received a pocket veto.

Veto power. The RIGHT not to approve an act passed by a legislative body. In the federal government, a vetoed act can still become law if two-thirds of the members of the Senate and the House of Representatives again approve it.

Vexatious litigation. > VEXATIOUS PROCEEDING.

Vexatious motion. A MOTION that is proposed in COURT for the purpose of delaying action on a controversy, rather than for the purpose of aiding justice.

Vexatious proceeding. A malicious COURT ACTION, begun not for the purpose of seeing justice done, but for the purpose of annoying and harassing the opponent in the case.

Viability. The ability to sustain life, such as the ability of an unborn child to live if it were not in its mother's womb; capable of working out, such as the viability of an enterprise; being able to survive; practicable.

Vicarious liability. The responsibility of one person for the acts of another. As an example, if a chauffeur of a car hits another car, the employer of the chauffeur is vicariously liable for the damages to the car which has been hit. > RESPONDEAT SUPERIOR.

Vice. **1.** Instead of; in place of, as a vice president. **2.** Immoral or sinful conduct; **3.** A defect or fault; an imperfection.

Vice consul. A commercial agent in a consulate of a government who assumes some of the duties of the CONSUL.

Vice president. A person who will serve as president in the president's absence or in the event of his death. In government, as well as in business, a vice president is frequently the officer immediately below the president in rank.

Vide. A word referring a reader to something else (Latin).

View of premises. A situation in which a JURY leaves the courtroom to visit the scene where an accident or crime took place. Such an excursion often aids a jury in coming to a VERDICT.

Vigilance. Alertness; precaution; promptness in carrying out one's rights and protecting them against possible violation.

Vindication. The act of being cleared of a suspicion or of a wrongdoing.
Vindicatory. The clause or clauses in a law that prescribe the PENALTIES for violations.
Violation of copyright. The act of infringing upon a COPYRIGHT, such as copying without permission a published article, treatise, book, or part of a book, that has been copyrighted. > INFRINGEMENT OF COPYRIGHT.
Violation of parole. Failure to follow the COURT's instructions upon being paroled, such as leaving the jurisdiction of a prescribed area, not reporting in to the authorities, consorting with known or suspected criminals, performing a criminal act, etcetera.
Violation of privacy. Interfering with one's basic RIGHT to privacy, such as exposing someone to unwanted public notice or publicity, photographing someone without his knowledge and publishing such photographs, etcetera.
Violent death. An unnatural death; death caused by an accident or by the violent actions of another. (MURDER is a violent death).
Violent presumption. Proof of a fact based upon the proof of circumstances that surround it; assuming something to be true because all the circumstances point toward it being true.
Vis-a-vis. **1.** Face to face. **2.** In relation to (French).
Visa. An endorsement on a PASSPORT or other official DOCUMENT allowing a person to enter another country.
Visitation. The act of visiting and investigating the premises of an institution or business by an official agency. Such visitation is usually carried out to determine if an institution is being managed properly. Prisons, state hospitals, and other institutions are often "visited" by specially appointed committees of observers or overseers. ≫ RIGHT OF VISITATION.
Vital statistics. Information on births, deaths, longevity, marriages, divorces, matters of health, etcetera, kept by the public authorities. Such data is kept in a hall of records.
Vitiate. To destroy the legal or binding effect of something.
Viva voce. TESTIMONY that a WITNESS gives in person, rather than that given by a transcript of previous testimony or testimony presented in writing (Latin).
Void. Having no legal or binding effect; null; ineffectual.
Void contract. A contract that is nonexistent and has no legal force; a contract in which neither party is or was bound because some essential element from a legal point of view is lacking.
Void judgment. A judgment that has no legal force or effect.
Void marriage. A MARRIAGE having no legal validity because it is prohibited by law, such as the marriage of a man presently married to another woman.
Void process. An ACTION of a COURT that is legally defective and therefore ineffectual; a process that is null and void because of a defect.
Voidable. Something that can be

declared VOID (not in effect) but is not automatically void.

Voir dire examination. An examination of potential JURORS to determine whether they are fit to serve or to determine if they should be challenged (French).

Volstead Act. The 18th Amendment to the U.S. CONSTITUTION, prohibiting the general sale of liquor. This Amendment was repealed in 1933.

Voluntary abandonment. The act of leaving someone without good reason and without the consent of the other party, such as a husband who, abruptly and without apparent or legal cause, leaves his wife without the intention to return.

Voluntary association. A group of people who voluntarily form an organization or society to carry out some public good; a not-for-profit organization, such as a benevolent society, a health insurance organization, a religious or social or political group, etcetera.

Voluntary bankruptcy. A BANKRUPTCY in which the bankrupt person (or company) initiates the proceedings to be judged bankrupt, as opposed to involuntary bankruptcy, in which the CREDITORS force someone (or a company) into bankruptcy.

Voluntary discontinuance. The willing (voluntary) withdrawal of a CASE from TRIAL by the PLAINTIFF; the taking of a nonsuit by a plaintiff. (A SETTLEMENT OUT OF COURT may stimulate a plaintiff to invoke a voluntary discontinuance.)

Voluntary liquidation. The winding up of the affairs of a solvent corporation, turning its ASSETS into money and distributing such funds to the shareholders.

Voluntary manslaughter. A killing associated with a sudden fit of rage, possibly for seemingly good reason (as when a person finds his or her spouse in bed with another). Such a killing, although intentional, is not PREMEDITATED nor motivated by a basic evil intent.

Voluntary nonsuit. A JUDGMENT against a PLAINTIFF who fails to press a suit in court.

Voluntary payment. **1.** Willingly paying a debt. **2.** The payment of an illegal demand, such as the giving of a bribe when it is requested or demanded.

Voluntary petition. A request by a DEBTOR to be declared BANKRUPT.

Voluntary statement. A willing STATEMENT by a DEFENDANT, completely free from coercion, admitting some damaging facts or attesting to his GUILT.

Voting trust. > TRUST, VOTING.

Voucher. A RECEIPT showing that one has paid a DEBT; a book of accounts containing the company's receipts; a DOCUMENT that gives evidence of an expenditure.

Wager. An AGREEMENT between two or more parties that they shall gain or lose upon the outcome of some uncertain event, such as an election, a game, etcetera. Those wagering have no interest except that arising from the possibility of a gain or loss, depending upon the outcome of the event; a bet.

Wagering contract. A bet; an AGREEMENT to WAGER.

Wages. Payment for labor.

Wages and Hours Act. > FAIR LABOR STANDARDS ACT.

Wagner Act. The National Labor Relations Act, a federal law giving the right to employees to organize, to form unions, and to bargain collectively with employers.

Waive. To relinquish or give up a RIGHT, PRIVILEGE, or BENEFIT. A WAIVER implies that the person knows what he is doing when renouncing his right, privilege, or benefit.

Waiver. The voluntary giving up or renouncing of a RIGHT, benefit, or PRIVILEGE. > WAIVE.

Waiver, express. The intentional giving up of a specific, known RIGHT.

Waiver, implied. An intention on the part of a person to give up a RIGHT, benefit, or PRIVILEGE, with conduct that can only be interpreted as meaning that a WAIVER of a right or advantage will be given.

Waiver of exemption. The intentional giving up, by a DEBTOR, of his RIGHT to exempt his PROPERTY, or part of his property, from the claims of a CREDITOR.

Waiver of immunity. The voluntary relinquishment by a WITNESS of his constitutional RIGHT to refuse to give evidence that might incriminate or be used against him. (WAIVER of the Fifth Amendment is such an act.) It is a fundamental right guaranteed by the U.S. CONSTITUTION that no one shall be forced to give evidence against him or herself.

Waiver of right to appeal. The giving up of the RIGHT to APPEAL from a decision of a COURT.

Waiver of tort. The act of an injured party (a PLAINTIFF) in which he gives up the RIGHT to sue someone on the basis that he has committed a wrong but, instead, sues merely to obtain REDRESS and SATISFACTION of his CLAIM. In other words, he sues as if there has been a BREACH OF CONTRACT but no wrongdoing on the part of the opposing party.

Wall Street lawyer. A popular term for an ATTORNEY who belongs to a large firm that handles large corporations and big business.

Want of consideration. A transaction in which no money, goods, or property were intended to pass from one party to another; absence of CONSIDERATION.

Want of jurisdiction. **1.** The lack

of authority to hear and try a case. As an example, a local city magistrate cannot try a case involving federal law. **2.** The overstepping of a judge's or court's authority in a particular case.

Wanton act. A reckless, careless, or malicious type of behavior that disregards the RIGHTS of others and causes them DAMAGE, whether physical or emotional.

Wanton negligence. The reckless disregard of the exercise of due care and regard for the welfare of others, resulting in physical or emotional injury. > NEGLIGENCE.

Ward. **1.** A child placed by a COURT under the care of a GUARDIAN. **2.** An election district or a precinct in a town or city.

Warden. A superintendant of a correctional institution or prison; a caretaker; a keeper; a guardian.

Wards of court. People whose rights and safety are guarded and protected by the courts. Small children, mentally ill people, etcetera, may be wards of court.

Warrant. **1.** A COURT ORDER giving authority to a SHERIFF OR POLICE OFFICER to arrest a person, to search a house, etcetera. ➢ WARRANT, BENCH; WARRANT, SEARCH. **2.** To state that something is true.

Warrant, bench. A WARRANT (court WRIT) for the arrest of someone charged with CONTEMPT or with some CRIMINAL OFFENSE. Such a warrant is issued by a judge, often when the person accused has failed to appear to answer the charges against him.

Warrant, death. An ORDER, usually issued by the chief authority of a state, for the appropriate officer to carry out a death sentence that has been passed by a court upon a convicted capital offender.

Warrant, search. A written ORDER of a COURT permitting the search of premises thought to contain stolen goods, illegal drugs, or other materials or documents that have been obtained unlawfully.

Warrant in bankruptcy. An ORDER of a COURT to a marshal, directing him to take possession of a BANKRUPT person's or company's PROPERTY.

Warrant of arrest. A COURT ORDER directing the arrest of an individual. The WARRANT states the grounds upon which the arrest is being made.

Warrant of extradition. The issuance of an ORDER to surrender a person ACCUSED or CONVICTED of a crime to the JURISDICTION where the crime is alleged to have been committed. This may involve transfer of such person from one county, state, or country to another.

Warrantee. Someone to whom a WARRANT is made.

Warranty. **1.** A STATEMENT that certain FACTS are true, made by one party to a CONTRACT and accepted by the other party as true. **2.** An AGREEMENT to make up for any DAMAGES that result from a false representation of FACTS.

Warranty, affirmative. A STATEMENT by an insured person that certain facts exist and are true, such statement (WARRANTY) appearing on the face of the insurance contract.

Warranty, collateral. A WARRANTY of a TITLE by someone who is a stranger to the title, such situation existing when the title was not gotten from a warranting ancestor.

Warranty, express. **1.** A WARRANTY that is bound by the explicit statements of the seller. **2.** A STATEMENT by an insured person, expressed in the INSURANCE POLICY, that certain FACTS are true.

Warranty, general. A written STATEMENT in a DEED that the purchaser of the PROPERTY is completely and fully entitled to accept the TITLE to the property, and that the seller of the property will defend the title against anyone who attempts to upset it.

Warranty, personal. An AGREEMENT by someone to pay a DEBT owed by another to a third person.

Warranty, special. A WARRANTY by the owner of PROPERTY to ensure and defend the TITLE that he has transferred (sold) to another person.

Warranty of fitness. An assurance by a seller to a buyer that the goods he has sold him are suitable and will be in conformity with his wishes.

Warranty of title. An assurance by a seller that he has the right to sell the goods or PROPERTY, and that the buyer will be free from CLAIMS against the goods or property.

Wash sale. Selling something and buying something that is similar to the thing that has been sold.

Wasting property. PROPERTY of which the contents are eventually used up or consumed, such as a gold mine, an oil well, etcetera.

Wasting trust. A TRUST in which the TRUSTEE has the RIGHT to use some of the principal if there is insufficient income.

Water pollution. The contamination of waters, such as streams, rivers, lakes, or oceans, with chemicals, sewage, garbage, industrial wastes, or other pollutants.

Water rights. The legal PRIVILEGE to use the water of a stream, river, or lake for one's own purposes, such as for the irrigation of land, to supply power for electricity, to supply drinking water, etcetera.

Water-tight case. A case that one is positive will be resolved in one's favor.

Watered stock. STOCK issued by a company as if it were fully paid up, when in reality the full PAR VALUE of the stock has not been paid in. Such stock is naturally not worth what the company pretends it to be worth.

Ways and means committee. A legislative committee whose function is to look into the ways and means of raising monies to run the government and/or one of its projects.

Weapon. An instrument used to injure another or to protect oneself. It may be a revolver or gun, or it may be a knife, club, or any other device for inflicting harm or for protecting oneself against an attacker.

Weight of evidence. Preponderance of truth; the weight of evidence is that which is more believable and is superior to the EVIDENCE submitted by the opposing side in a case. Thus, the weight of evidence convinces a JUDGE and/or a JURY that one party in a DISPUTE is right and the other party is wrong.
Welfare statutes. Laws to help support those who are unable to support themselves. Such laws may provide medical and hospital care, payment of rent, or money to buy food and clothing.
Welsh. To go back on one's word and fail to pay a DEBT, such as a gambling debt.
White. People of the Caucasian race.
Wholly. Completely; entirely; exclusively; the opposite of partially.
Widow. A married woman whose husband has died and who has not remarried.
Widower. A married man whose wife has died and who has not remarried.
Wildcat strike. A strike of workers that has not been authorized by the UNION.
Will. **1.** A DOCUMENT made in anticipation of eventual death, in which a person states what he wants done with his PROPERTY after he dies. Such a document must be made according to law, and is recorded and filed in a PROBATE COURT after the person has died. **2.** Desire or wish. **3.** Determination. **4.** The mental capacity to carry out a conscious act.
Will, ambulatory. A WILL in which the maker has the power to make changes while he is still alive.
Will, conditional. A WILL that states that certain things shall happen providing another event, uncertain in nature, occurs. As an example, certain PROPERTY may be willed to a particular person providing that person carries out some as yet unaccomplished act.
Will, double. > RECIPROCAL WILLS.
Will, holographic. A WILL that is entirely in the handwriting of the maker of the will.
Will, joint. A WILL that two people make and sign together. In other words, the same will serves as the DOCUMENT for both people.
Will, mutual. A WILL in which two or more people have provisions favoring each other or others. As an example, two people may provide that the survivor shall inherit all the money from the other.
Will contest. A legal ACTION to determine whether a will is legitimate and eligible to be probated. > PROBATE.
Willful. **1.** On purpose; intentional; deliberate; with full consciousness. **2.** Stubborn; obstinate; headstrong. **3.** With criminal intent.
Willful and malicious injury. INJURY to PROPERTY carried out intentionally and with a disregard of duty.
Willful misconduct. Intentional, conscious, deliberate disobedience and flaunting of the law.
Willful neglect. The deliberate and intentional NEGLECT of one's DUTY and OBLIGATION.

Willful negligence. Conscious, deliberate, intentional disregard of the safety of others. (This type of NEGLIGENCE implies bad faith on the part of the PERPETRATOR.)

Willful tort. A wrong intentionally committed with the knowledge and wish to hurt another.

Willfully and maliciously. A phrase frequently used to characterize the carrying out of an act intentionally and with a conscious desire to do harm to another.

Withdrawal of charges. A failure on the part of a PLAINTIFF to pursue his charges, resulting in the CASE being dropped.

Withdrawing a juror. A means of postponing a case by withdrawing one of the twelve JURORS. Since a case cannot be tried unless the JURY is complete, the withdrawal of one juror automatically causes the case to be postponed or tried again. When a JUDGE believes a MISTRIAL has taken place, he may withdraw one of the jurors.

Withholding evidence. Failure to give EVIDENCE that should be given; not disclosing information in a suit when that information is asked for.

Withholding tax. The holding of part of an employee's pay by an employer, in order to turn the money over to the government to prepay the employee's INCOME TAX.

Without defalcation. Without OFFSET, a phrase sometimes used in a document for the payment of money, preventing a SETOFF. (A setoff is a demand made to counteract an opposite demand.)

Without legal cause. Without justification. A DEFENDANT frequently uses this phrase in a PLEADING when he denies the charges made against him.

Without prejudice. A phrase implying that no RIGHTS of the contesting parties have been affected by the disposition of the matter before the court.

Without recourse. A phrase used by a person who endorses a check, a note, or some other negotiable paper, stating that he will not be responsible for payment if the party primarily liable does not pay. In other words, his endorsement is a qualified, limited one.

Witness. **1.** An individual who testifies under OATH at a TRIAL, a HEARING, or before a legislative body. **2.** To see or hear something take place. **3.** To be present, and often to sign, a legal DOCUMENT, such as a WILL or DEED. Having a witness sign lends authenticity to a document.

Witness, adverse. A WITNESS who is unfavorable to the person questioning him; a witness called purposely to give TESTIMONY that will favor the opposite side in a case.

Witness, competent. A WITNESS who is legally qualified to TESTIFY in a case. The competency of a witness does not necessarily mean that his TESTIMONY will be truthful.

Witness, credible. A believable giver of TESTIMONY.

Witness, expert. A WITNESS who has specialized knowledge of a particular field, such as an engineer, a chemist, or a physician.

Witness, hostile. A person who is antagonistic toward the party who summoned him as a WITNESS.

Witness, involuntary. A WITNESS who did not want to come to court to TESTIFY but, nevertheless, received a SUMMONS to do so.

Witness, prosecuting. The individual upon whose COMPLAINT or information a CRIMINAL ACTION is begun, and upon whose TESTIMONY the GUILT of the ACCUSED may be based.

Witness, voluntary. A WITNESS who gives TESTIMONY willingly.

Witness against himself. A provision in the U.S. CONSTITUTION that no person shall be forced to give TESTIMONY against himself in a criminal matter, or testimony that may lead to his being charged with a CRIME. This law constitutes the 5th Amendment to the Constitution.

Wittingly. With knowledge and planning.

Words of art. The special words of a particular science or profession. Technical legal terms are words of art.

Working capital. Monies used by a company to pay its current OBLIGATIONS. Such monies are usually kept on hand at all times so that the company doesn't have to wait for payments from its DEBTORS before paying its CREDITORS.

Working claim. A mining claim that is producing actively.

Workmen's Compensation laws. STATUTES that provide funds to pay workers hurt on the job, regardless of whether the injury was the fault of the worker. (Most states have enacted Workmen's Compensation laws.)

Wound. An INJURY to the body, usually involving the breaking of the skin or mucous membranes. However, a bruise, not accompanied by a breaking of the skin, is also considered to be a wound. Wounds can be caused by innumerable external objects, or by bites of animals or humans.

Writ. A formal ORDER of a COURT, in writing, ordering someone who is out of court to do something.

Writ of attachment. A WRIT that is issued to enforce obedience to an ORDER of the COURT. Often, it requires that the person who fails to comply with the court's order be brought to court to answer for the lack of obedience.

Writ of coram nobis. A WRIT requesting that a VERDICT be set aside because of errors of FACT that took place during the TRIAL (Latin).

Writ of coram vobis. Essentially the same as a writ of coram nobis (Latin).

Writ of debt. A WRIT in which a CREDITOR claims monies are due him by a DEBTOR, but such monies have not been paid.

Writ of dower. A COURT ORDER for a widow to receive her dower, her RIGHTS to the PROPERTY of her dead husband.

Writ of entry. A WRIT ordering that the PLAINTIFF be permitted to take POSSESSION of his PROPERTY, and that those presently occupying it shall leave.

Writ of error. An ORDER of a COURT OF APPEALS to the JUDGE or judges who tried a case in a lower court, to supply the appellate court with the records of the case. Such records will be examined by the appeals court to see if errors were committed on conducting the trial.

Writ of execution. An ORDER of the COURT that its JUDGMENT (DECISION) be carried out.

Writ of habeas corpus. An ORDER for a person to appear in COURT to determine his innocence or guilt.

Writ of inquiry. A COURT ORDER issued after a PLAINTIFF has won his case by default, the DEFENDANT not having appeared to defend himself. The WRIT instructs the SHERIFF, with the aid of a JURY, to determine the extent of DAMAGES and the amount of the plaintiff's CLAIM that should be awarded.

Writ of possession. An ORDER to enforce the court's JUDGMENT in regard to the POSSESSION of land.

Writ of restitution. If a higher court has overturned a lower court's decision, then an ORDER is issued to restore to the DEFENDANT what he lost in the SUIT. If what the defendant lost has been sold or disappeared, then the PLAINTIFF must make him whole again by giving him money equivalent in value to what he lost.

Writ of review. An ORDER from an APPEALS COURT to a lower court to supply records so that the case may be reviewed.

Write-off. A DEBT that cannot be collected.

Written contract. A CONTRACT in writing, as distinguished from a VERBAL CONTRACT.

Written interrogatories. A party to a LAWSUIT can compel an opponent to write down, under OATH, answers to written questions sent to him. Written interrogatories seek to obtain detailed information from the records the opponent has in his possession or under his control.

Wrongful act. An act that will in any way, physically or emotionally, DAMAGE another person. In most instances, a wrongful act is one that is done intentionally and willfully.

Wrongful commitment. The act of confining a person to a mental institution without proceeding lawfully, or committing someone who does not belong in such a facility; FALSE IMPRISONMENT.

Wrongful execution. The carrying out of a COURT ORDER incorrectly by going beyond the authorization of the order (WRIT); carrying out an irregular procedure.

Wrongful imprisonment. FALSE IMPRISONMENT; wrongfully depriving a person of his liberty.

X rays. Light rays of short length which are passed by an electric generator through a glass vacuum tube (the X-ray tube). Such rays have special penetrative powers through body tissue. Also called roentgen rays.

X rays, property of. X-ray films are the property of the physician, not the patient. The patient does not pay for the films, he pays for a report and interpretation of the findings of the X rays.

X-ray reports. Patients are entitled to a copy of the reports of the findings of the X rays.

X-ray technician. A person trained in the technique of taking X rays. The technician does not interpret the findings of the X rays.

Yea and nay. Yes and no.

Year and a day. 1. A not uncommon period for sentencing someone to jail. **2.** Death from wounding, in some JURISDICTIONS, must occur with a year and a day or the PERPETRATOR cannot be indicted for MURDER. The assumption is then that the person died from some other cause. **3.** The time period during which a person must claim a wreck, or the wreck shall become PUBLIC PROPERTY.

Yellow dog contract. An employment CONTRACT in which the newly hired employee agrees not to join a UNION, or if he already belongs to one, he agrees to resign from it. Such contracts are illegal.

Z

Zealous witness. A WITNESS who willingly and eagerly testifies in a case; a witness who is "friendly" to the party who called him to TESTIFY. > FRIENDLY WITNESS.

Zoning. The division of certain areas in a community into various categories for permission to build, or not to build, certain types of structures. For example, a certain area may be zoned for residential structures only, while another area permits business structures only.

Zoning commission. A group of people, appointed by a town or city government, to administer the ZONING LAWS and regulations.

Zoning exception. A special permission given by a town or city for a particular structure to be built, even though it does not conform to the ZONING LAWS and regulations of the area.

Zoning laws. ORDINANCES, RULES, REGULATIONS, and STATUTES governing the types of structures that can be placed upon lands in particular areas of a community, town, or municipality.

APPENDIX

DECLARATION OF INDEPENDENCE

The Declaration of Independence was adopted by the Continental Congress in Philadelphia, on July 4, 1776. John Hancock was president of the Congress and Charles Thomson was secretary. A copy of the Declaration, engrossed on parchment, was signed by members of Congress on and after Aug. 2, 1776. On Jan. 18, 1777, Congress ordered that "an authenticated copy, with the names of the members of Congress subscribing the same, be sent to each of the United States, and that they be desired to have the same put upon record." Authenticated copies were printed in broadside form in Baltimore, where the Continental Congress was then in session. The following text is that of the original printed by John Dunlap at Philadelphia for the Continental Congress.

IN CONGRESS, July 4, 1776.
A DECLARATION
By the REPRESENTATIVES of the
UNITED STATES OF AMERICA,
In GENERAL CONGRESS assembled

When in the Course of human Events, it becomes necessary for one People to dissolve the Political Bands which have connected them with another, and to assume among the Powers of the Earth, the separate and equal Station to which the Laws of Nature and of Nature's God entitle them, a decent Respect to the Opinions of Mankind requires that they should declare the causes which impel them to the Separation.

We hold these Truths to be self-evident, that all Men are created equal, that they are endowed by their Creator with certain unalienable Rights, that among these are Life, Liberty, and the Pursuit of Happiness—That to secure these Rights, Governments are instituted among Men, deriving their just Powers from the Consent of the Governed, that whenever any Form of Government becomes destructive of these Ends, it is the Right of the People to alter or to abolish it, and to institute new Government, laying its Foundation on such Principles, and organizing its Powers in such Form, as to them shall seem most likely to effect their Safety and Happiness. Prudence, indeed, will dictate that Governments long established should not be changed for light and transient Causes; and accordingly all Experience hath shewn, that Mankind are more disposed to suffer, while Evils are sufferable, than to right themselves by abolishing the Forms to which they are accustomed. But when a long Train of Abuses, and Usurpations, pursuing invariably the same Object, evinces a Design to reduce them under absolute Despotism, it is their Right, it is their Duty, to throw off such Government, and to provide new Guards for their future Security. Such has been the patient Sufferance of these Colonies; and such is now the Necessity which constrains them to alter their former Systems of Government. The History of the present King of Great-Britain is a History of repeated Injuries and Usurpations, all having in direct Object the Establishment of an absolute Tyranny over these States. To prove this, let Facts be submitted to a candid World.

He has refused his Assent to Laws, the most wholesome and necessary for the public Good.

He has forbidden his Governors to pass Laws of immediate and pressing Importance, unless suspended in their Operation till his Assent should be obtained; and when so suspended, he has utterly neglected to attend to them.

He has refused to pass other Laws for the Accommodation of large Districts of People, unless those People would relinquish the Right of Representation in the Legislature, a Right inestimable to them, and formidable to Tyrants only.

He has called together Legislative Bodies at Places unusual, uncomfortable, and distant from the Depository of their Public Records, for the sole Purpose of fatiguing them into Compliance with his Measures.

He has dissolved Representative Houses repeatedly, for opposing with manly Firmness his Invasions on the Rights of the ple.

He has refused for a long Time, after such Dissolutions, to cause others to be elected; whereby the Legislative Powers, incapable of Annihilation, have returned to the People at large for their exercise; the State remaining in the mean time exposed to all the Dangers of Invasion from without, and Convulsions within.

He has endeavoured to prevent the Population of these States; for that Purpose obstructing the Laws for Naturalization of Foreigners; refusing to pass others to encourage their Migrations hither, and raising the Conditions of new Appropriations of Lands.

He has obstructed the Administration of Justice, by refusing his Assent to Laws for establishing Judiciary Powers.

He has made Judges dependent on his Will alone, for the Tenure of their Offices, and the Amount and Payment of their Salaries.

He has erected a Multitude of new Offices, and sent hither Swarms of Officers to harrass our People, and eat out their Substance.

He has kept among us, in Times of Peace, Standing Armies, without the consent of our Legislatures.

He has affected to render the Military independent of, and superior to the Civil Power.

He has combined with others to subject us to a Jurisdiction foreign to our Constitution, and unacknowledged by our Laws; giving his Assent to their Acts of pretended Legislation:

For quartering large Bodies of Armed Troops among us:

For protecting them, by a mock Trial, from Punishment for any Murders which they should commit on the Inhabitants of these States:

For cutting off our Trade with all Parts of the World:

For imposing Taxes on us without our Consent:

For depriving us, in many Cases, of the Benefits of Trial by Jury:

For transporting us beyond Seas to be tried for pretended Offences:

For abolishing the free System of English Laws in a neighbouring Province, establishing therein an arbitrary Government, and enlarging its Boundaries, so as to render it at once an Example and fit Instrument for introducing the same absolute Rule into these Colonies:

For taking away our Charters, abolishing our most valuable Laws, and altering fundamentally the Forms of our Governments:

For suspending our own Legislatures, and declaring themselves invested with Power to legislate for us in all Cases whatsoever.

He has abdicated Government here, by declaring us out of his Protection and waging War against us.

He has plundered our Seas, ravaged our Coasts, burnt our towns, and destroyed the Lives of our People.

He is, at this Time, transporting large Armies of foreign Mercenaries to compleat the works of Death, Desolation, and Tyranny, already begun with circumstances of Cruelty and Perfidy, scarcely paralleled in the most barbarous Ages, and totally unworthy the Head of a civilized Nation.

He has constrained our fellow Citizens taken Captive on the high Seas to bear Arms against their Country, to become the Executioners of their Friends and Brethren, or to fall themselves by their Hands.

He has excited domestic Insurrections amongst us, and has endeavoured to bring on the Inhabitants of our Frontiers, the merciless Indian Savages, whose known Rule of Warfare, is an undistinguished Destruction, of all Ages, Sexes and Conditions.

In every stage of these Oppressions we have Petitioned for Redress in the most humble Terms: Our repeated Petitions have been answered only by repeated Injury. A Prince, whose Character is thus marked by every act which may define a Tyrant, is unfit to be the Ruler of a free People.

Nor have we been wanting in Attentions

to our British Brethren. We have warned them from Time to Time of Attempts by their Legislature to extend an unwarrantable Jurisdiction over us. We have reminded them of the Circumstances of our Emigration and Settlement here. We have appealed to their native Justice and Magnanimity, and we have conjured them by the Ties of our common Kindred to disavow these Usurpations, which, would inevitably interrupt our Connections and Correspondence. They too have been deaf to the Voice of Justice and of Consanguinity. We must, therefore, acquiesce in the Necessity, which denounces our Separation, and hold them, as we hold the rest of Mankind, Enemies in War, in Peace, Friends.

We, therefore, the Representatives of the UNITED STATES OF AMERICA, in General Congress, Assembled, appealing to the Supreme Judge of the World for the Rectitude of our Intentions, do, in the Name, and by Authority of the good People of these Colonies, solemnly Publish and Declare, That these United Colonies are, and of Right ought to be, Free and Independent States; that they are absolved from all Allegiance to the British Crown, and that all political Connection between them and the State of Great-Britain, is and ought to be totally dissolved; and that as Free and Independent States, they have full Power to levy War, conclude Peace, contract Alliances, establish Commerce, and to do all other Acts and Things which Independent States may of right do. And for the support of this declaration, with a firm Reliance on the Protection of divine Providence, we mutually pledge to each other our lives, our Fortunes, and our sacred Honor.

JOHN HANCOCK, President

Attest.
CHARLES THOMSON, Secretary.

SIGNERS OF THE DECLARATION OF INDEPENDENCE

Delegate and state	*Vocation*	*Birthplace*	*Born*	*Died*
Adams, John (Mass.)	Lawyer	Braintree (Quincy), Mass.	Oct. 30, 1735	July 4, 1826
Adams, Samuel (Mass.)	Political leader	Boston, Mass.	Sept. 27, 1722	Oct. 2, 1803
Bartlett, Josiah (N.H.)	Physician, judge	Amesbury, Mass.	Nov. 21, 1729	May 19, 1795
Braxton, Carter (Va.)	Farmer	Newington Plantation, Va.	Sept. 10, 1736	Oct. 10, 1797
Carroll, Chas. of Carrollton (Md.)	Lawyer	Annapolis, Md.	Sept. 19, 1737	Nov. 14, 1832
Chase, Samuel (Md.)	Judge	Princess Anne, Md.	Apr. 17, 1741	June 19, 1811
Clark, Abraham (N.J.)	Surveyor	Roselle, N.J.	Feb. 15, 1726	Sept. 15, 1794
Clymer, George (Pa.)	Merchant	Philadelphia, Pa.	Mar. 16, 1739	Jan. 23, 1813
Ellery, William (R.I.)	Lawyer	Newport, R.I.	Dec. 22, 1727	Feb. 15, 1820
Floyd, William (N.Y.)	Soldier	Brookhaven, N.Y.	Dec. 17, 1734	Aug. 4, 1821
Franklin, Benjamin (Pa.)	Printer, publisher	Boston, Mass.	Jan. 17, 1706	Apr. 17, 1790
Gerry, Elbridge (Mass.)	Merchant	Marblehead, Mass.	July 17, 1744	Nov. 23, 1814
Gwinnett, Button (Ga.)	Merchant	Down Hatherly, England	c. 1735	May 19, 1777
Hall, Lyman (Ga.)	Physician	Wallingford, Conn.	Apr. 12, 1724	Oct. 19, 1790
Hancock, John (Mass.)	Merchant	Braintree (Quincy), Mass.	Jan. 12, 1737	Oct. 8, 1793
Harrison, Benjamin (Va.)	Farmer	Berkeley, Va.	Apr. 5, 1726	Apr. 24, 1791
Hart, John (N.J.)	Farmer	Stonington, Conn.	c. 1711	May 11, 1779
Hewes, Joseph (N.C.)	Merchant	Princeton, N.J.	Jan. 23, 1730	Nov. 10, 1779
Heyward, Thos. Jr. (S.C.)	Lawyer, farmer	St. Luke's Parish, S.C.	July 28, 1746	Mar. 6, 1809
Hooper, William (N.C.)	Lawyer	Boston, Mass.	June 28, 1742	Oct. 14, 1790
Hopkins, Stephen (R.I.)	Judge, educator	Providence, R.I.	Mar. 7, 1707	July 13, 1785
Hopkinson, Francis (N.J.)	Judge, author	Philadelphia, Pa.	Sept. 21, 1737	May 9, 1791
Huntington, Samuel (Conn.)	Judge	Windham County, Conn.	July 3, 1731	Jan. 5, 1796
Jefferson, Thomas (Va.)	Lawyer	Shadwell, Va.	Apr. 13, 1743	July 4, 1826
Lee, Francis Lightfoot (Va.)	Farmer	Westmoreland County, Va.	Oct.14, 1734	Jan. 11, 1797
Lee, Richard Henry (Va.)	Farmer	Westmoreland County, Va.	Jan. 20, 1732	June 19, 1794

Delegate and state	*Vocation*	*Birthplace*	*Born*	*Died*
Lewis, Francis (N.Y.)	Merchant	Llandaff, Wales	Mar., 1713	Dec. 31, 1802
Livingston, Philip (N.Y.)	Merchant	Albany, N.Y.	Jan. 15, 1716	June 12, 1778
Lynch, Thomas Jr. (S.C.)	Farmer	Winyah, S.C.	Aug. 5, 1749	(at sea) 1779
McKean, Thomas (Del.)	Lawyer	New London, Pa.	Mar. 19, 1734	June 24, 1817
Middleton, Arthur (S.C.)	Farmer	Charleston, S.C.	June 26, 1742	Jan. 1, 1787
Morris, Lewis (N.Y.)	Farmer	Morrisania (Bronx County), N.Y.	Apr. 8, 1726	Jan. 22, 1798
Morris, Robert (Pa.)	Merchant	Liverpool, England	Jan. 20, 1734	May 9, 1806
Morton, John (Pa.)	Judge	Ridley, Pa.	1724	Apr., 1777
Nelson, Thos. Jr. (Va.)	Farmer	Yorktown, Va.	Dec. 26, 1738	Jan. 4, 1789
Paca, William (Md.)	Judge	Abingdon, Md.	Oct. 31, 1740	Oct. 23, 1799
Paine, Robert Treat (Mass.)	Judge	Boston, Mass.	Mar. 11, 1731	May 12, 1814
Penn, John (N.C.)	Lawyer	Near Port Royal, Va.	May 17, 1741	Sept. 14, 1788
Read, George (Del.)	Judge	Near North East, Md.	Sept. 18, 1733	Sept. 21, 1798
Rodney, Caesar (Del.)	Judge	Dover, Del.	Oct. 7, 1728	June 29, 1784
Ross, George (Pa.)	Judge	New Castle, Del.	May 10, 1730	July 14, 1779
Rush, Benjamin (Pa.)	Physician	Byberry, Pa. (Philadelphia)	Dec. 24, 1745	Apr. 19, 1813
Rutledge, Edward (S.C.)	Lawyer	Charleston, S.C.	Nov. 23, 1749	Jan. 23, 1800
Sherman, Roger (Conn.)	Lawyer	Newton, Mass.	Apr. 19, 1721	July 23, 1793
Smith, James (Pa.)	Lawyer	Dublin, Ireland	c. 1719	July 11, 1806
Stockton, Richard (N.J.)	Lawyer	Near Princeton, N.J.	Oct. 1, 1730	Feb. 28, 1781
Stone, Thomas (Md.)	Lawyer	Charles County, Md.	1743	Oct. 5, 1787
Taylor, George (Pa.)	Ironmaster	Ireland	1716	Feb. 23, 1781
Thornton, Matthew (N.H.)	Physician	Ireland	1714	June 24, 1803
Walton, George (Ga.)	Judge	Prince Edward County, Va.	1741	Feb. 2, 1804
Whipple, William (N.H.)	Merchant, judge	Kittery, Me.	Jan. 14, 1730	Nov. 28, 1785
Williams, William (Conn.)	Merchant	Lebanon, Conn.	Apr. 23, 1731	Aug. 2, 1811
Wilson, James (Pa.)	Judge	Carskerdo, Scotland	Sept. 14, 1742	Aug. 28, 1798
Witherspoon, John (N.J.)	Educator	Gifford, Scotland	Feb. 5, 1723	Nov. 15, 1794
Wolcott, Oliver (Conn.)	Judge	Windsor, Conn.	Dec. 1, 1726	Dec. 1, 1797
Wythe, George (Va.)	Lawyer	Elizabeth City Co. (Hampton), Va.	1726	June 8, 1806

CONSTITUTION OF THE UNITED STATES

The Original 7 Articles

PREAMBLE

We, the people of the United States, in order to form a more perfect Union, establish justice, insure domestic tranquility, provide for the common defense, promote the general welfare, and secure the blessings of liberty to ourselves and our posterity do ordain and establish this Constitution for the United States of America.

ARTICLE I.

Section 1—Legislative powers; in whom vested:

All legislative powers herein granted shall be vested in a Congress of the United States, which shall consist of a Senate and House of Representatives.

Section 2—House of Representatives, how and by whom chosen. Qualifications of a Representative. Representatives and direct taxes, how apportioned. Enumeration. Vacancies to be filled. Power of choosing officers, and of impeachment.

1. The House of Representatives shall be composed of members chosen every second year by the people of the several States, and

the electors in each State shall have the qualifications requisite for electors of the most numerous branch of the State Legislature.

2. No person shall be a Representative who shall not have attained to the age of twenty-five years, and been seven years a citizen of the United States, and who shall not, when elected, be an inhabitant of that State in which he shall be chosen.

3. *(Representatives and direct taxes shall be apportioned among the several States which may be included within this Union, according to their respective numbers, which shall be determined by adding to the whole number of free persons, including those bound to service for a term of years, and excluding Indians not taxed, three-fifths of all other persons.) (The previous sentence was superseded by Amendment XIV, section 2.)* The actual enumeration shall be made within three years after the first meeting of the Congress of the United States, and within every subsequent term of ten years, in such manner as they shall by law direct. The number of Representatives shall not exceed one for every thirty thousand, but each State shall have at least one Representative; and until such enumeration shall be made, the State of New Hampshire shall be entitled to choose three, Massachusetts eight, Rhode Island and Providence Plantations one, Connecticut five, New York six, New Jersey four, Pennsylvania eight, Delaware one, Maryland six, Virginia ten, North Carolina five, South Carolina five, and Georgia three.

4. When vacancies happen in the representation from any State, the Executive Authority thereof shall issue writs of election to fill such vacancies.

5. The House of Representatives shall choose their Speaker and other officers; and shall have the sole power of impeachment.

Section 3—Senators, how and by whom chosen. How classified. Qualifications of a Senator. President of the Senate, his right to vote. President pro tem., and other officers of the Senate, how chosen. Power to try impeachments. When President is tried, Chief Justice to preside. Sentence.

1. The Senate of the United States shall be composed of two Senators from each State, *(chosen by the Legislature thereof), (The preceding five words were superseded by Amendment XVII, section 1.)* for six years; and each Senator shall have one vote.

2. Immediately after they shall be assembled in consequence of the first election, they shall be divided as equally as may be into three classes. The seats of the Senators of the first class shall be vacated at the expiration of the second year, of the second class at the expiration of the fourth year, and of the third class at the expiration of the sixth year, so that one-third may be chosen every second year; *(and if vacancies happen by resignation, or otherwise, during the recess of the Legislature of any State, the Executive thereof may make temporary appointments until the next meeting of the Legislature, which shall then fill such vacancies.) (The words in parentheses were superseded by Amendment XVII, section 2.)*

3. No person shall be a Senator who shall not have attained to the age of thirty years, and been nine years a citizen of the United States, and who shall not, when elected, be an inhabitant of that State for which he shall be chosen.

4. The Vice President of the United States shall be President of the Senate, but shall have no vote, unless they be equally divided.

5. The Senate shall choose their other officers, and also a President pro tempore, in the absence of the Vice President, or when he shall exercise the office of President of the United States.

6. The Senate shall have the sole power to try all impeachments. When sitting for that purpose, they shall be on oath or affirmation. When the President of the United States is tried, the Chief Justice shall preside: and no person shall be convicted without the concurrence of two-thirds of the members present.

7. Judgment in cases of impeachment shall not extend further than to removal from office, and disqualification to hold and enjoy any office of honor, trust or profit under the United States: but the party convicted shall nevertheless be liable and subject to indictment, trial, judgment and punishment, according to law.

Section 4—Times, etc., of holding elections, how prescribed. One session each year.

1. The times, places and manner of holding elections for Senators and Representatives, shall be prescribed in each State by the Legislature thereof; but the Congress may at any time by law make or alter such regulations, except as to the places of choosing Senators.

2. The Congress shall assemble at least once in every year, and such meeting shall *(be on the first Monday in December,) (The words in parentheses were superseded by Amendment XX, section 2).* unless they shall by law appoint a different day.

Section 5—Membership, quorum, adjournments, rules. Power to punish or expel. Journal. Time of adjournments, how limited, etc.

1. Each House shall be the judge of the elections, returns and qualifications of its own members, and a majority of each shall constitute a quorum to do business; but a smaller number may adjourn from day to day, and may be authorized to compel the attendance of absent members, in such manner, and under such penalties as each House may provide.

2. Each House may determine the rules of its proceedings, punish its members for disorderly behavior, and, with the concurrence of two-thirds, expel a member.

3. Each House shall keep a journal of its proceedings, and from time to time publish the same, excepting such parts as may in their judgment require secrecy; and the yeas and nays of the members of either House on any question shall, at the desire of one-fifth of those present, be entered on the journal.

4. Neither House, during the session of Congress, shall, without the consent of the other, adjourn for more than three days, nor to any other place than that in which the two Houses shall be sitting.

Section 6—Compensation, privileges, disqualifications in certain cases.

1. The Senators and Representatives shall receive a compensation for their services, to be ascertained by law, and paid out of the Treasury of the United States. They shall in all cases, except treason, felony and breach of the peace, be privileged from arrest during their attendance at the session of their respective Houses, and in going to and returning from the same; and for any speech or debate in either House, they shall not be questioned in any other place.

2. No Senator or Representative shall, during the time for which he was elected, be appointed to any civil office under the authority of the United States, which shall have been created, or the emoluments whereof shall have been increased during such time; and no person holding any office under the United States, shall be a member of either House during his continuance in office.

Section 7—House to originate all revenue bills. Veto. Bill may be passed by two-thirds of each House, notwithstanding, etc. Bill, not returned in ten days, to become a law. Provisions as to orders, concurrent resolutions, etc.

1. All bills for raising revenue shall originate in the House of Representatives; but the Senate may propose or concur with amendments as on other bills.

2. Every bill which shall have passed the House of Representatives and the Senate, shall, before it becomes a law, be presented to the President of the United States; if he approves he shall sign it, but if not he shall return it, with his objections to that House in which it shall have originated, who shall enter the objections at large on their journal, and proceed to reconsider it. If after such reconsideration two-thirds of that House shall agree to pass the bill, it shall be sent, together with the objections, to the other House, by which it shall likewise be reconsidered, and if approved by two-thirds of that House, it shall become a law. But in all such cases the votes of both Houses shall be determined by yeas and nays, and the names of the persons voting for and against the bill shall be entered on the journal of each House respectively. If any bill shall not be returned by the President within ten days (Sundays excepted) after it shall have been presented to him, the same shall be a law, in like manner as if he had signed it, unless the Congress by their adjournment prevent its return, in which case it shall not be a law.

3. Every order, resolution, or vote to which the concurrence of the Senate and House of Representatives may be necessary (except on a question of adjournment) shall be presented to the President of the United States; and before the same shall take effect, shall be approved by him, or being disapproved by him, shall be repassed by two-thirds of the Senate and House of Representatives, according to the rules and limitations prescribed in the case of a bill.

Section 8—Powers of Congress.

The Congress shall have power

1. To lay and collect taxes, duties, imposts and excises, to pay the debts and provide for the common defense and general welfare of the United States; but all duties, imposts and excises shall be uniform throughout the United States;

2. To borrow money on the credit of the United States;

3. To regulate commerce with foreign nations, and among the several States, and with the Indian tribes;

4. To establish a uniform rule of naturalization, and uniform laws on the subject of bankruptcies throughout the United States;

5. To coin money, regulate the value thereof, and of foreign coin, and fix the standard of weights and measures;

6. To provide for the punishment of counterfeiting the securities and current coin of the United States;

7. To establish post-offices and post-roads;

8. To promote the progress of science and useful arts, by securing for limited times to authors and inventors the exclusive right to their respective writings and discoveries;

9. To constitute tribunals inferior to the Supreme Court;

10. To define and punish piracies and felonies committed on the high seas, and offenses against the law of nations;

11. To declare war, grant letters of marque and reprisal, and make rules concerning captures on land and water;

12. To raise and support armies, but no appropriation of money to that use shall be for a longer term than two years;

13. To provide and maintain a navy;

14. To make rules for the government and regulation of the land and naval forces;

15. To provide for calling forth the militia to execute the laws of the Union, suppress insurrections and repel invasions;

16. To provide for organizing, arming, and disciplining the militia, and for governing such part of them as may be employed in the service of the United States, reserving to the States respectively, the appointment of the officers, and the authority of training and militia according to the discipline prescribed by Congress;

17. To exercise exclusive legislation in all cases whatsoever, over such district (not exceeding ten miles square) as may, by cession of particular States, and the acceptance of Congress, become the seat of the Government of the United States, and to exercise like authority over all places purchased by the consent of the Legislature of the State in which the same shall be, for the erection of forts, magazines, arsenals, dockyards, and other needful buildings;—And

18. To make all laws which shall be necessary and proper for carrying into execution the foregoing powers, and all other powers vested by this Constitution in the Government of the United States, or in any department or officer thereof.

Section 9—Provision as to migration or importation of certain persons. Habeas corpus, bills of attainder, etc. Taxes, how apportioned. No export duty. No commercial preference. Money, how drawn from Treasury, etc. No titular nobility. Officers not to receive presents, etc.

1. The migration or importation of such persons as any of the States now existing shall think proper to admit, shall not be prohibited by the Congress prior to the year one thousand eight hundred and eight, but a tax or duty may be imposed on such importation, not exceeding ten dollars for each person.

2. The privilege of the writ of habeas corpus shall not be suspended, unless when in cases of rebellion or invasion the public safety may require it.

3. No bill of attainder or ex post facto law shall be passed.

4. No capitation, or other direct, tax shall be laid, unless in proportion to the census or enumeration herein before directed to be taken. *(Modified by Amendment XVI.)*

5. No tax or duty shall be laid on articles exported from any State.

6. No preference shall be given by any regulation of commerce or revenue to the ports of one State over those of another: nor shall vessels bound to, or from, one State, be obliged to enter, clear, or pay duties in another.

7. No money shall be drawn from the Treasury, but in consequence of appropriations made by law; and a regular statement and account of the receipts and expenditures of all public money shall be published from time to time.

8. No title of nobility shall be granted by the United States: and no person holding any office of profit or trust under them, shall, without the consent of the Congress, accept of any present, emolument, office, or title, of any kind whatever, from any king, prince, or foreign state.

Section 10—States prohibited from the exercise of certain powers.

1. No State shall enter into any treaty, alliance, or confederation; grant letters of marque and reprisal; coin money; emit bills of credit; make anything but gold and silver coin a tender in payment of debts; pass any bill of attainder, ex post facto law, or law im-

pairing the obligation of contracts, or grant any title of nobility.

2. No State shall, without the consent of the Congress, lay any imposts or duties on imports or exports, except what may be absolutely necessary for executing its inspection laws: and the net produce of all duties and imposts, laid by any State on imports or exports, shall be for the use of the Treasury of the United States; and all such laws shall be subject to the revision and control of the Congress.

3. No State shall, without the consent of Congress, lay any duty of tonnage, keep troops, or ships of war in time of peace, enter into any agreement or compact with another State, or with a foreign power, or engage in war, unless actually invaded, or in such imminent danger as will not admit of delay.

ARTICLE II.

Section 1—President: his term of office. Electors of President; number and how appointed. Electors to vote on same day. Qualification of President. On whom his duties devolve in case of his removal, death, etc. President's compensation. His oath of office.

1. The Executive power shall be vested in a President of the United States of America. He shall hold his office during the term of four years, and together with the Vice President, chosen for the same term, be elected as follows

2. Each State shall appoint, in such manner as the Legislature thereof may direct, a number of electors, equal to the whole number of Senators and Representatives to which the State may be entitled in the Congress: but no Senator or Representative, or person holding an office of trust or profit under the United States, shall be appointed an elector.

(The electors shall meet in their respective States, and vote by ballot for two persons, of whom one at least shall not be an inhabitant of the same State with themselves. And they shall make a list of all the persons voted for, and of the number of votes for each; which list they shall sign and certify, and transmit sealed to the seat of the Government of the United States, directed to the President of the Senate. The President of the Senate shall, in the presence of the Senate and House of Representatives, open all the certificates, and the votes shall then be counted. The person having the greatest number of votes shall be the President, if such number be a majority of the whole number of electors appointed; and if there be more than one who have such majority, and have an equal number of votes, then the House of Representatives shall immediately choose by ballot one of them for President; and if no person have a majority, then from the five highest on the list the said House shall in like manner choose the President. But in choosing the President, the votes shall be taken by States, the representation from each State having one vote; a quorum for this purpose shall consist of a member or members from two-thirds of the States, and a majority of all the States shall be necessary to a choice. In every case, after the choice of the President, the person having the greatest number of votes of the electors shall be the Vice President. But if there should remain two or more who have equal votes, the Senate shall choose from them by ballot the Vice President.)

(This clause was superseded by Amendment XII.)

3. The Congress may determine the time of choosing the electors, and the day on which they shall give their votes; which day shall be the same throughout the United States.

4. No person except a natural born citizen, or a citizen of the United States, at the time of the adoption of this Constitution, shall be eligible to the office of President; neither shall any person be eligible to that office who shall not have attained to the age of thirty-five years, and been fourteen years a resident within the United States.

(For qualification of the Vice President, see Amendment XII.)

5. In case of the removal of the President from office, or of his death, resignation, or inability to discharge the powers and duties of the said office, the same shall devolve on the Vice President, and the Congress may by law provide for the case of removal, death, resignation or inability, both of the President and Vice President, declaring what officer shall then act as President, and such officer shall act accordingly, until the disability be removed, or a President shall be elected.

(This clause has been modified by Amendments XX and XXV.)

6. The President shall, at stated times, receive for his services, a compensation, which shall neither be increased nor diminished during the period for which he shall have been elected, and he shall not receive within that period any other emolument from the United States, or any of them.

7. Before he enter on the execution of his

office, he shall take the following oath or affirmation:

"I do solemnly swear (or affirm) that I will faithfully execute the office of President of the United States, and will to the best of my ability, preserve, protect and defend the Constitution of the United States."

Section 2—President to be Commander-in-Chief. He may require opinions of cabinet officers, etc., may pardon. Treaty-making power. Nomination of certain officers. When President may fill vacancies.

1. The President shall be Commander-in-Chief of the Army and Navy of the United States, and of the militia of the several States, when called into the actual service of the United States; he may require the opinion, in writing, of the principal officer in each of the executive departments, upon any subject relating to the duties of their respective offices, and he shall have power to grant reprieves and pardons for offenses against the United States, except in cases of impeachment.

2. He shall have power, by and with the advice and consent of the Senate, to make treaties, provided two-thirds of the Senators present concur; and he shall nominate, and by and with the advice and consent of the Senate, shall appoint ambassadors, other public ministers and consuls, judges of the Supreme Court, and all other officers of the United States, whose appointments are not herein otherwise provided for, and which shall be established by law: but the Congress may by law vest the appointment of such inferior officers, as they think proper, in the President alone, in the courts of law, or in the heads of departments.

3. The President shall have power to fill up all vacancies that may happen during the recess of the Senate, by granting commissions, which shall expire at the end of their next session.

Section 3—President shall communicate to Congress. He may convene and adjourn Congress, in case of disagreement, etc. Shall receive ambassadors, execute laws, and commission officers.

He shall from time to time give to the Congress information of the state of the Union, and recommend to their consideration such measures as he shall judge necessary and expedient; he may, on extraordinary occasions, convene both Houses, or either of them, and in case of disagreement between them, with respect to the time of adjournment, he may adjourn them to such time as he shall think proper; he shall receive ambassadors and other public ministers; he shall take care that the laws be faithfully executed, and shall commission all the officers of the United States.

Section 4—All civil offices forfeited for certain crimes.

The President, Vice President, and all civil officers of the United States, shall be removed from office on impeachment for, and conviction of, treason, bribery, or other high crimes and misdemeanors.

ARTICLE III.

Section 1—Judicial powers. Tenure. Compensation.

The judicial power of the United States, shall be vested in one Supreme Court, and in such inferior courts as the Congress may from time to time ordain and establish. The judges, both of the Supreme and inferior courts, shall hold their offices during good behavior, and shall at stated times, receive for their services a compensation, which shall not be diminished during their continuance in office.

Section 2—Judicial power; to what cases it extends. Original jurisdiction of Supreme Court; appellate jurisdiction. Trial by jury, etc. Trial, where.

1. The judicial power shall extend to all cases, in law and equity, arising under this Constitution, the laws of the United States, and treaties made, or which shall be made, under their authority; to all cases affecting ambassadors, other public ministers and consuls; to all cases of admiralty and maritime jurisdiction; to controversies to which the United States shall be a party; to controversies between two or more States; between a State and citizens of another State; between citizens of different States, between citizens of the same State claiming lands under grants of different States, and between a State, or the citizens thereof, and foreign states, citizens or subjects.

(This section is modified by Amendment XI.)

2. In all cases affecting ambassadors, other public ministers and consuls, and those in which a State shall be party, the Supreme Court shall have original jurisdiction. In all the other cases before mentioned, the Supreme Court shall have appellate jurisdiction, both as to law and fact, with such exceptions, and under such regulations as the Congress shall make.

3. The trial of all crimes, except in cases of impeachment, shall be by jury; and such trial shall be held in the State where the said crimes shall have been committed; but when not committed within any State, the trial shall be at such place or places as the Congress may by law have directed.

Section 3—Treason Defined, Proof of, Punishment of.

1. Treason against the United States, shall consist only in levying war against them, or in adhering to their enemies, giving them aid and comfort. No person shall be convicted of treason unless on the testimony of two witnesses to the same overt act, or on confession in open court.

2. The Congress shall have power to declare the punishment of treason, but no attainder of treason shall work corruption of blood, or forfeiture except during the life of the person attainted.

ARTICLE IV.

Section 1—Each State to give credit to the public acts, etc., of every other State.

Full faith and credit shall be given in each State to the public acts, records, and judicial proceedings of every other State. And the Congress may by general laws prescribe the manner in which such acts, records and proceedings shall be proved, and the effect thereof.

Section 2—Privileges of citizens of each State. Fugitives from justice to be delivered up. Persons held to service having escaped, to be delivered up.

1. The citizens of each State shall be entitled to all privileges and immunities of citizens in the several States.

2. A person charged in any State with treason, felony, or other crime, who shall flee from justice, and be found in another State, shall on demand of the Executive authority of the State from which he fled, be delivered up, to be removed to the State having jurisdiction of the crime.

(3. No person held to service or labor in one State, under the laws thereof, escaping into another, shall in consequence of any law or regulation therein, be discharged from such service or labor, but shall be delivered up on claim of the party to whom such service or labor may be due.) (This clause was superseded by Amendment XIII.)

Section 3—Admission of new States. Power of Congress over territory and other property.

1. New States may be admitted by the Congress into this Union; but no new State shall be formed or erected within the jurisdiction of any other State; nor any State be formed by the junction of two or more States, or parts of States, without the consent of the Legislatures of the States concerned as well as of the Congress.

2. The Congress shall have power to dispose of and make all needful rules and regulations respecting the territory or other property belonging to the United States; and nothing in this Constitution shall be so construed as to prejudice any claims of the United States, or of any particular State.

Section 4—Republican form of government guaranteed. Each state to be protected.

The United States shall guarantee to every State in this Union a Republican form of government, and shall protect each of them against invasion; and on application of the Legislature, or of the Executive (when the Legislature cannot be convened) against domestic violence.

ARTICLE V.

Constitution: how amended; proviso.

The Congress, whenever two-thirds of both Houses shall deem it necessary, shall propose amendments to this Constitution, or, on the application of the Legislatures of two-thirds of the several States, shall call a convention for proposing amendments, which, in either case, shall be valid to all intents and purposes, as part of this Constitution, when ratified by the Legislatures of three-fourths of the several States, or by conventions in three-fourths thereof, as the one or the other mode of ratification may be proposed by the Congress; provided that no amendment which may be made prior to the year one thousand eight hundred and eight shall in any manner affect the first and fourth clauses in the Ninth Section of the First Article; and that no State, without its consent, shall be deprived of its equal suffrage in the Senate.

ARTICLE VI.

Certain debts, etc., declared valid. Supremacy of Constitution, treaties, and laws of the United States. Oath to support Constitution, by whom taken. No religious test.

1. All debts contracted and engagements entered into, before the adoption of this Constitution, shall be as valid against the United

States under this Constitution, as under the Confederation.

2. This Constitution, and the laws of the United States which shall be made in pursuance thereof; and all treaties made, or which shall be made, under the authority of the United States, shall be the supreme law of the land; and the judges in every State shall be bound thereby, any thing in the Constitution or laws of any State to the contrary notwithstanding.

3. The Senators and Representatives before mentioned, and the members of the several State Legislatures, and all executive and judicial officers, both of the United States and of the several States, shall be bound by oath or affirmation, to support this Constitution; but no religious test shall ever be required as a qualification to any office or public trust under the United States.

ARTICLE VII.

What ratification shall establish Constitution.

The ratification of the Conventions of nine States, shall be sufficient for the establishment of this Constitution between the States so ratifying the same.

Done in convention by the unanimous consent of the States present the Seventeenth day of September in the year of our Lord one thousand seven hundred and eighty seven, and of the independence of the United States of America the Twelfth. In witness whereof we have hereunto subscribed our names.

George Washington, President and deputy from Virginia.

New Hampshire—John Langdon, Nicholas Gilman.

Massachusetts—Nathaniel Gorham, Rufus King.

Connecticut—Wm. Saml. Johnson, Roger Sherman.

New York—Alexander Hamilton.

New Jersey—Wil: Livingston, David Brearley, Wm. Paterson, Jona: Dayton.

Pennsylvania—B. Franklin, Thomas Mifflin, Robt. Morris, Geo. Clymer, Thos. FitzSimons, Jared Ingersoll, James Wilson, Gouv. Morris.

Delaware—Geo: Read, Gunning Bedford Jun., John Dickinson, Richard Bassett, Jaco: Broom.

Maryland—James McHenry, Daniel of Saint Thomas' Jenifer, Danl. Carroll.

Virginia—John Blair, James Madison Jr.

North Carolina—Wm. Blount, Rich'd. Dobbs Spaight, Hugh Williamson.

South Carolina—J. Rutledge, Charles Cotesworth Pinckney, Charles Pinckney, Pierce Butler.

Georgia—William Few, Abr. Baldwin.

Attest: William Jackson, Secretary.

TEN ORIGINAL AMENDMENTS
THE BILL OF RIGHTS

In force Dec. 15, 1791

(The First Congress, at its first session in the City of New York, Sept. 25, 1789, submitted to the states 12 amendments to clarify certain individual and state rights not named in the Constitution. They are generally called the Bill of Rights.

(Influential in framing these amendments was the Declaration of Rights of Virginia, written by George Mason (1725–1792) in 1776. Mason, a Virginia delegate to the Constitutional Convention, did not sign the Constitution and opposed its ratification on the ground that it did not sufficiently oppose slavery or safeguard individual rights.

(In the preamble to the resolution offering the proposed amendments, Congress said: "The conventions of a number of the States having at the time of their adopting the Constitution, expressed a desire, in order to prevent misconstruction or abuse of its powers, that further declaratory and restrictive clauses should be added, and as extending the ground of public confidence in the government will best insure the beneficent ends of its institution, be it resolved," etc.

(Ten of these amendments now commonly known as one to 10 inclusive, but originally 3 to 12 inclusive, were ratified by the states as follows: New Jersey, Nov. 20, 1789; Maryland, Dec. 19, 1789; North Carolina, Dec. 22, 1789; South Carolina, Jan. 19, 1790; New Hampshire, Jan. 25, 1790; Delaware, Jan. 28, 1790; New York, Feb. 24, 1790; Pennsylvania, Mar. 10, 1790; Rhode Island, June 7, 1790; Vermont, Nov. 3, 1791; Virginia, Dec. 15, 1791; Massachusetts, Mar. 2, 1939; Georgia, Mar. 18, 1939; Connecticut, Apr. 19, 1939. These original 10 ratified amendments follow as Amendments I to X inclusive.

(Of the two original proposed amendments which were not ratified by the necessary number of states, the first related to apportionment of Representatives; the second, to compensation of members.)

AMENDMENT I.

Religious establishment prohibited. Freedom of speech, of the press, and right to petition.

Congress shall make no law respecting an establishment of religion, or prohibiting the free exercise thereof; or abridging the freedom of speech, or of the press; or the right of the people peaceably to assemble, and to petition the Government for a redress of grievances.

AMENDMENT II.

Right to keep and bear arms.

A well-regulated militia, being necessary to the security of a free State, the right of the people to keep and bear arms, shall not be infringed.

AMENDMENT III.

Conditions for quarters for soldiers.

No soldier shall, in time of peace be quartered in any house, without the consent of the owner, nor in time of war, but in a manner to be prescribed by law.

AMENDMENT IV.

Right of search and seizure regulated.

The right of the people to be secure in their persons, houses, papers, and effects, against unreasonable searches and seizures, shall not be violated, and no warrants shall issue, but upon probable cause, supported by oath or affirmation, and particularly describing the place to be searched, and the persons or things to be seized.

AMENDMENT V.

Provisions concerning prosecution. Trial and punishment—private property not to be taken for public use without compensation.

No person shall be held to answer for a capital, or otherwise infamous crime, unless on a presentment or indictment of a Grand Jury, except in cases arising in the land or naval forces, or in the militia, when in actual service in time of war or public danger; nor shall any person be subject for the same offense to be twice put in jeopardy of life or limb; nor shall be compelled in any criminal case to be a witness against himself, nor be deprived of life, liberty, or property, without due process of law; nor shall private property be taken for public use without just compensation.

AMENDMENT VI.

Right to speedy trial, witnesses, etc.

In all criminal prosecutions, the accused shall enjoy the right to a speedy and public trial, by an impartial jury of the State and district wherein the crime shall have been committed, which district shall have been previously ascertained by law, and to be informed of the nature and cause of the accusation; to be confronted with the witnesses against him; to have compulsory process for obtaining witnesses in his favor, and to have the assistance of counsel for his defense.

AMENDMENT VII.

Right of trial by jury.

In suits at common law, where the value in controversy shall exceed twenty dollars, the right of trial by jury shall be preserved, and no fact tried by a jury shall be otherwise re-examined in any court of the United States, than according to the rules of the common law.

AMENDMENT VIII.

Excessive bail or fines and cruel punishment prohibited.

Excessive bail shall not be required, nor excessive fines imposed, nor cruel and unusual punishments inflicted.

AMENDMENT IX.

Rule of construction of Constitution.

The enumeration in the Constitution, of certain rights, shall not be construed to deny or disparage others retained by the people.

AMENDMENT X.

Rights of States under Constitution.

The powers not delegated to the United States by the Constitution, nor prohibited by it to the States, are reserved to the States respectively, or to the people.

AMENDMENTS SINCE THE BILL OF RIGHTS

AMENDMENT XI.

Judicial powers construed.

The judicial power of the United States shall not be construed to extend to any suit in law or equity, commenced or prosecuted against one of the United States by citizens of another State, or by citizens or subjects of any foreign state.

(This amendment was proposed to the Legislatures of the several States by the Third

Congress on March 4, 1794, and was declared to have been ratified in a message from the President to Congress, dated Jan. 8, 1798.

(It was on Jan. 5, 1798, that Secretary of State Pickering received from 12 of the States authenticated ratifications, and informed President John Adams of that fact.

(As a result of later research in the Department of State, it is now established that Amendment XI became part of the Constitution on Feb. 7, 1795, for on that date it had been ratified by 12 States as follows:

(1. New York, Mar. 27, 1794. 2. Rhode Island, Mar. 31, 1794. 3. Connecticut, May 8, 1794. 4. New Hampshire, June 16, 1794. 5. Massachusetts, June 26, 1794. 6. Vermont, between Oct. 9, 1794, and Nov. 9, 1794. 7. Virginia, Nov. 18, 1794. 8. Georgia, Nov. 29, 1794. 9. Kentucky, Dec. 7, 1794. 10. Maryland, Dec. 26, 1794. 11. Delaware, Jan. 23, 1795. 12. North Carolina, Feb. 7, 1795.

(On June 1, 1796, more than a year after Amendment XI had become a part of the Constitution (but before anyone was officially aware of this), Tennessee had been admitted as a State; but not until Oct. 16, 1797, was a certified copy of the resolution of Congress proposing the amendment sent to the Governor of Tennessee (John Sevier) by Secretary of State Pickering, whose office was then at Trenton, New Jersey, because of the epidemic of yellow fever at Philadelphia; it seems, however, that the Legislature of Tennessee took no action on Amendment XI, owing doubtless to the fact that public announcement of its adoption was made soon thereafter.

(Besides the necessary 12 States, one other, South Carolina, ratified Amendment XI, but this action was not taken until Dec. 4, 1797; the two remaining States, New Jersey and Pennsylvania, failed to ratify.

AMENDMENT XII.

Manner of choosing President and Vice-President.

(Proposed by Congress Dec. 9, 1803; ratification completed June 15, 1804.)

The Electors shall meet in their respective States and vote by ballot for President and Vice-President, one of whom, at least, shall not be an inhabitant of the same State with themselves; they shall name in their ballots the person voted for as President, and in distinct ballots the person voted for as Vice-President, and they shall make distinct lists of all persons voted for as President, and of all persons voted for as Vice-President, and of the number of votes for each, which lists they shall sign and certify, and transmit sealed to the seat of the Government of the United States, directed to the President of the Senate; the President of the Senate shall, in the presence of the Senate and House of Representatives, open all the certificates and the votes shall then be counted;—The person having the greatest number of votes for President, shall be the President, if such number be a majority of the whole number of Electors appointed; and if no person have such majority, then from the persons having the highest numbers not exceeding three on the list of those voted for as President, the House of Representatives shall choose immediately, by ballot, the President. But in choosing the President, the votes shall be taken by States, the representation from each State having one vote; a quorum for this purpose shall consist of a member or members from two-thirds of the States, and a majority of all the States shall be necessary to a choice. *(And if the House of Representatives shall not choose a President whenever the right of choice shall devolve upon them, before the fourth day of March next following, then the Vice-President shall act as President, as in the case of the death or other constitutional disability of the President.) (The words in parentheses were superseded by Amendment XX, section 3.)* The person having the greatest number of votes as Vice-President, shall be the Vice-President, if such number be a majority of the whole number of Electors appointed, and if no person have a majority, then from the two highest numbers on the list, the Senate shall choose the Vice-President; a quorum for the purpose shall consist of two-thirds of the whole number of Senators, and a majority of the whole number shall be necessary to a choice. But no person constitutionally ineligible to the office of President shall be eligible to that of Vice-President of the United States.

THE RECONSTRUCTION AMENDMENTS

(Amendments XIII, XIV, and XV are commonly known as the Reconstruction Amendments, inasmuch as they followed the Civil War, and were drafted by Republicans who were bent on

imposing their own policy of reconstruction on the South. Post-bellum legislatures there—Mississippi, South Carolina, Georgia, for example—had set up laws which, it was charged, were contrived to perpetuate Negro slavery under other names.)

AMENDMENT XIII.

Slavery abolished.

(Proposed by Congress Jan. 31, 1865; ratification completed Dec. 18, 1865. The amendment, when first proposed by a resolution in Congress, was passed by the Senate, 38 to 6, on Apr. 8, 1864, but was defeated in the House, 95 to 66 on June 15, 1864. On reconsideration by the House, on Jan. 31, 1865, the resolution passed, 119 to 56. It was approved by President Lincoln on Feb. 1, 1865, although the Supreme Court had decided in 1798 that the President has nothing to do with the proposing of amendments to the Constitution, or their adoption.)

1. Neither slavery nor involuntary servitude, except as a punishment for crime whereof the party shall have been duly convicted, shall exist within the United States or any place subject to their jurisdiction.

2. Congress shall have power to enforce this article by appropriate legislation.

AMENDMENT XIV.

Citizenship rights not to be abridged.

(The following amendment was proposed to the Legislatures of the several states by the 39th Congress, June 13, 1866, and was declared to have been ratified in a proclamation by the Secretary of State, July 28, 1868.

(The 14th amendment was adopted only by virtue of ratification subsequent to earlier rejections. Newly constituted legislatures in both North Carolina and South Carolina (respectively July 4 and 9, 1868), ratified the proposed amendment, although earlier legislatures had rejected the proposal. The Secretary of State issued a proclamation, which, though doubtful as to the effect of attempted withdrawals by Ohio and New Jersey, entertained no doubt as to the validity of the ratification by North and South Carolina. The following day (July 21, 1868), Congress passed a resolution which declared the 14th Amendment to be a part of the Constitution and directed the Secretary of State so to promulgate it. The Secretary waited, however, until the newly constituted Legislature of Georgia had ratified the amendment, subsequent to an earlier rejection, before the promulgation of the ratification of the new amendment.)

1. All persons born or naturalized in the United States, and subject to the jurisdiction thereof, are citizens of the United States and of the State wherein they reside. No State shall make or enforce any law which shall abridge the privileges or immunities of citizens of the United States; nor shall any State deprive any person of life, liberty, or property, without due process of law; nor deny to any person within its jurisdiction the equal protection of the laws.

2. Representatives shall be apportioned among the several States according to their respective numbers, counting the whole number of persons in each State, excluding Indians not taxed. But when the right to vote at any election for the choice of Electors for President and Vice-President of the United States, Representatives in Congress, the executive and judicial officers of a State, or the members of the Legislature thereof, is denied to any of the male inhabitants of such State, being twenty-one years of age, and, citizens of the United States, or in any way abridged, except for participation in rebellion, or other crime, the basis of representation therein shall be reduced in the proportion which the number of such male citizens shall bear to the whole number of male citizens twenty-one years of age in such State.

3. No person shall be a Senator or Representative in Congress, or Elector of President and Vice-President, or hold any office, civil or military, under the United States, or under any State, who, having previously taken an oath, as a member of Congress, or as an officer of the United States, or as a member of any State Legislature, or as an executive or judicial officer of any State, to support the Constitution of the United States, shall have engaged in insurrection or rebellion against the same, or given aid or comfort to the enemies thereof. But Congress may by a vote of two-thirds of each House, remove such disability.

4. The validity of the public debt of the United States, authorized by law, including debts incurred for payment of pensions and bounties for services in suppressing insurrection or rebellion, shall not be questioned. But neither the United States nor any State shall assume or pay any debt or obligation incurred in aid of insurrection or rebellion against the United States, or any claim for the loss or emancipation of any slave; but all such debts, obligations and claims shall be held illegal and void.

5. The Congress shall have power to enforce, by appropriate legislation, the provisions of this article.

AMENDMENT XV.

Race no bar to voting rights.

(The following amendment was proposed to the legislatures of the several States by the 40th Congress, Feb. 26, 1869, and was declared to have been ratified in a proclamation by the Secretary of State, Mar. 30, 1870.)

1. The right of citizens of the United States to vote shall not be denied or abridged by the United States or by any State on account of race, color, or previous condition of servitude.

2. The Congress shall have power to enforce this article by appropriate legislation.

AMENDMENT XVI.

Income taxes authorized.

(Proposed by Congress July 12, 1909; ratification declared by the Secretary of State Feb. 25, 1913.)

The Congress shall have power to lay and collect taxes on incomes, from whatever source derived, without apportionment among the several States, and without regard to any census or enumeration.

AMENDMENT XVII.

United States Senators to be elected by direct popular vote.

(Proposed by Congress May 13, 1912; ratification declared by the Secretary of State May 31, 1913.)

1. The Senate of the United States shall be composed of two Senators from each State, elected by the people thereof, for six years; and each Senator shall have one vote. The electors in each State shall have the qualifications requisite for electors of the most numerous branch of the State Legislatures.

2. When vacancies happen in the representation of any State in the Senate, the executive authority of such State shall issue writs of election to fill such vacancies: Provided, That the Legislature of any State may empower the Executive thereof to make temporary appointments until the people fill the vacancies by election as the Legislature may direct.

3. This amendment shall not be so construed as to affect the election or term of any Senator chosen before it becomes valid as part of the Constitution.

AMENDMENT XVIII.

Liquor prohibition amendment.

(Proposed by Congress Dec. 18, 1917; ratification completed Jan. 16, 1919. Repealed by Amendment XXI, effective Dec. 5, 1933.)

(1. After one year from the ratification of this article the manufacture, sale, or transportation of intoxicating liquors within, the importation thereof into, or the exportation thereof from the United States and all territory subject to the jurisdiction thereof for beverage purposes is hereby prohibited.

(2. The Congress and the several States shall have concurrent power to enforce this article by appropriate legislation.

(3. This article shall be inoperative unless it shall have been ratified as an amendment to the Constitution by the Legislatures of the several States, as provided in the Constitution, within seven years from the date of the submission hereof to the States by the Congress.)

(The total vote in the Senates of the various States was 1,310 for, 237 against—84.6% dry. In the lower houses of the States the vote was 3,782 for, 1,035 against—78.5% dry.

(The amendment ultimately was adopted by all the States except Connecticut and Rhode Island.)

AMENDMENT XIX.

Giving nationwide suffrage to women.

(Proposed by Congress June 4, 1919; ratification certified by Secretary of State Aug. 26, 1920.)

1. The right of citizens of the United States to vote shall not be denied or abridged by the United States or by any State on account of sex.

2. Congress shall have power to enforce this Article by appropriate legislation.

AMENDMENT XX.

Terms of President and Vice President to begin on Jan. 20; those of Senators, Representatives, Jan. 3.

(Proposed by Congress Mar. 2, 1932; ratification completed Jan. 23, 1933.)

1. The terms of the President and Vice President shall end at noon on the 20th day of January, and the terms of Senators and Representatives at noon on the 3rd day of January, of the years in which such terms would have ended if this article had not been ratified; and the terms of their successors shall then begin.

2. The Congress shall assemble at least once in every year, and such meeting shall begin at noon on the 3rd day of January, unless they shall by law appoint a different day.

3. If, at the time fixed for the beginning of

the term of the President, the President elect shall have died, the Vice President elect shall become President. If a President shall not have been chosen before the time fixed for the beginning of his term, or if the President elect shall have failed to qualify, then the Vice President elect shall act as President until a President shall have qualified; and the Congress may by law provide for the case wherein neither a President elect nor a Vice President elect shall have qualified, declaring who shall then act as President, or the manner in which one who is to act shall be selected, and such person shall act accordingly until a President or Vice President shall have qualified.

4. The Congress may by law provide for the case of the death of any of the persons from whom the House of Representatives may choose a President whenever the right of choice shall have devolved upon them, and for the case of the death of any of the persons from whom the Senate may choose a Vice President whenever the right of choice shall have devolved upon them.

5. Sections 1 and 2 shall take effect on the 15th day of October following the ratification of this article (Oct., 1933).

6. This article shall be inoperative unless it shall have been ratified as an amendment to the Constitution by the Legislatures of three-fourths of the several States within seven years from the date of its submission.

AMENDMENT XXI.

Repeal of Amendment XVIII.

(Proposed by Congress Feb. 20, 1933; ratification completed Dec. 5, 1933.)

1. The eighteenth article of amendment to the Constitution of the United States is hereby repealed.

2. The transportation or importation into any State, Territory, or Possession of the United States for delivery or use therein of intoxicating liquors, in violation of the laws thereof, is hereby prohibited.

3. This article shall be inoperative unless it shall have been ratified as an amendment to the Constitution by conventions in the several States, as provided in the Constitution, within seven years from the date of the submission hereof to the States by the Congress.

AMENDMENT XXII.

Limiting Presidential terms of office.

(Proposed by Congress Mar. 24, 1947; ratification completed Feb. 27, 1951.)

1. No person shall be elected to the office of the President more than twice, and no person who has held the office of President, or acted as President, for more than two years of a term to which some other person was elected President shall be elected to the office of the President more than once. But this Article shall not apply to any person holding the office of President when this Article was proposed by the Congress, and shall not prevent any person who may be holding the office of President, or acting as President, during the term within which this Article becomes operative from holding the office of President or acting as President during the remainder of such term.

2. This article shall be inoperative unless it shall have been ratified as an amendment to the Constitution by the Legislatures of three-fourths of the several States within seven years from the date of its submission to the States by the Congress.

AMENDMENT XXIII.

Presidential vote for District of Columbia.

(Proposed by Congress June 16, 1960; ratification completed Mar. 29, 1961.)

1. The District constituting the seat of Government of the United States shall appoint in such manner as the Congress may direct:

A number of electors of President and Vice President equal to the whole number of Senators and Representatives in Congress to which the District would be entitled if it were a State, but in no event more than the least populous State; they shall be in addition to those appointed by the States, but they shall be considered, for the purposes of the election of President and Vice President, to be electors appointed by a State; and they shall meet in the District and perform such duties as provided by the twelfth article of amendment.

2. The Congress shall have power to enforce this article by appropriate legislation.

AMENDMENT XXIV.

Barring poll tax in federal elections.

(Proposed by Congress Aug. 27, 1962; ratification completed Jan. 23, 1964.)

1. The right of citizens of the United States to vote in any primary or other election for President or Vice President, for electors for President or Vice President, or for Senator or Representative in Congress, shall not be denied or abridged by the United States or any State by reason of failure to pay any poll tax or other tax.

2. The Congress shall have power to enforce this article by appropriate legislation.

AMENDMENT XXV.

Presidential disability and succession.

(Proposed by Congress July 6, 1965; ratification completed Feb. 10, 1967.)

1. In case of the removal of the President from office or of his death or resignation, the Vice President shall become President.

2. Whenever there is a vacancy in the office of the Vice President, the President shall nominate a Vice President who shall take office upon confirmation by a majority vote of both houses of Congress.

3. Whenever the President transmits to the President pro tempore of the Senate and the Speaker of the House of Representatives his written declaration that he is unable to discharge the powers and duties of his office, and until he transmits to them a written declaration to the contrary, such powers and duties shall be discharged by the Vice President as Acting President.

4. Whenever the Vice President and a majority of either the principal officers of the executive departments or of such other body as Congress may by law provide, transmit to the President pro tempore of the Senate and the Speaker of the House of Representatives their written declaration that the President is unable to discharge the powers and duties of his office, the Vice President shall immediately assume the powers and duties of the office as Acting President.

Thereafter, when the President transmits to the President pro tempore of the Senate and the Speaker of the House of Representatives his written declaration that no inability exists, he shall resume the powers and duties of his office unless the Vice President and a majority of either the principal officers of the executive department or of such other body as Congress may by law provide, transmit within four days to the President pro tempore of the Senate and the Speaker of the House of Representatives their written declaration that the President is unable to discharge the powers and duties of his office. Thereupon Congress shall decide the issue, assembling within forty-eight hours for that purpose if not in session. If the Congress, within twenty-one days after receipt of the latter written declaration, or, if Congress is not in session, within twenty-one days after Congress is required to assemble, determines by two-thirds vote of both houses that the President is unable to discharge the powers and duties of his office, the Vice President shall continue to discharge the same as Acting President; otherwise, the President shall resume the powers and duties of his office.

AMENDMENT XXVI.

Lowering voting age to 18 years.

(Proposed by Congress Mar. 8, 1971; ratification completed July 1, 1971.)

1. The right of citizens of the United States, who are 18 years of age or older, to vote shall not be denied or abridged by the United States or any state on account of age.

2. The Congress shall have the power to enforce this article by appropriate legislation.

PROPOSED EQUAL RIGHTS AMENDMENT

(Proposed by Congress Mar. 22, 1972; ratified, as of mid-1980, by 35 states: 5 voted later to rescind their approval. Total of 38 needed for approval before deadline, originally Mar. 22, 1979; extended to June 30, 1982, by Senate action Oct. 6, 1978.)

1. Equality of rights under the law shall not be denied or abridged by the United States or by any State on account of sex.

2. The Congress shall have the power to enforce, by appropriate legislation, the provisions of this article.

3. This amendment shall take effect two years after the date of ratification.

PROPOSED D.C. REPRESENTATION AMENDMENT

(Proposed by Congress Aug. 22, 1978; ratified, as of mid-1980, by 8 states.)

1. For purposes of representation in the Congress, election of the President and Vice President, and article V of this Constitution, the District constituting the seat of government of the United States shall be treated as though it were a State.

2. The exercise of the rights and powers conferred under this article shall be by the people of the District constituting the seat of government, and as shall be provided by the Congress.

3. The twenty-third article of amendment to the Constitution of the United States is hereby repealed.

4. This article shall be inoperative, unless it shall have been ratified as an amendment to the Constitution by the legislatures of three-fourths of the several States within seven years from the date of its submission.

FEDERAL ESTATE AND GIFT TAX

As a result of sweeping changes introduced by the Tax Reform Act of 1976, the federal government now taxes estates and gifts on an entirely different basis than previously applied. The major changes include the unification of estate and gift rates, the substitution of a unified credit for the previous estate and gift tax exemptions, and a new tax on generation-skipping.

ESTATE TAX

Instead of the specific exemptions which were subtracted from the total estate (previously $60,000) or the lifetime gift total (previously $30,000), the new law provides for a unified credit against combined estate and gift taxes. For estates of decedents who die in 1977, the unified credit is $30,000; in 1978, $34,000; in 1979, $38,000; in 1980, $42,500; in 1981 and thereafter $47,000. The 1977 credit is in general equivalent to an exemption of $120,660; by 1981, to $175,625.

Estate taxes are computed by applying the unified rate schedule, shown below, to the total estate (minus allowable deductions) plus taxable gifts made after 1976. Gift taxes paid are subtracted from tax due, and credit also may be taken for state death taxes. The amount of the state tax credit is determined by the schedule shown in the table below or the actual state taxes paid, whichever is less. No state tax credit is available to an adjusted taxable estate (i.e., taxable estate minus $60,000) smaller than $40,000.

Deductions may be taken from the gross estate for funeral expenses, administration expenses, debts, charitable contributions, and, within limitations, bequests to the surviving spouse. A special deduction is allowed for estates passing to orphans, up to $5,000 per child multiplied by the number of years by which 21 exceeds the child's age. For instance, two orphaned children aged 7 and 9 would be entitled to a deduction of $130,000.

The marital deduction for small and medium-sized estates is increased to the larger of 50 percent of the adjusted gross estate or $250,000. A fractional interest rule eliminates the previous requirement for a consideration-furnished test. In general, each spouse's interest will be one-half, where property is jointly held with rights of survivorship and joint tenancy is created by a transfer subject to gift tax provisions.

The new law provides for real property passed on to family members for use in a closely held business, such as farming, to be valued on basis of such use, rather than fair market value on basis of highest and best use. In no case may this special valuation reduce the gross estate by more than $500,000.

Generation-skipping transfers which occur after April 30, 1976, in general are now subject to taxes substantially equivalent to those which would have been imposed had the property been transferred outright to each successive generation. However, an exclusion is provided for transfers to grandchildren up to $250,000 for each child of the decedent who serves as a conduit for the transfer (not for each grandchild).

A return must be filed for the estate of every U.S. citizen or resident whose gross estate exceeds $120,000 ($60,000 if the decedent dies before 1977; $36,000 for the estate of a nonresident not a citzen). The return is due nine months after death unless an extension is granted.

GIFT TAX

Any citizen or resident alien whose gifts to any one person exceed $3,000 within a calendar year will be liable for payment of a gift tax, at rates determined under the unified estate and gift tax schedule. Gift tax returns are filed on a quarterly basis and ordinarily are due a month and a half following any quarter in which a taxable gift was made (i.e., May 15, August 15, November 15, and February 15). After 1976, however, quarterly filing is not required until cumulative taxable gifts during the year exceed $25,000.

Gifts made by husband and wife to a third party may be considered as having been made one-half by each, provided both spouses consent to such division. For gifts between spouses, there is an unlimited deduction for the first $100,000 of lifetime gifts.

Unified Rate Schedule for Estate and Gift Tax

If the amount with respect to which the tentative tax to be computed is:			The tentative tax is:	
Not over $10,000			18 percent of such amount.	
Over $10,000	but not over	$20,000	$1,800, plus 20%	of the excess over $10,000
Over $20,000		$40,000	$3,800, plus 22%	$20,000

Over $40,000	$60,000	$8,200, plus 24%	$40,000
Over $60,000	$80,000	$13,000, plus 26%	$60,000
Over $80,000	$100,000	$18,200, plus 28%	$80,000
Over $100,000	$150,000	$23,800, plus 30%	$100,000
Over $150,000	$250,000	$38,800, plus 32%	$150,000
Over $250,000	$500,000	$70,800, plus 34%	$250,000
Over $500,000	$750,000	$155,800, plus 37%	$500,000
Over $750,000	$1,000,000	$248,300, plus 39%	$750,000
Over $1,000,000	$1,250,000	$345,800, plus 41%	$1,000,000
Over $1,250,000	$1,500,000	$448,300, plus 43%	$1,250,000
Over $1,500,000	$2,000,000	$555,800, plus 45%	$1,500,000
Over $2,000,000	$2,500,000	$780,800, plus 49%	$2,000,000
Over $2,500,000	$3,000,000	$1,025,800, plus 53%	$2,500,000
Over $3,000,000	$3,500,000	$1,290,800, plus 57%	$3,000,000
Over $3,500,000	$4,000,000	$1,575,800, plus 61%	$3,500,000
Over $4,000,000	$4,500,000	$1,880,800, plus 65%	$4,000,000
Over $4,500,000	$5,000,000	$2,205,800, plus 69%	$4,500,000
Over $5,000,000		$2,550,800, plus 70%	$5,000,000

State Death Tax Credit for Estate Tax

Adjusted taxable estate				Of excess	Adjusted taxable estate				Of excess
from	to	Credit = +	%	over	from	to	Credit = +	%	over
$ 0	$40,000	0	0	$ 0	2,540,000	3,040,000	146,800	8.8	2,540,000
40,000	90,000	0	.8	40,000	3,040,000	3,540,000	190,800	9.6	3,040,000
90,000	140,000	400	1.6	90,000	3,540,000	4,040,000	238,800	10.4	3,540,000
140,000	240,000	1,200	2.4	140,000	4,040,000	5,040,000	290,800	11.2	4,040,000
240,000	440,000	3,600	3.2	240,000	5,040,000	6,040,000	402,800	12	5,040,000
440,000	640,000	10,000	4	440,000	6,040,000	7,040,000	522,800	12.8	6,040,000
640,000	840,000	18,000	4.8	640,000	7,040,000	8,040,000	650,800	13.6	7,040,000
840,000	1,040,000	27,600	5.6	840,000	8,040,000	9,040,000	786,800	14.4	8,040,000
1,040,000	1,540,000	38,800	6.4	1,040,000	9,040,000	10,040,000	930,800	15.2	9,040,000
1,540,000	2,040,000	70,800	7.2	1,540,000	10,040,000		1,082,800	16	10,040,000
2,040,000	2,540,000	106,800	8	2,040,000					

The adjusted taxable estate equals the taxable estate minus $60,000.

FEDERAL INDIVIDUAL INCOME TAX

WHO MUST FILE

Every individual under 65 years of age who resided in the United States and had a gross income of $3,300 or more during the year must file a federal income tax return. Anyone 65 or older on the last day of the tax year is not required to file a return unless he had gross income of $4,300 or more during the year. A married couple both 65 or older, need not file unless their gross income is $7,400 or more.

A taxpayer with gross income of less than $3,300 (or less than $4,300 if 65 or older) should file a return to claim the refund of any taxes withheld, even if he is listed as a dependent by another taxpayer.

FORMS TO USE

A taxpayer may, at his election, use form 1040 or Form 1040A. However, those taxpayers who choose to itemize deductions must use the longer form 1040.

DEDUCTIONS

A taxpayer may either itemize deductions or choose the zero bracket amount. For single taxpayers the zero bracket amount is $2,300. For married taxpayers filing a joint return it is $3,400. For married taxpayers filing separate returns the deduction is $1,700 each.

DATES FOR FILING RETURNS

For individuals using the calendar year, Apr. 15 is final date (unless it falls on a Saturday, Sunday, or a legal holiday) for filing income tax returns and for payment of any tax due, and the first quarterly installment of the estimated tax. Other installments of estimated tax to be paid June 15, Sept. 15, and Jan. 15.

Apr. 15 is final date for filing declaration of estimated tax. Amended declarations may be filed June 15, Sept. 15, and Jan. 15.

Instead of paying the 4th installment a final income return may be filed by Jan. 31. Farmers may file a final return by Mar. 1 to satisfy estimated tax requirements.

JOINT RETURN

A husband and wife may make a return jointly, even if one has no income personally.

One provision stipulates that if one spouse dies, the survivor may compute his tax using joint return rates for the first two taxable years following, provided he or she was also entitled to file a joint return the year of the death, and furnishes over half the cost of maintaining in his household a home for a dependent child or stepchild. If the taxpayer remarries before the end of the taxable year these privileges are lost but he is permitted to file a joint return with his new spouse.

ESTIMATED TAX

If total tax exceeds withheld tax by at least $100, declarations of estimated tax are required from (1) single individuals, heads of a household or surviving spouses, or a married person entitled to file a joint return whose spouse does not receive wages, who expects a gross income over $20,000; (2) married individuals with over $10,000 where both spouses receive wages; (3) married individuals with over $5,000 not entitled to file a joint return; and (4) individuals whose gross income can reasonably be expected to include more than $500 from sources other than wages subject to withholdings.

EXEMPTIONS

Personal exemption is $1,000.

Every individual has an exemption of $1,000, to be deducted from gross income. A husband and a wife are each entitled to a $1,000 exemption. A taxpayer 65 or over on the last day of the year gets another exemption of $1,000. A person blind on the last day of the year gets another exemption of $1,000.

Exemption for dependents, over one-half of whose total support comes from the taxpayer and for whom the other dependency tests have been met, is $1,000. This applies to a child, stepchild, or adopted child as well as certain other relatives with less than $1,000 gross income; also to a child, stepchild, or adopted child of the taxpayer who is under 19 at the end of the year or was a full-time student during 5 months of the year even if he makes $1,000 or more. A dependent can be a non-relative if a member of the taxpayer's household and living there all year.

Taxpayer gets the exemption for his child who is a student regardless of the student's age or earnings, provided the taxpayer provides over half of the student's total support. If the student gets a scholarship, this is not counted as support.

CHILD AND DISABLED DEPENDENT CARE

To qualify, a taxpayer must be employed and provide over one-half the cost of maintaining a household for a dependent child under 15, a disabled dependent of any age, or a disabled spouse.

Taxpayers may be allowed a credit of an amount equal to 20% of employment related expenses.

For further information consult your local IRS office or the instructional material attached to your return form.

LIFE INSURANCE

Life insurance paid to survivors is not taxed as income. Interest on life insurance left with the insurance company and paid to survivors at intervals is taxable when available. Surviving spouse has an exclusion of the prorata amount of principal payable at death plus up to $1,000 per year of interest earned when life insurance proceeds are payable in installments.

Regular payments under the Railroad Retirement Act, and those received as social security, are exempt.

DIVIDENDS

The first $100 in dividends can be excluded from income. If husband and wife both receive $100 on their joint return they can exclude $200.

The exclusion does not apply to dividends from tax-exempt corporations, mutual savings banks, building and loan associations, and several others.

Dividends paid in stock or in stock rights are generally exempt from tax, except when paid in place of preferred stock dividends of the current or preceding year, or when the stockholder has an option to take stock or property or when the stock distribution is disproportionate.

DEDUCTIBLE MEDICAL EXPENSES

Expenses for medical care, not compensated for by insurance or other payment for taxpayer, spouse, and dependents, in excess of 3% of adjusted gross income are deductible. There is no limit to the maximum amount of medical expenses that can be deducted.

Medical care includes diagnosis, treatment and prevention of disease or for the purpose of affecting any structure or function of the body, and amounts paid for insurance to reimburse for hospitalization, surgical fees and other medical expenses.

Only medicine and drugs in excess of 1% of adjusted gross income may be deducted.

One-half the cost of medical care insurance premiums up to $150 can be deducted without regard to the 3% limitation. The other half plus any excess over $150 is included with other medical expenses subject to the 3% limit.

Medical expenses for a decedent paid by his estate within one year after his death may be treated as expenses of the decedent taxpayer.

Medical and hospital benefits provided by the employer may be exempt from individual income tax.

Disability income payments are excludable only if the payee is totally and permanently disabled and under age 65 at the end of the tax year. Up to $5,200 can be excluded but must be reduced by income above certain limits.

DEDUCTIONS FOR CONTRIBUTIONS

Deductions up to 50% of taxpayers' adjusted gross income may be taken for contribution to most publicly supported charitable organizations, including churches or associations of churches, tax-exempt educational institutions, tax-exempt hospitals, and medical research organizations associated with a hospital. The deduction is generally limited to 20% for such organizations as private nonoperating foundations, and certain organizations that do not qualify for the 50% limitation.

Taxpayers also are permitted to carry over for five years certain contributions, generally to publicly supported organizations, which exceed the 50% allowable deduction the year the contribution was made.

Also permissible is the deduction as a charitable contribution of unreimbursed amounts up to $50 a school month spent to maintain an elementary or high school student, other than a dependent or relative, in taxpayer's home. There must be a written agreement between you and a qualified organization.

DEDUCTIONS FOR INTEREST PAID

Interest paid by the taxpayer is deductible.

To deduct interest on a debt, you must be legally liable for that debt. No deduction will be allowed for payments you make for another person if you were not legally liable to make them.

PRIZES AND AWARDS

All prizes and awards must be reported in gross income, except when received without action by the recipient. To be exempt, awards must be received primarily in recognition of religious, charitable, scientific, educational, artistic, literary, or civic achievement. (Nobel and Pulitzer prizes exempt.)

DEDUCTIONS FOR EMPLOYEES

An employee may use the zero bracket amount and deduct as well the following if in connection with his employment: transportation, except commuting; automobile expense, including gas, oil, and depreciation; however, meals and lodging are deductible as traveling expense only if the employee is away from home overnight.

An outside salesman—a salesman who works fulltime outside the office, using the latter only for incidentals—may use the zero bracket amount and deduct all his business expenses.

An employee who is reimbursed and is required to account to his employer for his business expenses will not be required to report either the reimbursement or the expenses on his tax return. Any allowance to the employee in excess of his expenses must be included in gross income. If he claims a deduction for an excess of expenses over reimbursement he will have to report the reimbursement and claim actual expenses.

An employee who is not required to account to his employer must report on his return the total amounts of reimbursements and expenses for travel, transportation, entertainment, etc., that he incurs under a reimbursement arrangement with his employer.

The expense of moving to a new place of employment may be deducted under certain circumstances regardless of whether the taxpayer is a new or continuing employee, or whether he pays his own expenses or is reimbursed by his employer. Reimbursement must be reported as income.

TAX CREDIT FOR THE ELDERLY

Subject to certain rules or exclusions, taxpayers 65 or older may claim a credit which varies according to filing status. Taxpayers should read IRS instructions carefully for full details. You may also be eligible for a credit if you are under age 65 and receive a taxable pension from a public retirement system.

The credit is limited to 15% of $2,500 for single taxpayers; 15% of $2,500 for married taxpayers filing a joint return when only one taxpayer is 65 or older; 15% of $3,750 for married taxpayers both 65 or older filing a joint return; and 15% of $1,875 for a married taxpayer filing a separate return.

NET CAPITAL LOSSES

An individual taxpayer may deduct capital

losses up to $3,000 against his ordinary income. However, it takes $2 of net long-term capital loss to get $1 of offset against other income. He may carry the rest over to subsequent years at the same rate, no legal limit on the number of years.

INCOME AVERAGING

Individuals with large fluctuations in their annual income may be able to take advantage of averaging provisions available to taxpayers whose income for a particular year exceeds 120% of their average income for the prior 4 years, if the excess is more than $3,000.

Returns with Itemized Deductions for 1978

Size of adjusted gross income	Total deductions		Zero bracket amount		Itemized deductions		
	No. of returns	Amount (thousands)	No. of returns	Amount (thousands)	No. of returns	%[1]	Amount (thousands)
Total, all returns	89,889,669	$303,871.125	59,777,260	$140,063,830	25,774,779	2.9	$163,807,295
(thousands)							
under $2	9,048,077	3,539,229	5,130,440	3,317,438	135,003	1.5	221,791
$2 under 4	9,260,108	15,875,309	8,586,505	15,493,028	177,290	1.9	382,281
4 under 6	8,400,764	19,135,357	8,001,625	17,869,920	342,686	4.0	1,265,437
6 under 8	8,263,096	21,177,876	7,720,276	18,942,626	540,639	6.5	2,235,250
8 under 10	6,943,938	18,996,563	6,128,201	15,555,001	815,708	11.7	3,441,562
10 under 12	6,096,515	17,922,145	5,083,435	13,470,303	1,013,080	16.6	4,451,842
12 under 14	5,603,534	17,481,290	4,423,419	12,095,009	1,180,115	21.1	5,386,281
14 under 16	5,016,424	16,748,856	3,566,848	10,004,231	1,449,576	28.9	6,744,625
16 under 18	4,682,500	17,090,464	2,907,594	8,376,021	1,774,906	37.9	8,714,443
18 under 20	4,277,380	16,851,073	2,268,349	6,721,312	2,009,031	47.0	10,129,761
20 under 25	8,554,843	37,989,909	3,409,297	10,311,251	5,145,546	60.1	27,678,658
25 under 30	5,384,966	27,749,503	1,493,945	4,619,162	3,891,021	72.3	23,130,341
30 under 50	6,534,412	44,325,312	948,201	2,954,085	5,586,211	85.5	41,371,227
50 under 100	1,468,912	17,374,761	97,905	299,743	1,371,007	93.3	17,075,018
100 under 200	285,161	6,511,085	10,028	31,006	275,133	96.5	6,480,079
200 under 500	60,075	3,093,774	1,118	3,421	58,957	98.1	3,090,353
500 under 1,000	6,872	1,009,788	74	217	6,798	98.9	1,009,571
1,000 or more	2,092	998,832	20	57	2,072	99.0	998,775

Individual Income Tax Returns for 1978

Size of adjusted gross income	All returns				Taxable returns		
	Returns		Adjusted gross income less deficit		Returns		Adjusted gross income less deficit
	Number	Percent of total	Amount ($000)	Average (dollars)	Number	Percent of total	Amount ($000)
Total	**89,889,669**	**100.0**	**1,304,188,847**	**14,509**	**68,805,961**	**100.0**	**1,242,436,934**
No adjusted gross income	506,017	0.6	−6,329,580	−12,509	13,284	(1)	−480,830
$1 under $1,000	3,509,421	3.9	2,037,534	581	2,346	(1)	710
$1,000 under $2,000	5,032,639	5.6	7,521,594	1,495	138,398	0.2	213,206
$2,000 under $3,000	4,684,163	5.2	11,709,712	2,500	139,895	0.2	358,964
$3,000 under $4,000	4,575,945	5.1	15,987,007	3,494	2,282,488	3.3	8,186,010
$4,000 under $5,000	3,990,373	4.4	17,937,631	4,495	2,571,709	3.7	11,601,562
$5,000 under $6,000	4,410,391	4.9	24,354,756	5,522	3,060,375	4.4	16,904,671
$6,000 under $7,000	4,391,512	4.9	28,538,388	6,499	3,389,991	4.9	22,066,055
$7,000 under $8,000	3,871,584	4.3	29,040,229	7,501	3,396,778	4.9	25,498,493
$8,000 under $9,000	3,701,698	4.1	31,386,245	8,479	3,456,339	5.0	29,311,111
$9,000 under $10,000	3,242,240	3.6	30,759,872	9,487	3,065,012	4.5	29,072,985
$10,000 under $11,000	3,156,654	3.5	33,135,913	10,497	3,006,172	4.4	31,556,142
$11,000 under $12,000	2,939,861	3.3	33,813,408	11,502	2,829,426	4.1	32,552,076
$12,000 under $13,000	2,928,858	3.3	36,590,126	12,493	2,869,143	4.2	35,844,896
$13,000 under $14,000	2,674,676	3.0	36,080,789	13,490	2,623,623	3.8	35,393,888
$14,000 under $15,000	2,560,594	2.8	37,151,846	14,509	2,516,250	3.7	36,511,022
$15,000 under $20,000	11,415,710	12.7	198,904,499	17,424	11,287,720	16.4	196,716,046
$20,000 under $25,000	8,554,843	9.5	190,968,905	22,323	8,496,442	12.3	189,667,995
$25,000 under $30,000	5,384,966	6.0	146,793,790	27,260	5,351,190	7.8	145,874,988

$30,000 under $50,000	6,534,412	7.3	238,845,792	36,552	6,498,889	9.4	237,511,649
$50,000 under $100,000	1,468,912	1.6	96,004,790	65,358	1,457,339	2.1	95,267,136
$100,000 under $200,000	285,161	0.3	37,471,450	131,405	284,197	0.4	37,349,418
$200,000 under $500,000	60,075	0.1	16,726,346	278,424	60,004	0.1	16,706,268
$500,000 under $1,000,000	6,872	(1)	4,572,184	665,335	8,954	(1)	4,567,156
$1,000,000 or more	2,092	(1)	4,185,621	2,000,775	**	(1)	4,183,317

	Taxable returns—continued					
	Taxable income	Income tax after credits		Total income tax		
Size of adjusted gross income	Amount ($000)	Number of returns	Amount ($000)	Amount ($000)	Percent of adjusted gross income	Average (dollars)
Total	**1,028,686,777**	**68,736,839**	**187,172,925**	**188,577,186**	**15.2**	**2,741**
No adjusted gross income	—	*28	*82	50,797	(1)	3,824
$1 under $1,000	*21	*2,137	*5,291	6,055	(1)	2,581
$1,000 under $2,000	393,165	137,997	8,415	9,043	4.2	65
$2,000 under $3,000	375,285	139,446	11,553	12,734	3.5	91
$3,000 under $4,000	6,525,919	2,281,424	144,645	146,723	1.8	64
$4,000 under $5,000	9,348,948	2,566,543	460,602	463,966	4.0	180
$5,000 under $6,000	14,035,215	3,056,284	954,625	959,631	5.7	314
$6,000 under $7,000	18,272,300	3,389,469	1,442,621	1,425,324	6.5	420
$7,000 under $8,000	20,756,787	3,393,897	1,758,641	1,761,545	6.9	519
$8,000 under $9,000	23,966,410	3,453,294	2,239,391	2,243,615	7.7	649
$9,000 under $10,000	23,794,422	3,064,664	2,426,149	2,429,346	8.4	793
$10,000 under $11,000	25,954,083	3,005,079	2,833,680	2,837,300	9.0	944
$11,000 under $12,000	26,758,578	2,828,126	3,063,307	3,065,189	9.4	1,083
$12,000 under $13,000	29,605,292	2,868,197	3,572,174	3,574,864	10.0	1,246
$13,000 under $14,000	29,345,154	2,622,354	3,686,331	3,690,141	10.4	1,407
$14,000 under $15,000	30,429,464	2,515,148	3,982,522	3,988,264	10.9	1,585
$15,000 under $20,000	163,342,052	11,280,887	23,410,856	23,440,513	11.9	2,077
$20,000 under $25,000	157,098,589	8,489,121	25,305,645	25,332,749	13.4	2,982
$25,000 under $30,000	121,424,158	5,348,744	21,914,906	21,961,430	15.1	4,104
$30,000 under $50,000	197,169,079	6,490,191	42,588,467	42,782,289	18.0	6,583
$50,000 under $100,000	78,719,319	1,452,092	24,021,669	24,343,970	25.6	16,704
$100,000 under $200,000	30,962,777	283,102	12,646,521	12,908,164	34.6	45,420
$200,000 under $500,000	13,653,105	59,726	6,734,932	6,944,938	41.6	115,741
$500,000 under $1,000,000	3,566,230	6,816	2,013,449	2,112,475	46.3	307,762
$1,000,000 or more	3,190,426	2,073	1,966,451	2,086,121	49.9	998,144

(1) Less than 0.05 per cent. *Estimate based on very small sample. **Sample too small for usage data.

JUDICIARY OF THE U.S.

Justices of the United States Supreme Court

The Supreme Court comprises the chief justice of the United States and 8 associate justices, all appointed by the president with advice and consent of the Senate. Salaries: chief justice $84,675 annually, associate justice $81,288.

Name; apptd from *Chief Justices in italics*	Service Term	Yrs.	Born	Died
John Jay, N.Y.	1789–1795	5	1745	1829
John Rutledge, S.C.	1789–1791	1	1739	1800
William Cushing, Mass.	1789–1810	20	1732	1810
James Wilson, Pa.	1789–1798	8	1742	1798
John Blair, Va.	1789–1796	6	1732	1800
James Iredell, N.C.	1790–1799	9	1751	1799
Thomas Johnson, Md.	1791–1793	1	1732	1819
William Paterson, N.J.	1793–1806	13	1745	1806
John Rutledge, S.C.	1795(a)	—	1739	1800
Samuel Chase, Md.	1796–1811	15	1741	1811

Name; apptd from *Chief Justices in italics*	Service Term	Yrs.	Born	Died
Oliver Ellsworth, Conn.	1796–1800	4	1745	1807
Bushrod Washington, Va.	1798–1829	31	1762	1829
Alfred Moore, N.C.	1799–1804	4	1755	1810
John Marshall, Va.	1801–1835	34	1755	1835
William Johnson, S.C.	1804–1834	30	1771	1834
Henry B. Livingston, N.Y.	1806–1823	16	1757	1823
Thomas Todd, Ky.	1807–1826	18	1765	1826
Joseph Story, Mass.	1811–1845	33	1779	1845
Gabriel Duval, Md.	1811–1835	22	1752	1844
Smith Thompson, N.Y.	1823–1843	20	1768	1843
Robert Trimble, Ky.	1826–1828	2	1777	1828
John McLean, Oh.	1829–1861	32	1785	1861
Henry Baldwin, Pa.	1830–1844	14	1780	1844
James M. Wayne, Ga.	1835–1867	32	1790	1867
Roger B. Taney, Md.	1836–1864	28	1777	1864
Philip P. Barbour, Va.	1836–1841	4	1783	1841
John Catron, Tenn.	1837–1865	28	1786	1865
John McKinley, Ala.	1837–1852	15	1780	1852
Peter V. Daniel, Va.	1841–1860	19	1784	1860
Samuel Nelson, N.Y.	1845–1872	27	1792	1873
Levi Woodbury, N.H.	1845–1851	5	1789	1851
Robert C. Grier, Pa.	1846–1870	23	1794	1870
Benjamin R. Curtis, Mass.	1851–1857	6	1809	1874
John A. Campbell, Ala.	1853–1861	8	1811	1889
Nathan Clifford, Me.	1858–1881	23	1803	1881
Noah H. Swayne, Oh.	1862–1881	18	1804	1884
Samuel F. Miller, Ia.	1862–1890	28	1816	1890
David Davis, Ill.	1862–1877	14	1815	1886
Stephen J. Field, Cal.	1863–1897	34	1816	1899
Salmon P. Chase, Oh.	1864–1873	8	1808	1873
William Strong, Pa.	1870–1880	10	1808	1895
Joseph P. Bradley, N.J.	1870–1892	21	1813	1892
Ward Hunt, N.Y.	1872–1882	9	1810	1886
Morrison R. Waite, Oh.	1874–1888	14	1816	1888
John M. Harlan, Ky	1877–1911	34	1833	1911
William B. Woods, Ga.	1880–1887	6	1824	1887
Stanley Matthews, Oh.	1881–1889	7	1824	1889
Horace Gray, Mass.	1881–1902	20	1828	1902
Samuel Blatchford, N.Y.	1882–1893	11	1820	1893
Lucius Q. C. Lamar, Miss.	1888–1893	5	1825	1893
Melville W. Fuller, Ill.	1888–1910	21	1833	1910
David J. Brewer, Kan.	1889–1910	20	1837	1910
Henry B. Brown, Mich.	1890–1906	15	1836	1913
George Shiras Jr., Pa.	1892–1903	10	1832	1924
Howell E. Jackson, Tenn.	1893–1895	2	1832	1895
Edward D. White, La.	1894–1910	16	1845	1921
Rufus W. Peckman, N.Y.	1895–1909	13	1838	1909
Joseph McKenna, Cal.	1898–1925	26	1843	1926
Oliver W. Holmes, Mass.	1902–1932	29	1841	1935
William R. Day, Oh.	1903–1922	19	1849	1923
William H. Moody, Mass.	1906–1910	3	1853	1917
Horace H. Lurton, Tenn.	1909–1914	4	1844	1914
Charles E. Hughes, N.Y.	1910–1916	5	1862	1948
Willis Van Devanter, Wy.	1910–1937	26	1859	1941
Joseph R. Lamar, Ga.	1910–1916	5	1857	1916
Edward D. White, La.	1910–1921	10	1845	1921
Mahlon Pitney, N.J.	1912–1922	10	1858	1924
James. C. McReynolds, Tenn.	1914–1941	26	1862	1946
Louis D. Brandeis, Mass.	1916–1939	22	1856	1941
John H. Clarke, Oh.	1916–1922	5	1857	1945
William H. Taft, Conn.	1921–1930	8	1857	1930
George Sutherland, Ut.	1922–1938	15	1862	1942
Pierce Butler, Minn.	1922–1939	16	1866	1939
Edward T. Sanford, Tenn.	1923–1930	7	1865	1930
Harlan F. Stone, N.Y.	1925–1941	16	1872	1946
Charles E. Hughes, N.Y.	1930–1941	11	1862	1948
Owen J. Roberts, Pa.	1930–1945	15	1875	1955

Name; apptd from *Chief Justices in italics*	Service Term	Yrs.	Born	Died
Benjamin N. Cardozo, N.Y.	1932–1938	6	1870	1938
Hugo L. Black, Ala.	1937–1971	34	1886	1971
Stanley F. Reed, Ky.	1938–1957	19	1884	1980
Felix Frankfurter, Mass.	1939–1962	23	1882	1965
William O. Douglas, Conn.	1939–1975	36	1898	1980
Frank Murphy, Mich.	1940–1949	9	1890	1949
Harlan F. Stone, N.Y.	1941–1946	5	1872	1946
James F. Byrnes, S.C.	1941–1942	1	1879	1972
Robert H. Jackson, N.Y.	1941–1954	12	1892	1954
Wiley B. Rutledge, Ia.	1943–1949	6	1894	1949
Harold H. Burton, Oh.	1945–1958	13	1888	1964
Fred M. Vinson, Ky.	1946–1953	7	1890	1953
Tom C. Clark, Tex.	1949–1967	18	1899	1977
Sherman Minton, Ind.	1949–1956	7	1890	1965
Earl Warren, Cal.	1953–1969	16	1891	1974
John Marshall Harlan, N.Y.	1955–1971	16	1899	1971
William J. Brennan Jr., N.J.	1956 —	—	1906	—
Charles E. Whittaker, Mo.	1957–1962	5	1901	1973
Potter Stewart, Oh.	1958 —	—	1915	—
Byron R. White, Col.	1962 —	—	1917	—
Arthur J. Goldberg, Ill.	1962–1965	3	1908	—
Abe Fortas, Tenn.	1965–1969	4	1910	—
Thurgood Marshall, N.Y.	1967 —	—	1908	—
Warren E. Burger, Va.	1969 —	—	1907	—
Harry A. Blackmun, Minn.	1970 —	—	1908	—
Lewis F. Powell Jr., Va.	1972 —	—	1907	—
William H. Rehnquist, Ariz.	1972 —	—	1924	—
John Paul Stevens, Ill.	1975 —	—	1920	—

(a) Rejected Dec. 15, 1795.

U.S. Court of Customs and Patent Appeals

Washington, DC 20439 (Salaries, $65,000)

Chief Judge—Howard T. Markey.

Associate Judges—Giles S. Rich, Phillip B. Baldwin, Donald E. Lane, Jack R. Miller.

U.S. Customs Court

New York, NY 10007 (Salaries, $61,500)

Chief Judge—Edward D. Re.

Judges—Paul P. Rao, Morgan Ford, Scovel Richardson, Frederick Landis, James L. Watson, Herbert N. Maletz, Bernard Newman, Nils A. Boe.

U.S. Court of Claims

Washington, DC 20005 (Salaries, $65,000)

Chief Judge—Daniel M. Friedman

Associate Judges—Oscar H. Davis, Shiro Kashiwa, Robert L. Kunzig, Marion T. Bennett, Philip Nichols, Jr., Edward S. Smith.

U.S. Tax Court

Washington, DC 20217 (Salaries, $61,500)

Chief Judge—C. Moxley Featherston.

Judges—William M. Drennen, Irene F. Scott, William M. Fay, Howard A. Dawson Jr., Theodore Tannenwald Jr., Charles R. Simpson, Leo H. Irwin, Samuel B. Sterrett, William A. Goffe, Cynthia H. Hall, Darrell D. Wiles, Richard C. Wilbur, Herbert L. Chabot.

U.S. Courts of Appeals

(Salaries, $65,000. CJ means Chief Judge)

District of Columbia—J. Skelly Wright, CJ; Carl McGowan, Edward Allen Tamm, Spottswood W. Robinson III, Roger Robb, George E. MacKinnon, Malcolm Richard Wilkey, Patricia M. Wald, Abner J. Mikva; Clerk's Office, Washington, DC 20001.

First Circuit (Me., Mass., N.H., R.I., Puerto Rico)—Frank M. Coffin, CJ; Levin H. Campbell, Hugh H. Bownes; Clerk's Office, Boston, MA 02109.

Second Circuit (Conn., N.Y., Vt.)—Irving R. Kaufman, CJ; Wilfred Feinberg, Walter R. Mansfield, William H. Mulligan, James L. Oakes, William H. Timbers, Ellsworth Van Graafeiland, Thomas J. Meskill, Jon O. Newman, Amalya Lyle Kearse; Clerk's Office, New York, NY 10007.

Third Circuit (Del., N.J., Pa., Virgin Is.)—Collins J. Seitz, CJ; Ruggero J. Aldisert, Arlin M. Adams, John J. Gibbons, Max Rosenn, James Hunter 3d, Joseph F. Weis Jr., Leonard I. Garth, A. Leon Higginbotham Jr., Dolores K. Sloviter; Clerk's Office, Philadelphia, PA 19106.

Fourth Circuit (Md., N.C., S.C., Va., W. Va.)—Clement F. Haynesworth Jr., CJ; Harrison L. Winter, Kenneth K. Hall, John D. Butzner Jr., Donald Stuart Russell, H. Emory Widener Jr., James D. Phillips Jr., Francis D. Murnaghan Jr., James M. Sprouse; Clerk's Office, Richmond, VA 23219.

Fifth Circuit (Ala., Fla., Ga., La., Miss., Tex., Canal Zone)—James P. Coleman, CJ; John R. Brown, Irving L. Goldberg, Robert A. Ainsworth Jr., John C. Godbold, Charles Clark, Thomas G. Gee, Paul H. Roney, Gerald B. Tjoflat, James C. Hill, Peter T. Fay, Alvin B. Rubin, Robert S. Vance, Phyllis A. Kravitch, Frank M. Johnson, Reynaldo G. Garza, Albert J. Henderson Jr., Thomas M. Reavley, Joseph W. Hatchett, Henry A. Politz, R. Lanier Anderson, Carolyn D. Randall, Samuel D. Johnson, Albert Tate Jr., Thomas A. Clark; Clerk's Office, New Orleans, LA 70130.

Sixth Circuit (Ky., Mich., Ohio, Tenn.)—Anthony J. Celebrezze, CJ; Paul C. Weick, Albert J. Engel, Pierce Lively, Gilbert S. Merritt, Damon J. Keith, Bailey Brown, Cornelia G. Kennedy, Boyce F. Martin Jr., Nathaniel R. Jones; Clerk's Office, Cincinnati, OH 45202.

Seventh Circuit (Ill., Ind., Wis.)—Thomas E. Fairchild, CJ; Luther M. Swygert, Walter J. Cummings, Wilbur F. Pell Jr., Robert A. Sprecher, Philip W. Tone, Harlington Wood Jr., William J. Bauer, Richard D. Cudahy; Clerk's Office, Chicago, IL 60604.

Eighth Circuit (Ark., Ia., Minn., Mo., Neb., N.D., S.D.)—Floyd R. Gibson, CJ; Donald P. Lay, Gerald W. Heaney, Myron H. Bright, Donald R. Ross, Roy L. Stephenson, J. Smith Henley, Theodore McMillian; Clerk's Office, St. Louis, MO 63101.

Ninth Circuit (Ariz., Cal., Ida., Mont., Nev., Ore., Wash., Alaska, Ha., Guam)—James R. Browning, CJ; Eugene A. Wright, Herbert Y. C. Choy, J. Clifford Wallace, Alfred T. Goodwin, Anthony M. Kennedy, J. Blaine Anderson, Procter Hug Jr., Thomas Tang, Joseph T. Sneed, Jerome Farris, Betty B. Fletcher, Mary M. Schroeder, Otto R. Skopil Jr., Harry Pregerson, Arthur L. Alarcon; Clerk's Office, San Francisco, CA 94101.

Tenth Circuit (Col., Kan., N.M., Okla., Ut., Wy.)—Oliver Seth, CJ; William J. Holloway Jr., Robert H. McWilliams, James E. Barrett, William E. Doyle, Monroe G. McKay, James K. Logan, Stephanie K. Seymour; Clerk's Office, Denver, CO 80294.

Temporary Emergency Court of Appeals—Edward Allen Tamm, CJ; Clerk's Office, Washington, DC 20001.

U.S. District Courts

(Salaries, $61,500. CJ means Chief Judge)

Alabama—Northern: Frank H. McFadden, CJ: Sam C. Pointer Jr., James Hughes Hancock, J. Foy Guin Jr.; Clerk's Office, Birmingham 35203. **Middle:** Robert E. Varner, CJ; Jane P. Gordon; Clerk's Office, Montgomery 36101. **Southern:** Virgil Pittman, CJ; William Brevard Hand; Clerk's Office, Mobile 36601.

Alaska—James A. von der Heydt, CJ; James M. Fitzgerald; Clerk's Office, Anchorage 99513.

Arizona—C. A. Muecke, CJ; William P. Copple, Mary Ann Richey, Vlademar A. Cordova, Richard M. Bilby; Clerk's Office, Phoenix 85025.

Arkansas—Eastern: Garnett Thomas Eisele, CJ; Elsijane Trimble Roy, Richard S. Arnold, William Ray Overton; Clerk's Office, Little Rock 72203. **Western:** Paul X. Williams, CJ; Elsijane Trimble Roy, Richard S. Arnold; Clerk's Office, Fort Smith 72902.

California—Northern: Robert F. Peckham, CJ; Lloyd H. Burke, Stanley A. Weigel, Robert H. Schnacke, Samuel Conti, Spencer M. Williams, Charles B. Renfrew; William H. Orrick Jr., William H. Schwarzer, William A. Ingram, Cecil F. Poole; Clerk's Office, San Francisco 94102. **Eastern:** Philip C. Wilkins, CJ; M. D. Crocker, Lawrence K. Karlton, Milton L. Schwartz; Clerk's Office Sacramento 95814. **Central:** Irving Hill, CJ; A. Andrew Hauk, William P. Gray, Warren J. Ferguson, Manuel L. Real, David W. Williams, Robert J. Kelleher, Wm. Matthew Byrne Jr., Lawrence T. Lydick, Malcolm M. Lucas, Robert Firth, Robert M. Takasugi, Laughlin E. Waters, Mariana R. Pfaelzer; Clerk's Office, Los Angeles 90012. **Southern:** Edward J. Schwartz, CJ; Howard B. Turrentine, Gordon Thompson Jr., Leland C. Nielsen, William B. Enright; Clerk's Office, San Diego 92189.

Colorado—Fred M. Winner, CJ; Sherman G. Finesilver, Richard P. Matsch, John L. Kane, Jim R. Carrigan, Zita L. Weinshienk; Clerk's Office, Denver 80294.

Connecticut—T. Emmet Clarie, CJ; T. F.

Gilroy Daly, Ellen B. Burns, Warren W. Eginton; Clerk's Office, New Haven 06505.

Delaware—James L. Latchum, CJ; Walter K. Stapleton, Murray M. Schwartz; Clerk's Office, Wilmington 19801.

District of Columbia—William B. Bryant, CJ; Oliver Gasch, John Lewis Smith Jr., Aubrey E. Robinson Jr., Gerhard A. Gesell, John H. Pratt, June L. Green, Barrington D. Parker, Charles R. Richey, Thomas A. Flannery, Louis F. Oberdorfer, Harold H. Greene, John Garrett Penn, Joyce Hens Green; Clerk's Office, Washington DC 20001.

Florida—Northern: Winston E. Arnow, CJ; William H. Stafford Jr., Lyle C. Higby; Clerk's Office, Tallahassee 32302. **Middle:** George C. Young, CJ; Ben Krentzman, Howell W. Melton, William Terrell Hodges, John A. Reed Jr., George G. Carr, Susan H. Black, William J. Castagna; Clerk's Office, Jacksonville 32201. **Southern:** C. Clyde Atkins, CJ; Joe Eaton, James Lawrence King, Norman C. Roettger Jr.; Sidney M. Aronovitz, William H. Hoeveler, Jose A. Gonzalez, James W. Kehoe, Eugene P. Spellman, Edward B. Davis, James C. Paine, Alcee L. Hastings; Clerk's Office, Miami 33101.

Georgia—Northern: Charles A. Moye Jr., CJ; William C. O'Kelley, Richard C. Freeman, Newell Edenfield, Harold L. Murphy, Marvin H. Shoob, G. Ernest Tidwell, Orinda Dale Evans, Robert L. Vining Jr., Robert H. Hall; Clerk's Office, Atlanta 30303. **Middle:** J. Robert Elliott, CJ; Wilbur D. Owens Jr.; Clerk's Office, Macon 31202. **Southern:** Anthony A. Alaimo, CJ; B. Avant Edenfield, Dudley Bowen Jr.; Clerk's Office, Savannah 31402.

Hawaii—Samuel P. King, CJ; Martin Pence; Clerk's Office, Honolulu 96850.

Idaho—Ray McNichols, CJ; Marion J. Callister; Clerk's Office, Boise 83724.

Illinois—Northern: James B. Parsons, CJ; Bernard M. Decker, Frank J. McGarr, Thomas R. McMillen, Prentice H. Marshall, Joel M. Flaum, John F. Grady, George N. Leighton, John Powers Crowley; Nicholas J. Bua, Stanley J. Roszkowski, James B. Moran, Marvin E. Aspen; Clerk's Office, Chicago 60604. **Central:** Robert D. Morgan, CJ; J. Waldo Ackerman, Harold A. Baker; Clerk's Office, Peoria 61650. **Southern:** James L. Foreman, CJ; William L. Beatty; Clerk's Office, E. St. Louis 62202.

Indiana—Northern: Jesse E. Eschbach, CJ; Allen Sharp, Phil M. McNagny Jr.; Clerk's Office, South Bend 46601. **Southern:** William E. Steckler, CJ; Cale J. Holder, S. Hugh Dillin, James E. Noland, Gene E. Brooks; Clerk's Office, Indianapolis 46204.

Iowa—Northern: Edward J. McManus, CJ; Donald E. O'Brien; Clerk's Office, Cedar Rapids 52407. **Southern:** William C. Stuart, CJ; Donald E. O'Brien, Harold D. Vietor; Clerk's Office, Des Moines 50309.

Kansas—Frank G. Theis, CJ; Earl E. O'Connor, Richard Dean Rogers, Dale E. Saffels; Clerk's Office, Wichita 67201.

Kentucky—Eastern: Bernard T. Moynahan Jr., CJ; Howard David Hermansdorfer, Eugene E. Siler Jr., Scott Reed; Clerk's Office, Lexington 40501. **Western:** Charles M. Allen, CJ; Eugene E. Siler Jr., Edward H. Johnstone, Thomas A. Ballantine; Clerk's Office, Louisville 40202.

Louisiana—Eastern: Frederick J. R. Heebe, CJ; Edward J. Boyle Sr., Lansing L. Mitchell, Fred J. Cassibry, Jack M. Gordon, Morey L. Sear, Charles Schwartz Jr., Adrian A. Duplantier, Robert F. Collins, George Arceneaux Jr., Veronica D. Wicker, Patrick E. Carr, Peter Hill Beer; Clerk's Office, New Orleans 70130. **Middle:** John V. Parker, CJ; E. Gordon West; Clerk's Office, Baton Rouge 70801. **Western:** Nauman S. Scott, CJ; Tom Stagg, W. Eugene Davis, Earl Ernest Veron, John M. Shaw; Clerk's Office, Shreveport 71161.

Maine—Edward Thaxter Gignoux, CJ; Clerk's Office, Portland 04101.

Maryland—Edward S. Northrop, CJ; Frank A. Kaufman, Alexander Harvey 2d, James R. Miller Jr., Joseph H. Young, Herbert F. Murray, C. Stanley Blair, Shirley B. Jones, Joseph C. Howard; Clerk's Office, Baltimore 21201.

Massachusetts—Andrew A. Caffrey, CJ; W. Arthur Garrity Jr., Frank H. Freedman, Joseph L. Tauro, Walter Jay Skinner, A. David Mazzone, Robert E. Keeton, John J. McNaught, Rya W. Zobel, David S. Nelson; Clerk's Office, Boston 02109.

Michigan—Eastern: John Feikens, CJ; Philip Pratt, Robert E. DeMascio, Charles W. Joiner, James Harvey, James P. Churchill, Ralph B. Guy Jr., Julian A. Cook, Patricia A. Boyle, Stewart A. Newblatt, Avern Cohn, Anna Diggs Taylor; Clerk's Office, Detroit 48226. **Western:** Wendell A. Miles, CJ; Douglas W. Hillman, Benjamin F. Gibson; Clerk's Office, Grand Rapids 49503.

Minnesota—Edward J. Devitt, CJ; Miles W. Lord, Donald D. Alsop, Harry H. MacLaughlin; Clerk's Office, St. Paul 55101.

Mississippi—Northern: William C. Keady, CJ; Clerk's Office, Oxford 38655. **Southern:** Dan M. Russell Jr., CJ; William Harold Cox, Walter L. Nixon Jr., Clerk's Office, Jackson 39205.

Missouri—Eastern: H. Kenneth Wangelin, CJ; William R. Collinson, John F. Nangle, Edward D. Filippine, William L. Hungate; Clerk's Office, St. Louis 63101. **Western:** John W. Oliver, CJ; William R. Collinson, Elmo B. Hunter, H. Kenneth Wangelin, Russell G. Clark, Harold Sachs, Scott O. Wright; Clerk's Office, Kansas City 64106.

Montana—James F. Battin, CJ; Paul G. Hatfield; Clerk's Office, Billings 59101.

Nebraska—Warren K. Urbom, CJ; Robert V. Denney, Albert G. Schatz; Clerk's Office, Omaha 68101.

Nevada—Roger D. Foley, CJ; Harry E. Claiborne, Edward C. Reed; Clerk's Office, Las Vegas 89101.

New Hampshire—Shane Devine, CJ; Martin J. Loughlin; Clerk's Office, Concord 03301.

New Jersey—Clarkson S. Fisher, CJ; Frederick B. Lacey, Vincent P. Biunno, Herbert J. Stern, H. Curtis Meanor, John F. Gerry, Stanley S. Brotman, Anne E. Thompson, D. R. Debevoise, H. Lee Sarokin; Clerk's Office Trenton 08605.

New Mexico—Howard C. Bratton, CJ; Edwin L. Mechem, Santiago E. Campos, Juan G. Burciaga; Clerk's Office, Albuquerque 87103.

New York—Northern: James T. Foley, CJ; Howard G. Munson, Neal P. McCurn; Clerk's Office, Albany 12201. **Eastern:** Jack B. Weinstein, CJ; Mark A. Costantino, Edward R. Neaher, Thomas C. Platt Jr., Henry Bramwell, George C. Pratt, Charles P. Sifton, Eugene H. Nickerson; Clerk's Office, Brooklyn 11201. **Southern:** David N. Edelstein, CJ; Edward Weinfeld, Lloyd F. MacMahon, Constance Baker Motley, Milton Pollack, Morris E. Lasker, Lawrence W. Pierce, Lee P. Gagliardi, Charles L. Brieant, Whitman Knapp, Charles E. Stewart Jr., Thomas P. Griesa, Robert L. Carter, Robert J. Ward, Kevin Thomas Duffy, William C. Conner, Richard Owen, Leonard B. Sand, Mary Johnson Lowe, Henry F. Werker, Gerard L. Goettel, Charles S. Haight Jr., Vincent L. Broderick, Pierre N. Laval, Robert W. Sweet, Abraham D. Sofaer; Clerk's Office N.Y. City 10007. **Western:** John T. Curtin, CJ; Harold P. Burke, John T. Elfvin; Clerk's Office, Buffalo 14202.

North Carolina—Eastern: Franklin T. Dupree Jr., CJ; Clerk's Office, Raleigh 27611. **Middle:** Eugene A. Gordon, CJ; Hiram H. Ward; Clerk's Office, Greensboro 27402. **Western:** Woodrow Wilson Jones, CJ; James B. McMillan; Clerk's Office, Asheville 28802.

North Dakota—Paul Benson, CJ; Bruce M. Van Sickle; Clerk's Office, Bismarck 58501.

Ohio—Northern: Frank J. Battisti, CJ; Don J. Young, William K. Thomas, Thomas D. Lambros, Robert B. Krupansky, Nicholas J. Walinski, Leroy J. Contie Jr., John M. Manos; Clerk's Office, Cleveland 44114. **Southern:** Carl B. Rubin, CJ; Joseph P. Kinneary, Robert M. Duncan, Clerk's Office, Columbus 43215.

Oklahoma—Northern: H. Dale Cook, CJ; Frederick A. Daugherty, James O. Ellison, Thomas R. Brett; Clerk's Office, Tulsa 74103. **Eastern:** Frederick A. Daugherty, CJ; H. Dale Cook, Frank H. Seay; Clerk's Office, Muskogee 74401. **Western:** Frederick A. Daugherty, CJ; Luther B. Eubanks, H. Dale Cook, Ralph G. Thompson, Lee R. West; Clerk's Office, Oklahoma City 73102.

Oregon—James M. Burns, CJ; Robert C. Belloni; Clerk's Office, Portland 97207.

Pennsylvania—Eastern: Joseph S. Lord 3d, CJ; Alfred L. Luongo, John P. Fullam, Charles R. Weiner, E. Mac Troutman, John B. Hannum, Daniel H. Huyett 3d, Donald W. VanArtsdalen, J. William Ditter Jr., Edward R. Becker, Raymond J. Broderick, Clarence C. Newcomer, Clifford Scott Green, Louis Charles Bechtle, Joseph L. McGlynn Jr., Edward N. Cahn, Louis H. Pollak, Norma L. Shapiro; Clerk's Office, Philadelphia 19106. **Middle:** William J. Nealon Jr., CJ; R. Dixon Herman, Malcolm Muir, Richard P. Conaboy, Sylvia H. Rambo; Clerk's Office, Scranton 18501. **Western:** Gerald J. Weber, CJ; William W. Knox, Hubert I. Teitelbaum, Barron P. McCune, Daniel J. Snyder Jr., Maurice B. Cohill Jr., Paul A. Simmons, Gustave Diamond, Donald E. Zeigler, Alan M. Bloch; Clerk's Office, Pittsburgh 15230.

Rhode Island—Raymond J. Pettine, CJ; Francis J. Boyle; Clerk's Office, Providence 02901.

South Carolina—J. Robert Martin Jr., CJ; Robert W. Hemphill, Charles E. Simons Jr.,

Solomon Blatt Jr., Robert F. Chapman, C. Weston Houck, Falcon B. Hawkins, Matthew J. Perry Jr.; Clerk's Office, Columbia 29202.

South Dakota—Fred J. Nichol, CJ; Andrew A. Bogue, Donald J. Porter; Clerk's Office, Sioux Falls 57102.

Tennessee—Eastern: Frank W. Wilson, CJ; Robert L. Taylor, C. G. Neese; Clerk's Office, Knoxville 37901. **Middle:** L. Clure Morton, CJ, Thomas A. Wiseman Jr.; Clerk's Office, Nashville 37203. **Western:** Robert M. McRae Jr., CJ; Harry W. Wellford; Clerk's Office, Memphis 38103.

Texas—Northern: Halbert O. Woodward, CJ; Eldon B. Mahon, Robert M. Hill, Robert W. Porter, Patrick E. Higginbotham, Mary Lou Robinson, Barefoot Sanders, David O. Belew Jr.; Clerk's Office, Dallas 75242. **Southern:** John V. Singleton Jr., CJ; Woodrow B. Seals, Carl O. Bue Jr., Owen D. Cox, Robert O'Conor Jr., Ross N. Sterling, Norman W. Black, James De Anda, George E. Cire, Gabrielle K. McDonald, George P. Kazen, Hugh Gibson; Clerk's Office, Houston 77208. **Eastern:** Joe J. Fisher, CJ; William Wayne Justice, William M. Steger, Robert Parker; Clerk's Office, Beaumont 77704. **Western:** Jack Roberts, CJ; William S. Sessions, Lucius D. Bunton 3d, Harry Lee Hudspeth; Clerk's Office, San Antonio 78206.

Utah—Aldon J. Anderson, CJ; Bruce S. Jenkins; Clerk's Office, Salt Lake City 84101.

Vermont—James S. Holden, CJ; Albert W. Coffrin; Clerk's Office, Burlington 05402.

Virginia—Eastern: John A. MacKenzie, CJ; Robert R. Merhige Jr., Richard B. Kellam, Albert V. Bryan Jr., D. Dortch Warriner, J. Calvitt Clarke; Clerk's Office, Norfolk 23501. **Western:** James C. Turk, CJ; Glen M. Williams; Clerk's Office, Roanoke 24006.

Washington—Eastern: Marshall A. Neill, CJ; Jack E. Tanner; Clerk's Office, Spokane 99210. **Western:** Walter T. McGovern, CJ; Morell E. Sharp, Donald S. Voorhees, Jack E. Tanner; Clerk's Office, Seattle 98104.

West Virgina—Northern: Robert Earl Maxwell, CJ; Charles H. Haden 2d; Clerk's Office, Elkins 26241. **Southern:** Dennis Raymond Knapp, CJ; John T. Copenhaver Jr., Charles H. Haden 2d, Robert Staker; Clerk's Office, Charleston 25329.

Wisconsin—Eastern: John W. Reynolds, CJ; Myron L. Gordon, Robert W. Warren; Clerk's Office, Milwaukee 53202. **Western:** James E. Doyle, CJ; Barbara B. Crabb; Clerk's Office, Madison 53701.

Wyoming—Clarence A. Brimmer; Clerk's Office, Cheyenne 82001.

U.S. Territorial District Courts

Canal Zone—Clerk's Office, Balboa Heights.

Guam—Cristobal C. Duenas; Clerk's Office, P.O. Box DC, Agana 96910.

Puerto Rico—Jose V. Toledo, CJ; Hernan G. Pesquera, Juan R. Torruella; Clerk's Office, San Juan 00904.

Virgin Islands—Almeric L. Christian, CJ; Warren H. Young; Clerk's Office, Charlotte Amalie, St. Thomas 00801.

LEGAL OR PUBLIC HOLIDAYS, 1981

Technically there are no national holidays in the United States; each state has jurisdiction over its holidays, which are designated by legislative enactment or executive proclamation. In practice, however, most states observe the federal legal public holidays, even though the President and Congress can legally designate holidays only for the District of Columbia and for federal employees.

Federal legal public holidays are: New Year's Day, Washington's Birthday, Memorial Day, Independence Day, Labor Day, Columbus Day, Veterans Day, Thanksgiving, and Christmas.

Chief Legal or Public Holidays

When a holiday falls on a Sunday or a Saturday it is usually observed on the following Monday or preceding Friday. For some holidays, government and business closing practices vary. In most states, the office of the Secretary of State can provide details of holiday closings.

Jan. 1 (Thursday)—New Year's Day. All the states.

Feb. 12 (Thursday)—Lincoln's Birthday. Alaska, Cal., Col., Conn., Ill., Ind., Ia., Kan., Md., Mich., Mo., Mon., N.C., N.J., N.Y., Okla., Pa., Vt., Wash., W.Va. In Ariz., Feb. 9; Del., Ore., celebrated Feb. 2 in 1981.

Feb 16 (3d Monday in Feb.)—Washington's Birthday. All the states except Fla. and Wyo. In several states, the holiday is called Presidents' Day or Washington-Lincoln Day. In Mo., Ut., celebrated Feb. 23, 1981.

Apr. 17—Good Friday. Observed in all the states. A legal or public holiday in Conn., Del., Ha., Ind., Ky., La., Md., N.J., N.D., Okla., Tenn., W.Va., P.R. Partial holiday in Wis.

May 25 (last Monday in May)—Memorial Day. All the states except Ala., Miss., S.C., (Confederate Memorial Day in Va., Decoration Day in Tenn.). Observed May 29 in Del., Md., N.H., Ut., Vt.

July 4 (Saturday)—Independence Day. All the states.

Sept. 7 (1st Monday in Sept.)—Labor Day. All the states.

Oct. 12 (2d Monday in Oct.)—Columbus Day. Ala., Ariz., Cal., Col., Conn., Del., D.C., Ga., Ha., Ida., Ill., Ind., Kan., La., Me., Mass., Mich., Mo., Mont., Neb., N.H., N.J., N.M., N.Y., N.C., Oh., Okla., Pa., R.I., S.D., Tenn., Tex., Ut., Vt., Va., W.Va., Wis., Wy., P.R.

Nov. 3 (1st Tuesday after 1st Monday in Nov.)—General Election Day. Col., Mo., Mon., N.J., N.Y., N.C., Okla., Pa., R.I., S.C., Va., Wyo. Primary election days are observed as holidays or part holidays in some states.

Nov. 11 (Wednesday)—Armistice Day (Veterans Day). All the states; N.C. celebrates Oct. 26.

Nov. 26 (4th Thursday in Nov.)—Thanksgiving Day. All the states. The day after Thanksgiving is observed as a full or partial holiday in several states.

Dec. 25 (Friday)—Christmas. All the states.

Other Legal or Public Holidays

Dates are for 1981 observance, when known.

Jan. 8—Battle of New Orleans. In La.

Jan. 15—Martin Luther King's Birthday. Conn., D.C., Ill., La., Md., Mass., N.J., Pa., S.C. Observed Jan. 19 by Mich., Oh. Many schools and black groups in other states also observe the day.

Jan. 19—Robert E. Lee's Birthday. Al., Ga., La., Miss., S.C.; Lee-Jackson Day in Va., Confederate Heroes Day in Tex.

Feb. 6—Arbor Day. In Ariz. (most counties).

Feb. 14—Admission Day. In Ariz.

Mar. 2—Texas Independence Day. In that state.

Mar. 3—Mardi Gras (Shrove Tuesday). Ala., La.; Town Meeting Day (1st Tuesday in Mar.) In Vt.

Mar. 17—Evacuation Day. In Boston and Suffolk County, Mass.

Mar. 25—Maryland Day. In that state.

Mar. 26—Kuhio Day. In Ha.

Mar. 30—Seward's Day. In Alas.

Apr. 3—Arbor Day. In Ariz. (5 counties).

Apr. 9—Patriot's Day. In Me.

Apr. 13—Thomas Jefferson's Birthday. In Ala.

Apr. 20—Patriot's Day. In Mass., Me. Easter Monday in N.C.

Apr. 21—San Jacinto Day. In Tex.

Apr. 22—Arbor Day. In Neb.

Apr. 24—Arbor Day (last Friday in Apr.). In Ut.

Apr. 25—Confederate Memorial Day. Fla.

Apr. 27—Confederate Memorial Day. In Ala., Ga., Miss. Fast Day (4th Monday in Apr.). In N.H.

May 4—Rhode Island Independence Day. In that state.

May 8—Harry Truman's Birthday. In Mo.

May 11—Confederate Memorial Day. In S.C.

May 19—Primary Election Day. In Pa.

May 28—Confederate Memorial Day. In Va. Decoration Day in Tenn.

June 1—Birthday of Jefferson Davis. Ala., Ga. (June 3), Miss., S.C. (June 3).

June 3—Confederate Memorial Day. In La.

June 11—Kamehameha Day. In Ha.

June 14—Flag Day. Observed in all states; a legal holiday in Pa. (June 15).

June 17—Bunker Hill Day. In Boston and Suffolk County, Mass.

June 19—Emancipation Day. In Texas.

June 20—West Virginia Day. In that state.

July 24—Pioneer Day. In Ut.

Aug. 2—American Family Day. In Ariz.

Aug. 3—Colorado Day. In that state.

Aug. 10—Victory Day (2d Monday in Aug.). In R.I.

Aug. 16—Bennington Battle Day. In Vt.

Aug. 21—Admission Day (3d Friday in Aug.). In Ha.

Aug. 27—Lyndon Johnson's Birthday. In Tex.
Aug. 30—Huey Long's Birthday. In La.
Sept. 9—Admission Day. In Cal.
Sept. 11—Defenders' Day. In Md.
Oct. 18—Alaska Day. In that state.
Oct. 31—Nevada Day. In that state.
Nov. 1—All Saints' Day. In La.
Nov. 27—Day after Thanksgiving. Fl., Me., Minn., Neb., Wash.
Dec. 24—Christmas Eve. In Ark.
Dec. 26—Day after Christmas. In S.C.

Days Usually Observed

All Saints' Day, Nov. 1. A public holiday in Louisiana.

American Indian Day (Sept. 25 in 1981). Always fourth Friday in September.

Arbor Day. Tree-planting day. First observed April 10, 1872, in Nebraska. Now observed in every state in the Union except Alaska (often on the last Friday in April). A legal holiday in Utah (always last Friday in April), and in Nebraska (April 22).

Armed Forces Day (May 16 in 1981). Always third Saturday in that month, by presidential proclamation. Replaced Army, Navy, and Air Force Days.

Bill of Rights Day, Dec. 15. By Act of Congress. Bill of Rights took effect Dec. 15, 1791.

Bird Day. Often observed with Arbor Day.

Child Health Day (Oct. 5 in 1981). Always first Monday in October, by presidential proclamation.

Citizenship Day, Sept. 17. President Truman, Feb. 29, 1952, signed bill designating Sept. 17 as annual Citizenship Day. It replaced I Am An American Day, formerly 3rd Sunday in May and Constitution Day, formerly Sept. 17.

Easter Monday (Apr. 20 in 1981). A statutory day in Canada and in N.C.

Easter Sunday (Apr. 19 in 1981).

Elizabeth Cady Stanton Day, Nov. 12. Birthday of pioneer leader for equal rights for women.

Father's Day (June 21 in 1981). Always third Sunday in that month.

Flag Day, June 14. By presidential proclamation. It is a legal holiday in Pennsylvania.

Forefathers' Day, Dec. 21. Landing on Plymouth Rock, in 1620. Is celebrated with dinners by New England societies especially "Down East."

Nathan Bedford Forrest's Birthday, July 13. Observed in Tennessee to honor the Civil War general.

Four Chaplains Memorial Day, Feb. 3.

Gen. Douglas MacArthur Day, Jan. 26. A memorial day in Arkansas.

Gen. Pulaski Memorial Day, Oct. 11. Native of Poland and Revolutionary War hero; died (Oct. 11, 1779) from wounds received at the seige of Savannah, Ga. Observed officially in Indiana.

Gen. von Steuben Memorial Day, Sept. 17. By presidential proclamation.

Georgia Day, Feb. 12. Observed in that state. Commemorates landing of first colonists in 1733.

Grandparent's Day (Sept. 13 in 1981). Always first Sunday after Labor Day. Legislated in 1979.

Groundhog Day, Feb. 2. A popular belief is that if the groundhog sees his shadow this day, he returns to his burrow and winter continues 6 weeks longer.

Halloween, Oct. 31. The evening before All Saints or All-Hallows Day. Informally observed in the U.S. with masquerading and pumpkin-decorations. Traditionally an occasion for children to play pranks.

Leif Ericsson Day, Oct. 9. Observed in Minnesota, Wisconsin.

Loyalty Day, May 1. By act of Congress.

May Day. Name popularly given to May 1st. Celebrated as Labor Day in most of the world, and by some groups in the U.S. Observed in many schools as a Spring Festival.

Minnesota Day, May 11. In that state.

Mother's Day (May 10 in 1981). Always second Sunday in that month. First celebrated in Philadelphia in 1908. Mother's Day has become an international holiday.

National Aviation Day, Aug. 19. By presidential proclamation.

National Day of Prayer. By presidential proclamation each year on a day other than a Sunday.

National Freedom Day, Feb. 1. To commemorate the signing of the Thirteenth Amendment, abolishing slavery, Feb. 1, 1865. By presidential proclamation.

National Maritime Day, May 22. First

proclaimed 1935 in commemoration of the departure of the SS Savannah, from Savannah, Ga., on May 22, 1819, on the first successful transatlantic voyage under steam propulsion. By presidential proclamation.

Pan American Day, Apr. 14. In 1890 the First International Conference of American States, meeting in Washington, was held on that date. A resolution was adopted which resulted in the creation of the organization known today as the Pan American Union. By presidential proclamation.

Primary Election Day. Observed usually only when presidential or general elections are held.

Reformation Day, Oct. 31. Observed by Protestant groups.

Sadie Hawkins Day (Nov. 14 in 1981). First Saturday after November 11.

St. Patrick's Day, Mar. 17. Observed by Irish Societies, especially with parades.

St. Valentine's Day, Feb. 14. Festival of a martyr beheaded at Rome under Emperor Claudius. Association of this day with lovers has no connection with the saint and probably had its origin in an old belief that on this day birds begin to choose their mates.

Senior Citizens' Day (Sept. 27 in 1981). Celebrated in Indiana on the fourth Sunday in September.

Susan B. Anthony Day, Feb. 15. Birthday of a pioneer crusader for equal rights for women.

United Nations Day, Oct. 24. By presidential proclamation, to commemorate founding of United Nations.

Verrazano Day, Apr. 7. Observed by New York State, to commemorate the probable discovery of New York harbor by Giovanni de Verrazano in April, 1524.

Victoria Day (May 18 in 1981). Birthday of Queen Victoria, a statutory day in Canada, celebrated the first Monday before May 25.

Francis Willard Day, Sept. 28. Observed in Minnesota to honor the educator and temperance leader.

Will Rogers Day, Nov. 4. In Oklahoma.

World Poetry Day, Oct. 15.

Wright Brothers Day, Dec. 17. By presidential designation, to commemorate first successful flight by Orville and Wilbur Wright, Dec. 17, 1903.

Youth Honor Day, Oct. 31. Iowa day of observance.

MARRIAGE INFORMATION

Marriageable age, by states, for both males and females with and without consent of parents or guardians. But in most states, the court has authority, in an emergency, to marry young couples below the ordinary age of consent, where due regard for their morals and welfare so requires. In many states, under special circumstances, blood test and waiting period may be waived.

State	With consent		Without consent		Blood test		Wait for license	Wait after license
	Men	Women	Men	Women	Required	Other state accepted*		
Alabama (b)	14	14	18	18	Yes	Yes	none	none
Alaska	16	16	18	18	Yes	No	3 days	none
Arizona	16(i)	16	18	18	Yes	Yes	none	none
Arkansas	17	16(j)	18	18	Yes	No	3 days	none
California	18(i)	18	18	18	Yes	Yes	none	none
Colorado	16	16	18	18	Yes	...	none	none
Connecticut	16	16(l)	18	18	Yes	Yes	4 days	none
Delaware	18	16(o)	18	18	Yes	Yes	none	24 hrs. (c)
District of Columbia	16	16	18	18	Yes	Yes	3 days	none
Florida	18	18	18	18	Yes	Yes	3 days	none
Georgia	16	16	18	18	Yes	Yes	none (k)	none
Hawaii	16	16	18	18	Yes	Yes	none	none
Idaho	16	16	18	18	Yes (n)	Yes	none (k)	none
Illinois (a)	16	16	18	18	Yes	Yes	none	1 day
Indiana	17(o)	17(o)	18	18	Yes (p)	No	3 days	none
Iowa	16(o)	16(o)	18	18	Yes	Yes	3 days	none
Kansas	14	12	18	18	Yes	Yes	3 days	none
Kentucky	18(o)	18(o)	18	18	Yes	No	3 days	none
Louisiana (a)	18(o)	16(j)	18	18	Yes	No	none	72 hours
Maine	16(j)	16(j)	18	18	Yes	No	5 days	none
Maryland	16	16	18	18	none	none	48 hours	none
Massachusetts	—(o)	—(o)	18	18	Yes	Yes	3 days	none
Michigan (a)	18	16	18	18	Yes	No	3 days	none
Minnesota	—	16(e)	18	18	none	...	5 days	none

Mississippi (b)	17	15	21	21	Yes	...	3 days	none
Missouri	15	15	18	18	Yes	Yes	3 days	none
Montana	15	15	18	18	Yes	Yes	3 days	none
Nebraska	17	17	18	18	Yes(n)	Yes	2 days	none
Nevada	16	16	18	18	none	none	none	none
New Hampshire (a)	14(e)	13(e)	18	18	Yes	Yes	5 days	none
New Jersey (a)	—	12	18	18	Yes	Yes	72 hours	none
New Mexico	16	16	18	18	Yes	Yes	none	none
New York	16	14	18	18	Yes	No	none	24 hrs. (g)
North Carolina (a)	16	16	18	18	Yes	Yes	none	none
North Dakota (a)	16	16	18	18	Yes	...	none	none
Ohio (a)	18	16	18	18	Yes	Yes	5 days	none
Oklahoma	16	16	18	18	Yes	No	none (f)(h)	none
Oregon	17	17	17	17	Yes	No	7 days	none
Pennsylvania	16	16	18	18	Yes	Yes	3 days	none
Rhode Island (a)(b)	18	16	18	18	Yes	No	none	none
South Carolina	16	14	18	18	none	none	24 hrs.	none
South Dakota	16	16	18	18	Yes	Yes	none	none
Tennessee (b)	16	16	18	18	Yes	Yes	3 days	none
Texas	14	14	18	18	Yes	Yes	none	none
Utah (a)	14	14	16	16	Yes	Yes	none	none
Vermont (a)	18	16	18	18	Yes	...	none	5 days
Virginia (a)	16	16	18	18	Yes	Yes (m)	none	none
Washington	17	17	18	18	(d)	...	3 days	none
West Virginia	(o)	(o)	18	16	Yes	No	3 days	none
Wisconsin	16	16	18	18	Yes	Yes	5 days	none
Wyoming	16	16	19	19	Yes	Yes	none	none
Puerto Rico	18	16	21	21	(f)	none	none	none
Virgin Islands	16	14	18	18	none	none	8 days	none

***Many states have additional special requirements; contact individual state.** (a) Special laws applicable to non-residents. (b) Special laws applicable to those under 21 years; Ala., bond required if male is under 18, female under 18. (c) 24 hours if one or both parties resident of state; 96 hours if both parties are non-residents. (d) None, but both must file affidavit. (e) Parental consent plus court's consent required. (f) None, but a medical certificate is required. (g) Marriage may not be solemnized within 10 days from date of blood test. (h) If either under 18, 72 hrs. (i) Statute provides for obtaining license with parental or court consent with no state minimum age. (j) Under 16, with parental and court consent. (k) If either under 18, wait 3 full days. (l) If under stated age, court consent required. (m) Va. blood test form must be used. (n) Applicant must also supply a certificate of immunity against German measles (rubella). (o) If under 18, parental and/or court consent required. (p) Statement whether person is carrier of sickle-cell anemia may be required.

GROUNDS FOR DIVORCE

Persons contemplating divorce should study latest decisions or secure legal advice before initiating proceedings since different interpretations or exceptions in each case can change the conclusion reached.

State	Breakdown of marriage/ incompatibility	Cruelty	Desertion	Non-support	Alcohol &/or drug addiction	Felony	Impotency	Insanity[1]	Living separate and apart	Other grounds	Residence time	Time between interlocut'y and final decrees
Alabama	X		X	X	X	X	X	X	2 yrs.	A-E	6 mos.	none-M
Alaska	X		X	..	X	X	X	X		C	1 yr.	none
Arizona	X		..	..	..	..	..	..			90 days	none
Arkansas	..		X	X	X	X	X	X	3 yrs.	C	3 mos.	none
California[2]	X		..	..	..	..	..	X			6 mos.	6 mos.
Colorado	X		..	..	..	..	..	..			90 days	none
Connecticut	X		X	X	X	X	..	X	18 mos.	B	1 yr.	none
Delaware	X[4]		..	..	..	..	..	..	6 mos.		6 mos.	none
Dist. of Columbia	..		..	..	..	..	..	..	6 mos.–1 yr.		6 mos.	none
Florida	X		..	..	..	..	..	X			6 mos.	none
Georgia	X		X	..	X	X	X	X		A-B-D	6 mos.	L
Hawaii	X		..	..	..	..	..	..	2 yrs.	K	6 mos.	none
Idaho	X		X	X	X	X	..	X	5 yrs.		6 wks.	none
Illinois	..		X	..	X	X	X	..			3 mos.	none
Indiana	X		..	..	..	X	X	X			6 mos.	none
Iowa	X		..	..	..	..	..	..			1 yr.	none-N
Kansas	X		X	..	X	X	X	X		H	60 days	none-M
Kentucky	X		..	..	..	..	..	..			180 days	none
Louisiana	..		..	..	..	X	..	..	2 yrs.	K	2 yrs.	none-N
Maine	X		X	X	X	..	X	X			6 mos.	none

State	Breakdown of marriage/ incompatibility	Cruelty	Desertion	Non-support	Alcohol &/or drug addiction	Felony	Impotency	Insanity[1]	Living separate and apart	Other grounds	Residence time	Time between interlocut'y and final decrees
Maryland	..	X	X	..	..	X	X	X	1–3 yrs.		1 yr.	none
Massachusetts	X[4]	X	X	X	X	X	X	..	6 mos.–1 yr.		1 yr.	6 mos.
Michigan	X	..	..	..	..	..	..	..			1 yr.	none
Minnesota	X[4]	..	..	..	..	..	..	..		K	180 days	none-O
Mississippi	X[4]	X	X	..	X	X	X	X		A-D-I	6 mos.	none-P
Missouri	X[4]	..	..	..	..	..	..	..			3 mos.	none
Montana	X	..	..	..	..	..	..	..			3 mos.	none
Nebraska	X	..	..	..	..	..	..	..			1 yr.	6 mos.
Nevada	X	..	..	..	..	..	..	X	1 yr.		6 wks.	none
New Hampshire[3]	X	X	X	X	X	X	X	..		K	1 yr.	none
New Jersey	..	X	X	..	X	X	..	X	18 mos.	E-K	1 yr.	none
New Mexico	X	X	X	..	..	..	..	..			6 mos.	none
New York	..	X	X	..	..	X	..	..	1 yr.	K	1 yr.	none
North Carolina	..	..	..	..	..	..	X	X	1 yr.	A-E	6 mos.	none
North Dakota	X	X	X	X	X	X	X	X		K	1 yr.	none
Ohio	X	X	X	..	X	X	X	..	2 yrs.	B-G-H-I	6 mos.	none
Oklahoma	X	X	X	X	X	X	X	X		A-B-G-H	6 mos.	none
Oregon	X	..	..	..	..	..	..	..			6 mos.	90 days
Pennsylvania	..	X	X	..	..	X	X	X		B-C-D-I	1 yr.	none
Rhode Island	X	X	X	X	X	X	X	..	3 yrs.		1 yr.	6 mos.
South Carolina	..	X	X	..	X	..	..	..	1 yr.		1 yr.	none
South Dakota	..	X	X	X	X	X	..	..			none	none
Tennessee	X	X	X	X	X	X	X	..		A-I-J-K	6 mos.	none
Texas	X	X	X	..	..	X	..	X	3 yrs.		6 mos.	none-O
Utah	..	X	X	X	X	X	X	X		K	3 mos.	none
Vermont	..	X	X	X	..	X	..	X	6 mos.		6 mos.	3 mos.
Virginia	..	X	..	..	..	X	..	..	1 yr.		6 mos.	none-P
Washington	X	..	..	..	..	..	..	..	2 yrs.		1 yr.	none-R
West Virginia	X	X	X	..	X	X	..	X	1 yr.	T	actual	none
Wisconsin	X[4]	..	..	..	..	..	..	..	1 yr.	K	6 mos.	none-O
Wyoming	X	..	..	..	..	..	..	X	2 yrs.		60 days	none

Adultery is either grounds for divorce or evidence of irreconcilable differences and a breakdown of the marriage in all states. The plaintiff can invariably remarry in the same state where he or she procured a decree of divorce or annulment. Not so the defendant, who is barred in certain states for some offenses. After a period of time has elapsed even the offender can apply for permission.

(1) Generally 5 yrs. insanity but: permanent insanity in Ut.; incurable insanity in Col.; 1 yr. Wis.; 18 mos. Alas.; 2 yrs. Ga., Ha., Ind., Nev., N.J., Ore., Wash., Wy.; 3 yrs. Ark., Cal., Fla., Kan., Md., Minn., Miss., N.C., Tex.,W. Va.; 6 yrs. Ida. (2) Cal. has a procedure whereby if the couple has been married less than 2 years, have no children, no real estate, little personal property, and few debts they can get a divorce without an attorney and without appearing in court. (3) Other grounds existing only in N.H. are: Joining a religious order disbelieving in marriage, treatment which injures health or endangers reason, wife without the state for 10 years, and wife in state 2 yrs. husband never in state and intends to become a citizen of a foreign country. (4) Provable only by fault grounds, separation for some period, generally a year, proof of marital discord or commitment for mental illness. (A) Pregnancy at marriage. (B) Fraudulent contract. (C) Indignities. (D) Consanguinity. (E) Crime against nature. (F) Mental incapacity at time of marriage. (G) Procurement of out-of-state divorce. (H) Gross neglect of duty. (I) Bigamy. (J) Attempted homocide. (K) Separation by decree in Conn.; after decree: one yr. in La., N.Y., Wis.; 18 mos. in N.H.; 2 yrs. in Ala., Ha., Minn., N.C., Tenn.; 3 yrs. in Ut.; 4 yrs. in N.J., N.D.; 5 yrs. in Md. (L) Determined by court order. (M) 60 days to remarry. (N) One yr. to remarry except Ha. one yr. with minor child; La. 90 days. (O) 6 mos. to remarry. (P) Adultery cases, remarriage in court's discretion. (Q) Plaintiff, 6 mos.; defendant 2 yrs. to remarry. (R) No remarriage if an appeal is pending. (S) Actual domicile in adultery cases. **Enoch Arden Laws:** disappearance and unknown to be alive—Conn., 7 yrs. absence, N.H., 2 yrs., N.Y. 5 yrs. (called dissolution), Vt. 7 yrs.

N.B. Grounds not recognized for divorce may be recognized for separation or annulment. Local laws should be consulted.

SOCIAL SECURITY PROGRAMS

Old-Age, Survivors, and Disability Insurance; Medicare; Supplemental Security Income

OLD-AGE, SURVIVORS, AND DISABILITY INSURANCE

Old-age, survivors, and disability insurance covers almost all jobs in which people work for wages or salaries, as well as most work of self-employed persons, whether in a city job, or in business, or on a farm.

Old-age, survivors, and disability insurance is paid for by a tax on earnings (for 1979 up to $22,900 and for 1980 up to $25,900; the taxable earnings base is now subject to adjustment when cost-of-living benefit increases have been made). The employed worker and his employer share the tax equally (cash tips count as covered wages if they amount to $20 or more from one place of employment. The worker reports them to his employer, who includes them in his social security tax reports, but only the worker pays contributions on the amount of the tips).

The employer deducts the tax each payday and sends it, with an equal amount as his own share, to the District Director of Internal Revenue. The collected taxes are deposited in the Federal Old-Age and Survivors Insurance Trust Fund and the Federal Disability Insurance Trust Fund; they can be used only to pay benefits, the cost of rehabilitation services, and administrative expenses.

H.E.W. REORGANIZED

Under a March 1977 reorganization of the Department of Health, Education, and Welfare, the federal-state assistance program of aid to families with dependent children became the responsibility of the Social Security Administration. The reorganization placed the Medicare program under the newly created Health Care Financing Administration, which also now administers Medicaid, the federal-state medical assistance program. The Social Security Administration continues to provide services, such as those relating to contributions and premiums and maintenance of beneficiary records, for the Medicare program.

In Medicare, following the required annual review of hospital costs under the program, increases were made in the hospital insurance deductible amount (what the patient must pay for hospital services before reimbursement can begin) and in the cost-sharing for days above the number specified in the law.

The Commissioner of Social Security is Stanford G. Ross. There are 632 district offices with 682 branch offices, and 30 teleservice centers where the public may obtain information about benefit rights.

BENEFIT INCREASES, JUNE 1979

Social Security checks delivered to beneficiaries in the first week of July 1979 reflected the fifth automatic cost-of-living increase in cash benefits under legislation enacted in 1972 and 1973. The 9.9-percent increase, which became effective in June, applied to benefits for all persons on the social security benefit rolls at the end of May.

Automatic increases are initiated whenever the Consumer Price Index (CPI) of the Bureau of Labor Statistics for the first calendar quarter of a year exceeds by at least 3 percent the CPI for the base quarter, which is either the first calendar quarter of the preceding year or the quarter in which an increase was legislated by Congress. In this case, the base quarter was the first quarter of 1978. The size of the benefit increase is determined by the actual percentage rise of the CPI during the quarters measured.

As a result of the benefit increase, average monthly benefits payable to retired workers were $323.43 for men (up $29.20) and $254.26 for women ($22.98 more). Average amounts for disabled workers rose to $349.97 for men and $257.13 for women, increases of $31.75 and $23.30, respectively. Average increases for entitled dependents of these workers ranged from $8.63 for children of disabled workers to $13.31 for wives and husbands of retired workers. Among survivors of deceased workers, average benefit increases were highest for nondisabled widows and widowers ($24.22) and lowest for disabled widows and widowers ($16.40), resulting in average benefits of $268.04, and $181.29, respectively.

Social security benefits are based on a worker's primary insurance amount (PIA), which is related by law to the average monthly earnings (AME) on which social security contributions have been paid. The full PIA is payable to a retired worker who becomes entitled to benefits at age 65 and to an entitled disabled worker at any age. Spouses and children of retired or disabled workers and survivors of deceased workers receive set proportions of the PIA subject to a family maximum amount. The PIA is calculated by applying varying percentages to succeeding parts of the AME. Whenever a cost-of-living benefit increase is implemented, these percentages are changed to reflect the percentage increase in benefits.

MEDICARE

Under Medicare, protection against the costs of hospital care is provided for social security and railroad retirement beneficiaries aged 65 and over (beginning July 1966) and, effective July 1973, for persons entitled for 24 months to receive a social security disability benefit, certain persons with chronic kidney disease and their dependents, and, on a voluntary basis with payment of a special premium, persons aged 65 and over not otherwise eligible for hospital benefits; all those eligible for hospital benefits may enroll for medical benefits and pay a monthly premium and so may persons aged 65 and over who are not eligible for hospital benefits.

Persons eligible for both hospital and medical insurance or for medical insurance only may choose to have their covered services provided through a Health Maintenance Organization (a prepaid group health or other capitation plan that meets prescribed standards).

Hospital insurance.—In the 11th year of operation (July 1976–June 1977) about $58.7 billion was withdrawn from the hospital insurance trust fund for hospital and related benefits. About 25,316,000 persons were enrolled under the program as of July 1976—2,392,000 of them disabled beneficiaries under age 65.

The hospital insurance program pays the cost of covered services for hospital and posthospital care as follows:

- Up to 90 days of hospital care during a benefit period (spell of illness) starting the first day that care as a bed-patient is received in a hospital or skilled-nursing facility and ending when the individual has not been a bed-patient for 60 consecutive days. For the first 60 days, the hospital insurance pays for all but the first $144 of expenses; for the 61st day to 90th day, the program pays all but $36 a day for covered services. In addition, each person has a 60-day lifetime reserve that can be used after the 90 days of hospital care in a benefit period are exhausted, and all but $72 a day of expenses during the reserve days are paid. Once used, the reserve days are not replaced. (Payment for care in a mental hospital is limited to 190 days.)
- Up to 100 days' care in a skilled-nursing facility (skilled-nursing home) in each benefit period. Hospital insurance pays for all covered services for the first 20 days and all but $18 daily for the next 80 days. At least 3 days' hospital stay must precede these services, and the skilled-nursing facility must be entered within 14 days after leaving the hospital. (The 1972 law permits more than 14 days in certain circumstances.)
- Up to 100 visits by nurses or other health workers (not doctors) from a home health agency in the 365 days after release from a hospital or extended-care facility.

Money to pay these benefits comes from special contributions paid by workers, their employers, and the self-employed.

Medical insurance. Aged persons can receive benefits under this supplementary program only if they sign up for them and agree to a monthly premium ($8.70 beginning July 1979). The federal government pays the rest of the cost. In December of each year the Secretary of Health, Education, and Welfare announces the premium payable starting in July of the following year. The premiums are to be increased only when there is a general benefit increase in the year and it will rise no more than the percent by which the cash benefits have been increased since the last premium increase.

About 140 million bills were reimbursed under the medical insurance program from Jan. 1976 to July 1977 for a total of $7.5 billion. As of July 1976, 24,614,400 persons were enrolled—2,168,500 of them disabled persons under age 65.

The medical insurance program pays 80% of the reasonable charges (after the first $60 in each calendar year) for the following services:

- Physicians' and surgeons' services, whether in the doctor's office, a clinic, or hospital or at home (but physician's charges for X-ray or clinical laboratory services for hospital bed-patients are paid in full and without meeting the deductible).
- Other medical and health services, such as diagnostic tests, surgical dressings and splints, and rental or purchase of medical equipment. Services of a physical therapist in independent practice, furnished in his office or the patient's home. A hospital or extended-care facility may provide covered outpatient physical therapy services under the medical insurance program to its patients who have exhausted their hospital insurance coverage.
- Physical therapy services furnished under the supervision of a practicing hospital, clinic, skilled nursing facility, or agency.
- Certain services by podiatrists.
- All outpatient services of a participating hospital (including diagnostic tests).
- Outpatient speech pathology services, under the same requirements as physical therapy.
- Services of licensed chiropractors who meet uniform standards, but only for treatment by means of manual manipulation of the spine and treatment of subluxation of the spine demonstrated by X-ray.
- Supplies related to colostomies are consid-

ered prosthetic devices and payable under the program.

- Home health services even without a hospital stay (up to 100 visits a year) are paid up to 100%.

To get medical insurance protection, persons approaching age 65 may enroll in the 7-month period that includes 3 months before the 65th birthday, the month of the birthday, and 3 months after the birthday, but if they wish coverage to begin in the month they reach 65 they must enroll in the 3 months before their birthday. Persons not enrolling within their first enrollment period may enroll later, during the first 3 months of each year but their premium is 10% higher for each 12-month period elapsed since they first could have enrolled.

The monthly premium is deducted from the cash benefit for persons receiving social security, railroad retirement, or civil service retirement benefits. Income from the medical premiums and the federal matching payments are put in a Supplementary Medical Insurance Trust Fund, from which benefits and administrative expenses are paid.

Medicare card. Persons qualifying for hospital insurance under social security receive a health insurance card similar to cards now used by Blue Cross and other health agencies. The card indicates whether the individual has taken out medical insurance protection. It is to be shown to the hospital, skilled nursing facility, home health agency, doctor, or whoever provides the covered services.

Payments are made only in the 50 states, Puerto Rico, the Virgin Islands, Guam, and American Samoa, except that hospital services may be provided in border areas immediately outside the U.S. if comparable services are not accessible in the U.S. for a beneficiary who becomes ill or is injured in the U.S.

AMOUNT OF WORK REQUIRED

To qualify for benefits for himself and his family, the worker must have been in covered employment long enough to become insured. Just how long depends on his date of birth (or if he dies or becomes disabled, the date of his death or disability).

A person is fully covered if he has one quarter of coverage for every year after 1950 (or year he reaches age 21) up to but not including the year in which he reaches age 62 or dies.

Certain provisions in the law permit special monthly payments under the social security program to persons aged 72 and over who are not eligible for regular social security benefits since they had little or no opportunity to earn social security work credits during their working lifetime.

To get disability benefits, the worker must also have credit for 5 out of 10 years before he becomes disabled. Persons disabled before age 31 can qualify with a briefer period of coverage.

WORK YEARS REQUIRED

The following table shows the number of work years required to be fully insured for old-age or survivors benefits, according to the year worker reaches retirement age or dies.

WHAT AGED WORKERS GET

When a person has enough work in covered employment and reaches retirement age (65 for full benefit, 62 for reduced benefit), he may retire and get monthly old-age benefits. If he continues to work and has earnings of more than $5,000 in 1980, $1 in benefits will be withheld for every $2 above $5,000. The amount that can be earned in a month without loss of any benefits is $270. The annual exempt amount and the monthly test are raised automatically or according to the rise in general earnings levels. The eligible worker who is 72 receives the full amount of benefit regardless of earnings.

A worker's benefit will be raised by 1% for each year after 1970 for which the worker between 65 and 72 did not receive benefits because of earnings from work. No increases are to be paid to the worker's dependents or survivors under this provision.

A special minimum benefit is payable to persons who worked 20 or more years under social security as an alternative to the regular minimum ($114.30 in June 1977) if a higher amount results. The highest minimum under this provision would be $252.80 a month, effective June 1979, for a person with 30 or more years of coverage.

When a person receives old-age benefits, payments can also be made to certain of his dependents, including a wife 62 or over, dependent children under 18 or who became totally disabled before age 22 or who are full-time students not yet aged 22, a wife (regardless of age) if caring for an eligible child, and a dependent husband 62 or over.

The special benefit for persons aged 72 or

Work credit for retirement benefits

If you reach 62 in	Years you need	If you reach 62 in	Years you need
1974	6*	1979	7
1975	6*	1981	7½
1976	6¼	1983	8
1977	6½	1987	9
1978	6¾	1991 or later	10

*For 1974 a woman needs only 5¾ years.

Deceased's work credit for survivor's benefits

Born after 1929, die at	Born before 1930, die before age 62	Years needed
28 or younger		1½
30		2
32		2½
34		3
36		3½
38		4
40		4½
42		5
44	1973	5½
45	1974	5¾
46	1975	6
48	1977	6½
50	1979	7
52	1981	7½
54	1983	8
56	1985	8½
58	1987	9
60	1989	9½
62 or older	1991 or later	10

Tax-rate schedule under old and new law

[Percent of covered earnings]

Year	TOTAL Old law	TOTAL New law	OASDI Old law	OASDI New law	HI Old law	HI New law
	Employees and employers, each					
1977	5.85	5.85	4.95	4.95	0.90	0.90
1978	6.05	6.05	4.95	5.05	1.10	1.00
1979–80	6.05	6.13	4.95	5.08	1.10	1.05
1981	6.30	6.65	4.95	5.35	1.35	1.30
1982–84	6.30	6.70	4.95	5.40	1.35	1.30
1985	6.30	7.05	4.95	5.70	1.35	1.35
1986–89	6.45	7.15	4.95	5.70	1.50	1.45
1990–2010	6.45	7.65	4.95	6.20	1.50	1.45
2011 and after	7.45	7.65	5.95	6.20	1.50	1.45
	Self-employed					
1977	7.90	7.90	7.00	7.00	0.90	0.90
1978	8.10	8.10	7.00	7.10	1.10	1.00
1979–80	8.10	8.10	7.00	7.05	1.10	1.05
1981	8.35	9.30	7.00	8.00	1.35	1.30
1982–84	8.35	9.35	7.00	8.05	1.35	1.30
1985	8.35	9.90	7.00	8.55	1.35	1.35
1986–89	8.50	10.00	7.00	8.55	1.50	1.45
1990–2010	8.50	10.75	7.00	9.30	1.50	1.45
2011 and after	8.50	10.75	7.00	9.30	1.50	1.45

over who do not meet the regular coverage requirements is $78.40 a month ($117.60 for a couple if both members are eligible). Like the monthly benefits, these payments are now subject to cost-of-living increases. The special payment is not made to persons on the public assistance or supplemental security income rolls.

Social security benefits are not subject to income taxes.

A woman worker is eligible for a full old-age benefit at age 65, but she may retire at 62 and get 80% of her full benefit for the rest of her life; the nearer she is to 65 when she begins collecting her benefit, the larger it will be. (Benefits for men retiring before 65 are reduced at the same rate as benefits for women retiring before 65).

A child can get benefits based on his mother's earnings on the same conditions as those entitling a child to benefits based on his father's earnings record.

OASDI	July 1979	July 1978	June 1977
Monthly beneficiaries, total (in thousands)	**34,673**	**34,106**	**33,333**
Aged 65 and over, total	22,858	22,154	21,447
Retired workers	16,729	16,126	15,549
Survivors and dependents	6,010	5,885	5,725
Special age-72 beneficiaries	120	143	173
Under age 65, total	11,815	11,952	11,886
Retired workers	1,924	1,901	1,831
Disabled workers	2,881	2,871	2,755
Survivors and dependents	7,010	7,180	7,300
Total monthly benefits (in millions)	**$8,871**	**$7,739**	**$6,933**

BENEFITS FOR WORKER'S SPOUSE

The wife of a man who is getting social security retirement or disability payments may become entitled to wife's insurance benefits in a reduced amount when she reaches 62, or she may wait until she reaches 65 and get the entire amount of the wife's benefit, which is one-half of the husband's benefit. Benefits are also payable to the divorced wife of an insured worker if she was married to him for at least 20 years (10 years eff. Jan. 1979) and he was contributing to or was ordered by a court to contribute to her support.

If a woman worker entitled to an old-age benefit has a dependent husband aged 65 or over, he may draw a benefit similar to a wife's benefit at 65 (or a reduced benefit at age 62).

BENEFITS FOR CHILDREN OF RETIRED OR DISABLED WORKERS

If a worker has children under 18 when he retires for age or disability they will get a benefit that is half his benefit, and so will his wife, even if she is under 62. Total benefits paid on a worker's earnings record are subject to a maximum and if the total paid to a family exceed that maximum, the individual dependents' benefits are adjusted downward. (Total benefits paid to the family of a worker who retired in 1975 at age 65 with average monthly earnings of $1,175 can be no higher than $1,098.)

When his children reach 18, their benefits will stop, except that a child permanently and totally disabled before 22 may get a benefit as long as his disability meets the definition in the law. In addition, child's benefits are payable until the child reaches his 22nd birthday if he is attending school as a full-time student. Benefits may now be paid to a grandchild or step-grandchild of a worker or of his spouse, in special circumstances.

WHAT DISABLED WORKERS GET

If a worker becomes so severely disabled that he is unable to work, he may be eligible to receive a monthly disability benefit that is the same amount he would receive as an old-age benefit if he were 65 at the start of his disability. When he reaches 65, his disability benefit becomes an old-age benefit.

Benefits like those provided for dependents of retired-worker beneficiaries may be paid to dependents of disabled beneficiaries.

SURVIVOR BENEFITS

If a worker should die while insured, one or more types of benefits would be payable to survivors.

1. A cash payment to cover burial expenses that amounts to 3 times the basic benefit but not more than $255, paid at the death of every insured worker.

2. A benefit for each child until the child reaches 18 (or up to age 22, if he is attending school). The monthly benefit of each child of a worker who has died is three-quarters of the amount the worker would have received if he had lived and drawn retirement benefits. A child with a permanent disability that began before age 22 may receive his benefit after that age.

3. A mother's benefit for the widow, if children under 18 are left in her care. Her benefit is 75% of the basic benefit and she draws it until the youngest child reaches 18. Payments stop then even if the child's benefit continues because he is attending school. They will start again when she is 62 (or 60), unless she marries. If she marries and the marriage is ended, she regains benefit rights. If she has a disabled child beneficiary aged 18 or over in her care, her benefits also continue.

Disabled widows and widowers qualify for benefits at age 50 at reduced rates that depend on age at entitlement. The widow or widower must have become totally disabled before or within 7 years after the spouse's death.

4. If there are no children entitled to receive benefits, the widow will receive a benefit that is 100% of the husband's basic amount, if it is first payable when she is 65. She may choose to get her benefit when she is 60; her benefit is then reduced by 19/40 of 1% for each month it is paid before she is 65. However, for widows aged 62 and over whose husbands claimed their benefits before 65, the benefit is the reduced amount he would be getting if he were alive but not less than 82½% of his basic benefit. Dependent widowers aged 60 or over are entitled to survivor benefits on same basis as widows.

5. Dependent parents may be eligible for benefits, if they have been receiving at least half their support from the worker before his death, have reached age 62, and (except in certain circumstances) have not remarried since the worker's death. Each parent gets 75% of the basic benefit except that if only one parent survives the benefit is 82½%.

The survivors of a woman worker receive benefits on the same basis as those of men workers. (Beginning March 1975, widowed father's benefits are payable on same basis as widowed mother's benefits).

MAXIMUM BENEFITS PAYABLE

The illustrative table on page 108 shows a column heading for average monthly earnings of $1,475, but the benefit amounts shown in the column are not in general payable yet, since it will be some time before workers can have an average that high (years when the maximum creditable amount of earnings was lower than $17,700—the 1978 maximum—must currently be included when the average is figured). Benefit amounts larger than those shown in the table will eventually be payable to persons who raise their average yearly earnings for social security purposes by earning, for a sufficient period, the highest creditable amount in years with the higher maximums specified in the law—$17,700 in 1978 and $22,900 in 1979 (higher amounts in the future whenever the base is raised under the automatic adjustment procedure).

Contribution and benefit base under old and new law

Calendar year	Old law[1]	New law[2]
1977	$16,500	$16,500
1978	17,700	17,700
1979	18,900	22,900
1980	20,400	25,900
1981	21,900	29,700
1982	23,400	31,800

(1) Estimated under automatic-adjustment provisions for 1979–82. (2) Stated in law for 1979–81. Estimated under automatic adjustment-provisions for 1982.

SELF-EMPLOYED

A self-employed person who has earnings of $400 or more in a year must report his earnings for income tax and social security tax purposes. If he is not a farmer he reports only net returns from his business. He need not add income from real estate, savings, dividends, loans, pensions or insurance policies if these are not part of his business.

A self-employed person who has net earnings of $400 or more in a year gets 4 quarters of coverage for that year. If his earnings are less than $400 in a year they do not count toward social security credits. The nonfarm self-employed person must make estimated payments of his social security taxes, on a quarterly basis, for taxable years after 1966, if combined estimated income tax and social security tax amount to at least $40.

The self-employed now have the option, comparable to that for farm workers, of reporting their earnings as ⅔ of their gross income from self-employment but not more than $1,600 a year. This option can be used only if actual net earnings from self-employment income is less than $1,600 and less than ⅔ of gross income and may be used only 5 times.

When a person has both taxable wages and earnings from self-employment, only as much of the self-employment income as will bring total earnings up to the current taxable maximum is subject to tax for social security purposes. A self-employed person pays the tax at a lower rate than the combined rate for an employee and his employer—about 1½ times what the employee alone pays.

FARM OWNERS AND WORKERS

Self-employed farmers whose gross annual earnings from farming are under $2,400 may report ⅔ of their gross earnings instead of net earnings for social security purposes. Cash or crop shares received from a tenant or share farmer count if the owner participated materially in production or management. The self-employed farmer pays contributions at the same rate as other self-employed, but he may make his tax returns annually.

Farm workers. Earnings from farm work count toward benefits (1) if the employer pays $150 or more in cash during the year; (2) if the employee works on 20 or more days for cash pay figured on a time basis. Under these rules a person gets credit for one calendar quarter for each $250 in cash pay in a year but no more than four quarters in any one year.

Foreign farm workers admitted to the United States on a temporary basis are not covered.

HOUSEHOLD WORKERS

Anyone working as maid, cook, laundress, nursemaid, baby-sitter, chauffeur, gardener and at other household tasks in the house of another, is covered by social security if he or she earns $50 or more in cash in three months from any one employer. Room and board do not count, but carfare counts if paid in cash. The job does not have to be regular or fulltime. The employee should get a card at the social security office and show it to the employer.

The employer deducts the amount of the social security tax from the worker's pay, adds an identical amount as his own tax and sends the total amount to the federal government, with the number of the employee's social security card.

SUPPLEMENTAL SECURITY INCOME

On Jan. 1, 1974, the supplemental security income program established by the 1972 Social Security Act amendments replaced the former federal grants to states for aid to the needy aged, blind, and disabled in the 50 states and the District of Columbia. The program provides both for federal payments based on uniform national standards and eligibility requirements and for state supplementary payments varying from state to state. The Social Security Administration administers the federal payments financed from general funds of the Treasury—and the state supplements as well, if the state elects to have its supplementary program federally administered. The states may supplement the federal payment for all recipients and must supplement it for persons otherwise adversely affected by the transition from the former public assistance programs. In July 1979, the number of persons receiving federal payments and federally administered state payments was 4,165,600, and the amount of these payments was $587.4 million. The average amount of combined federal payments and federally administered state payments was $141 for that month.

As a result of the 9.9 percent cost-of-living increase in social security benefits in June 1979, the federal SSI payment levels were raised in July 1979, from $189.40 per month for an individual and $284.10 for a couple to $208.20 and $312.30 respectively.

Minimum and maximum monthly retired-worker benefits payable to individuals who retired at age 65, 1940–79

Year of attainment of age 65[1]	Minimum benefit		Maximum benefit			
	Payment at the time of retirement	Payable effective June 1979	Payable at the time of retirement		Payable effective June 1979	
			Men[2]	Women	Men[2]	Women
1940	$10.00	$133.90	$41.20		$259.00	
1941	10.00	133.90	41.60		259.00	
1942	10.00	133.90	42.00		262.20	
1943	10.00	133.90	42.40		262.20	
1944	10.00	133.90	42.80		265.00	
1945	10.00	133.90	43.20		265.00	
1946	10.00	133.90	43.60		268.20	
1947	10.00	133.90	44.00		270.70	
1948	10.00	133.90	44.40		270.70	
1949	10.00	133.90	44.80		273.40	
1950	10.00	133.90	45.20		276.80	
1951	20.00	133.90	68.50		276.80	
1952	20.00	133.90	68.50		276.80	
1953	25.00	133.90	85.00		305.70	
1954	25.00	133.90	85.00		305.70	
1955	30.00	133.90	98.50		305.70	
1956	30.00	133.90	103.50		322.90	
1957	30.00	133.90	108.50		337.60	
1958	30.00	133.90	108.50		337.60	
1959	33.00	133.90	116.00		337.60	
1960	33.00	133.90	119.00		346.10	
1961	33.00	133.90	120.00		348.80	
1962	40.00	133.90	121.00	$123.00	351.90	$357.90
1963	40.00	133.90	122.00	125.00	354.90	363.30
1964	40.00	133.90	123.00	127.00	357.90	369.30
1965	44.00	133.90	131.70	135.90	357.90	369.30
1966	44.00	133.90	132.70	135.90	360.50	369.30
1967	44.00	133.90	135.90	140.00	369.30	380.30
1968	55.00[3]	133.90	156.00[3]	161.60[3]	374.90	388.20
1969	55.00	133.90	160.50	167.30	385.90	402.20
1970	64.00	133.90	189.80	196.40	396.60	410.50
1971	70.40	133.90	213.10	220.40	404.80	418.40
1972	70.40	133.90	216.10	224.70	410.50	426.70
1973	84.50	133.90	266.10	276.40	421.10	437.50
1974	84.50	133.90	274.60	284.90	434.50	450.90
1975	93.80	133.90	316.30	333.70	450.90	475.60
1976	101.40	133.90	364.00	378.80	480.20	499.80
1977	107.90	133.90	412.70	422.40	511.70	523.70
1978	114.30	133.90	459.80	459.80	538.20	538.20
1979	121.80	133.90	503.40	503.40	553.30	553.30

(1) Assumes retirement at beginning of year. (2) Represents benefit for both men and women until 1962. (3) Effective for February 1968.

Examples of OASDI Monthly Cash Benefits
(under the Social Security Act, effective June 1979)

Beneficiary family	Average monthly earnings of insured worker: $76 or less	$200	$400	$550	$750	$900	$1,100	$1,275	$1,475
Retired worker claiming benefits at age 65, or disabled worker:									
Worker alone	$133.90	$244.50	$369.30	$456.50	$560.60	$608.20	$668.50	$716.00	$764.30
Worker with spouse claiming benefits at—									
Age 65 or over	200.90	366.80	554.00	684.80	840.90	912.30	1,002.80	1,074.00	1,146.50
Age 62	184.20	336.30	507.90	627.80	770.90	836.30	919.30	984.50	1,051.00
Worker, spouse, and 1 child	200.90	366.80	673.40	826.10	981.10	1,064.20	1,169.40	1,252.90	1,337.40
Retired worker claiming benefits at age 62:									
Worker alone	107.20	195.60	295.50	365.20	448.50	486.60	534.80	572.80	611.50
Worker with spouse claiming benefits at—									
Age 65 or over	174.20	317.90	480.20	593.50	728.80	790.70	869.10	930.80	993.70
Age 62	157.50	287.40	434.10	536.50	658.80	714.70	785.60	841.30	898.20
Widow or widower claiming benefits at—									
Age 65 or over[1]	133.90	244.50	369.30	456.50	560.60	608.20	668.50	716.00	764.30
Age 60	95.80	174.90	264.10	326.40	400.90	434.90	478.00	512.00	546.50
Disabled widow or widower claiming benefits at age 50	67.10	122.40	184.80	228.30	280.40	304.20	334.30	358.10	382.20
1 surviving child	[2]133.90	183.40	227.00	342.40	420.50	456.20	501.40	537.00	573.30
Widow or widower aged 65 and over and 1 child[1]	200.90	366.80	646.30	798.90	981.10	1,064.20	1,169.40	1,252.90	1,337.40
Widowed mother or father and 1 child	200.90	366.80	554.00	684.80	841.00	912.40	1,002.80	1,074.00	1,146.60
Widowed mother or father and 2 children	200.90	336.80	673.40	826.10	981.10	1,064.20	1,169.40	1,252.90	1,337.40
Maximum family benefits	200.90	366.80	673.40	826.10	981.10	1,064.20	1,169.40	1,252.90	1,337.40

(1) Widow's or widower's benefit limited to amount spouse would have been receiving if still living but not less than 82½ percent of the PIA. (2) Sole survivor. **NOTE:** The higher monthly earnings shown in column headings on the right are not, in general, possible now, since earnings in some of the earlier years—when the maximum amount creditable was lower—must be included in the average. Therefore, the benefit amounts shown in these columns are not generally currently payable. (Effective June 1979, the highest average monthly earnings possible for a worker retiring at age 65 is $727).

SOCIAL SECURITY TRUST FUNDS

Old-Age, Survivors, and Disability Insurance Trust Funds, 1937–1979
(thousands)

Fiscal year	Receipts: Net contrib. inc., transfers, and reimb. from gen'l rev.	Receipts: Net interest received	Expenditures: Cash benefit payments and rehab. services	Expenditures: Transfers to R.R. ret. acct.	Expenditures: Administrative expenses	Total assets at end of period
1937	$ 265,000	$ 2,262	$ 27	$...	$ 26,840	$ 267,235
1940	550,000	42,489	15,805	...	12,288	1,744,698
1950	2,109,912	256,778	727,266	...	56,841	12,892,612
1955	5,087,154	438,029	4,333,147	-9,551	103,202	21,141,001
1960	10,829,664	564,040	10,798,013	573,606	234,291	22,995,939
1965	17,032,456	648,372	16,618,084	459,253	379,145	22,187,184
1970	34,554,182	1,572,375	29,062,772	589,257	623,055	37,719,951
1975	63,872,883	2,803,838	62,547,281	1,010,299	1,100,693	48,138,321
1976	67,867,099	2,815,197	71,462,416	1,238,669	1,200,326	44,919,209
1976 (July–Sept)[1]	18,264,899	93,726	19,459,572	...	304,448	43,513,811
1977	78,511,213	2,658,629	82,490,402	1,207,523	1,370,386	39,615,344
1978	87,192,105	2,403,128	90,828,787	1,618,461	1,413,414	35,349,916
1979 (Oct. '78–June '79)	72,919,080	2,072,954	73,866,540	1,477,438	1,111,725	33,886,245
Cum. 1937–June '79	**852,718,813**	**36,049,844**	**824,072,561**	**14,922,643**	**15,885,923**	**33,886,245**

(1) Transitional quarter. Beginning Oct. 1976, federal fiscal year begins Oct. 1.

Hospital Insurance Trust Fund, 1966–79

(thousands)

Fiscal year	Receipts: Net contribution income[1]	Receipts: Transfers from general revenues[2]	Receipts: Transfers from railroad retirement account[3]	Receipts: Net Interest[4]	Expenditures: Net hospital and related service benefits[5]	Expenditures: Administrative expenses[6]	Total assets
1966	$908,797	...	...	$5,970	...	$63,564	$851,204
1967	2,688,684	$337,850	$16,200	45,903	$2,507,773	88,848	1,343,221
1970	4,784,789	628,262	61,307	139,423	4,804,242	148,660	2,677,401
1973	7,663,119	429,415	61,222	197,844	6,648,819	192,839	4,368,666
1974	10,606,551	498,780	96,163	408,273	7,785,596	285,066	7,934,772
1975	11,296,773	529,353	126,749	614,989	10,355,390	256,134	9,870,039
1976	12,039,194	658,430	130,904	715,744	12,270,382	308,215	10,835,714
1976 (July–Sept.)[7]	3,367,940	...	135,863	11,951	3,315,251	88,408	10,947,810
1977	13,659,042	944,000	...	770,966	14,912,370	294,762	11,114,685
1978	16,689,361	830,938	196,506	797,209	17,415,132	417,537	11,796,031
1979 (Oct. '78–June '79)	14,444,121	874,849	175,600	873,215	14,764,472	302,400	13,096,943
Cum. July '66–June '79)	**116,209,516**	**8,211,676**	**1,224,940**	**5,111,773**	**114,742,926**	**2,918,046**	**13,096,943**

(1) Represents amounts appropriated (estimated tax collections with suitable subsequent adjustments), after deductions for refund of estimated amount of employee-tax overpayment. (2) Represents Federal Government transfers from general funds appropriations to meet costs of benefits for persons not insured for cash benefits under OASDHI or railroad retirement and for costs of benefits arising from military wage credits. (3) Represents receipts under the financial interchange with railroad retirement account with respect to contributions for hospital insurance coverage of railroad workers. (4) Represents interest and profit on investments after transfers of interest on administrative expenses reimbursed to the OASI trust fund and on amounts transferred from railroad accounts. (5) Represents (1) payment vouchers on letters of credit issued to fiscal intermediaries under sec. 1816 and (2) direct payments to providers of services under sec. 1815 of the Social Security Act. (6) Subject to subsequent adjustment among all 4 social security trust funds, for allocated cost of each operation. (7) Transitional quarter. Beginning Oct. 1976, federal fiscal year begins Oct. 1.

Supplementary Medical Insurance Trust Fund, 1967–79

(thousands)

Fiscal year:	Receipts: Premium income[1]	Receipts: Transfers from general revenues[2]	Receipts: Net interest[3]	Expenditures: Net medical service benefits[4]	Expenditures: Administrative expenses[5]	Total assets
1967	$646,682	$623,000	$14,052	$664,261	$133,682	$485,791
1970	936,000	928,151	11,536	1,979,287	216,993	57,181
1974	1,703,189	2,028,926	75,924	2,869,132	409,146	1,275,483
1975	1,886,962	2,329,590	105,539	3,765,397	404,458	1,424,413
1976	1,951,221	2,939,338	103,645	4,671,847	528,214	1,218,555
1976 (July–Sept.)[6]	538,648	878,000	4,420	1,269,038	132,077	1,238,508
1977	2,192,903	5,052,944	136,710	5,866,922	474,717	2,279,426
1978	2,431,133	6,385,503	228,848	6,852,252	504,234	3,968,425
1979 (Oct. '78–June '79)	1,952,405	5,096,780	352,803	6,078,129	411,911	4,880,371
Cum. July '67–June '79	**19,861,206**	**31,921,545**	**1,168,930**	**43,736,547**	**4,334,962**	**4,880,371**

(1) Represents voluntary premium payments from and in behalf of insured persons. (2) Represents Federal Government transfers from general funds appropriations to match aggregate premiums paid. (3) Represents interest and profit on investments after transfer of interest on administrative expenses reimbursed to the OASI trust fund (see footnote 5). (4) Represents payment vouchers on letters of credit issued to carriers under section 1842 of the Social Security Act. (5) Subject to subsequent adjustment among all 4 social security trust funds for allocated cost of each operation. (6) Transitional quarter. Beginning Oct. 1976, federal fiscal year begins Oct. 1.

EMPLOYMENT AND TRAINING SERVICES AND UNEMPLOYMENT INSURANCE

EMPLOYMENT SERVICE

The Federal-State Employment Service consists of the U.S. Employment Service and affiliated state employment services with their network of about 2,500 local offices. During fiscal year 1978, these offices made 6.6 million placements, 6.2 million in nonagricultural and 385,000 in agricultural industries. Overall, 4.6 million different individuals were placed in employment.

The employment service works to refer employable applicants to job openings that use their highest skills and helps the unemployed obtain services or training to make them employable. It also provides special attention to help older workers, youth, minorities, the poor, handicapped workers, migrants, seasonal farmworkers, and workers who lose their jobs because of foreign trade competition.

Veterans receive special services and absolute preference in placements at all employment service offices. During fiscal year 1978, these offices placed over 766,000 veterans in jobs.

COMPREHENSIVE EMPLOYMENT AND TRAINING SERVICES

The Comprehensive Employment and Training Act (CETA) of 1973 sets up a community system to give people training and job-related services and place them in jobs. Under this system all states and cities, counties, and combinations of local units with populations of 100,000 or more receive federal grants to plan and run comprehensive employment and training programs and provide public service jobs in their localities. Under the new Private Sector Initiative Program, every program sponsor sets up a Private Industry Council to help involve businesses in hiring and training economically disadvantaged workers. A major inducement for employers to hire certain disadvantaged workers is the targeted jobs tax credit, amounting to $3,000 for each eligible worker paid $6,000 or more for the first year of employment.

Besides operating comprehensive programs, local governments plan and provide public service jobs for unemployed workers.

NATIONAL ACTIVITIES

The federal role under CETA is to provide support and technical assistance to local programs, insure proper use of federal money, and serve groups with special job disadvantages.

In addition to continuing programs for Indians and migrant and seasonal farmworkers, there are new and expanded efforts for youth. These efforts include the Young Adult Conservation Corps, which hires unemployed young people to work on public lands; Youth Incentive Entitlement Pilot Projects, providing part-time jobs and training to youth attending school; Youth Community Conservation and Improvement Projects, which give unemployed youth paid work in community betterment; and Youth Employment and Training Programs to improve young people's job prospects. In addition, Job Corps, which was training disadvantaged youth at 90 residential centers at the end of fiscal year 1979, plans continued expansion so that it can serve 44,000 youth at any one time. The Summer Program for Economically Disadvantaged Youth supported over a million part-time jobs in 1978. The Employment and Training Administration also has programs to promote apprenticeship and to help employable people on Aid to Families with Dependent Children find jobs.

UNEMPLOYMENT INSURANCE

Unlike old-age and survivors insurance, entirely a federal program, the unemployment insurance program is a Federal-State system that provides insured wage earners with partial replacement of wages lost during involuntary unemployment. The program protects most workers in industry. During calendar year 1978, an estimated 86.2 million jobs in commerce, industry, agriculture, and government, including the armed forces, were covered under the Federal-State system. In addition, an estimated 500,000 railroad workers were insured against unemployment by the Railroad Retirement Board.

Each state, as well as the District of Columbia, Puerto Rico, and the Virgin Islands, has its own law and operates its own program. The amount and duration of the weekly benefits are determined by state laws, based on prior wages and length of employment. States are required to extend the duration of benefits when unemployment rises to and remains above specified state or national levels; costs of extended benefits are shared by the state and federal governments.

Under the Federal Unemployment Tax Act, as amended in 1976, the tax rate is 3.4% on the first $6,000 paid to each employee of employers with one or more employees in 20 weeks of the year or a quarterly payroll of $1,500. A credit of up to 2.7% is allowed for taxes paid under state unemployment insurance laws that meet certain criteria, leaving the federal share at 0.7% of taxable wages.

SOCIAL SECURITY REQUIREMENT

The Social Security Act requires, as a condition of such grants, prompt payment of due benefits. The Federal Unemployment Tax Act provides safeguards for workers' right to benefits if they refuse jobs that fail to meet certain labor standards. Through the Unemployment Insurance Service of the Employment and Training Administration, the Secretary of Labor determines whether states qualify for grants and for tax offset credit for employers.

Benefits are financed solely by employer contributions, except in Alaska, Alabama, and New Jersey, where employees also contribute. Benefits are paid through the public employment offices, at which unemployed workers must register for work and to which they must report regularly for referral to a possible job during the time when they are drawing weekly benefit payments. During the 1978 calendar year, $7.7 billion in benefits was paid under state unemployment insurance programs to 7,566,000 beneficiaries, representing compensation for 128,723,700 weeks of unemployment. They received an average weekly payment of $83.67 for total unemployment for an average of 13.3 weeks.

FEDERAL WORKER BENEFITS

Title 5, chapter 85 of the U.S. Code provided unemployment insurance protection during calendar year 1978 to about 2,922,600 federal civilian employees and about 2,167,800 members of the armed forces. Benefits for unemployed federal workers and ex-servicemen are financed through direct federal appropriations but are paid by the state agencies as agents of the federal government.

During calendar year 1978, a total of $175,498,200 was paid to 96,900 unemployed federal civilian workers for a total of 1,793,400 weeks of unemployment. The average weekly payment was $86.06 and was paid for an average of 16.5 weeks. A total of $277,681,690 was paid to 175,300 unemployed ex-servicemen for 2,863,400 weeks of unemployment. The average weekly benefit was $89.69 and was paid for an average of 15.8 weeks.

EMPLOYMENT SECURITY

Selected unemployment insurance data by state. Calendar year 1978, state programs only.

	Insured claimants[1] (1,000)	Beneficiaries[1] (1,000)	Exhaustions[3] (1,000)	Initial claims[4] (1,000)	Benefits paid[5] (1,000)	Avg. weekly benefit for total unemployment[P]	Funds available for benefits Dec. 31, 1978[6] (millions)	Employers subject to state law Dec. 31, 1978 (1,000)
Alabama	160	153	36	297	$101,255	$70.18	$88	64
Alaska	43	43	15	80	76,387	85.01	58	10
Arizona	55	37	11	115	31,854	73.82	138	47
Arkansas	129	81	17	220	54,482	72.00	34	48
California	1,553	1,134	275	2,513	962,998	75.84	1,756	515
Colorado	68	52	15	147	49,902	92.59	98	66
Connecticut	190	159	31	367	138,351	89.43	76	76
Delaware	30	25	6	63	30,068	93.56	16	13
District of Columbia	33	28	12	40	50,531	106.66	9	17
Florida	191	150	65	364	111,848	63.68	403	185
Georgia	248	181	48	367	104,077	73.39	347	96
Hawaii	37	28	9	57	37,392	93.29	38	20
Idaho	38	33	7	97	25,192	84.30	81	22
Illinois	390	370	124	768	608,959	97.68	−604	231
Indiana	203	137	38	352	95,081	75.75	358	90
Iowa	96	81	14	152	106,423	103.96	94	65
Kansas	60	45	12	90	47,335	84.47	200	54
Kentucky	153	120	26	253	101,259	79.30	166	62
Louisiana	139	97	32	208	123,472	91.62	124	72
Maine	66	62	17	173	40,737	73.33	25	29
Maryland	141	112	22	264	98,455	76.40	121	72
Massachusetts	264	234	66	550	263,381	84.00	215	115
Michigan	434	420	125	1,015	392,904	92.85	617	157
Minnesota	128	105	33	182	116,634	96.66	164	83
Mississippi	85	58	13	154	37,411	60.37	180	40
Missouri	222	169	49	436	125,883	75.62	211	108
Montana	40	29	7	63	26,696	84.14	15	22
Nebraska	45	31	9	58	24,487	79.54	66	36
Nevada	32	29	8	77	29,651	83.54	60	18
New Hampshire	38	27	1	52	14,389	74.35	60	21
New Jersey	432	338	134	739	515,675	87.68	148	159
New Mexico	27	20	5	62	19,047	68.71	55	27
New York	812	617	206	1,736	881,247	83.74	31	392
North Carolina	267	165	26	507	99,358	71.65	404	124
North Dakota	19	18	4	35	20,286	87.40	17	18
Ohio	353	266	58	682	336,028	100.32	452	192
Oklahoma	56	38	13	106	30,775	75.91	119	56
Oregon	120	93	18	274	86,718	81.18	194	63
Pennsylvania	679	599	110	1,390	730,759	97.83	193	208
Puerto Rico	112	127	47	244	73,108	45.53	36	46
Rhode Island	84	100	20	263	65,456	76.79	−88	24

EMPLOYMENT SECURITY

Selected unemployment insurance data by state. Calendar year 1978, state programs only.

	Insured claimants[1] (1,000)	Beneficiaries[1] (1,000)	Exhaustions[3] (1,000)	Initial claims[4] (1,000)	Benefits paid[5] (1,000)	Avg. weekly benefit for total unemployment[p]	Funds available for benefits Dec. 31, 1978[6] (millions)	Employers subject to state law Dec. 31, 1978 (1,000)
South Carolina	120	77	21	247	58,711	73.31	136	50
South Dakota	13	13	3	34	8,807	78.35	14	18
Tennessee	236	139	33	401	98,617	66.16	243	73
Texas	233	173	64	409	137,519	68.18	346	242
Utah	42	34	7	67	31,720	88.70	49	28
Vermont	25	19	4	43	16,909	76.10	16	14
Virginia	156	99	26	228	90,998	83.51	96	90
Virgin Islands	4	3	1	6	3,534	63.46[p]	2	2
Washington	152	129	33	440	134,482	86.80	104	90
West Virginia	208	94	12	154	74,517	75.22	57	32
Wisconsin	248	168	49	360	168,097	94.36	362	94
Wyoming	11	7	1	15	7,309	88.03	59	14
Total	**9,718**	**7,566**	**2,039**	**18,013**	**$7,717,173**	**$83.67[p]**	**$8,258**	**4,512**

(p.) Preliminary. (1) Claimants whose base-period earnings or whose employment—covered by the unemployment insurance program—was sufficient to make them eligible for unemployment insurance benefits as provided by state law. (2) Based on number of first payments. (3) Based on final payments. Some claimants shown, therefore, actually experienced their final week of compensable unemployment toward the end of the previous calendar year but received their final payments in the current calendar year. Similarly, some claimants who served their last week of compensable unemployment toward the end of the current calendar year did not receive their final payment in this calendar year and hence are not shown. A final week of compensable unemployment in a benefit year results in the exhaustion of benefit rights for the benefit year. Claimants who exhaust their benefit rights in one benefit year may be entitled to further benefits in the following benefit year. (4) Excludes intrastate transitional claims to reflect more nearly instances of new unemployment. Includes claims filed by interstate claimants in the Virgin Islands. (5) Adjusted for voided benefit checks and transfers under interstate combined wage plan. (6) Sum of balance in state clearing accounts, benefit payment accounts, and unemployment trust fund accounts maintained in the U.S. Treasury.

U.S. GOVERNMENT INDEPENDENT AGENCIES

ACTION—Sam Brown, dir. (806 Connecticut Ave., NW, 20525).

Administrative Conference of the United States—vacancy, chmn. (2120 L St., NW, 20037).

American Battle Monuments Commission—Mark W. Clark, chmn. (5127 Pulaski Bldg., 20314).

Appalachian Regional Commission—Albert P. Smith Jr., federal co-chmn.; Gov. John D. Rockefeller, 4th, states co-chmn. (1666 Connecticut Ave. NW, 20235).

Arms Control & Disarmament Agency—Robert Earle 2d, dir. (Department of State Bldg. 20451).

Board for International Broadcasting—John A. Gronouski, chmn. (1130 15th St., 20005).

Central Intelligence Agency—Adm. Stansfield Turner, dir. (Wash., DC 20505).

Civil Aeronautics Board—Marvin S. Cohen, chmn. (1825 Connecticut Ave. NW, 20428).

Commission on Civil Rights—Arthur S. Flemming, chmn. (1121 Vermont Ave. NW, 20425).

Commission of Fine Arts—J. Carter Brown, chmn. (708 Jackson Pl. NW, 20006).

Commodity Futures Trading Commission—James M. Stone, chmn. (2033 K St. NW, 20581).

Community Services Administration—vacancy, dir. (1200 19th St. NW, 20506).

Consumer Product Safety Commission—Susan B. King, chmn. (1111 18th St. NW, 20036).

Environmental Protection Agency—Douglas M. Costle, adm. (401 M St., SW, 20460).

Equal Employment Opportunity Commission—Eleanor Holmes Norton, chmn. (2401 E St., NW, 20506).

Export-Import Bank of the United States—John L. Moore Jr., pres. and chmn. (811 Vermont Ave. NW, 20571).

Farm Credit Administration—Ralph N. Austin, chmn. (490 L'Enfant Plaza East SW, 20578).

Federal Communications Commission—Charles D. Ferris, chmn. (1919 M St. NW, 20554).

Federal Deposit Insurance Corporation—

Irvine H. Sprague, chmn. (550 17th St. NW, 20429).

Federal Election Commission—Robert O. Tiernan, chmn. (1325 K St. NW, 20463).

Federal Emergency Management Agency—John W. Macy Jr., dir. (1725 I St., 20472).

Federal Home Loan Bank Board—John Janis, chmn. (1700 G St. NW, 20552).

Federal Labor Relations Authority—Ronald W. Haughton, chmn. (1900 E St. NW, 20424).

Federal Maritime Commission—Richard J. Daschbach, chmn. (1100 L St. NW, 20573).

Federal Mediation and Conciliation Service—Wayne L. Horvitz, dir. (2100 K St. NW, 20427).

Federal Reserve System—Chairman, board of governors: Paul A. Volcker. (20th St. & Constitution Ave. NW, 20551).

Federal Trade Commission—Commissioners: Michael Pertschuk, chmn., Paul Rand Dixon, Robert Pitofsky, David A. Clanton, Patricia P. Bailey (Pennsylvania Ave. at 6th St. NW, 20580).

General Accounting Office—Comptroller general of the U.S.: Elmer B. Staats. (441 G St. NW, 20548).

General Services Administration—Roland G. Freeman, 3d, admin. (18th & F Sts. NW, 20405).

Government Printing Office—Public printer: Samuel L. Saylor, act. (North Capitol and H Sts. NW, 20401).

Inter-American Foundation—Peter T. Jones, chmn. (1515 Wilson Blvd., Rosslyn, VA 22209).

International Communication Agency—John E. Reinhardt, dir. (1750 Pennsylvania Ave. NW, 20547).

Interstate Commerce Commission—Darius W. Gaskins Jr., chmn. (12th St. and Constitution Ave. NW, 20423).

Library of Congress—Daniel J. Boorstin, librarian (10 First St. SE, 20540).

Merit Systems Protection Board—Ruth T. Prokop, chmn. (1717 H St. NW, 20419).

National Aeronautics and Space Administration—Robert A. Frosch, admin. (400 Maryland Ave., SW 20546).

National Capital Planning Commission—David M. Childs, chmn. (1325 G St., NW, 20576).

National Credit Union Administration—Lawrence Connell, admin. (1776 G St. NW, 20456).

National Foundation on the Arts and Humanities—Livingston L. Biddle Jr. chmn. (arts). Joseph D. Duffey, chmn. (arts: 2401 E St. NW, 20506; humanities: 806 15th St. NW, 20506).

National Labor Relations Board—John H. Fanning, chmn. (1717 Pennsylvania Ave. NW, 20570).

National Mediation Board—Robert O. Harris, chmn. (1425 K St. NW, 20572).

National Science Foundation—Norman Hackerman, chmn. (1800 G St. NW, 20550).

National Transportation Safety Board—James B. King, chmn. (800 Independence Ave. SW 20594).

Nuclear Regulatory Commission—John F. Ahearne, chmn. (1717 H St. NW, 20555).

Occupational Safety and Health Review Commission—Timothy F. Cleary, chmn. (1825 K St. NW, 20006).

Office of Personnel Management—Alan K. Campbell, dir., (1900 E St. NW, 20415).

Overseas Private Investment Corporation—J. Bruce Llewellyn, pres. (1129 20th St. NW, 20527).

Panama Canal Commission—Dennis P. McAuliffe, adm. (in Panama); Thomas A. Constant, secy. (in Washington).

Pennsylvania Avenue Development Corporation—Thomas F. Murphy, chmn., Board of Directors (425 13th St. NW, 20004).

Pension Benefit Guaranty Corporation—Robert E. Nagle, exec. dir. (2020 K St. NW, 20006).

Postal Rate Commission—A. Lee Fritschler, chmn. (2000 L St. NW, 20268).

Railroad Retirement Board—William P. Adams, chmn. (Rm. 444, 425 13th St. NW, 20004), Main Office (844 Rush St., Chicago, IL 60611).

Securities and Exchange Commission—Commissioners: Harold M. Williams, chmn.; Irving M. Pollack, Philip Loomis Jr., John R. Evans, Stephen J. Friedman (500 N. Capitol St., 20549).

Selective Service System—Bernard D. Rostker, dir. (600 E St. NW, 20435).

Small Business Administration—A. Vernon Weaver Jr., admin. (1441 L St. NW, 20416).

Smithsonian Institution—S. Dillon Ripley, secy. (1000 Jefferson Dr. SW, 20560).

Tennessee Valley Authority—Chairman, board of directors: S. David Freeman. (400 Commerce Ave., Knoxville, TN 37902 and Woodward Bldg. 15th and H Sts. NW, Washington, D.C. 20444).

United States International Development Cooperation Agency—Thomas Ehrlich, dir. (320 21st St., 20523).

United States International Trade Commission—Bill Alberger, chmn. (701 E St. NW, 20436).

United States Metric Board—Louis F. Polk, chmn. (1815 N. Lynn St., Arlington, Va. 22209).

United States Postal Service—William F. Bolger, postmaster general (475 L'Enfant Plaza West SW, 20260).

Veterans Administration—Max Cleland, adm. (810 Vermont Ave. NW, 20420).

U.S. IMMIGRATION LAW

The Immigration and Nationality Act as amended by the Act of October 3, 1965, and the Immigration and Nationality Amendments of 1976 (P.L. 94-571) "marked the final end of an immigration quota system based on nationality." The latter amendments eliminated inequities in the existing law regarding the admission of immigrants from countries in the Western Hemisphere. The seven-category preference system, the 20,000 per-country limit, and the provisions for adjustment of status, all of which were in effect for Eastern Hemisphere countries, were extended to the Western Hemisphere.

The Immigration and Nationality Act, as amended, provides for the numerical limitation of most immigration. Not subject to any numerical limitations are immigrants classified as immediate relatives who are spouses or children of U.S. citizens, or parents of citizens who are 21 years of age or older; returning residents; certain former U.S. citizens; ministers of religion; and certain long-term U.S. government employees.

NUMERICAL LIMITATION OF IMMIGRANTS

Immigration to the U.S. is numerically limited to 290,000 per year. Within this quota there is an annual limitation of 20,000 for each country. The colonies and dependencies of foreign states are limited to 600 per year, chargeable to the country limitation of the mother country.

VISA CATEGORIES

Applicants for immigration are classified as either preference or nonpreference. The preference visa categories are based on certain relationships to persons in the U.S., i.e., unmarried sons and daughters over 21 of U.S. citizens, spouses and unmarried sons and daughters of resident aliens, married sons and daughters of U.S. citizens, brothers and sisters of U.S. citizens 21 or over (first, 2d, 4th, and 5th preference, respectively); members of the professions or persons of exceptional ability in the sciences and arts whose services are sought by U.S. employers (3d preference); and skilled and unskilled workers in short supply (6th preference); refugees (7th preference). Spouses and children of preference applicants are entitled to the same preference if accompanying or following to join such persons.

Except for refugee status, preference status is based upon approved petitions, filed with the Immigration and Naturalization Service, by the appropriate relative or employer (or in the 3d preference by the alien himself).

Other immigrants not within one of the above-mentioned preference groups may qualify as nonpreference applicants and receive only those visa numbers not needed by preference applicants.

LABOR CERTIFICATION

The Act of October 3, 1965, established new controls to protect the American labor market from an influx of skilled and unskilled foreign labor. Prior to the issuance of a visa, the would-be 3d, 6th, and nonpreference immigrant must obtain the Secretary of Labor's certification, establishing that there are not sufficient workers in the U.S. at the alien's destination who are able, willing, and qualified to perform the job; and that the employment of the alien will not adversely affect the wages and working conditions of workers in the U.S. similarly employed; or that there is satisfactory evidence that the provisions of that section do not apply to the alien's case.

EXTENSION OF ADJUSTMENT OF STATUS

The Act of October 3, 1965, excluded Western Hemisphere natives from adjusting their status to permanent residence under Section 245 of the Immigration and Nationality Act which allows a nonimmigrant alien to adjust to permanent resident without leaving the U.S. to secure a visa. The 1976 Amendments restored the adjustment of status provision to Western Hemisphere natives, and declared ineligible for adjustment of status aliens who are not defined as immediate relatives and who accept unauthorized employment prior to filing their adjustment application.

Immigrants Admitted from All Countries

Fiscal Year Ends June 30 through 1976, Sept. 30 thereafter

Year	Number	Year	Number	Year	Number	Year	Number
1820	8,385	1881–1890	5,246,613	1941–1950	1,035,039	1974	394,861
1821–1830	143,439	1891–1900	3,687,564	1951–1960	2,515,479	1975	386,194
1831–1840	599,125	1901–1910	8,795,386	1961–1970	3,321,777	1976	398,613
1841–1850	1,713,251	1911–1920	5,735,811	1971	370,478	1976 July-Sept.	103,676
1851–1860	2,598,214	1921–1930	4,107,209	1972	384,685	1977	462,315
1861–1870	2,314,824	1931–1940	528,431	1973	400,063	1978	601,442
1871–1880	2,812,191					**1820–1977**	**42,664,965**

NATURALIZATION: HOW TO BECOME AN AMERICAN CITIZEN

A person who desires to be naturalized as a citizen of the United States may obtain the necessary application form as well as detailed information from the nearest office of the Immigration and Naturalization Service or from the clerk of a court handling naturalization cases.

An applicant must be at least 18 years old. He must have been a lawful resident of the United States continuously for 5 years. For husbands and wives of U.S. citizens the period is 3 years in most instances. Special provisions apply to certain veterans of the Armed Forces.

An applicant must have been physically present in this country for at least half of the required 5 years' residence.

Every applicant for naturalization must:

(1) demonstrate an understanding of the English language, including an ability to read, write, and speak words in ordinary usage in the English language (persons physically unable to do so, and persons who, on the date of their examinations, are over 50 years of age and have been lawful permanent residents of the United States for 20 years or more are exempt).

(2) have been a person of good moral character, attached to the principles of the Constitution, and well disposed to the good order and happiness of the United States for five years just before filing the petition or for whatever other period of residence is required in his case and continue to be such a person until admitted to citizenship; and

(3) demonstrate a knowledge and understanding of the fundamentals of the history, and the principles and form of government, of the U.S.

The petitioner also is obliged to have two credible citizen witnesses. These witnesses must have personal knowledge of the applicant.

When the applicant files his petition he pays the court clerk $25. At the preliminary hearing he may be represented by a lawyer or social service agency. There is a 30-day wait. If action is favorable, there is a final hearing before a judge, who administers the following oath of allegiance:

I hereby declare, on oath, that I absolutely and entirely renounce and abjure all allegiance and fidelity to any foreign prince, potentate, state or sovereignty, to whom or which I have heretofore been a subject or citizen; that I will support and defend the Constitution and laws of the United States of America against all enemies, foreign and domestic; that I will bear true faith and allegiance to the same; that I will bear arms on behalf of the United States when required by the law; that I will perform noncombatant service in the armed forces of the United States when required by the law; that I will perform work of national importance under civilian direction when required by the law; and that I take this obligation freely without any mental reservation or purpose of evasion; so help me God.

U.S. PASSPORT, VISA, AND HEALTH REQUIREMENTS

Passports are issued by the United States Department of State to citizens and nationals of the United States for the purpose of documenting them for foreign travel and identifying them as Americans.

HOW TO OBTAIN A PASSPORT

An applicant for a passport who has never been previously issued a passport in his own name, must execute an application in person before (1) a passport agent; (2) a clerk of any federal court or state court of record or a judge or clerk of any probate court, accepting applications; (3) a postal employee designated by the postmaster at a Post Office which has been selected to accept passport applications; or (4) a diplomatic or consular officer of the U.S. abroad. Any children or brothers or sisters under age 13 may be included in the passport.

A passport previously issued to the applicant, or one in which he was included, will be accepted as proof of citizenship in lieu of the following documents. A person born in the United States shall present his birth certificate. To be acceptable, the certificate must show the given name and surname, the date and place of birth and that the birth record was filed shortly after birth. A delayed birth certificate (a record filed more than one year after the date of birth) is acceptable provided that it shows that the report of birth was supported by acceptable secondary evidence of birth.

If such primary evidence is not obtainable, a notice from the registrar shall be submitted stating that no birth record exists. The notice shall be accompanied by the best obtainable secondary evidence such as a baptismal certificate, a certificate of circumcision, or a hospital birth record.

A person in the U.S. who has been issued a passport in his own name within the last eight years may obtain a new passport by filling out, signing and mailing a passport by mail application together with his previous passport, two identical signed photographs and the established fee to the nearest Passport Agency or to the Passport Services in Wash., D.C. If, however, an applicant is applying for a passport for the first time, if his prior passport was issued before his 18th birthday, if he wishes to include a person other than himself in the passport, or if he is applying for an official, diplomatic, or other no-fee passport, he must execute a passport application in person.

A naturalized citizen should present his naturalization certificate. A person born abroad claiming citizenship through either a native-born or naturalized citizen must submit a certificate of citizenship issued by the Immigration and Naturalization Service; or a Consular Report of Birth or Certification of Birth issued by the Dept. of State. If one of the above documents has not been obtained, he must submit evidence of citizenship of the parent(s) through whom citizenship is claimed and evidence which would establish the parent/child relationship. Additionally, if through birth to American parent(s), parents' marriage certificate plus an affidavit from parent(s) showing periods and places of residence or physical presence in the U.S. and abroad, specifying periods spent abroad in the employment of the U.S. government, including the armed forces, or with certain international organizations; if through naturalization of parents, evidence of admission to the U.S. for permanent residence.

Under certain conditions, married women must present evidence of marriage. Special laws govern women married prior to Mar. 3, 1931 and should be investigated.

A person included in the passport of another may not use the passport for travel unless he is accompanied by the bearer.

Aliens—An alien leaving the U.S. must request passport facilities from his home government. He must have a permit from his local Collector of Internal Revenue, and if he wishes to return he should request a re-entry permit from the Immigration and Naturalization Service if it is required.

Contract Employees—Persons traveling because of a contract with the Government must submit with their applications letters from their employer stating position, destination and purpose of travel, armed forces contract number, and expiration date of contract when pertinent.

PHOTOGRAPHS AND FEES

Photographs—Identical photographs, sufficiently recent (normally taken within the past six months) to be a good likeness, both signed by the applicant, must accompany the passport application. An individual photograph of the passport bearer is required at all times. An additional photograph must be submitted showing other persons to be included in the passport.

Fees—The passport fee is $10. A fee of $4 shall be charged for execution of the application. No execution fee is payable where a passport is applied for by mail. All applicants must pay the passport fee and, where applicable, the execution fee unless specifically exempted by law.

The loss or theft of a valid passport is a serious matter and should be reported in writing immediately to the Passport Services, Dept. of State, Wash., D.C. 20524, or to the nearest passport agency, or to the nearest consular office of the U.S. when abroad.

FOREIGN REGULATIONS

A visa, usually rubber stamped in a passport by a representative of the country to be visited, certifies that the bearer of the passport is permitted to enter that country for a certain purpose and length of time. Visa information can be obtained by writing directly to foreign consular officials.

HEALTH INFORMATION

Smallpox—Some countries require an International Certificate of Vaccination against smallpox. Vaccination is not required for direct travel from the U.S. to most other countries.

Yellow Fever—A few African countries require vaccination of all travelers. A number of countries require vaccination if travelers arrive from infected or endemic areas. Vaccination is recommended for travel to infected areas and for travel outside the urban areas of countries in the endemic zones.

Cholera—A few countries require vaccination if travelers arrive from infected areas. Mozambique and Niger require vaccination of all travelers.

Plague—Vaccination is not indicated for most travelers to countries reporting cases of plague, particularly if their travel is limited to urban areas with modern hotels.

Malaria—There is a risk in the Caribbean, Central and South America, Africa, the Middle and Far East, and the Indian subcontinent. Travelers are strongly advised to seek information from their health department or private physician.

Return to the United States—No vaccinations are required to return to the United States from any country.

Vaccination Information—Yellow fever vaccine must be obtained at an officially designated Center, and the Certificate, valid for 10 years, must be stamped by the Center. The location of Centers is available from local health departments. Other vaccinations may be obtained from licensed physicians.

Travelers are advised to contact their local health department, physician, or agency that advises international travelers 2 weeks prior to departure to obtain the most current information.

CUSTOMS EXEMPTIONS AND ADVICE TO TRAVELERS

United States residents returning after a stay abroad of at least 48 hours are, generally speaking, granted customs exemptions of $300 each. The duty-free articles must accompany the traveler at the time of his return, must be for his personal or household use, must have been acquired as an incident of his trip, and must be properly declared to Customs. Not more than one liter of alcoholic beverages may be included in the $300 exemption.

If a U.S. resident arrives directly or indirectly from American Samoa, Guam, or the Virgin Islands of the United States, his purchase may be valued up to $600 fair retail value, but not more than $300 of the exemption may be applied to the value of articles acquired elsewhere than in such insular possessions, and 4 liters of alcoholic beverages may be included in his exemption, but not more than 1 liter of such beverages may have been acquired elsewhere than in the designated islands.

In either case, the exemption for alcoholic beverages is accorded only when the returning resident has attained 21 years of age at the time of his arrival. One hundred cigars and 200 cigarettes may be included (except Cuban products) in either exemption. Cuban cigars may be included if obtained in Cuba and all articles acquired there do not exceed $100 in retail value.

The $300 or $600 exemption may be granted only if the exemption, or any part of it, has not been used within the preceding 30-day period and your stay abroad was for at least 48 hours. The 48-hour absence requirement does not apply if you return from Mexico or the Virgin Islands of the United States.

Bona fide gifts costing no more than $25 fair retail value or $40 from American Samoa, Guam, or Virgin Islands, may be mailed to friends at home duty-free; addressee cannot receive in a single day gifts exceeding the $25 limit.

For a complete list of books available from Penguin in the United States, write to Dept. DG, Penguin Books, 299 Murray Hill Parkway, East Rutherford, New Jersey, 07073.

For a complete list of books available from Penguin in Canada, write to Penguin Books Canada Limited, 2801 John Street, Markham, Ontario L3R 1B4.